# THE CELY LETTERS
## 1472–1488

EARLY ENGLISH TEXT SOCIETY

No. 273

1975

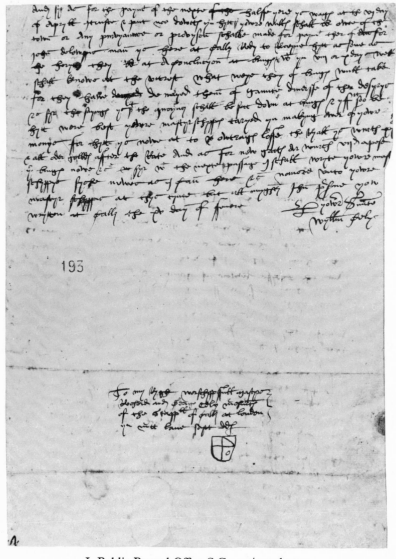

I. Public Record Office S.C.1 53/193 dorse
Letter no. 241, from William Cely

# THE CELY LETTERS

## 1472–1488

EDITED BY

ALISON HANHAM

*Published for*

THE EARLY ENGLISH TEXT SOCIETY
*by the*
OXFORD UNIVERSITY PRESS
LONDON   NEW YORK   TORONTO
1975

*Oxford University Press, Ely House, London W. 1*

GLASGOW  NEW YORK  TORONTO  MELBOURNE  WELLINGTON
CAPE TOWN  IBADAN  NAIROBI  DAR ES SALAAM  LUSAKA  ADDIS ABABA
DELHI  BOMBAY  CALCUTTA  MADRAS  KARACHI  LAHORE  DACCA
KUALA LUMPUR  SINGAPORE  HONG KONG  TOKYO

ISBN 0 19 722275 7

*Printed in Great Britain*
*at the University Press, Oxford*
*by Vivian Ridler*
*Printer to the University*

PR1119
.A2
no.273

SLTS

# CONTENTS

PLATES

  I. Public Record Office s.c.1 53/193 dorse      *Frontispiece*

  II. Public Record Office s.c.1 53/22      *Facing p.* 42

  III. Public Record Office s.c.1 59/16      ,,    50

  IV. Public Record Office s.c.1 59/5      ,,    55

  V. Public Record Office s.c.1 53/19A      ,,    185

INTRODUCTION      *Page* vii

TEXT      1

NOTES      250

BIBLIOGRAPHY      298

GLOSSARY      301

INDEX OF NAMES      349

# INTRODUCTION

THE Cely letters, often engaging enough in their own right, acquire a unique value from the social status of most of their writers. While the contemporary Pastons, Stonors, and Plumptons counted as 'gentry', the Celys were 'in trade'. That Sir William Stonor was engaged in exactly the same trade does not invalidate this distinction, which rests rather on the fact that the interests of the squirearchy were concentrated on the affairs of their country estates, while the Celys and their friends were, despite some minor landholdings, City men (in London or a provincial town such as York or Leicester), whose interests were predominantly in city affairs and in their business. In the case of wool merchants and merchant adventurers, this business was international, which meant that the businessman was in close touch with the Low Countries, in particular, and kept himself well informed about foreign affairs, so that his outlook was not exclusively parochial.

The Celys, less sophisticated but in a sense more modern than the Pastons, must thus be seen as representatives of the closely knit class of merchants, already important in the fifteenth century, whose social, political, and economic roles in the two subsequent centuries are now receiving a good deal of attention from historians. For the economic and social historian, the whole collection of Cely papers forms an incomplete but invaluable source of information about the life and commercial activities of the English wool merchant at a time when the wool trade, though in serious decline, still held a place of great importance in English economic and political life. More specifically, they are virtually the sole surviving source of information on the organization of a medieval English firm.[1] The papers also throw light on the financial activities of the merchant adventurers and of the Italian and Spanish merchants who acted as financiers in London and the Low Countries. In such respects they are unique in the period before 1500, and rivalled only by the still unpublished Johnson papers of the next century.

[1] 'The only considerable collection of medieval merchant papers known to survive in England': E. M. Carus-Wilson and Olive Coleman, *England's Export Trade 1275–1547* (Oxford, 1963), p. 26.

Linguistically, the collection occupies a special position as a record of the commercial English that had been developing over some four centuries of English involvement in international trade, and as a generally unselfconscious reproduction of the speech and writing habits of middle-class Londoners.

## 1. *The manuscripts*

The Cely papers came into the possession of the Public Record Office as the result of a dispute in 1489 between Richard Cely the younger and the widow of his brother George over payment of the debts arising from the brothers' joint trading ventures. The matter was taken to the Court of Chancery, and a mass of family letters and memoranda was collected as evidence in the suit, regardless of relevance. The resultant collection comprises two volumes of letters (Ancient Correspondence [s.c.1] vols. 53 and 59) and seven files of accounts and memoranda (Chancery Miscellanea [c.47] Bundle 37, Files 10–16), with two further letters in s.c.1 vols. 60 and 63. The accounts and memoranda, although full of individual items of interest, are disjointed and unwieldy, and contain some two hundred documents. This edition is therefore confined to the letters alone.[1]

The letters now mounted and bound together in s.c.1 53 and some of the memoranda were originally known as Tower Miscellaneous Roll No. 458. These letters were separated and bound about 1890.[2] The collection seems to have been first mentioned by Hubert Hall, in an article entitled 'The English Staple' in *The Gentleman's Magazine* for September 1883, which gives two letters in full, but inaccurately, and draws on some material from the memoranda.[3] In 1900 H. E. Malden edited a selection of 132 letters from approximately 194 known to him, and a few documents from the miscellaneous papers.[4] A further letter (**178** of the

---

[1] A loose definition of 'letter' has sometimes been employed. I have followed the P.R.O. in including **105** and **200** in the correspondence, and **92** has been added here as a parallel to **105**. No. **82** is my summary of a series of bills of lading which have become divided between the two P.R.O. volumes. s.c.1 53/196 has been omitted, since it is a mere fragment. No. **1** has been included, following the P.R.O., but no further financial instruments have been added.

[2] P.R.O. typewritten 'List of Chancery Miscellanea. Bundles 33–37' (1938), p. 59.           [3] Vol. cclv, 255–75.

[4] Henry Elliot Malden, ed., *The Cely Papers. Selections from the Correspondence and Memoranda of the Cely Family, Merchants of the Staple, A.D. 1475–1488*, Royal Historical Society (Camden Third Series, i, 1900). For

present edition) had been published in Bain's *Calendar of the Documents in Her Majesty's Public Record Office relating to Scotland*, iv, appendix 31, in 1888, and Malden re-edited this, with a correct ascription of authorship, under the title of 'An Unedited Cely Letter of 1482' in *Transactions of the Royal Historical Society* (Third Series, x, 1916), 159–65. A further file of forty-seven letters (now S.C.I vol. 59) was discovered at some date after this, and five of these have since been published.[1]

The 247 extant letters are a somewhat haphazard collection.[2] There are few unbroken sequences, and within these the correspondence is generally one-sided. They range between 1472 and early 1488, but the first two letters are isolated specimens from 1472 and 1474, and there is no correspondence for 1475. There is a further large gap from November 1482 to November 1483 (save for **200**, a cryptic note which appears to refer to events in June 1483), and another for the whole of 1485 and 1486. The correspondence ends in March 1488, over a year before the deaths of William and George Cely.[3]

The P.R.O. index suggests that the letters in S.C.I vol. 59 were George Cely's own file for the years 1476 to 1479.[4] There are some difficulties about this, however. The letters in this volume are not exclusively personal, and they intermesh with those now in vol. 53. It is true that this file was separated at an early date. The letters in it are numbered from 1 to 47 in Arabic numerals in a fifteenth-century hand, but the order is not chronological and the system, if any, is not apparent. The numbering may have been done by the writer who annotated many of the letters now in the larger

Malden's shortcomings as a textual editor, see Alison Hanham, 'The Text of the Cely Letters', *Medium Ævum*, xxvi (1957), 186–96. While much of the historical introduction to his volume is out of date, it should be said that his edition of the Cely letters was a basis for the important studies of the wool trade published by Eileen Power.

[1] By C. L. Kingsford in *Prejudice and Promise in Fifteenth-Century England* (Oxford, 1925), p. 29 n. 4 (**29** of the present edition), and by Laetitia Lyell in *A Mediaeval Post-Bag* (1934), pp. 303–10 (**19**, **43**, **74**, and **81** of this edition). Both Kingsford and Lyell made some mistakes in their transcripts.

[2] Documents in the memoranda (which will be referred to by File and folio number) touch on a wide range of the family's activities, but give even less consistent coverage, either chronologically or in subject matter. It is clear from the Chancery arbiters' notes in File 10 that they examined many of the firm's books. These, which would have given a clearer picture of the business, were probably returned to their owners.

[3] William died in or before May 1489: File 10 f. 25$^v$.

[4] 'List of Chancery Miscellanea. Bundles 33–37', p. 59.

volume while searching them for evidence in the Chancery suit of *c.* 1490.[1]

The standard size of a letter is a sheet of paper approximately 21 × 27 or 30 cm., but sometimes a double sheet is used, or a piece torn off for a shorter letter. The vast majority are the actual missives, not drafts. The finished letter was folded into a strip, addressed, tied with string or a strip of paper through slits, and sealed. On letters between members of the family, in addition to the address on the outside panel of the letter there is often a roughly drawn representation of the personal device of the sender, or more rarely of the recipient. The elder Richard's device consisted of a quartered shield with a diagonal bar in the upper and a circle in the lower right quartering (it can scarcely be described in heraldic terms). This badge formed the family's merchant mark. George used it on a fardel of goods left at Bruges to be shipped to London in 1486 (File 13 f. 27ᵛ), and it appeared on sarplers of wool sold by Richard 1 (e.g. File 15 f. 10; see frontispiece). William Maryon employed a rather similar mark, which he also had engraved on a signet ring. Richard Cely senior, however, used yet another pseudo-heraldic device on his signet, and letters written by him bear both mark and seal.[2] His sons sometimes used a mark derived from the device on his signet.

## 2. *The Cely family*

In 1474, when the correspondence proper begins, the Cely family consisted of Richard Cely 1, his wife Agnes, and their sons Robert, Richard, and George. Robert was probably the eldest, being already married in 1474, but by the time of his father's death in 1482 he had been virtually disinherited, and Richard inherited the principal properties and acted as chief executor. The brothers' ages are not known. The earliest accounts date from late 1473, and

---

[1] These annotations have been omitted here. A common one is the word *Nichill*, indicating that the letter contained no useful evidence. Others are résumés of business matters mentioned.

[2] A representation of the family's merchant mark formerly appeared on two of the stone corbels in St. Olave's, Hart Street, their parish church (A. Povah, *The Annals of the Parishes of St Olave Hart Street and Allhallows Staining in the City of London* (1894), p. 27, gives a reproduction). The roof was renewed shortly before the church was gutted in air raids in the Second World War. The new post-war decorations include shields to commemorate benefactors of the church, but the Celys' badge was not identified in time, and has been replaced by a coat of arms apparently granted to one of George's descendants in the next century.

since the Chancery arbiters who made the collection were interested exclusively in the affairs of George and Richard 2, it could be deduced that it was about that date that George began to take an active part in the family business. He may then have been about fifteen (see note to 50).

A brother of Richard 1, John Cely, was also a stapler and often acted as wool-gatherer for his brother,[1] and William Maryon, godfather of Richard 2, a grocer and merchant of the Staple, spent much of his time with the family. With Richard 1 they made up a loosely knit association of exporters, although these three older men were in no sense a partnership. It was usual for the senior members of the family to spend most of their time in England, buying the wool and fell and seeing to its packing and shipping, while a junior member of the firm attended to affairs at Calais. Apprentices helped in both sides of the business. It would appear from the memoranda that from at least 1472 to 1476 an associate, Thomas Kesten, was often in charge of the Calais end, assisted by Robert and (from 1473) George Cely. Probably Robert and George learnt the trade by serving an apprenticeship either to their father or to Kesten. The system of selling through attorneys or factors meant that the representative at Calais also handled wool on behalf of Maryon and John Cely, who shipped in their own names. But besides representing his father and other members of the family, from 1476 George operated a genuine partnership with his brother Richard, which lasted until his death in 1489.[2] By 1478 Kesten's services had been dispensed with, and George was in charge at Calais, assisted by the apprentice William Cely. William's precise relationship has not been determined; he was probably a family dependant, since after he became free of the Staple he remained in the position of factor, first to Richard 1 and then to George and Richard 2, to whom he always wrote with great deference.[3]

The origins of the family have not been traced. The name Cely or Sely is recorded in various parts of the country in the late

---

[1] John died before January 1483, leaving a son, John, a student at Oxford (will of Agnes Cely, P.C.C., 8 Logge).

[2] 'Fro the begynnyng of their occupying in comvne in anno domini M¹ iiij$^c$ lxxvj', File 10 f. 10$^v$.

[3] Like Richard 2, he was a godson of William Maryon. George was godfather to Maryon's nephew Robert Eyryk, and his mother Agnes Cely was godmother to Eyryk's daughter. Maryon in turn stood godfather to one of Richard 2's daughters.

medieval period, and a Sely family were London skinners between
at least 1281 and 1392.[1] No connection between these writers and
other families of the same name can, however, be proved, and it
is not known whether Richard 1 was a Londoner by birth.[2] The
only reference to a member of the previous generation is the
incidental information that Robert's grandmother was buried in
London (58). The first documentary reference to Richard 1 seems
to be a licence to him to ship wool and fell free of subsidy, together
with John Felde and Richard Bowell, merchants of the Staple, in
1449.[3] In 1453 he obtained exemption for life from holding various
offices and from jury service,[4] and in 1460 he was important
enough to be accused with other prominent staplers of abetting
the mayor and lieutenant in seizing the wool of another merchant.[5]
In 1481 he was a candidate for election as sheriff of London, but
was beaten by a better-known man, Sir Richard Chawry.[6] He
married Agnes, daughter of John and Lucy Andrew of Adderbury,
Oxfordshire, and sister of Richard Andrew, first Warden of All
Souls and of Sion College, a king's clerk by 1433, secretary to
King Henry VI from 1442 to 1455, and Dean of York from 1452
to his death in 1477.[7]

Richard Cely senior died on 14 January 1482. His will has not
been found, but details of some of his bequests are given in the
arbiters' accounts in File 10 of the Cely memoranda. His wife
Agnes died a little over a year later, leaving lands in Oxfordshire
and at 'Barton' in Northamptonshire enfeoffed to the use of her
son Robert for his lifetime.[8] Afterwards they were to go to Richard
and his heirs. Robert was also left 100 marks (£66. 13s. 4d.), of
which ten marks were to be delivered to him annually for ten years.

---

[1] See especially R. R. Sharpe, *Calendar of Letter-Books* (1899–1912), *passim*.
A number of references to our Celys, and to others of the same name, were
collected by Mr. F. Speer, F.S.A., F.R.Hist.S., who very kindly lent me his
notes on the subject.

[2] Malden did not explain the reason for his suggestion that the family 'was,
perhaps, Cornish in origin' (*Cely Papers*, p. vi). It led Zachrisson (*Pronunciation
of English Vowels*, p. 49) to the remarkable conclusion that the Celys' language
could be expected to show a mixture of Cornish ('southern') and Essex forms.

[3] *CPR 1446–52*, p. 315.                        [4] *CPR 1452–61*, p. 106.

[5] In the case of Richard Heron, cf. note to 129.

[6] No. 133.

[7] J. Otway-Ruthven, *The King's Secretary and the Signet Office in the XV
Century* (Cambridge, 1939), pp. 172-3, and J. Raine, ed., *Testamenta Eboracensia*
(Surtees Society, xlv, 1865), pp. 232-7.

[8] Will, P.C.C., 8 Logge, and Cely memoranda, File 10 f. 16ᵛ.

If he wished, the sum might be employed as a trading capital on his behalf, provided he obtained at least the same annual ten marks income from it. On her death bed she gave the furnishings of the house in Mark Lane to Richard 2 and his wife, as she had promised as part of the marriage settlement. They were worth £45. 4s. 8½d.[1]

Old Richard dominates the correspondence up to his death, worrying perpetually about prospects of war, about the price of wool and the difficulties of making a profit on it, and about his sons' remissness in writing. He was himself a careless and inelegant writer, and his meaning is not always clear. This is unfortunate, because his urge to give advice means that he often goes into details about operations of the wool trade that are not explained elsewhere. He was capable of showing real affection, as in his letters on the occasion of George's illness at Bruges (**67, 73**), but was inclined to be tyrannical. Richard 2 and George speak of him to one another with a mixture of kindliness and calculation (**4, 111**).

All three sons show signs of a rather easy-going disposition, in comparison with their father's carefulness, and in Robert's case parental misgivings proved amply justified. In 1478 his brother Richard threatened to have him arrested at Calais for debt. He had been given 30s. to pay his board and lost it all at dice (**32**). The following year he was still in debt, and Richard advised George to be very careful about lending him anything further, but in September 1480 Robert was again appealing to George to pay a bill of £14. 15s. (**47, 102**). The family were also involved in his matrimonial troubles. He was married by 1474, long before his brothers, and his wife died, along with six other people in the household, probably including the child mentioned in **39** and doubtless of the plague, on 19 July 1479 (**58**). By the following April he had been betrothed to a lady named Joan Hart and quarrelled with her. While he was changing his mind again, his father, who regarded the match as disastrous, persuaded the woman to call it off (**85, 86**). After this Robert is scarcely mentioned in the letters, and he seems to have dropped out of the wool business.[2] The accounts include various payments made by his

[1] File 10 f. 34.

[2] In 1481 a grant is recorded to Richard Sely, fellmonger, Robert Sele, fishmonger, and Walter Blunden, draper, citizens of London (*CCR 1476–85*, p. 213). If the two Selys are members of our family, this may mean that Robert had by then adopted another occupation.

brothers on his behalf for clothes, coals, and the mending of his chimney, for a physician and surgeon, and for a pilgrimage to St. James of Compostella.[1] There are some implications that his trouble was mental rather than moral. He died about 20 February 1485, leaving £3 to the church of St. Olave.[2] Stow mentions a monument there to 'Richard Cely and Robert Cely Felmongers, principall builders and benefactors of this Church'.[3] Did this inscription refer to members of an earlier generation, or did Stow miscopy that on the tomb that Richard 2 erected for his father, in which he and his mother were also subsequently buried?

George, as has been seen, served a normal apprenticeship in the firm at Calais. He makes an early appearance through a pamphlet of personal expenses in 1474-6, combining business with shopping sprees at the marts and lessons in music and dancing.[4] After his father's death he left William Cely in charge at Calais and moved to London, where it would appear that he was the more active partner in running the wool business. It seems likely that Richard 2 had little of his brothers' early training in the wool trade. He became a member of the Staple Company, as he was entitled to do by patrimony, and he occasionally helped at Calais at busy times, but does not show much experience of the Calais end of the business. As late as 1480 his father remarks that he has sent Richard to the Cotswolds to buy wool 'for ys leryng' (**87**). Richard's writing is not the usual merchant's hand of the period, and his language, especially early in the correspondence, shows a few northern traits not shared by other members of the family (see pp. xxiii–xxv). It is possibly significant in this connection that in 1481, after a trip to York, Northampton, and Leicester, Richard tells George of his visits to 'my [not 'our'] nowlde aqweyntans' in the north (**117**).

These rather imprecise pieces of evidence may indicate that Richard was educated apart from the rest of the family, possibly in the household of his mother's brother, Richard Andrew.

[1] File 10 ff. 16–17.

[2] Ibid. ff. 17–17$^v$.

[3] John Stow, *The Survey of London*, ed. C. L. Kingsford (Oxford, 1908), i. 132. Povah, the nineteenth-century historian of St. Olave's, cannot have been right in suggesting that our Celys erected the church: 'builders' must refer to repairs or additions. Richard 1 left money for building the steeple of the church and making an altar in St. Stephen's chapel there (File 10 f. 35).

[4] File 11 ff. 1–7$^v$; Alison Hanham, 'The Musical Studies of a Fifteenth Century Wool Merchant', *R.E.S.*, N.S. viii (1957), 270–4.

Andrew was made Dean of Newarke College, Leicester, in 1450 and became Dean of York in 1452, but he was such a devoted pluralist that it is difficult to say where he commonly resided after he ceased to be king's secretary in 1455. Little is known about Andrew, and still less about the background of Sir John Weston, Prior of the Knights of St. John of Jerusalem in England, and so premier baron of England, who figures prominently in the letters as an intimate friend of Richard 2 and patron of all the family.[1] I have not been able to trace any connection between Weston and Andrew, and there is no information about how Richard came to know him.

Richard and George were both looking for wives in 1481 (**117**). One of the best-known passages in the letters concerns Richard's brief and abortive wooing on May Day 1482, when he was in the Cotswolds to pack wool and was shown an eligible young lady at matins in Northleach church, with whom he exchanged wine and a roast heron, and had 'ryught gode comynecacyon' (**165**). Richard had previously favoured one of the Chester family, and nine days after his visit to Northleach his friend Harry Bryan urged on him another mercantile connection: with Anne, daughter of Richard Rawson. Rawson was a wealthy mercer from Yorkshire who became alderman and sheriff of London, and Anne had a dowry of 500 marks.[2] The wedding took place some time before the death of Agnes Cely about February 1483.[3]

George, with a series of mistresses at Calais, considered marriage with the sister of John Dalton, a fellow stapler, and instructed his brother to inspect her carefully when paying a visit to her mother in 1481 (**117**). But despite a good report, and his father's approbation, nothing came of the matter. He was still unmarried when in January 1484 Edmond Rygon, citizen and draper of London, and probably also a stapler, died leaving his second wife Margery as sole heir to his estates, which included property in Calais and its marches.[4] The young widow was immediately on the market. On 14 April (**215**) William Cely broke off a guarded report on George's progress in one matrimonial negotiation to congratulate him on being 'at apoynt' with 'þat oder gentyllwoman'.

[1] He was probably a brother of Edmond Weston of Boston, many of whose family belonged to the Order, and an uncle of the last prior, Sir William Weston.
[2] P.R.O. Ancient Petitions (c.1) 194/17.
[3] File 10 f. 34.
[4] Will of 19 January 1484, P.C.C., 22 Logge.

Her advisers were evidently expected to go carefully into George's income, for William assured him that sales at Calais had been double those of an unnamed rival. Richard's widow subsequently alleged, however, that George had spent more than his half share in the common stock of the two brothers on '[Je]wellys dyuers and many riche giftys and pleasurys geven to oon Margery Rygon then wydow and odyr her frendys tyme of his wooyng', on the expenses of his wedding, and on the purchase of land and other property for 'th'expedicion of his seid maryage'.[1]

George and Margery were married about 13 May 1484, and the accounts include William Maryon's bill for food and decorations at the festivities.[2] George died five years later, about 24 June 1489,[3] leaving four sons: Richard, Avery, George, and John, and a fifth (Edmond) 'in the moder bely'. He bequeathed £50 apiece to the five children, in addition to property in Essex, a house and garden in Mark Lane, and tenements in Mincing Lane. To his brother Richard he left 'the juell whiche I had of King Richard and the thirde part of the shippe callid Margaret Cely, forener'.[4] His widow later married, and predeceased, Sir John Halwell or Haleghwell, knight of the body, who held land and offices in Devon and Cornwall, including the stewardship of the Duchy of Cornwall from 1486.[5]

After George's death Richard made fruitless attempts to obtain payment of George's share in their joint debts, which were later claimed to have been £592. 11s. 8d., besides money owed Richard from the joint stock and profits.[6] In his own will he charged his executors with recovering and paying the money owed:

Item, whereas there belongith to me of ryght by the bequest of my brother George Cely a jewell with a balace [ruby] and v perlis hanging therby, and also as muche plate as shuld amounte vnto the some of Clxxx li. sterlingys toward the payment of suche debtys as we were joyntly bounde for, and I by survivourship stond yet charged [for], of the which jewell and plate nor also of the somme of M^l li. or theraboutys which as God knowith the said George . . . trewly ought vnto me,

---

[1] Ancient Petitions 194/17.

[2] File 12 ff. 41–3. In File 10 f. 34 an arbiter gives the date as April, but this must be wrong.

[3] File 10 ff. 7^v, 10^v.

[4] Will of 18 June 1489, P.C.C., 8 Horne, and Ancient Petitions, 300/15.

[5] Ancient Petitions 194/17 and 300/15. George junior was, by the time of the latter document (? 1513), the only survivor of the five children.

[6] Ancient Petitions 194/17.

I could neuer sith the death of the said George haue recouery of the same or of eny parte therof, I geue and bequeth the said jewell and plate to myne executours vnderwritten to th'entent that they with the same plate and jewell content and pay such debtys as I and the said George stood joyntly charged in, to any maner persone or persones as ferr as the said jewell and plate will extend vnto.[1]

By this time proceedings had already been started in Chancery. George's will was finally proved on 5 March 1497, with adminis-tration of everything apart from Margery's jointure granted to John Cutte, gentleman, and Avery Rawson, Richard's brother-in-law.[2] By February 1492 Richard was heavily in debt to his mother- and brother-in-law, and enfeoffed his landed property to their use until they were paid. On 3 June 1498, five years after Richard's death, his widow owed her brother Avery, on his own behalf and as executor of their mother, a total of £702. 11s. 2d.[3] This seems finally to have been discharged with a payment of one hundred marks from a sale of property by Richard's daughter and her husband in July 1509.[4]

By Anne, Richard had three daughters: Margaret, born c. 1489, Isabel, born in 1490, and Barbara, also called Anne, born in 1492 or early 1493.[5] Richard died on 5 July 1493.[6] His will is dated 4 July of that year, and it was proved on 30 July. His widow married Walter Frost, esq., of West Ham, 'sewar to Kyng Harry the eyght' (as Prince of Wales) and a commissioner of the peace for Essex, 1502–8.[7] She died on 23 October 1527. Their eldest daughter, Margaret, married John Kettleby or Ketylby, armiger, of Cotheridge (?), Worcs., and like her mother was buried in the church of West Ham.[8] Isabel married first Robert Warham, gent.,

---

[1] Essex Record Office, D/DL T1 528, with additions from P.C.C., 25 Dogett. The probate copy of George's will says nothing about any plate.

[2] P.C.C., 8 Horne.

[3] *CCR 1500–1509*, pp. 329–30.

[4] E.R.O. D/DL T1 589.

[5] *Calendar of Inquisitions Post Mortem, Henry VII*, i (1898), 379, and Maryon's will, P.C.C., 19 Vox (7 May 1493, proved 6 February 1494).

[6] Morant, in *The History and Antiquities of the County of Essex* (1768), i. 83, followed by Malden (*Cely Papers*, p. xlviii), makes a mistake in translating the regnal year, and gives the date as 1494. The inquisition post mortem apparently gives the right year, but has June in place of July (*Cal. Inq. P.M. Henry VII*, i. 379).

[7] John Weever, *Antient Funeral Monuments* (1767), p. 359, and *CPR 1494–1509*, p. 639.

[8] Weever, loc. cit., and *V.C.H. Worcestershire* (1901–26), iii. 552, 563.

and secondly (before 1531) Antony Cook or Coke, senior, of
Aveley, Essex.[1] By January 1532 Isabel and her second husband
had evidently obtained the shares of her two sisters in the family
property of Bretts Place in Aveley, which they then sold, with use
reserved to them for their lifetimes, to John Baker, recorder of the
City of London, along with other properties, including the third
part of the advowson of St. Olave, Hart Street.[2] Isabel was still
alive in 1560.[3]

### 3. *The financial background*

It is not possible to give here a detailed description of the operations of the wool trade,[4] but something should be said about the
Celys' financial dealings, which play a large, and sometimes rather
obscure, part in the correspondence. After inspecting a sample of
wool, the stapler made a written agreement with the woolman
to buy so many sacks, paying the same price for both good and
middle wool (the second-grade sortings of the fleece). The wool
was sorted and packed by a professional packer, and the sarplers
sent to London by wain. Here the wool was weighed in the
presence of both seller and buyer. The latter thereupon paid the
seller one-third of the price (four cloves per sarpler having been
rebated for canvas and the turn of the balance). The other two-
thirds were due, usually, in two instalments, the last perhaps
twelve months after the date of the agreement. To meet these
payments the Celys often borrowed a sum in sterling from an
English merchant adventurer in London, who received an obligation payable by their factor in Flemish money at a specified mart.
The exchange rate of the Flemish equivalent was agreed at the
time the loan was made, but the valuation of the coin in which it
was paid would be that obtaining at the mart.

Meanwhile, the factor had sold wool and fell at Calais at the

---

[1] Morant, i. 83; E.R.O. D/DL T1 586 and 616. The two elder girls were
married by July 1509.

[2] D/DL T1 616. The advowson of St. Olave's had probably been acquired
by Richard Cely 1 from Richard Andrew, as heir of Isabel, wife of Robert
Arnold, who had presented to the living in 1438–44 (Newcourt, *Repertorium*,
i (1708), 511–12).

[3] D/DL T1 653.

[4] For these see Eileen Power, 'The Wool Trade in the Fifteenth Century',
*Studies in English Trade in the Fifteenth Century*, ed. Eileen Power and M. M.
Postan (1933), pp. 39–90. Much of the detail in the chapter 'Thomas Betson'
in Eileen Power's earlier *Medieval People* (1924) is unfortunately not reliable.

price fixed (in marks sterling) by the Staple. The down payment, if any, was made at an exchange rate and in coin at a valuation dictated by the Staple. The further instalments, to be paid at stated marts, were computed at an exchange rate which was to some extent agreed between buyer and seller, and to some extent set by the Staple rules, but which was almost always, at this period, lower than that prevailing in Flanders. Payment was, again, made in coin at mart valuation (in the mixture of Flemish, English, French, Rhineland confederation and other coins that made up the currency in the Low Countries), or else in the form of drafts on a money-dealer-cum-banker in Bruges or Antwerp. Having paid any obligations due, and reserved enough money to pay any forthcoming dues at Calais, the stapler 'made over' his surplus by agreeing an exchange rate and terms with an English merchant who needed Flemish money to buy wares at the mart. Both in borrowing at London and in lending at the mart, these terms were expressed as 'so many shillings and pence Flemish for the noble sterling (6s. 8d. ster.), at so long (e.g. three months and six months)'. The factor at the mart noted the transactions as, say, 'made with W. Borwell £50 ster. at 8s. Fl., 3 months and 3 months'. In exchange loans, unlike credit sales, charging reasonable interest was not reprobated, on the ground that there was a clear risk involved. Accordingly, the rate for loans in London repayable at the mart would be fixed at something a little above par of exchange when the agreement was made, and loans at the mart were made at a rate slightly below par. The size of the loan and the terms for repayment were also taken into account, the smaller sum for the shorter time apparently costing the borrower relatively more. (But unless they were pressed for sterling at home, the Celys probably preferred to make fairly long-term loans, e.g. six and twelve months, since these brought more profit in absolute terms, and they were not interested in a quick turnover.) The selection of a reliable borrower was of paramount importance to them. In the few cases where probable interest charges can be deduced the usual basis seems to be about $2\frac{1}{2}$ per cent for one month.

Towards the end of the period covered by the letters, the Celys' business habits start to change. Turmoil in Maximilian's Burgundian dominions and English embargoes on trade there meant that the staplers' usual financial arrangements with English adventurers were seldom possible, and to make money over to

England they were forced to rely chiefly on 'Lombards' and Spaniards with connections in Bruges or Antwerp and London. Trade difficulties also meant that about 1483 the Celys and many other staplers began to break the regulations of their Company, which insisted that sales should be either cash down at Calais, or for obligations payable in Flemish money at one of the marts. Instead they dealt largely with customers like John De Lopez of Bruges who arranged to pay them in sterling at London.

No. **237** illustrates the temptation to diversify when conditions became difficult (many of the bigger London merchants had long traded as both staplers and mercers). The Celys eventually met the problem by engaging in the carrying trade, in partnership with William Maryon, and early in 1486 purchased a Breton fishing vessel known as the *Margaret of Penmarcke*, which they refitted and renamed the *Margaret Cely of London*. Some ten voyages are recorded in the accounts from 1486 to 1489. She went to Bordeaux for wine in the late autumn, to the Bay of Bourgneuf for salt, to Calais (but not, apparently, with wool), and on to Zealand with wheat and other grain, going on to Antwerp on at least one occasion and returning with a freight of miscellaneous goods for various merchants. The expenses of fitting out and victualling and of paying the crew of about fourteen were apparently paid haphazardly by one partner or another and shared out at the final reckoning for each voyage. The Celys also did some miscellaneous trading, joining with some Spanish merchants in exporting a cargo of wheat in 1487. It is possible that references to a ship called the *Anne Cely* mean that Richard acquired another vessel on his own account.[1]

It is impossible to reach an accurate estimate of the two brothers' average net annual income from trade, but curiously, two entirely independent calculations, neither very reliable, put it at about £100 ster. apiece.[2] The family also had some investments in land.

[1] e.g. *ACM*, p. 202.

[2] The first was made on behalf of Richard's widow, in Ancient Petitions 194/17. The document is damaged, and the exact financial position is a little unclear. The joint stock of merchandise apparently amounted to some £1,805 in value (this possibly included a stock inherited by the brothers from their father, worth £959 odd, and the 500 marks of Anne Cely's dowry). A half share of the total trading profit ('the moyte of the gayne of the same') over eight years (1482–9) was estimated to amount to £902. 13s. 8d. The second estimate is Malden's (*Cely Papers*, p. xliv), based on the statement (**215**) that within the twelve months up to April 1484 the Celys had sold £2,000 worth of wool, and

Besides his house in Mark Lane, near Leadenhall, Richard 1 had acquired Bretts Place, near Aveley, Essex, from his brother-in-law Richard Andrew in 1462.[1] This was used as a second residence, particularly in times of plague in the city, and Richard 1 farmed the land. Shortly after his father's death George listed land held by one or other of the two brothers in Essex, including Bretts Place (inherited by Richard 2), the manors of Manhall and Bumpsted (Aveley), the lordship of Aveley, Gaines, Upminster Hall, and land in Wennington and Dagenham.[2] George's country residence, also inherited from his father, was Mallins, Little Thurrock, where he later purchased 'Saccokkys', also known as Sacokkes Mershe, now Socketts Heath.[3] This part of Essex was much favoured by London merchants. Richard 2 also inherited his mother's property in Oxfordshire and Northamptonshire.[4]

### 4. *The language of the Cely papers*

I have discussed elsewhere some of the gaps in *OED* that would have been filled had all the Cely papers been available to the editors.[5] Since the papers fall outside the period covered by *MED*, proper coverage must await the compilation of a Tudor English dictionary. At a rough estimate, the papers supply nearly two hundred words, senses, or constructions either not found in *OED*, or, more often, first cited from the sixteenth century or later. While many of these (like *assist*) have now been documented by *MED* from considerably before the Cely period, very many belong to the special language of commerce, which has received little attention as far as English is concerned.

An important part of this sub-language involved the use of

allowing a profit of 10 per cent on the sale price. There is no way of knowing whether this year's trading was typical. My own calculation suggests that on sales of first grade wool only, allowing for taxes, freight, costs of travel to the Cotswolds, and other ascertainable expenses, but not overheads like board at Calais or wages or losses on exchange, a profit of 25 per cent might have been normal.

[1] E.R.O. D/DL T1 443. Andrew acquired the manor in 1447, possibly from Isabel Arnold, whose husband held it by grant in 1410 (ibid. 316). The house and property, now known as Bretts Farm, are still in existence.

[2] File 12 f. 34$^v$.

[3] P.C.C., 8 Horne; P. H. Reaney, *The Place-Names of Essex* (Cambridge, 1935), p. 173.

[4] D/DL T1 528.

[5] 'The Cely Papers and the Oxford English Dictionary', *English Studies*, xlii (1961), 129–52.

ordinary phrases with a special connotation. A sample of such expressions from the papers is *clear*, *clearness*, *comfort of payment* 'something on account', *content* or *please* 'pay', *do much to*, *do good over* (*upon*) 'make a profit from', *grow*, either 'accumulate' or 'fall due', *run to*, of money, 'be applied to a certain purpose', *run upon*, of costs, 'arise in connection with', *slack*, of the market, *standing upon* 'in account with', *write* a sum *upon* a bill 'deduct from', *write* (or *set*) someone *upon* somebody 'give a creditor a draft on (one's account with) a banker'. The mechanism of exchange loans had a whole vocabulary of its own in English: cf. glossary entries under *exchaunge*, *make*, *tacke*.

Many other English commercial terms were borrowings. The Celys kept their accounts in a mixture of English, French, and Latin, using terms such as *pro*, *memorandum*, *sum total*, *argent* 'total price', *le* 'per', *reste* 'there remains' and *feyt* 'makes in another currency'. Flemish and Middle Dutch had an early and long-continuing influence on the vocabulary of trade, giving English such words as *bettering*,[1] *budge* (**42,** note), *gruff*, *inship*, and *wrack* 'second-rate herring'. The wool trade, specifically, acquired *breckling*, *cloth* in the sense of 'bale', the curious device the *english* (**206,** note), *forehouse*, probably *blot*, *poke*, *poket*, and *sarpler*, and *shorling*.[2] Flemish was sufficiently close to English to make interchanges easy, and one might even speculate how far merchants like William Maryon were encouraged in their old-fashioned and often unetymological use of the prefix *y-* with past participles by hearing such Flemish participles as *gheper-petreert* and *ghecommittiert*.[3] Southern Englishmen in Bruges or Calais would hear *egges* from their many northern compatriots, but *eyren* from Flemish associates, and Caxton's *spoil* for 'wash'[4] may have been acceptable Bruges English, just as *overcorn* 'supplementary charge' came naturally to George Cely when he noted payments for board at Calais.[5]

Linguistically, Bruges may have had even greater importance

---

[1] *MED* oddly mistakes the sense: it meant 'compensation' (also, in Fl., 'fine'), not 'an increase in weight and hence in toll'.

[2] *OED* refers this to *shorn* ppl. adj.+*ling*, but it occurs in Scots with reference to the Low Countries *c.* 1400, and seems much more likely to be Flemish.

[3] Gilliodts–van Severen, *Inventaire des Archives de Bruges*, vi. 153.

[4] Not 'rinse': cf. 'nec spoelen nec sceren debet nec barbam alicujus . . . radere', Höhlbaum, *Hansisches Urkundenbuch*, i. 244.

[5] File 15 f. 32, File 16 f. 18ᵛ.

as a major centre of international trade and banking where the English met foreign terms, either from French or Italian merchants or indirectly through Flemish borrowings: probably they there encountered *a(ll) usanza* or *à usance*.[1] The international character of commerce makes it difficult to pin down the precise origin of many terms. Who originated the use of *nation* (and its cognates) in the sense 'the body of merchants of a particular nationality trading in a given centre'? In the absence of any early French instances, English (and Flemish) *net* in 'net price', 'net weight' (*OED* 1520, Cely papers 1486) should probably be derived from Italian *netto* (1262),[2] not French *nette*, and certainly not English *neat*. English *barter(ing)* probably derives indirectly from French through Flemish. Flemish *barteringhe* (unnoticed by *OED* or *MED*) occurs in one version of a document dated 1252.[3] Sometimes a vernacular equivalent throws light on the meaning of a borrowing. Richard 1's 'rebate for canvase and drathe' (File 15 f. 9) is surely the same as 'tare and tret', and confirms that *tret* was the *draught* allowed for inaccuracies in the scales.

It is not proposed here to discuss the language of the forty English writers represented in the letters, or even of the Cely family themselves in detail. To do so adequately would demand excessive space, and require consideration not only of the letters but of the entire collection of Cely papers. A few comments and notes on particular points must suffice.

The Celys (and still more their provincial correspondents like the Leicester Daltons and William Midwinter of Northleach) were far from writing a highly standardized English. Individuals among the younger members of the family can be observed to normalize certain habits in accordance with what was probably felt to be standard usage in London or Calais: Richard 2 drops his northern *qw(h)-* in favour of *wh-* and *at* in favour of *that*, and William Cely increasingly replaces the pronouns *hem* and *her* with

---

[1] The editors of *OED* forgot, or were unaware of, the importance of exchange loans between Bruges and London when they identified the *sheldes* of Chaucer's merchant as French *écus* instead of Flemish *scilden*, the contemporary money of account at Bruges. Suggestions that the merchant engaged in illegal money-changing at London are off the mark.

[2] Edler, *Glossary*.

[3] Höhlbaum, *Hansisches Urkundenbuch*, i. 150 (No. 435 (2)). *OED* quotes Fr. *barater* from 1373 and It. *barattare* from 1598 (Florio). Edler cites It. *barattare* from 1384. Fr. *baretter* occurs in a document from Ghent of 1359 (Höhlbaum, iii. 254).

*them* and *ther*[1] and adopts *ar* alongside other plurals of *be*, but much latitude is given to individual preferences.

This variety is clearly seen with regard to the third person present ending of verbs. In the singular, Richard 1 has approximately 18 -*t(h)* forms to 11 uninflected, and 17 *hath* to one doubtful *have*.[2] William Maryon has 20 -*t(h)* or -*d* to 7 zero. John Cely has only -*th* in the small sample available. Of the younger generation, Robert has 4 -*th* to 2 zero. Richard 2 has 6 -*th*,[3] 94 -*s* and 20 zero. George[4] has 23 -*th*, 34 -*s*, and 5 zero (excluding 26 *hath*, 23 *has*, 4 *have*). His use of -*s* in the sg. increases very greatly after 1486. William Cely appears to use only *hath* or *have*. There is a marked increase in -*th* forms in other verbs. The figures for three periods, 1479–82, 1483–4 and 1487–8, are:

| | | | |
|---|---|---|---|
| 1479–82 | 40 -*th* | 21 -*s* | 3 zero |
| 1483–4 | 48 -*th* | 8 -*s* | 4 zero |
| 1487–8 | 47 -*th* | 5 -*s*[5] | 7 zero |

William and George Cely thus change in opposite directions, George moving towards -*s* and William towards -*th*. It is possible that William regarded -*th* as the correct literary form, and it may be significant that most of George's extant writing after 1486 is in the form of accounts or memoranda. Richard's -*s* may derive from a different educational background.

In the plural, Richard 1 and Maryon diverge, Richard using -*th* only in 2 *hath* beside 2 *have*, and otherwise showing uninflected forms, and Maryon showing 9 -*th* to 2 zero. Both use only *be* in the plural of that verb.

Of the younger generation, Robert uses no plurals in his extant letters apart from *ben*. Richard 2 uses 23 -*s* to 25 zero, and 26 *be*; 20 *are*; 7 *is*. George has 7 -*th*, 11 -*s*, 11 zero, and 6 *be*; 7 *beth*; 6 *ben*; 8 *is*; 1 *are*. William Cely again shows changing habits:

---

[1] See note to **241**. Linguistic changes in other writers are demonstrated by Norman Davis in 'A Scribal Problem in the Paston Letters', *English and Germanic Studies*, iv (1951–2), 31–64, 'A Paston Hand', *R.E.S.*, N.S. iii (1952), 209–21, and 'The Language of the Pastons', *Proc. Brit. Acad.* xl (1955), 119–44.

[2] All these counts are taken from both letters and memoranda. Spellings are modernized.

[3] Only one, *abydythe*, in the letters. The other five are all of the verb *appear*.

[4] Figures exclude examples of the hybrid *pleaseth it* (? originating in a misunderstanding of *please it* as *pleaseth*), and of *appeareth* and *amounts*, which are nearly invariable forms.

[5] Including, surprisingly, *dar(e)s* twice.

| 1479–82 | 19 -th | 2 -s | 24 zero | 14 hath | 5 have |
|---|---|---|---|---|---|
| 1483–4 | 25 -th | 1 -s | 19 zero | 17 hath | 12 have |
| 1487–88 | 9 -th | — | 18 zero | 10 hath | 11 have |

In the verb *to be* the figures are:

| 1479–82 | 42 be; | 11 is; | 3 beth (ye are once) |
|---|---|---|---|
| 1483–4 | 27 be; | 12 is; | 3 beth; 3 ben; 5 are |
| 1487–8 | 7 be; | 5 is; | 3 beth; 1 ben; 9 are |

In the plural, Richard 2 again displays northern influence, although *are* does not entirely displace *be*. William begins to discard *-th* in favour of the modern zero ending after 1484, and starts to use *are* in 1483, apart from an earlier isolated occurrence in the second person (**189**).

## 5. *Spelling*

Much earlier work on English pronunciation, which seized on 'significant occasional spellings' (or often supposed spellings) from fifteenth century writers like the Celys in a careless and unsystematic way, is now discredited. Useful discussion of their spelling remains extremely difficult because there are so many variables: we do not know what the writers heard, what they thought they heard, or how far they might (or could) attempt to render the second phonetically. Nor can we always be sure what phonetic value, if any, they attached to a given symbol. There is no need to labour the point, but three examples might be adduced.

George's servant Nicholas Best, writing a domestic account,[1] regularly uses the spellings *bod* and *med* for 'boat' and 'meat'. In copying the same document he changes to *botth* and *metth*, and keeps these forms thereafter. It would be far-fetched to suppose that he had a cold on the first occasion. Did George or his wife correct his spelling? George and William Cely and John Dalton frequently refer to a Burgundian coin which they term a *nemyng* or *nymhekyn* groat. Two separate employees render this *lymon* or *lymmyn* groat. Did they both mishear the word, which seems to occur only in the Cely papers? Thirdly, what private analogy lies behind William Maryon's almost invariable *fyght* 'fish' (once *fytht*, once *fysscheys*) in the memoranda?

Syntax is often as unfixed as spelling and morphology. One result of this is that although the Celys and their correspondents

---

[1] File 16 ff. 30–35ᵛ, 36–7.

tend to write in clichés, and certain words, often coupled with a particular modifier, like *good* or *great cheer*, *poor honesty*, occur monotonously in certain contexts, within the general framework of a conventional phrase the writer often has various choices of syntax or word order available to him. One could 'do good' *over*, *upon*, or *with* the commodities of trade; be *in way to* or *in a way to* do something or else *in the way of* doing it; or, when an activity once started was going well, be *in good way of* it. One could also act *in all haste*, *in all the haste*, *in all the haste possible*, or *in as possible haste as may be*. A debt 'lies upon my honesty' (or 'lies my honesty upon'), equally, with a switch in the syntactical relationships of the components of the phrase, 'my honesty lies upon the payment'. Syntactical uncertainty, however, can produce such clumsy constructions as Richard 1's 'and I were intrete for asvrte of a comforde of paymen⟨t⟩', 38 (apparently 'if I were offered the assurance of some payment on account'), or 'all hoder men there as he ys intreted to', 11 ('everyone else with whom he is in negotiations'), and the idiom *set by* notably resists George's apparent attempt to use it in a double construction in 4.

There is little striving for literary effect in the letters. At best the writing is governed by the rhythms of ordinary speech; at worst it lapses into long formless sentences, in which the dash sometimes seems the best method of imposing punctuation. It is difficult to single out words as 'colloquial' at this period, but certain expressions have the ring of spoken rather than literary English: *this reckoning* (persecution by the mob); *cross* 'coin'; *go on wheels* 'be topsy-turvy'; *that pleased him nothing*; *as for the hawks that be dead, all our evil go with them*; *I shall upon him for them*; *take it sore at your stomach*; *ye may say ye have a homely fellow of me*; *what* 'well then'; *too outrageous out of the way* 'impossibly expensive'. Interestingly enough, many of them come from the rather precise William Cely, who seems to have been linguistically more sophisticated than his masters, and experimented with different opening and closing formulae, and with minor spelling variations, like the doubling of final *-e*. One would like very much to have the lost letter with what he described as 'myn lewde and ontrewe Englysche' (cf. 203).

In this edition capitalization and punctuation have been supplied, but virgules and double virgules (/, //) in the original are retained. The usual abbreviations have been expanded, as far as possible in accordance with the writer's spelling in full forms. The modern spelling has been followed in the expansion of a flourish as *er* or *ar*. The three abbreviations of plural endings, in the form of looped long *s*, ȝ (virtually confined to Callȝ, fellȝ), and superior ⁹ (very rare) are expanded respectively to *-ys*, *-es* and *-us*. Letters or words lost by damage are supplied in square brackets where a plausible reconstruction can be offered; otherwise a gap, regardless of length, is indicated by [. . .]. Interlineations are indicated by half-brackets. Cancellations of more than a single letter are noted at the foot of the page. A few emendations have been made in the interest of sense, usually by supplying letters or words which the writer has omitted. These additions are placed in angle brackets ⟨ ⟩. In one or two cases a more radical emendation has been made, e.g. 23 line 4 reads in the manuscript 'I have none schepynt*er*'. In this text 'schepynt*er*' has been replaced by 'schepyn⟨g⟩', and the manuscript reading is given in a footnote. Some uncancelled miswritings and accidental repetitions have also been removed to the footnotes. Modern word division has been adopted, except where a writer has transferred *n* from the indefinite article *an* to the following noun.

Among the many people who have been generous with help and comment I especially wish to thank Professor Norman Davis, Dr. P. O. E. Gradon, R. W. Burchfield, Professor E. J. Dobson, Professor H. J. Hanham, Professor H. G. Koenigsberger, Professor Peter Ramsey, and Professor T. S. Willan. Dr. Renée Doehaerd, Dr. N. J. M. Kerling, and Professor F. J. Warne very kindly gave assistance with the translation of Dutch and French material in the papers. On matters concerning coinage I have drawn heavily on the goodness of Professor Philip Grierson. I am also grateful to the Public Record Office for permission to reproduce the plates. The late Miss S. I. Tucker supervised the preparation of the University of Bristol dissertation on which this edition is based. I here acknowledge in deep gratitude her tuition and her friendship.

# THE CELY LETTERS
## 1472-1488

## 1. John Dycons to John Wode at London, 8 December 1472

s.c.1 53/1

### Jhesus

Ryght worschipfull *and* reuer*e*nt mayster, I recomaunde me vnto
you, etc. Pleaseth hit you to wytt I haue rec*eyu*ed by exch*a*unge
of Thom*a*s Kestevyn, attor*n*ey of Ric*hard* Cely, m*e*rch*a*unt of the
Stap*le* at Caleis, fourety poundez sterlyng*ys* to be paid to the said
Ric*hard* Cely or to bryng*er* of þ*ys* lett*r*e at London the xij day of 5
Feue*r*er next comyng. The which xl li. st*er.* I pray you may be
well *and* truely content *and* paid at þe day aforesaid, by this my
first *and* seco*n*de lett*r*e of payem*e*nt. In wytnesse hereof, I, the said
John Dycons, haue wretyn þ*ys* bill w*yth* myn owne hande *and*
haue sett hereto my maist*er*s seall, the viij day of Decembre, in þe 10
yeer of oure Lord God, M¹iiijᶜlxxij.

By yo*ur* attorney
John Dycons.

*Dorse*: To my ryght worschipfull maister John Wode, m*e*rch*a*unt
of þe Stap*le* at Caleis, at London, soit doon. *Drawing of shield.* 15

## 2. Richard Cely the elder at London to Robert Cely at Calais, 5 July 1474

s.c.1 53/2

### Jhesu M¹iiijᶜlxxiiij

I grete the wyll, and I haue resayuyd a letter from the, wryte at
Caleys the xxiiij day of Jun, the weche I haue wyll understand, and
that ye [haue] solde youre fellys the sopesans, for the weche I am
wyll plesyd, a[n]d [. . .] haue resayuyd a letter from Thomas
Kesten and charge for [. . .] he hath send to me for you a letter 5
of payment of Grace, mecer, [. . .] xl li. st*er.* payable the x day of
September at London, and I understand nothyng of resayvyng
of woll, of no good rvlys of the Place, nayder in a sale nor in hoder
wyse, for the weche ȝe be sloe in wrytyng. And saye to Thomas
Kesten I was at Geteryng feste on Sonday after Send Peter day, 10
for a mater that I for to doe there, and the pryse of ⌐woll⌐ ys

2. 2 Caleys the] the *repeated*

xxviij d. a stone, as men tell me. John Ranys can tell you. And as
for Wyll Derlyngton, he sele ys londe at Barton, but I haue non
nor non wyll haue of hym, and soe saye to my mayster Wetyll or
15 to ys men. I [wryte] no mor, but Jhesu kepe you. And saye to
Jorge Cely I hadde [no word f]rom hym of youre comyng to
Caleys, and youre wyfe thyng [ye] schuld haue wryt to here. Ye
forgete youreselve, wat y[s] for [to do]. Slothe ys a grete thyng
and dothe lyttyll good hottymys ther[e as] good besynes dothe
20 esse. Wryte at London the v day of Jule, in [haste].

per Richard Cely.

*Dorse*: To Robard Cely at Caleys be thys delyuer. *Shield*.

### 3. Robert Cely at London to George Cely, *13 April 1476*
s.c.1 53/3

Aº lxxvj

Welbelouyd brother, I recomaund me herttely to yow, fferthermore informynge yow that the xiij day of Aprell the ʒeere aboue
sayd, I Robard Cely haue ressayuyd off Wylliam Eston, mersar
of London, xij li. ster. to pay at Andewarpe in Sencyon martte the
5 xxiiij day of June, for euery nobyll of vj s. viij d. ster., vij s. x d.
Fllemeche, and I pray yow to delyuer to the sayd Wylliam Eston
xij li. ⌐starlynge⌐ at the same ratte, takynge a byll of ys honde to
paye at London the sayd xij li. at a day as longe hafter ⌐þe day⌐ as
I toke the mony wp beffore. In wettnes herof I sette my seell at
10 London the xiij day of Aprell.

per Robard Cely.

*Dorse*: A George Cely.

### 4. George Cely at Antwerp to Richard Cely the younger at Calais, *27 September 1476*
s.c.1 59/17

Ryght whellbelovyd brothyr, I recomeavnde me vnto as lowyngly
as I con or may. Fordyrmor, plesythe yt yow to vndyrstonde I
hawe resseywyd an letter ffrom yow, the wheche I hawe rede and

---

**3. 7** starlynge *over canc.* Flemeche

do whell vndyrstonde/ I hawe wrytt owr ffathyr an answer therof,
etc. Owr ffathyr wold that I showd hy me vnto Calles. Ytt ys so 5
I resseywyd of Thomas an byll of an Cxxj li. vj s. vj d., wherof
I con resseywe but lxx li. Fl., that hawe I resseywyd and Thomas
Kesten hathe promyssyd me to delyuyr me the rest, and mor to.
Allso ther ys an veryavns bytuyxt Kesten and John Vandyrhay
ffor ix sarplers woll. Thys ys an shrowd ⟨matter⟩: I whas at 10
Mekyllyn and saw yt yll woll. Yt ys thys ys bytuyxt Kesten and
hym. In owr ffathyrs dewte he hathe payd me truly, and he con
none ffardyr go but to me, and the mater ys soyche I trow I conot
ȝese hym / Brothyr, owr ffathyr ys now at Calles, and ys whorshyppffull, and so takyn, and ffor owr honesteys latt vs se that all 15
thyng anbowt hym be honest and clenly. He ys nott now at Allay,
and the mor whorshyppffull as he ys at Calles, the better belowyd
shall whe be, and the mor sett by thys actys the world / Brothyr,
Y vndyrstonde he hathe no mo to whaytt vppon hym but yow.
Do yowr dewte, and at my comyng to Calles I shall do myne. 20
I thynke hewry owr iij tyll com to Calles. I hoppe to be wyth yow
shorttly. I pray recomeavnde me to owr ffathyr, and to owr
brothyr, and say vnto owr ffathyr the next trosty man that comyth
shall bryng hym x li. Wrytt at Andewarpe xxvij day of Septembyr
lxxvj, in grett hasst. 25

per yowr brothyr, George Cely.

*Dorse*: A my brothyr Rychard Cely, beyng at Calles at host wyth
Thomas Kesten, soit dd.

## 5. *William Maryon at London to George Cely at Calais, 28 September 1476*

s.c.i 53/4

### Jhesu

Ryght reuerent syre and my specyall frend, I recomaund me vnto
you. Ferdermor, and yt plesse you, ye schall vnderstond that
Y haue schypped in the George of London, Wylliam Wellson
beyng master, ix packys d. of fellys contaynyng iij M¹ viijᶜl fellys,
the whych fellys leyyt in the for-rom of the sayd schyppe, v packys 5
iijᶜ d., and the remenant leyyt abaft the mast vpon John Tamys

4. 4 wrytt] my *canc.*    10 ⟨matter⟩: *ms.* martter    11 yll *canc.*?
17 as] as *canc.*

fellys, the wyche fell*ys* war Thomas Kestenys, and thay war
arested be Thomas Hadam for the som of lx li. Syr, ye schall
vnderstond that Tho*mas* Kesten hat y-wreten vnto me that Y
10  schuld fynd the way and the men to saff the cortte harmeles her,
and taake the fell*ys* for myn own, that Y schuld be sewyr of that
som in dyschargyng of the sewyrteys and allso in p*a*rty of payment
of seche goodys as he ys owyng vnto me, as ye know well, and
therfor, syr, I pray you that ye woll ressayue them as myn own
15  proper good, and so yt ys, and allso I pray you that ye woll pay
the freyght and all hoder scostys theroff. Syr, Y pray you that ye
woll reco*m*aund me vnto my mastere youre fader, and allso vnto
youre broder Rechard, and ye may say vnto hem that Hary
Seyseld reco*m*aunde hem vnto yowre brodere Rechard Cely, and
20  he prayd hem harteley that he would bey for hem ij vernakelys,
seche as youre broder Roberd hatt y-yeuen vnto Sent Tolowys
scryssche. No mor vnto you at thys tym, but the Trenyte haue you
in hys kepyng. Wreten at London the xxviij day of Septembere,
a*n*no lxxvj.

25                      Be youre owne, Wyll*ia*m Maryon.

*Dorse*: Wnto George Cely, marchant of the Stapull at Calles, thys
lettere be delyuerde. (*Seal, partly covered by binding.*)

## 6. *Thomas Kesten to George Cely, 1476*
s.c.ı 53/6

### Jhesis Mˡiiijᶜlxxvj

Goode ande speceall ffrende, I beseche you to recomaunde me
vnto my mays*ter* your ffader, and to my gosse Robert Cely, ande
to your broder ande my goode ffrende Ric*har*d Cely. It*em* ande
I haue wretton to my wyffe ⌐to take an acteon⌐ by ande w*yth* the
5  adwisse of you as my speceall ffrende vpon Thom*a*s Adam the
elder ys god*ys*, vpon a reconeng for l li. Fl., ande vpon the god*ys*
of Wyll*ia*m Adam for the som of xl li. Fl., and I pray y[ou] to
delyu*er* my wyffe the xl s. that I delyu*er* you. It*em* I pray [you] to
be ⌐good⌐ ffrende to my wyffe in helpeng her in all s[e]che theng
10  as sche hathe to done, as in that at may be ffor the plessure of my

6. 4 wyffe] to *canc.*

mayst*er* yowre fader ande yowre ande my f⟨r⟩end*ys*, and Jh*e*sis
kepe you, amen.

per Thom*a*s Kesten.

*Dorse*: A Jorge Cely soit del*ivré*.

## 7. *Thomas Miller* (?), [*1476*]. *Copy in G. Cely's hand*
s.c.1 53/202

Syr, and yt pless yowr mast*e*rschypp [. . .] thys man has sayd
ffor hymsellf as whell as he con. I besek ȝe gew me l[e]f[fe to
say for m]yselffe, etc.

Syr, and yt plessyth yowr mast*e*rshypp [the]re beth devars of
my mastyrs her ⌈*þat*⌉ thynk*ys* that at I do ys ffor none othyr but 5
to deffravde thys man, thynkyng that thes fell*es* wher shyppyd
by collar in the name of Wyll*i*am Maryon. Syr, I wholl nott say
the contrary but they wher Thomas Kestenys fell*es*, but I woll
do ytt good as an Crestyn man how to do. Wyll*i*am Maryon hade
nevyr i-delt w*yth* them but ffor soyche dewte as whas bytuyxt 10
Thom*a*s Kesten and hyme, and norhowyr Wyll*i*am Maryon
stondyth chargyd by the men of thes fellys to sawe the suyrteys
that bethe bovnde vnto Thom*a*s Adam and Wylliam Adam harmles, and moreovyr syr, I do yt good, the Kyng hawyng hys cost*u*m
and thes suyret*ys* savyd harmeles ancordyng/ The rest whyll nott 15
sarwe Wyll*i*am Maryon by xx li. Y trost to God yowr cousan woll
not that Wyll*i*am Maryons good showld pay Thom*a*s Kestenys
dett*ys*.

Syr, and ytt pless yowr mast*e*rschypp, I pott an casse: thes fell*es*
hade bene drovnyd by the whay or takyn w*yth* henmyys, who 20
showld a ben callyd vppon ffo*r* costom and sobsyde?

I beseke yowr mast*e*rschypp and my mastyrs all ȝe whyll
menystyr yowr law vnto me so that I shall nott nede to seke none
hodyr ways.

*No address or subscription.*

**7.** 12 chargyd] vn *canc.*     13 vnto *repeated*

**8.** *Richard Cely the younger at London to George Cely at Calais, 28 October* [*1476*]

s.c.1 53/204

Welbelouyd brother George, I recomend me harttely onto you. Lyke yt you to wet the cauys of Thomas Mylars com*m*yng ys to se how he may be dyschargyd, for he ys sewyrte for lx li. for the fell*ys* that my godfather schyppyd last, lyke as he wyll inform you
5 at hys com*m*yng, and as for the tother ij, dar not schew ther hedd*ys*, and as for Thomas Myller wyll do nothyng in thys mat*er* byt as my father and ʒe wyll awys hym. Also my godfather onderstond that ʒe haue sent to Thomas Kesten for the lett*er* that he wrat. And ʒe haue that lett*er* then he prayes you that ʒe wolld take
10 the lett*er* that ys closyd in thys lett*er*, ewe ʒe thynke yt be beste so for to do, and ryed to Bregys to Thomas Kesten, and desyer hym to make another lett*er* bett*er* then thys ys aft*er* your intent, acordyng to the lett*er* that ys in my lett*er* at I wrat to my father— Kyrstower Brvn ys ma*n* was the brynger therof. And eve so be
15 that Thomas Kesten make yt danger so to wrytte, my godfather wolde that ʒe schuld intret hym, and gewe wnto hym x or xij li., or more, and ʒe se that yt wolld make all the remna*n*[t] sew[er . . .] godfathers tryst ys nov on you a[. . . godfa]ther letters and thes lettyrs at ʒ[e wot] not w[hat] be yn thym. My godfather ys hewe
20 [and] wyl be tyll he he[yr] better tydyng*ys*. I wryt no mor to you a[t] thys, byt I porpos to wryt mor schortly. Jh*e*su kepe you. Wryt at London the xxviij day of Octobur.

per Rychard Cely.

I pray you recomend me to my brother Robard, and yt ys teld me
25 owr ger ys in Temys. And my syst*er* hys wyef ys in good hell, byt Wyll*i*am hys prentes ys sor syke.

*Dorse*: Wnto my brother George Cely at Cales, be [t]hys delyu*er*yd.


**9.** *William Maryon at London to George Cely at Calais, 5 November* [*1476*]

s.c.1 53/5

Jhesu

Ryght reuerent syr and my specyall frende, I reco*m*aund me vnto you. Ferdermor, and yt plesse you ye schall vnderstond that I haue

ressayued a lettere from you, wreten at Calles the second day of
Nou*em*bere, and anoder lettere i-closed in youre lettere of Thomas
Kestenys hand, wreten at Breges. The wyche boothe letterys 5
I haave well vnderstond, and how that Thomas Kesten ys dys-
sposed for to put me sclen away from the fell*ys* the wyche Y
schypped last at London, that Y schuld haue no *pre*ferment be
them in the neyhyng of my mony. Syr Y vnderstond by youre
wrytyng that Thomas Kesten woll co*m* vnto Callys schorteley, 10
and wan that he comyt, syr, Y pray you harteley that my master
youre fadere and ye woll labor vnto Thomas Kesten, ⌐yeff ye
thynke yt best so for to do,¬ seyng Thomas Adam y-serued and
Thomas Mellere y-dysscharged, then Y wovld that Thomas
Kesten and you mytht acorde and agree togedere for the forsayd 15
fe[ll], Thomas Ad[am] y-served, that ye myt haue of the sayd
fell*ys* a ij M¹ [. . .] party of payment of the mony [. . .] as for the
rest of the mony [. . .] and he can agree, and Y woll hovld me
plesed. And yeff that [Thomas] Kesten woll nat be agreabell vnto
thys b[arg]en he [b]e neydere Goddys man nayder manys, but 20
the de[w]e[llys . . .] that thys be a good way for to doo Y pray you
[. . .] as [my] trust ys in you, etc. Syr I pray you that ye woll
recom*a*und me vnto my mast*er* youre fadere, and ye may say vnto
hem that my maysterys youre modere haue i-ressayued from John
Cely ys viij sarpelerys of woll, and Y vnderstond he woll send 25
v sarpelerys yt morre. Y lokt for them eu*er*y day. Wreten at London
the v day of Nouemb*er*.

Be youre owne
Wylli*a*m Maryon.

*Dorse*: Wnto Georg Cely, ma[rchant] of the Stapull at [Calles, 30
thys] letter be delyuerd.

## 10. *John Spencer at London to George Cely at Calais, 2 December [? 1476]*

s.c.1 53/35

Ryght worschypfull s*ir and* my faythfull frend, I recomaund me
vnto yowe, dyssyrynge to heyr of y*our* welfayr, hertely thankyng
yowe of the greht cheyr *and* welfayr þat I had w*yth* yowe at many
*and* dyuers tymys, also of y*our* greit labor *and* besynes seth my
dep*ar*ture, the whych at my power I schall dyssaruf at sych tyme 5

as þat ʒe *and* I meyt togedure. Lettynge yowe wyt that I haue
mayd exchange w*yth* Thom*a*s Abram of London, grocer, for xx li.
st*er*., wherof I haue receuyd x li. st*er*., and schall receyf the rest
at sych days as he *and* I be agreyd of. Wherfor I p*r*ay yowe þat ʒe
10 pay vnto hyme xxv li. Fl. of sych mony as ʒe haue of myn, and
þ*a*t ther be no defaut of payment of the sayd xxv li. to the sayd
Thom*a*s or his atto*ur*ney in no man*er*, for I haue fond hym so
curtes in his delyng þ*a*t I wold not for twyse the walur he were
dysspontyd at the syght of hys byll. No mor at þys tym, bot the
15 Trenyte haue yowe in hys kepyng. Wryttun at London the secund
day of December, etc.

                              Y*ou*r awne Jhon Spenc*er*.

Also sir, I p*r*ay yow to tacke of Thom*a*s Abram the byll wherin
I am bonde*n*; also a byll the whych he schall mayke vnto yowe for
20 the odur x li. the which byll muste [be payde wythin] xiiij after
Candellmase, etc.

*Dorse*: To the ryght worschipful George Cele, merchand of the
Stapull at Cales be þys delyu*er*d.

*In G. Cely's hand*:

Item vppon the Fr⟨i⟩day in Estyr wyeke I delyuyrd vnto my
25 ffadyr my byll off x[. . .] off hosscloth [bo]the p*aya*bull the last
day of Jovne next comyng. I delyueryd at vij s. x d. Sum xj li.
xij s. vj d. Fl. Item, I most set thys in my new reconyng. Item,
I lewe w*yth* my brodyr Ry*char*d to by ffell*es*—x li. st*er*.

**11.** *Richard Cely the elder at London to George Cely at
Calais, 26 January 1476/7*
s.c.1 53/197

                    Jh*e*su M¹iiij*c* lxxvj

I grete the wyll, and I haue grete marvele that ye wryt not to me
no letters of syche ty⟨dy⟩ngys as ⌐ye⌐ haue at Caleys, the weche
ys meche speche of at London, for the weche I cannot wryt to the
nothyng for lake of vnderstan⟨d⟩yng how it stand in the pertys
5 of the Dewke of Borgens londys and the Kyng of Franse, for here
ys strange spekyng, for the weche I pray the be wyse, and be not
or-haste in sale *and* delyueryng of good into Flanders, for I fere
me sore of ware, and the Dewke be dede, as it ys sayd, and the

**10.** 13 curtes] þat *canc.*     24 the *repeated*     **11.** 4 lake *ch. from* loke

Kyng of Franse enterd into Pecardy, as men saye, for the weche
I pray the se wyll to. And also say to Thomas Kesten that he    10
promysyd to me that the x s. of sarplere scholl be payd to John
Tate, the weche ys not payd, for the weche I haue grete callyng
for the payment there, and Wyll Maryon *and* Robard Cely for
there perte, for the weche I am not wyll plesyd wyt Kesten for
that mater, werefor wryt me answere wat he saythe, and also wat   15
pontment makyt wyt Byfylde and all hoder men there as he ys
intreted to, and saye to Thomas Kesten I tryste to hym that he
wyll haue in rememborans ys promyse mayde to me wan I
delyuerd hym plate, that I schall be plesyd wyt som payment of
hym wyt hoder men. And he wyll do soe I schall be ys good    20
frende, and that he schall wyll understand in tyme to com, for
the weche I wyll be glade for to doe for hym and wyll hymselve.
I wryt no more to the at thys tyme, but Jh*e*su kepe you. Wryt at
London the xxvj day of Jeneuer in grete haste.

p*er* Rychard Cely.    25

*Dorse*: To Jorge Cely at Caleys be thys delyuer. (*Seal and drawing
of shield.*)

## 12. *Richard Cely the elder at London to George Cely at Calais, 23 May 1477*

S.C.1 53/7

Jh*e*su M¹iiij<sup>c</sup> lxxvij

I grete the wyll, and I understand there com no marchauntys to
Caleys for to bye woll nor fellys, for the weche ys ryght heuy⌐nese⌐
for the marchauntys of the Stapyll, for the weche I fere me euery
man wyll fende the mene for the sale *and* delyuer ys woll *and* fellys
into svre men ys handys be the mene of sale to marchauntys    5
strangers the weche haue repayryd to Caleys afor thys tyme, for
the weche I wolde ye hadde commyngaschon wyt syche marchauntys as ye haue fonde svre men *and* good men, for to aventer
som of my woll *and* fell in there handys be the mene of sale at long
dayys, for I fele men schall do so at thys seson, for the weche   10
I wolde thynke taht John Underhaye were a good man for ⌐to⌐
tryste *and* hoder men syche as ye thynke good men. Spare not for

11. 15 answere wat] wat *repeated*    and *repeated*
12. 11 to *over canc.* the

a long day, for I fere me it wyll com thereto, for I understande
wyll there be dyvers men of the Felychepe of the Stapyll of Caleys
15 haue solde woll for iij ȝere day, the laste payment, *and* the pryse
kepyt, *and* the money xxij s. viij d. for the li. Also for money be
exchonge at London ys vij s. x d. Fl., for vj s. viij d. st*er*., *and* for
to resayue at London in hand *and* for to delyuer at Bregys at
a monyth day after, vij s. x d. Fl. for vj s. viij d. st*er*., for the weche
20 I can thynke money wyll better thys marte noe, for the weche doe
as wyll as ye can, for I haue not schargyd the wyt a peny. Nor send
me no st*er*. money, for the lose ys to grete at thys seson. I wryt
no more at thys tyme, but Jhe*su* kepe. Wryte at London the xxiij
day of May in haste.

25                              *per* Rychard Cely.

*Dorse*: To Jorge Cely at Caleys be thys letter delyuerd. (*Shield*.)

## 13. *Richard Cely the elder at London to George Cely at Calais, 26 June 1477*

s.c.1 59/46

Jhe*su* M¹iiijᶜ lxxvij

I grete the wyl, and I thynke long tyl I haue wrytyng from the of
syche maters as ye haue to doe for me at the marte. God send you
a good marte, *and* me also. Ye schall understand that Robard Cely
*and* Thomas Folbord my pryntys be comyng to Caleys, for I muste
5 make the forsayd Thomas Folborne, my prentys, freman of the
Staple wytin iiij ȝere of ys terme, the weche ys viij ȝere as aperyt
be ys endentur, for the weche I wyll ye doe youre pert for me to
make hym freman. I wryt no more to you at thys tyme, but Jhe*su*
kepe you. Wryt at London the xxvj day of Jun in grete haste.

10                              *per* Rychard Cely the elder.

*Dorse*: To Jorge Cely at Caleys be thys delyu*er*. (*Seal and shield*.)

## 14. *Jan Vanderheyden at Mechlin to George Cely at Calais, 9 October 1477*

s.c.1 53/8

Ghemynde wrient, wet dat Ic U se*ere* groete messter Soersse
ende Ic late U wette*n* by myn hant ghescryft*e* hoe dat ghy wel wet

dat wy te gaeder ghesproke*n* hebbe*n* ⌐van⌐ wollen die ghy my
sendden sout by Ryke*n* Joes Wranx factoer ghelijc also ghy wel
wet. En*de* daer um scrywe Ic Jan Vanderheyde*n* aen U Soersse 5
Seely goede wrient en*de* late U wette*n* dat ghy my wylt senden iiij
sacken myddel Cutsewout schoen ghebont ghelyc als Ic my toet
U betrowe: te wettene, iij nwe en*de* j out. Item, wet Soersse
soe sulle*n* wy te Bergghe*n* alle dynch wel eens sijn wylt God. Sent
my de beste Soersse en*de* scrijft my ghelieft U yet dat Ic doir U 10
doe*n* maech. Ghescreue*n* te Mechele*n* a*n*no lxxvij ix in October.
                                      By Jan Vanderheyde*n*.

*Dorse*: De*n* erbaren Soersse Seely, coepma*n* vande*n* Stappel at
Caelijs, sal[ut]. (*Merchant's mark*.)

[Dear friend, I greet you well, master George, and confirm in
writing that, as you will remember, we agreed that you should
send me some wool by Ryken, factor of Joes Wranx. So I, Jan
Vanderheyden, write to you, my good friend George Cely, and
let you know to send me four sarplers middle Cotswold, good
packing: that is three new and one old, as I trust you. And God
willing, I shall pay you [literally, 'we shall see all well'] at Bergen-
op-Zoom. Send me the best, George, and let me know anything
that I can do for you. Written at Mechlin, 9 October 1477.

To the worshipful George Cely, merchant of the Staple of Calais.
Greeting.]

## 15. *Robert Cely at London to George Cely at Calais, 19 November 1477*

s.c.i 53/9

### A*n*no lxxvij

Ryght welbelouyd brother, I recomaunde me herttelly to yow.
Farthermore pleesse yt yow to wette that I heue ressayuyd fro
yow a lett*er* wrette at Calles the xxx day of Octobor, in the weche
lett*er* wer clossyd iiij lett*erys* of paymentte, werof ij ben dyrect
to Rychard Twege, merc*er*, of London, bothe lett*erys* contaynynge 5
lij li. Item, allsso ij lett*erys* of paymentte dyrecte to John Cowlard,
merc*er*, contaynynge bothe xx li. The dayys ben longe ∥ I care for
nothynge saue butt ffor my ffellmen of Barmessay Strette, ffor
thay wyll be nedy and call faste on me for mony er M[arc]he be

10 paste. Brother Gorge, I pray yow sp⟨e⟩ke scharply to John
Raunsse of Gynys for the fferme of Senttercasse, ffor Wylliam the
parsson ys man ys att London and cawlthe faste on me for mony,
and alsso I honderstonde that ȝee haue lentte to the Plasse for me
xx li. I moste preste here at London x li., *and* howr father xx li.
15 Yt ys a scherewde werke, God amende yt. Item, brother, as apon
the Sonday afore the datte of thys letter my brother Rychard Cely
*and* I wer at Pollys Crosse to here the sarmon, and ther we herde
fforste word that howr wncull the Dene of Ȝorke ys passyd to God,
and the prechar prayyd for hym by name, and ther sate that tyme
20 v bochoppys at Pollys Crosse // No more to yow at thys tyme, bott
howr Lorde kepe yow. Wrette at London the xix day of Nouember.

> By yowr brother,
> Robart Cely.

*Dorse*: A George Cely, marchande of the Staple at Calles, thys be
25 delyuerd.

### 16. *Draft in the name of Richard Cely, 28 February 1477/8*

s.c.1 53/198

Honorable *and* worshipfull sir, after all humble *and* due reuerence
had as apparteyneth / Y recomaunde me vnto you, desyring to
here of your prosperous welfare, which Jhesu preserue to th'ac-
complysshment of your hertys desire / Please it your mastership
5 to haue noticion and knowleche that late Y receyved a lettre beryng
date atte Caleys the x^th day of this present moneth of Feuerer to
me depected by the right worshippfull the Lyeftenaunt of the
Staple of Caleys, by the which lettre Y vnderstond þat ⌐it was
enformed your saide maystership⌐ that Y shold report vngodely
10 language by you *and* youres / Wherof Y gretly marvayle that eny
suche synistre or wrong suggestion shuld be ⌐made or⌐ reported
of me vnto your saide mastership / Wherfore Y call allmyghty God
to ⌐wittnes *and*⌐ record ⌐þat⌐ Y never made report ⌐to any maner
persone⌐ of any suche or other vngodely language by you ⌐sade
15 maystership nor any of yours by⌐ the which ⌐ye⌐ shuld take any

---

**16.** 2 as] appareth *canc.*          8 þat] your saide mastership is enformed *canc.*
13 made] any *canc.*          14 by you] nor youres thurgh *canc.*          15 ⌐ye⌐
*subst. for* you ar any of youres owe or

displeser ayenst me/ and therupon ⌜Y am⌝ *and* will be redy atte all
tymes to do theryn as a trew Cristen man. And as Y am enformed
there ⌜was⌝ bytwene Thomas Blakh*am* *and* my wyf causes vrgent,
for the which Y haue had her in ⌜sharp⌝ examynacion. Nat-
w*yth*stondyng Y ca*n*nat haue none o*þ*er vnderstondyng but *þ*at    20
suche language *þ*at was reported to *þ*e saide Thom*as* Blakh*am* was
not by her spoken nor seyde, for *and* yf Y cowde haue had due
knowleche *þ*erof Y wold haue had corrected her *þ*at she shuld haue
remembred it dury*n*g her lyf, wherfore s*ir* Y hertly beseche *and*
pray you atte *þ*e reu*er*ence of Jh*es*u co*n*sidery*n*g *þ*e feithfull love    25
*þ*at Y owe *and* bere towardys you *and* so will do dury*n*g my lyf,
that ye will vouchesaif to set asyde all siche sinstre suggestions *and*
seyingys ayenst me in *þ*at behalf, *and* to shew to me *and* myne *þ*e
fauo*ur* *and* hertly love of yo*ur* saide maystership, as my s*er*uice
shall be to you redy at yo*ur* comm*and*ement, *and* as Y *and* myne    30
shall be bounde to pray to God for yo*ur* pr*e*seruacion in felicite to
be pr*e*serued oure lyfys dury*n*g. Wrete atte Lee *þ*e xxviij day of
Fev*er*er a*n*no lxxvij by yo*ur* owne Rich*ard* Cely.

                                                        T. P.

*No address.*                                                      35


**17.** *Draft of letter in the name of Richard Cely to the*
*Lieutenant of the Staple, 28 February 1477/8*

s.c.1 53/198 dorse

Right worshipfull s*ir*, Y recomm*au*nde me vnto your gode maystyr-
ship, desiryng to here of your pr*o*sperous welfare, which Jh*es*u

16 therupon] yam *canc.*          17 man] owith to do / and therfore Y beseche &
pray you to take none displesir w*yth* me, but to owe me your gode fauo*ur* &
hertly love in suche wyse as ye haue done hereafore / trustyng in God ye shall
have none other cause *canc.*          18 ⌜was⌝ *subst. for* hathe bene          19 examyna-
cion] & Y can not vnderstond, prevy ne appert, *þ*at any suche language as was
reported to Thomas Blakh*am* was by her spoken or seyde / and yf Y cowde haue
⌜had⌝ vnderstondyng therof *þ*at she had so done Y shuld haue geven her suche
correccion therfore that she shuld haue bene remembred therof dury*n*g her lyf
/ Wherfore s*ir* Y desyre & hertly pray (ys *canc.*) ⌜you⌝ atte reu*er*ence of Jh*es*u to
owe me & myn your gode fauo*ur* & mastership in suche wyse as ye haue done
afore / So that Y & myn shall be bounde to pray God for the pr*e*seruacion of
yo*ur* saide mastership, in felicite to be pr*e*served oure lyfes dury*n*g. Wrote atte
London the *canc.*          20 *þ*at *over* as          23 her] as *canc.*          25 you]
ayenst me on *þ*at behalf *interl. and canc.*

*prese*rue to yo*ur* cordyall desyre, thankyng you hertly of yo*ur*
grete gentilnes ⌐*and* tender fauo*ur*¬ to me hereafore shewde wherof
5 Y beseche you of co*n*tynuance. Certefyn[g] ⌐you¬ that I receyved
a *lett*re from you wreten atte Caleys the x*th* day of this *pres*ent
moneth off Feue*r*[er] for the which Y hertly thancke you that it
pleasyd you so to doo, and I trust to God in tyme com*m*yng to
dese*r*ue it to yo*ur* ⌐saide¬ mastership. The teno*ur* of which *lett*re
10 Y vnderstode ryght wele *and* therupon haue wreten ⌐to mayster
T. Prout¬ myn excuse of þe wrongfull suggestion þer ys made
ayenst me/ and s*ir*, eny se*r*uice that Y ⌐can or¬ may do for yo*ur*
maystership ⌐here¬ is and shall be r⟨e⟩dy atte yo*ur* desyre, as oure
Lord God knowith, who Y beseche to *prese*rue you and youres in
15 felicite long duryng.

*No address.*

### 18. *John Dalton at Calais to George Cely at London, 24 March 1477/8*

s.c.1 53/10

Right welbeluffyd brother, I recomaunde me vnto you, s*er*tyffyeng
you that her was Daneyll Van the Rayde, and yt was soo he
desseryd j s*arp*eller of yo*ur* olde wooll for redy money. I myght
noot deny hym yt, and so he hayth won, the n° xxxij, j sac di.,
5 xviij cl. of goode Co*tty*swolde acordyng to þe *pr*ice and ordenance
for redy money, wych amontyd vnto xxv li. and od money, and
her was Jois Francke, and he dessereyd to haue hayd such olde
woll as you hayd leyeft, the ton hallff in havnde, the todor at
Syncyon next, and I tolde hy*m* he schulde geyff me redy money
10 or he went owt of Cales or ell*ys* he schulde haueff no wooll of me
at thys tyme, and soo we dep*ar*tyd. Alsoy s*ir*, ȝe schall ond*er*stond
that I intende to dep*art* into Ynglond as sone as the martt y*s* done,
wherfor yff you come not yo*ur*sellff I *pr*ay you sende me word
whom you wyll that I schall leyff such thengk*ys* of you*r*s as my
15 brother Wyll*ia*m D. leyfft w*yth* me of you*r*s. No mor to you at

**17.** 3 preserue] of th *canc.*     4 to me] shewde *canc.*     8 doo] for the
which *canc.*     11 T. Prout: *reading conjectural.*     12 ayenst me] as God
know*yth* who Y beseche to *prese*rue you *and* yours in felicite long durying *canc.*
eny] thyng *canc.*

**18.** 7 such] *4 letters canc.*     13 yff] you *canc.*

thys tyme, but Jhesu kep you. Wretton at Cales the xxiiij day of March, Anno M¹iiij⁣ᶜ lxxvij⁣ᵗʸ.

Be your B.

John Dalton.

*Dorse*: To Jorge Cely at London, marchaunt of the Staple at 20 Cales, be thys letter lyuerd.

## 19. *Richard Cely the younger at London to George Cely at Calais, 26 March 1478*

s.c.1 59/38

Jhesu M¹iiij⁣ᶜ lxxviij

Ryught reuerent and harttely welbelouyd brother, I recomend me wnto you, and I thanke you for the grete coste that ȝe dyd on me at your departyng. Fordermor informyng you, at the makyng of thys owr father and mother wher in good heyll, thankyd be God, and sendys yow ther blessyngys. Allso owr father has ressauyd 5 from yow ij lettyrs and the rekenyng of the sale of hys Cotsolde f⟨e⟩lles, the qweyche he doys well wndyrstond, etc. Syr, your horse farys well and ys in good plyte, byt ȝeyt I cannot sel hym. I schaull do my beste therto, and ther cum a locky man. Syr, I pray ȝe remembyr me, for ȝe know my nessesyte. Hyt ys greyt now, that 10 knowys God.

Syr, heyr ys Rychard Prowde, the bryngar of thys letter, that sent you and me the wenson, has made labor to owr father and me to wryte to you to be good master and frend to hym in helppyng hym to sowme good sarwes at Calles tyll he be better 15 akeayntyd ther.

Syr, I haue beyn at Awelay almoste ewer syn ȝe departyd, and my Loorde of Sent Jo[nys] lay at B. Pasmars iij dayes, and I wos ther wyth hym, and I browt hym from owr father ij grette lawmprays, and he toke them thankefully, and euery nyte I had iij of 20 hys gentyllmen home to ly vyth me, and I mad them good scher, and syne that tyme I had the wycwr of Awelay, and the preste of Awelay, and the preste of Berweke vyth ⌜me⌝ iij nytys, and dynyd and suppyd, and lay wyth me, and thay be good schotterys and manarly fellows avll iij, and wyl be redy to do for me at all tymus. 25

Thay ar con[tr]ay men born in Walys, in my*n* oncles paryche at Gresford.

Syr, the xxij day of Marche I saw iij as greyt harttys in owr whete as eu*er* I sau in my lyue, abowte none dayes, and the same
30 day at euy*n* I hard a fesaunte koce crow. Owr whelpys wax fayr, and Ect*er* ys a far hond, and a fat. Hys soor ys hooll. Syr, I wryte to you of aull thyng*ys*, as well of japys as sad mattars, lyke as I promysyd you at owr departyng, etc. Now a lett*er* from you to me wer grette cu*m*forde. Syr, owr father wolde that ʒe wolde send
35 hym wrytyng how that ʒe heyr of owr inbasseturs, and whate ansfor thay haue of the Dewyke. Owr father sayes he cannot wryt to you tyll he heyr what thay haue don, a trestys to yowr wysdu*m* that ʒe wyll do at the next mart w*yth* that at ys growyn, to the leste lose tat may be. No mor to you at thys tyme. Jh*es*u kepe you.
40 Wryttyn at London the xxvj day of Marche

                                        *p*er yowr brother, Rychard Cely.

*Dorse*: Syr, owr brother Robard*ys* mane come to me and sayd that hys mast*er* leuyd a cheste w*yth* me at hys departyng. Syr, I pray ʒe say to hym I had none, ner he delyu*er*yd me none: ʒe
45 war at hys departyng as well as I // Wyll*i*am Cely tellys me that he was v*yth* owr brother at hys departyng from Bottons, and ther he sawe a lyttyll cheste in hys chambur, and owr brother lockyd hys bokys therin, and sent you the caye be Wyll*i*am Cely, byt he leuyd the cheste at Bottons. Syr, and he had byd me farwell
50 I wolde a prayd you to a co*m*mendyd me to hym.

I praye you to recomend me ⌜to⌝ owr ostes and aull the felly-schyp. Syr, owr father desyr you, and I pray you, to be frendlly in speky*n*g for a sarwes for Rychard Prowde. Hys labor ys gret to vs, and he trestys myche in you, and owr father gawe hym xx d.
55 at hys departyng.

A my welbelouyd brother George Cely, m*er*chante of the Stapull at Call*es*, beyng at oste v*yth* Bornell*es* whedow in Call*es*, so hyt dd. (*Seal, the same as that of Richard Cely senior.*)

**19.** 26 my*n*] no *canc.*        37 a] th *canc.*

**20.** *Richard Cely the elder at London to George Cely at Calais, 1 May 1478*

s.c.1 53/199

Jhesu M¹iiij° lxxviij

I grete the wyll, and I wryt to the at thys tyme as I understand we sshal ⌈paye⌉ howre custon *and* subsete at Caleys to the sodears sterlyng money, xxiiij s. for the li. Were we payd xxj s. iiij d. Flemyche, we schall paye from henys forwarde after the rate of ster., that ys, ij ryallys for a li., hoder goldys after the rate *and* 5 the valve of the same. I was wyt the Mayar of the Stapyll *and* the felychepe wyt the Kyng and ys lordys of ys Consell for thys mater, and there the mater was declarede be the Recordar of London *and* the answere was playnely schol be non hoder wyse— the acte of Parlement ys to paye them in sterlyng money, and so 10 thay wyll be payd. The cavse I wryt to the ys for to beware ⌈of⌉ resayuyvng of syche goldys as gryte lose ys in at Caleys. The schepyng ys begone at London, but I doe notyng tyll the tyme I haue wrytyng from the, the weche ys long of comyng as me semyth. The laste day of Apperell I haue resayuyd ij letters from 15 the, a let[ter wrete] at Caleys the xvij day of Apperell, be the weche I understande youre comyng t[o] Caleys, the toder letter wrete at Caleys the xxiiij day of Apperell, the weche I understand wyll. Ye schall understand the mater be thys letter of t[he] concleseon notyng for the welle of the Felychepe of the Stapyll, but men 20 schepe faste at London, werefor I am avysyd for to schepe xix sarplerys *and* a poke of my Cottyswolde woll, the weche was of John Busche gaderyng, of the same that ys to selle at Caleys, for the weche I wyll ye make som sale and ye may doe wyll *and* svere, for I fere me men ⌈will⌉ sele schortely wan the plete com to Caleys. 25 John Cely hathe bogwyt for me iij M¹ fell, but thay be not com to London yete. I pray the send me wrytyng as sone as ye can of youre avyse, for I wyll aponte me thereafter in schepyng of my woll, *and* as I haue conford from you. I wryte no more to you at thys tyme, but Jhesu kepe you. Wryte at London the fryste day 30 of May in haste.

*per* Rychard Cely.

*Dorse*: To Jorge Cely at Caleys be thys delyuer. (*Seal and shield.*)

**20.** 18 Caleys the] toder *canc.*          31 in *repeated*

**21.** *Robert Cely at London to George Cely at Calais, 5 May 1478*

S.C.I 53/11

Anno lxxviij

Ryght trosty syr and brother, I comaunde me to yow, fertherm[or]e
inf[or]mynge yow [that] at the [ma]kynge of thys let[t]er howrre
father [and] mother and all howr good frendys wer in goode
hell[the], blessyd be God, and so we hope that ʒee be ‖ Brother

5   George, the cawsse [necess]ery of my wrytynge to yow at thys
tyme ys tys: for sothe ther ys grette chepynge now at London of
ppellys and wollys to Calleswarde, God be ther spede, and I
cannatte schepe no ffellys before the ffeste of Wyttsontyde, botte
sone haufeter I hope to God to doo ‖ I ham notte well intredyd,

10  ffor I haue notte mony by me to pay the xvj s. viij d. of the sarpler
hafter the ratte, for of the secutorys of Cowlarde I haue no comffortte of paymentte ‖ And as for Rycharde Twge ys notte corttes
yn ys dellynge, for hee hathe payd me [b]y xx s. *and* by xl s.
lewde payment, and wen I wolld haue x li. I cowde notte haue ytt

15  att my nede bott I mo[st]e geue hym viij d. for a galon of wyne
ande ʒette hee kepe in hys honde xx s. st*er*. the weche ʒee schowlde
haue of Wyytte ys man. I pray yow sende me worde wether yt be
soo or nott, for moche sorow and angere haue I hade *wyth* hym
for ressayuynge of my mony. I pray yow delyuer hym no more of

20  my mony: he saythe yow lettyll worchepe, that yow schowlde
howe ys man xx s. and abatte ytt of my dewtte. I pray yow tell
ytt hym. No more to yow at thys tyme, bott allmyty God haue ws
all in ys blessyd kepynge. Wrette att Londo[n] the v day of Maye.

By yowr brother, Robart Cely.

25  *Dorse*: A George Cely ma⟨r⟩chand of the Staple at Calles thys
let*er* be delyuerde, etc.

**22.** *George Cely at Calais to Richard Cely the elder at London, 8 May 1478*

S.C.I 53/12

Jhesu M¹iiijᶜ lxxviij

Ryght whorshyppffull ffadyr, afftyr all dew recomendassyon pretendyng I recomeavnd me vnto yow yn the most lowlyest whysse
that I con or may ‖ Fordyrmor plesyth yt yow to vndyrstonde Y

resseywyd an lettyr ffrom yow wrytt at London the fforst day of
May, the wheche lettyr I hawe rede and do whell vndyrstonde /  5
I ffelle be yowr sayd letter ytt ys conclewdyd wyth the Kyng and
hys Covnsell that whe shall pay the sowdyar starlyng mony.
Whe wher at losse ynowe affore, thow ytt be no mor. Mony ys stylle
at Calles ij s. vj d. ⌐lowar¬ than ytt ys in Flavndyrsse, and now
starleng mony, to that ytt ys to grett an losse // Whe most soffyr  10
ytt, whe may nott chesse // Me semyth yff ytt cowd be browght
anbowght that whe myght hawe an quyne at Calles agen, and lat
none hodyr mony go in the towne of Calles but starlyng mony,
than showld whe make bettyr shyfft and ytt showld nott torne vs
to so grett losse // For now as the casse stondythe at thys tyme ⌐ther  15
ys no merchant þat¬ spende an grott in the towne of Calles but
they lesse an halpeny, and men of the Stapell breng the mony to
Calles that ys browght. ᴈe may se what losse ys in grett somys, but
yff the Mayre and the Fellyshyp seke an remedy herffor ytt
whyll be ffor the Fellyshyp to grett an losse, etc. // Plesyth ytt  20
yow to whett Y ffelle by yowr wryttyng the shyp at London; and
ᴈe wold shyp and ᴈe myght hawe any comeffortt. In good ffayth
ytt wher whell done that ᴈe sheppyd; also ᴈe shall stonde in as
good casse as any hothyr man, and whan ytt ys at Calles the venter
ys borne. I thanke God ᴈe hawe growyn at Calles to answer the  25
costys and ⌐chargys¬ of the same, and houyr and abowe that I trost
to God to make yow houyr at thys marte C li. ster. and mor, and
I may be whell payd as my hoppe ys Y shall be. In any whysse
latt yowr ffellys come thys next sheppyng, and yowr xix sarplers
and a poke / and afftyr, yff God send ffayr whedyr and good  30
tydyngys, ᴈe may dayly send mor, etc. I woll be the grasse of God
vnto thys Syngsyon martte, and ther I woll speke wyth John
Vandyrhay and soche merchantys as I am acostom to delle wyth.
Y most do as hothyr men dothe, ar ellys Y most kepe stylle.
[Dorse] I vndyrstode by John Daltonys wryttyng at London whan  35
ytt come to me ther þat he myght an sowlde all yowr woll, halffe
in honde, the tothyr halffe at Whyttsontyde/ Ytt whas no mor but
all yowr howld woll, and as ffor the new, ytt ys the iij^{de} peny, vj
monthys and vj monthys, and so myght Y a done syn I come vnto
Calles. The day ys long: Y woll knowe hym ryght whell þat shall  40

---

22. 6 conclewdyd] that canc.              9 ij s. vj d.] lowar over hyar in an canc.
13 starlyng mony] ytt canc.       16 they canc. spende] nott canc.          25 I]
ho canc.         28 In any whysse] thys canc.

hawe any at that day. Y shall se at the marte what Y may do: yff
I can do none bettyr Y most do as hothyr men dothe, etc. Whe
hawe chossyn Robard Tate to be howyr Leffetennavnt and he
most be at Calles wythin thys mony[th]. No mor vnto yow at thys
45 tyme, but Jhesu hawe yow and all yowrs in hys blessyd kepyng,
Amen. Wrytt at Calles the viijᵗʰ day of May, lxxviij.

per yowr son,<br>
G. Cely.

Vnto my ryght whorshypffull ffadyr Rychard Cely, merchant of
50 the Stapell off Calles, dewellyng at London yn Marte Lane, soit
done, etc. (*Shield*.)

### 23. *Richard Cely the elder at London to George Cely at Calais, 18 May 1478*

s.c.1 53/13

Jhesu Mˡiiijᶜ lxxviij

I grete the wyll, and the xviij day of May I resayuyd a letter from
the wryte at Caleys the viij day of May, the weche letter I haue
wyll understande, and as for schepyng of woll or fell, I haue non
schepyn⟨g⟩ at thys day, but be the grace of God I am avysyd for
5 to schepe a perte of my woll; a xx sarplerys or more, *and* fell iij
or iiij Mˡ at thys neste schepyng, the weche ys not as ʒete begone,
nor I soppose schall not tyll thys scheppys com agane from Caleys.
*And* also men wyll here *and* understand of thys Synsson marte,
for the toder marte was not good for the Stapyll—I hope thys
10 schall be good. Thomas Bvrgane, mecer, wylled me to wryte to
the: and ys man wyll haue money at thys marte he wolde haue ⌐of¬
me, for the weche I wyll ye delyuer to ys man before hony hoder
man. As the money in the marte, doe as wyll as ye can. God send
vs a good marte, and good ty⟨d⟩yngys of the warthe, *and* send vs
15 pese; and I pray the kepe ⌐the¬ in good felyschepe to the marte
warde, and in the marte, *and* from the marte to Caleys warde, for
there ys moste drede. I wryte no more, but Jhesu kepe you. Wryte
at London the xviij day of May in haste.

per Rychard Cely

20 *Dorse*: To Jorge Cely at Caleys be thys delyuerd. (*Shield*.)

**23.** 4 schepyn⟨g⟩: *ms. has* schepynt *with* (*meaningless?*) *flourish on the final
letter*        18 at] Caleys *canc.*

### 24. Richard Cely the elder at London to George Cely at Calais, 17 June 1478

s.c.1 53/15

Jhesu M¹iiij<sup>c</sup> lxxviij

I grete the wyll, and I haue resayuyd a letter from the wrete at
Bregys the ix day of Jun, the weche letter I haue wyll understande
euery ponte, and I haue resayuyd closyd in the sayd letter iij
letters of payment acordyng to youre wrytyng be Thomas Granger
bryngar, and I understand wyll the ʒeyng of money be exchange  5
at the marte ys not good, and also I understande be Thomas
Granger the sodears at Caleys wyll not be plesyd for take for ther
payment viij s. Fl. for the nobyll st*er*., for the weche it ys to grete
a lose for the Stapyll to bere after there desyar, for the weche
I am ry⟨ght⟩ sory that I haue chargyd me so sore and so meche,  10
but I wyll understande more of that mater or I schepe woll or fell.
I bogwyt a v M¹ fell in Cottyswolde and they be good. I am
avysyd not for to schepe neder woll nor fell tyll I haue wrytyng
from the of syche maters and resaytys of money at Bregys, that
be the grace of God ye sa[ll] and haue done fuill wyll, and Jhesu  15
for ys grete mersy send a good pesse in the Dvke of Borgans londys,
for ellys wyll be no good marchantys warde. I wryte no more, but
Jhesu kepe you. Wryt at London the xvij of Jun in grete haste.

per Rychard Cely.

*Dorse*: To Jorge Cely at Caleys be thys delyuer. (*Shield*.)    20

### 25. Richard Cely the younger at London to George Cely at Calais or Bruges, 18 June 1478

s.c.1 53/203

Anno Jhesu M¹iiij<sup>c</sup> lxxviij

Ryught harttely welbelouyd and myn aspecyaull good brother,
I recomend me wnto you, informyng you at the makyng of thys
letter owr father and mother fard well, and sendys you ther
blessyngys. Syr, we wndyrstond be Thomas Granger and be your
wrytyng that ʒe far well, thankyd be God, and ys myry at Bregys.  5
Syr, our father woulld that ʒe taryd ther tyll new collecturs wer
schosyn at Calles, for we fer that ⌜ther chargys⌝ wyll be gret the

25. 7 chargys] ʒe *expunged*

next qwartter. S[yr] I haue ressauyd of our fathers gyffte to by
a M¹ fell*ys* w*yth* for you and me, xxx li., and I haue bowyt xij^c
10 good Cottys fell*ys*, pryse le C, iij li., and the caryayge of eu*ery*
lod, xx s. Syr, ther ys not mony ynow for another lod. Syr, I dar
charge ws no farder tyll I haue wrytyng from you: I pray you send
me word hov I schaull be demenyd in byeng of mo fell*ys*. Syr, my
syngler good Loord of Sent Jhonys recomendys hym onto you,
15 and ys glad wen he herys any word from you be me, and he
desyerd me to wryt to you and pray you wen ʒe know eny tydyng*ys*
for certayn that ʒe wold wryet them to me at I myt inform hym,
and that wold be to hym a gret pleseur. Syr, he has geuyn me
a longe gown clothe of hys leueray, and he wolde be wrothe and
20 I cum into Esex and be not w*yth* hym dayly at Meandry [. . .]
   Syr, I onderstond that Thomas Folborn has bovt fell*ys*, and he
wyll wryte to you to do for hym, and at hys fell*ys* may be schyppyd
in yo*ur* name. Syr, me thynk the kenred ys kumbrus, and therfor
hyt wer bet*er* for you not to dell v*yth* them, houbehyt I fynd hym
25 curtes. Byt Syr, I wndyrstond that ovr brother Robard and ʒe and
I ar sewyd at Westmyst*er* for [a fr]ay at wos mad betwen Fulborn,
Petyt, Maudyslay and the gentylma[n a]nd hys men at Myllʒend
in Estyr weke, and ar lyke w*yth*owt G[od hel]pe to be indyty[d],
howbehyt we wer not ther, byt I treste to God to f[yn]de [the]
30 mene to schrape you and me w*yth*. No mor to yow at thys tyme,
Jh*e*su haue you and yours in kepyng. Wrettyn at London the xviij
of Jun.

                                           by your brother,
                                           Rychard Cely.

35 *Dorse*: Vnto my welbelouyd borother George Cely, m*er*chand of
the Estap*e*ll, beyng ⌐at⌐ Calles or at Brgys.


**26.** *Richard Cely the elder at London to George Cely at
Calais, 10 July 1478*
s.c.1 53/200

                        Jh*e*su M¹iiij^c lxxviij

I grete the wyll, and I haue resayuyd a letter from the wryt at
Caleys the xxix day of Jun, the weche letter I haue wyll understand: of youre demenyng at thys marte, the clerenesse, for the

25. 14 Sent] Joh *canc.*

weche I am wyll plesyd, and of the sale of my woll: a poke solde
to John Borsse, marchant of Ryssyll, and to John Delopys, 5
Cornelys Vandorne and Gysbryght Van Whynsbeyg vj sarplerys
of good woll Cottyswolde, *and* ij sarplerys *and* a poke of medell
woll Cottyswold, for the weche I am wyll plesyd, and the waythe
and the sum of money, *and* the iij<sup>de</sup> peny at xxv s. for the li., *and*
to resayuyd at Bamys marte neste com, and the secon payment 10
vj monyht, *and* the reste vj monyht after that. The schepyng of
woll *and* fellys ys begone at London, for the weche I am avysyd
for to schepe my woll *and* fell at thys tyme, for the weche kepe
money for the frayght and costom *and* subsete. There was l li.
lent beforhand and my parthyschom of iiij s. the li. schall halpe 15
to. And ȝete I may doe no more good, neder in byyng of woll nor
fellys nor in byldyng, for defayte *and* lake of money, for the weche
I schall thynke long tyll Bamys marte com. [*Written later*:] At
thys day I haue schepyt x sarplerys woll and dayly do schepe, God
send them wyll to Caleys *and* save, for yt ys lyke to be a grete 20
schepyng of woll *and* fell at London. I wryt no more, but Jhesu
kepe you. Wryte at London the x day of Jule in grete haste.

　　　　　　　　　　　　　　　　　　*per* Rychard Cely.

*Dorse*: To Jorge Cely at Caleys be thys delyuer. (*Shield*.)

## 27. *Richard Cely the elder at London to George Cely at Calais, 20 July 1478*

s.c.1 53/16

### Jhesu M<sup>l</sup>iiij<sup>c</sup> lxxviij

I gre[te the wyll a]nd I send the a letter wryt at London the xiij
day of Jule of the answare ⌐of⌐ ȝoure letter, but I fele wyll ye
haue not that letter as ȝete. I wryte to the that I haue schepyt
*and* wyll schepe xl sarplerys of Cottyswolde woll and x packys of
fell or more, for the weche I wyll ye schall make porveons for 5
frayth *and* hossyng as ye schall vnderstand be my fryste letter
afor wryte, and ye schall porvay for hossyng for Rychard ⌐Cely⌐
and thyselve for viij packys fell, wereof I haue a perte wyt you in
the same fellys as ye schall understand be thy broder Rychard Cely
at ys comyng to Caleys schortely, for the schepyng ys ner doe, *and* 10
schall be wytin vj dayys, for the weche I wryt to the schortly and
in grete haste, *and* also, in good faythe, for lake of money I forgoe

　　27. 2 *ms.* answare of youre ⌐of⌐ ȝoure

many good barganys of fell, for the weche I am ryght sory, but
I pray the haue thys mater yn my[nd] and lete me understande
15 wat redy mony I haue at Brygys of myn in hand that I may scharge
the, and I may doe hony goo[d] therewyt, as I fele wyll I schall.
I wryt no more, Jh*e*su kepe th[e]. Wryte at London the xx day
of Jule in haste.

per Rychard Cely.

20 *Dorse*: To Jorge Cely at Caleys be thys letter delyuerd. (*Seal and
shield*.)

### 28. *John Dalton at Leicester to George Cely at Calais, 24 July 1478*
s.c.1 59/44

Welbeluffyd brotheyr, I recomaund me vnto you, pr*a*yng you for
do so mvch for me noo at thys tyme, to pay the freyght for a xviij
s*a*rpl*e*rys wooll and ffell*y*s of Thom*a*s Wigestons tyll my brod*er*
Wyll*i*am Dalton or ell*y*s I come, the wych schal be ryght schortely
5 the ton or ell*y*s booyth of vsse. Alsoy they said Thom*a*s Wygeston
hasse sent ouy*r* ys schylde for to ress*e*y*u*e it *and* hosse it tyll owr
comyng, and yff ther be ony theng that I may doy I am yo*u*rs to
my poyer, that knowys God, who kep you. Wretton at Leycett*er*
the xxiiij^t day of Jully, a*n*no M^liiij^c lxxviij^t

10 Be yo*u*r brod*er*, John Dalton<br>of Leyc*e*tter.

*Dorse*: A Jorg*e* Cely m*e*rchaunt of they Staple at Calles, lowgyd
at Bornell*y*s wyedows, be thys lyu*e*rd, dd. (*Seal*.)

### 29. *Challenge to an archery match, from the married free-men of the Staple to the bachelors, Calais, 17 August 1478*
s.c.1 59/47

And it wold pleyse yow for your dysport and plesur opon Thursday next comynge to meyt w*yth* vs of the est syde of thys towne,
in a place called The Pane, ʒe shall fynde a p*e*re of prykys of lenght
betwyx the on and the other xiij^xx tayllyo*u*r ʒard*y*s met owt w*yth*

27. 16 and *repeated*          17 London *repeated*
28. 4 come] to *canc.*

a lyne // Ther we vndyrwretyn shall meyt w*yth* alls many of 5
yow*r* ordyr and shot w*yth* yow at the same pryk*ys* for a dyner or
a supper, p*ry*ce xij d. a man. And we p*ra*y you of you*r* goodly
answher w*yth*in xxiiij owrse. Wretyn at Cale*s* the xvij day of
August, a*n*no Jes*u* lxxviij.

                              Redy to dysport w*yth* yow:        10

|            | Rob Adlyn         | Willi*a*m Bondeman |    |
|            | John Ekyngton     | John Dyars         |    |
| Weddyd     | Phelip Willi*a*mson | Ric*har*d Wylowly |    |
| men        | Seman Granth*a*m  | Rob Besten         |    |
|            | Thom*a*s Sharpe   | Thomas Layne       | 15 |
|            |                   | John Wryght        |    |
|            |                   | Rob Knyght         |    |

*Dorse*: To owr welbelufed good Brodyr Thom*a*s Wryght and all
other Bachelery*s* beyng Fremen of the Stap*le* be this delyuerd.
(*Fine seal with man's head with laurel wreath and initials* R.A.)    20


**30.** *Richard Cely the elder at London to George Cely at*
*Calais, 17 August 1478*

s.c.1 53/17

                    Jh*e*su M¹iiij^c lxxviij

I grete the wyll, and I marvele meche wat ys the cavse that ye send
me no lett[er] from Caleys, neder thy broder nor thyselve, for the
weche I thyng ryght strange, insomeche as I am so schargyd for
thys good late schepyt it were grete comford for me to here howe
ye doe, and in wat case my good ys in at Caleys: my fell, the bacons 5
for to be deperde, *and* make all sengyll fell, *and* sorte Cottyswolde
on themselve, *and* London somor fell of themselve, wynter in lyke
wyse. There ys non askvse but ye may wryt at all tymys as hoder
men doe to there maysters *and* frendys. I wryt no more, but Jh*e*su
kepe you. Wryt at London the xvij day of Auguste in haste.        10
                              *per* Rychard Cely.

*Dorse*: To Jorge Cely at Caleys, thys letter delyuerd. (*Seal and*
*shield*.)

29. 12 John] Ekyngs *canc.*    15 Layne] Thomas *canc.*

**31.** *Richard Cely the elder at London to George Cely at Calais, 25 August 1478*

s.c.1 53/18

Jhesu M¹iiijᶜ lxxviij

I grete the wyll, and I haue resayuyd from the a letter wryte at Caleys the xiij day of Auguste, the weche letter I haue wyll understand, and ye haue solde vj sarplerys of my good Cottyswolde woll, pryse the sacke xix marke, to Peter Van de Rade *and* Danyell Van
5 de Rade, marchantys of Bregys: the poyse, the argent *and* the dayys I clerely understand, and also I understand ye haue solde to John Delopys *and* Cornelys Van Dorne, *and* Gysherybyrt Van Wehnysbarge, marchauntys of Bregys, vj sarplerys of my good woll Cottyswolde, pryse the sacke xix marke: the poyse, argent
10 *and* dayys I understand wyll, for the weche I am wyll plesyd. I understand ye haue resayuyd my woll late schepyt—xlvij sarplerys and a poke, all Cottyswolde, *and* my fell—in savete, I thanke God, and the fraygh[t] payd, for the weche I praye you send me a cope of the payyng of the frayfte, that I may wryt in
15 my bogke the passelys, and for the costom and subsete, pay yt as hoder men doe. There ys l payd befor, *and* my pertyschon hellpyt to, *and* as for the reste, I wyll ye paye yt, for I understand wyll we schall paye the costom *and* subsete ster. mony. Doe as hoder men doe, schortely. I haue not schargyd the wyt a peny to
20 paye for me, neder at Caleys nor Bregys, nor at the marte, for the weche I pray the doe in thys pertys as wyll as ye can, as my very stryte ys in the, and take the warled as yt ys in sale and exschange. *And* payyng of custom *and* subsete, take you no thowe therefore. I understonde that mater before youre wrytyng, for the weche
25 I haue bogwyt not j sacke woll thys seson, but I haue payd my woll marchauntys in Cottyswolde for the woll I haue in Caleys *and* fell, John Cely *and* all, and ⌐they⌐ schall doe there beste for me for a tyme, werefor I pray the make salle to svre men, and ye can, for the warled ys not good, werefor it ys as good for to lese in the
30 begeyn⟨yn⟩g as in the ende. Save as meche as ye may, for the exshange be syche it wyll be heuy to bare, the weche I praye God amente yt. I wryt no more to you at thys tyme, but Jhesu kepe you. Wryt at London the xxv day of Auguste in grete haste.

Also I wyll ye delle wyt Borganys man at the marte, for ys pay-
35 ment ys good to me at all tymys befor the day, as Rychard Cely

can enforme you. The man of Lyne ys good payment, and that ys mery for to dele wyt syche men. Take good men *and* doe the better to them rader.

*per* Rychard Cely.

*Dorse:* To Jorge Cely at Caleys be thys letter delyuerd.

40

## 32. *Richard Cely the younger at Calais to George Cely at Bruges [? 27 August] 1478*
s.c.i 53/14

Jh*e*su M¹iiij<sup>c</sup> lxxviij

Right whelbelouyd brother George, I recomend me to you, informyng you that I haue beyn to seke your blacke goune at Redhod*y*s, and hyt wos at Bondmans, and I haue ressauyd hyt and put hyt yn your schest, and as for your barell v*yth* pound garnett*y*s, ar not ʒeyt cu*m* to Call*e*s. Syr, I haue spokyn w*yth* 5 Tomas Adam, and I towl[d] hym that I porposyd to stope Robard from hys passayge, and he has desyryd me to spar Robat, for and I reyst hym the⟨r⟩ ys no mane that wyll helpe hym owt of preson, and so he ⌐Tomas⌐ has promysyd me in hys brothers name that hys brother schaull agre w*yth* me at Lond*o*n. Hary Whayt de- 10 lyu*e*ryd to the sayd Robard a xxx s. to pay hys ostes, and he has playd hyt at dys, euery *farthing*, and so Tomas ys fayn to go to mast*e*r Lefetenant to pray hym to pay Robard*y*s cost*y*s to London. S*y*r, in thys mat*e*r I wyll do my beste for you. Syr, the m*e*rcha[ntys] ys cu*m* owt of Frauns, and whe say the peys ys not lyke 15 to lat longe betwen Frauns and ws. No mor to you. Wryt at Call*e*s the Thursda aft*e*r your departyng.

I pray ʒe recomende me to aull good fr⟨e⟩nd*y*s.

*per* Rychard Cely.

*Dorse:* A George Cely at Bregys be thys dd.

20

## 33. *The Vicar of Watford to George Cely [? 1478]*
s.c.i 59/9

Reu*e*rend *and* worschipfull S*i*r, after dev recommendacyon I recom*m*and me vnto ʒou. Ferthermore, I pray you to remembre ⌐me⌐ in thys seson for a goshavke or a tarsel, the wyche lykyth

beste ⌐you¬, ffor I wote wele I schall haue ⌐non¬ but hyt come
5 from yow / werfor I pray ȝou, thowe Y be ferre from yow in
sythe lette me be ny to ȝou in hert, as I schall deseruit vnto ȝou
in tyme commyng. Also I pray you to send me a bylle of your
wellfare, *and* the prys, and hyt schall be content by the grace of
God, ho have ȝou in his kepyng.

10                                        By your Chapelayn, the
                                         Vycar of Watford.

*Dorse*: This bylle be delyuerd vnto maister George Cely marschaunt
of the Stapyll.

## 34. *Richard Cely the younger at Calais to George Cely at Bruges or Antwerp, 25 September 1478*

s.c.1 53/20

Jhesu M¹iiij° lxxviij

Welbelouyd brothe⟨r⟩, I recomen[d] me harttely onto you. Plese
hyt you to wet at the makyng of thys my godfadyr and I wer in
good hell at Calles. Syr, whe had no wrytyng ovt of Ynglond syn
Wylliam Cely went. Syr, her ys marchantys of Roon, and thay
5 wolde by good Cottyswold woll, and thay spake to me, and
desyryd to haue had iij sarpelers, ij partys in hand of the payment
xxv s. iiij d. my li., and halfe ȝer daye of the therd *penny*, mony
corant in Flandyrs. And I ansford them and thay wold geue me
redy mony xxv s. iiij d., mony corant in Calles, and the rembnant
10 at xxiiij s. my li. redy mony, that ys to say the Ryan[s i]iij s. iiij d.,
vyth all odyr gowldys as thay ȝeyd at Cowlld Marte, thay schould
hau[e i]ij or iiij. And wat thay wyll do I wot not ȝeyt. Syr, the
woll ys tornyd and mend[yd a]nd ther ys a myddyll sarpeller
ȝeyt—No. xvj. Syr, her be com iiij felysch[yp of Ho]ll[a]ndars—
15 thay be the harddeste men that euer I spake wyth. Syr, my g[od-
fadyr Ma]ryon has soullde hys owld fellys—xiiij noblys xx d.—to
Wylliam Gow[ldsmith an]d hys felyschype. Syr, I wos in hand
wyth them for owr fellys, and [se]t the Cottyswold at xiiij ⌐noblys¬
xx d., or not, and contre at xiij noblys xl d., or not, and then tay
20 wold refewy a scarttayn and I wald not, and wat thay wyll do
I wotte not ȝeyt. Syr, I haue not the praysment of my brothers
Robarddys fellys, nether of Wylliam Daulltons owlde fellys, wher-

34. 20 refewy *over* praise      scarttayn] at *canc.*      do] y do *canc.*      22 fellys]
nor *canc.*

for I wold haue wrytyng how I schuld be demenyd. Syr, I pray
ʒe recomend me to Wyll*i*am Robard*ys* that ys logyd w*yth* w*us*
wen he ys in Calles, and say to hym that we knowe now that he 25
lefte a gret fardell in hys wolhus in Schewstre⟨t⟩, the qwyche be
a thefe or theuys wos opynyd and a casket takyn owt and brokyn,
and that at was in hyt born away, and what a had more I wote nat.
A sarwant of the felbyndars ʒed into the ʒard to es hym, and save
the wyndov opyn, and lokyd in, and sawe canuas, lynnyn clothe, 30
bankars, knyuys, v*yth* od*er* stofe, and marwellyd, and com to the
Lewetenaunt and tellyd hym. And so the Lefetenaunt and Fely-
schyp went thyedyr, and ther hyt was pakyd togyddyr and had
into the Stap*e*ll, ellys we trow hyt had be gone th[e] same neyte.
No mor to you at thys tyme, Jh*e*su kepe ʒe. Wryt at Callys the 35
xxv day of Septembyr.

p*er* Rychard Cely junor.

*Dorse*: [. . .] brother [. . . m]archant [. . .] of Calles, be thys dd.


## 35. *Robert Cely at London to George Cely at Calais, 6 October 1478*

s.c.1 59/39

An*n*o lxxviij

Reuerentt syr and brother, I recomaunde me herttelly to yow.
Ferthermore infformynge yow that at the makynge of thys llett*er*
howre ffather and mother wer in good helle, blyssyd be God, and
soo I hope that ʒee be alsso. Brother, plesse ytt yow to wette that
I ressayuyd ffrome yow by Wyll*i*am Cely a lett*er*, the weche 5
I haue well undurstonde, and of the prayssementte of my ffell*ys*,
God sende them good sale / ‖ and brother, God thake yow for
the goode wyll and goode loue ʒee schowe *and* haue schewyd to
me at my laste beynge at Calles. And ther be any thynge that
I can do for yow in Ingelonde I wyll do yt w*yth* all my hartte, and 10
it ly in my power, the weche conowthe God, ho haue yow in ys
kepynge, amen. Wrette at London in haste, the vj day of October.

By yowr brother,<br>Robartt Cely.

**34.** 33 to] dyr *canc.* [gyddyr　　　**35.** 4 yow] the wett *canc.*　　　7 yow] for
yow *canc.*　　　12 October] by yowre brother *canc.*

15 Item brother, I sende to yow herw*yth* yowr indent*ter*.

*Dorse*: A George Cely marchand of the Staplle at Calles thys be delyu*er*d.

### 36. *Richard Cely the elder at London to George Cely at Calais, 10 October 1478*

s.c.1 53/201

Jh*esu* M¹iiij° lxxviij

I grete the wyll, *and* I haue resayuyd the wrytyng of the salys of woll solde to Joh[n] Descermer of Gante: iij sarplerys of my medell woll, *and* to Jacobe Pottry of Bregys: j sarplere *and* a poke of my medell woll Cottyswolde, pryse the sacke xiij marke, *and*
5 the same man: j sarplere *and* a poke of refvse woll Cottyswolde, pryse the sacke x marke, *and* John Under Hay *and* ys felyschepe of Mekelyn: xx sarplerys of my medell woll Cottyswolde— x sarplerys of the newe woll *and* x of olde woll—pryse the sacke xiij marke, the iij^de peny in hand at xxv s. iiij d. Flemeche for the
10 li. st*er*., and ij partys at xxiiij s. the pond Flemeche, *and* vj monyht*ys* *and* vj monythys, for the weche I am wyll plesyd. But I understand the exschonge ys not good at the marte: viij s. *and* viij d., that ys a grete lose for the marchant*ys* of the Stapyll, nerthelese I here saye the money in Flanderys schall be sete at a loar pryse schortely,
15 for the weche be wyll ware kepe no money be the, for there schall be a grete lose to all them that hathe meche Flemyche money in hand, for the weche be ware betyme. I understand thys schall be schortely in hand and in com*m*yng, for the speche ys grete in Inglond of thys mater, *and* I can thynke there schall be grete
20 hotterans of woll *and* fell schortely for the same entent, for the weche in my consayt better unsolde nor solde. For that cavse I fere me of grete ⌐lose¬ of Flemyche money in thys tyme of settyng done of the golde. I wyll ye ȝeue my money to good men, *and* the longgar days, and ⌐that¬ ys leste lose. I wryt no more to
25 you at thys tyme, but Jh*esu* kepe you. ⌐Wryt¬ at London the x day of Octobor in grete haste.

*per* Rychard Cely.

*Dorse*: To Jorge Cely at Caleys, be thys delyu*er*. (*Seal and shield*.)

**37.** *Richard Cely the elder at London to Richard Cely the younger at Calais, 28 October 1478*

s.c.1 59/34

Jhesu M¹iiij<sup>c</sup> lxxviij

I grete you wyll, and I understand that youre moder send a letter
to the wyllyng that ȝe scholld be stylle ⌈at⌉ Caleys for a tyme tyll
I send you wrytyng, for the weche I wyll ye com home wyt Wyll
Maryon, for there schall be no besynese at Caleys thys marte
tyme. I sopose Jorge ty broder gothe to thys Colde marte. I pray  5
you se a fayre weder or ye take youre passage for onny haste, for
the weche I tryste to God Wyll Maryon *and* ȝe wyll se that weder
*and* wynde be fayre. At the wrytyng of ⌈thys⌉ letter youre moder
*and* I were in good helle, thankyd be God, and all my hosseso⟨l⟩d
also. I wrote to Jorge Cely late, my woll *and* fell were better unsolde  10
nor solde, weneyng to me there scholde a be more labor for to sete
done Flemeche money nor I can ⌈here⌉ of, the weche I wyll that
Jorge Cely selle my woll *and* woll fell acordyng to the ordenanse
of the Plase, and doe as hoder men doe, for I here of no remedy,
God send vs a ⌈good⌉ sale buthe for woll *and* fell. The pryse of  15
woll ys rese in Cottyswolde—a marke in a sacke in schorte tyme.
Also youre gosehawke, the weche was delyuerd to my Lorde of
Send Johnys, ys dede for defayte of good kepyng, for the weche
I wolde we hadde kepyt the hawke the weche Wyll Cely bravthe
home *and* ys delyverd to the Vekery of Watforde. I wryt no more  20
to you at thys tyme, but Jhesu kepe ⌈you⌉. Wryte at London the
xxviij day of Octobor in haste.

*per* Rychard Cely.

*Dorse*: To Rychard Cely the ȝongar at Caleys be thys letter
delyuerd. (*Seal and shield.*)      25

*In Richard Cely junior's writing:*

| | | | | |
|---|---|---|---|---|
| A meser alantarn | - vj d. | | A rasar of ot*ys* | - xix d |
| A kettyll | - xxij d. | | iiij brom*us* | - ob. |
| A harskob amane | - iiij d. | | | |
| A loke | - ij d. | | | |
| A donge forke | - iiij d. | | | 30 |

**37.** 28 harskob] *?* e *canc.*      amane: *reading uncertain.*

**38.** *Richard Cely the elder at London to George Cely at Calais, 6 November 1478*

s.c.1 59/43

Jhesu M¹iiij° lxxviij

I grete ⌈the⌉ wyll, and I haue resayuyd from the ij letters be Wyll
Maryon, j lett[er wryt] the xxiiij day of Octobor, the weche I wyll
understand, the toder letter wryt frysth day of Novembor, the
weche I understand wyll, and of the sale of woll—xxxj sarplerys
5 good woll Cottyswold, *and* j sarplere medell woll, all ys solde.
Dayys be comyng, for the weche I am wyll plesyd: the marchaunt*ys* be good. Also I understand youre beyn[g] at Bamyse
marte and the ʒeueyng of money be exschonge: viij s. viij d.
Flemyche for vj s. viij d. st*er*., the weche ys grete lose. I haue
10 resayuyd of Wyll Maryon, the bryngar of the letters, a boxkys,
therein ix letters of payment acordyng to youre wrytyng. Also
I wrote to you in my laste wrytyng of the money, saiyng of in
Flemders I harde of no labor at that tyme, but yt ys novne the
Mayar of the Staple and the Felyschepe of marchaunt*ys* make
15 grete svte to the lordys of the Kyngys Consell, of the weche ys
lyke to be a conclesyon, and that mater schall be reformede, as
I onderstand, to more profete for the Stapyll, for the weche kepe
no money be the, for there wyll be meche lose to them that haue
meche money in there handys. I pray the beware of lose, for
20 I understand wyll there wyll be grete lose. Also I haue payd my
byll of xvj s. viij d. the sarplere—xlvij li. xviij s. iiij d.—*and*
youre byll—iiij li. xv s. x d.—*and* Wyll Maryons byll—ix li.
vij s. vj d. I understand that I schall ⌈haue⌉ anoder byll in doket
of my custom at Caleys, for the wech[e] I wolde understand befor
25 the comyng of the s*u*m that I make the sayd money redy, for I love
not the scharpe callyng on at London, for I understode not ij
dayys befor I payd the byll of xvj s. viij d. to John Tate. I am not
payd of John Raynolde at the ⌈day⌉ nor a monythe after thys byll.
Send to me as sone as ye may clere my byll of custom *and* payd
30 them schortely: I wyll understand the clerenese of my delyng *and*
clere my boke. I wyll Rychard Cely com home: lette hym wat
a fayar weder, for Wyll Maryon was sore aferd for the grete myste,
*and* [as for d]ede at London, ys no syche fere of syche thyng as
youre moder wrote of, but in the Weste Contre ys gret. I pray
35 you speke to Thomas Kesten: say to hym I loke that he wyll kepe

the promyse he made to me at syche tyme as I delyuerd to ⌜hym⌝
ys plate and all syche sthofe as I hade areste. I was the fryste that
relesyd my acschon *and* delyuerd the good the weche I hadde in
warde to hymselve. Hoder men were conten⟨t⟩ be agremen⟨t⟩
agrete and sete in a waye, but I am not spoke wyt nor intrete lyke    40
the promyse made to me at that tyme be Thomas Kesten, for the
weche and Thomas Kesten wyll sete me in worse case of asvrete
nor be ⌜do⌝ toder men, he kepe not ys faythefull promyse. I here
meche thyng sayd be hym, for the weche *and* I were intrete for
asvrte of a comforde of paymen⟨t⟩ I code doe *and* say for hym, the    45
weche wolde be for ys profete *and* worschepe. I onderstand that
wyll be dyverse men that I speke wyth *and* spere of me the gydyng
*and* the desposycheon of Thomas Kesten, for the weche I wyll
ye rede all thys clase to hym. Yt be for ys worschepe to remembor
thys mater. I wryt no more to iou at thys tyme, Jh*e*su haue iou in    50
kepeyng. Wryt at London the vj day of November in grete
haste.

*per* Rychard Cely.

*Dorse*: To Jorge Cely at Caleys be thys delyue*r*. (*Shield*.)

**39.** *William Maryon at London to George or Richard Cely*
*the younger at Calais, 8 November [1478]*
s.c.i 59/35

### Jh*e*su

Ryght reuerent syr and my specyall ffrende, I reco*m*aund me vnto
you. Ferdermor, and yt plesse yow to wete, the sam day that Y
dep*ar*ted fro Calles Y londed in the Dovnys at iij a clokt at afternon,
and Y cam to London the Freyday at non aft*er*. Ser, ye schall
vnderstond that Y delyu*er*ed the sam day vnto my mast*er* youre    5
fadere, youre boxkt wyt all youre lette⟨r⟩ys, wyt the wyche he wosse
ryght well plesed. Also syr, ye schall vnderestond that my mast*er*
yowre fadere hat y-payd vnto John Tatte all hys bell, yowre bell
*and* my bell, and Y vnderestond Robard Cely hat y-payd hys bell
allso, of xvj s. viij d. of the sarpp*ler*. Syr, as for John Cely ys bell,    10
Y can her nothyng therof, and Y haue spoken vnto John Tatte

therof, and he answar me he hat no seche yt y-comen. Syr, Y
vnderstond that ye mad seche a bell of John Cely ys of xxx s. for
hys xvj s. viij d. of the sarpp*ler*. Syr, Y pray you that ye woll spekt
15 vnto Thomas Scharpe therof, war the bell ys becomen. Also syr,
Y haue ynformed my mast*er* that he most pay a xx or a xxx li.
mor her now in Ynglond schortlay for hys costom, and ye schall
vnderstond that plesse yowre fader nothyng, for he had levere for
to paye yt at Calles a grette dell then for to pay yt here at London,
20 but Y answard hem aȝyn yt myt nat so be. *And* also syr, I pray
you that ye woll recommeund me vnto Rechard Cely, and Y pray
you that ye woll schow hem thys lettere, for my mast*er* youre fadere
and my masterys yowre moder wovld fayn that Rechard Cely war
her at hom, for, blessed be God, her ys no seche dethe as wos
25 spoken of at Callys. Syr, they wovld in no wysse that Rychard
Cely schuld take pasage but at a morow tyd and a feyer set wedere,
as Y soppeowse my mast*er* the Leffetenant and hoder of the Feleschyppe that be y-porposed for to com hovere woll doo. Also syr,
ye schall vnderstond that Rechard Cely ys gosshavke, the wyche
30 that he gaave vnto my Lord of Sent Jonys, for the fawte of good
kepyng, ys ded, and Y vnderstond that my Lord sayd that he had
lever a lost xx markt than the havke schuld a be so y-lost in hys
kepyng, and therfor my mast*er* yowre fader wovld that Rechard
Cely schuld bryng hover anoder govshawke wyt hem, yeff ye covd
35 bey any at Calles for viij or ix s., and he wovld pay for the sayd
havke hemselffe for the pleser of my Lord, and my mast*er and* my
maysterys sayt vnto me that they repented them xx tymys that they
had nat kept styell the hawke that Wyll*i*am Cely broght fro Calles,
etc. Also syr, ye schall vnderstond that my master youre fader
40 and my maysterys yowre moder faryt well, yowre broder Robard
Cely and hys wyffe faryt well, blessed be Good, and sche ys gret
wyt chylde, and all hoder good frendys faryt well, blessed be
Good. No mor vnto yow at thys tym, but Y pray you that ye woll
recomm*m*end me vnto myn houst Thomas Kesten and to hys wyffe,
45 and to Wyll*i*am Byfeld, and to Thomas Grangere. Wreten at
London the viij day of Novemb*er*.

By youre owne,
Wyll*i*am Maryon.

*Dorse*: Wnto Georg Cely or to Rechard Cely, marchant*ys* of the
50 Stapull at Calles thys letter be delyu*er*ed, etc. (*Shield*.)

*G. Cely's writing*: To Kay

>Item, p*ayd* ffor W. Maryon  --- xviij d.
>pr*o* my brodyr Ry  --- vj d.
>ffor postorne  --- xix d.
>ffor menydyng [?]  --- ij d.  55
>          su*m* - iij s. vij d. Fl.

**40.** *William Maryon at London to Richard Cely the younger at Calais, 23 November [1478]*

s.c.i 59/45

### Jhe*s*u

Ryght reuerent syr, Y reco*m*meund me vnto yow. Ferdermo
plessed yow to wete that my mast*er* yewre fader and my massterys
yowre moder, yowre broder Robard and ⌐al⌐ faryt well, blessed
be God, and as for any dehet her, thanked be God, set Y cam hom
her hat ben non, and therfor my mayssterys yowre moder loked  5
for yow dayley, but yt sche wovld nat that ye schuld covm, nat
tyell my mast*er* the Leffetenant Robard Taatte cam, and that ye
take a morow tyde and a lyght mone for any hasste. Syr, Y haue
spoken vnto my masterys yowre moder for a govn clothe to makt
yow a reydyng govnne for to co*m* hom in, and sche bed yow that  10
ye schulld borow on of Georg Cely yowre broder, and he schall
have anoder therfor ayenst Ester of clothe in grayne, sche saythe.
Allso syr, ye schall vnderstond that my mast*er* hat y-boght the
Rector ys woll of Abendon hys ij yerys woll set Y cam hom. Also
syr, ye schall vnderstond that my Lord of Sen Jonys bedfelowe  15
wosse her wyt my mayssterys yowre moder now late, wytin thys
iij dayes, and he sayd that my Lord sent hem heder for to wete
wheder that ye war y-comen hom or non, for he sayth my Lord
thynket long for yow, and as for yowre hauke that my Lord had
of yow, yt ys ded, and therfor my mast*er* yowre fader would, lyke  20
as Y wrote vnto yow affor, yeff ye covde bhey anoder havke at
Calles for viij or ix s., he wovld pay therfor hemselffe, and so he
wovld fayn that ye broght anoder hauke wyt yow, and as for the
Fekerey ys hawke of Watford, yt prevyt well: yt hat y-cautte thys
sam yer vpon a lx fenanys and malardys, and the Fekerey sayt he  25
woll nat yeffe hem, nat for xij nobelys, to no man. Also syr, Y pray

**39.** 54 xix d. *over canc.* xviij d.

yow harteley that ye woll reco*mm*eund me vnto Georg Cely. No
mor vnto yow at thys tym, but the Trenyte haue yow in hys blessed
kepyng. Wreten at London the xxiij day of Nouembere.

30                                              *per* Wyll*ia*m Maryon.

*Dorse*: Wnto Rechard Cely, marchant of the Stapull at Calles at
osthe w*yth* Bornell the wedew, thys letter be delyuered, etc.
(*Shield*.)

## 41. *George Cely at Calais, to Richard Cely the elder at London, 23 November 1478*

s.c.i 53/21

### Jh*e*su M¹iiij*c* lxxviij

Ryght rewerent and whorshipffull ffadyr, aff*ter* all dew recomen-
dasyon p*re*tendyying I recomeavnd me [vn]to yow in the moste
lowlyest whysse that I can or may. Fordyrmor, plesyth yt you
to vndyr[stond] that I hawe resseyuyd an lett*er* ffrom yow beryng
5  date at London the vj^th day of Novemb[y]r, [whech I] do whell
vndyrstond. Also Y ffelle by yowr sayd wryttyng that ȝe vndyrst[ond . . .] to John De Lopis and his ffellowys and of the salle
made vnto Jois Franke of Mekelyn [. . . I vndyr]stond by yowr
sayd wryttyng that ȝe hawe resseywyd the charge wheche I sent
10 vnto yow [by] Wyll*ia*m Maryon ∥ Also plesyth ytt yow to vndyrstond that Y ffelle allso be yowr wryttyng ȝe hau[e] p*a*yd yowr
byllys and howrs whyche I sent howyr vnto yow, etc/ Plesythe
yt yow to whett that I hawe made annodyr byll in yowr name allso
of xxx li. st*er*. wheche most be p*a*yd at the syght allso ∥ And whan
15 that ys p*a*yd yowr costu*m* and sobsyde ys ffull content and payd,
as ȝe shall ffynd by an byll closyd in thys lettyr, how ytt ys p*a*yd
and by what men heu*er*y [som] vppon ∥ And I hade nott recond
w*yth* the collectors so sone as I dede ȝe hade p*a*yd the [whole] of
that hade bene vnpayd ȝe hade ⌐p*a*yd⌐ ytt yn Ynglond, and as
20 many as bethe to pay at [ . . . ] shall pay the v^the peny of ther
costu*m* and sobsyde in Ynglond at the syght / Y vndyrs[tond] that
ȝe be lothe ⌐to⌐ pay any of iowr costu*m* and sobsyde in Ynglond,
wherffor I hawe endev[eryd] myselffe that ȝe pay so lyttyll as ȝe
do, but whan ȝe se my byll closyd in thys lett*er* I deme ȝe whyll
25 thynke ytt hade bene mor porffett that mor hade bene p*a*yd in
Ynglond. Now ytt conott helpe, ytt ys passyd, etc. ∥ The rekenyng

whyll ⌜be⌝ better now heuery day ffor [mony is] amendyd in
Flavndyrs ij s. vj d. in an povnd ‖ Ther has bene moche hewyng
[. . .] betwext the Kyngys Covnsell and vs ffor thys haillwe ʒer
whaygys, as my brod[er Rychard] con ynfforme yow. Whe wolld 30
an takyn dyvars whays wyth them, but they woll no [oder] whay
but as the wher payd last, sawyng whe hawe browght ytt that they
shall [hawe] ij manyr a gowldys, ij d. derar in an pesse than they
dyde, that ys the crovne and the Ryn[ysh] gylderne, etc. ‖ Y send
vnto yow now her in the⌜is⌝ as ys anffor wrett, the cleyrnesse of 35
yowr costu[m] and sobsyde, and be the grasse of Goode as sone
as the marte ys done I shall cleyr vp my boke of myn acovmpt:
and Y se yt ffayyr whedyr and but lyttyll besynesse toward neydys
Y wyll bryng ytt my selffe vnto yow, etc. ‖ Plesythe ytt yow to
vndyrstond that I h[awe] latly made an ssalle vnto men of Deffe 40
of my brodyrs Rychard Cely ys Cottys ffellis, M¹xvj solld [at]
xiiij noblis xx d., my sayd brodyr con shew yow the reconyng of
the same, etc. ‖ Also plessythe y[t] yow to vndyrsstond that my
brodyr and I hawe spokyn wyth Thomas Kesten, and he saythe
vnto v[s as] my brodyr con infforme yow, a connott kepe the 45
promysse that a made vnto yow, wh[erfor] Y vndyrstond by hym
that he wyll take my brodyr an lettyr wherby ʒe sh[all se] hys
intent mor cleyrly. He saythe whell, as my brodyr con ynfforme
yo[u]. [God] gewe hym grace to ⟨do⟩ theraffter. No mor vnto yow
at thys tyme, but Jhesu haue yow [and] all yowrs in hys kepyng, 50
amen. Wrettyn at Calles the xxiijᵗʰᵉ day of Novemby[r] lxxviij.

per yowr son,<br>George Cely.

*Dorse*: Vnto my ryght whorshy[pf]full ffadyr Rychard Cely,
merchant of the Stapull of [Calles] d[ew]elyng at London.    55

*In G. Cely's hand, partly obscured by modern mounting*: Thesse byllys
[. . .] my ffaders blakke [. . .]

## 42. *Robert Radclyff at Calais to George Cely, 11 December* [1478]

s.c.1 59/8

Brothur George, I comaund me vnto you, etc./ Prayng you hertely
that ʒe will vowchsaff to take the payne as to by ffor me such stuff
nessessary as I most nedes occupy, *and* to lay owte the money vnto

your comyng, the qwych wyth Godus leve 3e schall trewly be payd
5 at your next comyng. And yf het ly in my power I schall do as
moch that schal be vnto your plesure, as knoweth owre Lord, qwou
send you good fortune wyth þe accomplichment off your goodly
desyrys. At Cales þe xj day off ⌐Decembre⌐ wyth þe hand off your
faythfull felow,
10                                le filz Sir John Radclyff, Robert.

Thes be the parcellys þat hereaffter folow:
    Fyrst lx boge skynnes off vij d. or viij d. þe pece.
    Item vj sugurre loves off iij cuet.
    Item xij pownd off raysens off Coraynce.
15 And yff 3e can ffynd hany fayre furre off marten tayles for a long
gowne, I praye you by for me j ‖ And such cariage as 3e can best
fynd, þat hit myght best come heder before this tyme, I requere
you hertely ‖ Brothur, I am bold to desyre you to do thus mekull,
but I schall aquytte you in takyng dowble the payne for your sake
20 in hanything 3e desire to do for you, or hany frynd off yours.

Dorse: To my right trusty brothur George Cely, marchaunt off
þe Staple.

## 43. Richard Cely the younger at London to George Cely at Calais, 15 December 1478

s.c.1 59/36

### Jhesu M¹iiij⍧ lxxviij

Ryught welbelouyd brother George, I recomend me harttely
wnto you, thankyng you of the grette kyndnes that 3e schewyd to
me at my beyng wyth ⌐you⌐ at Calles, and for your russet gowyn
furryd wyth blake lambe that I had in the schype wyth me, for
5 I trow I had beyn loste for kowlde byt for hyt. Syr, I delyueryd
the same gowyn to John Lambe, wolpackar, to conway hyt to you
agayn, and he hyt me so to do. Syr, owr father and modyr ys, and
whe aull be, in good heyll, thankyd be God, and ar ryght glad
that 3e pwrpos yow to be wyth them thys Kyrstemes, and as for
10 deythe, her ys noyn, thankyd be God. I harde of noyn syn I com
to London. Whe loke for you eueri fay3er wy⟨n⟩de, I pray God
send you well hydyr, and in sauete. Syr, whe be sewyd at Weste-

42. 8 day off] Nouembre canc.        12 lx] xx canc.        15 yff] 3e canc.

myst*er* styll, and ther be ij panell*es* schosyn agaynys ws agaynste
the nexte terme, wherfor I wolde whe wer bothe heyr to ansfor.
I haue payd to Torowllde viij s. aullredy. Syr, Brandon ys in the 15
Flete styll, and schaull be tyll he gre w*yth* Dankowrt, and he says
that the Wycur of Awelay was caus*er* of hys cu*m*myng to Dankort*ys*,
wherfor ha schaull leys hys wekerayge. Sy⟨r⟩, I schulde a sent an
hat be John Lambe to Twesylton, byt he wos goy*n* ʒeyr I cam to
London. No mor to you, byt I pray you to recomend me to my 20
nostes and all goyd frend*ys* a be name. Wrytt at London the xv
day of Desembur. Syr, our mother and I pray ʒe to conway su*m*
of yor powd ga*r*nett*ys* hyddyr.

p*er* yowr brother, Rychard Cely.

*Dorse*: A my welbelouyd brother George Cely, m*er*chand of the 25
Stap*ell* at Call*es*, be thys delyuerydd. (*Same seal as his father's*.)

### 44. *John Dalton at Calais to George Cely at London, 12 February 1478/9*

s.c.1 59/40

Right inteyrly and welbeluffyd brod*er*, aft*er* all dew recomen-
dacyons hayd I recomaunde me vnto you. Furthermor ʒe schall
ond*er*stond that I haue sold vnto Pett*er* Johnsu*n* of Delff and is
felyschip y*our* fayd*er*ys Cotty*s*wold ffeell*ys*, the wych ffell*ys* lay
wher my brod*er* Wyll*ia*m Dalton ffell*ys* lay—p*ra*ysyd at xiiij 5
no*bl*es, sold for xiiij no*bl*es v s. Alsoy I haue sold Wyll*ia*m May-
ryons ffell*ys* wych lay by Thom*a*s Kesteyns in the thackyd howsse
to the same men, for xiiij no*bl*es, etc. Furthermo[r] ʒe schall
ond*er*stond that Py y*our* horsse doys weyll, God saue hym. I p*ra*y
you þat I may be recomandyd vnto y*our* brod*er* ⌈Rychard⌉ Cely, 10
and God knowys we haue a gret myesse of you. I hayd leyu*er* then
þe best gowne that I haue that you myght abydyn styell her w*yth*
husse. ʒe schall ond*er*stond mor at y*our* comyng—yt ys of meyrth
the cavsse I woold haue you for / Alsoy ʒe schall ond*er*stond that
mayst*er* Levetenaunt tell*ys* me that you and my brod*er* Wyll*ia*m 15
Dalton mvst breng into they Place syn you wher tressorars x li.,
for he says that you haue dyschargyd you w*yth* a tone wyne the

---

**43.** 18 sent *over canc.* beyt

**44.** 6 haue sold] of *canc.*      14 Alsoy ʒe] schall *canc.* ʒe *repeated*      16 wher]
colett*ys canc.*      17 he *repeated*

wych ȝe hayd of hym that was tresorar afor you, and not schargyd
you wythall. No mor to you at thys tyme, but Jhesus kep you.
20 Wretton at Calles the xij day of Feueruell anno M¹iiijᶜ lxxviij.

                    Be your b.      John Dalton.

Alsoy I haue wretton to my broder Wylliam Dalton of the same
maytter, and I suposse he wyl be at London or you come frome
theyns hyder, but I pray you as goodly as you may and in as schort
25 space, your beysones done in Ynglond, to speed you tooward
husse, etc.

Dorse: A my welbeluffyd Gorge Cely, merchaunt at the Staple of
Calles, dwellyng in Marcke Layne be thys letter delyuerd dd.

## 45. George Cely at Calais to Richard Cely the elder at London, 12 March 1478/9

s.c.i 53/22

Ryght rewerent and whorshypffull ffadyr, afftyr all dew reco-
mendasyon pretendyng, I recomeavnd me vnto yow in the most
lowlyest whisse that I con or may. Fordyrmor, plesythe ytt yow
to vndyrstond that I come vnto Calles the Thorsseday afftyr my
5 departyng ffrom yow, in saffte Y thanke God, and Y whas whelcom
vnto my ffrendis, ffor tyll my brodyr com to Calles ther whas none
hodyr tydyngys ther but I whas dede // etc. // Plesythe ytt yow to
vnderstond ther ys now none merchantys at Calles nor whas but
ffew thys monythe / and as ffor any hodyr tydyngys I con none
10 wrytt vnto yow as ȝett tyll Y her mor, and be the next wryttyng
þat I sent ȝe shall vndyr⟨stond⟩ the salle of yowr ffellis wyth mor,
be the grasse of God, who hawe yow and all yowrs in hys kepyng,
amen. Wrytt at Calles the xijᵗʰ day of Marche, anno lxxviij.

                         per yowr son,
15                         G. Cely.

Dorse: Vnto my ryght whorshypffull ffadyr Rychard Cely,
merchant of the Stapell of Calles at London in Marte Lane, soit dd. (Shield.)

44. 28 be repeated
45. 2 the] mo canc.        12 God] whah canc.

II. Public Record Office S.C. ɪ 53/22. Letter no. 45, from George Cely

**46.** *George Cely at Calais to Richard Cely the elder at London, 21 March 1478/9*

s.c.1 53/23

Jhesu M¹iiijᶜ lxxviij

Ryght rewerent and whorshipffull ffadyr, afftyr all dew reco-
mendasyon I recomeavnd me vnto yow in the most lowlyest
whisse that I con or may ∥ Fordyrmor plesythe ytt yow to vndyrstond that I hawe hade comynycasyon w*yth* Thom*a*s Kesten, and
he w*yth* me, and Thom*a*s Kesten whan I come vnto Calles, he  5
axyd me yff Y hade browght hym any wryttyng ffrom yow. He
sayd vnto me that he sent wryttyng be my cossyn Maryon and
be me wheroff he hade whent Y ⌜had⌝ browght hym an answer ∥
I sayd vnto hym agen that at my comyng houyr se yowr besynesse
whas soyche ȝe myght nott hawe non laysar to wrytt vnto hym,  10
wherffor ȝe comeavndyd me to say vnto hym / That ȝe ⌜wyll⌝ wrytt
vnto hym and to me schorttly of an answer of theke lett*er*ys and
how that ȝe whollde that I showld be demenyd in that casse, etc.
Ytt wholl be whell don yff ȝe sode ∥ Plesyth ytt yow to vndyrstond
that in this sayd lett*er* ȝe shall ffynd closyd the salle of yowr  15
Cott*y*s ffellis and how they wher sowlld. Ther wher sowlld no mor
⌜but⌝ iij M¹ixᶜ lxxj ffor Cott*y*s ffellis and the remenavnt of theke
ffellis bethe anwhardyd by the whardars ffor Contre ffellis, ȝett
they kepe the prysse of xiiij noblis, etc. As ȝett Y connott wrytt
vnto yow of none newis, yff ther come any ȝe shall vndyrstond.  20
No mor vnto yow at this tyme, but Jh*e*su kepe yow and all yowrs,
amen. Wrytt at Calles the xxj day of M*a*rche, *anno* lxxviij, etc.

per yowr son George Cely.

*Dorse*: Vnto my ryghtt whorshippffull ffadyr Rychard Cely,
m*er*chant of the Stapell of Calles devellyng at London in M*a*rte  25
Lane, soit dd. (*Shield.*)


**47.** *Richard Cely the younger at London to George Cely at Calais, 9 April 1479*

s.c.1 53/24

Jh*e*su M¹iiijᶜ lxxix

Ryught reuerent and welbelouyd brother, I recomende me wnto
you as harttely as I can dewyse or thynke, informyng you that

46. 9 comyng *ch. from* comyny ;      19 etc.] aȝ *canc.*      21 all *repeated*

I haue ressauyd a letter from you wryttyn at Calles the xxvij day
of Marche, ⌈be⌉ the qweche I do well onderstonde the demenyng
5 of owr brother Robard, and of hys neyd, and how ʒe haue holpyn
hym and howe ʒe be lyke to helpe hym mor, and ʒe wryte to me
for covnsell. Syr, me thynkys hyt wel done to lene hym now at hys
neyd, so that ʒe may stond sewyr. I wndyrstond be your wrytyng
that ʒe be schargyd wyth an offe. I pray God make yow well
10 qwyte therof, and owʒre father wold ⌈be⌉ sory that he has chargyd
hym so sor, or begone on hys byldyng, byt at he trystys of comforte from you, etc. Whe heyr saye that our brother has wrettyn
for hys wyfe, and sche has askewyshyd hyr that ther be so many
Flemyng and Fraynchem apon the see that sche dar not com.
15 Syr, ther was a mane wyth my godfadyr, and askyd hym for owr
brother Robard, and sayd he wosse sory of hys losse. The caws
of hys askyng for hym ⌈was⌉ for he ys owr brother Robardys
sewyrte for xv li. that owr brother mwste pay at marte, besyd x li.
that ys to Wylliam Eston. Qwat ys mor God know. Whe heyr say
20 that hys wyfe has sent to hym for mony. ʒe wryt to me a clawys
in your letter ‖ The mor ys done for hym the more ys he beholdyng ‖ byt me thynky the mor comfort that sche haue of hym,
and the mor helpe he haue of you, the les wyll sche sette by ws.
Be well ware how that ʒe ⌈do⌉: hyt ys better to pyttye than be
25 pyttyd. I awyse you to lene hym no mony, ne do no thyng wyth
hym byt afor record. ʒe knowe the onstedfastenes of hym well
inow. I cannote thynke how ʒe schawll stond sewyr of that ʒe
haue lente hym, byt ʒeue ye can geyte parte of hys felles transporte
be the covrt, and ʒeyt hyt wyl be sayd be hyr frendys that ʒe haue
30 ondone hyme. Whe be informyd that owr brother Robarde chyld
ys goyn to Calles ageyn: whe marwell in so myche as he browyt
lettyrs, at he desyryd none ageyn. Syr, I wryt the playnear to yow
for owr father sawe your letter er hyt come to my handys, and wos
resenably wel plesyd therwyth, so that ʒe stonde sewyr. Owr father
35 rydys into Cotsold vythin viij dayes, and I go to my Loorde [. . .].
Syr, I pray ʒe remembyr my Loordys hosse clothe, he [. . .] [Dorse]
Syr, I haue made Robarde Eryke a byll of xvj s. Fl. payabull at
sye[t] the qweche ys my dewte. I pray you harttely that hyt may
be ansforde. Syr, yowr hors ys in good plyte, and he hawltyd sor
40 syn ʒe departyd, byt whe haue made bathe thys for hym, and so
he ys hoyll he wyll playe wyth a straw. Now mor to you. Godd

47. 7 lene or ph. leue    12 that] ʒe canc.    41 Godd ch. from good

se[nd] me a goyde market for owr hors, and you a good market
for owr fell*es*. Jh*e*su kepe yow. Wryt at London on Good Fryday,
and I go to my Lord on Est*er* Ewe. Syr, I pray 3e recomende me
to owr ostes and aull good frend*ys*, and grete well Bawlser.      45
p*er* yowr brother, Rychard Cely.

*Dorse*: A my welbelouyd brother George Cely, m*er*chand of the
Stap*ell* at Call*es*, at oste w*yth* Bornell*es* whedow.

## 48. *Richard Cely the elder at London to George Cely at Calais, 15 April 1479*

s.c.1 59/32

Jh*e*su M<sup>l</sup>iiij<sup>c</sup> lxxix

I grete the wyll, and I wyll ye understande that I haue resayuyd
a letter from Thomas Kesten, the weche I haue wyll understand,
in lyke wyse as ye sayde to me be mothe, as ⌐for¬ the iiij<sup>c</sup> li. the
weche Thomas Kesten howyth to me, and for to 3eue to hym viij
3ere day of payment. For to resayve a C li. in woll *and* fellys at   5
Caleys, the pryse of the Stapyll, and I for to delyuer to Kesten
l li. in redy money at the resayyng of the woll *and* fell, allwaye
the costom *and* subesete ⟨to⟩ be payd be Thomas Kesten, *and*
frayghtys and all hoder costys at done at Caleys before the
resayuy⟨n⟩g of the woll *and* fellys, the weche schall be the s*u*m   10
of a C li. clerely to me above all costys dvryng the viij 3ere. That
ys to me, for to resayve 3erely a C li. *and* I 3erely after the ressau*yng*
for to delyuer to Kesten l li. in money. For thys mater I wyll ye
make thys bargan wyth Thomas Kesten in my name: I wyll
stan[d] thereto, be God grace. And Thomas Kesten wyll kepe thys   15
bargan wyll *and* trwely I wyll be a frende to hym or thys be all
at a ende, at he schall wyll fynde me a good frende. I thyngke long
after wrytyng of comforde from you, the weche I praye God send.
I wryt no more, but Jh*e*su kepe you. Wryt at London the xv day
of Apperell in haste.                                20
p*er* Rychard Cely.

*Dorse*: To Jorge Cely at Caleys be thys delyu*er*d. (*Seal and shield.*)

48. 5 3ere day] day canc.      12 resayve] 3e canc.

**49.** *John Dalton at Calais to George Cely at Bergen-op-Zoom, 28 April [? 1479]*

s.c.1 59/19

Brothir Jorge, I recomaunde me vnto you, etc. Furthermor ȝe schall onderstond that I haue soold your B. Rychard ffellys to John Cleys Hewson and hys felyschip, xl d. aboweff the prasement in euery C. That is to witt, I haue sold them for xiij nobles v s. the
5 C. ij M¹ by your byll ys in the sayd chamber. No mor to you at thys tyme, but Jhesus kep you. Wretten in hast at Calles the xxviij day of Aperell.

> Your brothir
> John Dalton.

10 *Dorse*: To Gorge Cely, merchaunt at the Staple of Calles, no beyng at Barowgh, be thys delyerd dd.

*In G. Cely's hand, scattered over the dorse*:
Je boy Avous mademoy selle / Je vous plage movnsenyuevr //
Poirsse ke vous l estes se belle / Je boy, etc.
Je sens lamor rensson estyn selle ke me persse par me
15    le kowre / Je boy a [. . .] Je voue plege movnsenywr /
de davns wyth in / de horsse wyth hov[te] Bosonye besy //
shavnte // syng / // vn shavnssovne / an song
lere / Rede   vn shen an doge / shovtt hott
ffrett covld
20 Je le vous hay de kavnt je Raye / I have sayd yow whan
I go // Je swy hovntesse / shamed Je swy hovntesse //
I am shamyd //

**50.** *Richard Cely the elder at London to George Cely at Calais, 30 April 1479*

s.c.1 53/25

Jhesu M¹iiijᶜ lxxix

I grete you wyll, and I haue resayuyd a letter from you wryt at Caleys the xix day of Apperell, the weche letter I haue wyll under-stande, and ye haue hadde comyng wyt Gylbar Pamar, Borganys man, and lese nor ix s. vj d. *and* iiij monthys or v monthys he wyll

---

**49.** 12 Je nott Je boy a voȝe *canc. before* Je boy    13 etc.] Je ssue sseur *canc.*

no lese, werefore ye haue made non wyt hym. For sothe, I can 5
haue of Rychard Tywne, mecer, at London ix s. viij d. I to resayue
in hand *and* ⌐pay¬ hym in Wysson marte neste, l li. or more, for
the weche I am avysyd for take oppe at London as meche as
I schall nede there for thys tyme. I haue resayuyd of the bryngar
of the letter, xij li. st*er*. in Carleche grotys, xij d. lese, the weche 10
xij li. st*er*. ys vj li. waythe, di. unse. The lose ys grete in the
my⟨n⟩te: I schall resayue but xj li. xviij d. ob. for the same, werefore send me no more, for I can not understand that ys not good
for me. I am in speche wyt Hewe Brone, mecer, for money: to
resayve at London l li. st*er*. and I to delyuer at Wysson marte 15
ix s. viij d. Fl. for vj s. viij d. st*er*., the weche ys grete lose to me,
werefor make me a l li. st*er*. as wyll as ye can *and* as schorte day
as ye can. I haue packyde my woll in Cottyswolde; xxvij sarplerys
good packyng, the weche com to London dayly. As for all maters
long⟨in⟩g to me, do as wyll as ye can, as my tryste ⟨is⟩ in the, and 20
doe as moste men doe. Ye schall understande at the marte weche
ys beste to doe. At the makyng of thys letter we were in good helle,
all my hossolde, I thanke God, and ȝete the sekenese ys grete at
London, God for ys mersy sessyde. I wryte no mor at thys tyme,
but Jh*e*su kepe you. Wrete at London the laste day of Apperell in 25
grete haste.

p*er* Rychard Cely.

*Dorse*: To Jorge Cely at Caleys be thys delyu*er*. (*Shield*.)

## 51. *John Dalton at Calais to George Cely, 8 May 1479*
s.c.1 59/7

Brothir Jorge, I recomaunde me vnto you, and ȝe schall ress*aue*
by þe breng*er* herof ij corss*ys*, won harnysyd and anod*er* vnharnyssyd, and of that that is vnharnyssyd I wold you bowght vj
of them. It cost iij s. or xl d., I wott not wheyd*er*. Thowffe the be
not past ij of a color or iij it skyllys not—blew, or tawne, or grene, 5
or vyolet⫽ Alsoy I woold you bowght iiij such as hasse the harnysse
apond, and the harnyss seet on as it is. It cost but ij s., the corsse
and the harnys togyd*er*. Thowff they od*er* colers as is afor wretten
it skyll*ys* not. Alsoy I p*ra*y you yff you may not by them that you
wyll dysyr Raff Lemengton to do it for me, for it schal be for my 10

51. 9 I *repeated*.

Laydy Skot. Wretten in hast at Calles, viij day of Maye, *anno* lxxix.

Be John Dalton.

*Dorse*: A Gorge Cely, me*r*chaunt at the Staple of Calles.

## 52. *Richard Cely the elder at London to George Cely at Calais, 13 May 1479*

s.c.1 53/26

Jhesu M¹iiij<sup>c</sup> lxxix

I grete you wyll, and at the makyng of thys letter we were all in good helle at Brytys Plase in Esexkys, youre moder *and* I, Wyll Maryon, but Rychard Cely youre broder ys wyt my Lorde of Send Johnys at Sotton, all mery I thanke God. The sekenese ys
5 sore in London, werefor meche pepyll of the Sete ys into the contre for fere of the sekenese. I wrot to you answere of the letter ye send to me lat ⟨by⟩ John Stokars man, *and* of the xij li. of Carlyche grotys I schall haue but xj li. *and* xviij d. in the Torwer, for the weche that ys not good. Also I wrote to you I may ⌐haue¬ money at
10 London for ix s. *and* viij d. to paye at Synschon marte, but tary *and* haue non take tyll I haue wrytyng from you, but I can thynke I moste take som, for my woll ys com hom from Cottyswollde—xxvij sarplerys. I loke dayly for the men of Cottyswolde for to wey at Ledehalle, *and* than I mvste haue money for them. I may
15 haue of Hewe Brone *and* Rychard Tewek. Also S*i*r Wyll Stoker, Mayer of the Stapyll, send to the marchaunt*ys* at London for to wyte wat euery man wyll schepe, werefor I can ȝeue non answere tyll I haue wrytyng from you. Also youre broder Rychard hath solde ys sorell horse for iiij marke *and* lent hym the money tyll
20 Mechelmesse, *and* I haue ys hoder horse to carthe and I schall paye for hym as he coste at Ȝorke, and soe the horse ys wyll solde. And as for youre horse, ys no sale at London. The horse ys fayer, God saue hym and Send Loye, werefore God send you a schapeman for hym and redy money in hand. I wryte no more to you,
25 but Jh<i>e</i>su kepe you. Wryt at London the xiij day of May in haste.

per Rychard Cely.

*Dorse*: To Jorge Cely at Caleys be thys delyuer. (*Seal and shield*.)

**51.** 11 viij *over canc.* ix
**52.** 8 grotys *ch. from* grodys

**53.** *Richard Cely the elder at London to George Cely at Calais, 21 May 1479*

s.c.1 53/27

Jh*e*su M¹iiij^c lxxix

I grete you wyll, and ye schall understand I haue resayuyd be excheaunge of John Hosyer, mecer, of London a C li. st*er*., I for to paye to John Hosyar in marte ix s. vj d. for euery vj s. viij d. st*er*., and I schall delyuer to John Hossyer anoder C li. st*er*. ix s. vj d. for euery vj s. viij d. st*er*. and iiij monthes day after the 5 resayuy*n*g in the marte, for the weche C li. st*er*. ye schall haue a letter of payment of John Hossyer to be payd to me at London in Octobor next com, and soe I haue wryt a letter of payme*nt and* derckyt to you some ij^c li. st*er*. for to ⌐payd⌐ in thys Synschon ⌐mart⌐ to John Hossyer in thys manar forme befor wryt, for the 10 weche I praye you se my letter be wyll payd, for I haue bu⟨n⟩de me streydly for the payment thereof. Also I schall payd to Rychard Haynys, mecer, of London, for John Perys of Norlache more than lx li. st*er*., for the weche Rychard Haynys mecer wyll haue money of me in thys Synchon marte be excheaunge as the markyt gothe, 15 *and* I haue promysyd ye schall delyuer hym lyke as ys man and ʒe can gree in the marte, for that schall be good payment for me in Octobor or Novembor, and it be iiij^xx li. or C li. st*er*. Thomas Cryspe hath spoke to me for haue xl li. or l, for the weche I wyll ye delyuer to Rychard Cryspe ys son as ye can agree in the mart. 20 I wyll ⌐be⌐ glade and ye can resayue my money and delyuer yt be excheunge to svre men for I ⌐wyll⌐ not schepe tyll I haue my money hom in letters of payment, be the dayys ner so long. By for me v^c or vj^c Baras canvase for to packe woll wyt: Robard Hereke wyl helpe you to by yt. I wryt no mor, but Jh*e*su kepe you. Wryt [at 25 Lo]ndon the xxj day of May. At wrytyng of thys be in good elle at Brytys Plase in Esexkys.

per Rychard Cely.

*Dorse*: To Jorge Cely at Caleys be thys letter delyuer.

**54.** *Clare — to George Cely* [? *before 26 May 1479*]

s.c.1 59/41

Trèschier et especial, je me reco*m*mande à vous, Jorge Sely. Sachies q*ue* je suy en très bon point et je prye à Dieu q*ue* ainsy

soiet il de vo*us*. Sachies q*ue* je vo*us* ay amé lo*n*geme*n*t, mais je ne
le vo*us* ossoye point dire. Sachies q*ue* je vous enuoye vne reco*m*-
5 mandatio*n*, et je vous prye q*ue* il vous souuiegne de moy, et je
vo*us* en p*r*ie q*ue* vo*us* m'enuoyes vne souue*n*anche ainsy co*mm*e
je fais à vo*us* par bonne amour. Et je vo*us* laisse sąuoier q*ue* mo*n*
coeur n'es mis sur aultre ho*mm*e q*ue* sur vo*us*, mais je pense q*ue*
vo*t*re amo*ur* n'est point sur moy. Mais je vous en p*r*ie q*ue* vo*us*
10 m'e*n*uoyes vne lettre le plus tos q*ue* poees, car mo*n* coer ne sera
point à son repos tant q*ue* je veray vne lettre venas de vous, car
de ceste ensaingne q*ue* je vo*us* dissoye à la table q*ue* je vous
enuoraye vne lettre. Aul*t*re chose ne vo*us* say q*ue* j'escrie po*ur*
le pressent, sino*n* q*ue* Dieu soiet garde de Jorge Sely et de Clare.
15                    Tout le coer de Clare est à vous, Jorge Sely—
                       tous jour en mon coer.

Sachies q*ue* j'enuoye vne ainsaigne à Biet*r*emeulx vo*t*re serviteur,
et se me recoma*n*de à lui. Je lui promis cai*n*t il estoiet pardecha.

*Dorse*: Desen brief zy ghegeuen tot Jorge Sely. (*Indistinct seal.*)

## 55. *Richard Cely the younger in Essex to George Cely at Calais, 26 May 1479*

s.c.1 59/16

Anno Jhesu M¹iiij*c* lxxix

Riught interly welbelouyd brother, I recomende me onto you as
harttely as I may dewyse or can thynke. Plesythe hyt you to
vndyrstond that I haue ressauyd frome you ij lettyrs. I vndyrstond
them ryught well. The laste wos wryttyn the xx day of Ap*r*ell and
5 therin was iiij nobullys st*er*., and therof I delyu*er*yd to my godfather xx s. and I thankyd hym acorddyng to your wrytyng. Syr,
owr brother Robard ys com to London, and owr father sent to
hym to wete ʒeyffe ʒe sente ony wrytyng*ys* be hym, and he ansford
that he was not sew*er* betryste, qwherfor I longe to hey*r* of hys
10 delyng in payeng you, and of hys departyng from you // Owr
father has beyn in Cottyssold, and packyd hys woll: I wos nat
w*y*th hym ther becaws of deythe. Plese hyt you to wnde*r*stond of
my passyng of tyme syn ʒe departyd: tyll Tenebyr Weddynysday

54. 7 fais *over* fay          9 point] sur *canc.*
55. 5 st*er*. *over* iust

III. Public Record Office S.C.1 59/16
Letter no. 55, from Richard Cely junior

I wos at Auvelay, and I departyd from London on Estyrn Ewyn,
and I cowd not get frome my Loord of Sent Jonys not paste iij   15
days togyddyr syn Estyr Ewe. iij dayes afor the wrytyng of thys
I departyd from my Loord, and come to se my father and my
mother, and the morow after ⌜thys⌝ I pwrpos be grasse of God to
goo ageyn. Syr, owr father and mother ys in good heyll ⌜and⌝
myrry in Essex, thankyd be Good, and heyr has beyn Cowldall   20
and hys wyfe, and dyuer of my Loordys mene, and dynyd wyth
owr father and wer merry. Syr, I had your hors into Kent to schow,
and ther wos none that bad me to no porpos. Browmer profurd
v marke for hym, and that wos the moste. Hottys be deyr—I by
none in Essex ner Kente vndyr ij s. viij d. Yowr hors had a sor   25
ey, but hyt mendys well. I pray ʒe send me wrytyng how I schavll
be demenyd wyth hym. My Loorde recommendys hym to you and
prayys you to remembyr hys clothe for hossyn, for he porpos to
make noyn tyll hyt cum. Syr, he prayes you to pvrway hym of
a peys of Hollond clothe of xxx Englys ellys or mor, of a xiiij d.   30
the eylle. Gladman wyth aull my Lordys sarwanttys recomendys
them to you. Syr, I pray ʒe send me word qwedyr thay dy at
Calles or not // As towchyng the mater in your letter of the pour
woman, I saw her nevyr syn byt as I com by her fathers dor I saw
the mayde stond wyth her modyr. Me thynke sche ys lyttyll and   35
ʒeung, qwerfor I spake no mor of the matter. I pray you send me
word how ʒe do in tho maters, and qwate your profur wos, and
wyth hom, and ther schawl be nothyng be doyn heyr byt ʒe schaull
haue knowlege. Syr, I pray ʒe geue Robard Eryke as myche
Flemysche mony for the nobull starllyng as ʒe geue of owr fathers.   40
I ow hym a marke: he has no byll of me byt thys letter. At the
wrytyng of thys her wos Gladman and Tomson to feche me. No
mor to you at thys tym, Jhesu kepe yow. Wryt at Bryttys the xxvj
day of Maye.

per your brother,   45
Rychard Cely.

Dorse: A my welbelouyd brother George Cely, merchand of the
Estapell of Calles, beyng at oste wyth Bornelles whedowe, be thys
delyueryd.

**56.** *Richard Cely the elder at London to George Cely at Calais, 14 June 1479*

s.c.1 53/28

Jhesu M¹iiij<sup>c</sup> lxxix

I grete you wyll, and I haue resayuyd a letter from you wryt at
Caleys the xxxj [day] of May, the weche letter I haue wyll understande, *and* also the same day I haue resayuyd a boxkys, therein
v letters of payment, acordyng to youre wrytyng, *and* I haue
5 schewyde the letters of John Domynyco Barthelomeo, Lombarde,
to ys clarke, and he saythe the letter schall be payd at the day, *and*
I haue schewyd to John Spyngyll, Lombard, ys letter *and* hathe
promysyd payment at the day, but as for Phyllypys Seller of
Dorney, ye mvste wryte to me were I schall speke wyt hym at ys
10 comyng to London. The xiiij day of Jun I schewyd the Lombardys
letters at London. I wrote to you a letter I send to you be John
Rose, *and* of ij salt salers of sylver of the weythe of x unse or xj,
or there abode, bothe wyt a qweryng, and I spake to John Rose
for to ⌈speke to⌉ you for to bye for me a carthe at Caleys for j horse,
15 a schorte carthe, bare unschoide: the wyllys for I haue hyar of my
wolde Caleys carthe. Se the carthe body be good hassche, *and*
hexsyd rydy for goe to worke, for I haue gret nede therto. I sopose
it wyll coste a vj s. or vij s., clotys, lynys pynys *and* all. Praye
John Parcar for hellpe you, or Thomas Granger, for I traywe ye
20 can but lytyll skyle of syche ware. I wrote to you in the letter send
be John Rose, as for all syche money as ye haue resayuyd for me
*and* schall resayue in thys marte, I wyll ⌈ye⌉ make home to me as
meche as ye can, for I here saye there schall goe schepys of war
to the see, werefor God ⌈send⌉ vsse pese. Ye schall here myche
25 more in thys pertys nor I can at Brytys. I wyll ye bye for me v or
vj<sup>c</sup> of good Baras canvase at the marte, for I am avysyde for to
⌈by⌉ more woll. I haue marvele that ye send me no wrytyng be
Randofe of syche maters as he com to London for. I fere me ys
comyng ys for grete maters for the Plase, and here ys but strange
30 warlede for to sve nou. The sekenese raynyd sore at London, God
sesyd wan ys wyll ys. At the wrytyng of thys letter ⌈we⌉ were all
in good helle, I thanke God. Wryte at London the xiiij day of
Jun in grete haste.

*per* Rychard Cely

**56.** 15 haue] ha *canc.*    31 the *repeated*    32 I *repeated*

*Dorse*: To Jorge Cely at Cale[ys] be thys letter delyuerd. (*Shield.*) 35

*In G. Cely's writing*:

| | | |
|---|---|---|
| John Smethe ----------------- | [ . . . ] | |
| [Ja]cob de Bloke---------------- | ix li. xix d. Fl. | |
| xxix Andre*us* iiij s. vj d., s*um*------- | vj li. x s. vj d. Fl. | |
| xxx Rynyshe iiij s. iiij d., s*um* ------ | vj li x s. Fl. | |
| xij Huitryshe iiij s., s*um* ----------- | xlviij s. | 40 |
| an lewe ------------------------ | vj s. viij d. | |
| v postlatys ij s. vj d., s*um* --------- | xij s. vj d. | |
| iiij crovnys at v s. iiij d., s*um* ------ | xxj s. iiij d. | |
| iij Arnovldes ij s. ij d., s*um* -------- | vj s. vj d. | |
| An Gyldars rydar ----------------- | iij s. vj d. | 45 |
| Item vj docat*ys* ------------------ | xxxiij s. | |
| Item in plak*ys* v li.---------------- | v li. Fl. | |
| Su*m* page -------------------- | xxxiij li. xiij s. vij d. Fl. | |
| Item Ryc' Crysp ----------------- | xlvij li. xij s. Fl. ⎫ | |
| Item *receyued* *per* John Mell ------- | xxiiij li. ⌜xij s.⌝ Fl. ⎬ s*um* | 50 |
| Su*m* ------------------------- | lxxj li. Fl. | |
| G. Palmer in redy mony ---------- | l li. Fl. ⎫ | |
| Vpon Loyssor Moy -------------- | l li. Fl. ⎬ C li. Fl. | |

## 57. *John Roosse at Calais to George Cely, 14 June [1479]*
s.c.1 59/4

Ryght worchepffull syr, I recomend me vnto your goode master-
schep, deysyryng eu*er* to herre of your good helle and prosperyte,
the wysch I beseche allmyty God to kep and p*r*esarffe vnto hys
most plesor and to your most hartys deysyre, and yf yt ples you
to here of myn, at the makyng of thys lett*er* I was in goode helle, 5
and all good masters and ffrend*ys*, blesbe Jh*e*su. Fyrste laytyng
you wyt that your ffather and mother and all your good ffrend*ys*
be in goode hell, blesbe Jh*e*su. Syr, yt ys so that I browte a llett*er*
w*yth* me ffrom your ffather to you, of the wyche lett*er* your ffather
had hopyd that I schold a browte hym a answer of from you. Also 10
syr, he leyde arnd*ys* on me by mothe to sey to you: on ys that you
moste by hym a Call*es* carte, onschod for he hathe tyre at hom to
scho yt w*yth*all, and he wolde haue yt schortly, etc. Item, laytyng
you wyt that my chef comyng to Callys was to a spokyn w*yth* you,
for I had browte for you a jentyll lytyll haumlyng horrs, the 15

56. 53 Moy] li. *canc.*

wysche I purpos to haue howom ageyn wythhowte I met wyth
som good merchant for hym. Master Gorge, I tryste veryly in you
to haue a goshauke of you as you promysyd me at London; and
20 syr, yf yt ples you that I schall haue j, when that you wyll wryte
for me to com for hyr I wyll com, and yf you wyll that I bryng
a haumlyng hors wyth me I wyll, and wryte me your intent of
what prys and I troste to God to ples you. Allso syr, yf yt ples you
to haue ony woll or ffell to your hone behoffe yf you wyll haue my
25 ssaruys you schall haue yt before hony man. Syr, yf you wyll wryte
a letter to me you most wryte to me dwyllyng in Lowyke besyd
Hyham Ferrys in Norhamtonscheyr. No more to you at thys tym,
but Jhesu haue you in hys kepyng, amen. Wreton at Callys the
xiiij day of Jun,
30　　　　　　　By your saruant in þat I can, John Roosse.

Dorse: To my ryght worchepffull master Gorge Celly mercha⟨n⟩t
of the Stapull at Callys thys be delyuerd.

## 58. *William Maryon at London to George Cely at Calais,* *22 July [1479]*

s.c.1 59/1

Jhesu

Ryght reuerent syr and my specyall frende, I recomaund me vnto
you. Ferdermor, and yt plesse you ye schall vnderston⟨d⟩ that
Y haue ressayved j letter fro yow, wreten at Bregys the xj day of
Jowlle, the wyche lettere ys derecked vnto yowre broder Rechard
5 Cely, the wyche letter, syr, Y haue ressayved and redde and well
vnderstond. And as for yowre broder Rechard Cely he ys in
Warwykescher wyt my Lord of Sent Jhonys at a town ther that
callyt Baltyssall beseyd Contre. Yt ys nat past a xiiij dayes set he
departyd thederward. Syr, ye sschall vnderstond that my Lord
10 hemselffe cam to my masterys plasse in Hesext for to deseyer of
yowre fader and of yowre moder that yowre brodere Rechard myt
reyd wyt hem into that conterey. Syr, ye schall vnderstond that we
lokt for hem her ayen wytin thys iij wekys, etc. Syr, Y vnderstond
bey yowre wrytyng that they dey sor at Calles, and that ye wovld
15 haue knowlec how that we do in Hessex. Syr, ye schall wnderstond
how that we do in Hesex: as yt Y thanke God ⌐yt ys⌐ ressnabell
well, for ther haue nat y-deyed ther as yt, Y thanked God, nat

57. 27 Norhamton] sy *canc.*

IV. Public Record Office S.C. I 59/5. Letter no. 59, from Richard Cely senior

past a vj personys, and therfor, Syr, my master yowre fadere and
my maysterys yowre moder would awyes yow that ye wovld com
howre vnto them into Hessex, and nat for to com at London, and   20
for to be mery ther wyt them thys hervest, and so for to do youre
pylgrymage. Also syr, ye schall vnderstond that yowre broder
Robard hat y-beryed owte of hys housse her at London by a vj
personys, and the xix day of Jovlle he beryed hyss wyffe. Sche
deyed at Stratford and beryed at London by yowre grandam, and   25
he schall com and dwell ayen in hys hovsse in Mart Lan, etc. Also
syr, I pray yow as my trust ys in yow, that ye woll se well vnto my
fellys at Callys, that they may be scast hoft ynow, for hels they
woll take harm; and wan that ye com houere the se, I pray you that
ye woll makt som good man yowre atorney for to do seyell them,   30
for Y wovld fayn they ware y-sould, for the lengar that Y keppe
them ther the worsse woll the fellys be. Syr, Y pray you that ye
woll remember my ryng, the wyche Y sent you by Robard Eyryk.
No mor vnto you at thys tym, but the Trenyte haue you in hys
kepyng. Wreten at London the xxij day of Jovlle.                 35

per Wylliam Maryon.

*Dorse*: Wnto George Cely, marchant of the Stapull at Calles, thys
letter be delyuerde, etc. (*Shield*.)


**59.** *Richard Cely the elder to Agnes, Richard, and George
Cely* [*12 August 1479*]

s.c.i 59/5

I grete you wyll. I late you wyt of seche tytyng as I here. Thomas
Blehom hatth a letter from Caleys, the weche ys of a batell done
on Sater⌐day⌐ last paste besyde Tyrwyn be the Dwke of Borgan
*and* the Frynche Kyng, the weche batell begane on Saterday at
iiij of the cloke at afternon, and laste tyll nyght, *and* meche blode-   5
schede of bothe pertys, and the Dwke of Borgan hathe the fylde,
and the worschepe. The Dwke of Borgan hathe gette meche
ordenons of Frenche Kyngys, and hathe slayne v or vj Mˡ Frenchemen. Wryte on Thorysday noe in haste.

per Rychard Cely.     10

*Dorse.* To Annese Cely, Rychard Cely, Jorge Cely. (*Trace of seal.*)

**58.** 19 my *repeated*.

### 60. *R. Coldale to George Cely, 21 September* [*1479*]

s.c.1 59/22

Ryght wyrschypfull cossyn, I commaunde me to yow, praying yow
to send me halfe a doson quysschyns *and* viij yerd*ys* ov banker*ys*
acordyng þareto, of Ynglyssche yerd*ys*, verdure þe colowr; and
a fur of bugyschankys ffor my dame, and a fur of calabyr ffor
5 mysselfe yf yt be gode cheper þare. And a desen elnys Ynglysche
of Holand clothe, þe ⟨one⟩ to haue xij þe elne, *and* þe tothyr xvj
di. þe elne, and wryte to my cosyn Rechard what all drawys to,
*and* I schall contente hym w*yth* Godd*ys* grace, who haue you in
hys kepyng. At yow fadyrs place on Saynt Matthew Day.
10                                                                yowr R. Coldale.

I pray you buge for coler *and* sleuys for my wyfe.

*Dorse*: To my ryght wyrschypfull *and* hertly belouyd cosyn George
Selye, be þis delyu*e*red.

### 61. *John Roosse at Calais to George Cely at the mart,* *22 September* [*1479*]

s.c.1 59/21

Ryght worchepffull syr, I recomend to your goode mast*er*schep,
etc., laytyng your mast*er*schep wett the caus of my comyng to
Callys was to com vnto you for a goshauke, as you p*ro*mysyd me
at my laste beyng w*yth* ⌐you¬ in London. Syr, your ffather and
5 mother be in goode ⌐hell¬ and sen⟨d⟩ you Godys blesyng and
thers// And my mast*er* your brother Rechard infformyd me that
you had a hauke in Callys as you tolde hym: he sayd that you
powyntyd ffor me, and that causyd me to com ou*er* seye, and
therfor syr, I beseche you, and you haue onny, to lett me haue
10 hyre as sche ys worthe, and yf you haue non here, thatt you wolde
by on ther w*yth* you now, and send hyr to Call*es*. Or ellys and you
wyll that I com to you, I prey yow to lett me haue worde by the
next man that com bytwyne; for syn I am com so ffar, I wyll haue
on, and yt coste me more then sche ys worthe by large mony. Syr,
15 I wyll not departe ffrom Callys tyll I haue worde ffrom you, *and*
that I beseche you yt may be schortly, for her I haue nothyng to
do but to wayte on a nanswer herof ffrom you. Syr, yf yt ples you

**60.** 7 and] my *canc.*      8 contente hym] wh *canc.*      12 cosyn] Rec *canc.*

to do thys ffor me you schall haue my ssaruys as I am tru Cresten
man, as long as eu*er* I leue. No more to yow, but Jh*e*su kepe ⌐you⌐,
amen. Wreton in Call*es* on the mowro affter Sen Mathew.    20

By your ssaruant, John Roosse.

*Dorse*: To my synggular good mast*er* Gorge Celle, mercha⟨n⟩t of
the Stapull of Callys, beyng in the m*a*rte, þes be delyu*e*ryd, dd.

## 62. *Waterin Tabary to George Cely* [? *before 12 October 1479*]

s.c.i 59/33

Mon treschier et bien ame Maistre Jorge Siliat, je me reco*m*ma*n*de
a v*o*tre bon*n*e grasse; et vous plaise savoir que je vous e*n*voie vng
hom*m*e porteur ⌐decheste⌐ po*ur* co*n*duire l'om*m*e as hotoirs, et
luy ay promys iij stoitrez, et sy do*n*nez au fauco*n*nier vng pot de
vin a v*o*tre vole*n*te pour ses despens. Et se n'eust este po*ur* l'amo*ur*    5
de v*o*us, led*y* hotoirs ne fuchent point venu dechy achy, car il
ont este depuis v*o*tre parteme*n*t requernt du ge*n*tilhom*m*e de
mo*n*seigne*ur* de Bewrez, et ausy de mo*n*seigne*ur* le Lieutenant.
No*n* plus pour le present, synon que Dieu vous ayt en sa sainte
garde. Et paiez led*y* porteur lesd*y* iij stoitrez.    10

Le tout v*o*tre<br>Waterin Tabary

*Dorse*: Soyt don*n*e a Maistre Jorge Silait, demeu*rr*a*n*t aupres de
Mo*n*seigne*ur* Maistre Portier.

## 63. *John Roosse at Calais to George Cely at Bruges, 12 October 1479*

s.c.i 59/15

Ryght worchepfull syr, I recomaunde me vnto you, laytyng you wett
that Thom*a*s Granger infformyd me that you wolde that I scholde
com to Breges to you for to helpe to conuey your haukys into
Eynglond. Syr, I beseche you to pardon me, for by my trothe and
I mowte gett xl s. therby I may not, my besynes ys so at thys tym,    5
butt and your haukys com to Callys or I departe ffrom then*n*s,
I wyll helpe to conuey them ther as yt ples you. And yf yt ples

63. 7 them] the *canc.*

you that I may haue j or ij of them at a resnabyll prys and asyn me
in Eynglond to whom that you wyll that I schall pay at the prys
10 that you do sett of them. And ʒet I bowte a mewd hauke in Callys
syn I cam: sche coste me xl s. and more, the wysche I haue sent
into Eynglond, and ʒett I wyll haue a coppyll of yours and you
wyll, and therfor and yt ples you that I schall haue onny of them,
or and you wyll that I schall helpe to cary them into Eynglond, lett
15 them be sentt to Callys schortly, for I wyll into Eynglond schortly,
by the gras of Jhesu, who haue you in hys kepyng, amen. Wreton
at Calles the xij day of Octobur, anno xix.

By your sseruant,
John Roosse.

20 *Dorse.* To my reuerent Gorge Celly, marchant of the Stapull at
Breges, thes letter be delyueryd. (*Good seal.*)


## 64. *Thomas Granger at Calais to George Cely at Bruges, 20 October 1479*

S.C.I 59/12

Ryght trusty frende, I hertely comaunde me vnto yow, desyreng
euermor to her of your welfar, whyche I pray God contynew vnto
his pleser, amen./ Ferthermor sir, lyke yt yow to wyt how I haue
done your erand vnto Jhon Ros, and I haue desyred hem to com
5 to Brugys vnto yow, and ye sholde haue payd ffor his costys and
haue rewardyd hym so þat he sholde haue holde hym ryght well
plesyd / and sir, he answerd me agayn and sayd how þat he wolde
do also myche ffor yow as lay in his power to do / but ffor sarten
and he shold wynne therby xl s. he myght not com vnto yow at
10 this tyme / and so he hath wryte j lettre vnto yow of his intent,
whyche is bownde vnto þis lettre/ Forthermor sir, ye shall resseue
your ffox gowne of Thomas, on of þe Stapull carters, and Wylliam
Dalton gowne togeder / Morovir sir, I haue ffetched your packe of
ares clothes home vnto me, and my wyfe hathe vndon them
15 euerychon, and shake them, and serched / and blissid be God, ther
is no harme amonge them/ Morovir sir, as ffor the dethe her,
blissid be God, it is passyng well sesid. It is not j quarter as it
was/ and that knowthe the blissid Lorde, who ffor his mercy haue

63. 16 kepyng] ane *canc.*

vs eu*er* in his gydeng, and sende yow good hele, amen. Wryten
at Callys the xx day of Octobir, a*nn*o lxxix.                    20

By yo*ur* to my power,
Thom*a*s Graunger.

*Dorse*: To my ryght trusty ffrende George Cely, march*a*unt of the
Stapull at Callys, beyng now at Brug*ys* at the syne of þe Sterr*e*.

## 65. *Robert Radclyff at Calais to George Cely at Bruges,* [? *1479*]
s.c.1 59/10

Brothur George Sely, I com*a*und me vnto you, etc., lettyng you
haue yn knowlege that I vnderstond by my felow Gilbert Hussy
that a flecked spaniell off myn was late at yo*ur* logyng at the Sterr*e*,
the q*w*ych I wold be loth to forgoo, *and* specially this seson,
pr*a*yng ⌐you¬ to help that my s*er*uau*n*t this berer myght haue hym   5
delyu*er*ed // I haue non othur cause to send hym fore bott only
þat // Sauyng I requer*e* you *and* ʒe see any goodly fedurs to by for
me twayn; j to wer*e* myselff, *and* another for an hors, *and* at yo*ur*
comyng I schall co*n*tent you, both for thaym *and* for þat ʒe haue
layd owte for me heretofore. I p*r*ey you gyffeth cr*e*dence to Golbrond   10
this berer. In hast w*yth* þe hand off yo*ur* brothur *and* felow this
Wedunsday at Cales /

Le filz s*ir* John Radclyff, Robert.

*Dorse*: To my right trusty ffelow George Cely, marchand off þe
Staple.                    15

## 66. *Richard Ryisse at Calais to George Cely at Bruges,* 6 November 1479
s.c.1 59/14

Jh*e*s*u*s, at Calais, the vj[th] day of November, l'an lxxix.

Ryght trusty and welbelouyd brother, I comaunde me vnto you
in the best wyisse I can or may, deseryng to here of yo*ur* good
welfar, the which I beseche allmyghtty Jh*e*su to preserve and kepe
vnto his plesur and youris, etc. Furthermor brother, ye shall
rec*e*y*u*e a lett*er* by Gilberd Palm*er*, the bryng*er* herof, the which   5
cam owt of Inglond at the last passage, the which I receyvid of

a sauldio*ur*, and bycause I know not what mate*rs* of charge may be therin, therfor I send it to you. Item brother, I haue cleryd the bill owt of the tresory for the l li. ster. that we had into the col-
10 lectry, and any servis that I can or may do for you here, ye shall fynde me as redy to do it and as glad as any man on lyve, that knowith the blessid Trynyte, whom I beseche to p*r*eserve you into good helthe, amen. Item brother, the dethe here is well sesid, for ther dyed non here of the sekenesse, not this iij dayes, thankid be
15 Jh*e*su. Wrytyn in hast as afor said.

By yo*ur* lou*er and* brother,<br>Richard Ryisse.

*Dorse*: To my ryght welbelouyd brother George Cely, m*er*shaund of the Staple at Brug*ys*, soit doné.

## 67. *Richard Cely the elder at London to George Cely at Calais or Bruges, 6 November 1479*

s.c.i 53/29

Jh*e*su M¹iiij<sup>c</sup> lxxix

I grete you wyll, desyryng for to here of youre reqvreng, for I und*er*stande be John Rose ȝe were sore seke at Bregys, werefor youre moder *and* bothe youre breon *and* Wyll Maryon *and* I were sory *and* hevy for you. The laste day of Octobor I haue resayuyd
5 a letter from you, wrete at Bregys the xxiij day of Octobor, the weche letter I haue wyl understand, and I tryste to God ȝe be reqvrede and wyll amendyd. Youre letter cam to me the Sonday befor Alhalon Day at dynar tyme at London, and Wyll Eston, mecer, *and* Wyll Medewynter of Norlache ⌜dynde wyt me at tyme⌝
10 and the comford of youre letter cavsyd me for to bye of the forsayd Wyll Medewynter lx sacke of Cottys woll, the weche ys in pyle at Norlache. And John Cely hath gadered and bogwyt for me in Cottyswolde xxxvij sacke be the toode *and* sacke *and* halfe sacke, for the weche I schall hoape meche canvase, for the weche and
15 ye can bye for me iiij or v<sup>c</sup> of Borgan canvase or Barase canvase of good brede, as brode as Normandy canvase, and iij dosen packe trede of Caleys trede, it were good for me. And ȝe cannot I mvste purvae at London for the same, but I am avysyd for to packe ⌜the⌝ forsayd woll after Crystemese, towarde Candelmese. I tryste in
20 ⌜God⌝ ye schall be at the packyng of the sayd woll in Cottyswolde.

**66.** 7 bycause] I *canc.*

I wyll not seppe no woll afor Marche, as I am avysyd at thys tyme.
I wryt no more at thys tyme, but Jhesu kepe you. Wryt at London
the vj day of Novembor in haste.

per Rychard Cely.

Dorse: To Jorge Cely at Caleys or Bregys thys letter delyuerd.  25
(Shield and seal.)

## 68. John Sambach at London to George Cely at Calais, 6 November 1479

s.c.i 59/18

Jhesus 1479

Ryght trusty and welbeloved, I recommaund me vnto you as
hertily as I can, praying you hertily, if it please you, to send me
word by writyng howe ye haue doon wyth John Robert, for Godd
knoweth I wold gladly be quyte wyth hym. He told me when I was
ther at this last Synxon mart that as sone as ye shuld a comen  5
from the marte he wold haue paid you my money, or ellys a
deliuered you fellys of his therfor at a reasonable price. I pray you
send me word how ye doo wyth hym, and Jhesu haue you in
kepyng. Wreten at London the vj day of Nouember, anno lxxix.

By yourys to his power,    10
John Sambach.

Dorse: To my right trusty and welbeloved ffreend George Cely,
merchauntt of the Staple at Caleis, soo it dd.

## 69. William Maryon to George Cely [? before 8 November 1479]

s.c.i 53/108

Jorge Cely, I pray you that wan ye com to Calles that ye woll
remember you for to sell my refussche fellys, for ther schuld be of
them iijᶜ, wytowte my xl blake, for I knowe well that Thomas
Kesten ys lothe for to sell them, for I woust hem neuer for to selle
non of myn but yeff that Y war there mysellfe. And wan that ye  5
haue sould them, I pray you that ye woll by me j pyesse of Holond

sclothe for schertys, and a noder pyesse of Haustar sclothe for
schetys, of xxx ar a xl yerdys. I pray you harteley.

*Dorse, in George Cely's writing*: Wyllıam Maryon.

## 70. *William Maryon at London to George Cely at Calais, 8 November* [*1479*]

s.c.1 53/31

### Jhesu

Ryght reuerent Syr and my specyall frende, I recomaund me vnto
you, euermor deseyryng to her of yowre wellfare, for yt hat be
sayd vnto vs her that ye hath be sore seke, but Y trust to Good ye
be now amended. My master yowre fader and my maysterys yowre
5 modere hat ben ryght heuy for yow. After tym that they hard that
ye war seke ther covde nothy⟨n⟩g make them mery, nat tyell yt
warre Alhalowhyn Heuen that my master hat wrytyng from yow.
Also my maysterys yowre mader and yowre broder Rechard thay
haue had a lytell fette of sekenes to, but now Y thanke God they
10 be amended and all holl, and so Y trust to God ye be also. Syr,
I pray yow that ye woll remembere my bellys of the Holondorys
the wyche that be payabell now at thys Covld mart, and yeff so be
that ye ressayved Y wovld pray yow that ye wovld bestowhyd in
mader of thys sam yerys growyng yeff so be that ye can bey hyt for
15 a nobell the C, and yeff ye can nat bey for a nobell a C, than Y
pray yow that ye woll by me non, but yeff yt owte vnto som good
man. And yeff Rechard, Robard Eyryk ys schyld, haue any ned
of any mony now at thys mart, I pray yow that ye woll delyuer vnto
hem as mesche as he woll haue. And Y pray yow, lyke as Y have
20 wreten vnto yow dyuerys tymes her beforn, that ye woll bey for
me now at thys mart a xx or a xxx yellys of fyn Halfftar for to make
me schetys therwyt, and also that ye woll bey for me a dagar seche
as ye thynke ys good for me. Also Syr, yeffe my wenter fellys be
nat y-sovld wan ye com houere into Hynglond now at Screstemas,
25 Y pray yow that ye woll speke vnto Thomas Gra⟨n⟩ger and yeff
hym the chard and the gydyng of my fellys ⌐the⌐ wylys that ye be
here in Ynglond. Also Syr, ye schall vnderstond that Feleppe

**70.** 7 Heuen] Heven *repeated*        9 Y] trust to good *erased*.        22 seche]
sche *canc.*        25 vnto] *ms.* tho Thomas

Seller ys desesyd her at London and therfor my master yowre
fader wovld that ye wovld nat lat seche thynkys as ye have in yowre
handys in plege for to departe owte of yowre handys tyell ye be  30
sewere of seche mony as ye schuld haue of hem, etc. Wreten at
London the viij day of Nouember, etc.

per Wylliam Maryon.

*Dorse*: Wnto Georg Cely marchant of the stapull at Calles thys
letter be delyuerde, etc. (*Shield*.)                                      35

**71.** *Richard Cely the younger at London to George Cely
at Bruges, 8 November 1479*

s.c.1 53/30

Jhesu M¹iiijᶜlxxix

Whelbelouyd brother, I recomend me harttely wnto yow, desyryng
to heyr of your whelfar and good heyll, etc. Informyng you at the
makyng of thys owr father and mother wher, and whe aull wher,
in good heyll, thankyd be God. Syr, owre father commawnddyd
me to wryte and informe yow that Pelyp Sellar ys dyssessyd and  5
has not payd owr father no peny of hys dwete, qwerfor owre father
wyll that ꝣe kepe the pawyn in yowr handys tyll tyme that ꝣe haue
wryttyng from owr father. Whe ondyrstond that hys wyffe ys
sente for hyddyr: hyt wher whelldoyn to enqwer and ondyrstond
of hys frendys ther how h⟨i⟩t mythet be payd. Syr, ower mother  10
desyer you to by for hy⟨r⟩ a lofe of iij or iiij li. sewgyr and bryng hyt
w*yth* yow at thys Kyrstemes. Owr father sayes he can do nothyng
in Phelype Sellars matter tyll tyme he ha wrytyng frome yow.
I longe sor for William Fawkene⟨r⟩, for Meyge ys sor syke of the
cray and the crampe. I pray yow remembyr my rynge. No moyr  15
to you at thys tyme, byt I pray Jhesu send yow heyll, and bryng
yow wheyll to London, and in sauete. Wryttyn at London the
viij day of Nowembyr. Syr, heyr ys game of betors inow, byt Mege
ys syke: whe lette hyr fly to erly and that ys seyn by hyr now.

per yowr brother,   20<br>Rychard Cely.

*Dorse*: A my welbelouyd brother George Cely merchantt of the
estapell of Calles beyng at Bregys. (*Seal*.)

**71.** 11 hy⟨r⟩: *ms*. hyt

### 72. Ralph Lemyngton at Calais to George Cely at Bruges, 8 November 1479

s.c.1 59/23

Jhesus anno lxxix

Trusti sir, I recommend me wnto yow, desiryng gretly to here of yowr gud welfare, the which I beseche allmyghty God inkrese to his plesure ‖ Also sir, I spake wnto yow for Carroldus grotys at Andwarp, and ye tolde me ye had at Calles wppon ijᶜ li. And if it
5 plese yow to departe wyth all or parte of them, how many soeuer ye will, and I shall giff yow in euery li. acordyng as ye desir⟨e⟩ becawse þat master Levetenaunt callyth so fast apon for custem and subsete ye shall ⌐haffe⌐ in euery li. vj d., etc. Ye shall not fawte of your mony in the Colde marte: the be such men as I shall haffe
10 my mony of in that marte as I dare make me fast apon—it is Jacob Yong Jocobson and Laurans Lambryghtson wyth Peter Martson: the be fast men/ If I may be sped of yow, I pray yow send the kay of your conter to John Dalton or whom that it pleis yow for to delyuer me, and I shall make yow a bill as atornay of Thomas
15 Burton and Thomas Marshall. I pray yow of answere by the next man at cums bytwyn, for if I be not sped of yow I must goo seke farther ‖ Also sir, I haffe sent to William Dalton to reseyue for me—the which I thynke shal be payd this weke—xxxj li. and od syluer. If ye desire þat of hym I haffe wreton wnto hym to delyuer
20 it yow. I pray yow let me haffe shortly word from yow agayn, and God kepe yow. Wreton at Calles the viij day of November.

yowrs Raffe Lemyngton.

Dorse: To George Cely, merchaunt of the Stapull at Calles, beyng at Brugys this don.

### 73. Richard Cely the elder at London to George Cely at Bruges, 11 November 1479

s.c.1 53/32

Jhesu Mˡiiijᶜlxxix

I grete you wyll, and youre moder and I desyer for to here of youre reqvryng and amenyng, as I tryste in God ye schall ryght wyll. Be as mery as ye can and spare for no coste of syche tyngke as may be

72. 3 plesure] ferther canc.    6 desir⟨e⟩: ms. desiruer    7 Levetenaunt] calles canc.

good for you in good mete ⟨and⟩ dryke; and youre fessychons, doe
be there consell and plese them at my coste, and take no gret labor 5
in rydyng tyll ye be stroke. And for that cavse I send Wyll Cely to
you for to do for you wyt the hoversyth of som ⌐good⌐ man, for
I wyll not that ye labor to the marte: kepe youreselve wyll in onny
wyse. I haue lever my money be note resayuyd tyll anoder tyme
radar nor ye schall labor youreselve and not holle, werefor the 10
brenar of thys letter schall enforme you of hoder maters of Phelep
Selar, and hoder maters syche as ye wyll desyer for to here of. Wyll
Cely schall wate on you *and* tend to as long as schall plese you, and
I tryste to God ye schall com home to London or Crystemese.
I wryt no more to you, but Jhesu kepe you. Wryt at London the 15
xj day of Novembor in grete haste.

*per* Rychard Cely.

*Dorse*: To Jorge Cely at Bregys be thys letter delyuerde. (*Seal and
shield.*)

## 74. *Richard Cely the younger at London to George Cely, 11 November 1479*

s.c.1 59/6

Jhesu M⌐iiij⌐ᶜlxxix

Ryught interly belouyd brother, I recomend me harttely onto yow.
Fordermor brother, I haue ressauyd from yow ⌐a leter⌐ wr⟨i⟩ttyn
at Bregys apon Aulhalon Day, wherby I wndyrstond of your grehyt
seckenys, thankyng God of yowr amendment, trystyng the whorste
be passyd. Syr, I haue beyn ryught seyke in Essex afor Halontyd: 5
I thanke God and good dyet I ⌐am⌐ qwyte therof now; and in that
sesun Meyge tooke a seykenes qwherof sche dyed at London; and
when I come to London amonge aull my gownys my beste blake
gown whos gnawyn w*yth* rattons abowte the skyrttys; and i the
nexte mony that I ressauyd for owyr father whos xxx li. qwherof 10
I loste xx s. in gowlde, a my sowll I whot not qwheyr. Thys I wryte
to you of my payne and grefe as ʒe haue doyn ⌐vn⌐to me of yowrs.
I pray yow to come hoom at thys Kyrstemes, and be the grays of
Jhesu whe schaull be myry aftyr all thys trybelassyon and whexsasyon of sekenes. Syr, owr cosyn Cowldayll recomendys hym and 15
hys wyffe to yow, and thay thanke yow of your greyt labor in byeng

74. 1 brother *repeated*          12 doyn to] to *repeated*

of ther stowe, and as for the bankers, thay pray yow that ȝe wyll
by them wyth flowyrs and no sylke, wyth vj cossyons of the same
wharke of the bankers: [they] mwste be in ij peyssys, the toyn
20 v Englysche ȝeardys and the other vj, and the cosyons onstofyd
of the same wharke, etc. Syr, I ame sory that ȝe haue beyn so
combyrd wyth Wylliam Fawkener, byt hyt help not, and as for
the haukys that be deyd, aull owr ewyll go wyth them. When
Wylliam ys mendyd I pray you send hym home. My Lorde of
25 Sent Jonys has wryttyn me a letter wherin he recomendys hym
to yow, and dyssyers me to cum wyth my hawke, for ther ys myche
fowll abowt hym. I longe soor for Wylliam Fawkenar. Syr, owr
father and mother sendys to yow Wylliam Cely to whayt apon yow
and to go and ryd at yowr commawndeme⟨n⟩t acordyng to yowr
30 wrytyng. Syr, owyr ⌈father⌉ and mother ys ryught heuy for yow
and goys ⌈a⌉ pillgrymage dayly for you, and my godfather recomendys hym to yow, and thankys yow for yowr rememberans of
hys stofe, and whe pray yow be myrry and take a good hartte to
you. Owr father and mother desyer yow not to labor nowher tyll
35 ȝe be hoy⟨l⟩. Syr, I pray yow of yowr goodly ansfor scorttly. I had
byt thys letter frome you syn whe departyd. I go nowher ne ryd
tyll I haue a nansfor from yow. And haue my ryng in remembrans.
No mor to you at thys tyme. Jhesu kepe you and send yow heyll.
Wryttyn at London the xj day of Nowembyr.
40                              per yowr brother,
                               Rychard Cely.

*Dorse*: A my ryught whelbelouyd brother George Cely.

## 75. *John Goldson at Calais to George Cely, 30 November 1479*

S.C.I 59/11

### Jhesu anno lxxix

Ryght worschypffull sur, after all due recomendacions had I
herttely recomaund me vnto you, euermore dessyryng to here of
your wyllfare. Forthermore serteffyyng you that your man wyth
your akys com sowre seyk to Calles, and sow my ostys keped hyme
5 a day and a nyght, and thyne we herd ij womon in the towne and

---

**74.** 17 and *repeated*      18 them] of *canc.*      20 Englysche] e *canc.*

the keped hyme at anoder howsse in the towne, *and* sow he ys
deyd *and* theparded to God, God haue marsse on ys sowlle, *and*
I *and* my ostys haue bereed hyme, *and* he had ys masse [*and*] derge
*and* all ys ryghtys as a Cresten man schuld haue. Item, as ffor your
ij akys I haue leyt a man kep thyme that con good skylle of akys,   10
*and* theye lyek wyll, *and* sur, lok what I maye do for you here *and*
hyt schall be redde to my powhere be the grase of God, how haue
you in ys kepe. Wrytte at Calles the xxx day of November vt super.

Be your servant,<br>John Goldson.   15

*Dorse*: To Gorge Selle be thys letter delyuerd. (*Seal representing
gowned and hatted figure.*)

## 76. *Thomas Kesten at Calais to George Cely* (*at Bruges*), *30 November 1479*

s.c.i 59/13

Jhesu M¹iiijᶜ lxxix

Reuerent ande worschepffull syr ande my speceall ffrende ande
gossep, I recomaunde me wnto yow hertely/ dessireng to here of
yowre welffare, the ⌐wyche⌐ Jhesu sende yow to his plessure ande
to yowre hertes esse ande wyll. I wnderstonde that yow haue ben
sore seke ande now well rewiwid, ⌐in⌐ the wiche ⌐Jhesu⌐ cownfort   5
yow ande make yow strong for his mercy, etc. Syr, enformeng yow
that in this towne ther hathe ben gret dethe and yet I thanke Gode
my chelderen ande wyffe stonde, but my mayde ys dedde, etc. //
Syr, enformeng yow that I am remevid ande haue taken me a lesse
lodgeng ande Bondeman dwellethe in my howsse / ande if yow   10
leste to haue yowre hors stelle ther, ar what he can ar may do,
I hope yow schall fynde hym goode ande gentyll, etc. Syr, in
my lytyll lodgeeng that I am now in I haue a fayre stabyll
[*Dorse*] ande a fayre rome and chambur for all my gode maysteres
ande frendes yf yt plesse any of them to se me in my pouerte.   15
A lyttyll forther fſrom the market yt ys / Ande if ther be any
theng that I can do ar may ffor yow I am ande schal be at yowre

comandement, ande Jhesu kepe yow. Wretton at Calles the xxx
day of November.

20
Per yowre owne to his pore pover
T. Kesten.

To the reuerent syr Gorge Cely merchaunt of the Stapell of
[Ca]lles. This be delyuerd. (*Fine seal.*)

## 77. William Cely at Bergen-op-Zoom to George Cely at Bruges, 7 December 1479

s.c.1 59/2

Jhesu M¹iiijᶜ lxxix

Ryght worschyppffull syr, affter dew recommendaschon I louly
recommend me vnto yowre masterschypp. Enfformyng yowre
masterschypp that the Saterday after I departyd ffrom yowre
masterschypp I came to Barow yn saffte wyth all my thynggys,
5 thanckyd be God, etc. Syr, enfformyng yow as ffor Howllonders,
ther be butt ffew comvn to the marte yett. Ther ys non com that
I hawe to do wyth all but Peter Johnson and hys ffellowys, but now
thys weke they saye ther wull come as many as wull come thys
marte, and as ffor mony I hawe receyued none yett off no man,
10 nor non off owre ffellyschypp that I can here syn they cam to the
marte, and as ffor gevyng hower off mony I can nott tell how hit
wyll be yett, ffor I here off non exchaunge makyng yett. Men ffeyr
hytt wyll be nawght ffor ther ys but lycull ware heyr ffor men to
bestow her mony apon: they wene the schyppys schall goo hom
15 halff onladyn, etc. Syr, as schortly as I can receyue my thyngys
I schall make me redy and com vnto ⟨yow⟩ wyth h⟨y⟩tt, wyth the
grace ⌜of⌝ God hytt schall not be long erst, who hath yow yn hys
kepyng. Wrytten at Barow the vij day off December.

per yowre seruaunt,
Wylliam Cely.

20

*Dorse*: Vnto that worschypffull syr George Cely, marchante off
the Stappell at Caleys at Bregys wyth Master Jacob the Vesyschon
be thys dd. (*Shield.*)

77. 9 marte] as *canc.*

**78.** *Richard Cely the younger at London to George Cely at Calais, 9 December 1479*

S.C.I 53/33

Jhesu M¹iiij^c lxxix

Ryught interly whelbelouyd brother, I recomend me wnto yow wyth aull my harte, desyryng grehytly to heyr of your amendment and good heyll. Informyng you at the makyng of thys owr father and mother, brother, godfather and all owr howssowld wher in good heyll, thankyd be God, and desywr grehytly to her of yours. 5
Syr, whe marwell grehytly that whe haue no wrytyng from yow. Syn Wylliam Cely departyd whe had no letter from hym byt whone, and that wos wryttyn at Calles heuer a cam at yow. Syr, heyr ys Phelype Sellar ys factors come. The ton has weddyd Phelypys dowtyr, hos name ys John Forner, and the tother ys 10
name ys Herry Demorres. Be the meyn of a brocar hos name ys John Jacope, a Lombar, whe bar them on hand at the byll wos prodeste and owr father pwt the matter in John Jakopys hand, and he has labord for payment, and the viij day of thys present monythe of Desembyr I ressayuyd iij^c crowny, the qweych ar chosyn be the 15
brocar howt of j iiij^c, euery crown iiij s. The Kynge payd them euery crown at iiij s. vj d. The brocar has awardyt that I schaull ryd to owr father into Essex and bryng a letter of hys hand to them, derectyd to you, that 3e may delyuer them the fardell wyth arras that Pelype Sellar leffyt wyth you, and I schawll haue v li. for the 20
prodest and aull hother costys; byt the brocars parte wyl be myche, etc. I pray yow say to them at fette the arras from you at the byll wos prodest. Syr, whe loke for yow dayly: I ⌜pray God⌝ send yow a fayre passage. Syr, my Lord has wryttyn to me to cum se hym thys Crystemas. I pwrppos to go to hym iij days afor Cryste me⟨s⟩ 25
and be ther iiij dayes and cum agen. And 3e cum not to London iiij dayes afo⟨r⟩ Crystemes I pray you send me my ryng be sum trwsty man. Owr mother lokys for the cas for the peny that 3e toke mesur of. I pray Jhesu send you hydyr in sawete euer I go to Bawlsall, for than I schawl be better besene than I am lyke. No 30
mor. Wrettyn at London the ix day of Decembyr.

per your brother,
Rychard Cely.

**78.** 15 of] Sep *canc.* 26 not] be *canc.*

Syr, I spake to you for hawlue a dosyn payr of Frenche glouys,
35 iij for men and iij fo⟨r⟩ whomen.

*Dorse*: Wnto my Ryught whelbelouyd brother George Cely,
merchantt [of the Esta]pell of Calles be thys dd.

### 79. *Richard Cely the elder at London to George Cely at Calais, 10 December 1479*

s.c.1 53/34

Jhesu M¹iiij<sup>c</sup> lxxix

I grete you wyll. I lete you wyte I haue resayuyd of John Forner
and Hary Demorys for the full payment of Phelepe Seller ys letter
of payment, werefor I wyll that ȝe delyuer to the sayd John or
Hary, the bryngar of thys byll, the plege of Harys the weche
5 Phelype Seller lefete wyt you at Caleys. Wryt at London the
x day of Desembor.

Be youre fader,<br>Rychard Cely.   (*Shield.*)

*Dorse, in Richard Cely junior's hand*: Wnto George Cely at Calles.

### 80. *Richard Cely the elder at London to George Cely at Calais or Bruges, 11 December 1479*

s.c.1 53/36

Jhesu M¹iiij<sup>c</sup> lxxix

I grete you wyll and I desyar for to here of youre recvryng *and*
of youre good hele, as I tryste in God ȝe be. I haue resayuyd a
letter from ⌈you⌉ wryt at Bregys the xxj day of Novembor the
weche letter I haue wyll understande, the weche was to youre
5 moder *and* me and bothe youre brethon *and* Wyll Maryon a gret
comford. *And* fele be youre wrytyng that Wyll Cely was com to
you at that day, for the weche I was wyll plesyd that ⌈he was⌉ wyt
you *and* he can doe onnythyng for youre hesse in thys marte tyme
as I tryste he wyll. Also the vj day of Dessembor I was payd of
10 Phelepe Seller letter of payment, all in cronys at iiij s. ster. a crone,
for the weche I wyll ȝe delyuer the plegys to ys faturs, ⌈for⌉ the
weche I haue delyuer to them a byll wryt wyt my hand for to
delyuer to you for the sayd plegys. But I understand ye delyuerd

a byll of youre handewrytyng to Phelepe Seller at the resayuy⟨n⟩g
of the plegys, the weche byll ys loste, as thay saye, werefor ys   15
faturs hath promysyd for ⟨to⟩ make you a quytons under nottarys
syne. See wyll to that mater for youre dysecharge of the forsayd
plegys, for John Forner *and* Hary Demorys payd me at London for
sayd letter of payment. I wryt no more at thys tyme, but Jh*e*su
kepe you. Wryt at London the xj day of Dessembor in hast.          20

                              p*er* Rychard Cely.

*Dorse*: To Jorge Cely at Caleys or Bregys be thys letter delyuerd.
(*Shield*.)


**81.** *Richard Cely the younger at London to George Cely
at Bruges, 12 December 1479*
s.c.1 59/3

                    Jh*e*su M¹iiijᶜ lxxix

My ryught interly wheylbelouyd brother, I reco*m*mend me vnto
you as harttely as I can dewyse or thynke, thankyng God hyly of
yowr amendemente. Informynge ⌐you⌐ the ixᵗʰᵉ day of Desembyr
I ressauyd ij lettyrs from you: the tone wos wryttyn at Andwarpe
in Octobur and the tother wos wryt at Bregys the xxj day of   5
Nowembyr, the qweche ʒe delyu*er*yd to Wyll*ia*m Fawkenar to
a browhyt, on hos sowyll Jh*e*su haue marsy. Syr, Tomas Grawng
has wryttyn a lett*er* to owre fady*r* and info*r*myd hws of the dysses
of the sayd Wyll*ia*m and how he has pwte the ij goshaukys in good
kepyng tyll yowr comyng to Call*e*s. I pray Jh*e*su sende yow and   10
them hyddyr in sauete and schorttely. Ther ys a claws in your
lett*er* that ʒe wrate laste, trystyng to God that whe schawl be so
myry at owr mettyng that aull sorrowys schavll be forgettyn:
I treste the same. I pray you labor yowselue not to sor tyll ʒe fynd
yoursellfe stronge, and then at ʒe wylle come hyddyrwarde. I wolde   15
wryte to yow of many thyng*ys*, byt I tryste to telle yow them
meryly be movthe. Syr, of aull Phelype Sellars matters I haue
wryttyn you in another lett*er*, sawe I hard Herry Demorrs, that
wos Phelypys mane, say that ʒe delyu*er*yd to the forsayd Pelype
a lett*er* of your hande of seche thyng*ys* as he leuyd w*yth* yow, byt   20
thay wot not wher hyt ys. I tryst to yowr wysdome that ʒe wyll se
to whell inow. No mor to you at thys tym, byt I pray to the

Ternyte sende yow heyll and brynge yow whell hyddyr. Wryttyn
at London the xij day of Decemby⟨r⟩.
25          p*er* yowr brother,
               Ry*chard* Cely, that thynke longe tyll he se yow.

*Dorse*: Ther wos neu*er* mor game abowt ws then the⟨r⟩ ys now.
I treste ȝe wyll nat tary longe at Call*es* at yow comyng ȝeyfe ther
be any sewyr passayge.

30 Wnto my whelbelouyd brother George Cely, m*er*chand of the
Estap*e*ll beyng at Bregys, thys dd.

## 82. *William Cely at London to George Cely or Thomas Granger at Calais, 23 March 1479/80*

s.c.1 53/37;
     59/24 to 31 (excerpted)

Jh*e*su M¹iiij꜀ lxxix

Worschyppffull Syr, affter dew reco*m*mendaschon I louly recommend me vnto yowre mast*er*schypp, enfformyng yowre mast*er*-
schypp that ye schall receyue off the Mary off Raynam, John
D[a]nyell beyng master, iiij sarplers wull: nᵒ vij; nᵒ viij; nᵒ xxv;
5 nᵒ xxiij, the whych ye muste receyue and paye the ffrayte, etc. No
more vnto yowre masterschypp at thys tyme, but almyghty Jh*e*su
hath yow yn hys blessyd kepyng. Wrytten at London the xxiij
day off Marche.
                              *Per* Wyll*i*am Cely.

10 *Dorse*: To George Cely or Thom*a*s Graynger, merch*au*ntys off the
Stapp*e*ll at Calese so hit dd. *Reversed*: John Da*n*ye[ll].

59/24 . . . ye schall receyue off the Mary off Bryckyllsaye, Wyll*i*am
Rechirdley mast*er*, iij sarplers: nᵒ iiij; nᵒ xiij; xxiiij, the whych ye
muste receyue and paye the ffrayte, etc. . . .

15 59/25. . . . off the Antony off London, John Cottyn beyng mast*er*,
iiij sarplers; nᵒ xix; nᵒ ij; nᵒ xx; nᵒ xij . . .

59/26. . . . off the Mary off London, Wyll*i*am Wylson beyng
mast*er*, iiij s*ar*plers wull: nᵒ xiiij; nᵒ xxj; nᵒ vj; nᵒ xxij . . . almyghty
Jh*e*su hath yow yn hys kepyng and bryng hit well vnto yow . . .

**81.** 23 yow] hell *canc.* [heyll
**82.** 3 Raynam] iiij sarplers wull *canc.*          10 Cely] me *canc.*

59/27. . . . off the Blythe off London, Robard Mvncke beyng 20
mast*er*, ij sarplers: n° xvij; n° xviij . . .

59/28. . . . off the Clement off London, Wyll*i*am Phylpott mast*er*,
j serpler and a poke, n° j; n° xxvij . . .

59/29. . . . off the Fortune off London, John Maryett master, iij
sarplers: n° xvj; n° xv; n° v . . . *Dorse*: J. Marrett.                25

59/30. . . . off the Crystover off London, John Leyche master, ij
serplers: n° ix; n° xj . . .

59/31. . . . off the Mary off Redryth, Dave Wyll*i*am master, iij
serplers: n° iij; n° x; n° xxvj . . .


**83.** *Richard Cely the younger at London to George Cely
at Calais, 7 April 1480*
s.c.1 53/38

### Jh*e*su M¹iiijᶜ iiijˣˣ

Ryught enterly whelbelouyd brother, I recomend me harttely
onto yow, and I thanke yow for aulle kyndnes schewyd be yow
to me at yowr laste beyng heyr. Syr, whe wndyrstond be a lett*er*
frome my godfathyr of yowr comyng to Call*es*, and the woll flete,
thankyd be God // Whe haue sente yow be a mane of mast*er* 5
Thewhaytys the whete of the wolle and sch⟨y⟩pys namys acordyng
to yowr desyr. Whe ar aull mery: my Loord has cepeyd hys
Estyrn at Sente Johnys in London and I hav[e] bene w*yth* hym
ther aull the tyme. He and hys howssowlde recomend*ys* them
harttely onto yow. The morne aft*er* the wrytyng of thys howre 10
father depart*ys* to Awelay and ⌐I in⌐to Cottyssowlde. Syr, ther is
a deuysyon fawllyn betwen owr brother Robard and sche that
schowlde a be hys wyfe, and he has geuyn hyr ower, and he
pwrpos to absente hymsellfe and com to Call*es* schorttly, and as
for John Rawns mat*er*, I haue spokyn w*yth* the Kyng*ys* bowȝer, 15
and a sayes he has sent the syngnete to Call*es*, and heyr has bene
Lenarde Boys, and thay has fonde the menys at the mony schawll
be payd at Call*es*. Bawll ys in good plyte: he mornyd tyll he had
felleschype, and the smythe has geuyn hym a drynke for the kow,
and I haue sente hym to Awelay be Lontelay till I cwm agen. No 20

**83.** 15 bowȝer: *or* bowzer

mor to you at thys tym. Jhesu kepe yow. Wryttyn at London the
vij day of Apryll.

per your brother,<br>
Rychard Cely.

25 *Dorse*: Wnto my ryught whellbelouyd brother George [Ce]ly
merchant of the Estapell beyng at Calles.

## 84. *Richard Cely the younger at London to George Cely at Calais, 29 April 1480*

s.c.i 53/39

Jhesu M¹iiijᶜ iiijˣˣ

Ryught interly welbelouyd brother, I recomende me wnto yow
as tendyrly as harte con thynke, informyng yow at the makyng of
thys howre father and mother wher in good hell, and whe aull,
thankyd be God. Syr, I hawe bene in Cottyssowlde and packyd
5 xxix sarpellerys woll for howr father, and in the mene sesun howre
father ressauyd a letter frome yow to me derectyd, and of Lokyngton a carte and a cower qwherin I haue lokyd and fwnde aulthyng
acordyng to yowr wrytyng. Howr father has payd for the kustum
v s., and Lokyngton haskys for frayte vj s. viij d.—a ys not ȝeyt
10 payd. Syr, I haw bowte no felles ȝeyt. I departe to Addyrbery te
fyrste day of May and qwen I cwme agene I wyll wryte to you mor
playnely. I pray yow se my godfathers leter and lete hyme se yowrs.
Howr father marwwellys that he haue no wrytyng frome you.
I pray yow wryt byt for hoype in ws to a whor dyscwmfortys for
15 heuer, ant therfor lete ws indewer ws to plese, as Jhesu geue ws
grase to do, ho haue ws and howre good frendys ⟨in⟩ kepyng.
Wryttyn at London the xxix day of Aprell.

per yowr brother<br>
Rychard Cely.

20 *Dorse*: Syr, my Lord of Sente Jonys commende hym to you, and
thankys yow for yowr tydy[ngys], and prays you of contynewans.
He ys ryught glad of them, and he prays yow to remembyr hys
sadyllys, styropys and spwrs, and clothe for hosyn. Aull tys a[t]
thys Whytsuntyd he pray yow that hyt may be had.

25 Wnto my ryught whelbelouyd br⟨o⟩ther George Cely merchande
of the Estapell beyng at Calles so dd. (*Seal*.)

## 85. *Richard Cely the elder at London to George Cely at Calais, 3 May 1480*

s.c.i 53/40

Jhesu M<sup>l</sup>iiij<sup>c</sup> iiij<sup>xx</sup>

I grete you wyll, *and* I haue resayuyd of Lokynton schepe a pype *and* the stofe therein, *and* a carthe, *and* ix dosen packe threde, *and* I payd v s. for the fraythe *and* v s. for the custom, for Rychard Cely was at Norlayge at that tyme, and hathe packyd my woll wyt Wyll Medewynter—xxvj sarplerys *and* iij sarplers at Westewell— 5 and ys com hom in savete. I understand ȝe be at Bregys, I pray God be youre spede in the maters that ȝe goe for. I fele Robard Cely ys at Bregys for fere of fytyng at Caleys into Beschepys corte for the lvde mater of Jonne Harthe, the weche ys meche adoe for at London. The frendes of here hath spoke wyt me for that mater, 10 but all they wyll not grant a grote for ⟨to⟩ ȝeve them, werefor I haue sayd to them I wyll not ȝeve them a peny of my good, werefore I understand sche wyll falle of for to haue all the ȝetys that Robard hath delyuerd her, *and* to ⌐haue⌐ all Robard Cely hathe of herys; and I understand S*ir* John the pryste hathe promysyd 15 for to make thys ende. But and Rabard Cely were wyse and wylle avysyd, all thys wyll be layd aperte wyll noe, for ys undoe and he wede her, but I may not saye, werefor I haue wryt a letter of thys mater to Wyll Maryon more clerely, for the weche I pray you ȝeve hym good consell and send me wrytyng, for I may doe notgh. 20 But prevely kepe thys maters preve and lette me understand ys entent, and after that I schall wre⟨te⟩ more to you. No more at thys tyme, Jh*e*su kepe you. Wryt at London iij day of May.

p*er* R*ychard* Cely.

*Dorse*: To Jorge Cely at Caleys be thys letter delyuerd. (*Shield*.)   25

## 86. *Richard Cely the younger at London to George Cely at Calais, 15 May 1480*

s.c.i 53/41

Jhesu M<sup>l</sup>iiij<sup>c</sup> iiij<sup>xx</sup>

Ryught int*er*ly whellebelouyd and my syngeler good brother, I recomend me wnto yow in as louynge whyse as harte cone

85. 15 I *repeated*

thynke, enformyng ⌜you⌝ at the makyng of thys howr father and
mother, my godfather Maryon, and whe awll wher in good heyll,
5 thankyd be the good Loord. Syr, hyt is so be grehyt labor that
the whoman that howr brother Robard whos tangyllyd wyth, sche
has made hyme a qwyetans, and sche has aull her awne good that
was browhyt to howr brothers ageyn, and aull the good that howr
brother leuyd wyth her, saue a gyrdyll of goulde wyth the bokyll
10 and pendawnte sylluer and gylte, and a lyttyll golde ryng wyth
a lyttyll dyamond, and a typete of damaske. Sche has awll hother
thyngys that he leuyd wyth her, and wyll haue. Syr, howr father
and mother wolde that ꝫe payd for hys bord at Calles and delyuer
hym v s. ⌜or mor⌝ in hys pors, and ꝫe to take a byll of hys hande of
15 as mwche mony as ꝫe lay houte for hyme; and whe wolde that
he wolde come to Hawelay and be ther tyll the mater be better
hessyd. Howr father thynkys he neddys not to be large of spendyng,
remembyryng aulleth⟨y⟩ng. Syr, I pray you lette hyme not se thys
letter ne tell hym note of tys ꝫend byt of the qwetans, and hy hyme
20 to Hawelay in as gret haste as ye can. No mor to you at tys tyme.
Jhesu kepe you. Wryttyn at London the xv day of Maye. Syr,
I pray yow send my doblet by hym, or be the nexte frend that com.
Hyt ys not for hyme to come in London ꝫeyte.

per yowr brother,
25                                                 Rychard Cely.

Dorse: Wnto my ryught whelbelouyd brother George Cely,
merchand of the Estapell at Callys, be thys dd.

## 87. Richard Cely the elder at London to George Cely at Calais, 22 May 1480

s.c.1 53/42

Jhesu Mˡiiijᶜ lxxx

I grete you wyll, and I haue resayuyd a letter from you wryte at
Caleys the xiij day of May, the weche letter I haue wyll understande, of youre beyng at the martys, and of the sale of my medell
⌜woll⌝ desyred be John Descermer and John Underhay, werefor
5 be the grace of God I am avysyd for to schepe thys forsayd xxix
sarplerys, the weche I bogwyt of Wyll Medewynter of Norlayche
xxvj sarplerys, the weche ys fayre woll, as the woll packar Wyll

86. 19 ꝫend] byt canc.          25 George canc. [Ryc

Breten saythe to me. And also the iij sarplerys of the Recturs ys
fayre woll—meche fynar woll nor was the ʒere before, the weche
I schepede afore Ester laste paste. The schepyng ys begone at 10
London, but I haue non schepyde as yete, but I wyll after thys
halydayys, for the weche I wyll ye orden for the frayth and hoder
costys. Thys same day youre broder Rychard Cely ys rede to
Norlay for to se and caste a sorte of fell for me and anoder sorte
of fell for you *and* Rychard Cely. Wyll Cely ys fore wyt hym, God 15
be there spede. And as for syche maters that the Felysche[p] cam
to London for, I can wryt to you nothyng, for I was in the contre.
Thomas Burgan, mecer, send to me for to a delyuerd me money
be exschanchege befor hand, but I haue take non of hym nor of
no man, but I wyll ye dele wyt Borganys man: he send anoder 20
man—Gilberde Pamar ys from Borgan. I pray you doe as wyll as
ye can in makyng hover of money, for I fere me Rychard Cely wyll
scharege me wyt fell in Cottyswolde and he lyke the passell wyll,
werefore I haue send hym for ys leryng. Also youre horse Bale ys
fayre, werefor I wolde ye send for hym, here ys no sale of horse. 25
I wryt no more to, but Jhesu kepe you. Wryt at London the xxij
day of May.

*per* Rychard Cely.

*Dorse*: To Jorge Cely at Caleys be thys delyuerd. (*Shield*.)

**88.** *John Cely at London to George Cely at Calais,*
[*? 25 May 1480*]

s.c.1 53/70

Right wursull and welbelouyd cosyn, Y recomavnde me vnto wyth
all myne harte, desiring to here off youre gode hele and welfare,
the wiche allmyghty Jhesu mayntene and encrece euer to his
plesur and to youre hartis desire. Firthermore Cosen, and hit plese
you to vnderstand, ther wasse in tyme paste a verians and a jarre 5
betwyne Richard Bowell and my maystur youre fadur for a dute
that he schulde owe to my said maystur youre fadur, and yt ys so
now be my labur Y haue made my sistur and ⌐my⌐ maystur youre
fadur acordyd and agreid for that mater, and a parte is forgevin,
and the todir parte ye and my cosen Richard youre brodur shall 10
haue to *p*arte betwyne you/ and my sistur hath spokyn to my

87. 8 also] iij *canc.*

maystur youre fadur that ye myght helpe to calle vppon Fythian
for a riknyng off ⌜suche⌝ godis as ys in his handis, and also she wull
pray you so to do. Y wasse fully purposid to haue comyn ouer to
15 Caleis now, lyke as Y promysid Fidyan; but, as I vnderstande, ye
be purposid to the marte in shorte space, wherfor Y wull abyde.
Ytt wyll be nere Mydsomer ere I come and be that tyme the marte
wull be don. And Y pray you saye to Wylliam Fidyan what is þe
cause of my tarying/ Y shall bringe wyth me power for vs bothe
20 to take ryknyng of hym, etc. Y pray you recomavnde me to myn
oste John Parker and telle hym Y send hym a chese be þe wull
shippis. No more to you at this tyme, but þe Holy Goste be wyth
you. Wrete at London the Thursday in Whisson weke.

Be John Cely.

25 *Dorse*: To my wursull and welbeloued cosin Jorge Cely marchant
off the Staple att Caleis, be this delyuerd.

### 89. *William Cely at London to George Cely and Thomas Granger at Calais, 1 June 1480*
s.c.1 53/43

Jhesu M¹iiij° lxxx

Worschyppffull syr, affter dew recommendaschon I louly recommend me vnto yowr masterschypp, enfformyng yowre masterschypp that ye schall receyue at ⌜the commyng off⌝ thys fflete
xvij sapplers woll, the whych my master schyppyd at the porte off
5 London the laste day off Maye yn *anno* abowe sayd, and thes be
the schyppys namys they ley yn:

Item yn the Anne off London, Patryck Mychellson master,
v serplers:

N° xl—ss xx cll. ⌜M.⌝　　N° lj—ss xj cllys.
10 N° xxxvj—ss xviij cll.　　N° xxx—ss. xiij cll.
N° ⌜M.⌝ lij—ss xiiij cll.

Item yn Crystower off London, Rechard Grene master, v serplers:
N° xxxix—ss xiiij.　　N° xlvj—ss xv cll.
M. N° xlj—ss xiiij cllys.　　N° xlij—ss xx cll.
15 N° xxxvij—ss xj cll.

Item yn the Mary John off London, John Costentyne master, iij
serplers:

88. 12 to] ca *canc.*　　16 marte] shortly *canc.*

M. N⁰ xxxij—ss xx.    N⁰ xxviij—ss di. iiij cll.

N⁰ xxxviij—ss xx cll.

Item yn the Antony of Myllhall, John Hawll*us* master, iiij serplers: 20
N⁰ l—ss j cll.    N⁰ xxxj—ss xxij.    N⁰ xlviij—ss xiiij.

N⁰ liij—ss xviij cll. Etc.

No more vnto yow at thys tyme, but almyghty Jhesu hath yow
yn hys kepyng. Wrytten at London the ffyrste day off Jun.

per Wyllyam Cely.    25

*Dorse*: To George Cely and Thom*a*s Gran[ger], marchantes of
the Stapp*e*ll at Caleys, so hit dd.


## 90. *Richard Cely the elder at London to George Cely at Calais or the mart, 2 June 1480*

s.c.i 53/45

Jhesu M¹iiij° iiij××

I gret you wyll, *and* I haue resayuyd a letter from you wryt at
Caleys the xxix day of May, the weche I haue wyll understand,
and that ye haue solde vj sarplerys and pok[e] of my medell woll
Cottyswolde to John De Sclermer of Gante, pryse the sacke xiij
marke, for the weche I am wyll plesyd, werefor I haue schepyd at  5
London the laste day of May, xvij sarplerys of my Cottyswolde
woll, wereof be vj clotys medell woll, in grete haste, for the cokyys
were made the same day and the schepys depertyd ij day of Jun,
and my Lorde Levetenanthe depertyd the same day, I pray God
send my Lorde *and* the woll schepys wyll to Caleys. Rychard Cely  10
hath be in Cottyswolde and hath bogwyt xv° fellys for you and
hymseve *and* xv° for me of Wyll Medwynter, the weche cam to
London thys same day. I wyll ye bye for me v or vj° of canvase
at the marte for to packe wo[ll] wyt, of a good brede, not elle
brode—halfe quarter lese, *and* not of the smaleste, but prathy rond  15
canvase for to packyng in woll. I pray you send me wrytyng of all
syche maters as schall long to me, for [I] thynke ye mythe wryt
meche more nor ye doe, for my Lorde of Send John[ys se]nd to
me for ty⟨d⟩yng euery weke, for the weche my Lorde takyt for
a [grete] ple⟨s⟩ar for to haue syche ty⟨d⟩yng as ye here in thys  20
partyys, for the weche ye may no lese doe but wryt meche the

90. 5 at *repeated*        9 I] pa *canc.*

more of ty⟨d⟩yng, for my Lordys sake, for in good faythe he ys
a curtes lord to me *and* to you *and* Rychard Cely. I wryt no more,
but Jh*e*su kepe you. Wryt at London the ij day of Jun in grete
25 haste.

per Rychard Cely.

*Dorse*: To Jorge Cely at Caleys or the mart, thys letter delyuerd.
(*Shield*.)

**91.** *Richard Cely the younger at London to George Cely
at Calais or the mart, 2 June 1480*
s.c.1 53/46

Jh*e*su M¹iiijᶜ iiijˣˣ

Ryu*g*ht interly whelbelouyd and my syngeler good brother,
I recomende me wnto yo*u* in as louyng whys as hartte con thynke.
Plese hyt yow to wndyrstonde at the maky[ng] of thys howr father
and mother, my godfather Maryon and whe aull ⌐wher⌐ at London
5 in good heyll, thankyd be the good Loorde. Syr, I haue bene in
Cottyssowlde and bohut for hus xxvᶜ pell*ys*, pryse le C of xvᶜ:
iij li., and of a M¹: heu*ery* C iij li. iij s. iiij d., and I haue payd and
a mwste pay v*yth*⌐in⌐ thys v days in parte of p⟨a⟩ym*ent* of thes
fell*ys* and for caryayge, xl li. and aboue, and I mwste pay to
10 Wyll*ia*m Mydwynt*er* at Bartyllmewys tyd xx li., and at Hallontyd
xx li. for the forsayd fell*ys*. Syr, I pray yow haue theys dayes in
rememerans, my powr honeste lyes ther apon. And at my com-
*my*ng*ys* howte of Cottyssowlde apone a schorte pwrpos howr father
has schypyd xvij sarp*ellerys* of hys wooll that whos packyd at Nor-
15 lache syn Est*er*, and ther ⌐ys⌐ vj of theme myddyll, and that ys aull
the myddyll woll of that soorte. I know hyt whell, ther come not
bett*er* myddyll woll of howr fathers thys vij ʒeyr; and at the next
schyppyng howr father wyll schype the remenand of good whooll
of thys sorte, and hawlle hys fell*ys*, and so wyll I howrys. And
20 I haue ressauyd ij lettyrs frome you, whon of howr brother
Robarde, and therin whos of hys own hande contanyng iiij li.
starlyng payabull the iiij day of ⟨June⟩. I pray God send ws good
paym*ent*, and another Edwhard Lenawll*ys*, the qweche I do whell
wndyrston⟨d⟩. I pwrpos be the gras of God to be at Lontelays
25 whoddyng on Sonday next, and my godfather to. Syr, heyr ys
yowr blake hors and you*er* gray at London: thay ar in good plyte.

Ther ys no mane byd no mony for them, and thay stond you to
grete coste dayly. As for horsse and hawkys, I pwrpos neu*er* to
haue paste whon at onys. Syr, I wndyrstond be yowr wrytyng that
ȝe haue leuyd Thom*as* Grayngar to be your atornay at Call*es*  30
whyll ȝe go to the marte. I do send hym a lett*er*, and therin the
schypys namys and the whette of howr fathers, and nwmbyr that
he schawlle ressaue hyt by, be the grasse of Jh*esu*, haue you in
hys blessyd kepyng. Wrytyn at London the sekund day of June.

Be your brother,    35
Rychard Cely.

*Dorse*: Wnto my ryught whelbelouyd brother George Cely
m*er*chand of the Estap*ell* at Calleys or at the marte be thys
delyu*er*ydd.

## 92. *George Cely: memoranda for Thomas Granger*, c. *2 June 1480*

Ch. Misc. C. 47 37/12 f. 6

Jh*esu* M¹iiij*ᶜ* iiij*ˣˣ*

A reme*m*bravns ffor Thom*as* Graynger ffor George Cely.

Forst syr, and ȝe con, sell iiijᶜlvj wynt*er* London of my ffadyrs
Rychard Cely hys: they be praysyd at xij noblis, xx d., and they
be howlde ffelys. They ly in the nedyr chambyr houyr my Lady
Clar.                                                                      5

Syr, ther ys in the same chambyr iijᶜ xlix Cot*ys* of my fadyrs in
the sayd chambyr, praysyd xiiij noblis, howlde ffellys allso.

Syr, ther ys in the sayd chambyr of my neme John Celys viijᶜ
d. xlij contre pel*es* pra*y*syd at xiij noblis xx d.

Syr, ther ys in garett abawe vjᶜ xl whynt*er* ffell*es* of Wyll*i*am  10
Maryons praysyd xij noblis d.

It*em*, ther ys an Cxlix Cott*ys* ffellis of Wyll*i*am Maryons that ys
the ȝend of an sortt pr*a*ysyd at xiiij noblis. They ly in the hopper
garett.

Syr, all thes bethe howlde ffellys abowe wrettyn ‖ I pray yow  15
sell them as whell as ȝe con, etc.

Ther lyys in an stabull theras Thom*as* Kesten dewellyth now,
vᶜ xxv som*er* ffellis London praysyd at xvj noblis d.

It*em*, ther ys in an garratt in that same plasse, ij M¹ lxxv wynt*er*

20 London praysyd at xiij noblis v s. // This sortt lyys in ij lytyll
garatt*ys* togedyr. All thes bethe newe ffellis.

Thom*a*s, I pray yow sell som of myn good Cott*ys* woll that com
at Estorn and ʒe con, and as ffor that at com syns I pray yow lat
ytt alon tyll Y com, but yff John Vandyrhay of Mekelyn com, ffor
25 he most hawe all the medyll wholl that I hawe: I hawe mony in
my hondys of hyssyn that Y browt w*yth* me ffrom ther. That woll
that com last ys nott awhardyd ʒett, and ʒe shall know the todyr
be the nombyrs, ffor all that woll that ys no*m*byrd anbovyn xxvij
com last //

30   Syr, yff ther com any woll or ffell to Calles ffrom my ffadyr or
brodyr or W. Maryon, howsse the woll in Provd*ys* whollhowsse,
and hyr som of the garat*ys* houyr the sayd whollhowsse yff any
ffelis com. I dem ther woll com none tyll I com ffrom the m*a*rte
agen, etc. //

35   Syr, I lewe w*yth* John Cay the cayys of my ffelchambyr to the
entent he shall cast my sayd ffellis, and whan he has done he shall
bryng the cayys vnto yow.

Syr, yff any wollys of my ffadyrs comys, I pray yow lat the
ffrayght be p*a*yd and send me wryttyng of the comyng therof, as
40 ʒe woll Y shall do yow plesur in tyme comyng, and wherto I am
bovnde.


**93.** *George Cely* [*at Antwerp*] *to Richard Cely the elder
at London,* c. *June 1480* (*Draft*)

s.c.i 53/44

Jh*e*su M¹iiijᶜ iiijˣˣ

Ryght reverent and whorschypffull ffadyr, aff*ter* all dewe reco-
mendasyon p*re*tendyng, I recomavnd me vn⟨to⟩ yow in the most
lowlyest whisse that I con or may. Fordyr mor, plesythe ytt yow
to vnd⟨e⟩rstond that at my comyng vnto this Syngsyon m*a*rte
5 I spake w*yth* John Descyrmer of Gavnt, and he hawe made vnto
me, and to dyvars of my fellyschyppe heuyr I come to the m*a*rtte,
grett complaynt of yowr medyll woll wheche Y sowlde vnto hym.

92. 20 v s. //] thes *canc.*      lytyll] y *canc.*      36 whan he] as *canc.*      38 any]
go *canc.*

93. 4 comyng *repeated*

He swerys vnto me largely that he has hade of yowrs in tyme
passyd bet*ter* medyll yowng Cott*ys* than this woll whas. They lay
vnto me grett vnkyndenesse that Y delle w*yth* them vnd*er* this 10
maner/ they say vnto me that ȝe myght an takyn howght of this
vj sarpl*eris* and the poke, ij sarpl*eris* medyll yowng. Ytt ys so,
becavsse they wollde nott strywe w*yth* me, they do hodyrwhysse
than they wher porposyd—they bowght ytt ffor ⌐þer⌐ own drapery,
and now ther ys no man wholl drap*er* none of theke sarpl*eris* at 15
Gav*n*t nor at Breg*ys*, but he ys ffayne to bryng them to the m*ar*te
and sell them ther, wherffor I am ryght sory // In good ffayþe
Y connott say ⌐wher Y⌐ wrytt vnto yow or no heroff // Y hade
moche whorke at Calles heuyr I covde hawe ytt anwhardyde ffor
Cott*ys*, and moche stekyng whas anȝenst ytt anmon⌐ge⌐yst the 20
Fellyschyp. In the reverens of Good se bet*ter* to the pakyng of
⌐yowr⌐ woll that shall com, or ellis yowr woll ys lyke to ⌐lesse⌐ that
name that ytt has ⌐hade⌐ heuyr anffore ⌐in tyme passyd⌐ // I nevyr
whyst yow sent cursar woll to Calles ffor the contre than this last
whas/ I am porpossyd to com hovyr vnto yow whan this m*ar*te 25
ys done, and than schall Y tell yow mor playnle be movthe.

*No address or subscription.*

## 94. *Robert Good at London to George Cely at Calais,* 24 *June 1480*
s.c.1 59/37

### Jh*e*su M¹iiij° lxxx

Ryght reu*er*entt and worshypffull mast*er*, aftyr dwe recom-
*m*endacon I lowly recom*m*ende me vnto you, dysyry*n*g eu*er*more
to ȝer of y*our* welfar*e*, the ⟨which⟩ allmythy Jh*e*su pr*e*ser hyt to hys
plesyr and to y*our* most hart*ys* desyr*e*, etc. Doy*n*g y*our* mastershyp
to vnderstondon, at the maky*n*g of thys lettyr my mast*er* and my 5
mast*er*s, my mast*er* Rychard Cely, *and* Wylli*a*m Maryon, and all
owre howssowld be yn goode helle, thankyd by God, etc. I⟨f⟩ hytt
plesse y*our* mastershyp to wnd*er*stond, my mast*er* *and* my mast*er*s
*and* all ou*er* houssowld by yn Esex, they by byssy at maky*n*g of
hay now. As for my mast*er* Rychard ys much at my Lord of Sentt 10

---

**93.** 22 yowr woll that] yowr *subst. for* the       23 hade *in marg., ch. from* dade

Johns *and* som*e* tyme w*yth* my master, etc. No mor*e* vnto you at
thys tyme, bud the Holy T*r*enyte haue you yn hys kepy*ng*. Wrytt
at London the xxiiij day of Jun yn hast*e*.

*p*er *your* sa⟨r⟩uand*e*,

Robard Good.

15

*Dorse*: To my worshypffull most*er* Jorge Cely, m*er*chaunt*e* of the
Estap*e*ll of Caleys, thys lettyr by delyu*e*rd.

## 95. *Richard Cely the younger at London to George Cely at Calais, 30 June 1480*

s.c.1 53/47

An*n*o Jh*e*su M¹iiij° iiijˣˣ

Ryught enterly whelbelouyd brother, I recomende ⌈me⌉ wnto yow
as louyngly as harte cane thynke, enformyng you at the makyng of
thys hour father, mother, and whe aull wher in good ⌈hell⌉,
thankyd be God, and the xxvj day of thys monthe I resauyd ij
5 lettyrs frome you, whon to houre father, another to myselue, the
qweche I do whell wndyrstonde, and heyr I sende yow closyd in
thys a byll of mast*er* Rychard*ys* hand from the Mayar of the
Estap*e*ll for the dyscharge of the xxiij s. iiij d. of the sarpler, for
xvij sarp*ellerys* xix li. xvj s. viij d. And I feyll be your lett*er* at the
10 woll sch⟨y⟩pyd at your departyng frome hens vhos not so good as
I wholde hyt had bene. Howr father whos at the packyng therof
hymselfe. I trwste to God thys wholl schaull plese you bett*er*;
and as for myddyll wooll, ჳe haue aull that belong*ys* to that sorte.
Syr, I haue resauyd not ჳeyt byt xv° of howr fell*ys*, byt thay be
15 good. I wndyrstonde be your wrytyng that ჳe wyll come into
Inglond schortely—I pray you kepe your porpos and whe schaull
be myrry, be God*ys* grase. My Loorde comend*ys* hym to you and
lokys dayly for the geyr that ჳe promysyd to pwruay hym, and
Gladman prayse yow to purway a saddyll for hyme, sumwhat lesse
20 then my Loord*ys* schall be. A lyes styll at Berwyke, and I thynke
wyl do aull thys som*ar*. Syr, I h⟨a⟩ue ressauyd at the day whell and
trewly the iiij li. st*er*. of hour brother Robarde. And now the
sch⟨y⟩pe heyr, byt houre father powrpos not to schype tyll hyt
be ny Myhellmas, and therfor whe wyl loke for yow dayly, and syr,

**95.** 2 louyngly as] har *canc.*

I pray yow brynge w*yth* yow a the rekenyng that I am indettyd 25
to y*ou*, and ⌐whe⌐ schaull se a way therin, be the grase of Jh*e*su
kepe you and bryng you into Yngelond soyn and in safete. Wryttyn
at London the laste day of Juyn.

Syr, howr father has ben dysesyd sor. I tryste hyt be byt an
axys, byt I wolde fayne that ʒe whor her tyll he be bett*er* mendyt. 30

p*er* you brother,
Rychard Cely.

*Dorse*: Wnto my ryught whellbelouyd brother George Cely,
m*er*chand of the Estap*e*ll at Callyes be thys dd.


## 96. *Richard Cely the younger in Essex to George Cely,*
*5 July 1480*
s.c.i 53/48

Jh*e*su M¹iiij<sup>c</sup> iiij<sup>xx</sup>

Ryught interly whelbelouyd brother, I recomende me wnto yow,
informyng yow at the makyng of thys howr father ys aull hooll
and ryugtht merry, thankyd be God, as my neym the bryngar of
thys can informe you. Syr, howr father wyll that ʒe be not ou*er*
haste in comyng into Ynglonde, for thys cauys: he wndyrsto*n*dys 5
whell that the woll that whos schyppyd at your departyng from
London ys not lyke of goodnes to that at ys of the laste ʒeyrs
growythe, and therfor he whoulde not that ʒe schulde sell them
togeyddyr, byt as for the myddyll woll at ⌐vos⌐ laste schypyd, he
wyll that John Wandyrhay haue hyt acordyng to your wrytyng, 10
and hour father whowlde fayne that ʒe mythet make salle of the
good woll of the furste sorte as whell as ʒe can. He dar not sende
no moor to Calleys tyll he heyr of the salle of the forsayd. Syr,
hour father wndyrstond*ys* of owr brother Robard*ys* chyldysche
dellyng. And Wylli*a*m Browell has beyn w*yth* hym and me, and 15
he says that Cowlton or ʒe haue a speceaulte of xiij li. Fl. payabull
at Bammys marte next, whenyng to hym that hyt had bene
payabull at Senchan m*ar*te laste, and that made hym so bowlde,
as he says, byt howr father wyll that ʒe ⟨se⟩ the clernes and send
ws whoord hou hyt ys. No mor to you. Wryttyn at Byrtt*ys* the 20

---

**95.** 27 kepe: *ms.* hepe    **96.** 11 ʒe] co *canc.*    12 the] fur *canc.*
18 payabull at] so[.]w *canc.*

v day of Juyll. Tomorrow I go *wyth* my Loorde to Grauys End
to brynge in my Lady Marget.

*p*er your brother,
Rychard Cely.

25  *Dorse*: Wnto my ryught whelbelouyd brother George Cely.

### 97. *Harold Stawntoyn at Calais to George Cely at Bruges, 19 July [? 1480]*

s.c.i 53/128

Jhe*s*u M

Me*st*er Cely, I p*r*ay yow let yowr man do so myche ffor me as to
go to the syne off the Ster next onto Flemmyng*ys* Dame wheras
daggers be maid, *and* I p*r*ay yow let hym resc*ey*ue a dagg*er* off
hym *and* pay therffowr ij s. vj g*r*. by the same tokyn that I payd
5  hym vj g*r*. in arnst. Allsso I p*r*ay yow that he may go to the cap-
maker next beyond Willi*a*m Kenett*ys* on the same synd to
Flemyng*ys* Dame warde, *and* let hym resc*ey*ue off hym vj sengell
bonot*ys* off dyu*er*s colors as I bespake ffor, *and* I p*r*ay yow let hym
be p*a*yd ffor them, *and* at yowr comyng to Cales ye shall be co*n*tent
10  w*yth* Godd*ys* grace. Syr, ye may say ye haue a howmly ffelow off
me, ffor ye haue don so myche ffor me that hit lyse not in me to
deserue hit, but ye shall haue my s*er*ues, *and* that God knows, how
p*r*eserue. At Cales the xix^th day off Juylly.

by yowr owne to my power,

15

H. Stawntoyn.

*Dorse*: To the ryght worshipffull Jorge Cely, m*er*chant off the
Stap*e*ll, soitt dd. (*Seal.*)

### 98. *Richard Cely the elder at London to George Cely at Calais, 1 September 1480*

s.c.i 53/49

Jhe*s*u M^l iiij^c iiij^xx

I grete you wyll, and I haue resayuyd a letter from you wryt at
Caleys the xxij day of Auguste, the weche I haue wyll understand,
and ʒe haue solde iiij^c lvj fell, for the weche I am wyll plesyd, but

97. 2 to the] ster *canc*.    5 gr.] on *canc*.    6 next] to *canc*.    16 worship-
ffull] syr *canc*.

I understand ȝe can sele no woll as ȝete. I tryste to God ȝe schall
full wyll. We schall schepe at London woll *and* fell nowe dayly, 5
for the weche I am avysyd for to schepe my woll *and* fell, werefor
ȝe mvste se wyll to the resayyng at Caleys, for I haue no man for
to sende wyt the schepys, for Wyll Cely ys fore wyt Rychard Cely
wyt my Lorde of Sent Jonnys into Franse, God be there spede,
for the weche I tryste to you for the resayyng of my woll *and* fell, 10
and allsoe for youre fell *and* Wyll Maryons fell. I sopose ȝe haue
not meche adoe at thys marte, for the weche I praye you send me
wrytyng of youre goyng to thys marte or not, for and ye be at
Caleys at the londyng of my woll *and* fell I wyll be wyll plesyd
and ye may so doe. I haue resayuyd of Mondedanell iiij sadellys 15
*and* a grane *and* payere of styropys, and be the grace of God Wyll
Maryon *and* I schall lade ys schepe wyt fell. The schepyng ys not
as ȝete begon, as it gothe fore I schall wryt to you. And ye here of
ware send me wrytyng schortely, for I wyll not be the fryste that
schall schepe. I wryt no more to you, but Jhesu kepe you. Wryt 20
at London the fryst day of Septembor in haste.

per Rychard Cely.

*Dorse*: To Jorge Cely at Caleys thys letter delyuerd. (*Shield.*)

## 99. *Richard Cely the younger at Dover to George Cely at Calais, 2 September 1480*

s.c.1 53/50

Jhesu M¹ iiijᶜ iiijˣˣ

Ryught whelbelouyd brother, I recomend me wnto you, and I pray
you hartely to be at Bolen the iij day of Septembyr, for my Loord
wyll be ther, and I pray yow to brynge *wyth* yow your crosse and
v ar vj li. Flemysche for me, and at howr metyng I wyll tell you
mor. No mor to you. Wryt at Dowyr the sekunde day of Sep- 5
tembyr.

per your brother,<br>Rycharde Cely.

Plomtton p⟨r⟩ays you to delyuer thys byll to hys brother Nowell
ȝer ȝe cum to Bolen.                                          10

*Dorse*: A my whelbelouyd brother George Cely at Calles, so-
hyt dd.

**99.** 4 me] W *canc.*

**100.** *John Cely at London to George Cely at Calais, 6 September 1480*

s.c.1 53/52

Right wurshipfull and welbelouyd Cosen, I recomavnde me vnto you, and also my sistir youre avnte comavndyth her vnto you as hartyly as she can or may, allway thankyng you off youre grett labur and besinesse that ye hadd for ⌐her⌐ now at this tyme, for
5 the wiche she hopeth to rewarde you in suche wise as ye shal be plesid, wyth the grace off Godd, etc. Item, sir, Y haue byn wyth maystur Ylam, and he hath promisid to paye this lxx li. vj s. viij d.: it is redy for her. Also sir, ye shall vnderstande that my sistir youre avnte hath made her exchange wyth John Mathew,
10 mercer, of London for the iiijˣˣ xj li. Flemmyshe, the wiche is in your hand, and she shall reseyue here of the said John Mathew at suche dais as they be agreid, lxxv li. xvj s. viij d. ster., and heruppon she hath delyuerd to the said John Mathew the bylle of youre hand, the wiche mone she prayeth you hartly to paye to the
15 said John or to his atorney *and* bringer of youre said bylle, now at this nyste marte, as her very truste is in you that ye wull so do, etc. Firthermore sir, as for the byllis of John Eton þat Fedyan axith, in gudd fayth we cannott yett fynde them; Y trowe nor neuer shall. Yf we can he shall haue them, and so saie to Fydian.
20 No more to you at this tyme, butt allmyghty Jhesu haue you in keping. Wrete at London þe vj day off September anno Mˡiiijᶜ iiijˣˣ.

Be John Cely.

*Dorse*: To my cosen Jorge Cely merchante off the Stapull att
25 Caleis, be this delyuerd.


**101.** *John Cely at London to George Cely at Antwerp, 6 September 1480*

s.c.1 53/51

Right wurshipfull Sir and welbelouyd cosyn, I recomavnde me vnto you wyth all myne harte. Plese it you to wete that my sistir youre aunte hath made a bargen wyth John Mathew, mercer, of London, and shall reseyue off hym at suche days as she and he be
5 agreid, lxxv li. xvj s. viij d. ster., and she hath delyuerd hym youre

bylle of youre hand, be the wiche he must reseyue of you now att
this marte, iiij$^{xx}$ xj li. Flem*m*ysshe, the wiche she praith you to
paie to the said John Mathew or to his atorney or bringer off youre
bylle, acordyng to her couinavnte and promysse, etc. No more at
this tyme, but allmyghty Jhe*s*u haue you in keping. Wrete at 10
London the vj day off September, a*nn*o M$^l$iiij$^c$ iiij$^{xx}$.

Be John Cely.

*Dorse*: To my cosen Jorge Cely att Anwarp marte be this lettir
delyuerd. (*Drawing of heart-shaped device.*)

## 102. *Robert Cely at London to George Cely at Calais, 6 September 1480*

s.c.1 53/53

A*nn*o lxxx

Ryght reuerentte and worchepffull broder, I herttelly recomaunde
me to yow. Farthermor, plesse yt yow to wette that at the makyng
of thys lett*er* howr ffather *and* mother wer mery and in god hell,
blessyd be God, and so we hop that ȝe be. And as for howr broder
Rychard Cely, ys departtyd w*yth* my Lorde of Sentte Johnys w*yth* 5
þe inbassetorys into Frawnce, werof I soposse yow wndorstonde
ryght well, and I ham att London, and haue ben grettely desshessyd allmoste heuer sen yow departtyd fro Alluelay, and moste
partte haue kepte my bedde, for I hafe ben so seke *and* sore that
I goo w*yth* a staffe. I thanke God I ham now daylly amendynde // 10
Item, Brother George, the causse of my wrytynge ys thys, and
I pray yow herttelly of yowr good broderhod that ȝe wyll do so
moche for me to see that Wyll*ia*m Borwell, merc*er*, of London, be
contentte of ys byll of xiiij li. xv s., and wat mony yow lay howtt
for me I wyll conttentte yow herefor. And I had natte haue hade 15
þat mony of Wyll*ia*m Borwell at that tyme, I had loste all my
platte; werfor, good brother, remember me, *and* I shall dessaruytte
to yow w*yth* the grasse of God, hoo haue yow and all ws in ys
blessyd kepynge, amen. Wrette at London the vj day of Sep-
tembe⟨r⟩ w*yth* grette payne.                                      20
[*In George Cely's hand*:]                    Be yowr brother,
Domyne heny[. . .]                            Robard Cely.

*Dorse*: To my welbelouyd Brother George Cely, marchand of the
Staple at Calles. (*Shield.*)

**103.** *Edmond Bedyngfeld at Calais to George Cely, 24 September [? 1480]*

S.C.1 59/20

Wurshipfull sir and my ryght specyall frende, I recomande me vnto you as hertyly as I can, thankyng you of your good will shewed vnto me at all seasons // And as for my mony, I hope veryly to be purveyd be ⟨the⟩ Leutenaunt of the Stapill / and ellys I wold
5 haue ben bold to haue called vpon you / But I must pray you to take summe labour for me in this martt // for to bie for me—yf ther be eny—worn long gowne of chammelet, damaske or sateyn, that be not but of a small pryce of iiij nobill or ther aboute. I pray you bie me on / but I had leuest haue chammelet, so it be blak,
10 tawne or violet, but non other coler // Ferþermore, I pray you to bie for me ij ⌜dosyn⌝ peyre of glovys for women: on dosyn of the largest assyse, and another dosyn, the on half lesser than the tother / And also to bie me a sheff of good quarell for a bowe of xiiij li., and a wyndas for bothe handys for a bowe of vj or vij li.,
15 and let the quarell be sent to Lynne or to Boston wyth my gere that Bondeman sendes, and that my quarell may com hom that ye boute for me the last mart, weche I wold had be sent to Lynne or to Boston also, and ellys I pray you let them com eder and this stuff bothe, as ⌜sone as⌝ ye may / And yf ther be eny manerly
20 dagers or ponchys at the mart, that I may haue summe to geve away. And hour Lord kepe you. At Calais þe [*Dorse*] xxiiij day of Septembre.

your Edmond Bedyngfeld.

Vnto Jeorge Sely marchauntt of the Stapill.

**104.** *Richard Cely the elder at London to George Cely at Calais, 25 September 1480*

S.C.1 53/54

Item, be the grace of God I haue schepyt woll *and* fell at Porte London in my name:—

Item, in the Thomas of Raynam, Hemonde Danyall mayster, vj packys contening xxiiijᶜ ij fe[ll].
5 Item, in the Blethe of London, Laryns Bordon mayster, vij packys *and* ijᶜ fell contening xxx⟨ᶜ⟩ fell.

**103.** 11 ⌜dosyn⌝ *over canc.* peyre

Item, in the Anne of London, Patryke Mechelson mayster, ----
ij sarplers.

N° xxxiiij ----ss xviij cll.     Sum iiij sacke d. x cll.
                                 Rebate ------- ix cll.            10
N° xxxv -----ss xviij cll.       Sum clere, iiij sacke d. j cll.

Item, in the Thomas of London, Thomas Horne mayster:
----- ij sarplers.

N° xxix ----- ss xv cll.         Sum iiij sacke d. viij cll.
                                 Rebate -------- ix cll.           15
N° xlv -------- ss xix cll.      Sum clere, iiij sacke xxv cll.

Item, in the Mary of Mallyng, John Underwode mayster:
------- ij sarplers.

N° xliiij ----- ss xvj cll.      Sum iiij sacke d. ij cll.
                                 Rate ---------- ix cll.           20
N° xxxiij ----- ss xij cll.      Sum clere, iiij sacke xix cll.

Item, in the Edward of Mylale, Thomas Arnolde mayster:
----- ij sarplers.

N° xliij ------ ss xvj cll.      Sum iiij sacke d. iiij cll.
                                 Rebate -------- ix cll.           25
N° xlix ------ ss xiiij cll.     Sum clere, iiij sacke xxj cll.

Item, in N⟨i⟩colas of Colchester, John Smythe mayste⟨r⟩:--------
ij sarplers.

N° liiij ------ ss ix cll.       Sum iiij s⟨a⟩cke xvj cll.
                                 Rebate -------- viij cll.         30
N° lv -------- ss vij cll.       Sum clere iiij sacke viij cll.

Item, in the Mary of Brekellyssay, Wyll Recherdlay mayster: - - -
j sarpler.

N° xlvij ------ ss xiiij cll. Rebate iiij cll. Sum clere ss sacke x cll.
        Sum toall      ------------ xj sarplerys.                  35
        Sum toall in sackys -------- xxiiij sacke vj cll.

I cannot haue my woll packyd the weche lythe in pyle at London
in no wyse, for the weche it schall abyde tyll the neste schepyng.
I understande be youre letter that ye schall packe my woll; xx
sarplerys the weche was schepyt in Marche. I wolde fayne under-    40
stand the packyng of that sorte. I send to you wyt schepys Robard
Good for to helpe to londe my fell and youre xviij° fell and hode⟨r⟩
fell and Wyll Maryons fell. I wyll ye se scharly to hym, and wan
the schepys be dyschargyd, send hym home be water to London,
for I haue grete myse of Rychard Cely and Wyll Cely at thys tyme, 45
in good faythe. I may not dele ⌈wyt⌉ woll and fell and my hosbanry

in the contre bothe, but I may ⌈haue⌉ helpe. I was never soe wery
of delyng wyt worde as I am at thys tyme, and shyt that my Lorde
of Send Jonnys cam to Bollen I hadde no wrytyng from you but
50 j letter noue late, for the weche I understod not veryly for ⌈ye⌉
were in Franse or at the marte. I hadde so many sayyng of men
that cam from Caleys and no letters, for the weche I was gryly
astonyd, *and* grete lettyng in my besynese, for the weche I pray
the wryt *and* send be svre men that I may understande my delyng.
55 Also ye wryt not to me of the reste of my fell, weder thay be refvse
or nay, *and* wat sum of fell there be, for I wat ⟨not wat⟩ fell the
reste schold be. I wryt no more to you at thys tyme. Jhesu kepe you
*and* hvse. Wryte at London the xxv day of Septembor in haste.
                                        *per* Rychard Cely.

60 *Dorse*: To Jorge Cely at Caleys delyuerd. (*Shield*.)

*In G. Cely's hand*:
The costum and sobsede of
       my ffadyrs ------------- iij×× xiij li. iij s. xj d. ster.
       Wylliam Maryons ------- xxij li. ster.
       Rychard Cely jonyor ----- xv li. vj s. vj d. ster.
65                             Cxxx li. x s. v d. ster.


**105.** *Copy of memoranda by G. Cely for Thomas Granger,*
*and notes by George for William Cely, c. 25 September 1480*
s.c.1 53/55

*In W. Cely's hand*:

                    Jhesu M¹iiijᶜ lxxx

A remembraunce ffor Wylliam Cely.
       Syr I pray yow to sell souche howlde ffellys as I haue as ny as
ye can. Ther ys off my ffaders in the lower chamber iijᶜ xlix Cottys
praysyd at xiiij noblys. In the vppyr chambyr: Ther ys off Wylliam
5 Maryons CC xxvj praysyd at xij noblys di. Ther ys off Wylliam
Maryons C xlix praysyd at xiiij noblys.
       Thes be all the howld ffellys that I hawe. Ytt ys sayd that many
off them bethe reffewys. When the prayssers hath sen them, as
they awarde ytt I am plesyd. Yff the prysse be to meche they to
10 sett ytt lower—I woll be content because I wolde hawe them
gone, etc.

New ffell*ys*. Ther ben in Thomas Kestens xij<sup>c</sup> lxxv wyn*ter* ffell*ys* London, p*ray*syd at xiij noblys v s. I pray yow sell them and ye can.

Syr, I pray yow sell sum off my ffaders Cott*ys* woll and ye con.  15 Sell off that at beryth nombyr abowe xxvij, and all that ys vndyr xxvij shall at my co*m*myng to Callys be packyd aȝeyn. Ther ys x *s*arplers goode Cott*ys* bers nombyr abowe xxvij. Sell them and ye con, I pray yow, and all tymes my *s*ervyse as moche.

Syr, I pray yow reseyve off John Eldyrbecke or at Wyll*i*am  20 Bondmans the key off the wollhowsse nexte Wyll*i*am Bondemans, ffor ther moste be parte off Wyll*i*am Maryons ffell*ys* when they come.

Syr, I lewe w*yth* yow xx li. Fl. to pay ffrayght w*yth*all, yff any off my ffaders woll and ffell com yn the men seson. Syr, I prayow  25 lat Kay fforhowsse the xx sarplers off my ffaders owte off John Prowdys wollhowsse vnto the wollhowsse besyde my stabull. Ytt ys theke xx that moste be packyd aȝen. They bere no*m*byr vndyr xxvij. I pray yow that ⌜that⌝ woll at ys co*m*myng may be howssyd yn John Prowd*ys* wollhowsse w*yth* the x *s*arplers, etc.  30

And my ffaders ffell*ys*, as many as woll ly ower the woll be my stab*u*ll I pray yow ley there, and gett howssyng ffor the remnant, and my brodyrs ffell*ys* howyr my Lady Clare. Wyll*i*am Maryons ffell*ys* nexte Wyll*i*am Bondemans. I woll send Wyll*i*am Cely to vnto yow in all the haste that I can.  35

[55 B] Syr, I pray yow yff any wryttyng com owte off Ynglonde to me, loke appon ytt and kepe hit by yow tyll I com. Ytt schall nott be longe but Wyll*i*am Cely schall com vnto yow, and Kay and my ladde that kepe my horsse schall be redy yff any thyng com to wayte vppon yow, etc.  40

The kay off my ffell chamber ower my Lady Clare, John Wurme hathe ytt. I pray yow reseyue hit off hym.

It*em* I pray yow receyue off Randolffe ij oblygaschons, on off my neme John Cely off xj li. viij s., and on off Wyll*i*am Maryons off viij li. xiiij s. v d. ob. Fl. They be off Cleyss All Wynson and  45 hys ffellowys off Laythe.

[*In G. Cely's hand*:]                              Pro W. Cely.

Se whell to the londyng of thes ffellis, and as sone as they be londyd, tell them and se that ȝe hawe yowr talle of them all, and of yowr wholl.  50

**105.** 32 stab*u*ll *ch. from* stapull          34 ffell*ys*] ow *canc.*

And as sone as all ys londyd, send Robyn home. And as ffor all hodyr thyng*ys*, Y remytt to yowr whysdome ‖
[55 C. *In W. Cely's hand*:]
Item the last day off September p*a*yd to the howssers ffor the fforhowssyng off xxj s*a*rplers, eu*e*ry sarpl*e*r ij d.—iij s. vj d.
55 [*In G. Cely's hand*:] Thom*a*s Grayng*e*r at my dep*a*rtyng ⌐in⌐ to Av[. . .]

### 106. *Richard Cely the elder at London to George Cely at Calais, 13 October 1480*
s.c.1 53/56

Jh*e*su M⌐iiij*c* iiij*xx*

I gret you wyll, and I lette you wyt I haue payd for xxiij s. iiij d. of the sarplere for xxij sarplerys woll *and* fell to S*ir* Wyll Stoker, Mayar of the Stapyll, the xiij day of Octobor—s*u*m xxvj li. xiij s. iiij d., as aperyt be the waront the weche I haue in my hand.
5 I schall send the waront to you wat tyme I understande ʒe be at Caleys. I send to you wrytyng of my schepyng at London at thys tyme be Robard Good my schylde, the weche I mygth not wyll a myssyd hym *and* Wyll Cely bothe, for the weche youre moder *and* I were not soe sarvyd thys xx ʒere, for the weche I purpose
10 me ⌐to⌐ more esse, be the grace of God, the weche haue you in ys kepyng. Wryt at London the xiij day of Octobor in grete haste.
*per* Rychard Cely.

*Dorse*: To Jorge Cely at Calys thys letter delyuerd. (*Shield*.)

### 107. *Richard Cely the elder in Essex to George Cely at Calais, 29 October 1480*
s.c.1 53/57

Jh*e*su M⌐iiij*c* iiij*xx*

I gret you wyll, and I haue resayuyd a letter from yow wryt at Caleys the xvj day of Octobor, the weche letter I haue understand wyll, and that ye haue solde a sarplere of my good woll Cottyswolde, pryse the sacke xix marke, and vj sarplerys of my medle
5 woll Cottyswolde, pryse the sacke xiij marke, all solde to John Van Underhay of Mekelyn for redy money in hand, as I understand.

The poyse *and* sum argent I understand be the byll. I understand
be Wyll Cely ys letter that my woll, xj sarplerys, and my fell
schepyth at London late, rysythe ryght fulle at Caleys, for the
weche the fellys mvste be made, werefor I wyll that Wyll Cely be   10
style wyt you at Caleys for to make my fellys wyll and to helpe
to packe my xx sarplerys woll, the weche was schepyt in Marche
laste paste. And as Robard Good, I wyll he com home as sone as
he may haue a fare passage. I haue grete myse of hym. Also my
xxiij s. iiij d. of the sarplere ys payd at London, and the waronte   15
send to Caleys be a marchant of Berelay. I understand be youre
wrytyng yt ys lyke be ware wyt Frase, for the weche I wyll avyse
you for to purchese a save condyte in onny wyse or that ye pase
the se, for dyverse cavsys, the weche I wyll wryt to you of or ye
com hover the se, and yt be ware as I fere me yt wyll be, for the   20
weche wryt to me as ye can here and understand in syche maters,
for I haue not as ȝete packyd my woll at London, nor I haue not
bogwyt thys ȝere a loke of woll, for the woll of Cottyswold ys
bogwyt be Lombardys, werefor I haue the lese haste for to packe
myn woll at London. I haue a grete scharge at Caleys of my woll   25
there at thys day, God send vs good sale. I wryt no more to you
at thys tyme. Jhesu haue in kepyng. Wryt at Brytys the xxix day
of Octobor in haste.

per Rychard Cely.

*Dorse*: To Jorge Cely at Caleys be thys lett*er* delyuerd. (*Shield*.)   30

## 108. *Richard Cely the younger at London to George Cely at Calais, 15 November 1480*

s.c.i 53/59

Jhesu M¹iiijᶜ iiij×ˣ

Riught interly whelbelouyd brother, I recom*m*end me harttely
wnto you, and I thanke you of your grehyte coste and scheyr that
ȝe dyd to me and my fellouys at howr laste beyng w*yth* yow at
Calleys. Syr, whe had a faȝeyr passayge, and the Satter*day aftyr
howr departtyng whe come to the Kyng to Helttame, to home my   5
Loorde whos ryught whelcu*m*, and ther whe tarryd tyll the
Kyng*ys* dowt*er* whos kyrstynd, hos name ys Bregyt, and the same
nyte ryught late whe come to London, and heyr I fownd hovr
father, brother Robar⟨d⟩, and my goddefather Maryon, and thay

10  ar myry. Howr mother ys yn Essex: I se har not ʒeyt. My godfather
Maryon tellyd me that he has wryt lettyrs to yow: I ondyrstonde
a part of them. Robyn Good tellyd howr fathe⟨r⟩ tha⟨t⟩ ʒe had
v hors, and I tellyde hym ʒe had byt iiij, and how ʒe haue sowlde
Py j to Syr Vmf[ry] Tawlbot, and he whos welle content. I towllyd
15  howr fathe⟨r⟩ of the lose of Twesyltonys mewyll. Syr, howr father
wyll not schype tyll Marche, and he wolde fayne that the vooll
ᴵvherᴵ packyd. I feyll by hym that he wolde not that ʒe come home
at Crystemas, for he thynkys ther wyll be salle abohut xij tyde.
Ther ys gret dethe of schepe in Engelond. Syr, I wollde wryte
20  more to yow byt I depart into Essex thys same day to fet howr
mother. No mor to yow. Wryt at London the xv day of Nowembyr.
                                        per your brother, Rychard Cely.

And the mewyll m⟨a⟩y be gityn, send hym to howr father, for he
whoulde fayne haue hym.

25  *Dorse*: Wnto my ryught whelbelouyd brother Geoorge Cely
merchand of the Estapell at Calleys.

[*In G. Cely's hand*:] Domyne ffyat p[ax] cum vyrtute.

## 109. *George Cely at Calais to Richard Cely the elder at London, 16 November 1480*

s.c.1 53/60

Jhesu Mᴵiiijᶜ iiijˣˣ

Ryght rewerent and whorshypffull ffadyr, affter all dewe recomendacyon pretendyng, I recomeavnd me vnto yow in the most
lowlyest whysse that Y con or may/ Fordyrmor, plesythe ytt yow
to vndyrstond that I hawe resseywyd an letter ffrom yow beryng
5  date at London the xiij day of Octobyr in hast/ wheche Y do
whell vndyrstond, and I hawe resseywyd yowr warant, and ys
anlowyd appon yowr byll ancordyng. As towchyng hodyr clavsys
in yowr sayd letter, Y vndyrstond them ryght whell, and as ffor
Robyn, ye vndyrstond ᴵbe thisᴵ how whell he has done none thyng
10  but put ʒe to cost, etc. As towchyng me, bothe be yowr sayd letter
and be my cossyn Maryons, I am sory, and Y connott be mery tyll
that Y hawe ben wyth yow, and Y whollde a ben wyth yow shorttly,
savyng my besynesse ys soche that Y connott, as ʒe know // Indede

109. 5 at London *repeated*          13 know //] Imd *canc.*

Y hawe bene long awhay, and therffor my besynesse ys the mor.
Y this day Y begon to pake yowr wholl. Y thanke Good ytt rysythe 15
ffull ffayr, and som medyll woll ӡe shall hawe, but and ytt rysythe
as ytt do, ytt shall nott be moche. I hawe men apon yowr ffellis
dayly, in good ffaythe Y nevyr sawe yowr good so lond in my dayys,
and so dyd all mens. ӡe shall hawe abowe an M¹ made ffellis/ and
yowr woll ys lykewhysse arayd. Be the grace of Godd Y sshall 20
fenyshe all thyng*ys* heuyr that Y go vnto the m*a*rte ‖ As tovchyng
my clawis afore, I hawe ben long hens, as ӡe know, nevyrthelesse,
and my debyteyys had done ther devteys, Y myght so a ben ffor
that sesson ryght whell / Now Y hawe sen that at Y desyryd long
to se Y toke this seson, wheche tyme Y wollde that Y hade lyne 25
syke in my bede yf ӡe be dysplesyd therw*yth*. Y hawe hade lettyrs
dyvars to an kept Wyll*ia*m Cely styll at Calles: indede he dep*a*rtyd
heuyr any wryttyng, [60 B] and allso Y shall nott nede hym grettly,
Y hawe helpe ynow. Y am in good whay of my besynesse now, ӡett
whas ther ryght lytyll done therto whan he dep*a*rtyd. 30

Ytt ys so that her whas grett ado at Calles ffor that woll that come
in the last schyppyng, becawis the dokat*ys* bare nott dat of the
xiiij day of Septembyr, dyvars men wold an hade ytt but newe
woll. Ther ys derectyon takyn that ytt shall nedyr be new nor
howllde, but yt shall hawe that lysens that yt shall passe w*yth*- 35
howght howlde woll, appon yt selffe. Men hade whent that the
ffellis showld a bene howlde, ӡett whe connott tell: ther ys replyyng
ther anӡenst. Y thynke that whe shall sett them in the sam kasse
as the wholl stondys: whe shall do moche therto / Y whas to swefft
in wryttyng to my cosyn Maryon, Y wrott hym they wher howllde 40
ffellis. It ys so that the xiiij ⌈day⌉ of Nove*m*byr ytt whas conclevdyd
be Cortt that ⌈from⌉ Candyllmesse ⌈forþe⌉ no man shall sell but
ffor xxvj s. le li. I thynke ytt shall cavsse an stope. ӡe most now
wrytt me yowr hadvysse how Y shall be demenyd: wher Y shall
howlld hand tyll than, or sell affore, and Y con / Ther ys but lytyll 45
Cotty*s*wolld woll at Calles, and Y vndyrstond Lombardys has
bowght ⌈yt⌉ vp yn Ynglond, and ӡe vndyrstonde what sobstons is
at Londo*n* to shyppe. I hope ther whas nott a bett*er* m*a*rkett
toward ffor Cotty*s* woll many a day ‖ I woll nott avysse ӡe to shype
in the dede of wynt*er*: ytt ys long lyyng, ffowlle whedyr, and 50
jepardes ffor stormys. Of tydyng*ys* I con none wryght yow ffor
sarten as ӡett, but at myn howllde Lady ys comyng ffrom Bynus

109. 32 becawis] yt *canc.*    42 *ms.* at ⌈from⌉    47 is *ch. from* of

D 148    H

to Sent Tomers, and the ambassettors bothe of Inglond and
Fravnsse. Y connott say what whorlld whe shall hawe: some of
55 the Devkys Covnsell wholld hawe whar and som pesse—the very
grovnde most come howght of Ynglond. The Frenche Kynge has
fforneshed his garysons appon the ffrontys all redy, etc. [60 C] My
lady porposythe to ly at Sent Tomers and the Frenche ambassett shall
ly at Tyrwhyne iij lekys thens, etc. || Her ys but ffewe merchantys
60 at Calles nowe. I am in whay wyth Gyshbryght Van Whennysbarge
ffor an ij of yowr sarpleris: Y hope Y shall go thorow wyth hym /
I woll tha[t] Y myght vndyrstond be wryttyng wher the Kyng
porposythe to hawe whar wyth Fravnsse or no: my brodyr
Rychard may vndyrstond that of my Lorde. Yff Y vnd[yr]stode
65 betymus Y myght, yf nede be, porvay me off saffecondytt. Y
whollde fforst vndyrstond how the Kynge take my Lordys answar,
etc. No mor vnto yow at this tyme, but Jhesu hawe yow and all
yowrs in his kepyng, amen. Wrettyn at Calles the xvj^th day of
Novembyr, Anno iiij^xx.

70                                           per yowr son,
                                              George Cely.

*Dorse*: Vnto my ryght whorschyppffull ffadyr Rychard Cely,
merchant of the Stapell of Calles, dwelling at London in Marte
Lane, soit dd. (*Shield*.)

## 110. *William Maryon at Aveley to George Cely at Calais,* *19 November [1480]*
s.c.i 53/62

### Jhesu

Ryght reuerent syr and my specyall good frend, Y recommeund
me vnto you. Ferdermor, plessed you to wete that Y haue ressayued
a lettere fro you wreten at Calles the xij day of Novembere, the
whyche lettere I haue red and well vnderstond that ye haue
5 ressayued a letter fro me wreten at London the ix day of Novembere. Yn the wyche lettere I wrote a clausse of youre horsse, the
wyche Y vnderestond ye taked sor at yowre stomakt. Syr, in good
fayth Y am sory therefor, for and Y had west that ye would a taked
so sor Y would nat a wreten so vnto you, nat and Y schuld a gette
10 therbey xx nobelys, but ye schall vnderstond wat caused me so
for to wryte vnto you. Syr, ye wrote vnto my master that ye

sophosed be lyklyhod yt schuld be ware; and yeff yt so be yt
schuld be war, ther schuld be gret rydyng and mekell ado abowte
Calles; and yeffe ye be well horssed, Y feyr me that seche sowdyerys
as ye be aqu⟨a⟩y⟨n⟩ted wytall schulld causse yow for to put yowre 15
body in aventere; and yeff ther com anythyng to yow hoderwysse
then good, in good faythe a grete parte of my mastys gey in thys
world wayere y-do. Syr, thys caused me in good fayt for to wryte
so vnto yow as Y dod; for Y know well and ye haue no good
horsse they woll nat deseyere yowte of the toun. Syr, in good 20
faythe my mastere youere fader neder my maysterys yowre modere
knowe no thyng of my wrytyng, and in good faythe ye shull
vnderstond that Y wrote nat so vnto you for no spyte, neder for
no hewell well that I haue to yow, but for gret loue; for in good
faythe, sauyng my master [y]oure fadere and youere broder 25
Rechard, in good faythe there ⌈ys⌉ no man in Iynglond Y would
do so meche for, and that ye schuld know and ye had ned. And
that caused me to be so bovld to wryte so to yow, the wyche Y
would yt had be vndo the wylys ye taked so as ye doo. No mor
vnto you at thys tym, but the Trenyte haue you in hys kepyng. 30
Wreten at Aluerley the xix day of Novembere.

                              per Wyllam Maryon.

*Dorse*: Wnto George Cely, marchant of the Stapull at Calles ⌈thes⌉
lett[er] be delyuerd.


**III.** *Richard Cely the younger at London to George Cely
at Calais, 22 November 1480*
s.c.1 53/61

                    Jhesu M¹iiij° iiij××

Whelbelouyd brother, I recomende me harttely onto you.
Plessythe hyt you to wndyrstond at the makyng of thys howyre
father and mother and aull the howshowlde ⌈ar⌉ in good heyll at
London, and merry, thankyd be God // Sir, I haue ressauyd a letter
from yow wrytt at Calleys the xij day of Nowembyr, wherby 5
I wndyrstonde yowr greve, qwerof my godfather has wryttyn to
yow // He saw howr father pensyffe and heve at Robyn Godys
comyng home ⌈and afore⌉, as ʒe know hys condyssyon of howllde,

110. 21 modere] moder *repeated*
III. 8 know] gys *canc.*

and that causyd hym so to wryte. Syr, howre whyen ys commyn
10  and ys ryught good as of that contre; whon hagyshed vyll gene
xx s., and the rembenant ys lyke to be dronk her and at Auvelay.
For frayte, costome and caryayge, my godfather has geuyn
towarde. Syr, as towchynge the matter of your hors, I harde howr
father neuer speke whorde of them more then I whrote to yow in
15  a letter that I sente be Asschelay Bacar, and as for the blynde
hors, I pray yow selle hym, whatsomeuer 3e gehyt for hym. As
for ij or iij hors, ys not myche as 3e be pwrwayd. Qwheras ⌈3e⌉
wryte at thay haue yow in jelosy, I cannote parsaue hyt: thay
thynke as 3e ar horssyd and aqwayntyd that and any whar be, 3e
20  schulde be desyryd forthe wyth other; and as fortewyn a whar ys,
3e to be takyn or sclayn, the leyste of bothe wher j dethe bothe to
father and mothe⟨r⟩. Whe mwste tendyr thayr ayge and haue a ny
to hour own whell. 3e ar goyng to a marte that I know well has not
bene heyllfull ner mery to yow in tyme paste, qwerfor I schaul not
25  be were myr⟨y⟩ ner qwyhet tyll I heyr of your good comyng to
Callys ageyn. Howre father schype at thys tyme byt ij packys
fellys that he cowde not haue no rome for at the laste schypyng,
and as for hys woll, schaull abyde to Marche. Syr, whe how to
my godfather xiiij li. ster. qwerof my Lorde howys ws x li. I se
30  hyme not thys viij days. Petter recomendys hym ow⟨n⟩to yow and
thankys ⌈yow⌉ of yowr grette cheyr at Calleys. He has hys deyd
of my Loord. And as for whar betwene ws and Frawns I can
thynke 3e schawl haue noyn: ther goys houer inbassette schorttely
—what thay ar I connot tell. Thys day begyn the Counssell at
35  Whestemynster. Syr, whe loke not for yow at thys Crystemes for
becawys of the wheddyr, and in aspessyaull that howre father and
whe tryste at 3e schull make sum good salle aftyr the hallydayes of
wooll and fell, as I pray God send ws. Ther ys lyke to be many
fellys, for scheype begynys to dy faste in diuerys contrey, and
40  I wholde whe wher doyng among hodyr men. Syr, I pray yow
sende me the rekenyng of my Loordys stoufe, and Coldallys, and
the spor rowell. No mor to yow at thys tyme, Jhesu kepe yow.
Wryttyn at London on Sente Clementys 3ewyn.

per your brother,

45                                                    Rycharde Cely.

*Dorse*: Wnto my ryght whellbelouyd brother George Cely,
merchant of the Estapell at Calles, be thys dd.

**111.** 18 yow in] go *canc.*          39 in *repeated*

**112.** *George Cely at Calais to Richard Cely the elder at London, 24 November 1480*

s.c.1 53/63

Jhesu Mⁱiiijᶜ iiijˣˣ

Ryght rewerent and whorshypffull ffadyr, affter all dew recomendacyon Y recomeavnd me vnto yow in the most lowlyest
whysse that Y con or may. Fordyrmor plesythe ytt yow to vndyrstond that Y hawe sowllde vnto Gysbryght van Wenysbarge ij
sarpleris good Cottys. He has takyn hon of the xx that ys pakyd 5
agen and anodyr of the todyr sortt, as be an byll closyd herin
makys mensyon, etc. / Yt ys so that Y hawe nott ȝett made an ȝend
of the pakyng of yowr ⌐sort⌐ of xx sarpleris. Ther ys xj pakyd all
redy. The cawis of the taryyng of the remnavnt ys ther whas
moche bettyn wholl, and as sone as that con be whonde and made 10
rede ytt shall be entyrdyd in þat at ys to pake. Ther ys in the
pakekyng of thes xj sarpleris mor nan an sarpler medyll wholl cast
howght. As son as ytt ys pakyd ȝe shall vndyrstonde be the next
how ytt ys // etc. // Yowr wholl ys all y-clowsyd and nevyr a hone
pakyd agen saweng that at ys ffowllest arayyd ys takyn togydyr, 15
and whan yowr woll ys pakkyd ytt shall be cast howght and whardyd, and so pakyd agen /// Yowr ffellis bethe ny made—ȝe shall
hawe mo made thane Y wrott to yow of // Whan all thyng ys
ffeneshyd than shall ȝe hawe the clernesse of all thyngys. Her ys
as now but ffewe merchantys. Ther shall be som ffett done betwene 20
Crystmesse and Candyllmasse becavsse of the ordynavnsse, wherffor now Y porposse me to tarry and com nott to yow tyll
Candyllmasse. As of any tydyngys her Y con none wrytt yow
as ȝett. Ther ys, but Y connott hawe the trewthe therof / ther
has ben an varyavnsse betw⟨e⟩ne the Devkys men of whar 25
and hys Allmaynus, and ther ys many of his Allmaynus slayne,
and therffor he takys grett desplesure. þer ys dyvars of his
jentyllmen stollyn away therffor, and som ar comyn to Calles
and hone of them ys sent to owr soweren Lorde the Kynge,
and som [Dorse] and som ben ren Frenchemen when that the 30
Frenche Kynge has gottyn lattly [dyuars] of the best men of
whar the Dewke hade, wherof he makys hym now bowllde.
No mor vnto yow at this tyme, but Jhesu hawe yow and all

112. 1 ffadyr] ffadyr *canc.*

yowrs in his kepyng, amen. Wrett at Call*es* the xxiiij day of
35 Nove*m*byr a*n*no iiij*ˣˣ*.

p*er* yowr son,
George Cely.

Ytt ys so that Y do send Harry my boye to whayght appon my
brodyr this Crystmesse // etc. //

40 Vnto my ryght whorschypffull ffadyr, Rychard Cely, m*er*chant of
the Stapull of Calles, being at London yn M*a*rte Lane, soit dd.
(*Shield.*)

### 113. *Richard Cely the younger at London to George Cely or Thomas Granger at Calais, 12 December 1480*

s.c.1 53/64

Jh*e*su M¹iiij*ᶜ* iiij*ˣˣ*

Riught whellbelouyd syr, I recomend me harttely wnto yow.
Plesythe yow to wndyrstonde that I haue schypyd at London in
the Grase à Dew of Calles, John Markeso*n* beyng mast*er*, M¹iiij*ˣˣ*
xiij fell*ys*, qwherof be iiij*ᶜ* xlvj Cottyssowlde onmarkyd, and the
5 rembnant be som*er* and wh⟨i⟩nt*er* of London, and thay be markyd
w*yth* an O. Aull iij sortys lyes togyddyr whon w*yth* anothyr befor
the maste wndyr the hachys. Syr, ꝫe schaull ressaue of Mondanyell
a lett*er* and a fardell w*yth* pelltys. The mast*er* of the Grase à De
schulde an had them, byt he whos awalyd and goyn. No mor to
10 yow, Jh*e*su kepe yow. Wryt at London the xij day of Decembyr.

p*er* yowr brother,
Rychard Cely.

*Dorse*: Wnto my whelbelouyd brother George Cely or Thomas
Grayngear at Calleys, be thys dd.

### 114. *Richard Cely the younger at London to George Cely at Calais or Bruges, 26 January 1480/1*

s.c.1 53/67

Jh*e*su M¹iiij*ᶜ* iiij*ˣˣ*

Riught whellbelouyd brothyr, I recomeawnd me vnto yow as
louyngly as harte can thynke. Ples hyt yow to wndyrstond at the

113. 6 O.] the Cottys *canc.*

makyng of thys howr father and mothe⟨r⟩ and whe aull ar in good
heyll, and prays to God send yow a fayr passayge and bryng yow
whell hyddyr. Syr, I haue resauyd a letter frowm yov wrytyn at 5
Calles apon Sent Steuyns Day, the qweche I wndyrsto⟨nd⟩ riught
wh⟨e⟩ll, both yowr beyng at the mart and what the marte whos, and
how ȝe porpos to be at Br⟨e⟩gys at thys Candyllmes. I pray God
speyd yow and sende yow good men to make yowr mony wyth.
Syr, I ondyrstonde be the same lettyr that ȝe haue sowlde howre 10
fellys, I thanke God, and I treste God whe schawll haue heuer
Whytsuntyd mo. And syr, as for yowr ij wyrkyns, whon of samon
and the tothyr of tony, thay ar not com ȝeyt—Gylbard Paulmar
tellys me thay be ȝeyt in Selond wyth geyhyr of hys. And syr,
I haue spokyn wyth Bongay and he spekys of you myche whor- 15
schype. Syr, th' xxiiij day of Geneuer I resauyd ij lettyrs frome
yow of Harrowlld Stawnton, whon to howr father, another to me.
ȝe whrote to howr father that he schawll fynd clossyd in hys letter
the sayll of ij sarpelers wholl. I opynd hyt at London byt I fond
non therin. I sent Hane thys same day to howre father to Aulay 20
wyth yowr letter. Syr, ȝe schaull ressaue closyd in thys letter howr
fathyrs wharant of hys fellys laste sch⟨y⟩pyd—hyt amowntys l s.
ster. And as tochyng yowr laste letter, my Lorde ys sende for be
the Lorde Master, byt the Kyng wyll not lat hym departe. The
Kynge has wry⟨t⟩ an ansfor to the Lorde Master. My Loorde prays 25
yow when ȝe cwm to Brygys that ȝe wyll enqwer of the Whenysyans and Florantynys of tydyngys of the Rodys. And the Kyng
has comandyd my Lord Rewars, my Loord Schambyrlen and
my Loorde of Sente Jhons to go to the Towyr and se hys hordenans
and to amyt gonars and se that awll thyngys be made redy, and 30
as for hors, my Loorde Reuerys sendys dayly abhowte to inqweyr
for. Syr, gentyll hors ar whorthe myche mony hey[r], I whowlde
awyse yow brynge houer aull yowr trottyng hors and Geoys to
kepe them. I harde you say that ȝowr harnes whaxyd to lyttyll for
yow. And ȝe bryng hyt ⟨hyt wyll⟩ be whell sowlde. Syr, I haue 35
a p⟨a⟩yr of as fayr bregenders as ony in London. I pray yow by me
a fayer and sewyr bycoket, a standarde, a payr scleuys a⟨s⟩ ȝe
haue, and a fowld of mayll, and then I treste to Jhesu that I am
whelharnest to kepe London wyth. [Dorse] Syr, as for tydyngys
I can whryte none byt ther come inbassyturs howt of Skoteland. 40
The Kyng whoullde not let them cowm no nar byt sent ther ansfor

**114.** 35 bryng] the *canc.*        37 a⟨s⟩: *ms.* af

to Newcastell. Whe say heyr that my Loord Schambyrlen comys
to Calles schortly. No mor to you at thys tym. Jhesu kepe you.
Whryt at London the xxvj d[ay] of Genewer.

45                              per yowr brother, Rychard Cely.

Syr, I whould awyse yow to brynge not paste ij or iij horse wyth
you, byt and ʒe coude conwhay a barell or an hogyshed foull of
sewyr fowlldys, flankardys and sum standardys of mayll whelbhowte ther whoulde be done good ouer the[m], and I pray yow
50 bryng the peys for doblet clothys that I whrot to you for afor
Kyrstemas, syche as Hynys ys of. I haue a gowyn clothe of
mostyrdewyl[l] of my Lordys leueray for you agayn ʒe cwm.

*Address*: Wnto my brodyr George Cely merchand of the Stapell of
Calleys, be thys delyuyrd at Calleys or at Bregis in haste.

**115.** *William Cely at Calais to George Cely at Bruges,*
*13 May 1481*
s.c.1 53/69

Jhesu M¹iiijᶜ iiijˣˣj

Ryght worshyppffull syr, afftyr dew recommendaschon I louly
recommend me vnto yowre masterschypp, etc. Furdermore plese
hit yowre masterschypp to vnderstonde that I hawe receyued an
letter ffrom yow the whych I hawe redd and well vnderstond all
5 thyngys theryn, ⌐and⌐ as ffor yowre debenters I hawe delyuerd
hem to Wylliam Bentham acordyng to yowre commavndement,
and he hath promysyd me as sone as he ys ffurnyschyd wyth money
I schall be payd and content ffor the partyschon off x s. off the
pownde wyth the ffyrste, and as ffor yowre warantys off xv s. off
10 the pownde, I hawe spoken to master Lefftenaunte ffor them, and
he hath promysyd me that at yowre commyng to Caleys they schall
be sett vppon yowre byllys of costom and subsede, etc. Item, syr,
plese hit yow to wytt that on the xij day of Maye ther was ij
Frenschemen chasyd an Englysch schypp affore Caleys, and
15 Federston, and John Dave and Thomas Owerton ley yn Caleys
rode, but themsellffe were a londe, and as sone as they sawe them
they gote botys and ʒede aburdde, and soo dydd master Marschall,
and Syr Thomas Eueryngham, and master Nesseffylde wyth
deuersse sowdeers off Caleys, and rescudyd the Englysch schypp

**115.** 6 Bentham *or* Beucham          16 as they] sethe *canc.*

and toke the Frenschemen and browght on ⌜off them⌝ ynto Caleys  20
hawen. The toder was so grett sche myght nott commyn, but ⟨they⟩
browght the master and the capteyn to my Lorde, and they saye
ther ys Scottys amonggyst hem, and they say that Federsston and
hys ffellowys be gon wyth the bygger Frenscheman ynto Ynglonde,
etc. Item, syr, hytt ys sayd here that afftyr thys day, the xij day  25
off Maye, ther schall no man kepe noo logyng off gestys, straungers
nor Englyschemen, wythowte the gatys of Caleys excep ij howssys
synyd, that ys Serche and the Water Baylys, and euery man that
hath howssynge wyth⟨owt⟩ the gatys ys warnyd to remeve hys
howsse as schorttly as he can ynto the towne and sett hytt there  30
where hym plese that he hath grownde; and yff he do nott soo,
stond at hys owne aventture at syche tyme that schall ⌜come⌝ to
be pluckyd schorttly down, or ellys burnyd ffor the schortter
warke, and betwyxte thys and that tyme, non off them be soo hardy
excep the ij plasys affore rehersyd to loge noo man ower an nyght,  35
payne off treson, etc. Item, syr, plese hit yow to wytt that Syr
Wylliam Chanon that was logyd wyth John Fowlle, ys ded. He
was beryd as on Sonday last was, and Syr Wylliam Stappell,
pryste, hath ys benyveysse grauntyd be my Lorde, etc. Syr oder
tydyngys hawe we non, but almyghty hawe yow yn hys kepyng.  40
Wrytten at Caleys the xiij day off Maye.

per yowre servaunte,<br>Wylliam Cely.

*Dorse*: To my worshyppffull master George Cely, marchaunte off
Stappull off Cales, being at Bregys at the Scape ys Clawe, soo hit  45
dd. (*Shield.*)

## 116. *Richard Cely the elder in Essex to George Cely at Calais, 4 June 1481*

s.c.1 53/71

Jhesu M¹iiijᶜ iiijˣˣj

I grete you wyll, *and* I haue resayuyd a letter from you wryte at
Caleys the xxvj day of May, the weche I haue wyll understand, and
that my xvj sarplerys *and* a poke of woll ys com to Calys in sauete,
I thanke God, *and* of a sale of woll of ij sarplers *and* poke of my
Cottyswolde woll. I fele be youre wrytyng that the ȝeueyng of  5

money was ix s., ix s. ij d.; for the weche ye avyse me to speke at
London to som man. That were not good, for the weche I haue
spoke to no man for that mater. Do as wyll as ye can. Also thy
broder Rychard hath be at ʒorke and at Laysetter—he hade grete
10 schere for youre sake, for the weche mater in aspeschall I wyll be
wyll plesyd to here more of [*Dorse, reversed*] for the weche ye may
haue in youre my⟨n⟩de and good rememrens for to meve *and*
labor at Caleys at thys tyme. I wryt no more. Jhesu kepe you.
Wryt at Brytys the iiij day of Jun.

15                                                   *per* Rychard Cely.

To Jorge Cely at Caleys thys byll delyuerd.


**117.** *Richard Cely the younger at London to George Cely
at Calais, 4 June 1481*
s.c.1 53/72

Jhesu Mˡiiijᶜ iiijˣˣj

Riught interly whelbelouyd brother, I recomend me harttely onto
you, thankyng you of aull good brotherhod that ʒe haue scheuyd
to me at aull tymus. Syr, ʒe know whell that I haue bene in the
Northe Contre, and ther I haue had grette scheyr of my nowlde
5 aqweyntans, as the bryngar heyrof can informe you; and as for
my noncle ys exseketurs has promysyd me and Plomton be the
faythe of ther bodys to be wy*th* howr father her Myhellmes, and to
make a neynd wy*th* hym. And as I whente northewharde, I met
Roger Wyxton a thys syd Northehamton, and ⌈he⌉ desyryd me to
10 do so myche as drynke wy*th* hys whyfe at Laysett*er*, and aft*er*
that I met wy*th* Wylli*am* Daulton, and he gaue me a tokyn to hys
mother, and at Laysett*er* I met wyth Rafe Dawlton, and he brohut
me to hys mother, and ther I delyuyrd my tokyn, and sche prayd
me to come to brekefaste on the morow, and so I ded and Plomton
15 bothe, and ther whe had a gret whelfar, and ther whos Freyr
Este, and I pray yow thanke them for me. Syr, and ʒe be remembyrd, whe thaulkyd togydyr in hour bed of Dawltonys syst*er*, and
ʒe ferryd the condyscyons of father and brethyrn, byt ʒe neyd not.
I saw hyr and she whos at brekefaste wy*th* hyr mother and ws.
20 Sche ys as goodly a ʒenge whomane: as fayr, as whelbodyd and
as sad as I se hony thys vij ʒeyr, and a good haythe. I pray God

117. 9 ⌈he⌉ *over canc.* thay

that hyt may be inpryntyd in yur mynd to sette yowr harte ther.
Syr, howr father and I comende togydyr in the new orchard on
Fryday laste, and ⌐a⌐ askyd me many qwestyonys of gyu, and
I towlde hym aull as hyt whos, and he whos ryught sory for the 25
dethe of the sch⟨y⟩lde, and I toulde hym of the good whyll that
the Whegystons and Dawltons hows to yow, and how I lykyd the
ȝenge gentyllwhoman, and he commaunded me to whryte to yow
and he whowlde gladly that hyt whor brohut abohut and that ȝe
labyrde hyt betymys, and I haue towllyd hour father of Schestyrs 30
dowter, how that I whowlde fayne be ther, and howur father whos
ryught glad of thys comenycacyon. Daultons mother comendys
hyr to you and thankys yow for the knyuys that ȝe sente to hyr.
Howr father has ressauyd a letter frome yow wherby he wndyrstond of the salle: ij sarpellys and a peke. As for the mony at ys 35
by you, he whyll that hyt ly be yow tyll Sencyon marte, and lette
the mersars haue the lengar days, bothe Browell and Paullmar,
and ther mony acordyng. [Dorse] Syr, I thanke you at hyt
plesehyd you to leue me Goos, for he has d[on] to me good sarues
in thys gornay, and I haue delyuyrd to him ix [s.] to brynge hym 40
to you, etc. My godfathyr has be syke byt he ys whell mendyd,
thankyd be God. [Thys same] day my Loord ys comyn to London
to aske the Kyng leue to go to the Rodys for he ys sent for. Syr,
I send you be Goos a purs seche as whos gewyn me at ȝeorke, and
I pray yow b[y] for Alyson Myhell a mantell of fyn blake schankys, 45
for I haue mony therfor, and sche comendys hyr to you. No mor
to yow at thys tyme, Jhesu kepe you. Wrytyn at London the
iiijᵗʰᵉ day of Juyn.

per yur brother,
Rychard Cely.        50

Wnto my riught whelbelouyd brother George Cely, merchand of
the Estapell of Calles be thys dd.

**118.** *Richard Cely the younger at London to George Cely at Calais or the mart, 24 June 1481*

s.c.1 53/73

Anno Jhesu Mˡiiijᶜ iiijˣˣj

Riught whelbelouyd brother, I recomend me onto you in as louyng
whyes as hart con thynke, informyng you at the makyng of thys

howr father and mothe⟨r⟩ ar in good heyll, thankyd be God ∥
I marwhell grettely that I haue ⟨no⟩ wrytyng frome you syn Geyos
5 departyd. I whot not whethyr he be come to yow or note. Syr, my
Loorde and the Turkepler goys to the Rodys togyddyr. Thay
pwrpos to be at Calles the xv day of Juylle. He ys porposyd to take
be exchonge of howr father an C li. or ij, and ȝe to delyuer hyt at
Bregys or Calles. My Loord prays you to gette hym as mony
10 doketys and Rynysche gyldyrns as ȝe may. I whoulde wryte mor,
byt thys day I departe into Cottssowld. No more, Jhesu kep you.
Wryte at London the xxiiij day of Juyn.

per Rychard Cely.

Dorse: Wnto my brother George Cely marchand of the Estapell
15 at Calles or the marte, be thys dd.

## 119. *Richard Cely the younger at London to George Cely at Calais, 21 July 1481*
s.c.i 53/74

Jhesu M¹iiijᶜ iiijˣˣj

R⟨y⟩ught interlly whelbelouyd brother, I recomend me wnto yow
wyth aull myne harte, informyng yow that at the makyng of thys
howr father and mother ar in good heyll, and sendys you ther
blessyngys. Syr, I send you Hayne; and I haue bohut a nox for
5 yow, hyt coste xvj s., and I pwrpose to sell hys tallow and skyn
and by therwyth candyll, and I haue sent yow by Hayn a borell of
candyll wherin ys xiiij dosyn and an hawlfe a dosyn of x the li.,
and ij dosyn vj le li., and aull the remenant cownter candyll of di.
quarter the li. I send yow by Hayne yowr whyt fryse, and ij bytys,
10 and a barell befe and wyrkyn wyth the same. Syr, my Loord has
made howyr vᶜ li. to resaue of Lombardys at Bregys in Flemysche
mony, the qweche ys payabull wythin vj days after the syt. My
Loor pwrpos to send yow hys lettyrs to schev and ȝe to ressaue
hys mony. I porpos to be wyth you at my Lordys comyng and then
15 I schau[l] informe yow of many thyngys. Syr, as for Haynys
passayge ys payd for, and yowr gere aullso. No mor to yow, Jhesu
kepe yow. Wryttyn at London xxj day of July.

118. 5 whethyr] I *canc.*
119. 4 Hayne] in Mwndanyell ys schyp *canc.*        8 of] j *canc.*

I pray you se to yowr befe at hyt take no harme when hyt cwm
to Call[es].

per your brother, Rychard Cely.          20

*Dorse*: Wnto my whelbelouyd brother George Cely, merchant of
the Estapell at Calles.

**120.** *Richard Cely the younger* [*at London*] *to Joyce
Parmenter at Calais* [c. *21 July 1481*]

S.C.I 53/75

I gret yow whell, and I pray yow heve my brother George Cely
be not coum to Calles that ȝe wyll sende thys box and my letter
to hym in aull the haste, or hellys and ȝe know none sewyr man
that goys, I pray you to take an hors and go yowrsellfe to Bregys
to my brother and delyuer hym them. I haue sent Hayne wyth  5
the wol flet, and ⟨a⟩ barell and a wyrkyn of befe and a barell candyll.
I purpos to be wyth scoostely.

per Rychard Cely.

*Dorse*: Thys letter be delyuyrd to Goos, saruant wyth George
Cely, merchand of the Stapell at Calles.          10

**121.** *Richard Cely the younger at London to George Cely
at Calais or Bruges, 26 July 1481*

S.C.I 53/99

Jhesu Mˡiiijᶜ iiijˣˣj

Riught interly whelbelouyd brother, I recomend me harttely onto
yow, informyng you at the makyng of thys howr father and mother
ar in good hell, and sendys yowu ther blessyngys. Syr, my Loord
comendys hym harttely wnto yow, and thankys yow of your letter,
and syche tydyngys as he knowys a wryttys yow parte, and he  5
prays you harttely that ȝe wholl be good factur for hym at thys
tyme as ȝe haue beyn in tyme passy, as heuer he may desarue hyt.
Syr, he has made howyr wyth Lombardys to Brogys apon vᶜ li.
qwherof he sendys to you iij lettyrs of exchonge, the qwyche he
prays yow to schow them, for thay ar payabull vythin viij days after  10

120. 6 candyll] I *canc.*

the syhyt, and ther ys in the same box ij lettyrs myssyue. My
Loorde prays yow to delyuer them to the sayd Lombardys at
Brogys. I whollde not awyse yow to ressaue none of thys mony
tyll my Loor cum hymselfe. He prays you to dessyer them to make
15 hym fayr payment at the day, and he whowlde fayne that ȝe wher
at Calles at hys c⟨o⟩myng. He pwrpos to brynge wyth hym ij or
iijᶜ li. of starlyng mony. Has a letter of passayge for the serche for
hymselfe and l parsonys. He prays yow that ȝe wyll make serche
in the Coletry or ony syche plasse as ȝe thynke that docettys
20 Wenycyans may be getyn. He powrpos to be at Calles the vj day
of Augwste at the fardest, and ther comys vyth hym master
Twrkepler, Syr Wyllyam Wheston, Syr Tomas Dane, wyth many
mo god fellows, and at that tymy I schaull tell yow many thyngys.
I longe sore to speke wyth yow. No mor to you at thys tyme. Wryt
25 at London on Sent Tanys Day.

per yowr brother,
Rychard Cely.

*Dorse*: Wnto my whelbelouyd brother George Cely, merchant of
the Estapell beyng at Calles or Bregys, be thys letter and box dd.

**122.** *Richard Cely the elder at London to George Cely at*
*Calais or Bruges, with note by Richard junior, 31 July 1481*
s.c.1 53/76

Jhesu M¹iiijᶜ iiijˣˣj

I gret you wyll, and I haue resayvyd a letter from you wryte at
Caleys the xxv day of Jule, the weche I haue wyll vnderstand, and
that ye haue be at the marte and resayuyd pert of my detys and
ȝeue hover be exschange to mersers my money, for the weche
5 I am wyl plesyd, and I haue resayvyd of John London, Robard
Brone, purser, a packe of canvase acordyng to youre wrytyng.
Also I fely be youre letter ye avyse me for to by woll in Cottyswolde. For sothe I schall haue of John Cely ys gaderyng xxx sacke,
and of Wyll Medewynter of Norlache lx sacke, and I am avysyd
10 for to by more, but woll in Cottyswolld ys at grete pryse: xiij s.
iiij d. a tode, and gret rydyng for ⌐woll⌐ in Cottyswolde as was onny
ȝere thys vij ȝere. I fele be youre wrytyng that my Lorde of Sent
Jonns wolde haue a C or to Flemeche be exschounge for ij ȝere

121. 25 *ms.* os on

day. For sothe I promysyd to my Lorde for vij s. the nobyll s*ter*.
but I here no more thereof, werefor at the comyng of my Lord 15
at Caleys or at Brygys I wyll ye make an exschaunge wyt my Lorde
of Send Johnns: and he wyll desyar for to haue a C li. s*ter*. or
more, I wolld fayne plese ys Lordschepe for to hese hym lyke as
ye wry[t] to me.

[*Richard Cely junior's writing*:] Syr, howr father has whryt to yow 20
hys intent in the forparte of thys lett*er*, and my Loord whowl pray
yow to take the labor to Bregys for hys matt*er*, and he pwrpos for
whery sartten to departe frome London the iij day of Auguste, and
at hys cowmyng I schawll informe yow of many thyng*ys*. No mor
to yow. Whryttin at London the laste day of Jully.    25

*Dorse*: Wnto my riught whelbelouyd brother George Cely
me*r*chand of the Estapell at Calleys or Bregys be thys dd.


## 123. *Roland Thornburght at the Hospital of St John of Jerusalem, Clerkenwell, to George Cely, 4 August [1481]*
s.c.1 53/77

Bedfelow, I comaund me to you, and I thank you hertely of the
good lodgeng that ye fand vs at Derford/ I had forgettyn to haue
spokyn with you that, and ye myght, for to a provyded for me
a fur of boge, on of the fynest that ye can feynd in Byrgesse. I trust
be the cownsell of my cosyn y*our* brother and you that and ther 5
be any fyne in Byrgesse, that ye will fynd hit/ and at y*our* comyng
ye shal be trewlye payed therfore, whatsomeu*er* it cost/ And
I p*ra*y as hertely as can that as sone as ye may, that ye hast yow
homward, for heyr is a heve howseold/ consyderyng that my Lord
and his feloship ys dep*ar*ted. No more to you at this tyme, but 10
almyghty God haue yow in hys kepyng/ At Seynt*es* John*es* the
iiij^th day of August.

I p*ra*y you lat maist*er* William, my Lord Chapelen, vndo*ur*stond
prevelye that the parson of the church within Newgate that is in
my Lord*ys* gyfte ys dessesced this howre.    15

By y*our* bedfelow s*ir* Roland Thornburght.

*Dorse*: To my worshipfull bedfelow George Sele, this be delyu*er*ed.

**124.** *George Cely at Calais to Richard Cely the elder at London, 5 August 1481*

S.C.I 53/78

Jhesu M<sup>l</sup>iiij<sup>c</sup> iiij<sup>xx</sup>j

Ryght rewer⟨e⟩nt and whorschypffull ffader, affter all dew recomendacyon *pre*tendyng I recomeavnd me vnto yow in the most
lowlyest whysse that I con or may ‖ Fordermor plesythe ytt yow
to vndersto*n*d that it ys now condessendyd that ⌜ther⌝ shall be an
5 *par*tysseon of xv s. of the pownd/ of the debentyrs, and byllis of
xviij monthis and xviij and obyllygacyons of whollis b⟨r⟩owght all
in hon casse, etc. ‖ Her ys moche ado w*yth* vs at Calles and ther
ys gret vttravnsse of wholl, as Thom*a*s Graynger con infforme
yow. Her ys none hottravnsse of ffellis nor whas nott sen the m*ar*te.
10 I sawe newer Hollendars make whorsse paym*en*t in my dayys,
God ame*n*d ytt. Зe shall resseywe an byll clossyd herin of the
salle of iij sarp*leris* sowlld to John Vander Hay of Mekelyn of
yowr medell Cott*ys*. Ytt ys so that I loke ffor my Lord of Sent
Jonys dayly, and at his comyng I wholl breng ⌜hym⌝ appon the
15 way or do as my brod*er* shall avysse me to do/ ffor the Mayr ys
porpossyd to dep*ar*te an Fryday com viij dayys and I am porpossyd to com houyr to yow that same tyme myselffe; and than
shall I show vnto yow þe mowthe many thyng*ys* etc./ and so con
the breng*er* herof. Plesythe ytt yow to vndyrstond that yowr wholl
20 ys anwhardyd ffor good Cott*ys* be Wyll*ia*m Bretten and Harry
Jon. Ther whas non sarpler cast howght but sen in þe showe. Of
hoder tydyng*ys* I kon non wrytt vnto yow, but Jh*e*su kepe yow,
amen. Wrett at Calles the v day of Augost.

*per* yowr son,
25 George Cely.

*Dorse*: Vnto my ryght whorschypffull ffader Rychard Cely,
m*er*chant of the Stapull of Call*es* at London in M*ar*te Lane, soit
dd. (*Shield*.)

---

**124.** 4 ⌜ther⌝ *over canc.* heuery m*a*n

**125.** *John Dalton at Calais to George Cely, 22 September 1481*

s.c.1 53/79

Jhesus Anno M<sup>l</sup>iiij<sup>c</sup> iiij<sup>xx</sup>j

Right worchepffull syr and broder, after all dew recomendacyon hayd, I recomaund me vnto yow and vnto my broder and yours, Rychard Cely. Furthermor, syr, plese yow to wit that here hase be Gysbreth Van Wynbarow and I haue sold hym the vj sarplers of the Cottysold wooll, that freeth hymsellff acordyng to your 5 remembrance. Alsoy syr, wenyng to me that they wold haue hayd of your new wooll, for they cavsyd me to kep hyt iiij or v dayes, and then the sayd the staple therof was to schoortte, nottwyth-standyng hayd they not bene I hayd soold partt therof vn⟨to⟩ Arnold Johnson of Andwarpe. And as for ffell I cane seell non ytte: 10 God knowes I wold be ryght glayd to do that that myght be plesur vnto yow in sayellys or oder wayes, and yff ony Holonderes come done I schall do my best in sayellys to my otterst poyer, boyth in wooll and ych ffeellys. I remember well that yow desered to ⟨do⟩ my best ffor Wylliam Maryon ffellys, and syr, ytt schall not be 15 forgetton and Gud wyell. And syr, wat plese yow that yow wyll schal be don wyth such money as I haue by me, yt schal be redy for yow whersumeuyr ʒe wyll haue yt, wheder yt be at Calles, Brugys or Andwarpe. Syr, they laytter end of the next weke I pur-pose into Flaunderes. Alsoy syr, I haue wretton yow affor thys 20 that I haue sent yow your gounysse, the wych I trvst ʒe haue reseyvyd or thys tyme. Alsoy syr, your horson doyth weell, God save them, and syr, thys weke haue we hayd in iij loodys heey for yow. Syr, as towchynge all oder maytterys I schall do my best, and hayth done to sum of them, and I haue reseyvyd of Prestun xx s. 25 Fl. anwardys, and I spokon wyth the ader that ow yow money but yette can I geet no more therof. Syr, I haue lent vn⟨to⟩ Andrew Hawes iiij li. but I hauue gud swerte thereof that I [*Dorse*] [s]chalbe content at my plesur, and the byll ys mayd in my name, and he sayeth wher yow come ʒe schvld haue a bargyn of hym to pay me 30 agayne, etc. Syr, I pray yow that I may be recomaundyd vnto my mayster your fayder and moder. No mor to yow at thys tyme, but owr Lord send you long lyff and gud to hys plesur and yours. At Calles wythowt gattes, the xxij day of September.

your B., John Dalton.    35

**125.** 22, 25 reseyvyd: resvyd *with stroke through tail of* s

Alsoy syr, I forgeet not your hawkes, but her comys non, but the furest that I may geet for money I schall send yow wyth Godys grace.

*Dorse*: To my inteirly beluffyd brother Jorg Cely, merchant at the
40 Staple of Calles, so it don.

**126.** *Richard Cely the younger at London to Joyce Parmenter at Calais, 16 October 1481*
s.c.1 53/80

Anno Jhesu M¹iiij<sup>c</sup> iiij<sup>xx</sup>j

Whelbelouyd, I grehyt yow whell, and as for yowr pesse of gowlde whe cannot fynd hyt ʒeyt, nethyr heyr no whord of my bowhay. I haue a cheys frome my mother to send yow. I marwhell grettely that whe haue no whrytyng of my brothers comyng to Calleys,
5 and as for Py ys whell mendyd. And the Thorsday aftyr yowr departtyng the gray beche whelpyd, and had xiiij, and on the Sattyrday next aftyr sche dyed sodenly, and x of her whelpys, and so iiij be kepyd as whell as thay can be. Geoos, I pray the send me the aulmen dagar that my brother gaue me, and send me whorde
10 ʒefe Twesylton sellyd hony of my brothers hors whyll he wher heyr or not, and comende me to Twhessylton and aull good fellows. No mor. Whryt at London the xvj day of Octobur.
                                        per Rychard Cely the ʒeungar.
I pray the sende my brothers letter to hym in haste.

15 *Dorse*: Wnto Geos, sarwhant wyth George Cely, marchand of the Estapell at Calleys.

**127.** *Richard Cely the younger at London to George Cely at Calais or the mart, 24 [October] 1481*
s.c.1 53/81

Anno Jhesu M¹iiij<sup>c</sup> iiij<sup>xx</sup>j

Riught interly whelbelouyd brother, I recomend me harttely wnto yow, informyng you at the makyng of thys howr father and mother wher in good heyll, and aull ther howssowllde, thankyd be God. Syr, I haue ressauyd ij lettyrs from yow derectyd to howre
5 father. The fyrste I schowyd to hym, and thys I wyl ber hym.

I hawe schypyd of howr fathers xxv packys and a hawlfe all redy,
and I haue iij packys of hys to schype, and I haue schypyd iiij
packys of howrs, vj packys and hawlfe of my godfathyrs. I [sc]hawll
send yow the nowmbur in heu*er*y schype, and schypys nameys,
and [how] many be Cottsowlde, and how many som*er* London and   10
hou many whynt*er* [London], and how thay be markyd. Syr,
I ame goyng to labor to Syr Tomas [Mongo]mbre, for howr father
and ʒe and I ar indyttyd for scleyng [an hartt] and sartten hynde
cawluys, and thys whosse doyn be the mein [of . . . an]d Syr
Tomas Tyrryll, scherefe, byt I tryste to Good whe schaull [. . .   15
h]ow as I speyd I schaull wh⟨r⟩ytte to you. Syr, I pray [yow
remem]byr the x li. and the mantell of schank*ys* for Myhyllys
[wyfe]. [No m]or to yow. Jh*es*u kepe yow. Whryttyn at London
the xxiiij [Octobe]r.

p*er* yowr brother,   20
Rychard Cely.

*Dorse*: A my whelbelouyd brother George Cely, m*er*cha⟨n⟩t of the
Estap*ell* at Calleys or at the martte, be thys dd.

## 128. *William Cely at London to George Cely at Calais, 26 October [1481]*

s.c.1 53/82

Ryght worschyppffull syr, affter dew reco*m*mendaschon I louly
reco*m*mend me vnto yow, doyng yow to wytt that be the grace
off God ʒe schall receyue off the Mary Grace off London, John
Lokyngton, mast*er*, vj pack*ys* ffell, whych lyeth nex the maste
affterwarde lowesste, and nexte abowe them lyeth v pack*ys* ffell   5
off Thom*as* Graunger. Off the vj pack*ys* ffell beth v*c* xxxviij cast
small tale wynter ffell*ys* off London markyd wyth ynccke—the
marke ys a C, and certeyne somer ffell*ys*—the marke ys off them
a O—whych vj pack*ys* ʒe muste receyue and paye the ffrayte, etc.
No more vnto att thys tyme, but Jh*es*u kepe yow. Wrytte att   10
London the xxvj day off October.

p*er* yowr s*er*ua*u*nte,
Wyll*ia*m Cely.

*Dorse*: To George Cely m*er*cha*u*nte off the Stapp*ell* off Callys, soo
hit dd. (*Shield*.)   15

**127.** 10 London and] and *repeated*

**129.** *Sir John Weston at Rome to George Cely at Calais,*
*27 October 1481*
s.c.1 53/83

### Jhesus

Worshypfull coyssyn, wyth du recomendassyonus premysset, it
is so I come to Rome the xv day of Octobre, and was ryt welcome,
wyth euer nobleman saying thay sawe not thys C yer so lequelly
a felychyppe for so manny *and* in þat aray come howte of Ynglonde.
5 The Popes Hollynes made me gret cher, *and* wallde a sente me
home agayn *and* asollet me of al manner abedyensses or comandement made to me or motte be made, bot I desyret is Hollynes at
I motte do my vayage sennes I was so far forthe, *and* so is Ollynes
sendes me as is inbassador wyth materis of gret inportansse. I treste
10 do be the sonner at ome, be Godys grace.

Coyssyn, as tossyng the mater of the Staple *and* Ryscharde
Herron, the Kyngys proctor and I as don in þat mater as meche
as motte be don to fulfylle the Kyngys intente *and* the wel of the
marchantes of the Staple; for I take God to recorde, *and* the
15 brynger of thys, a frere, at I dede in is as messe as I wolde affe
don *and* they ad gyn me a gret gud. As thay sal se al the remedyis
*and* demandys at the sayde Herron makys, I sende thayme be the
sayde frere. I promesse 30w he is gretly favorret, *and* he wolde
a made a fol werke *and* remedy ad not son be fonde.
20 Coyssyn, I pray 30w sende me worde of 30ur welfare and
comande me to my fader and 30urs, *and* 30ur moder, *and* Jhesus
keppe 30w.

At Rome, the xxvij day of Octobre 1481, be 30ur coyssyn Sir
John Weston, Pryor of Sant Johns.

25 *Dorse*: To is worshypfull coyssyn Jorge Sellay, thys leter be
deleverde at Callez.

**130.** *William Maryon at London to George Cely at Calais,*
*28 October 1481*
s.c.1 53/84

### Jhesu

Ryght rewerent syr and my specyall good frend, Y recommend me
vnto you, eueremor deseyryng to her of yowre wellfar. Ferdermor,

**129.** 7, 8, 13 motte *or perhaps* mette     7 *ms.* s desyret

plessed yow to wete that Y haue schypped in the Mare of Raynam, John Danyell beyng mast*er*, vj packys halffe lvij somer London fell*ys*, co*n*taynyng M¹M¹vj^c lvij ffell*ys*, the wyche be bystowyd in  5 the sayd scheppe, all afor the mast and lowyst abafte the mast, and yowre broder Rechard Celyys ys ⌐fell*ys*⌐ be stowyd abaft the mast vpon myn, and ther haue no more men fell*ys* in the sayd schyppe but yowre brodere and Y. ⌐Ther be of hys fell*ys* iiij packys xlj fell*ys*.⌐ The wyche fell*ys* Y pray you that ye woll ressay⟨ue⟩ for  10 me and to do hovsse them, the on halffe yn on hovsse and the toder halffe in anoder housse, and that wer met for the marchant beyere; and Y pray you that ye woll pay the freyght and all scheche oder sostys as schall ron vpon them. No mor vnto you at thys tym, but the Trenyte haue you in hys blessed kepyng. Wreten at Lon-  15 don the xxviij day of Octobere a*n*no Jh*e*su M¹iiij^c iiij^xxj.

per Wylliam Maryon.

*Dorse*: Wnto George Cely, marchante of the Stapull at Calles, thys lettere be delyuerde, etc. (*Shield*.)

### 131. *William Cely at London to George Cely at Calais, 31 October 1481*

s.c.1 53/85

Jhesu M¹iiij^c iiij^xxj

Ryght worshyppffull syr, affter dew reco*m*mendaschon I louly reco*m*mend ⟨me⟩ vnto yow, lettyng yow vnderstonde that my mast*er* hath shyppydd hys ffell*ys* at the portte off London now att thys shyppyng yn October yn the yere abowesayde, whych ffell*ys* ȝe muste receyue and paye the ffrayghte. Fyrste, be ⌐the⌐ grace off  5 God, yn ⌐the⌐ Mary off London, Wyll*ia*m Sordyvale master, vij pack*ys*, s*u*m ij M¹ viij^c ffell, lying be affte the maste—j ⌐packe⌐ lyeth vpprest—and s*u*m off that packe ys somer ffell*ys* markyd w*yth* an O, and than lyeth iij pack*ys* ffell*ys* off Wyll*ia*m Daltons, and vnder them lyeth the toder vj pack*ys* off my masters // Item  10 yn the Crystover off Raynam, Harry Wylkyns master, vij pack*ys* *and* a hallffe, Cott*ys* ffell, s*u*m iij M¹ pell lyinge be affte the maste, and vnder them lyeth a ij^c ffell*ys* off Wetherffyld*ys*, Wyll*ia*m Lyndys man off Northhampton, and the p*ar*tyschon ys made w*yth* small cordys, etc. // Item, yn the Thom*a*s off Maydeston,  15 Harry Lausson mast*er*, vj p[a]ckys, s*u*m ij M¹iiij^c pell, wheroff

lyeth v pack*ys* nexte beffore the maste vnder hatchys, noo man
abowe them, and j packe lyeth yn the sterne schete. Off the vj
pack*ys* ffell*ys* beth sum somer ffell*ys* markyd w*yth* an O lykewyse,
20 etc. Item, yn the Mary Grace off London, John Lokyngton
mast*er*, vj pack, s*um* ij M¹iiij*c* pell lying be affte vnder the ffell*ys*
off Thom*a*s Graunger—the p*ar*tyschon ⌜betwyxte⌝ them ys made
w*yth* rede. S*um* off the ffell*ys* my mast*er* hath schyppyd at thys
tyme—xxvj pack*ys* and a hallffe, wheroff be wynt*er* ffell*ys* off the
25 contrey, v*c* lvj ffell, and they be markyd w*yth* a C, and off somer
ffell*ys* ther schuld be vj*c* and moo, butt parte off hem be leffte
behynde, ffor we hawe ij pack*ys* we cowde hawe noo pwoyntment
ffor them, and all the somer ffell*ys* be markyd w*yth* an O, etc. Item
syr, ye shall receyue off the Mary off Raynam, John Danyell
30 mast*er*, yowr male w*yth* yowr gere, and a Esex chesys m*ar*kyd w*yth*
my mast*er*s marke. Item syr, ye schall receyue off the Crystover
off Raynam, Harry Wylkyns mast*er*, a ffardell off pellt*ys* m*ar*kyd
w*yth* yncke, my godffader Maryons marke, and w*yth* chavke my
mast*er* marke, etc., and parte off them be my mast*er*s, and p*ar*te
35 my godffader Maryons, and my mast*er*s be markyd w*yth* a ᶜ etc.
No more vnto yow at thys tyme, ⌜but Jh*e*su kepe yow⌝. Wrytten
at London the laste day off October.

                    p*er* yowre s*er*va*u*nte, Wyll*ia*m Cely.

Item syr, ye shall receyue be the grace off God, off the Myhell off
40 Hull, Andrew Goody*s* mast*er*, j pack ffell conteynyng iiij*c* ffell*ys*,
wheroff sum ⌜off them⌝ be off the vj*c* xliij somer ffell*ys* and ⌜ȝe⌝
muste paye noo ffrayte ffor them, ffor the ffrayte was payd at
London, etc. [*Written later*:] Item syr, ȝe schall receyue, be the
grace off God, off the Thom*a*s off New Hythe, Robard Ewen mast*er*,
45 j pack hallffe a C xiiij ffell*ys* lying nexte the maste afftewarde
vnder the ffell*ys* off Thom*a*s Bettsons, and a ffew broken ffell*ys*
and pesys bownde togeder, markyd w*yth* my mast*er* marke, and
they lyeth vprest, nexte the maste, and they be the laste end off all
my mast*er*s ffell*ys*, s*um* to*t*all yn pack*ys*—xxviij pack*ys* and a hallff,
50 lxiiij ffell.

*Dorse*: To George Cely m*er*chaunte off the Stapell off Caleys, be
thys dd. (*Shield*.)

131. 20 etc.] Item *canc.*      22 ⌜betwyxte⌝ *over canc.* off      33 chavke my]
go *canc.*      35 a ᶜ] C *canc.*

## 132. *William Cely at London to George Cely at Calais, 2 November 1481*

s.c.1 53/86

Jhesu M$^l$iiij$^c$ iiij$^{xx}$j

Ryght worschyppffull syr, affter dew recommendaschon I louly recomend me vnto yow, lettyng yow wytt that, be the grace off ⌐God⌐, ye schall receyue off the Thomas off New Hythe, Robard Ewen master, j pack hallff a C xiiij ffell*ys* and a lytyll ffardell off ffell*ys* that ys alowyd ffor iij ffell*ys* w*yth* the costomer, and the   5 sayd ffell*ys* lyeth nexte be affte the maste lowest vnder the ffell*ys* off Thomas Bettson, and the lytyll ffardell lyeth iuste to the maste vprest off my masters ffell*ys*, whych ffell*ys* ye muste receyue and paye the ffrayght. No more vnto yow att thys tyme, but Jhesu kepe yow. Wrytten at London the secon day off November.      10

per your servaunte,
Wylliam Cely.

*Dorse*: To George Cely, merchaunte off the Stappell off Caleys, be thys letter delyuerd. (*Shield*.)

## 133. *Richard Cely the younger at London to George Cely at Calais, 5 November 1481*

s.c.1 53/87

Anno Jhesu M$^l$iiij$^c$ iiij$^{xx}$j

Riught whellbelouid brother, I recomend me wnto yow w*yth* aull myne hart, informeyng yow at the makyng of thys howr fathe⟨r⟩ and mother wher whell comforttyd and sendys yow ther blessyng*ys*. Hyt whos so that be the menys of Brandon howr father and I wher indytted for scleyng of an hartte that whos dreuyn into Kent, the   5 qwheche whe newyr se ner knew of, and thys day I haue ben w*yth* mastyr Mwngewmbre, and geuyn hym the whalew of a pype whyn to haue ws howt of the boke heuir hyt be schewyd the Kyng, and so he has promysyd me, and to be good master to howr father and ws in the matter betwhene Brarddon and hus. John Froste, foster,   10 brohut me to hys mastyrschyp and aqwaynttyd me w*yth* a genttyll-mane of hys hos name ys Ramston, that ys a ny mane to master Mongewmbre, and so I mwste informe hym my matters at aull

tymys, and he whyll sche⟨w⟩ them to hys master, etc. Syr, I haue
15 ressauid a letter frome yow wryte at Calleys, wherby I wndyrstonde
ȝe haue pwrwayd x li. in Carolus grottys. I pray yow send them at
the next passay[ge], for I pwrpos schorttely into Cottyssowllde,
and ⌈I⌉ haue informyd my godfather that ȝe haue made for hym
wyth Wylliam Browell xxxj li., and I thanke God that he pwt hyt
20 in yowr mynd to haue the C xxx li. howt of the whystelers handys
when I whos laste wyth yow at Bregys. Syr, hyt whos so that when
Whykyng whos deyd and another whos chosyn, howr father whos
sor kawlyd apon, and byt at Chary whos bettyr knowyn, howre
father hade beyn ⌈scheryfe⌉, etc. Howre father wyll that ȝe by vjᶜ
25 stykys more canuas at thys marte. And I wndyrstonde that ⌈ȝe⌉
haue sowlde yowr grehyt gray hors, and I am ryught glade therof,
for ij ys as good as xx. I wndyrstonde that ȝe haue a fayre hauke.
I am ryught glade of hyr, for I trwste to God sche schall make yow
and me ryught grehyt sporte. Ȝefe I whor sewyr at what passayge
30 ȝe whollde send her I whowlde fett hyr at Dowyr and kepe hyr
tyll ȝe cwm. A grehyt inforttewin ys fawlyn on yowr beche, for
sche had xiiij fayr whelpys, and aftyr that sche hade whelpyd sche
wholde newyr hett mette, and so sche ys deyd and aull her
whelpys, byt I tryste to pwrwhay agayn yowr comyng as fayr and
35 as goode to plesse that genttyllman. [87B, headed Jhesu Mˡiiijᶜ
iiijˣˣj] I wndyrstond ȝe pwrpos to be wyth ws afor Crystemes, and
therof whe be riught glade, and whe schaull make mery whethyr
Brandon wyll or not, be the grasse of God. And as for Py, ys as
hartty as heuir I sau hym, and in ressenabull good plyte and hole.
40 Whylliam Cely do ys partte whell in kepyng of hym. And as for
howr pensyon in Fornyngwhallys In schaull be payde wythin thys
iiij days. Syr, heyr aftyr aperythe howr father schypyng and
schypys namys and mastyrs.

Item, in the Mary of London, Wylliam Sordywoll master, vij
45 packys Cottsowlde fellys be stovyd behynde the maste: vj be
wndyr holl, and a packe lyes wpwrmwste apon Dawlttons behynd
the maste - - - - - - - - - sum—xxviijᶜ felles.
Item, in the Crystowyr of Rayname, Hary Wylkyns master, vij
packys and an hawlfe Cottsowlde: thay ly behynd the maste and
50 no mane abowe them - - - - - - - sum—xxxᶜ felles.
Item, in the Tomas of Maydston, Hary Lawson master, vj
packys Cottysowlde medyllyd wyth somer London fellys markyd
wyth O. Thay ly befor the maste wndyr hatchys, and parte

behynde ȝeuyn next the maste, in a pyle as brod as ij fellys be
long - - - - - - - - - - - - - - - - - - - - - - - - - - - - sum—xxiiij^c felles. 55
Item, in the Mary Grasse of London, John Lokyngton master, vj
packys fellys, qwherof be v^c lvj whynter London—thay be markyd
wyth C, and the rembnant be Cottsowlde. Thay ly behynde the
maste and Granger apon them, and rede betwyn them - - - sum—
- - - - - - - - - - - - - - - - - - - - - - - - - - - - - - - - - - - xxiiij^c felles. 60
    Item, in the Myhell of Holl, Andrew Good master, j packe felles
Cottsoulde, meddyllyd wyth somer London markyd wyth O. Thay
ly behynde the maste wpurmoste, and I hawe payde hyme hys hole
frayte for that packe fellys. - - - - - - - - - - - - iiij^c felles.
    Item, in the Thomas of New Hythe, Robard Hewan master, a 65
packe lxiiij felles Cottyssowlde. Thay ly behynde the maste and
Bettsonys felles ly abowe them - - - - - - - - iiij^c lxiiij felles.
    Sum totall of howr fathers felles - - - - - xj M^l iiij^c lxiiij felles.

[87C, *headed* Anno Jhesu M^l iiij^c iiij^{xx}j]
    Item, in somer London felles - - - - - - - - - - vj^c lxiij felles.      70
    Item, in whyntter London - - - - - - - - - - - - - v^c lvj felles.
    Item, in Cottsowlde - - - - - - - - - - - x M^l ij^c xlv felles.
    Item, in the Mary of Rayname, John Danyell master, I schypyd
iiij packys ⌈xlj⌉ felles of yowrs and myn. Thay ly behynd the
maste: iij packys of them be Cottsowlde, and whon packe xlj 75
felles be Wharwykeschyre—thay ly wppurmwste. I pray yow lay
them by themselfe for hurtteyng of the tother sorte - - - - - - - - - - -
- - - - - - - - - - - - - - - - - - - - - - - - - - - - - - - - xvj^c xlj felles.
    Item, my godfather has vj packys a hawlfe lvij felles in the same
schype, and no mane has a fell in that schype byt whe, my god- 80
fadyr and I - - - - - - - - - - - - - - - - - - - sum xxvj^c lvij somer London.
    And I haue spokyn wyth Whylliam Dawlton a⟨n⟩d schewyd hym
the clawys that ȝe whrat of Laysetter in, and he whos riught glade
therof. I whosse hys ges[t] on Hawlhalon Heuyn in Howlde
Fysche Strette at dynar wyth hym and Charlly[s] Wyllars. I pray 85
yow thanke the⟨m⟩ at ther comyng to Calles. Syr, I who[w]lyd
fayne heyr some good tydyngys of yowr matter that Claysse
Demowll ha[s] in hande. No mor to yow at thys tym. Jhesu kepe
yow. Whr⟨i⟩tte at London the v day of Nowembyr.
                                        per yowr brother,      90
                                        Rychard Cely.

**133.** 54 behynde] the *canc.*       59 apon them] the *canc.*       61 Holl:
H *ch. from* Lo

Wnto my whellbelouyd brother George Cely, merchant of the
Stapell be⟨yng⟩ at Calleys, so dd.


**134.** *Richard Cely the younger at London to George Cely
at Calais* [? *14 November 1481*]

s.c.1 53/90

Riught whelbelouyd brother, I recomende me wnto yow as
louyngly as harte can deuyse or thynke. Plese hyt yow to wndyrstond thys same day I ressauyd a letter frowm yow be Kay, and
the fayreste sor hawke thys day wythin aull Yngelond, the qwheche
5 schaull be as whel kepyd tyll ȝe cwm, be the grase of God, and
I haue yowr box wyth saulwe—hyt schall be whell kepyd tyll ȝe
cwm, and I am ryught glade of yowr apwnttemente and pwrpos to
be heyr at Sente Tomas tyde. Syr, I sente yow a lettyr by Robard
Flemyngys man, by the qwyche ȝe myte ⌐heyr⌐ of aull howr
10 schypynge and many hother maters at has beyn to me laborus and
howr father and ws cwstelew. Syr, I pray yow send me the x li.
that ȝe whrate to me ȝe had pwrwhayde in Carlys grottys. I porposyd to be in Cottyssowlld wythin iij days after the dat of
thys, byt for taryng for that x li. Byt hyt cwm wythin thys xij
15 dayes I am hawlfe schamyd hellys be my promys, and therfor
I pray yow for God sake rememyr my pwr honeste. Syr, howr
father whryttys to yow an letter—I awyse yow loke theron and
wndyrstonde hyt whe[ll], for he thynkys the whorllde qwhessy and
ȝe ar whelknowyn, and therfor he whowlde that ȝe gebart not
20 yowrselfe to hofton to Bregys, rather he had leuyr ȝe sent Geos.
And as for tydyngys I can whrytte yow noyn, byt hyt ys sayd ther
schawl be a Cownsell and a Parlemente sone after. Syr, I haue
ressauyd my Loorddys hoby, and I schawll haue the hawke and
I haue a good kepar of my nowyn pwrwyans, byt I pwrpos to
25 haue hym and that hauke to Melcheburne, and lewe yowr Mehyg
wyth Whatkyn Fawkyner at Bwschay, or hellys to haue her wyth
me into Cottyssould. Plumar has promysyd me to brynge me to
my Loorde of Essex, and I to schew hym that my Loorde gaue
me at Barwyke. I wndyrstond that my sayd Loorde sayes that he
30 newyr gaue Brandon no powher. I schall whryte mor playnely to
yow be my next letter. I haue delyuyrd Kay ij s. acordyng to yowr
whryttyng, and vj d. mor becaus he says ⟨he⟩ whos robbyd be the

whay of iij s., byt the theuys gaue hym viij d. agen. [Syr], he
delyuyrd ⌐me⌐ the hawke in sauete, and he sayd that ʒe spake to
mast*er* [Depu]te and Marschaull for yowr sarwant*ys*, and ʒe had   35
them grawntty*d*; [but] vᶜ Doche pepwll whos pwt hut of Calles. No
mor. Whryt at Londo*n* [. . .] day of Nowhembyr.

p*er* yowr brother,
Rychard Cely.

*Dorse*: Wnto my whellbelouyde brother George Cely, marchand of   40
the Stap*ell* at Calleys, dd.

## 135. *Harry Bryan at London to George Cely at Calais, 16 November [? 1481]*

s.c.1 53/156

Jh*esu*

Ryght worschipffull syr, I recomand me vnto yow, eue*r*more
dyssyeryng to her off yowre wellffare, and I thanke yow, syr,
hertely off yowr gret labore that ʒe haue done ffor me, os brynyng
my ij oblygacions of the Stapyll to Cales, and I pray yow, syr,
hertely to send me word whowe that ʒe haue done w*yth* them,   5
whedyr ʒe haue resayvyd my mony off tham or not, and yff ʒe
haue not ressayvyd hyt at the comyng off thys lett*er* to yow, that
ʒe wyll do so myche ffor me to ressayve hyt. And I had had my
oblygacions at the marte, dyu*er*ys men of yowr Plase wolde haue
gyffyn me Flemmyche mony ffor tham—xxvj s. vj d. Flemmyche   10
ffor the povnd—John Hatfeld was on, *and* oder dyu*er*ys,—but
I had lever yowr masterschipe had tham than any oder man that
I knowe of yowr Plase. And syr, yff ʒe haue ressayvyd the mony
of tham, ovder in yowr custu*m* or in schey⟨c⟩he mony os the Plas
payis owt, that ʒe wyll kepe my oblygacions styll in yowr handys,   15
and yff thay be ffull content *and* payd, and late the colectors canssell
tham, ffor I must delyu*er* tham to the sam man that owys tham,
ffor thar be dyu*er*ys men that has ressayvyd morre ⌐mony⌐ off
tham than I, and I knowe not whow myche mony that I haue
ressayvyd of tham tyll I se the oblygacions, and that ys causse that   20
I wryt to yow off tham. And I bes⟨e⟩che yow syr, and yff ʒe haue
not ressayvyd my mony of tham, that ʒe wyll ressave hyt and do
so to send me the oblygacions in all the hast by the next soore man

**135.** 4 my] ne *canc.*

that comys, for I muste delyuer my reke⟨n⟩yng vp of tham to
25 hym that owys tham, that knowys Jhesu, who haue yow in hys
blyssyd kepyng, amen. At London the xvj day off November last
passyd, and I bes⟨e⟩che yow syr of a answer of thys letter in all
haste.

By yowr sarvand,
30                                                    Harre Bryan.

*Dorse*: To my ryght worschipffull Gorge Cele, marchand off the
Stapull at Cales, thys letter be delyuerd.

## 136. *Richard Cely the younger at London to George Cely at Calais, 22 November 1481*
s.c.i 53/88

Jhesu M¹ iiij$^c$ iiij$^{xx}$j

Riught whellbelouyd brother, I recomende me harttely wnto yow,
informyng you at the makyng of thys howr father and mother, and
whe aull, ar in good heyll, and so whe treste that 3e be. Syr, I haue
whryttyn to yow dyuarys lettyrs, byt I haue of them none ansfor.
5 The laste I sente be Kay; therin wher many maters, and amonge
aull I pray you rememyr the x li. that 3e pwruayd at the laste marte,
and send hyt at the nexte passayge, for I had beyn in Cottyssowlde
heuer thys, byt for tarryng on that mony. And as for howre matter
that howr father and I and Lontlay wher indyttyd for, whos be
10 Brandons sormyse that whe schullde dryue an harte houyr Temys,
the qwheche whos sclayn at Darteford, and that whe schulde scle
ij hynde caulluys; and aull thys he dyde hymsellfe, w*yth* myche
mor, and ys indyttyd hymselfe for the detthe of ij hartt*ys* and sartte
cawluys. Hyt ys so that Syr Tomas Mongehowmbre ys comynge
15 to Calleyswharde, and so he whyll to Sent Tomers for to fete my
Lady. I pray yow at hys comyng whate apon hym and thanke hym
for ws, for he has beyn howr spessyall good master in thys mater,
and has promysyd me to contenew, and labord sor for ws, and
thorrow hys labor I am cwm in qwayntans of dyuars whowr-
20 schypfull men that w⟨y⟩ll ⌐do⌐ myche for ws for hys sake. I gawhe
hym of howr fathers pwrs an C s., and Ramston, a genttyllmane of
hys, iij s. iiij d. I pray yow make hym good scheyr, for he has beyn
good cellyssytor for ws, and he bryngeys yow a letter frome me,

**136.** 9 whos] for *canc.*     19 cwm in] k *canc.*

and whe whoulde be ryught glade and ʒe myhyt be redy to cowm
in cowmpeny of my Lady *wyth* master Mwngewmbre, for he 25
pwrpos to be heyr afor Cyrstemes. And as for howre forsayde
matter, whe haue howre supersedyas for aull iij; and howr father
ys fully agreyd that ʒe schawll hawe howyr at yowr depattyng
ageyn, Hectyr and son for the Lewheuftenaw⟨n⟩t of Grauenyng in
recwmpense of yow⟨r⟩ beche, for he wyll kepe no mo grewand*ys*. 30
A whyll be g⟨r⟩eabyll to kepe a hauke and spaynellys, and so I haue
my Loordys hauke and ⌈a⌉ kepar, byt he cwmys not heyr tyll I cum
howt of Cottyssowlde, for he and sche goys *wyth* me to Attyrbery.
And as for yowr hawke, I cowde not kepe hyr, my besynes whos so
gret. I hawe sowlde hyr for vij nobullys, byt whone nobyll ys pwt 35
on yowr wyll at yowr comyng. Sche whos not hawlfe insamyde.
I whowlde awyse yow to brynge anothyr *wyth* yow and ʒe may
gehyt hyr gowd schepe. Hyt ys informyd howr father at ther ys
myche Normandy canwhas at Calles: he wyll that ʒe by for hym
iijᶜ awnys and send them be the wholschypys. And as for tydyng*ys* 40
I cane none, byt my ʒeunge lady of ʒeurke ys deyd. No mor to
yow. Whryttyn at London the xxij day of Nowhembyr.

                                   *per* yowr brother, Rychard Cely.

Howr mothe whowllyde that ʒe wyllyd by for hyr mor greyn
gynger, and a qwhattyrn safron.                                    45

*Dorse*: Wnto my riught whellbelouyd brother George Cely
merchand of the Estapell, beyng at Calleys, so dd.


**137.** *Richard Cely the younger at London to George Cely
at Calais, 28 November 1481*

s.c.1 53/89

                Anno Jhesu Mˡiiijᶜ iiijˣˣj

Riught whellbelouyd brother, I recomend me wnto yow. Plesse
hyt yow to whete that I haue tarryd heyr in London for whryttyng
frowme yow thys xiiij days, heuyr syn Kay departtyd, and thys
day I ressauyd a letter frowme yow be Randowlfe, the Stapell
clarke. I sent yow a letter be Flemyng*ys* mane, a nothyr be Kay, 5
the thyrd be Benet Trotter—aull iij sowndyng whone matter, etc.

               **136.** 29 son *ch. from* for    34 hyr] for *canc.*

Syr, I wndy[r]stonde be yowr letter that aull the whowlschypys
ar cwm to Calles sauyng vij, qwherof ij be spent. I trwste to God
that the Crystowyr of Rayname be cwm to Calleys be thys. And
10 as for howre matter of indyttemente, whe ⌜be⌝ thoro and haue
howr sewpersedyas wndyr sele of hoffes of my Loorde of Essex,
the Kyngys Lewhetenawnt of the forreste, byt hyt haue coste
myche mony; byt and Sur Thomas Mongewmbre had not beyn
howr good master hyt wholld a coste myche mor, and my Loorde
15 of Essex hasse confermyd and subseryvyd hundyr hys syngnet the
same whryttyng that my Loorde of Sent Johnys gaw[e] me. And
thys same day I departe into Cottyssowllde—I may tarry no
lenger—and ther rydys wyth me Wylliam Cely apon Py yowr hors,
and I haue wyth me my fawkener wyth my Lordys hawke that
20 noyn of howr hows ken of. I sau heyr newyr fle ȝeyt. The fawkener
and hawke schawll be wyth howr father and hus at my cwmyng
home. Schepe dys wpe in Engelonde. No mor wnto you at thys
tyme, Jhesu kepe yow. Wh⟨r⟩yttyn at London the xxviij day of
Nowhembyr.

25                                         per yowr brother, Rychard Cely.

*At bottom of page, in Richard's writing*: Not myry [?] in hartte.

*Dorse*: Wnto my whellbelouyd brother George Cely, merchand of
the Stapell at Calleys be thy⟨s⟩ delywirdd.


**138.** *William Dalton at Bergen-op-Zoom to George Cely
at London* [? *end of December 1481*]
s.c.1 53/66

Brother George, I recommaunde me vnto you, prayng that ye will
delyuer this letter to my Lorde, fir I have writ that ye shal bryng
hit hym, thoff ye yede to Wynsour to hym. I thynke he will thank
you. *And* that I may ⟨be⟩ recommaund to my maister your fader
5 *and* moder, your brethern *and* my George Cely. At Barow the
morow after departyng.

                                        your B., W. Dalton.

*Dorse*: To ⟨my⟩ tr[u]sty brother George Cely, merchant of the
Staple at Cales, soit don. London.

**139.** *John Dalton at Calais to George Cely at London,*
*1 January 1481/2*
s.c.1 53/93

Right worchipffull broder, after all dew recomendacyon hayd
I recomaunde me vnto yow. Syr, I send yow herwyth a letter
came frome my B. Wylliam Dalton and letter in hys letter closyd.
Alsoy I send yow by Harold Stanton your leyder poch and your
corall beydys, and your man Joyse doyth weell, and your horssys,  5
and as for Andrew ys content. Syr, as in all ader maytterys I schall
do my best. I pray yow that I may be recomaundyd vnto my
mayster your faider and moder and your brother. No mor to yow
at thys tyme, but Jhesus kep yow. At Calles on Neweresday.

your owne to poer,    10
John Dalton.

*Dorse*: To my broder Goerg Cely, merchaunt at þe Staple of
Cales, so it don. London. (*Well-preserved seal.*)


**140.** *John Dalton at Calais to George Cely at London,*
*19 January 1481/2*
s.c.1 53/94

Jhesus

Worchipffull broder, after all dew recommendacyon hayd, I recomaunde ⟨me⟩ vnto yow, etc. Furthermor syr, it ys so that we lack
pelltys her, and we haue sent for to Sent Tomos and ther we bene
promesyd to haue ij° for yow, and I haue sent to Brygys and to
Sandwych for mo peltys, for we mvst haue mo for yow / And syr,  5
Robard Byngam sent to me for iiij nobles of queyt rent for the
grovnd ʒe haue bowght of Andrew Hawes, and I told hym I knew
not therof; yff it wher your dewte to ⌐do⌐ I wold onswer thertto,
wherffor I pray yow of onswer. Alsoy syr, it ys soo that Botrell
hase be vncurtese in hys dedis, for he hayth thrawen in at your  10
woollhovsse wendow dongke among your ffellys, and syn that
tyme he hase geffun a man that spredyd the dongke abrood iij or
⟨iiij⟩ stripys, and toke hys forke frome hym. Albeit I haue spoken
wyth hym, and he hys vncurtes in hys sayeng. For the sayd Botrell

139. 4 leyder] spo *canc.*

15 hase bene owt of towne vnto thys same day; and no I schall schow
the maytter to þe Lewtenant, and so forth to þe consell I purpossyd.
No mor to yow at thys tyme, but Jhesus kep yow. At Calles the
xix day of Jenuar, anno M¹iiijᶜ iiijˣˣj.

your to my poeier,<br>John Dalton.

20

*A line has apparently been cut off the bottom here.*

*Dorse*: To my inteirly beluffid brother Gorge Cely, merchaunt at
þe S[taple o]f Cales, no beyng in London in Marke Layne, so it
don. (*Seal.*)

### 141. *John Dalton at Calais to George Cely at London, 27 January 1481/2*

s.c.1 53/95

Jhesus

Ryght inteirly beluffyd broder, after all dew recomendacyon hayd,
I recomaunde me vnto yow as hartely as I can or may. Furthermore syr, I haue receyued ij letterys from yow, by the wych letter
I onderstond of your grett hevenes of your faider, on whose sole
5 God haue mercy. Furthermore syr, it ys so that Gysbreth Van
Winbragh hayth bene her syn yow departyd, and he wyl be here
agayne, he telles me, wythin xiiiij dayes after Candellmes, and fyech
the xj sarpllerys Cotys woolle of yours, on the wych I haue takon
a Godys peny of hym, for alsoy syr here came non Holanderys
10 syn yow went but won felyschip of Delff, the wych I kod seell non
ffell vnto. Alsoy syr I haue mayd the byllys of costum and subsede
payabull in Marche next, and no syn we haue mayd byllys of
xiij s. iiij d. on the sarpellys, the wych mvst be sent ouyr into
Ynglond, and ther payd at plesur. Your faders byll at plesur
15 amontys vnto xv li. vj s. viij d. ster., your broder Rychard xliiij s.
ster., and Wylliam Maryon byll iij li. x s. viij d. ster.
Alsoy syr syn tyt ys soo as it ys of my mayster your fayder, in
the reverens of God take it pacyenly and hvrte nott yoursell, for
that ⌜God⌝ wyll haue done no mane may be gense. Alsoy syr all
20 your ffellys here don weell, but ȝe schall onderstond that we lacke

140. 15 no] up *canc.*    141. 17 of] me *canc.*

peltys, and here ys non / Thow that bene be at xx d. a dosseren.
Alsoy syr syn yow departyd I haue bene wyth my broder William
Dalton at Brugys, and ther I bowgh⟨t⟩ vjᶜ peltys after iiij s. iiij d.
a C and lytyll moor, the wych ȝe schall allwaye haue the ton halff
of as long as I haue ony. The wych peltys schall be here schortely, 25
sum of them, and betwyxt thys and Fast I trow to haue a Mˡ
peelltys. Syr I schall do my best for yow in all maner of theng
belongyng vnto yow as I wold do for owr broder William Dalton,
so helpe me Jhesus. Alsoy syr I trowe to haue of Gysbreth Van
Wynesbragh xl or l li. of Caroldys at ys comyng. He told me that 30
he wold do ys best to geet them for me at xvj d. þe pond. In case
be that yow wyll that I schall send them ouyr to yow or to ony
oder for yow, send me worde and it schal be don, and that I can
do for yow or maye do in ony oder maytter / Your horsyn do weell,
God save them. Alsoy syr, wher as we ette the good podyngys, the 35
womon of the hosse that mayd them, as I onderstond sche ys wyth
schylde wyth my broder that hayd the Irysch skeyne of me. Syr
all owr howswold by nam recomaund them vnto yow, and the
bene ryght sore of your hevenes in gud fayth. Syr I pray yow that
I may be recomaunddyd vnto your broder Rychard Cely, and ych 40
of yow cheere oder in þe reuerens of owr Layde, who preserue
yow. At Calles the xxvij day of Jenuar.

　　　Your broder to my poer, John Dalton, that I can or may.

Dorse: To my intierly beluffid brother Gorge Cely merchant [at
th]e Staple of Calles, no beyng [in Lo]ndon in Marke Layne. 45
(Celys' shield.)

## 142. Joyce Parmenter at Calais to George Cely at London, 30 January 1481/2

s.c.1 53/96

### Jhesu

Ryghte worshipfull maystir, I recommand me vnto yow, lattyng
yow wyt þat I haue reseyuyd ij lettyrys þat cam frome yow, be the
whiche writtyng I ondirstond my mayster your fadir is discesyd,

---

**141.** 21 be] mayd canc.　　　dosseren: dossen with stroke through tail of second s
23 and repeated
**142.** 2 I] res canc.

on whose sowle God haue mercy. Lattyng yow wyt þat your woll
5 *and* fell ar in good savete. We lak no thyng but onely pelt, for we
can haue none her onder xx$^{ti}$ d. a dosen. If it please yow to send
me M$^l$ w*yth* nexte shippyng þat comys betwene I wold pray yow.
Also your brodir Dalton hathe promysyd ⌜me⌝ iij$^c$ pelt þat he hathe
boghte in Flawndyrys. þay be not suffysient. Also I lat yow wyt
10 þat Bottrell hathe brok vp a wyndew of the weste syde off your
wolhowse, *and* þer he hathe caste in horsse dong vppon your fellys.
I dyd make a man w*yth* a donge forke in hys hond to caste the
donge asyde. Bottrell cam in *and* tuke þe forke fro hym *and* bete
hym wele *and* ithryftyle. I seynge hys vncurtesse delynge, I prayd
15 John Ekynton, Robert Turney, John Ellyrbek *and* William Hyll
w*yth* moo to brekefaste in your chamber: for this entent to see
the hurtys *and* harms he dyd yow vppon your good, þat þay myghte
beyr record ane othir day, whatsoere ye wold sey þerto. Doyng
yow to wyt þat þer be no Holanderys come vnto þe day þat þys
20 byll was mayd, *and* þan þer cam one cartt. Also I latt yow wyt
þat your brodir Dalton hathe sold xj sarplerys of woll to a man off
Brggys, *and* he hathe mayd promyse to be her w*yth*in xiiij days
after Candylmesse to fet þayme away, *and* he hathe promysid to
helpe yow of l li. of Caruluss grottys for xvj d. in þe pownd change.
25 Also I lat yow wyt þat Charlys hathe offyrd viij li. Flemyshe for
Bayerd your horse. I haue grantyd hym for ix li., wharfor I pray
yow to send me word how ye wyl be disposid þerin. Also I lat
yow wyt, þer ye go *and* ete puddyngys the woman is withe child,
as I ondirstond. Also I pray ȝou to puruay yow off oottys, for we
30 can haue none ondir ij s. iiij d. the rasur, and to puruay you bothe
of whete vj rasurys. I can no mor to yow, but I beseche yow to
recom*m*and ⌜me⌝ to my good maystres your modir, to all my
maysturys your brethyrne, *and* to Hankyn; *and* all your howsehold is in sauety, blissid be Jhesu, who preserue yow bothe body
35 *and* sowle. At Calice, xxx$^{ti}$ day of Jeneuer.

Be your seruaunt,
Joysse Parmenter.

*Dorse*: To my ryghte worshipfull maystir Georg Seely in Marke
Layne in London, this byll be delyuerd in goodly haste.

**143.** *Thomas Kesten at London to George Cely at London,*
*13 February 1481/2*

s.c.1 53/97

### Jhesu M¹iiijᶜ lxxxj

Reuerent syr ande my speceall frende and gossep, all dewe recomendacon had, plesse it you to vnderstond that I am latte comen to London, ande for deyueres causses ande matteres, also well agayn Wylliam Brerely as oder, I wolde speke wyth you / Ande I do com to you to my heuy mastres I scholde renew her hewynesse 5 and nat elles / Ande also I ⌈dare⌉ nat well be sen in London / I thanke God and the Keng I myght, but I wyll nat, ande I may do oderwisse, put my pertecseon in ewre in London, for it scholde be a gret noysse theroff; wherfore I beseche you to do so meche to com to Saynt Laurence Pouteny before ij of the cloke at afternon, 10 and ellys the [nexte] morne in the morneng at vij of the clok at the furthest. Ther I schall wayte vpon you justely, by the grace of Jhesu. Wretton in London the Wedonysday the xiij day of Feuerell, the day after the kepeng, as I wnderstond, of your fader my gode mayster ys monthis mynd. Besecheng you to kepe this lettre closse 15 tyll I haue spoken wyth you.

By all your,<br>Thomas Kesten.

*Dorse*: To the worschepfull syr Gorge Sely, merchaunt of the [St]apell, he beeng at his [fade]rs place in Marke L[ane in] 20 London, so dd.

**144.** *Thomas Kesten at London to George Cely at London,*
*21 February 1481/2*

s.c.1 53/98

### Jhesu M¹iiijᶜ lxxxj

Reuerent syr, all dewe recomendacon hadde, plesse it you to wnderstond that I haue spoken wyth Wylliam Segon that whas the atto⟨r⟩ny of Wylliam Brereley, ande I fynde hym the same man that he whas in his sayeng that that mony ys the dewte of Wylliam Brereley ande nat hessen / Syr, he dessirethe to know to whom the 5

143. 6 ⌈dare⌉ *over* doo *canc.*          9 be] agre *canc.*
144. 3 atto⟨r⟩ny of] the *canc.*

bylles wher madde ande when they wher payabyll, the wiche ys
nat fresche in my remembraunce. In the reconeng ⌜of my⌝ honde
delyuerd to my master your fader I hope you schall fynde remembraunce of the same, if it plesse you to serche, ande if you fynde
10 yt of any remembraunce I pray you lette me haue knowleche from
you be your chelde to the same place ther you spake wyth ⟨me⟩ any
day this iiij dayes, in the morneng from vij of the cloke tyll viij of
the cloke/ ande Jhesu kepe you ande all your. Wretton ⌜on⌝ Asche
Wedonysday, anno lxxxj.

15                                    per your owne Thomas Kesten.

*Dorse*: To the reuerent syre Gorge Cely the son of Richard Sely,
in Marke Lane on Lond[on], this be delyuerd.


## 145. *Thomas Kesten to George Cely at Calais, 14 March 1481/2*

S.C.1 53/100

Jhesu M¹iiij° lxxxj

Worschepfull syr, I recomaunde me vnto you, etc., and I dowte
me that it wyl be meche after Owre Lade Day [ere] I com whom,
wherffore I sende you a bylle of Wylliam Bereley is honde of all
the stuffe that he hath of myn for the som of vj li. v s., the wiche
5 ys worthe als meche more; the wiche I beseche you to take into
yovre hondes, and I promysse you as I am Cresten man to descharge yt schortely and elles you to haue yt at the same prys.
I hadde leuer you hade a proffet by me r[a]der th[a]n he. Ande
sende me worde of the bylles of Brereleyes that I may speke wyth
10 Segeon at Westemyster, and Jhesu kepe you/ All the sayde
thenkys ben in a gret bage ande sellid by me, all saue iij pesses:
ij govnys, j furre ys owght. I beseche you to be my gode frende
ande gossep now in this matter and in all oder, ande I schall owe
you my sarves my liffe devreng, that know[eth] Jhesu, who kepe
15 you. In haste the xiiij day of Marche.

                              per Thomas Kesten, your ovne servaunt.

*Dorse*: To the reuerent syr Gor[g] Cely, merchaunt of the St[a]pell
at [C]alles, this be delyuerd in hast.

144. 9 serche] I hope you sch *canc.*     11 ⟨me⟩: *ms.* you     13 / ande] of
*canc.*     ⌜on⌝ *over canc.* the

**146.** *Richard Cely the younger at London to George Cely at Calais, 21 March 1481/2*

s.c.i 53/101

Anno Jhesu M<sup>l</sup>iiij<sup>c</sup>iiij<sup>xx</sup> j

Riught whelbelouyd brother, I recwmend me wnto yow w*yth* aull my hart, info*r*myng you that I hawhe resawyd ij lettyrs frome John Dawltton, thay bothe derecttyd to yow, wherby I wndyrstond he desyrys to hawhe bohwt for hym iij ʒeard*ys* of blake pewyke, and I hawhe pwrwhayd hyt for hym, byt I can gehyt no caryayge 5 tyll Robard Heryke cw*m* at Estyr. Syr, thys day I spake w*yth* Bryan, and he says at that ys not the bastard swherd at he whowlde hauhe, hyt ys yowr gylte swherd. And my Loord Schambyrlen pwrpos to be at Calles befor Est*er*, and thys day I departe into Cottysowldewhard be the grase of Jh*e*su kepe yow, and send ws 10 goode tydyng*ys* frome yow. Whryt at London the xxj day of Marche.

p*er* yowr brother,<br>Rycha*rd* Cely.

Syr, I hawhe bene spokyn to for a whyfe in ij plassys syn ʒe 15 departtyd: whon whos be the praysayrs, as schawll whryt to yow mor playne in my next lett*er*.

*Dorse*: A my whelbelowyd brother George Cely, m*er*chand of the Stap*e*ll, beyng at Calles, thys dd.

**147.** *Richard Cely the younger at London to George Cely at Calais, 29 March 1482*

s.c.i 53/102

Anno Jhesu M<sup>l</sup>iiij<sup>c</sup>iiij<sup>xx</sup> ij

R⟨y⟩ught whellbelouyd brother, I recomende me wnto yow as lowyngly as I con or may, informyng yow that the xxviij day of M*a*rche I resawyd a lett*er* frome yow whryt at Calles the Twysday aft*er* howr departtyn*g*, qwherby I ondyrstonde ʒe be howyr in safette, thankyd be God, and ʒe fynde aull thyng acordyng to 5 yowr intent. And as for Tomas Kesten, ys lett*er* ys delyuyrd, and as for aull thyng in Essex, I schawll do for yow as I do for my nowyn. Syr, I wndyrstonde be Wyll*ia*m Celys lett*er* that aull howre ⌜Cott*ys*⌝ wholl ys sowlde in Calles: hyt ys good tydyng*ys*; I pray

10 God sende ws sum sall of howr fel*es*. I hawhe beyn at Abynton
syn I whrat my laste lett*er*, and spake w*yth* Wyll*ia*m Bretten, and
he myte go no fardar w*yth* me for packyng of Lombard*ys* wholl at
Hamton, the qwheche mwste departe into Gean at thys Est*er* in
the Kyng*ys* schypys, and he has promysyd to met w*yth* me at
15 Norlache on Low Sonday. Syr, I pray you sende me a lett*er*
schorttely how I schawl be demenyd in ansfor to Wyll*ia*m Mydwyntt*er* of hys fellys, for and ʒe make any salle hyt wyl be whysdo*m*
to be sewyr of mo. Heyr ys Wyll*ia*m Dawlton now, and I thynke
heffe he hawhe any wente at Calles hyt wyll cawse hym do the lese
20 w*yth* yow. Syr, heyr has beyn John Croke of the Tempyll w*yth*
howr mother, and informyd hyr that he hard the Exchett*er* of
Essex say that he moste go into Essex to syt in an enqwery of howr
londys, qwhether howre father dyed sesyd in hys lond, or qwethyr
whe be of lawfull ayge, and of home howr londe ys howlldyn; and
25 ʒeystyr day I whente to mast*er* Molenars and bare w*yth* me the
laste made deyde of Brett*ys* and yowr laste madedys of Malyns,
and whe schewyd hym that the londe stode in fefes hand*ys*; and
hyt whos informyd hym that Malyns whos holdy*n* of the Kyng,
and awll londe howldyn of the Kyng schulde be exchettyd for the
30 Kyng tyll the hayre has made hys fyne w*yth* the Kyng, byt whe
hafe no londe that holld*ys* of the Kynge. Be the awyse of mast*er*
Molenars I gawhe the Exchett*er* xl s. for ws bothe, and so whe be
thorow w*yth* hym for aull matters and parellys, byt Y mowste
brynge hym at laysar a byll of the day a the dysses of owr fathe⟨r⟩,
35 owr ayge, and of home owr londe ys howldyn, at he may sett hyt
in the Kyng*ys* bokys. [*Dorse*] And on the xxvij day whos Byfelde
berryd, and on the morow herly hys whyfe toke the manttell and the
rynge, and at aftyrnoyn the same day whos the grehyte ⌈nev⌉ gone
of brasse schott at Myleʒeynde, at vhos mad in the Towyr, and
40 hyt braste awll to pessys. Syr, I hawhe lettyrs fromy Lorde wryte
in Napwll*ys*, byt I red them not ʒeyt. Whane I se them I schawll
wh*r*yte to yow of syche thyng*ys* as ys in them, be the grasse of
Jh*e*su, ho kepe yow. Wrytte at London the xxix day of M*a*rche.

p*er* yowr brother,
45 Rychard Cely.

A my whellbelouyd brother George Cely, m*er*chand of the
Stap*e*ll beyng at Call*es*, so thys dd.

**147.** 26 madedys of] L *canc.*       36 xxvij] and *canc.*

**148.** *Richard Cely the younger at London to George Cely at Calais, 2 April 1482*

s.c.1 53/103

Anno Jhesu Mˡiiijᶜiiijˣˣ ij

Riught whellbelouyd brother I recomend me wnto yow as hartte con thy*n*k, informeyng yow that I hawhe resauyd a lletter from yow whryt at Callys the xxvij day of Marche, wherby I wndyr-sto⟨nd⟩ of yor salle, w*yth* many hother thyng*ys*. And ȝe schawll resaue of Wylliam Dawlltom iij ȝeard*ys* pewyke for howr brother John Dawltton. And as for felle*s*, I troste whe schawll haue as good as any schawll com howt of Cottyssowld; for as ȝe whryte to me wholl wyll be skante, I pwrpos to ryde into Cottyssowlld on Tewysday in the Ester Wheke for to pake. Now whyll I am a whryttyng of thys letter, Wylliam Mydwyttyrs mane ys com to fet mony, and I pwynte my tyme w*yth* hym. As for tydyng*ys* frome my Lord, I sende yow my Lord*ys* letter, and an letter frome Syr Wylliam dyrectyd to yow, and I send yow the copy of my Lordy byll that he made me closyd in thys. And hystyrday the inbaseturs of Frawns wher ressauyd into London / and thys day I depart into Essex. Wh⟨r⟩ettyn in haste at London the sekunde day of Aprell.

per Rychard Cely.

*Dorse*: A my riught whelbelouyd brother George Cely, merch⟨a⟩nt of the Stapell, beyng at Calle*s*.

*G. Cely's hand*: ijᶜxxxvj li.                    20
xxxvj li.
xviij li.

**149.** *William Maryon at London to George Cely at Calais, 2 April 1482*

s.c.1 53/104

Jhesu Mˡiiijᶜiiijˣˣ ij

Ryght reuerent syr and my specyall good ffrende, I reco*m*aund me vnto you. Ferdermor, and yt plesse yow, ye schall vnderstonde that Y haue ressayved a letter from you wreten at Calles the xxviij day of M*a*rche, the wyche letter Y haue well vnderstonde: that ye haue sowlld vnto Henryc Page and to Jacob Tymanson and hys

148. 1 hartte] hart *interlineated*.        20 ijᶜ lxxij li. *canc.*        21 xlij li. *canc.*

feleschype of Laythe, xxiij<sup>c</sup> of my new somer ffellys London ffor
xvj noblis halffe le C—argente Clxiiij li. ix s. Fl., werof ye haue
ressayued in hand, and schall ressayve at thys next martt, iiij<sup>xx</sup>
ij li. ix s. Fl., and the xxvj day of September next—xlj li. Fl., and
10 the xxvj day of Marche, the rest—xlj li. Fl. And so, syr, ⌜Y⌝
vnderstond ther remayng behynd wheche be mad and sore brent,
ij<sup>c</sup>xxv felles, the wyche ye woll do yowre best to put away wyt
yowre fell*y*s, for the wyche, syr, Y thanke yow hartley. Also syr,
Y vnderston⟨d⟩ that Y schall leyesse cler of my brent fell*y*s, the
15 wyche woll neuer be mad, s*u*m Cxxxij ffell*y*s. Syr, Y thankt Good,
as the casse requered, that Y lesse no mo. Also syr, Y vnderstond
that a lytell befor yowre comyng to Calles John Dallton had sovud
all myn hoder fellys the wyche Y had in Calles, for the wyche, syr,
Y thankt yow and hem bothe hartteley, and Y pray to God that
20 Y may deserued ayenst yow, for God sent you now lokeley to Calles
for to do so son so gret a fette as ye haue don set ye cam to Calles,
thanked be God. Syr, yowre broder Rechard Cely a ij dayes afor
Owre Lady Day, he wasse at Habendon and wayted vpon Wyll*i*am
Breten for to goo vnto Norlagh, but Wyll*i*am Breten myt nat
25 atendyt, and in that men tym com Wyll*i*am Medwenter to London, and so non of them spakt wyt hodere, and so Rechard Cely
porposet be the leffe of God for to reyde into Cotyswoldward vpon
Wedynysday or on Thorysday in Hester Weke, I pray to God be
hys sped. Syr, vpon Palm Sonday the Frensche inbaset co*m* into
30 London, and they war worschyppefull-ley ressayved wyt the
Mayhere and all the craftys of London. Also syr, ye schall vnder-
ston⟨d⟩ that my mayesterys youre moder ys in good hell, so
ressonabeley, and wext all strong as of a woman of har age, thanked
be Good, and sche reco*m*aund har vnto you, and sendyt vnto you
30 Godys blessyng and harys. Alsso syr, ye schall vnderstond that all
the hooll hovssovlld faryt well, thanked be God. No mor vnto you
at thys tym, but the Trenyte haue you in hys kepyng. Wreten at
London the ij day of Aperell, etc.

Be youre owne,
40                                        Wyll*i*am Maryon.

*Dorse*: Wnto Georg Cely, marchant of the Stapull at Calles, thys
letter be delyuerde, etc. (*Shield*.)

*In G. Cely's hand*: Thes ben lettyrs done M<sup>l</sup>iiij<sup>xx</sup>j *and* ij.

149. 31 Also syr] Y thanke *canc*.

**150.** *Richard Cely the younger at London to George Cely at Calais, 8 April 1482*

S.C.I 53/105

Jhesu M$^l$iiij$^c$iiij$^{xx}$ ij

Riught interly belouyd brother, I recomend me harttely wnto yow, etc., informyng yow that I hawhe ressauyd an letter frowme yow, wherby I wndyrstonde the dethe of my yow⟨n⟩ge Lady of Borgen and of the treson at Sent Tomors. I pray God kepe hyt and sawhe Flawndyrs. I wndyrstonde be a letter that cam to me frome 5 Wylliam Cely now lat that ʒe hawhe sowlde vj M$^l$vj$^c$ d. of Cottys-sowlde fellys; and thay ar into Hollonde in safete, as he whryttys to me, thankyd be Jhesu, and as for tydyngys I can none wrytte. The Kynge, the Qwehyn and the Prynse lyes at Eltam, and I pwrpos to departe into Cottysowlde the ix day of thys monthe, 10 and the xj day I wndyrstond ʒe pwrpos to Bregyswhard, the Holy Trenyte sped ws bothe. And I pray yow thynke apone howr bowys, for I hawhe brokyn the bastard bow that ʒe lefte heyr as I ʒeyde to Hawelaywhard. And Lonttelay and Lasse has beyn at yowr plasse Malyns ⟨and⟩ mendyd yowr hege. Heuyry letter that I 15 ressawe frome yow ys to me a grehyt cumfortte. Wryte at London the viij day of Aprell.

per ʒor brother,
Rychard Cely.

*Dorse*: A my riught whellbelowyd brother George Cely, merchand 20 of the Stapwll at Calleys, so dd.

**151.** *William Maryon at London to George Cely at Calais, 14 April 1482*

S.C.I 53/106

Jhesu M$^l$iiij$^c$iiij$^{xx}$ ij

Ryght reuerent syr and my specyall ffrende, I recomaund me vnto you. Ferdermor, and yt plesse you, ye schall vnderstonde that Y haue ressayued a letter from you wreten at Calles the xxviij day of Marsche, leyke as Y wreten vnto yow in my last lettere, that Y well vnderstond that ye haue sould all my fellys at Calles, 5 saffyng ij$^c$xxv ffellys, for the wyche salys, syr, Y thanke yow harteley, etc. Also syr, Y pray you that ye woll delyuer vnto Robard

Eyryk xxx or xl li. st*er*., lyke as ye and he can agre, and as ye do
wyt hoder men; for lyke as ye do, Y hovld me greyd both in mony
10 and in dayes, saffyng he hat promysed me x li. her in hand at my
plessere, and therfor Y wold that he had the lengar day of the
rest, they yt be Mehellmas day. And as for yowre broder Rechard
Cely, ye schall vnderstond that he ys at hys plasse in Hesext, for
he wos y-porposed for to a be at thys day in Cottysswold, saffyng
15 Wyll*ia*m Breten sent hem word fro Hamton that he myt nat atend
vnto hem, nat tyell yt be xiiij dayes after Estere, and be that day
yowre brodere porposed be the leue of God to be at Nortlacht, an
at that day Wyll*ia*m Breten hat y-promesed therfor to met hem.
Also, ye schall vnderstond that my masterys yowre modere ys in
20 good hell, thanked be God, sauyng har leghe ys nat yt all holl, but
Y truste to God yt stondyd in good casse. Syr, sche reco*m*aund
har vnto you, and sche send you God ys blessyng and harys, and
so sche doyt, in good fayyt, eu*er*y day seyt ye departed. Yowre
broder Robard and all the houssould faryt well, thanked be God.
25 Wreten at London the xiiij day of Aperell, etc.

Be youre owne
Wyll*ia*m Maryon.

*Dorse*: Wnto Georg Cely, marchant of the Stapull at Calles, thys
letter be delyuerde, etc. (*Shield*.)

*In George Cely's hand*:
30          Of Claysse Pet*er*son and his ffellowys.
iiij d. ob. ------------------------- xxj li. Fl.
iiij d. ob. ------------------------- xiij li. x s. Fl.
xxxiiij lewis vij s. ----------------- xj li. xviij s. Fl.
xl Andr*us* iiij s. viij d. -------------- ix li. vj s. viij d. Fl.
35 xxvj new crovn*us* v s. viij d. --------- vij li. vij s. iiij d. Fl.
xxj owlld crovn*us* v s. vj d. ---------- v li. xv s. vj d. Fl.
xxx postlaty*s* ij s. viij d. ------------- iiij li. iij d. Fl.
                    S*um* --------- lxxij li. xvij s. ix d. Fl.
iiij d. ob. ------------------------- v li. v s. Fl.
40 ij d. qr. ------------------------- ij li. xiiij s. Fl.
ix lewys vij s. --------------------- iij li. iij s. Fl.
iiij d. ob. ------------------------- vj li. Fl.
ix lewys vij s. --------------------- iij li. iij s. Fl.

**151.** 12 & *erased*          21 God *ch. from* Good          35 col. 2 vij s. iiij d.
*over* vij s. viij d.

iij crownys v s. vj d. ---------------- xvj s. [vj d.]
vij Andreus iiij s. viij d. ------------- xxxij s. viij d. Fl.        45
iiij r[y]darus iij s. x d. -------------- xv s. iiij d. Fl.
an Rynyshe gyldorn---------------- iiij s. vj d. Fl.
ij d. qr. -------------------------- v li. Fl.

Logged at the howyser in Barow.*
iij postlatys ----------------------- viij s. Fl.        50
xij Hettryus iiij s. ij d. -------------- ij li. x s. Fl.
in pensse ------------------------ x s. Fl.
iiij d. ob. ------------------------ vij li. xix s. Fl.
    Sum ---------------------- xl li. xij d. Fl.

ij d. qtr. ------------------------- xxj s. Fl.        55
xxxj rydars Gyll. iij s. x d. le pese ----- v li. xviij s. x d. Fl.
In whyght mony ------------------- xvij d. Fl.
        Sum --------- vij li. xv d. Fl.
        Sum totall ---- Cxx li. Fl.

## 152. Robert Eyryk at London to George Cely at Calais, Bruges or Bergen, 18 April 1482

s.c.1 53/107

Jhesus M¹iiijᶜ lxxxij, the xviij day of Aprell in London.

Right reuerent and worschepfull ser, I recommavnd me vnto yow
wyth all my hart, desyryng to heer of your welfare, the wheche
I beseche God to preserue to his blessud plesure and to your most
proffyt both of body and soulle. Ser, yf hyt plesith yow to wete
that my mastras your moder and my maysters both your bredurne,   5
my em Wylliam Maryon, and all your hovssold faryn well, and
my mastras is in gud heell, thankyd be Jhesus, and mery; God kepe
her long soo // Also ser, pleseth hyt yow to wyt that my em and
I be agreed that I schold haue xl li. that schold be delyueryd by
yew. Ser, hit is so that I porposed to a byn wyth yow in the   10
Esterne weke, but in trouth I haue a let that hath kavsed me to
tare, and ʒyt I haue not done. But ser, I porpose to be at Bryggys
mart yf I may, and els I prey yow that hyt may be redy when
I come, for I tryst to haue hyt redy, as my em tellyth me, whenso

* Written sideways along the figures column below this point.
151. 56 v li. over iij li.

15 I com. I had lever to haue hyt at Bryggys or at Barow than at Cales,
yf hyt plese yew to provyde so for me. Also ser, I prey yew to be
my gud godfader in the mater that spake vnto, and I wyll evyr do
yew seruys in eny thyng that I can, by the grace of God, who haue
yew in his blessud kepyng. Wryttyn in hast.

20
　　　　　　　　　　　　　　　　　　By your owne,
　　　　　　　　　　　　　　　　　　　Robert Eyryk.

*Dorse*: To my right reuerent *and* trysty ffrend Jorge Cely marchaunt of the Staple, be this letter delyueryd in Cales, at Bryggys
or at Barow mart.


## 153. *William Maryon at London to George Cely at Calais, 20 April 1482*

s.c.1 53/109

### Jhesu

Ryght worschyppfull and reuerent syr and my specyall good
ffrende, Y recomaund me vnto you. Ferdermor, and yt plesse you,
ye schall vnderstond that Y haue ressayved j letter from yow,
wretten at Calles the xv day of Aperell, the wyche letter Y haue
5 rede and well vnderstond, etc. Also syr, Y vnderstond that ye haue
sovld now latte for me the rest of my fellys, for the wyche, syre,
Y thanke you harteley. Y pray to God that Y may deserved ayenst
you. Also syr, Y vnderstond that ye war porposed at the makyng
of youre letter schortely to the martward. Syr, Y pray you that ye
10 woll do for me in the latyng owte of my mony that ys growyn at
thys tym, as ye do wyt yowre owne, sauynd that ye woll keppe vnto
the comyng of Robard Eyryk xxx or xl li. ster., and that ye yeffe
yt owte vnto hem as ye do vnto hoder men, sauyng he hath promysed me that Y schall haue x li. ster. her at my plesere. Syr, he
15 had porposed for to a be wyt yow or thys tym, but he hat seche
lettyng her that he may nat com yt thys xiiij dayes. Also syr, ye
schall vnderstond that the xix day of Aperell yowre broder
Rechard Cely departed owth of London into Cottyswouldward
at iij of the byell at afternon, and as he wasse takyng hys horsse,
20 wrytyng cam from you, the wyche was wreten at Calles the xv day
of Aperell, the wyche wrytyng, syr, he myth nat well tarey for to
red, and therfor, syr, he hat boren them wyt hem into Cotyswovld.
Syr, yowre broder Rechard sayed: as for the matter of my Lord

of Canterbery ys cortte, ye schall haue no nede for to com hasteley
hom, for he hat spoken wyt Marynare, and Marynar sayyt vnto   25
hem and ye be her be Medsomere ye ned nat dowte theroff, etc.
Syr, my mayesterys yowre moder ys in good hell, thanked be
Good, and sche sendyt vnto you God ys blessyng and harys.
Yowre broder Robard and all the hovssould faryt well, blessed be
God. Wreten at London the xx day of Aperell, etc.                    30

*per* yowre owne,
Wyll*ia*m Maryon.

*Dorse*: Wnto George Cely, marchant of the Stapull at Calles, thys
lettere be delyuerde, etc. (*Maryon's shield*.)

### 154. *Robert Eyryk at London to George Cely at Bergen-op-Zoom, 20 April 1482*

s.c.1 53/110

J*he*sus M¹iiij<sup>c</sup> lxxxij, the xx day of Aprell in London.

Ryght reuerent and worschepfull sur, I reco*mm*avnd me vnto
w*yth* all my hart, desyryng to heer of youre welfare, the wheche
I beseche J*he*sus longe to pre*ser*ue *and* kepe. Also ser, lettyng yow
wete that at the makyng of this letter my mastras your modir *and*
my masters your bredurne, *and* all your hovssold faren well,   5
blessud be God // Also ser, my em Wyll*ia*m Maryon *and* I be
agreed as for xl li. that I schold ress*eyue* of yew, the whech I prey
yew yf that ӡe come hom or I com, that hyt may be left at Brygg*ys*
or at suche a place as I may haue hyt redy when I com, or els w*yth*
Wyll*ia*m Cely at Cales. Ser, in trouth I p*or*posed to a be w*yth* yow   10
in Esturne weke, but I haue suche a lettyng that I cannot come
ӡyt, but odir I wyl be at Brygg*ys* mart or els at Synksen betymes,
by the grace of Gud, who haue yew ɪn his blessud kepyng.
Wryttyn in hast.

Ser, yf hyt wold plese yew to send me word in a lytell byll by   15
Thomas Clarke that was my broder Richard*ys* man wher that
I schall ress*eyue* hyt, I prey yew hartly, for I trowe he wyll come
home hastely.

By your owne,
Rob*er*t Eyryk.   20

153. 25 for *repeated*
154. 4 makyng of] your *canc.*

*Dorse*: Wnto my right reuerent *and* worschepfull George Cely marchaunt of the Stapull, beyng in the howeyser at Barow.

### 155. *William Cely at Calais to George Cely at Bruges, after 20 April 1482*

S.C.1 53/111

Jh*e*su M¹iiij<sup>c</sup> iiij<sup>xx</sup>ij

Ryght worshyppffull syr, afftyr dew recom*m*endaschon I louly recom*m*end ⌐me⌐ vnto yowre masterschypp, etc. Furthermore, plese hit yowre mast*er*schypp to vnderstonde that I hawe receyued an letter ffro*m* ⌐yow⌐ be Hayne that was yowre s*er*ua*u*nte, the
5 whych I hawe redd and well vnderstonde, and all thyng*ys* schall be don acordyng to yowre wryttyng, etc. Item syr, ple⟨s⟩hit yow to wytt I hawe receyued an lett*er* ffro*m* Robard Heryck, and he wryt*ys* me he was purpossyd to a ben at thys Passe Martt, but hys besynesse was syche ⌐that⌐ he myght nott, wharffor he prayth yow
10 that the xl pownde st*er*lyng that he schulde a receyued off yow at the sayd martte ffor my godffader Maryon, as I wrotte vnto yowre mast*er*schypp yn annoder lett*er*, he prayth yow that ʒe wyll kepe hit bye yow tyll he com*m*e, ffor yn Whyttson weke he purpose to [be wyth yowre mast]*er*schyp at Caleys wyth the [gra]ce off Godd
15 and [. . .] sake, etc. [*Rest torn off.*]

*Dorse*: To my worshyppffull mast*er* George Cely, m*er*chau*n*te off the Stapell off Caleys, he beyng at Bregys, soo hit dd. (*Shield.*)

### 156. *William Cely at Calais to George Cely at Bergen-op-Zoom, 23 April 1482*

S.C.1 53/112

Jh*e*su M¹iiij<sup>c</sup>iiij<sup>xx</sup> ij

Ryght wurshyppffull syr, afftyr dew recom*m*endaschon I louly recom*m*end me vnto yowre masterschypp, etc. Plese hit yowre mast*er*schypp to vnderstond that John Dalton and I hawe spoken to mast*er* Lefftena*u*nte ffor payme*n*t off yowre warrantt*ys*, and he
5 sayth we schall hawe payment wyth*y*n v or vj days, but he sayth

we cannott hawe all at thys tyme, and we desyryd to hawe them
sett apon yowre byll*ys* off costom and subsede, and he sayth hit
may nott be, ffor ther be mor soo don than may be p*er*fformyd;
ffor the whych they shall bryng yn sterlynge mony ynto the
Collectry agayn and hawe her payme*nt* owte off the Tressery, etc.   10
Syr, plese hit yow to wytt her be many Hollonders, butt they bye
noo noder ffell*ys* off bott London and contrey ffell*ys*, and as ffor
woll, I can sell here non w*yth*owte I hadd olde wull, ffor they can
hawe no olde wull but where they bye new wull, etc. Syr, I hawe
receyuyd noo letters owte off Ynglonde syn yow dep*a*rtyd, but   15
I hawe sent ynto Ynglond at eu*er*y passage, etc. Syr, Bayarde
yowre horsse doyth well, and so doys yowr toder horsse at Twys-
sulltons too. And I here nobody that makys any do ffor hym,
Joysse wolde ffayne hawe hym home ynto hys stabull. I pray yow
send ⌈vs⌉ worde how we schall be demenyd w*yth* hym, etc. Syr,   20
oder tydyng*ys* hawe we none here, but I pray almyghty Jh*e*su kepe
yow. Wrytten at Calys the xxiij day of Apryll, p*er* yowre s*er*ua*u*nte,
Wyll*ia*m Cely.

*Dorse*: To my wurshyppffull master George Cely, m*er*chaunte off
⌈þe Stappell of⌉ Caleys, he being at the martte at Barrowe, be þis   25
delyu*er*ed.

### 157. *John Dalton at Calais to George Cely, 23 April [1482]*

s.c.1 53/113

Intierly beluffyd brother, I recomaunde me vnto yow aft*er* all dew
recomendacyon hayd, etc. S*yr*, plese it yow to wytt that in casse
be that yow haue natt bowght no horse, I wolde ȝe bowght non,
for at yo*ur* comyng ȝe schall ⌈know⌉ wher won *ys* or may that wyll
be solde as gud for iiij li. and ond*er* as Tweseltons *ys*. S*yr*, no more   5
to yow at thys tym, but Jh*e*su*s* kep yow. At Calles on Sent Jorge
Day at nyght,
yo*ur* B., John Dalton.

*Reversed, in George Cely's writing*:
Item, p*a*yd be me to Hary Bryan be John
    Delopis byll     - - - - - - - - - - - - - - - - -   xxviij li. ix s. x d.   10

---

**156.** 6 them] them *canc.*      9 ffor the] st*er canc.*      15 Ynglonde]
synss *canc.*

Item, in v d. ob. le pesse    -------------    vj li.xij s. Fl.
Item, in ij d. ob.            -------------    viij li. Fl.
Item, in ij d. qr.            -------------    v li. v s. Fl.
Item, in pensse               -------------    xxx s. Fl.
15 Item, in pensse            -------------    iij s. ij d. Fl.
                              Sum ---------    l li. Fl.

*Dorse*: To my intierly beluffyd brother Gorge Cely, merchaunt at
the Staple of Calles.


### 158. *William Cely at Calais to George Cely at the mart, 29 April 1482*

s.c.1 53/114

Jhesu M¹iiijᶜiiijˣˣ ij

Ryght wurshyppffull syr, affter dew recommendaschon I louly
recommend me vnto yowre masterschypp, etc. Furthermore, plese
hit yowre masterschypp to vnderstond ther ys bonde vnto thys
lettere serteyn letters selyd that comme ffrom my Lord off Sent
5 Jonys, but oder letters owte of Ynglonde hawe I receyued none
syn yowre masterschypp departyd ffrom Calys, etc. Syr, plese hit
yow to wytt that yowre horssys be all yn gode pwoynte, and Bayard
ys all hole off hys maledy, and he was newer better to labor than
he ys now, etc. Syr, Joyse prayis yow to send hym worde when
10 ʒe thyncke ʒe schall be redy to com to Calys that he myghte
send yow lyccwll Bayarde to comme home on, etc. Syr, we hawe
tydynggys yn Calys that my Lorde Chamberleyn ys at Dower,
and they loke afftyr hym at Calys at euery tyde, etc. Syr, all
thyngys at Calys doys well, thaunkyd be Godd. Syr, oder
15 tydyngys hawe we non, but Jhesu kepe yow. Wrytten at Calys the
xxix day off Apryll,

> per yowre seruaunte,
> Wylliam Cely.

*Dorse*: To my worshyppffull master George Cely merchaunte off
20 the Stappell off Calys, being at the martte, soo hit dd. (*Shield*.)

**157.** 11 col. 2 v *canc.* [vj li.        17 brother] Wyll *canc.*

**159.** *Nicholas Knyveton to George Cely* [c. *May 1482*]
s.c.1 53/92

Brodur Jorge, I hertely pray you to doe for me as anodur tyme
I shal be as glad to do you pleser *and* iff I kan. To bye a bed, tester
*and* sellere *and* coueryng therto, *and* lett þe coueryng be large *and*
þe bed as hyt plese you best—off god warkus as ye wold doe for
yourselffe, *and* off þe strangyusst warke. *And* also yff ye kan fynd   5
a hangyng off þe same warke *and* off lyk pryse, thre yardus deppe
*and* xxx yerdus of lengkhe, I pray you to bye hyt acordyng to þe
same. See what ye may doe, hyt shal be treulle onsward euery
peyny. I pray you maystur Jarge, doe for me as I wold doe for
you: hyt shal be quyt by thys ⌐my⌐ wryttyng.          10

> Your verey ffrynd
> Nycolas Knyveton.

*Dorse, in G. Cely's hand*:
  The goblettys xxxiiij ovns v d.
  iiij sylwyr xxvj ovns xv d.


**160.** *William Cely at Calais to George Cely at the mart,
2 May 1482*
s.c.1 53/115

> Jhesu M¹iiijᶜiiijˣˣij

Ryght worschyppffull syr, afftyr dew recommendaschon I louly
recommend me vnto yowre masterschypp, etc. Furthermore, plese
hit yowre masterschypp to vn⟨der⟩stond that my Lord Chamberleyn cam to Calys as on the ffyrst day off May, and he was wor-
schyppffully receyued ther, etc. Syr, plese hit yow to vnderstond   5
I hawe receyued a letter derectyd to me ffrom my godffader
Maryon whych was wrytten at London the xxij day Aprell, be
the whych I vnderstond that hit wyll be a xiiij days or Robardd
Heryck commys to the martt, wherffor my godffader Maryon prays
yow that ȝe wull kepe a xl li. ster. ⌐off⌐ hys mony tyll the sayd Robard   10
Herycke comys, etc. Syr, as ffor thys payment off the sowdeers, we
be yett at no sertente, but men suppose hit schall be starlyng
mony, etc. Syr, master Mayer and sarten off the Felyschypp off

---

**159.** 6 lyk] ht *canc.*     13 v d.] the pott (?) *canc.*

**160.** 6 ffrom *over canc.* was     10 ster.] of my *canc.*     13 and] ma *canc.*

London hath wrytten to master Lefftenaunt and to the Felyschypp
15 at Calys that they be yn a wey wyth the Kyngys gode Grace, and
hopyth ⌐ffor⌐ to stablysch hit ffrom thys payment fforwarde that
⌐the Felyschypp off the Stappell⌐ schall pay ffor ⌐her⌐ costom and
subsede as myche ffor the pownde ⌐ster.⌐ as they recheyuyth ffor
thyr pownde sterlyng, and non oderwyse, but as thys payment ys
20 put at the descreschon off my Lorde, etc. Also syr, I vnderstond
that hit ys grauntyd to the Kyngys gode Grace vj thowchand
marke ffor surplysage, wherffor I vnderstand ther schall be a commavndement sent that euery man schall schy[pp] syche godys as
he hath by hym schorttly; and ⌐all⌐so the Kynge w[yll] hawe ⌐yff
25 ther be any man⌐ off the Stapell and ys off abylyte to ocupye an[d
he do]th nott, that he schall schypp be an sarten day, or e[ls . . .]
⌐ffall⌐yn an penwalte, ffor the Kynge wyll hawe a ffr[. . .]. They
hawe amyttyd at London master Stocker to [. . .] Mayer yn hys
absens, and they haw i-chosen [. . .] solyster, and he ⌐hath⌐
30 wrytten to master Lefftenaunt [and the Felly]schypp at Calys to
ffynd a mene that thys syrplysa[ge . . .] Syr, Joysse recomavndytys
hym vnto yowre mas[terschypp and prays yow] to bye hym
a dublett clothe at the martt. [Syr oder tydyngys] hawe we non,
but almyghty Jhesu hath yow y[n hys kepyng. Wrytten at] Calys
35 the ij day off Maye.

[*Signature torn off.*]

*Dorse*: To my worshyppffull master George Cely merchaunte off
⟨the⟩ Stappell off Calys, he beyng at the martte, soo hit dd. (*Shield.*)


**161.** *Harry Bryan at Calais to George Cely at Bruges,*
*2 May [1482]*

s.c.1 53/68

Ryght trusty and welbelouyd ffrend, I recommaund me vnto you,
acertynyng you sens your departyng ther hath ben laboure mad
ayenst you and your brother for the mater ye knowe, but my ffortune was to be by my Lord whan it was question, and I remem-
5 beryd my Lord wiche had fforgotyn the sayd mater. And so after
my rememberaunce my Lord mad suche a aunswer as shal be to

---

160. 17 the Felyschypp off the Stappell *over canc.* euery man          her *over*
*canc.* hys          18 subsede] any *canc.*          24 hawe] euery man *canc.*
27 They] a *canc.*

your plesure, in so muche as my Lord hath promysid his singuler
good lordshipe vnto you and youre brother, all men recervid, and
in any thing els he can do for you or youre brother he wul be youre
good lorde // And to my power I shal be your ffrend duryng my    10
lyff // Felow George, I require you bespeke me xij dosin payre of
⌜Loven⌝ glovis: ij dosin of the marke of ij, iij dosin of the mark
of iiij, ij dosin of the mark of iij, and iiij dosin of the mark of ij /
I must wythin this viij dayes send you wurd to pray you to ley
owth mony for vj hor⟨s⟩harnese for my Lord of Bokyngham, and    15
I shall pay you for it at Calis. I p⟨r⟩ay you send me wurde how ye
wul do for me in thes maters by the next that comyth, to the wiche
tyme I shall think long to, as knowith Jhesu, who have you in his
keping. From Calis the ij day of May wyth the hand of your tru
loving ffrend    20

yourys Bryan.

*Dorse*: Item my xij dosin payre of glovis. Item iij stykkys of tavny
sateyn or els vyelett sateyn of Brugys.

To my ryght hertly belouyd ffrend George Sely, marchaunt, being
at Brugys be thys letter deliueryd.    25


**162.** *William Cely at Calais to George Cely at the mart,*
*5 May 1482*
s.c.1 53/116

Jhesu Mⁱiiijᶜiiijˣˣij

Ryght worshyppffull syr, afftyr dew recommendaschon I louly
recommend me vnto yowre masterschypp, etc. Plese hit yowre
masterschypp to vnderstond that master Lefftenaunte hath had
commynnecaschon wyth my Lordd Chamberleyn and wyth the
Kyngys Consell ffor the payment off thys hallff ʒerys wagys, and    5
they demavndyd all starlyng money to be payd at Calys, but master
Lefftenaunte and the Fellyschypp at Calys hath greyd wyth my
Lorde and the Kyngys Consell and be ffully concludyd apon the
same: that they schall paye ffor thys hallff ʒerys wagys, ⌜the ton⌝
hallff sterlyng money yn Ynglond to be payd the last day off Jule,    10
and the toder hallff to be payd at Calys be mydsomer yn Flemysche

**161.** 19 Calis the] ffurst *canc.*

money att xxvj s. v[iij d.] the pownde, and soo ffor to send byll*ys*
ower ynto Ynglonde off the ton hallff; but he that hath sterlyng
money here and wyll paye hit here, hit schall be deductyd off hys
15 byll yn Ynglond, etc. Syr, my mast*er* Lefftena*u*nte says he ffynd
my Lordd hys godd and graci*us* lordd ffor the Stapp*e*ll, etc. It*em*,
syr, mast*er* Debyte reported yow to mast*er* Lefftena*u*nte affore
my Lorde Chamberleyn—that ther was a dewte off st*er*lyng money
betwyxte pore Henley and yow, and he says ʒe wold receyue no
20 money off hym benethe xxviij s. the pownde st*er*., etc. It*em*, syr,
as ffor yowre gode detters here, I can receyue no money off hem
ʒett. They ascuse hem that I most tarry tyll they be p*a*yd off her
wagʒ*ys*, etc. It*em*, syr, John Dalton hath ben at a ffeyr yn Flaunders,
and he hath bowght hym a ffeyr yonge horsse, and he standyss yn
25 yowre stabull, etc. It*em*, syr, all yowre horsse be yn goode state,
thanckyd be God, who hath yow yn his kepyng. Wrytten at Calys
the v day off Maye.

per yowre s*er*ua*u*nte,
Wyll*i*am Cely.

30 *Dorse*: To my worshyppffull mast*er* George Cely, m*er*chau*n*te off
the Stapp*e*ll off Caleys, he beyng at the martt, soo hit dd. (*Shield*.)

### 163. *William Cely at Calais to George Cely at the mart, 7 May 1482*
s.c.i 53/117

J*h*e*s*u M¹iiijᶜiiij××ij

Ryght worshyppffull syr, afftyr dew recom*m*end[aschon I louly
recommend me vnto yowre] mast*er*schypp, etc. Furthermore plese
hit yowre [mast*er*schypp to vnderstond that] I hawe receyued
a letter ffrom yow whych [I hawe rede and do] well vnderstond,
5 and as towchyng ʒowre [. . .] schall yndewer me to hym acordyng
to yowre letter [. . .]. It*em*, syr, I vnderstonde that yowre mast*er*-
schypp wold [th]at John Dalton schuld bye the horsse that he
wrote to yow off. Syr, he hath bowght won as on Synt Telen Day,
besyde Odenborow at a ffaʒer, and he standys yn yowre stabull.
10 Hys color ys maner off a gray coler, and he ys but yong, ffor he

162. 12 money] att *ch. from* (?) and        18 was a] dews *canc.*
163. 5 towchyng] the *canc.*        8 as on] holy *canc.*

was neuer broken yett, and he ys almoste as moche as yowre grett
Bayardd, etc. Item, syr, hit ys grauntyd to the Kyng be the
Fellyschypp at London vj thowsand marke ffor hys syrplysage;
and apon that the Lefftenaunte and the Fellyschypp here hath
agreyd, as be an semble the vj day off Maye, that all the woll and  15
ffellys that schall be schyppyd at London at thys nexte schyppyng
schall be kockyttyd yn affore the vj day off Aprell last past, and
⌐hit⌐ schall paye the costom yn Ynglonde at syche days as they
can gett off the Kynge and to ryn to the payment off the sayd
syrplysage; and that that ys schyppyd more than the syrplysage  20
schall be cokettyd yn afftyr the vj day of Apryll last past, and pay
nott tyll hit com to Calys, and all the woll and ffellys that ys
schyppyd at all oder porttys schall paye nothyng tyll hit comme
to Calys noder, and all that schall ryn to the payment off the nexte
hallffe yerys wagys, etc. Item syr, hit was agreyd that thys hallffe  25
yerys wagys schold a be payd hallff yn Ynglonde sterlyng money
be the last day off Jule, and the ⌐toder⌐ hallff at Calys be Mydsomer
yn Fl. money at xxvj s. viij d. le pownde. Syr, now I vnderstonde
we most pay all here be Whyttsontyde at xxvj s. viij d. the pownde,
ffor the sowdeers hath lewer to be payd here at xxvj s. viij d. than  30
hawe yn Ynglonde sterlyng ⌐money⌐, ffor they mystruste her payment there, etc. Syr, oder tydyngys hawe we none here, but Jhesu
kepe ⌐you⌐. Wrytten at Calys the vij day off Maye.

per yowre seruaunte,<br>
Wylliam Cely.                    35

*Dorse*: To my worshyppffull master George Cely, merchaunte off
the Stappell off Caleys, he beyng at the martt, soo hit dd. (*Shield*.)

*In G. Cely's hand*:
Item dyner an *peny* ⎫
at Andewharp        ⎭
At And ----------- x s. vij d. qtr.                    40
At Gent soper [?] -- v s. iij d.
And abatyd be yow ⎫
at dener ---------⎭ iiij s. x d. Fl.
Layd owght per me G. C.

163. 33 Wrytten] you *interl. and canc.*

**164.** *William Cely at Calais to George Cely at the mart,*
*10 May 1482*

s.c.1 53/118

Jhesu M¹iiij°iiij×ⁱⁱⁱⁱj

Ryght worshyppffull syr, afftyr dew recommendaschon I louly
recommend me vnto yowre masterschypp, etc. Syr, plese hit yowre
masterschypp to vnderstond that John Dalton and I hawe spoken
many tymes vnto master Lefftenaunte ffor payment of yowre
5 warrantys off xv s. off the pownd, and he hath dreven vs off ⌐many
tymes⌐ and dessyryd vs to fforbere but vj or vij days and we schulde
hawe payment, but as on the x day off thys month we spake to hym
agayn and dessyred ⌐hym⌐ that we myght hawe payment off them,
or ellys that they myght be sett apon yowre byllys off costom and
10 subsede, and he dessyryd vs to tarry tyll ye comme and than they
schall be sett apon yowre byllys off costom and subsede, etc. Syr,
as ffor yowre horsse that Twyssullton hath, I wolde a hadd hym
home to yowre stabull, but Joysse says hit ⌐ys⌐ nott best soo ⌐to do⌐
tyll ye comme, ffor he says John Dalton wyll myssedeme than and
15 take hit att a grett onkyndnesse, etc. Syr, I pray yow send me
wordde how I schall be demenyd wyth hym, etc. Syr, Joysse prays
yow to send hym worde when he schall send yow yowre horsse to
come home on, etc. Syr, no more vnto yowr masterschypp at thys
tyme, but almyghty Jhesu hath yow yn hys kepyng. Wrytten at
20 Caleys the x day off Maye.

per yowre seruaunte,
Wylliam Cely.

*Dorse*: To my worshyppffull master George Cely, merchauntt of
the Stappell off Caleys, he being att the martt, soo hit dd. (*Shield*.)

**165.** *Richard Cely the younger at London to George Cely*
*at Calais or the mart, 13 May 1482*

s.c.1 53/119

Anno Jhesu M¹iiij°iiij×ⁱⁱⁱⁱj

Riught interly whelbelouyd brothe⟨r⟩, I recomende me harttely
wnto yow, informing yow at the makyng of thys howr mother,
brother, my godfather and the howsowlde ar in goode heyll,
thankyd be the good Loorde. Syr, the same day that I departtyd

into Cotesowlde I ressauyd a letter frome yow wryte at Calles the 5
xiiij day of Aprell, wherein I fynd the inuiatory of syche godys
that whos howr fathers and mony on that syd of the see. Syr, I
spake not wyth the Byschopys ofesars syn that I resauyd yowr
letter. When I spake laste wyth them thay sayd that awl thyng
schullde abyd yowr cwmyng. I wndyrstonde be yowr letter that 10
3e wyll make howyr abowe vᶜ li. I hawhe beyn in Cottyssowllde
thys iij whekys, and packyd wyth Wylliam Mydwyntter xxij
sarpellys and a poke, wherof be iiij mydyll. Wylliam Bretten says
hyt ys the fayreste wholl that he saw thys 3eyr, and I packyd iiij
sarpellys at Camden of the same bargen, wherof ar ij good, ij 15
mydyll. Ther wyl be in all, wyth blottys, apon xxvij or xxviij
sarplers wholl. Syr, I cannot hawhe Wylliam Mydwynttyrs fellys
wndyr iij li. xl d. the C. And I schaull go to that pryse I pray yow
send me a letter schorttely. Syr, I hawhe bohyt in Cottysowlde
apon the poynt of vij Mˡ resenabyll good felles, and I pay iij li.; 20
I can gehet noyn wndyr. Syr, I whryte to yow a prosses: I pray
God sende therof a good heynd. The same day that I come to
Norlache, on a Sonday befor mattens frome Burforde, Wylliam
Mydwyntter wyllcwmyd me, and in howr comynycacyon he askyd
me hefe I wher in any whay of maryayge. I towlde hyme nay, and 25
he informeyd me that ther whos a ⌈3eunge⌉ genttyllwhoman hos
father ys name ys Lemryke, and her mother ys deyd, and sche
schawll dyspend be her moter xl li. a 3e⟨r⟩, as thay say in that
contre, and her father ys the gretteste rewlar a⟨n⟩d rycheste mane
in that conttre, and ther hawhe bene grete genttyllmen to se ⟨h⟩yr 30
and wholde hawhe hyr, etc. And hewyr matens wher done,
Wylliam Mydwynter had meuyd thys mater to the gretteste mane
abot the gentyllman Lemryke, and he 3eyd ⌈and⌉ informyd the
forsayd of aull the matter, and the 3ewng gentyllwomane bothe;
and the Sattyrday aftyr, Wylliam Mydwyntter whent to London, 35
as aull wholl getherars wher sent for be wryt be the mene of Pettyt,
for inwynde and grete markyng, and thay hawhe day to cwm agen
at Myhellmas. [New page, headed Anno Jhesu Mˡiiijᶜiiijˣˣij] When
I had packyd at Camden and Wylliam Mydwyntter departtyd,
I came to Norlache ageyn to make a nende of packyng, and on the 40
Sonday nexte aftyr, the same mane that Wylliam Mydwy⟨n⟩ter
brake fyrste to cam ⟨to⟩ me and telde me that he had brokyn to hys

165. 12 Mydwyntter] and canc.    16 apon] xij or canc.    18 schaull]
hawhe ⌈them⌉ I p canc.    27 ms. and and sche    40 and repeated

master acordyng as Mydwyntter desyryde hym, and he sayd hys
master whos ryght whell plessyde ther whothe. And the same mane
45 sayd to me hefe I whowllde tary May Day I schulde hawhe a syte
of the ȝewnge gentyllwhoman, and I sayd I wholld tary wyth a
good wyll, and the same day her father schul⟨d⟩ a syttyn at Norlache for the Kyng, byt ⌜he⌝ sente whon of hys clarkys and rod
hymselfe to Wynchecwme. And to mattens the same day come the
50 ȝewnge gentyllwhoman and her mother-i-law, and I and Wylliam
Bretten wher sayng mattens when thay com into chyrche, and
when mattens vhos done thay whente to a kynnyswhoman off the
ȝewnge genttyllwhomane; and I sent to them a pottell of whyte
romnay, and thay toke hyt thankefully, for thay had cwm a myle
55 a fote that mornyng; and when Mes whos done I come and whellcwmyd them, and kyssyd them, and thay thankyd me for the
whyne, and prayd me to cwm to dyner wyth them, and I ascwysyd
me and thay made ⌜me⌝ promys them to drynke wyth them after
dyner. And I sent them to dyner a galon whyne and thay sent me
60 a heronsew roste, and aftyr dyner I com and dranke wyth them and
toke Wylliam Bretten wyth me, and whe had ryught gode comynecacyon, and the person plesetheyde me whell as be the fyrst
comynycacyon: sche ys ȝewnge, lytyll, and whery whellfauyrd and
whytty, and the contre spekys myche good bye hyr. Syr, aull thys
65 matter abydythe the cowmyng of her father to London, that whe
may wndyrstonde what some he wyll departte wyth, and how he
lykys me. He wyll be heyr wythin iij whekys. I pray send me a letter
how ȝe thynke be thys matter. (New page headed Anno Jhesu etc.,
as above] Heyr has beyn whyt my mother Myhell Koke and hys
70 whyfe from Ȝeorke, and my mother and I hawhe made them gret
scheyr, and my mother has gewyn to Myhelles wyfe a cremsyn
gov[ne] of hyr wheryng, and sche has prayd me to whrayt to yow
to by for her a for of calla[b]yr for to lay in the same gowne,
and Kokys whyfe and scho prays yow to by for them x as fyne
75 mynkys as ȝe cane fynde in the marte, and ȝe schawl be plesyd
for them. I schawll ⌜send⌝ to Calles be Robard Heryke at thys
Whyttesontyd the byll of xiij s. iiij d.: hyt am[o]wntys to xv li.
vj s. viij d. and payde. I ondyrstonde be Wylliam Celys letter that
ȝe hawhe whryttyng frome my Lorde of Sent Jonys. I pray yow
80 send me partte of yowr tydyng: I sent to yow the laste that I had.
Syr, thay hawhe begwn to schype at London, and aull howr wholl

**165.** 43 sayd] and *canc.*    74 *ms.* ho Kokys

and fell ys hyt in Cottyssowllde, sawhe iiij sarpllerys; therfor whe
can do nothyng at thys tyme. Syr, I thynke mony wyll be gode at
thys marte, for the Kyng has sente to the mercars and lette them
whet that he wy[l] hawhe iij whystyllys; whon at Bregys, another  85
at Calles, the thyrd at London; and as I am informyd, what
merchand of the Stapell that sellys hys wh[oll], he may by what
whar that he wyll ageyn. And thay that by no whar schaull brynge
in ther mony into the Kyngys wystyll at Bregys ar Calles, and be
payd at London at a monythe day, and the mony schawl be  90
stablyschyd at viij s. The mercars be not conttent therwyth. I pray
yow rememyr howr bowys. No mor. Wrhryt at London the xiij
day of May.

per Rychard Cely.

*Dorse*: A my riught whelbelouyd brother George Cely, merchand  95
of the Stapell at Calles, or at the marte, be thys dd.

### 166. *William Adam at Langham to George Cely at Calais, 14 May [1482]*

s.c.1 53/120

Right worshipffull sir, I recommawnd me vnto you. Forthermore
sir, lyke it you to wytt þat at my last beynge at Calles John Dalton
and I hadd certeyn comunicacon for your horse, and if I might
a spoken wyth you I wold a boght hym of you, so þat ȝe wold a ben
resvnabyll, for he shuld be for a ⌈grett⌉ gentylman of whom you  5
might deserue grett thanke, if it be so þat you thynke þe horse
wold serue hym. Praynge you to owe me þerin your goode wyll,
and send me worde by the brynger heroff your disposicon of
answere by writyng, and you shall haue my seruice at all tymes,
that knowyth God, who euer preserue you. Written at Langham  10
the xiiij day of May.

yours,<br>Wylliam Adam.

*Dorse*: To the worshipffull George Cely, merchaunt of þe Stapell
at Calles soit dd.                                                    15

### 167. *William Cely at Calais to George Cely, 20 May 1482*
S.C.I 53/121

Jhesu M<sup>l</sup>iiij<sup>c</sup>iiij<sup>xx</sup>ij

Ryght worschyppffull syr, afftyr dew recommendaschon I louly recommend me vnto yowre masterschypp, etc. Furthermore plese hit yowre masterschypp to vnderstond that here at Caleys be many Hollonders, but they be all off Laythe sawe on man, and he ys off
5 Dellffe, but he hath nomoo ffellowys but hymsellffe, and ⌈he⌉ sawe yowre ffell*ys* but he lokyd but lyghtly on hem. We saye they wyste where to abyde or they cam at Caleys, ffor they sawe nott, all the ffellyschyppys off hem, but iij or iiij mens ffell*ys* or they were spedd, etc. John Dalton hath solde to John Marttyson and hys
10 ffellowys x M<sup>l</sup> ffell*ys*, etc. Syr, I am hallff afferdd to make any sale tyll yowre masterschypp commyth, ffor men talke yn Caleys marvell*ys*ly, as Joysse can enfforme yowre masterschypp well inowe, etc. Item syr, as ffor yowre warr*au*nt*ys*, Master Lefftenaunt sayth ȝe schall be plesyd at yowre commyng to Caleys, and as ffor yowre
15 partyschon off x s. off the pownde, Wyll*ia*m Bentham hath hadd yowre boxe w*yth* debenters a grett whyle, and I hawe spoken to hym many tymes to hawe owt yowre partyschon, and he puttys me off allweys, but he sayth I schall be ffyrst that schall be seruyd, etc. Item syr, I vnderstonde that they schypp at London and hath
20 don thys viij days and more, as Rechard Chester sayth and dyuersse that com ffrom London, but I hawe receyued noo letters ffrom London off noo syche thyng ȝett, etc. Syr, oder tydyng*ys* hawe we non here, but that Joysse can enfforme yowre masterschypp be mouth well inowth, etc. No more vnto yowre masterschypp at thys
25 tyme, but almyghty Jhesu saue yow and kepe yow. Wrytten at Caleys the xx day off Maye.

　　　　　　　　　　　per yowre seruaunt,
　　　　　　　　　　　Wyll*ia*m Cely.

*Dorse*: To my worshyppffull master George Cely, merchaunte off
30 the Stappell off Caleys, soo hit dd. (*Shield*.)

---

**167.** 4 Hollonders] the *canc.*　　11 men] talke *canc.*　　16 yowre] yowre
*canc.*　　23 that] Joh *canc.*

**168.** *Richard Cely the younger at London to George Cely at Calais or Bruges, 22 May 1482*

S.C.1 53/122

Anno Jhesu M$^l$iiij$^c$iiij$^{xx}$ij

Riught interly belouyd brother, I recomend me wnto yow w*yth* aull myne harte, informeyng yow that I hawhe ressauyd an le*tter* frome yow whryttyn at Barow, the wheche I do whell wndyr-ston⟨d⟩. And as for wholl and fell, loke aftyr noyn of howrs at thys schypyng, for whe hawhe not cwm to London byt vj sarp*ellerys*  5 frome Kyng*ys* Sotton and not a fell. I hawhe bohut at Chepyng Nortton vj M$^l$ fell*es*—iij li. le C. I hawhe caste them and I fynd them resnabyll good. I cannot deyll w*yth* Wyll*ia*m Mydwynt*ter* wnd[er] iij li. iij s. iiij d.: he has apon iiij M$^l$. I pray yow send me whorde how I schawll be demenyd. Howr mother longys sor for  10 yow: Wyll*ia*m Cely wrat that whe be lyke to hawhe whar w*yth* Frawns, and that makys hyr ferde. Syr, Harry Bryan, the bryngar of thys, laburs me soor to goo and se Rawson[s] dowttyr. I am beheldyng to hym for hys labur, for I know whell that he whowlde I dyd whell, and I pray you delyu*er* hym some mony ⌐at⌐ thys tyme  15 and do whel by hym, for hyt ys seuyr inow. I hawhe many thyng[ys] in my mynde byt I hawhe no laysar to whr⟨y⟩tte. Зe may wndyrstonde partte be my le*tter* that I sente yow befor thys / Syr, I wndyrstond as I ryd in the cwnttray many thyng*ys*: whone ys that howr brother Wyll*ia*m Dawltton schaull be maryd to whon  20 of the nexte kynyswhomen that Kyrstowyr Brown has. Syr, I hawhe sowlde Py. I konnot get for hym byt v marke on my faythe, and зehyt he that has hym thynkeys hymselfe full begyllyd. I pray yow harttely sped yow into Ynglonde, for many thyng*ys* abyd*ys* yow cwmyng. I hawhe whorkmene a settyng in Berwyke parke  25 abouhe xij M$^l$ stakys. No mor. Whryttyn at London the xxij day of May.

per R*ychard* Cely.

*Dorse*: A my riught whellbelouyd brother George Cely, mer-ch⟨a⟩nd of the Stap*ell* beyng at Call*es* or at Brogys, so dd.          30

**168.** 1 belouyd: *ms.* belouydwyd          22 kon] get *canc.*

**169.** *Richard Cely the younger at London to George Cely at Calais or Bruges, 25 May 1482*

s.c.1 53/123. *Stained and damaged by damp*

Anno Jhesu M¹iiij°iiij××ij

Riught interly whelbelouyd brother, I recomende me harttely wnto yow, informyng yow at the makyng of thys howr mother ys in good heyll, and aull the howso[olde], thankyde be the good Loorde; and howr mother sendys yow har blyssyng, and 3e mwste
5 pwrwhay for hyr a potte of greyn gynger. 3e are ofttyn in har mynde: sche says to har madys at 3ewr comyng home many thyng*ys* schawl be mend amonge them. Whe loke for Geos and yowr geyr be thys whollschypys, and for yow [a]for mydsom*ar*. Howr mother says at yowr cwmyng sche wyll go to Auwheley.
10 Syr, hyt ys so that a chawns ys fawllyn that lyes ap[on] myne oneste, byt I cannat kepe no cwnsell frome yow, for be polesy 3e and I may fynd the meyn to sawhe awl thyng cler[e] at yowr comyng. Hyt ys so that Em ys w*yth* schyllde, and as Godde knoweys byt that whons that hyt wh[as] gettyn I desarwyd for
15 [m]yn. Hyt whos gettyn on Schrofe 3euyn, and sche has beyn seke heuyr syn 3e departtyde of the axsys. Syr, 3e whryte to me that 3e hawhe a good tassell*ys*, and I ame in a whay to hawhe Whatkyn Fawkene⟨r⟩ to my sarwhant. A neste of gosehawk*ys* that whe myte gewhe an hawke or ij schuld caus ws to lyue in grehyt reste in
20 Essex, for the genttyllmane ys byt strayngely dysposyd, as I schawll whryte yow mor play*n*ly in my nextte lett*er*. Whone of the Kyng*ys* dowttyrs, my Lady Mary, ys desessyd. Whord is heyr that Tyrwhenyng ys byrnyd be Frenschmen, and Gawnt and Bregys ys pattyschyd to the Frensche Kyng, and that cause howr mother
25 to be the ferdar for yow. I wh⟨r⟩ate to yow a lett*er* be Harry Bryan; and 3e wyll that whe schaull by any wholl the next 3eyr, make parte of yowr mony to be payd befor Barttyllmew Tyde. No mor to yow, my gostely brother, byt I pray Jh*e*su that aull thyng*ys* may be whell conwhayd. Whryttyn at London on Whytson Heuyn.
30 <center>*per* y⟨o⟩wre brother,</center>
Rychard Cely, and ⌐your⌐ lowar.

*Dorse*: A my riught whellbelouyd brother George Cely, m*er*chand of the Stapell beyng at Call*es* or Bregys, thys be delyuyrdd.

**170.** *William Cely at Calais to George Cely at Bruges,*
*26 May 1482*

s.c.1 53/125

Jhesu M$^l$iiij$^c$iiij$^{xx}$ij

Ryght worshyppffull syr, afftyr dew reco*mm*endaschon I louly
reco*mm*end me vnto yowre mast*er*schypp, etc. Plese hytt yowr
mast*er*schypp to vnderstond that I hawe receyued an lett*er* ffro*m*
yow be Joysse, be the whych I vnderstond ye be well mendyd off
yowre grett sycknesse, wheroff I am ryghyt gladd, and I thanke 5
God off yowre goode rekewer, etc. Item, syr, I hawe ⌜receued⌝ off
the sayd Joysse yowre kascett w*yth* all thyng*ys* acordyng to yowre
wryttyng. Item, syr, yowre mast*er*shypp wryttyth me that I shall
receyue off John Lemyngton xxx li. Fl., the whych yowre mast*er*-
schypp schuld a receyued off Raff at the martte. Syr, I hawe nott 10
spoken w*yth* hym ʒett theroff, but I shall today and Godd wull.
Item, syr, the rest off ⌜all⌝ yowre byll*ys* off costom and subsede
dew be y⌜ow⌝ to the Plase amovntyth an Cx li. v s. viij d. st*er*.,
wheroff the ton hallffe most be payd here schorttly. For on Thursday, the last courtte day, hytt was agreyd here be the Fellyschypp 15
—ffor dyuersse consederraschons, as ffor dewtes owyng be the
Plase yn Ynglond—whereas men shulde a payd ther hole costom
and subsede here at Caleys at xxvj s. viij d. le li., we shall paye
now—as was agreyd allso affore be assemble—but the ton hallffe
here at Calles at xxvj s. viij d. le li., and the sayd money to be payd 20
w*yth*yn xiiij days than alemetyd, payn off fforffett to paye the
hole yn Ynglon*d* st*er*lyng money, and the toder hallff off the sayd
byll*ys* to be p*ay*d yn Ynglond st*er*lyng ⌜money⌝ at the last day off
Jule, and he that hath st*er*[lyng] money here and wyll paye hytt
ynto the Plase, hytt schall [be deductyd] off hys byll*ys* that shall 25
go ynto Ynglond. Item, syr, the same day I spake to mast*er*
Leffetenau*n*t ffor paym*en*t off yowre warranty*s*, or elly*s* that they
myght be sett vppon yowre byll*ys* off costom and sobsede ⌜as he
promysyd me beffore⌝; and he sayd they may nott, but I most pay
redy money and receyue redy money, and he sayth now I maye 30
nott be p*ay*d but off the ton hallff at thys tyme off yowre warranty*s*,
ffor he sayth ther ys but ij$^c$ li. yn the treserry, and eu*er*y man that
be behynde w*yth* her warranty*s* most be p*ay*d part lyke eu*er*y man

---

**170.** 5 wheroff *ch. from* wher ffor     6 receued *over canc.* an letter ffrow*m*
be Joysse     9 yowre] mh *canc.*     25 byllys] yn *canc.*

afftyr hys quantette off hys prynspall sum, etc. Syr, he ys noo
35 stydffast man, nor he owyth yow noo goodd wyll thow3th he make
a ffayer fface, ffor I hawe spoken to hym ffor yowre warrantys xx
tymys, and ⌐he⌐ gyffyth ⌐me⌐ at euery tyme a contrary answer; but
I shall apon hym today ffor them agayne affore Wylliam Dalton.
Item, syr, I am purp⟨o⟩syd to paye yowre byllys off costom and
40 subsede as tomorow, the ton hallff wyth parte off the money that
3e hawe sent, be the vyce off Wylliam Dalton, and wrytt hytt
vppon the byllys, etc. Item, syr, hytt was lemetyd be the courtte
that euery man that hath any wull or ffellys yn Calys shuld bryng
yn an byll, payne off lesyng off the benyffete, be Saturday last
45 past; how myche wull and ffell he hath yn Caleys at that day,
euery contrey apon hyt selffe, and whych ys old and whych ys
newe, and soo to depose on a boke ffor the same, and I hawe born
yn a byll ffor yow acordyng off al thyngys, etc. Item, syr, 3e shall
receyue off Joysse [*Dorse*] ij letters ffrom master Rechard and an
50 letter ffrom Wylliam Adam. Item, syr, I hawe receyued ij letters
ffrom master Rechard wheryn he wrytys he hath bowght vj
thowsand gode ffellys at Chepyng ⌐Nortten⌐ but he can nott hawe
Wylliam Mydwynters vnder iij li. xl d. an C. Item, syr, he wrytys
he hath schyppyd nothynge yn thys fflete that ys comyng, ffor he
55 hath but vj sarplers wull commen to London, etc. Item, syr, we
send yow be Joysse an ambelyng horsse off Thomas Haywardys
ffor ⌐yow⌐ to come to Caleys on. He wyll be glad yff he may ese
yow. Hytt ⌐ys⌐ butt lyccull: *and* yff hytt be nott byg inowe ye may
hawe Wylliam Bondmans horsse. He ys at Bregys at the Starr, and
60 Wylliam Bondman hath sent an letter to hys man be Joysse to
delyuer yow the horsse to comme home on, etc. Item, syr, here ys
Harry Bryan—he wold ffayn speke wyth yow, I thyncke hytt ys to
hawe sum money off yow. He browght the lesser letter ffrom
master Rechard, etc. Syr, oder tydyngys hawe ⌐we⌐ non here, but
65 I beseke almyghty Jhesu kepe yow and bryng yow well to Cales,
ffor here be many off yowre gode ffrendys that be sory ffor yowre
grett sycknesse. Wrytten at Caleys the xxvj day off Maye.

> per yowre seruante,
> Wylliam Cely.

70 To my worshyppffull master George Cely marchaunt off the
Stappell off Calles at Bregys be thys dd.

**170.** 34 Syr] hyr *canc.*          43 bryng: *ms.* bryngys          55 but] iiij *canc.*
57 ffor] ys glad to come *canc.*          67 Maye] per youre ser *canc.*

**171.** *William Dalton at Calais to George Cely at Bruges,*
*26 May 1482*

s.c.1 53/124

Jhesu 1482

Brother Cely, after ffull hartely recommendacon plese hit you to
witte that I sende you be Joyes your servaunte Thomas Heywarde
amblynge horse. Also ye shal reseyue closed in this letter j letter
to William Bondman servaunte to tak his horse if hy[t] lest you
bet. I send you this because Thomas Heywarde tellethe me that 5
W. Bondman horse will stomble, *and* this is lityll *and* easye / Item
⌐brother⌐, I vnderstonde that my Lorde will vpon Wenesday next
comyng to Gynese, wherfor ye may com a day later from Brgys if
ye thynke it for your yeasse. Item, my Lorde haythe good tythyngys
come of Englonde, copye of letter sent f[rom my] Lorde off 10
Gloceter *and* my Lorde of Northomberlonde [that] late ⌐[were]⌐
sent to [the] Kynge⌐. The messenger that brought them I herde
hym sey he departede from the Kynge at þe Tower of London
vpon Frydey last past. No more to you at this tyme, but I pray
Jhesu sende you gode helthe, whe preserve you. Wreten at Callys 15
the vpon Whesensondey.

Your in that I can,<br>William Dalton.

*Dorse*: To my right good Brother George Cely at Brugys, merchant
of the Staple at Callys. Brugys.                                          20


**172.** *Thomas Colton to George Cely [? before 31 May 1482]*
s.c.1 53/186

Brother Jorge, I pray you, as my speceall trust ys in yow, that ye
wyll remembre me for to pay to Wylliam Norton of London,
draper, for me xl or l li., what ye may spare me, but for xij or xiiij
dayes, for I ow hym iiij*ˣˣ* li., of the whyche he hathe a byll of my
hand; for I loke yeuery day for tydyngys owte of Holand for my 5
schyp *and* my presoners. *And* brother thes payment lyethe my
pore onestie apon, wherfor I beseche yow to remembre me, as
my speceall trust ys in yow aboue all other. *And* by thes my

**171.** 6 Item] sire *canc.*          10 come *ch. from* from          13 Tower: *ms.* tow3
15 helthe: t *over* f          16 the] x *canc.*          vpon] Whesensondon d *canc.*

handwryteng I promes yow to answer yow at yowre pleseur
10 what ye delyuer the seyd Wylliam.

>From yowres to my power,
Thomas Colton.

*Dorse*: A remembrans of Thomas Colton.

*In G. Cely's hand*:
Jacob Wylliamsone and hys ffelow de Delffe -- xiiij li. xix s.
15                                                    viij d. [Fl.]
John Wyllmson and hys ffellowy of Laythe ---- vij li. xij s. Fl.
Mavryn Claysson of Laythe --------- xxvj li. xvj s. iij d. Fl.
Idem ---------------------------- xxij li. x s. viij d. [Fl.]
Of Jacob Wylliamson, iiij d. ob. ------ vij li. iiij s. Fl.
20 Yn ij d. ob. ---------------------- iij li. Fl.
iiij d. ob. ------------------------ iiij li. xvj s. Fl.


**173.** *Note by George Cely for 'Hugh', [? 1482]*
s.c.1 53/65

De George Cely.

Hew, Y pray yow remembyr to speke to John Wylliamson and
hys ffellowes ffor my oblygacyon of vij li. xij s. Fl. Y pray yow
resseywe ytt of them, and ȝe con, etc.

*In another hand*:
x In di. lymvn grotys wyth x grottys     ij li. v s.
5 x In pensse --------------------     xlj s. v d.
x In blankys --------------------     x s. iij gretys.
x In ij d. the pesse --------------     x s. vj d.
x In iiij d. a pesse --------------     xvij s. vj d.
x In brasse pensse --------------     iiij s. ij d.
10 x Item iij Felyppys at iij s. iiij d. ---     x s.
x A lew at vij s. iiij d. -----------     vij s. iiij d.
x In lymon grotys *and* pensse ------     v s. x d.
                                         vij li. xij s. gr.
*No address.*

172. 9 handwryteng] to p *canc.*     20 Item *canc.* [yn

**174.** *Richard Cely the younger at London to George Cely at Calais, 1 June 1482*

s.c.1 53/126

Anno Jhesu M¹iiijᶜiiijˣˣij

Riught interly belouid brother, I recomende me wnto you as louyngly as hart cane thynke, heuyrmor thankyng the good Lorde of yowr amendmente. I wndyrstonde ⌜by⌝ Wylliam Celys letter that ȝe hawhe beyn riught sor syke, and a whryttys to me that ⌜a⌝ has sent to yow an awmbeler to brynge yow to Calles, and that 5 ȝe pwrpos to cwme schorttely into Ynglond. I pray yow sende me an letter and I whyll sende my hoby to Douyr to mehyt yow, and many mattars abydys ywr comyng. Syr, I hawhe hyrryd Wh⟨a⟩tkyn Faukenar for thys ȝeyr, and I hawhe tylars at Awhelay wyth many hother wharkemene. I neuyr longyd so sor for yowr cwmpany. 10 I pray Jhesu brynge yow whell hythyr and send yow heyll. Whryt-tyn at London the fyrste day of Juyn.

per yowr brother,
Rychard Cely.

*Dorse*: A my riught whellbelouyd brother George Cely merchand 15 of the Stapell at Calles, dd.

**175.** *Richard Cely the younger at London to George Cely at Calais, 24 June 1482*

s.c.1 53/127

Anno Jhesu M¹iiijᶜiiijˣˣ ij

Riught whelbelouyd brother, I recomend me harttely wnto yow, informyng yow that I hawhe resauyd an letter frome yow be Robard Heryke wherby I wndyrstond that ȝe wyll send owyr an ȝewng horsse. Whe schaull kepe hym wyth grasse a⟨s⟩ whell as whe can tyll ȝe cwm, acordyng to yowr whryttyng. Syr, hyt whos 5 tellyd Robard Heryke at Calles that howr mother schowlde be maryd or in the whay of maryayge, into so myche that thay sayd howr mother schulld go on preschesyon on Corpys Kyrste Day in a cremysyn gown and hyr mayny in blake, and a my sowyll howr mother whe[nt] at that day byt as sche whent at owr fathers 10 monthys mynd, and therfor I whowlde hyt wher tryd howt the

bryngar of that to Calleys. Syr, whe ar grehytly envyd: I trwste ⌈to⌉
Jhesu whe schaull be abbull to wythstonde howr enmys. Syr John
ys in grehyt trobull, and God knowys full whrongefowlly, and
15 parte of them that whe gawhe gownys to labors moste agayne hym:
I had leuer then a good med that ȝe whor heyr. No mor to yow.
Whryt at London the xxiiij day of Juyn. I pray Jhesu send yow
safe hythyr and sone: Robard Eryke whos schasyd wyth Scottys
betwheyn Calles a⟨n⟩d Douer—th⟨e⟩y schapyd narow.
20                                                    per Rychard Cely.

Dorse: A my riught whellbelouyd brother George Cely merchand
of the Stapell at Callys soit dd.


**176.** *William Cely at Calais to George Cely at Bruges,
4 July 1482*
s.c.1 53/129

Jhesu Mˡiiijᶜiiijˣˣij

Ryght worshyppffull syr, afftyr dew recommendaschon I louly
recommend me vnto yowre masterschypp. Forthermore plese hit
yowre masterschypp to vnderstond that I hawe receyued an letter
ffrom yowre masterschypp, the whych I haue redd and well
5 vnderstonde. And as ffor tydyngys here, we haue non but goode
yett; but that we loke afftyr the Kyng at Dower schorttly, and my
Lordd Chamberleyn lokyth allwey when he schall be sent ffor,
etc. Furdermore syr, plese hytt yow to vnderstond that I hawe
sold all yowre ffellys that leye yn the howse nexte Bondmans to
10 master John Johnson and hys ffellowys off Dellffe ff[or] xiiij
nobullys the C, and hallffe redy mony yn honde, the rest at Colde
martt and Passe nexte ensewyng. They be nott yett delyuerd. Syr,
they desyre to borow x or xij li. theroff tyll Balmus martt, but
I wolde nott graunte hem; but I sayd thys vnto them: I lokyd
15 afftyr yow wythyn ij or iij days, and yff yow wold do so myche
ffor them as to graunte hem, that I was content, or ellys I wold
hawe the hole ton hallffe at Callys, x s., etc. Syr, I hawe receyued
yowre gere off John Wyxstons man, all sawe an towell whych John
Dalton tellyth me that ⌈master⌉ John Wyxston hadd nott, butt he
20 hath hit hymsellffe and wyll ddelyuer hit, etc. Syr, as ffor yowre

175. 12 whe ch. *from* wher
176. 3 that] that *canc.*     6 Kyng] the *canc.*     19 John] M *canc.*

lyvelode, ys nott yett cleryd, but the warddysmen hath sen yowre
lyvelodd and enteryd hit ⌐yn⌐ her bok*ys*, and ⌐w*yth*yn⌐ thys ij
days yowre evydensse most be schewyd affore the comyschoners.
I hawe them styll by me, ffor John P*a*rker prayd me soo ffor to do;
ffor he sayd hit was so best and most redyest, ffor when they   25
co*m*me to that warde they schall be send ffor, etc. No more vnto
yowre mast*er*schyp at thys tyme, but Jh*e*su kepe yow. Wrytten
at Calles the iiij day off Jull*e*.

p*er* youre s*er*uau*n*te,
Wyll*ia*m Cely.        30

*Dorse*: To my worshyppffull mast*er* George [Ce]ly m*er*chau*n*te off
the Stap*e*ll off [Ca]lles, beyng att Breg*ys* so hit [dd.].

### 177. *William Cely at Calais to Richard or George Cely at London, 31 July 1482*

S.C.I 53/130

Jh*e*su M⌐iiij*c*iiij*xx*ij

Ryght worshyppfull syrs, affter dew reco*m*mendaschon I louly
recommend me vnto yowre mast*er*schyppis. Furd*er*more, plese hit
yowre ⌐mast*er*schyppis⌐ to vnderstond off syche tydyng*ys* as we
hawe here at Calys. Hytt ys so that the town off Ary ys geven vp
to the Frenschmen, and anoder castell w*yth*yn a Dowche myle   5
off Sent Thom*er*s be the menys off treson, acordyng as hit specy-
ffyeth yn my toder lett*er*, and the Frenschemen purposyth to be
at Graveny⟨n⟩g, and they be nott lettyd, w*yth*yn thys ij days and
lesse. And ther comys eu*er*y day ffro*m* Sent Thom*er*s to my Lord
a mes⟨e⟩nnger dessyryng off my Lord Chamb*er*leyn help and   10
rescew owte off Ynglond, and my Lordd hath promysyd hem þ*a*t
they schall lacke no men nor vettell, wherffor we loke afftyr here
that ther schall com a ffellyschypp owte off Ynglond schorttly, etc.
It*e*m, syr, we ffere here that ther woll be schrode passage to thys
Ballm*us* martt and yff the Frenschemen hawe Grawenyng, as men   15
ffere they schall hawe hytt, ffor they hawe all the passagys to hit
redy, etc. No more vnto yowre mast*er*schypp at thys tyme, but
Jh*e*su kepe yow and all owre ffrendd*ys*. Wrytten at Call*e*s the last
day off Jowll.

yowr s*er*uau*n*t,        20
Wyll*ia*m Cely.

*Dorse*: To my worshyppffull master Rechard or George Cely, merch*aunt*ys off the ⟨Stappell⟩ off Call*es* at London yn Martt Lane so hit dd. (*Shield*.)

### 178. George Cely to Sir John Weston (*draft*) [*? July 1482*]
s.c.1 60 f. 94

Jh*e*su Mˡiiijᶜiiijˣˣij

Ryght whorshypffull syr and myn essynglar good Lord, aff*ter* all dew recomendacyon p*re*tendyng Y recomeavnd me vnto yowr good Lordshyp yn the most lowlyest whysse that I co*n* // Fordyrmor plesythe ytt yow*er* Lordshyp to vndyrstond that Y hawe ressaywyd
5 an lettyr ffrom yowr Lordshyp beryng datte at Napull*us* the last day of Nove*m*byr derectyd to my broder Rychard and me. ⌐Whe¬ vndyrstond // my Lord by yowr sayd lett*er* of yowr ryall resseywyng at Napull*us* and of yowr grett p*re*sent*ys*, wheche whas to vs glad tydyng*ys* and grett rejoyssyng to her of // etc. //
10    Plesythe ytt yowr Lordshyp to vndyrstond that the Dewke of Abany ys comyn ynto Ynglond and he ys sworne to the Kyng*ys* good grace // and the Kyng hasse sent hym ynto Scottlond w*yth* lx Mˡ men yn iij battelles and many lord*ys* of Ynglond w*yth* hym, Jh*e*su be his ⌐good¬ spede. W*yth*yn an mony⟨th⟩ ther hasse ben //
15 ⌐w*yth*¬ xliiij town*us* and velayg*ys* brent en Scottlond and many lord*ys* takyn and slayne // Donfryss ys brent / Alsso my Lord the Kyng*ys* eldest dowt*er* sawe hone ys dede / now latt // The ⌐yov*ng*¬ Dowchesse of Borgon ys dede and that lond ys in grett ro*m*byr // Of hodyr tydyng*ys* Y con none wryt.
20                  Jh*e*su Mˡiiijᶜiiijˣˣ

### 179. William Cely at Calais to George Cely at London, 3 August 1482
s.c.1 53/131

Jh*e*su Mˡiiijᶜiiijˣˣij

Ryght worshyppffull syr, afftyr dew reco*m*mendaschon I louly reco*m*mend me vnto yowre mast*er*shypp. Furdermore, plese hytt

178. 6 me] wheche whe do whell *canc.*          8 whas to] my broder *canc.*
12 wyth] iiij *canc.*          17 dede] in *canc.*          18 *over* grett *a cross in a circle, and a circle with vertical line through centre, both canc.*

yowr masterschypp to vnderstond that I hawe told all yowre ffellys
that remayned yn Calles at yowre departyng ffrom Callys, and ther
ys off hem ij M¹iijᶜ xij ffellys yn all, wheroff schuld be lx ffellys off 5
my godffaders Wylliam Maryons, as he wrote vnto me; and off
yowrys ther be ij M¹ijᶜ lij ffellys, and so hit comyth even owte
wyth yowre boke here, wherffor I pray ⟨y⟩owre masterschypp to
refforme the som off ⌐the⌐ ffellys yn the endenter, etc. Item, syr,
plese hytt yow to wytt that yowre yong horsse ys sore apayard syns 10
yowre masterschypp departyd ffrom Calles, ffor he wull ete noo
mete yett but grasse and grene tarys, ffor off hardd mette he wyll
non, and he ys but bare yn plyght—I cannott thyncke that he
maye be laboryd schorttly—but Grett Sorell ys yn good plyght,
God sawe hym, but I suppose he wyll nott be sold here, etc. Item, 15
syr, plese hytt yowre masterschypp to vnderstondd that I hawe
⌐nott⌐ receyued yowre poll axe whych schulde come ffrom Brege,
nott yett. I askydd Wylliam Dalton off hit at hys comyng home,
and he tellyd me hit was nott comen to Bregys ⌐all the⌐ whyle he
was theyr, etc. Syr, oder tydyngys hawe we non here, but that the 20
Dewke of Burgeyne lyeth styll at Ypur wyth a grett oste, and as
ffor the Frenschemen, hytt ys sayd here thaye hawe vetellyd and
mannyd the town off Ary and the remmnante be gon backe agayne,
as hytt ys sayd here. No more vnto yowre masterschypp at thys
tyme, but almyghty Jhesu hath yow yn hys blessyd kepyng. 25
Wrytten at Cales the iij day off Auguste.

per yowr seruaunte,
Wylliam Cely.

*Dorse*: To my worshyppffull master George Cely, marchaunte off
the Stappell off Cales at London yn Mart Lane sohit dd. (*Shield*.) 30

## 180. *John Dalton at Calais to George Cely in England,*
*12 August 1482*

s.c.1 53/132

Ryght intierly beluffyd broder, I recomaunde ⟨me⟩ vnto yow after
all dew recomendacyon hayd, and vnto my maystres your moder,
wyth ower broder Rychard. Furthermor syr, at they makyng heroff

179. 4 remayned: d *added later*     at] thys de *canc.*     9 som off] yowre
*canc.*      26 at] London *canc.*

all that nov bene in Leyceter in recomaunde them vnto yow and
5 desyred me so to wreet, *and* that we wold ffayne haue yow heere
agayne, etc. Furthermore syr, plese yt yow I askyd Wylliam Cely
no after your departyng yff yow hayd tolde hym wat yow wold that
he schvlde do wyth your hosse wher ase your stabyll hyse, and he
tolde me yow sayd nothyng to hym theroff. Syr yff yt plesse yow
10 that yow will lett hit owt, I pray yow that I may haue ij of the
romes off the stabull; *and* yff yt plesse yow 3e schall haue at your
comaundement at all tymus the fforsayd romus agayne, and wyth
the grace of Gode 3e schall ffynde haye *and* ottys ffor your horssys
at your comyng. Wheyder I haue the fforsayd hosse or not, 3e
15 schall not ffavte of non thyng that I haue ne may do ffor yow to
my vterst poyer / But syr won ⌈thyng⌉ I pray yow off, that in case
be that yow wyll that I schall haue the fforsayd hose, that I may
know wat I schall pay therffor. For wythowt that I may pay
therffor lyke as yow may leet yt to anoder // ellys // I wyll pray yow
20 to take non displesur, ffor ellys I wyll not haue yt. And yff I haue
yt, lyke as I haue wretton yow, 3e schall at your comyng allwaye
haue yt and do therwyth that schall plese yow, that knowes
God, who preserue yow. At Calles the xij day of Agust in anno
M¹iiijᶜiiijˣˣij.

25          Your owne at all tymus, John Dalton, to my poyer.

*Dorse*: To my intierly beluffyd Gorge Cely merchaunt at the
Staple of Calles, so it don.

**181.** *William Cely at Calais to George Cely at London,*
*13 August 1482*
s.c.1 53/134

Jhesu M¹iiijᶜiiijˣˣij

Ryght worschypp⟨full⟩ syr, afftyr dew recommendaschon I louly
recommend me vnto yowre masterschypp. Furdermore, plese hytt
yowre masterschypp to vnderstond that thys day we hawe schyppyd
bothe yowre horsse, and I hawe delyuerd Joysse v s. x d. Fl. ffor
5 al maner costys here, as hallff passage and brege money, etc., and
ffor hys costys yn Ynglond, xx s. ster. acordyng to yowre wrytyng,
etc. Furdermore, plese hytt yowre masterschypp to be enfformyd

---

**180.** 4 all] Leyc' *canc.*          8 he *ch. from* ye          stabyll *ch. from* stapyll

that Margery commavndyþ her vnto yowr masterschypp, and
sche tellyth me sche schulde hawe rayment—as a gowne and oder
thyngys—agaynest her chyrchyng, as sche hadd the toder tyme, 10
wheroff sche prays yow off an answer, etc. Item, syr, John Dalton
desyryth to hawe ij romes yn yowre stabull, and he wold paye ffor
hit, and he tellyd me he wold wryte to yow ffor the same, but
Joysse tellyd me that yowre masterschypp hadd grauntyd hym the
stabull and the howsse at hys commyng agayne to Calles ffor to 15
occupye hytt, and yowre masterschypp to hawe yowre rome at
yowre comyng, etc. Syr, pray yowre masterschypp off an answer
off thys, etc. Syr, as ffor yowre oder stuffe, I schall send hytt vnto
yowre masterschypp be on off the wollers, etc. No more vnto
yowre masterschypp at thys tyme, but Jhesu kepe yow. Wrytten 20
at Calles the xiij day off Auguste.

per yowre seruaunte,<br>Wylliam Cely.

*Dorse*: To my worshyppffull master George Cely, merchaunte off
þe Stappell off Calles, at London yn Martt Lane, soohit dd. 25
(*Shield.*)

### 182. William Cely at Calais to Richard and George Cely at London, 13 August 1482

s.c.1 53/135

Jhesu M$^l$iiij$^c$iiij$^{xx}$ij

Ryght worshyppffull masters, after dew recommendaschon I louly
recommend me vnto yowre masterschyppys. Furdermore, plese
hit yowre masterschyppys to vnderstond that thys day I receyued
an letter ffrom yowre masterschyppys whereyn ys wrytten the
nombyr *and* poyse off yowre wull and the tale off yowre ffellys 5
whych ȝe hawe schyppyd at London yn thys fflete, and the namys
off euery schypp, etc. Item syrs, I vnderstond be ⌐the⌐ sayd letter
that yowre masterschyppys woll hawe yowre wull howssyd yn
yowre wullhowsse be the Est Wache Howsse, and yowre ffellys
yn yowre howsse be Sent Nycolas Chyrche, whych at the ryvyng 10
alond shall be howssyd acordyng, etc. Furdermore, plese hytt
yowre masterschyppys to vnderstond that master Lefftenaunt and
dyuersse off the Felleschypp hathe hadd commenyng wyth my

**181.** 11 Dalton] tellyth *canc.*　　　13 me] he *ch. from* ye　　　19 be] fo *canc.*

Lordd Chamberleyn and the Kyng*ys* Conssell ffor the paym*ent*
15 off thys hallffe ȝerys wagys, and I vnderstond they wull be p*ay*d
at xxvj s. viij d. ffor the pownd, and they wull hawe noo noder
money than Nemyng grot*ys* at iiij d. ob. le styc. Syr, I vnderstond
the goode that comys nowe ffro*m* London *and* Ypyswyche most
paye partt off the same paym*ent*. Syr, hytt woll be a schrode losse
20 to receyue the Nemyng grot*ys* at v d. and paye hytt yn ⌈to þe
Place⌉ at iiij d. ob., etc. Item syr, plese hytt yow to vnderstond that
I am nott payd ffor non off yowre waraunt*ys* of xv s. off the pownd,
nott ⌈yett⌉, but hytt ys co*m*mavndyd be courtt that eu*er*y man that
hath any warant*ys* off xv s. off the pownde moste be browght ynto
25 the cowrt the nexte courte day, and ther the court to ffynde syche
menes that all the waraunt*ys* schall be p*ay*d owte, etc. Syr, as ffor
tydyng*ys*, we hawe non here ffor very sarten, but that the Frenschemen lyeth styll yn garysons apon the borders, and gadryth and
encresyth dayly, as hytt ys sayd; and as ffor the Dewke off Bor-
30 gayne, hytt was sayd he was a thys syde Ypur w*yth* a grett ost off
men, and schuld a be at Sent Tomers or thys tyme, but we here
nott off hym yett—som men sey he ys gon backe agayne, etc. No
more vnto yowre mast*er*schyppys at thys tyme, but Jh*e*su kepe
yow. Wrytten at Calles the xiij day off Auguste.
35                                         p*er* yowre s*er*ua*u*nt,
                                          Wylli*a*m Cely.

*Dorse*: To my worschyppffull masters Rechard *and* George Cely,
m*er*chauntes off the Stapp*e*ll off Call*es* at London yn Martt Lane,
soo hit dd. (*Shield*.)


**183.** *William Cely at Calais to Richard and George Cely
at London, 16 August 1482*
s.c.1 53/136

Jh*e*su M¹iiij^c iiij^xx ij

Ryght worschyppffull syrs, afftyr dew reco*m*mendaschon I louly
reco*m*mend me vnto yowr masterschyppys. Furdermore plese hit
yowre mast*er*schypp*ys* to be enfformyd that thys day, the xvj day
off Auguste, the wull fflete came to Call*es*, bothe off London and
5 Ypysweche, yn saffte, thanckyd be Godd; and thys same day was
partt londyd, and hytt rysyth ffayer yett, thanckyd be Godd, etc.

Syrs, oder tydyng*ys* hawe ⌐we⌐ non here but that cam owte off Ynglond ⌐don apon þe Scott*ys*⌐, ffor the whych my Lordd com-mavndyd a gen*er*all *pro*seschon, and at nyght bonffyers to be made att eu*er*y mans dorre, as was att Myddsomer Nyghte, and all   10 the gvnnes yn the bollewarkys ⌐and abowte the wall*ys*⌐ were schett ffor joye. And as ffor the Dewk off Borgayne, ys at Bregys and hys *com*pany yn Brabon. I vnderstond they co*m*me but slowly on, and the Frenschemen lyeth styll yn garysons apon the borders, etc. No more vnto yowre mast*er*schyppys at thys tyme, but Jh*es*u   15 kepe yow. Wrytten at Calles the xvj day off Auguste.

p*er* yowr s*er*ua*u*nt,<br>Wylli*a*m Cely.

*Dorse*: To my worshyppffull masters Rechard *and* George Cely, *m*erchant*ys* off the Stapp*e*ll off Call*es*, at London yn M*a*rtt Lane   20 soo hit dd. (*Shield.*)

## 184. *William Cely at Calais to Richard and George Cely at London, 19 August 1482*
S.C.1 53/137

Jh*es*u M<sup>l</sup>iiij<sup>c</sup>iiij<sup>xx</sup>ij

Ryght worschyppffull mast*er*s, affter dew reco*m*mendaschon I louly reco*m*me*n*d me vnto yowre mast*er*sschyppys. Furd*er*more, plese hit yowre mast*er*schyppys to vnderstond that all yowre wull whyhch was schyppyd in thys fflete ys londydd and howssyd, all sawe v s*ar*plers whych schall be howssyd as schortly as I can. And   5 thanckyd be Godd, hit ys drye, and non hurtt w*yth* non burny*n*g, sawe iiij or v s*ar*plers be rent w*yth* hysyng owte off the schypp. And as ffor yowre ffell*ys*, be londyd and howssyd all sawe iiij pack*ys*, whych schal be londyd tomorow betymes, and Godd wull, and thanckyd be Godd they ryse resonnabull ffeyr yett, but they   10 were hott yn the schypp and began to swete, but non off them that I hawe landyd that be peryschydd. And I hawe Robard Rover to ffollow the cartt*ys*, and he ffollowythe eu*er*y cartt, etc., and as sone as I can I schall send yow the clernesse off them. And on Fryday

---

183. 10 made att] wa *canc.*    was] att *ch. from* on       11 gvnnes *ch. from*<br>gonnes       15 mast*er*schyppys] ath *canc.*

184. 4 whyhch *ch. from* sch       14 And on] *two words erased*

15 at affternone the wull fflete cam to Calles, as I wrote vnto yowre
masterschyppys yn anoder letter, wrytten the xvj day off August,
etc. No more vnto yowr masterschyppys at thys tyme, but Jhesu
kepe yow. Wrytten at Calles the xix day off August.

per yowr seruaunt,

20 Wylliam Cely.

*Dorse*: To my wurshyppffull masters Rechard and George Cely,
merchauntys off [the] Stappull, at London yn Martt Lane, sohit
dd. (*Shield.*)


### 185. William Cely at Calais to Richard and George Cely at London, 20 August 1482

s.c.1 53/138

Jhesu M$^l$iiij$^c$iiij$^{xx}$ij

Ryght worshyppffull masters, affter dew recommendaschon I louly
recommend me vnto yowr masterschyppis. Furdermore, plese hit
yowre masterschyppys to vnderstond that on the xx day off Auguste
was redd yn courtt a letter that cam ffrom Syr Wylliam Stocker
5 and dyuersse off the Fellyschypp, howe that the Kynge wull hawe
ij M$^l$ pownd ffor hys syrplyssage off all soyche wullys and ffellys
that hath ben schyppyd ffrom the vj day off Apryll ⌈last past⌉ tyll
the vj day off October nexte, and ffor the whych he wull hawe made
vj oblygaschons payabull at vj monthys and vj monthis, the styc
10 conteynyng v$^c$ marke. To the whych the Fellyschypp hath agreydd
here be courtt that ther schall be made vj oblygaschons vnder the
Stappell seall—iij payabull yn Feuerell next, and the toder thre
payabull yn Auguste nexte affter that, etc. Item, plese hytt yowre
masterschyppys to wytt that all they that were beffore yn the
15 wagys off master Robardd Raddclyffe, Porter off Calles, be putt
owte off wagys and warnyd to voyde the town be Fryday nexte
com, and as ffor Botterell, ⌈he⌉ schall owte off preson, and all that
were theryn ffor the same mater, and they all be warnyd to voyde
the town off Cales and the Marches, wyffe, chyldern and goodes,
20 be Fryday nexte com, payn off deth, ffor the whych I trow Botrell
woll ⌈nott⌉ dyshease yow off yowre howsse noo lenger, etc. No

---

**185.** 7 ffrom the] last *canc.*        21 dyshease yow] off *ch. from* ffor

more vnto yowre masterschyppys at thys tyme, but Jhesu hath
yow yn hys kepyng. Wrytten at Calles the xx day off August.

> per yowr seruaunte,
> Wylliam Cely.    25

*Dorse*: To my worshyppffull master Rechardd and George Cely,
merchauntys off Sta[pell] off Calles, at London yn Martt Lane soo
hit dd. (*Shield*.)

**186.** *William Cely at Calais to Richard and George Cely
at London, 23 August 1482*

s.c.1 53/139

Jhesu M<sup>l</sup>iiij<sup>c</sup>iiij<sup>xx</sup>ij

Ryght worschyppffull masters, affter dew recommendaschon I louly
recommend me vnto yowr masterschyppys. Furdermore, plese
hytt yowre masterschyppys to wytt that all yowre wull ys howssyd
drye, and thanckyd be God, ye hawe non that ys sore broken; and
as ffor yowre ffellys I hawe serchyd hem and told hem ower, and  5
ye hawe all yowr tale, and ther ys none off hem that ys hurtt wyth
burnyng, but ther ys an ij<sup>c</sup> rent wyth þe londyng and the howssyng,
whych schall be made as schortly as I can, etc. Item, plese hit
yowre masterschyppys to wytt that on Monday last was, Robard
Hobard was at Bregys, and he sayth the same day he sawe the  10
Dewke off Burgeyne departe owte off Bregys, but wyth x horsse,
ynto Selond, ffor they off Gaunte and off Bregys wyll nott graunt
hym syche thyngys as he askyth ffor. The Dewke askyth noothyng
off hem but mony, and he wyll take syche men wyth hym to goo
vppon the Frenschemen as plesyd hym, but þe Gaunteners and  15
they off Bregys wyll nott 3eve hym noo money wythowte he take
syche men as they wull asyne hym, ffor the whych he departyd
ynto Selond; but I vnderstonde the Frenschemen lyeth styll yn
garysons appon the Marc[hes] and encrece dayle wyth new men
owte off Hye Fraunce, etc. No more vnto yowre masterschyppys  20
at thys, but Jhesu kepe yow. Wrytten at Calles the xxiij day off
Auguste.

> per yowre seruaunte,
> Wylliam Cely.

*Dorse*: To my worshyppffull masters Rychard and George Cely,  25 merchantes off the Stappell off Calles, at London yn Martt Lane, so hit dd. (*Shield.*)

### 187. *William Cely at Calais to Richard and George Cely at London, 29 August 1482*

s.c.1 53/140

Jhesu M$^l$iiij$^c$iiij$^{xx}$ij

Ryght worshyppffull masters, afftyr dew recommendaschon I louly recommend ⌐me⌐ vnto yowre masterschyppys. Furdermore, plese hytt yowre masterschyppys to be enfformyd that the xxviij day off Auguste hytt was agreydd here be courtt that euery ⌐man⌐ that
5 hadd any goode comvn ffrom London or Ypyswyche wyth thys last fflete schall bryng yn hys byllys off costom and subsede off ⟨the⟩ sayd goodys be that day senyght, payne off xij d. off the pownde, and that we moste make ij byllys, yche off them off the hallffe, the ton payabull the xx day off October nexte and the toder
10 payabull the xx ⌐day⌐ off Feuerell nexte, and we moste make a byll off xx s. off the sarpler made payabull at plesyr, whych schall be sent ower ynto Ynglond and wrytten vppon won off the byllys affore rehersyd, etc. Fordermore, plese hytt yowre mastersschyppys to vnderstond that master Lefftenaunt and syche off the
15 Fellyschypp as were apwoyntydd be the courtt hath agreydd wyth my Lordd Chamberleyn and the Kyngys Conssell what mony we schall paye ffor costom and subsede to ⌐the payment off⌐ thys hallffe yerys wagys. Fyrste, we schall paye xxvj s. viij d. ffor the povnde ster.; and thes be ⌐the⌐ goldys and whyte mony that
20 ffollowyth that ys apoynttyd ffor the payment, as they were corrant affore the Doches dyedd ffyrst:

The new crowne, at v s. vj d. The old crowne at v s. iiij d.
The Lewe at a vj s. viij d. The Andreus gyldern at iiij s. vj d.
The Ryder at v s. viij d. The Gylhellmus at iiij s.
25      The salew at v s. vj d. And ij or iij oder goldys affter þe same rate.
The olde nobull, at xj s. And the Nemyng grotys at iiij d. ob.
The ryall at xiij s. iiij d. And the old sengull plack at ij d. ob.

And as ffor any oder goldys and ⌐oder⌐ syluer, they wyll non, etc.

**187.** 4 courtt that] all *erased*          16 Lordd] what mony that w *canc.*

No more vnto yowre mast*er*schyppys at ⟨thys⟩ tyme, but Jh*e*su
kepe yow. Wrytten at Calles the xxix day off Auguste.                30

*per* yowre s*er*ua*u*nte,
Wyll*ia*m Cely.

*Dorse*: To my worshyppffull mast*er* Rechard and George Cely,
m*er*chau*n*t[*ys* of] the Stappell off Call*es*, at London yn M*ar*tt Lane,
sohit dd. (*Shield*.)                35

## 188. *William Cely at Calais to George Cely at London, 29 August 1482*

s.c.1 53/141

Ryght worshyppffull syr, affter dew rec*om*mendasch*on* I louly
rec*om*mend me vnto yowre mast*er*schypp. Furd*er*more, plese hett
yowre mast*er*schypp to be enfformyd that Margere ys dowghter ys
past to Godd. Hytt was berydd thys same daye, on whoys sowle
Jh*e*su hawe marsy. Syr, I vnderstond hytt hadd a grett pang: what  5
sycknesse hytt was I cannott saye, etc. Item, syr, Bottrell ys
dep*ar*tyd owte off Calles and ys yn Ynglond, and thys day hys
wyff goyth to ⌐hym⌐ w*yth* all her stuffe, and they be c*om*mavnded
that they schall nott come w*yth*yn the town off Call*es* as long as my
Lordd Chamberleyn ys Lefftena*u*nte off Calles, etc. No more vnto  10
yowre mast*er*schypp at thys tyme, but Jh*e*su kepe yow. Wrytten
at Call*es* the xxix day off Auguste.

*per* yowre s*er*ua*u*nte,
Wyll*ia*m Cely.

*Dorse*: To my worschyppffull mast*er* George Cely, m*er*cha*u*nte  15
[of] the Stappell off Call*es*, at London y*n* Martt Lane sohit dd.
(*Shield*.)

## 189. *William Cely at Calais to Richard and George Cely at London, 3 September 1482*

s.c.1 53/142

Jh*e*su M¹iiij*ᶜ*iiijˣˣij

Ryght worschyppffull mast*er*s, affter dew rec*om*mendasch*on* I
louly rec*om*mend me vnto yowre mast*er*schyppys. Furd*er*more,

**188.** 8 goyth *altered from* ? geth

plese hit yowre masterschyppys to be enfformyd that I hawe
receyued a letter ffrom yowre masterschyppys be Wylliam Daltons
5 man, whych I hawe redd and well vnderstond, and I schall do
all thyngys acordyng to hytt as nye as I can, and as ffor yowre
chamberynge that was at makyng at Bregys, when Andryan yowre
oste was at Calles I delyuerd hym mony to paye ffor the makyng
off hit, and he hath sent hytt to Calles redy, and I hawe receyued
10 hytt euerythyng acordyng to yowre remembravnce, sawe the cor-
tens be stayned but on the ton syde, and ther ys no demy corten
but they be all hole that ʒe maye slytte whych ye thyncke best;
and as sone I can hawe any schypp that come to London I schall
send hytt vnto yowre masterschypp, etc. Syr, as ffor a gossehawke
15 I can gett non here yett, ffor all that come to Calles my Lordd
Chamberłeyn beyth hem vpp and they be anythyng wurth, etc.
And ⌐as⌐ ffor yowre man that ʒe delyuerd yowre mony to ffor
hawkys, I here nott off yett, etc. Furder more, plese hytt yowre
masterschypp to vnderstond that here ys an ordynaunce made be
20 all the Fellyschypp the last courte day that we schall receyue ffrom
that day fforward redy mony yn Calles, and xxvj s. viij d. Fl. ffor
the pownd ster.—mony as hytt was corrant affore the Dowches off
Borgayne dyed—ffor all wull and ffell that shall be sold at Calles
ffrom hencefforwardd; but they off the town off Laythe and Dellffe
25 schall paye but hallffe yn hondd at Cales at xxvj s. viij d. the li.,
mony as hytt was corrant affore the Dowches a Borgeyn dyed, and
the rest at vj monthys and vj monthys at xxviij s. the pownd, mony
as hytt ys corant at the martt, etc. Furdermore, plese hytt yowre
masterschyppys to vnderstond that I hawe born ynto the Plase
30 yowre byllys off costom and subsede whych be abelyd yn courtt,
and I hawe borne yn yowre byll off xx s. off the sarpler made
payabull at plesur: hytt amovntyth—xxxv li. x s. ster., and hytt ys
wrytten vppon yowre last byll payabull the xx day off Feuerell, as
all oder mens ys yn lyke case, and the byllys of xx s. off the sarpler
35 schall be sent ynto Ynglond to the solyster schorttly, etc. And as
ffor yowre byll off costom and subsede that ys payabull the xx day
of October, hit amovntys lxxix li. xiij s. v d. ob. ster., whych
[Dorse] moste be purveyd ffor agaynest thys payment yn thys nexte
martt. For the mony the whych I schuld a receyued owte off the
40 Plase ffor yowre warrantys off xv s. off the pownd, I can hawe but

xiiij li. Fl. yett, ffor hytt hawe be spoken off yn courtt, and ther
ys dyuersse that be yn casse lyke as ye ar, and the courtt sayth
they can take noo derecsch[on] ffor ⌐hytt⌐ tell hytt be grown yn
tresory, ffor the whych they say ye moste fforbere a seson, etc.
No more vnto yowre mast[er]schyppys at thys tyme, but Jhesu   45
kepe yow. Wrytten at Cal[les] the iij day off September.

per yowre seruaunte,
Wylliam Cely.

To my worshyppffull masters Rechard *and* George Cely, merchauntes off the Stappell off Calles, at London yn Martt Lane so   50
hitt dd. (*Shield.*)


**190.** *William Cely at Calais to Richard and George Cely
at London, 8 September 1482*

s.c.1 53/143

Jhesu M¹iiijᶜiiijˣˣij

Ryght worshyppffull masters, afftyr dew recommendaschon I louly
recommend me vnto yowr masterschyppys. Furdermore, plese hytt
yowre masterschyppys to vnderstondd that I hawe cast owte
a sarpler off yowre wull, No. xij, and the packer commend hit
grettly, be the whych hytt schall be awardd the nexte warde day;   5
and I hawe sett all yowre ffellys r[edy] ffor to prese, etc. Item syr,
plese hit yowre masterschyppys to vnderstondd that here ys noo
gossehawkys to gett, ffor all that commys my Lordd Chamberleyn
bye hem vpp, etc. Here hath come dyuersse hawkys, but they be
so dere that no man byethe hem but my Lordd—they be at iiij   10
nobullys, v nobullys an hawke, etc. Syr, oder tydyng[ys] hawe we
non here yett, but allmyghty Jhesu hath y[ow] yn hys blessyd
kepyng. Wrytten at Calles the viij da[y] off September.

per yowre seruaunte,
Wylliam Cely.                              15

*Dorse*: To my worshyppffull masters Rechard and George Cely,
mer[chauntes] of the Stappell at Ca[lles], at London yn Martt Lane,
soo hit dd. (*Shield.*)

**190.** 4 the] the *erased*              9 but] *word expunged and canc.*       they] bye
*expunged and canc.*              13 off] Augu *canc.*

**191.** *William Cely at Calais to Richard and George Cely at London, 12 September 1482*

S.C.I 53/144

Jhesu M<sup>l</sup>iiij<sup>c</sup>iiij<sup>xx</sup>ij

Ryght worshyppffull masters, affter dew recommendaschon I louly recommend me vnto yow masterschyppys. Furdermore, plese hit yowre masterschypp to vnderstond that yowre ffellys be sett and presyd at xiiij nobullys the C, but as ffor yowre wull, ys nott yett
5 awarddyd, but hitt schall as schortly as I can, etc. Furdermore, plese hit yowre masterschyppys to vnderstond that we hawe tydyngys here that the Frenschemen hath goten the cyte off Lewke, and slayne the Boschoppe off Lewke, and we hawe tydyngys here nowe that men off the londde of Lewke wyth the
10 helpe off Braboners hathe broken vpp all the burgys betwyxte Fraunce *and* them, and ⌐hath⌐ beseghyd ⌐the⌐ town off Lewke agayne, and lyckly to recover the town agayne, etc. Furdermore, plese hyt yowre masterschyppys to vnderstond that we hawe tydyng[ys] here that the town off Gaunte *and* the town off Bregys
15 be at a fferyaunce betwyxte hemsellffe, yn so mekyll that they off Gaunte hathe sent to the Englysch naschon, and to euery naschon ⌐yn Bregys⌐, commavndyng them to sett styll and doo her merchaundyes and entermete wyth noo party, payne off that wull comme theroff, etc. No more vnto yowre masterschyppys at thys
20 tyme, byt Jhesu kepe yow. Wrytten at Callys the xij day of September.

per yowre seruaunte,<br>Wylliam Cely.

*Dorse*: To my worshyppffull masters Rechard Cely and George
25 Cely, merchauntes of the Stappell at Calles, at London yn Martt Lane so hit dd. (*Shield*.)


**192.** *William Mydwynter at Northleach to Richard Cely the younger at London, 20 September [1482]*

S.C.I 53/145

Ryght reuerent and worchupfull syr, Y reykecommand me vnto yow, desyryng to here of yowr wellefare. Furdurmorr, I thank yow of the grette cher the⟨t⟩ ye deydde me at my laste beyng wytthe

yow. Syr, Y made a bargyn wytthe yow at that seysyn, the wycche
I wolde Y hadde sleppyd the wylys; for theke costemerys that  5
Y trosty⟨d⟩ moste for to a sowyld theme, and Y trostyd that I solde
nat a bowte ther wolle aboffe—xiij s. viij d. a tod, *and* nowye Y
co*n*nat bey ther woll hondor xiiij s. *and* xiiij s. *and* vj d a tod. The
pryse ys that Y bey at aboffe that I solde yow ryght mycche; *and*
to recckyn the reffys, Y salle lesse, be my trothe, a noboll or x s. in  10
effyry s*ack*, *and* as my trothe helpe ma, and they moste haffe
reddy mo*n*ney bey and bey: they that werr wonte to leffe in my
honde moste parte of ther mo*n*ney, nowe they moste nedys haffe
halle ther mo*n*ney, *and* now Y moste troste to yowr cortesy. *And*
Y prye yow co*n*sedyr thys well, as ye maye haffe my sarfys, and  15
I moste t⟨r⟩oste to yow that I may haffe the ij*c* li. that ye sayde
Y solde nat haffe hytte tyll Nowhembyr: I praye as hartely as Y
ca*n*ne that ⌜ye⌝ make hytte reddy wytthein xiiij dayys haff*ter*
Myhelmas, or helse I ha*m*me hottely sa*m*myd, for I made myselfe
neffyr so barr wytthehowte money, and therfor I pray yow that  20
ye make hytte reddy. No morr to yow at thys tyme, botte Jh*e*su
kepe yow. Wrytty*n* at Northelacche the xx day of Septembyr.

> Bey Wyllya*m* Mydwynt*er*.

*Dorse*: Thys lett*er* be delyuyrt to Ryc*hard* Cely in London in
Marke Lanne.   25

**193.** *Richard Cely the younger at London to George Cely
at Calais or the mart, 26 September 1482*
s.c.1 53/147

> Jh*e*su M¹iiij*c*iiij*xx*ij

Riught whellbelouyd brother George, I recomend me wnto yow
w*yth* aull myne hartte, informeyng yow that I hawhe yowr ʒeu*n*ge
horsse at London, and I hawhe spokyn w*yth* the beste cossars and
smytthys in Smethe Fellde, and thay gewhe me cownsell to lette
hym ron in a parke tyll Hallontyd, and then take hym wpe and
ser hym, and lette hym stand in the dede of whyntt*er*, and let ren  5
the next som*ar*, and then he schawll be sawhe whell he ys hors.

**192.** 7 Y] haue *canc.*   8 *ms.* xiiij s. & a & xiiij s. & vj d.   13 they] w
wolle *canc.*   17 praye as] ye *canc.*   22 yow] wy *canc.*   25 Marke]
Lanz *canc.*

D 148   N

No mor to yow at thys tym. J*h*esu kepe yow. Wryt at London the
xxvj day of Septemby⟨r⟩.

10                                                                    p*er* yowr brothe⟨r⟩,
                                                                    Rychard Cely.

I schawll seke the sewreste plas in Essex for yowr ȝewnge hors, and
I pray yow remembyr an hawke.

*Dorse*: A my whellbelouyd brother George Cely, m*er*chand of the
15  Stap*ell* at Calleys or the Martte, be thys dd.


**194.** *William Cely at Calais to George Cely at the mart,
30 September 1482*
s.c.1 53/148

J*h*esu M¹iiij°iiij*ˣˣ*ij

Ryght worschyppffull syr, affter dew rec*om*mendaschon I lowly
rec*om*mend me vnto yowr mast*er*schypp. Furdermore, plese hit
yowre masterschypp to vnderstond that Joysse and yowre horsse
cam to Calles the Wedonsday nexte afft*er* ȝe dep*ar*tyd ffro*m* Calles,
5  all yn saffte thanckyd be Godd, etc. Syr, as ffor any m*er*cha*u*ntes
strangers or Hollonders, ther cam non syn ȝe dep*ar*tyd, etc. Syr,
ȝe schall receyue off the bryngger heroff a lett*er* derectyd to yow
ffro*m* mast*er* Rechard, etc. Syr, I hawe sent ower yowre lett*er* ynto
Ynglond that ȝe lefte ⌐here⌐, but hit was v days affter ȝe dep*ar*tyd
10  ffyrst, ffor here was noon passage no sonner, the wynd was so
contrary and the see soo trublys, passage was hallffe see ower wonys
or twyse, and was ffayne to co*m*me to Call*es* agayne, etc. Item syr,
yowre mast*er*schyp most reme*m*ber to bryng home w*yth* yow an
Cvj li. Fl. ffor to paye yowre costom and subsede, etc. Syr, the
15  begyny*ng* off thys next weke I purpose that Joysse schall come
fforward w*yth* yowre horssys toward yowre mast*er*schypp, etc. No
more vnto yowr mast*er*schypp at thys tyme, but J*h*esu kepe yow.
Wrytten at Call*es* the last day off Septe*m*ber.

                                                          p*er* yowre s*er*ua*u*nt,
20                                                          Wyll*ia*m Cely.

*Dorse*: To my worshyppffull master George Cely, m*er*cha*u*nte off
the Stap*ell* at Call*es*, he beyng at þe m*ar*tte, soo hit dd. (*Shield*.)


**194.** 8 ffrom] gm mast*er canc.*

**195.** *Richard Cely at London to George Cely at Calais or the mart, 3 October 1482*

s.c.1 53/149

Anno Jhesu M$^l$iiij$^{xx}$ij [*sic*]

Riught whelbelouyd brother, I recwmende me harttely wnto yow, informeyng yow that howr mother and whe ar in good heyll, thankyd be God, and so whe truste that ȝe be. I hawhe byn at Raylay and gewyn them iij s. iiij d., and now whe hawhe day of doyng of howr homayge tyll Myhellmas nexte cwm. Syr, I send 5 to yow Wylliam Mydwynttyrs letter clossyd in thys letter. I whotte not how to ansfor hyt, and howr fathers towmbe ys a settynge wp, and howr heyme ys heyr for mony, and thys day I departte into Cottesowlde, and how sone thay wyll cawll apon for the xx s. of the sarpller I connot say. I am at my whyttys end w*yth*⌐hwt⌐ yowr 10 cwmfortte. Syr, I hawhe pwt yowr ȝewnge gray hors in Thondyrlay Parke, and ther he has pastyr inow, and ther ar byt iij horse goynge in aull the parke. And ȝe mwste pay the parcar for hys paster iiij d. a wheke, and I hawhe promysyd hym a bow, and I trwste that he wyll se whell to yowr hors and make yow sportte at yowr cwmyng. 15 He ys a man of master Mongewnbres. No mor to yow at thys tym, Jhesu kepe yow. Wh⟨r⟩yt at London the iij$^{de}$ day of Octobur.

*per* yor brother,
Rychard Cely.

I pray yow sende me whryttyng in as schortte spas as ȝe may.    20

*Dorse*: Wnto my brother George Cely, merchand of the Stapell, at Calles or the marte, so dd. (*Shield.*)

**196.** *William Cely at Calais to George Cely at the mart, 6 October 1482*

s.c.1 53/151

Jhesu M$^l$iiij$^c$iiij$^{xx}$ij

Ryght worshyppffull syr, affter dew recommendaschon I louly recommend me vnto yowre masterschypp. Furdermore, plese hytt yowre masterschypp to vnderstond that John Tate whych schall be Lefftenaunte off the Stappell ys come to Calles, etc. Syr, as ffor any salys off wull or ffell, I hawe made non syn yowre masterschypp 5

**195.** 2 heyll] of bo *canc.*      8 *ms.* in into

departyd, ffor here cam noo merchaunttys straungers syns, wherffor yowre masterschypp most remember ffor yowre costom and
subsede yn the martt, etc. Syr, as ffor all yowre thynggys here
doyth well, but as ffor the wull fflete off London, ys nott common
10 yett. I vnderstond be men that comme thens they be nott all
poynttyd vpp yett, and wheder master Rechardd schyppyth any
ffellys or nott at thys tyme I wott nott, etc. Item syr, I hawe
delyuerd Joysse ffor hys expens ffor the horssys *and* hymsellff
vj s. ix d. Fl., etc. Item syr, plese hit yow to vnderstond that my
15 Lordd Chamberleyn gooyth over ynto Yngelond wythyn day or
twayne wyth all hys howssold mayne, etc. No more vnto yowre
masterschypp at thys tyme, but Jhesu kepe. Wrytten at Calles the
vj day off October.

*per* yowre seruaunte,
20          Wylliam Cely.

Item, syr, ȝe schall receyue off Joysse iiij quarters *and* ij slevys off
yowre blacke gowne, and a black bugge ffurre to the sayd gowne.

*Dorse*: To my worshyppffull master George Cely, merchaunte off
the Stappell at Call[e]ys, at the Mart be thys delyuerd. (*Shield.*)

*Dorse, in G. Cely's hand*:
25 Of Jacob Wylliamson and hys ffellous.

| | |
|---|---|
| C xxiij Hettrytus—iiij s. iiij d. sum ----- | xxvj li. Fl. xiij s. |
| Item, ij Ryallys xiiij s. vj d. ---------- | xxix s. |
| Item, an Phellypus ----------------- | iij s. iiij d. Fl. |
| Item, in plakkys ------------------- | xxvj d. |
| 30                    Sum ----- | xxviij li. vij s. vj d. Fl. |
| Item, in Nyme Egyn grottys --------- | xiiij li. Fl. |
| Item, ij d. ob. --------------------- | xxx s. |
| Item, in pensse -------------------- | xx s. |
| Item, xxij Andreus v s. -------------- | v li. x s. Fl. |
| 35 Item, vj Rydars vj s. iiij d. ---------- | xxxviiij s. |
| Item, ij crow⟨n⟩us v s. viij d. --------- | xj s. iiij d. |
| A Rynyshe and ij d. ---------------- | v s. |
| ij postlatys ij s. viij d. -------------- | v s. iiij d. |
| An Dawethe ----------------------- | iiij s. |
| 40 ij Arnowldys ij s. iiij d. ------------- | iiij s. viij d. |
| ij parttys of an sallewe -------------- | iiij s. j d. |

**196.** 9 London] I here *canc.*     35 Item] xxx *canc.*

| | | |
|---|---|---|
| An pesse gowld of ------------------ | xx d. | |
| In ij d. ob. ------------------------ | xx s. | |
| Of vj le pesse ---------------------- | xiiij s. | |
| In v d. ob. ------------------------- | v s. vj d. | 45 |
| In v d. ----------------------------- | iij s. iiij d. | |
| v d. -------------------------------- | x s. viij d. | |
| Sum ------ | xxviij li. vij s. vj d. Fl. | |
| Item, in v d. le pesse -------------- | v li. Fl. | |
| Item, of iij d. ---------------------- | xx s. | 50 |
| Item, in vj le pesse ---------------- | xij s. | |
| Item, in ij d. ob. ------------------- | viij s. | |
| Item, xviij Hettry*tus* iiij s. iiij d. ------ | iij li. xviij s. | |
| Item, v Rynyshe iiij s. x d. ---------- | xxiiij s. ⌜iiij d.⌝ | |
| Item, rydars ---------------------- | xij s. ⌜viij⌝ d. | 55 |
| An salewe ------------------------- | vj s. ij d. | |
| An Davyd ------------------------- | iiij s. | |
| ij Andre*us* ------------------------ | x s. | |
| An Rynyshe ----------------------- | iiij s. x d. | |
| An ------------------------------- | xvj d. | 60 |
| Item, in v d. ob. -------------------- | xxviij s. vij d. | |
| Item, in ij d. ob. -------------------- | xxxv s. | |
| Item, ij ryallys --------------------- | xxix s. | |
| Item, in grott*ys* ------------------- | iiij s. v d. | |
| sum ------ | xviij li. xviij s. vj d. Fl. | 65 |
| Sum To*tall* ---- | lxxv li. xiij s. vj d. Fl. | |
| Item, iiij*ˣˣ*xvj Andre*us* v s. ---------- | xxiiij li. Fl. | |
| Item, and Andre*us* ----------------- | v s. | |
| Item, --------------------------- | xx d. | |
| s*um* ------ | xxiiij li. vj s. viij d. Fl. | 70 |
| s*um* to*tall* ---- | C | |

To be done heuyr þat Y go hens: to ffeche my xxv li. x s. of Florde,
to hawe in my byll*es* of Nycolas Hont/ to make xx st*er*. at the syght.

*In different ink and written larger*: P*er* Clays my sarvant. John de
Bott of Barow, an hoggy*s*hed w*yth* this token (*a merchant's mark*). 75

196. 60 An] s*um* xvj li. x s. j d. Fl. *canc.*

**197.** *Richard Cely at London to George Cely at Calais or Bruges, 17 October 1482*

S.C.I 53/153

Jhesu M<sup>l</sup>iiij<sup>c</sup>iiij<sup>xx</sup>ij

Ryght whellbelouyd brother I recomend me wnto yow, informeyng yow that thys day I resauyd a letter frome yow whryt at Andwarpe the fyrste day of Octobur, the qwheche I do well wndyrstond, and I am sory that the whar ys so grett in that partteys at Hollondars
5 may not cwm dowyn. I hawhe beyn at Chepyng Nortton and sett awll thyng in good whay, and wyth my neym John Cely, and he has gatheryd xvj sacke of fayr wholl, and now heyr ys cwm Wylliam Mydwyter, byt I spake not wyth hym ʒeyt. How that I do wyth hym I schawll wryt to yow in my nexte letter. Howr mother ys at
10 Byrttys ʒeyt myry, thankyd be God. The Kynge ys at the Towr and hys Lordys in cwnsell dayly. I pray God send ws a myrry whorllde: hyt ⌜ys⌝ euyll for a mane to scharge hym far now a days, for I heyr of none ottyrans. Ʒeyffe I may departte fayr frome the bargin wyth Wylliam Mydwytter that ʒe and I made, I wyll do
15 my beste. Me thynke hytt wyll be whel done, for howr detturs ar sclow payars, etc. I wndyrstonde be Robard Eryke that ʒe hafe ij fayr hawkys. I whowld fayne that ʒe whoullde spede yow into Ingelonde: whe longe sor for yow. Bayard yowr hors dos whell, and as for yowr ʒenge gray hors, ronys in as good an parke as any
20 in Essex, as Levynge, the bryngear of thys letter, can informe yow. Syr, ottys be deyr, and so ys aull othyr corne. I hawhe resauyd yowr hangynge of yowr schambyr from Wylliam Cely. No mor to yow: Jhesu kepe yow. Wryt at London xvij day of Octobur.

per Rychard Cely.

25 Ʒe mwste remembyr to by canwas to packe in.

*Dorse*: Wnto my riught whellbelouyd brother George Cely, merchand of the Stapell, at Calleys or Bregys, so dd.

**198.** *William Cely at Calais to George Cely at the mart, 19 October 1482*

S.C.I 53/154

Jhesu M<sup>l</sup>iiij<sup>c</sup>iiij<sup>xx</sup>ij

Ryght worschyppffull syr, affter dew recommendaschon I lowly recommend me vnto yowre masterschypp. Furdermore, plese hytt

yowre ⌐masterschypp⌐ to vnderstond that the xviij day off October
Joysse and yowr iij men cam to Calys wyth iij hawkys, all yn saffte
thanckyd be Godd, and I hawe receyued ffrom yowre masterschypp 5
be þe sayd Joysse an letter, the whych I well vnderstond, and
acordyng to yowre letter at the next passage they schall goo owyr
wyth yowre hawkys, etc. Syr, the wull schyppys be comme to
Calles all sawe iij, wheroff ij be yn Sandwyche hawen; and oon ys
at Oste End, and he hath cast ower all hys wull owyrburdd. Syr, 10
ʒe hawe noo wull nor ffell comme at schyppyng, wherffor I am the
gladar, ffor wull and ffell ys passyng ffowle arayd at thys tyme, etc.
Syr, as ffor the crayer that ʒede to London wheryn yowre chamberyng was, was nott reffelyd on þe see, but annoder schypp that
ʒede wyth hym was ryffylyd wyth Flemyngys, ffor the crayer that 15
hadd yowre chamberyng yn hath ben at London and dyschargyd,
and ys come to Callys agayn ladyn wyth wull, etc. Syr, the next
schypp that goyth to London I schall send home the beyr bye,
etc. Syr, my Lord Chamberleyn ys ower ynto Ynglond, and ther
was at Dower to abyde hym vᶜ men all yn whyte gownys to bryng 20
hym home, etc. No more vnto yowre masterschypp at thys tyme,
but Jhesu kepe yow. Wrytten at Calles the xix day off October.

per yowr seruaunt,<br>Wyllïam Cely.

Dorse: To my worshyppffull master George Cely, merchaunte off 25
the Stappell at Calles, at the martt so hit dd. (Shield.)

### 199. William Cely at Calais to George Cely at the mart, 20 October 1482

S.C.I 53/155

Jhesu Mˡiiijᶜiiijˣˣij

Ryght worschyppffull syr, affter dew recommendaschon I lowly
recommend me vnto yowre masterschypp. Furder, plese hitt yow
to vnderstond that I hawe receyued off the hackeney man ij letters,
oon ffrom yow and anoder ffrom master Rechard, the whych I well
vnderstond. And where yowre masterschypp wrytyth that ʒe sent 5
a letter be Robard Heryck and be oder dyuersse, and he, ⌐Robard⌐,
tellyd me that he hadd noon to me: Syr, I receyuedd noo letter

---

198. 3 day off] Octobr smudged [October      20 men] yn canc.

ffrom yow syn that ȝe departyd ynto Flaunders tyll that Joysse
cam, etc. Syr, yowre hawkys cam all yn saffte to Callys, but syr,
10 on Satarday at affternone, betwyxte iiij and v, the ffawckener when
noon off vs was bye, dyd call the lest hawke that ys nott reclamyd
wyth a creaunce, and the creaunce brake, and the hawke fflew
awaye ower the wallys. Than cam a sowdoer off town, and toke
her vpp and wold a browghter ynto town agayne, but master
15 Porter mett hym and toke her ffrom hym. And I hawe ben wyth
master Porter ffor her, and ther was Syr Raff Hastyngys, and
I pray them to hawe her agayne, but master Portter ys lothe to
departe ffrom her, but he sayd he wold geve me as myche as sche
cost, and yow myche thancke, and master Syr Raff sayd affore
20 master Porter þat he wylld nott kepe yowr hawke agaynyst yowre
wyll ffor an C li., and soo master Syr Raffe badd me that I schuld
wayte vppon hym thys day. And he sayd that he wold see that
I hadd as myche mony as sche cost, and more to, or ellys the hawke
agayne, etc. Syr, as ffor yowre premer, hytt ys nott yn yowre
25 ffawckeners bage. Syr, I hawe delyuerd Joysse yowre letter to
master Rechard, and I trow tomorow wee schall hawe passage,
etc. Syr, yff any merchauntys com I schall do my best to make som
sale; syr, I plehytt, and wyll doo as nye as I can. Syr, as ffor all
oder thyngys, ys don acordyng. No more vnto yowre masterschypp
30 at thys tyme, but Jhesu kepe yow. Wrytten at Calles the xx day off
October.

per yowre seruaunte,
Wylliam Cely.

Dorse: To my worshyppffull master George Cely, merchaunte off
35 the Stappell at Callys, at the martt, soo hytt dd. (Shield.)


**200.** *Note of events [June 1483], and memoranda [? 1482],
by George Cely*

S.C.1 53/19

Ther ys grett romber in the Reme/ The Scottys has done grett yn
Ynglond / Schamberlayne ys dessesset in trobell. The Chavnseler

199. 8 ffrom ? ch. from ffrow       11 call] hys canc.       28 plehytt (?) ch. from
plyhytt

200. 1 over romber a cross in a circle       over done fig. resembling the abbrev. for
per       2 over dessesset an arabic 4

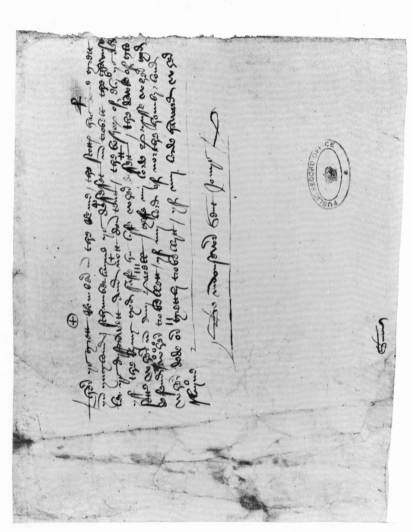

V. Public Record Office S.C. 1 53/19A. Letter no. 200, June 1483

ys dyssprowett and nott content / The Boshop of Ely ys dede /
Yff the Kyng, God ssaffe his lyffe, wher dessett / The Dewke of
Glosetter wher in any parell / Geffe my Lorde Prynsse, wher God 5
defend, wher trobellett / Yf my Lord of Northehombyrlond wher
dede or grettly trobellytt / Yf my Lorde Haward wher slayne.

   De Movnsewr Sent Jonys.

                         Summus      (*Rest of page torn off.*)

[19 b *dorse*]

(*Cancelled*: The som of Nycolas                                      10
Brystall hys partyshon of bothe
oblygacyons amovntys ------------    xxxj li. vii[j s.] vij d. Fl.
Item thys amovntys in Fl. at xxvj s.
le li. ----------------------------  xl li. xv[ij s.] j d. Fl.)
Item Nycolas Brystallys partyshon of                                 15
bothe oblyggacyons amovntys vnto --  xxxj li. iiij s. v[ij d. ster.]
Item ytt amovntys in Fl. at xxvj s.
le povnd ------------------------    xl li. xj s. xj d. Fl.
The rest of bothe oblygacyons
amovntys vnto --------------------   x li. viij s. jd. ster.          20
Item Y most pay vnto Hary Bryan
at Syngsyon marte be an byll of
my hond ffor his wharrant and the
rest of his oblygacyons ------------ l li. Fl.

## 201. *William Cely at Calais to George Cely at London, 13 November 1483*

s.c.1 53/157. *Torn at top of page*

                         Jhesu M[. . .]iiij

Ryght worschyppffull syr, affter dew recommend[aschon I lowly
recommend] me vnto yowre masterschypp. Furdermor [plese
hytt] yow[re master]schypp to vnderstond that I hawe [receyued
a] le[tter ffrom yowre] masterschypp beryng date the v day off
November, the [whych] I hawe redd and well vnderstond, an[d 5
t]hat yowre m[asterschypp] marwellyd that I wrytyth non offtener.

200. 3 *over* nott *a cross.*     *over* Ely *a* b.        4 *over* dessett *a double* tt
5 *over* parell *three vertical strokes*     6 *over* wher trobellett C *canc. and three
circles*      7 *over* grettly *two vertical strokes*     *over* slayne *a circle*
201. 6 that I] am *canc.*

I th[yn]cke yow [. . .] knowe the cause, ffor off a monyth day we covd[e] haw[e] noo conveyaunce off noo letters to London be noo maner m[an], ffor ther was ⌐noo⌐ man that ȝede that wold beyr
10 any letters ffor serchyng, etc. Syr, as ffor John Delowppys, yff he be a trewe man he hathe wrytten to Petter Bayle & Delete, ffor he promysyd me be hys ffaythe that as sone as he cowde hawe any conveyaunce off hys letter he wold wryte to Peter Bayle that he schuld delyuer yow as myche mony as ye schuld nede at thys
15 tyme, and therffor I trowe Peter hath wryttyng off hytt be thys tyme. Syr, as ffor yowre iij sarppellys off Cottyssold wull, re-maynyth here styll. John Delowppys and Gyesbryght wold hawe them, but they ⌐wold⌐ hawe them as they hadd the toder, and I wold nott delyuer them wythowte I hadd redy mony, ⌐wherffor⌐
20 they wyll nott off them nowe, but I hope ffor ⌐to⌐ sell schorttly to som oder merchauntys, etc. Syr, as ⌐ffor⌐ the wull fflete, cam heder all yn saffte, thanckyd be Godd, and soo I wrote vnto yowre masterschypp yn annoder letter be Benett Trotter. Item, syr, I vnderstond yowre masterschypp wold ⌐hawe⌐ a ton off goode
25 Gascon wyne, bothe redd and clarett. Hytt ys resonably goode chepe, but the counssell off the towne wyll suffer none passe owte off towne, ⌐nott yett⌐, wythowte he be yn ffawer to hawe a lysens off my Lordd. Syr, I schall ⌐a⌐seye yff I can gett a lysens ffor a ton, etc. Syr, as ffor all oder thyngys, I schall see as well to as
30 I can. I hawe byn a lykull dyssesyd, but I thancke Godd I am amendyd and walkynge, and Joysse hathe ben syke allso, butt nowe he ys well mendyd, thanckyd be Godd, whoo hath yow yn hys blessyd kepynge. Wrytten at Calles the xiij day off November.

per yowre seruaunte,
35                      Wylliam Cely.

*Dorse*: To my worshyppffull master George Cely, merchaunte of the Stappell at Calles, at London yn Martte Lane, soo hit dd. (*Shield*.)

**201.** 14 mony] ye *canc.*    16 tyme] etc. *canc.*    17 hawe] hav *canc.*
22 yn] th *canc.*    27 lysens] off *canc.*

**202.** *William Cely at Calais to Richard Cely the younger at London, 13 November* [*1483*]

s.c.1 53/58. *Badly torn at top of page, and year missing*

Ryght wurschyppff[ull] syr, affter [dew recommendacyon I lowly] recommend me vnto yowre masterschypp. Fur[dermore plese hytt yowre] masterschypp to vnderstond that I hawe [reseyued a letter ffrom yowre] masterschypp wrytten at London the [. . .] the whyche I doo well vnderstond, and where [yowre master-  5 schypp] wrytyth that ȝe marvell I am soo slowe i wry[. . .] know the cawsse whye, ffor I thyncke ther hathe no[t come any] wrytynge ffrom Calles to London, nott thys monyth, nor [no man] that browght any letters. ⌈And⌉ as ffor yowre byll off Pe[yrs Joye I] sent hytt to the martt be Wylliam Hyll, and ther was [no man] ffor  10 Peyrs Joye, nor ffor Crystower Collyns neder, that [w]olld paye the byll; nor noo man yn the martt cowde [t]ell off n[oo] attorney that Peyrs Joye hadd theyr, whatsomewer Peyrs Joy[e] saythe, etc. And whereas yowre masterschypp wrytytyth that I remember lytyll that ye badd me speke to John Delowppys that he schuld  15 wryte to Peter Bayle & Delyte; syr, I haw remember hytt ⌈as myche⌉ as leye yn mye power to doo, ffor I hawe wrytten to hym and allsoo I hawe ben theyr and spoken wyth hym, and he tyllyd me that he hath wrytten to Petter Bayle & Delyte that he schuld delyuer yow beffore Crystemasse a iijᶜ li. ster. more, bysyde that  20 ȝe hawe. And I wott well Petter hadd had the letter or thys tyme, but ther myght noo letters passe, but I thyncke he hathe hytt be thys tyme, or ellys he schall schorttly, etc. Syr, I hawe delyuerd Joysse iiij li. Fl. lyke as ye commavndyd me more than a monyth agon. Also syr, I vnderstond ȝe wyll that I schuld delyuer Joysse  25 yowre x li. Fl. that ys receyued, and the byll off x li. that ⌈ys⌉ to receyue. Syr, heryng ys at viij li. a last bothe at Oste End and Dame, and ⌈Joysse⌉ lye syke yn hys bedd. And allsoo syr, I cannott spare thys mony tell tyme I hawe made a sale, ffor all schall be lykyll inowe to paye yowre costom and subsede; and yett I schall  30 leye owte xx li. off my mony, ffor yowre costom and subsede amowntys iiijˣˣix li. iiij s. ix d. ster. whyche moste be ⌈payd⌉ here wythyn thys xiiij days, and I ffeyr me we schall ⌈nott hawe⌉ the warantys off þe preste mony that was prestyd to the payment off the crew alowyd tyll the nextte schyppynge, ffor hytt wyll be  35

**202.** 4 at] Calles *canc.*    34 to the] thee *repeated*

lykull inow3ght ffor thys hallff yerys wag*y*s, etc. No more vnto
yowre mast*er*schypp at thys tyme, but allmyghty Jh*e*su pr*e*ser*u*e
yow. Wrytten at Call*es* the xiij day off Nove*m*ber.

per yowre seru*au*nte,

40 Wyll*ia*m Cely.

*Dorse*: To my worschyppffull master Rechard Cely, m*er*cha*u*nte
off the Stappull at Call*es*, at London yn M*a*rtt Lane, soo hit dd.
(*Shield*.)

### 203. *William Cely at Calais to Richard and George Cely at London, 18 November 1483*

s.c.1 53/158

Jh*e*su M¹iiij*c*iiij*xx* iij

Ryght worschyppffull masters, affter dew reco*m*mendacyon I lowly
reco*m*mend me vnto yowre mast*er*schypp. Furd*er*more, plese hytt
yowre mast*er*schypp*y*s to vnderstondd that I hawe receyued a
lett*er* ffro*m* yowre mast*er*schyppys beryng date the xiiij day off

5 November, wherby I vnderstond yowre mast*er*schypp hath
receyuedd ij letters lattly fro*m* me, wher*o*ff I beseche yowre
mast*er*schypp to take noon dysplessur off myn lewde and ontrewe
Englysche that I wrote, ffor att that tyme ⌐my¬ mynd was nott
quyett, ffor I was syke, but howsomewer I wrote I ment well. But

10 syr, whereas I wrote to yowre mast*er*schypp*y*s that I trowyd that
3e myght hawe ower owte off yowre charg*y*s here a xxx or xl li.
st*er*.: syr, hytt can ⌐nott¬ now bee sparydd w*y*thowte Godd fforten
yow sale, ffor at that tyme that I wrote yowre mast*er*schypp*y*s, soo
ffolke thowght here that they schuld a hadd a sparynge off a grett

15 partt off ther costom and subsede tyll Aprell, ffor hytt was sayd
⌐at that tyme¬ that Boston fflete wold a ben here schorttly, whyche
schuld a borne a grett partt off thys hallffe yere wag*y*s; and hytt
ys nott ⌐yett¬ comen, wherffor the goodd*y*s that ⌐came¬ at thys last
schyppynge moste bere the charg*y*s off thys hallffe yerys wag*y*s.

20 Wherffor syr, all the mony that ye hawe grown at thys day ⌐here¬
and schall be grown at thys martt wyll be lykull inow3th to answer
yowre costo*m* and subsede and my goddffader Maryons togedder,
etc. Item, syr, I vnderstond be yowre lett*er* yowre mast*er*schypp ys
well content that I hawe delyuerd Joysse the iiij li. Fl. and that he

203. 13 tyme] I *canc.*

⌐hath⌐ receyued yowre mony off Mayhew hackney man ⌐and þat 25
ȝe be content þat Joysse schall occupye þe mony⌐, wheroff I am
ryght gladd, etc. Item, syr, I vnder⟨stond⟩ be yowre sayd letter
that and heryng were at vj li. Fl. a last master Rechard wold hawe
hys mony bestowyd theryn. Syr, herynge ys at viij li. a last and
abowe, etc. Item, syr, I vnderstond yowre masterschyppys wold 30
hawe a ton off goodde Gaskon wyne. Syr, yett ys noon sold here
more than ys retaylyd yn town. They ley hytt all yn sellers wythyn
town and wull suffur noon goo owte, nott as ȝett. Goode Gaskon
wyne ys at vj li. a ton and soo the vyntners off the towne byeth,
etc. No more vnto yowre masterschyppys at thys tyme, but 35
allmyghty Jhesu preserue. Wrytten at Calles the xviij day off
November.

per yowre seruaunte,
Wylliam Cely.

*Dorse*: To my worschyppffull masters Rechard and George Cely, 40
merchauntys of the Stappell at Calles, at London yn Martt Lane,
soo hytt dd. (*Shield*.)


**204.** *William Cely at Calais to Richard and George Cely
at London, 5 December 1483*

s.c.1 53/159

Jhesu M¹iiijᶜiiij×× iij

Ryght worschyppffull syrs and my specyall goode mast[er]s, affter
all dew recommendacyon hadd I lowly recommend me vnto yow.
Furdermore, plese hytt yowre masterschyppys to vnderstond that
⌐I sent⌐ vnto yowre masterschyppys ⌐at the last schypp[yng]⌐ be
George Reede seruaunte wyth my Lordd off Sent Jonys ij letters, 5
oon derectyd to master Rechardd, the toder to yowre masterschypp, the whyche I vnderstond be my goddffader Maryons
wrytyng that the sayd letterys at that tyme were nott receyued,
wheroff I marvell grettly, etc. Item, syr, plese hytt yowre masterschyppys to vnderstondd that Gyessebryght Wan Wynsbarge hath 10
ben here at Calles lattly, but he bowght noo wull, but he was here
ffor matters þat he hadd to doo yn owre courtt, and I spake wyth
hym and I askydd hym wheder John Delowppys hadd wrytten to

203. 33 suffur] now *canc.*
204. 6 derectyd to] yowr *canc.*

Pet*ter* Bayle & Delytte lyke as he promysyd me to doo, and
15 Gyesbryght sayd to ⌜me⌝ that John Delowppys sayd vnto hym at
hys comy*ng* ffourthe that he hadd wrytten to Pet*ter* Bayle to
delyuer yowre mast*er*schyppys as myche mony as he myght spare;
and allsoo John Delowppys sayd vnto Gyesbryght that he wold
make ower a⟨s⟩ myche mony yn thys m*a*rtt as schull content the
20 hole som off yowre byll*ys*, trustyng that ʒowre mast*er*schyppys wyll
doo them as grett plesser yn tyme to come, etc. It*em*, syr, plese
hytt yowre mast*er*schyppys to vnderstondd that oon Tewysday
the ij day off Decemb*er* hytt was agreyd here be courtt that byll*ys*
off xx s. off the s*a*rppler payabull at plessur off the goodd*ys* that
25 cam last ffro*m* London, and allsoo off that ys come now ffrom
Boston, schall be sent ower to answer syche charg*ys* as ben grown
yn Ynglondd. And syr, yff the byll*ys* off plessur com ower I schall
send ower to yowr mast*er*schyppys as myche mony as schall content yowr byll, but wheder thes byll*ys* schall com ower or nott ʒett
30 wee cannott tell. Yff we paye the hole costom here I can send ower
noo mony as yett: I hawe p*a*yd hallffe yowre costom here allredy
and hallff my goddffader Maryons, and I hawe taken Rechard
P*a*rker, John P*a*rkers son off Call*es*, ffor to receyue yn thys martt
all syche specyallt*ys* off yowr*ys* payabu*ll* yn thys martt: ffyrst an
35 oblygacyon ⌜off⌝ Allbryght Allbryghtson *and* Cleys Pet*er*son *and*
ther fellowys, cont*aynyng* xxxij li. st*er*., item, a byll off Jacobb
Gyesbryghtson and Jacob Harmanson whyche I lent them to paye
at thys martt, cont*aynyng* xiij li. st*er*., and the byll off Crystower
Collyns *and* Peyrs Joye cont*aynyng* x li. Fl., whyche he wyll
40 receyue and bry*ng* w*yth* hym home to Call*es* to answer the rest
off yowre costom, etc. It*em*, syr, plese hytt yow to vnderstond that
the alowaunce ys come ower to Call*es* wherby [y]e schall recayue
vppon ⌜yowre⌝ costom *and* subsede yowr condyte mony—iij s.
iiij d. st*er*. off the s*a*rpler whyche ʒe p*a*yd y*n* Ynglondd, and alsoo
45 the ij s. viij d. st*er*. off þe s*a*rpler whyche we p*a*yd here to John
Narsbye, etc. [159 B] It*em*, syr, plese hytt yow to vnderstond that
Boston fflete ys come to Call*es* all yn saffte, thanckyd be Godd,
sawe the Battowll, whych ys ʒett behyndd, and sche hathe yn an C
s*a*rppller*ys* wull *and* ffell, and they here noothynge off her here yett:
50 I pray Godd send her well heder, etc. It*em*, syr, plese hytt yow to

204. 19 martt] al *canc.*          22 that] they *canc.*          23 ij day] the *canc.*
28 ower *ch. from* yowre          35 Allbryght] son *canc.*          38 Crystower] off
*canc.*          43 subsede] the *canc.*

vnderstond that here ⌜ys⌝ a veryaunce ffall betwyxte owre oste
Thomas Graunger and the ffellyschypp off owre logynge, ffor
Thomas Graunger promysyd vs at hys comyng ynto owre logynge
that we schuld paye noo more ffor owre burdd but iij s. iiij d. Fl. a
weke at the hye tabull, and ij s. viij d. at the syde tabull, and nowe  55
hee saythe he wyll hawe noo lesse than iiij s. a weke at the hye tabull
and xl d. at the syde tabull, wherffor the ffellyschypp here wyll
departe ynto oder logyngys; som to oon plase and som to annodder.
Wylliam Dalton wyll be at Robard Torneys, and Raff Lemyngton
and master Brownys man off Stamfford schall be at Thomas  60
Clarkys, and soo all the ffellyschypp departyth sawe I, wherffor
I lett yowre masterschyppys hawe knowlege that ȝe maye doo as
hytt schall lyke yow best, etc. No more vnto yowre masterschyppys
at thys tyme, but allmyghty Jhesu preserue yow. Wrytten at Calles
the v day off December.  65

per yowre seruaunte,
Wylliam Cely.

Dorse: To my worshyppffull masters Rechardd and George Cely,
merchauntys of the Stappell at Calles, at London yn Martt Lane
soo hit dd. (Shield.)  70

## 205. William Cely at Calais to Richard and George Cely at London, 5 January [1483/4]

S.C.I 53/191

Ryght worschyppffull masters aff[ter dew recomendacyon hadd
I lowly recomend] me vnto yowre masterschyppys. Furder[more
plese hytt yowre masterschyppys to] vnderstondd that yowre
Kesten wull [. . .] contrey, but ther ys schett owte off [. . .] viij
clovys meddyll wull, and ther ys sche[tt owte . . . of my god]ffader  5
Maryons that was new packyd [. . .] the wull that was wett wyth
salt watter vij [. . .] very bare, etc. Item syr, yowre iij M¹ijᶜl pellys
[. . .] be sett [a]nd [praysyd] be the prayssers off the Plase at xiij
nobellys an C, a[nd] ther ys wastyd and brent xx ffellys, etc. Item
syr, plese hytt yowre masterschyppys to vnderstond that I hawe  10
ben att Brugys, ffor the case was soo that yowre byll off costom
and subsede off the whych the oon hallffe was ⌜to⌝ payd, and my

204. 53 comyng] to canc.
205. 11 ffor] that canc.

godffader Maryons allso, and oder sarten byll*ys* off the Fellyschyp-
pys, were sent to the martt ffor to be answeryd theyr, ffor to paye the
15  v<sup>c</sup> m*ar*ke that was taken vppe be exchaunge yn Ynglond be mast*er*
Stocker and the solyster ffor the Plase. And I wrote to Rechard
P*ar*ker, i whych I delyuerd sarten specyalt*ys* payabull at the sayd
m*ar*tt, ffor to content the sayd byll*ys*, and he wrote me agayne that
he hadd receyued all that mony y*n* Englysche grotys and Carowll*ys*
20  grot*ys*; and Harry Wayte that y[s] s[ol]esseture ffor the Plase that
schuld paye the mony, and he wolde nott receyue the mony affter
the rate ffor hytt schuld be a grett losse to the Plase, ffor hytt was
nott soo goode as xxx s. the li. Wherffor Rechardd P*ar*ker wrote
that I schuld ffynde the menys that the mony schuld be conveyd
25  home ⌐shortly⌐. Soo I hawe ben at Brug*ys* and schyfftyd the mony
and p*ay*d yowre byll, ffor hytt ⌐ys⌐ caswell bryngyng to Call*es*, the
serche ys soo strayghte at Gravenynge, ffor master Grafftons man
lost l li. st*er*. comy*ng* ffro*m* thys martt, taken ffro*m* hy*m* at Grave-
ny*ng*, etc. Item syr, I spake vnto John Delowpys and I schewyd
30  vnto hym lyke as yowre mast*er*schyppys wrote vnto me, and he
sayd vnto me that Pet*er* Bayle hadd wrytten hym off the same,
howe ⌐he⌐ hadd answeryd yowre masterschyppys. But Peter wrote
John Delowpys that he knew nott at that tyme that John Delowppys hadd sentt ower syche charge as he dydd, ffor John Delowppys
35  saythe he sent ower ij M<sup>l</sup> li. yn letters of paym*en*t. And he hath
sent ower now at thys tyme iij M<sup>l</sup> li., and he hath wrytten a lett*er*
to Pet*er* Bayle, the whyche lett*er* he schewyd me, that Peter schall
content yow at syche tyme as ȝe schall aske it. And John Delowpys
schewyd theyr vnto me that he hathe [191 B] [. . .] me ffor to
40  answer the v<sup>c</sup> m*ar*ke that [was taken vppe be exchaunge yn
Y]nglond, iij<sup>c</sup> li., the whyche he schall [. . .] hathe sent Wyllykyn
hys man [. . .] geder ffro*m* Brug*ys* ffor to bestowe that [mony]
w[hych] he browght w*yth* hym yn wull, and soo he wold haw[e
some o]ff yowre wull w*yth* that he myght hawe a lyk[e respyt]e yn
45  paym*en*t off som off the mony, but I wold graunte hy[m] none
w*yth*owte redy mony all gr. What he wull doo [I] wotte nere, etc.
Item syr, plese hytt yowre masterschypp*ys* to vnderstond that oon
Sonday beffore Twellffeday the Breten fflete and the Frenschemen
cam togeder toffore Call*es* ffrom Sclewse, and that same nyghte
50  sarten schyppys that was mannyd owte off Call*es*, w*yth* the Carvyll

**205.** 18 that] hath *canc.*          22 rate ffor] the lose *canc.*          34 Delowppys]
for *canc.*          44 hawe] some *canc.*

off Hewe, ʒede amongyste hem and toke a xxx<sup>ty</sup> sayll*ys* off Frenschemen, but all the Bretens be scapydd, ffor ther was non off all the
oder schyppys off Englyschemen that hath don any goode, w*yth*-
owte that the Westerne men wyll doo anythynge to the Bretteyns,
ffor all owre oder schyppys when theye sawe the fflete, ⌐they⌐ ran   55
w*yth* the Downys, ffor ther was Brettens and Frenschemen vij<sup>xx</sup>
and xvj sayll*ys*, etc. No more vnto yowre masterschyppys at thys
tyme, but allmyghty Jh*e*su pr*e*ser*u*e and kepe yowe. Wrytten at
Call*es* the v day off Jenyveyr.

                                        p*er* yowre s*er*ua*u*nte,        60
                                        Wyll*ia*m Cely.

To my worshyppffull masters Re*char*d and George Cely, m*er*-
ch*au*ntt*ys* of the Stapp*e*ll at Calles, at London y*n* Martt Lane, soo
hytt dd. (*Shield*.)


**206.** *William Cely at Calais to Richard and George Cely
at London, 29 January 1483/4*

s.c.1 53/160

Ryght worschyppffull syr, aff[ter dew recomendacyon hadd 1 lowly
recommend me] vnto yowre mast*er*schyppys. [Furdermore, plese
hytt yowre master]schyppys to vnderstond tha[t I hawe receyued
from yowre] mast*er*schypp be John Byllsby [a letter whych I hawe
rede] and well vnderstond; and as [towchyn]g yowre warrant [of   5
the] prest mony, hytt ys deductyd vppon yowre costom and
su[b]sede acordyng as oder mens was yn case lyke, a[nd] soo wa[s
the] condyte mony that yowre mast*er*schypp p*a*yd yn Ynglond
alsoo, etc. Item syr, yowre mast*er*schypp wrytyth that ye wyll that
I sch[all] be styll at Graungers tell yowre mast*er*schypp*ys* wrytyth   10
co[ntra]ry. Syr I am glad off the same, ffor I knowe noo plase yn
a[ll] Call*es* that I can be soo well logyd, nor w*yth* a sadder man,
etc. Item syr, as towchyng yowre matt*er* off John Delowppys,
I thyncke that he menys trewly, howbehytt he ys gre[tt]ly chargyd
dyuersse ways; but sartenly, lyke as I hawe wrytte[n] to yowre   15
mast*er*schyppys beffore, he sayd vnto me, and nowe when I was
last at Brug*ys* he schewyd me an lett*er* whyche he sent to Peter
Bayle be Wyll*ia*m Roo, m*er*cer, howe [he] sent ower s*er*ten

        **205.** 51 ʒede] and *canc.*        55 sawe] them *canc.*

specyall*tys* off exch*a*unge and how he wuld ȝe schuld be content
20 and plesyd affore all oder. Wherffor I hope yowre mast*er*schyppys
schall stand yn noo gebardd*ys* off that þat ys betwyxte yowre
mast*er*schyppys and hym, ffor he ys a man that ys yn grett credens
amongyst the Fellyschypp here nowe, and doyth grett ffett*ys*, and
- now Wyllykyn hys man ys here, whyche I am sewer that he wyll
25 bye myche wull or he goo. And allsoo, as ffor warre w*yth* Flaunders
I trust to God we schall nott nede to drede hytt, ffor I vnderstond
they ar nott dysspossyd to hawe noo warre agaynst Ynglond, ffor
ther ys sarten Englysche men that ⌜cam⌝ lattly owt off Flaunders,
and they saye Flaunders wyll hawe noo war, wherffor ther schall
30 come owte off Flaunders, as they saye, an ymbasett to the Kyng*ys*
goode grace off Ynglond. And as ffor the schyppys that were taken
to Sandwyche whyle yowre mast*er*schypp was theyr, hytt ys sayd
here that they were ffrayght w*yth* Brettayns goodd*ys*. Wee here
noo tydyng*ys* off theke schyppys from Brug*ys*, nott ȝett, wherffor
35 wee thyncke here yff the schyppys maye be delyuerd agayne ther
schall noo dysspleser [160 B] [. . . Engl]yschemen resorte to
Brug*ys* [. . .] man trublyd, ffor they that were [. . .] lorddys off
Gaunte wrate to the borow [. . .] to be delyuerd agayne, wherffor
hytt ys th[ought they] wyll nott breke, but syr, syche tydy*n*g*ys* as
40 I can here I schall wrytythe yowre mast*er*schyppys theroff. Item
syr, plese hytt yow to vnderstond that I hawe sold to Wyll*ia*m
Kenett the xxvij day off Jenyvere ij s*a*rppll*erys* off yowre Cott*ys*
wull that came last, and I sold beffore to hym a s*a*rpler medyll
Cott*ys*, off the whyche s*a*rpler off medyll wull I hawe sent vnto
45 yowre mast*er*schypp yn a lett*er* be Robardd Stockers man the
poysse and the n*o*mbyr and rekeny*n*g off hitt. And the poysse *and*
nomb*er* off the ij s*a*rppll*erys* ffyne Cott*ys* ys here vnder ys wrytten.
And Wyll*ia*m Kynett hath promysyd ⌜me⌝ to be at Call*es* w*yth*yn
xiiij or xv days, and than he wyll haue more off yowre Cott*ys* wull,
50 as myche as he can gett old wull ffor, etc. He wold a hadd vj
s*a*rppll*erys* off hytt at thys tyme yff I wold a resspyte hym off ij
p*a*rtys off the mony tyll Est*er*, and he wold a sett me good sewerte
off owre Fellyschypp, but I wold nott, etc. No more vnto yowre
mast*er*schypp*ys* at thys tyme, but allmyghty Jh*es*u pr*e*ser*u*e you.
55 Wrytten at Call*es* the xxix day off Jenyvere.

*per* yowre s*er*ua*u*nte,
Wyll*ia*m Cely.

**206.** 32 masterschypp] ys *canc.*     33 Wee] thyncke *canc.*     55 the] xv *canc.*

Memorandum. The xxvij day off Jenyvere anno iiij$^{xx}$iij sold per me
Wylliam Cely yn the name off my masters Rechard and George
Cely to Wylliam Kynett and Allysaunder Mvnstron, merchauntys   60
off Brugys, ij sarppllerys ffyne Cottys wull, pryce le sacc xx$^{ti}$
marke, nomber and poysse affter wrytten.

No. ij  ------------------  sss j cll.
No. j  -------------------  ss di. xliij cll.
Sum yn saccys  -------------  v sacc hallff, xliiij cll.          65
Sum argent  ----------------  lxxix li. xviij s. o ● ster.

To my worschyppffull masters Rechard and George Cely,
merchauntys off the Stappull at Calles, at London yn Martt Lane
soo hytt dd. (Shield.)


### 207. William Cely at Calais to Richard and George Cely at London, 10 February 1483/4

s.c.1 53/161

Jhesu M$^{l}$iiij$^{c}$iiij$^{xx}$ iij

[Ryght] worschyppffull masterys, affter dew recommendacyon
hadd I lowly recomme[nd m]e vnto yowre masterschyppys.
Furdermore, plese hytt yowre masterschyppy[s] to vnderstond
that Wyllykyn, John Delowpys man, ys here at Calles, and hath
schewyd me that John Delowppys dydd w[ryte] vnto Petter Bayle  5
& Delyte to speke wyth yowre masterschyppys that [John]
Delowppys myght hawe all yowre Cottys wullys that remaynyth
here at Calles, and paye yow ffor hytt yn Ynglond as he hath don
yn tymes past. And soo Wylykyn sayth that Peter Bayle hath
wrytten vnto John Delowppys that he hath spoken wyth yowre  10
masterschyppys ffor hy[tt], and how that yowre masterschyppys
answeryd Peter Bayle that [I] schuld be demenyd lyke as yowre
masterschyppys wrote me. Wherffor Wyllykyn sayth that John
Delowppys prayd me that I wuld se[ll] no more off yowre Cottys
wull tell yowre masterschyppys wrate me off the same matter. And  15
I hawe answeryd hym agayne I wold kepe noon ffor hym, but take
the markett as hytt comyth wythowte yowre masterschyppys
wrytyth me the contrary, ffor I tellyd hym he hath nott deseruyd
yn payng off the last, to hawe resspyte off thys; but he sayth to me
hytt schall be schorttly payd, etc. Item, plese hytt yowre master-  20
schyppys to vnderstond that here ys come to Calles, whyche ys

purpossyd to come ynto Ynglond, sarten merchauntys off Flaunders, the whych sarten off the gooddys belonggyth vnto that was
taken yn the schyppys that were browght ynto Sandwyche hawen
25  at the seson the Kynggys goode Grace was theyr; wherffor the
sayd merchauntys hath browght a letter ffrom the yong Dewk
Phellyppus and the Councell off Flaunders, derectyd vnto the
Mayer and Fellyschypp off the Stappell at Calles, dessyryng them
to wryte vnto the Kyngys goode Grace that he wyll be ffaverabull
30  vnto hys sewgyettys and ⌜that⌝ hys goode Grace wyll see they maye
hawe restytyschon off ther gooddys that ys taken be hys sewgeyttys,
lyke as he hath don yn hys londd off Flaunders: dyschargyd the
Kynggys sewgettys and made hem restytyschon off ther gooddys.
And soo thes merchauntys comyth ower ynto Ynglond and schall
35  hawe wryttyng ffrom the Fellyschypp off the Stappell here to
Kyngys goode Grace, and allssoo to the Mayer off the Stappell
ffor to labour ffor them yn ther matter, etc. Item, syr, plese hytt
yow too vnderstond that the Councell off Flaunders hath lett crye
yn euery towne to be redy yn harnesse as sone as the towne bell
40  rynggyth, and allsoo, he that wyll take wagys to entter hys name
to the Regent [Dorse] [f]or to wythstandd the Dewke Maxymelyanys, ffor they ff[eyr . . .] because he hath gooten ij townes
off Flaunders: Rovbey and Lyell; but as ffor as wee knowe here,
they wyll hawe pese wyth Ynglond, etc. No more vnto yowre
45  masterschyppys at thys tyme, but allmyghty Jhesu preserue yow.
Wrytten at Calles the x day of Feuere.

                                         per yowre seruaunt,
                                         Wylliam Cely.

Item syr, here beth dyuersse merchauntys off Brugys, and they
50  hawe bowght myche wull, and they hawe ben yn handd wyth me
ffor yowre Cottys wull, bott I can sell them none wythowte they
maye hawe Passe day off payment as they hawe off oder men, wherffor hytt ys to thyncke they put noo mystruste yn Flaunders, etc.

To my worschyppffull masters Rechard and George Cely,
55  merchauntys off the Stappell at Calles, at London yn Martt Lane,
soo hit dd. (Shield.)

207. 23 the whych] owte canc.    31 hys] seg canc.    43 Flaunders] Dov
canc.    and] lyll canc.    52 as they hawe] Passe day off payment canc.

**208.** *William Cely at Calais to Richard and George Cely at London, 24 February 1483/4*

S.C.I 53/162

Jhesu M¹iiijᶜiiijˣˣ iij

Ryght worschyppffull masters, affter all dew recommendacyon I lowly recommend me vnto yowre masterschyppys. Furdermore, plese hytt yowre masterschypp[ys] to vnderstond that I hawe sold yowre iij [th]owsand ijᶜ and oodd ffell off Cottyssold whych cam wyth the last fflete ffor xiiij nobullys the C, to Claysse Petterson 5 *and* Wylliam Ardson off Dellffe. Syr, [they] be nott yett all delyuerd, but as sone as they be delyuerd I schall send yo[wre] masterschyppys the rekenyng off hem, etc. Item, plese hytt yow[re] masterschyppys to vnderstond that Gyesbryght Van Wynsbarg[e] ys com to Calles, and soo he hath spoken to me to wytt yff I hadd 10 any wrytyng ffrom yow off the matter that Peter Bayle spake to yowre masterschyppys off, and I tellyd ⌐hym⌐ naye, lykewyse as hytt ys, that I hawe noo wrytyng ffrom yow, nott lattly, wherof he sayd he marvellyd. Never the less, he dysyreth to hawe the rest off yowre Cottyssold woll, and he wold make me a byll yn the name 15 off John Delowpys and hymsellffe off the hole som off mony that the wull schuld draw, made payabull at plesur, and yowre master-schyppys schuld chese wheder ȝe wold be payd yn Ynglond or here. Yf yow wold hawe ⌐hit⌐ yn Ynglond ȝe schuld be payd wythyn ij monthys or lesse: yff ȝe wyll be payd here ȝe schall be 20 payd be Ester and schorttlyer, ⌐and⌐ ȝeff yowre masterschyppys wyll hawe hytt soo. And I answeryd hym agayne þat I myght nott sell non to no man wythowte redy mony, nor wyll nott wythowte yowre masterschyppys commavnd ⌐me⌐ to doo. Than he sayd he trowyd I schuld hawe wrytyng ffrom ⌐yow⌐ schortly ffor that matter, 25 ffor he sayd he supposyd yowr masterschyppys were content and plessyd, or ellys schall be schorttly; ffor he saythe he hath sent ower lattly to Petter yn byllys iijᶜ li. ster. and now wyth thys passage, ijᶜ li. ster. Syr, I thyncke he menys trewly, ffor he ⌐sayth⌐ yff ȝe myssetrust hym he wyll sett yow yn asewerte, how that euer the 30 world goyth, etc. But as ffor Flaunders, I thynke they wyll nott breke wyth vs; but syr, ther be sarten banyschyd Englyschmen that be oon the see, hath taken v or vj sayle off Spaynarddys ladyn wyth wyne comyng yn to Flaunders, etc. Furdermore, plese hytt yowre

**208.** 7 they be] all *canc.*    11 Bayle] sap *canc.*    29 ster.] ffor yowre *canc.*

35 masterschyppys to vnderstond that ther ys an ordynaunce made
here be courtt ffor the alldormen off Calles whyche be ffremen off
the Stappell, how tha[t] they schall lewe ther alldermanschypp and
all oder jurdyccyons yn Calles be ⌈a⌉ day exprest, and be only off
the Stappull, or ellys to be crossyd the Plase. And soo oon Saterday
40 last was, they all were comavnded to be at courtt vppon payne off
ther haunsse; [162 B] and soo all thes that ther names heraffter
ffollowyth were there at court: ffyrst, John Chawley, Harry
Achamber, Thomas Benett, Alyn Redeman, Romenett Dessall,
Wylliam Fethyan, Robard Byngham, Wylliam Muston, John
45 Deram. And there the Lefftenaunt schewyd vnto them how that
the Fellyschypp ffownd them grewyd wyth the[m] becawse they
were sworne ffyrst vnto the Stappell and browght vpp theyr, and
syns sworne vnto the jurdyccyon off the towne, and obserue that
yn many thyngys contrey the welth off the Plase, wherffor ther ys
50 an ordynaunce made they schall come yn and sche[w] hem al
ffremen off the Place and fforsake ther alldermanschypp and
jurdyccyon off the town; or ellys yff they wold nott, they schuld
schewe hytt theyr, and they schuld be dyschargyd off ther ffredome
off the Stappell. And soo they promysyd all theyrffor to dyscharge
55 them off ther towne, and toke hem oonly to the ffredom off the
Stappull, sawyng only twayne—Romenett Desall and Wylliam
Fethyan—whyche beythe crossyd the Plase, etc. Item, syr, I
beseche yowre masterschypp to remember to send ower the
pampelett that I schall make my rekenyng bye, that I myghte
60 clere hytt, etc. No more vnto yowre masterschyppys at thys tyme,
but allmyghty Jhesu preserue yow. Wrytten at Calles the xxiiij
day off Feuerell.

per yowre seruaunt,<br>
Wylliam Cely.

65 Item, syr, my master Rechard wrate me that I or Joysse schuld
purvey ffor onyvn seedd off Sent Thomar. Syr, hytt ys soo wee can
gett non, ffor hytt ys at xx s. a pownde.

Dorse: To my worschyppffull masters Rechard and George Cely,
merchauntys off the Stappell at Calles, at London [y]n Martt
70 Lane, soo hitt dd. (Shield.)

**209.** *William Cely at Calais to Richard and George Cely
at London, 29 February 1483/4*

S.C.1 53/163

Jhesu M<sup>l</sup>iiij<sup>c</sup>iiij<sup>xx</sup> iij

Ryght worschyppffull masters, affter all dew recomendacyon I
louly recom[mend] me vnto yowre masterschyppys. Furdermore,
plese hytt yowre masterschyppys to vnderstond that I hawe
receyued a letter lattly ffrom yowre masterschyppys beryng date
the xvj day off Feuere, be ⌐the⌐ tenor wheroff I vnderstond that  5
Peter Bayle hathe ben wyth yowre masterschyppys ffor that John
Delowpys myght hawe the rest off yowre Cottys wull, and how
that yowre masterschyppys hath graunttyd hym wyth that ȝe maye
be payd off the oon hallff ⌐at London⌐ betwyxte thys and Ester,
and the rest wythyn iiij monthys affter the delyuerey off the sayd  10
wull, etc. Syr, hytt ys soo that Gyesbryght and Wyllykyn bethe
here, and thys letter that yowre masterschypp sen[t] vnto me was
hadd to Brugys wyth sarten letters off John Delowppys; and soo
John Delowppys sent hytt heder agayne, and a letter to Gyesbryght
and Wyllykyn how that Peter Bayle wrate vnto hy[m] how that  15
he hath a promyse off yowre masterschypp lyke as ȝe hawe wrytten
yn yowre letter to me. But I sayd vnto them that I hawe promysyd
the wull beffore to anoder man, but never the lesse I hawe taken
a Goddys peny off hem acordyng to the pryce off the Place, and
when hytt ys wayedd they schall make a byll yn John Delowppys  20
name and Gyesbryght, off the hole som off mony that the wull
schall drawe ⌐vnto; *and* the byll⌐ made payabull at London at
yowre pleser. And allsoo Gyesbryght hath promysyd me that hytt
schall be payd be Ester, the hole sum at the ffarthest. Syr, I hope
hytt ys sewer inowȝth, ffor they ar ffast men, and allsoo that Peter  25
Bayle hath promysed to content yowre masterschyppys how-
someuer the world goys. And allsoo, I thyncke Flaunders wyll nott
breke wyth vs, ffor we putt hem yn noo myssetruste here, ffor ther
ys noo man here that sellythe new wull but hytt schall be Ester
martt or he schall hawe hys mony, etc. Item, syr, yowre master-  30
schypp wrytyth me that I wrate yow nott whatt mony I receyuedd
ffor the iij sarppllerys wull I sold vnto Wylliam Kenett. Syr, hytt
was all yn Nemyng grottys sawe xxiiij li. ster. yn Carowllys, whych
I schall send ower vnto yowre ⌐masterschypp⌐ yff yee wyll that

209. 7 hawe] yowre *canc.*

35 I schall soo doo, and I trow I schall gett more yff ȝe wyll hawe
more, etc. Item, syr, plese hytt yowre master [163 B] schyppys to
vnderstond that the Dewke Maxymelyanys ys yn Flaunders wyth
myche pepull, and he hathe sarten townys yn Flaunders submyttyd
vnto hym; and as on Tewysday the xxv day off Feuere, he was
40 wyth a thowsand horssys at Brugys gattys ffor to a comvn yn, but
they schytte the gattys and wold nott lett hym com yn. Than he
sawe that, and sent a messonger to the gattys desyryng that ⌐som⌐
off the rewlers off the town schuld come to the gatys and speke
wyth hym, but noon wylld come, wherffor he retornyd backe
45 agayne vnto hys oste. And soo he lyethe styll wythyn iiij Dewche
meyll off Brugys, and hys desyre ys no more but to hawe vj
persones at hys wyll: that ys, iij off Brugys, ij off Gaunte, and oon
off Iper; wherffor the comen pepull wold haue hym ffull ffayne,
sawe v or vj off the hedys be off a contrary apenyon, but ffolkys
50 that cam ffrom Brugys sayth that they thyncke hytt schall nott be
long or they wyll lett hym yn at Brugys, etc. Item, ⌐syr⌐, on
Fryday the xxvij day off Feuerell cam passage ffrom Dower, and
they saye that oon Thursday affore cam fforth a passonger ffrom
Dower to Calleswardd, and sche was chasyd wyth Frenschemen
55 and drevyn ynto Donkyrke hawen, etc. Item, syr, plese hytt yow
to vnderstond that I hawe sold to Claysse Petterson and hys
ffellows off Dellff yowre Cottys ffellys that cam last, and they hawe
cast owte iiijˣˣ reffewse ffellys, and the rekenyng off the sayd ffellys
ys on the toder syde wrytten. No more vnto yowre masterschyppys
60 at thys tyme, but allmyghty Jhesu preserue an⟨d⟩ kepe yow. Wrytten at Calles the xxix day off Feuere.

per yowre seruaunt,
Wylliam Cely.

[163 C. *Third page of folded sheet*]

Jhesu Mˡiiijˣˣ iij

Memorandum. The xxviij day off Feuere anno vt suppra, sold per
65 me Wylliam Cely yn the name off my masters Rechard and George
Cely to Claysse Petterson, Wylliam Ardson, John Wylliamson,
Derycke Johnson off Dellff, iij Mˡjᶜ l Cottys pell, prys le C xiiij
nobullys sterlyng. Argent---- Cxlvij li. ster.
Item, to be receyuedd yn redy mony the on
70 hallff, sum --------------------------- lxxiij li. x s. ster.

209. 51 on] Thurs *canc.*

Item, lent them be an oblygacyon to pay
þe xx day off August nexte ensewyng ----- xxxvj li. xv s. st*er*.
    Item, lent them be anoder oblygacyon,
payabull þe xx day off Feuere nexte, oder ---- xxxvj li. xv s. st*er*.
    Item, syr, as ffor the lxxiij li. x s. st*er*. whyche I schuld ⌐a⌐ 75
receyuedd yn hondd, I hawe receyued theroff but xx li. x s. st*er*.
yn Nemy*ng* grott*ys*, and crownys, and the rest ys liij li. st*er*.,
whyche I lent them be a byll off her hond to paye at Passe, ffor they
browght butt lyttull mony heder w*yth* hem because off trublyng
be the waye w*yth* sowdears off Maxymelyanys; but the men ar 80
sewer inow3th: they hawe bowghte here abowe xvj M¹ ffell*ys* ⌐at
þis tyme⌐.

[163 D]: To my worschyppffull masters Rec*hard* and George Cely,
marchaunt*ys* off the Stappell at Call*es*, at London yn Martt Lane,
soo hitt dd. (*Shield.*)      85

### 210. William Cely at Calais to Richard and George Cely at London, 3 March 1483/4

s.c.1 53/164

Jh*e*su M¹iiij*ᶜ*iiij*ˣˣ* iij

Ryght worschyppffull masters, affter all dew recommendacyon
hadd I lowly reco*m*mend me vnto yowre mast*er*schyppys. Furdermore plese hytt yowre mast*er*schyppys to vnderstond that I send
vnto yow be the brynger heroff, whooys name ys John Clyffton,
atorney ffor Harry Kebyll, clossyd yn thys lett*er*, a lett*er* off 5
paym*ent* off John Delowpys and Gyesbryght Wan Wynsbarge,
m*er*chaunt*ys* off Brug*ys*, payabull at Est*er* nexte comy*nge*, con-
teyny*ng* ij*ᶜ*xlij li. xvij d. st*er*lyng, etc. Item, syr, I send to yowre
mast*er*schyppys wrytten yn thys sayd lett*er* the nombyr and wayght
off vj s*ar*pll*erys and* a poke wull sold to the fforsayd m*er*chaunt*ys*, 10
as herevnder þe tenor wheroff ffollowythe. *And* no more vnto
yowre mast*er*schyppys at thys tyme, but allmyghty Jh*e*su pr*e*ser*u*e
yow. Wrytten at Call*es* the ⌐iij day off M*ar*che⌐.

p*er* yowre s*er*ua*u*nt,<br>Wylli*a*m Cely.    15

M*e*morand*u*m. The xxviij day off Feuere a*n*no iiij*ˣˣ*iij, sold p*er* me

**210.** 13 Calles the] xxviij day off Feuere *canc.*

Wylliam Cely yn the name off my masters Richard and George
Cely to John Delowppys and Gyesbryght Van Wynsbarge,
merchauntys off Brugys, vj sarppllerys and a poke ffyne Cottys
20 wull prys le sacc xxᵗⁱ marke sterlyng; nomber and poysse affter
apperyth.

No. iij — ss. lij cllys.                        Sum totall yn saccys—
No. v — ss. lxvij cllys.                        xviij sacc xiiij clls.
*No. xxij — ss. di. xl cllys.                   Sum totall argent—
25 *No. x — ss. di. xxxv cllys.                 CCxlij li. xvij d. ster.
*No. xv — ss. lij cllys.
No. iiij — ss. lviij cllys.
No. vij — s. di. xxv cllys.

The whych som off ijˡᶜ xlij li. xvij d. ster. to be payd at London at
30 Ester nexte comyng. Item, syr, No. x and No. xv and No. xxij ys
the iij sarppllerys the whych was the rest off the xix sarppllerys
schyppydd yn Jun laste, etc.

[*Written in later by G. Cely:*]
Cxxix li. xviij s. vj d. o ● ster.
Cxj li. xvij s. v d. o ● ●

35 *Dorse*: To my worschyppffull masters Rechard and George Cely,
merchauntys off the Stappell at Calles, at London yn Martt Lane
soo hytt dd. (*Shield.*)


**211.** *William Cely at Calais to Richard and George Cely*
*at London, 17 March 1483/4*
s.c.1 53/165

Jhesu Mˡiiijᶜiiijˣˣ iij

Ryght worschyppffull syrs and my specyall good masters, affter
all dew recomendacyon I lowly recommend me vnto yowre masterschyppys. Furdermore, plese hytt yowre masterschyppys to
v[nde]rstond that I sent vnto yow at the last passage be oon Roger
5 Kynton, a letter conteynyng the rekenyng off þe sale off iij Mˡ jᶜl
pellys sold ⌐to⌐ Claysse Peterson and hys ffell[ysch]ypp. Item,
I sent vnto yowre masterschyppys at the sayd passage b[e] oon
John Clyffton, a letter off the sale made to John Delowpys and
Gyesbryght Van Wynsbarge off vj sarppllerys and a poke ffyne

210. 24 xxij *ch. from* vij

Cottys, and I sent vnto yowre masterschyppys closyd yn the sayd 10
letter a le[tter] off payment off the ⟨sayd⟩ John Delowpys and
Gyesbryght payabull at Ester ne[xt] conteynyng CCxlij li. xvij d.
ster., etc. Item, syr, oder salys I hawe mad[e] non ʒett, but I trust
I schall doo schorttly. Here hathe ben Hollo[nders], moo I vnderstond wyll be schorttly. I myghte a sold yowre old [fellys] but 15
I wold sell som off yowre new ffellys wythall, etc. Item, syr, [her]
ys myche adoo betwyxte the Dewke Maxymelyanys and sarten
townys off Flaunders. The Dewke hathe ben affore Brugys,
wherffo[r] Gaunte and Brugys and oder townys off Flaunders be
afferdd off hym, ffor they kepe strayght watche and wardd yn 20
euery towne dayly, and they off Brugys hath beheddyd v or vj off
the dwellers off Brugys tha[t] toke Dewke parte. But noo man
saythe nor doyth nothyng to noon Englyscheman, but that they
maye resorte too and ffroo as they hawe doon yn tymes past;
saweng only men ben affardde off Frenschemen, ffor they hawe 25
taken ij Englyschemen comyng ffrom Brugys betwyxte Donckyrcke
and Gravenyng: on ys John Eston and the toder ys oon Jamus,
Robard Stockers man. Item, syr, on Fryday last past, on Rychard
Awrey, that was master off my Lord Dennam schypp, ʒede fforthe
a warffare yn a schyppe off hys owne, and toke yn merchauntys and 30
sett hem alond at Dower, and at Dower toke yn passage to Calleswardd agayne. And as he cam to Callesward, ij men off warre off
Frensche mett wyth hym and ffawghte wyth hym, and theyr he
was slayne and dyuersse moo off hys company: they saye viij or
ix persones, oon whoois sowllys Jhesu hawe mercy. And soo on 35
Fryday at affternone the Frenschemen browghte hem ynto Donkyrke hauen, and Wylliam Bryerley ys yn the same schypp, and
dyuersse londmen moo: what they ar I cannott tell ʒe⟨t⟩. [Dorse]
[Item syr], I vnderstond that schyppyng ys begon at London. Syr,
I pray God ther may be ynowghe schyppyd to pay thys hallff 40
ʒerys wagys that ys grown at the vj day off Apryll nexte, ffor that
most be payd all off thys schyppyng, ffor here ys nothyng toward
hytt; and allsoo a grett partt off the prest mony, that was prestyd
yn October to pay the flete wyth, most be repayed off the same,
ffor myche off hytt ys oonpayd, but yowrys ys repayd. Wherffor 45
syr, all syche goodys that comyth now at thys schyppyng moste
paye hole costom at þe ryvall off hytt, etc. Furdermore, plese hytt
yow to vnderstond that Roger Wyxtan off Laysetter ys chosen
Lefftenaunt ffor the next seson affter thys man, and he to be here

50 at Calles be the last day off Apryll, etc. No more vnto yowre
masterschyppys at thys tyme, but allmyghty Jhesu preserue yow.
Wrytten at Calles the xvij day off Marche.

per yowre seruaunt,
Wylliam Cely.

55 To my worshyppffull masters Rechard and George Cely, merchauntys off the Stappell at Calles, at London yn Martt Lane, soo
hit dd. (*Shield.*)

### 212. *William Cely at Calais to Richard and George Cely at London, 25 March 1484 (misdated 1483)*

s.c.i 53/166

Jhesu M¹iiij^c iiij^xx iij

[R]yght worschyppffull and my specyall goode masters, affter all
dew recommendacyon hadd I lowly recommend me vnto yowre
masterschyppys. Furdermore, plese yowre masterschyppys to
vnderstond that I hawe sold iij M¹ off yowre Cottys pell, wheroff
5 ij M¹v^c beythe off yowre vij M¹ ffellys schyppyd at the portt off
London the x day off Junn, anno iiij^xxiij, and the rest ys off yowre
v M¹iiij^c pell schyppyd at the portt at London the xxiiij day off
Jowll, anno iiij^xxij, etc. Syr, I wold ffayne a sold moo new ffellys
wythall, but I kowde nott, ffor ther ys grett plenty off old ffellys
10 yn town: iij old agaynest on new, and allsoo the vij M¹ pell schyppyd
yn Jun anno iiij^xx iij were sorre blemeschyd, as brent yn the
schyppys bothe tymes, as they were schyppyd twyse, etc. Syr, the
rekenyng off the fforsayd sale off iijM¹ pellys hereaffter yn thys
letter ys conteynyd, etc. Furdermore, plese hytt yowre master-
15 schyppys to vnderstond that thys day, Owre Lady Day, all the
Fellyschypp w[ere] asemlyd yn the hall, and ther was my Lord
Dennam and master Donsta[l] and master Marschall, wyth oder
off þe Councell that be made ffree off the Stapp[ell] now late, and
soo theyr the old Mayer was dyschargyd, and ther was putt yn
20 alecschon off the new Mayer Syr Wylliam Stocker, master Yorcke,
and master Wymbysche; and soo Syr Wylliam Stocker ys choosen
Mayer off the Stappull ffor thys yere fforthe, etc. Furdermore syr,
plese hytt yow to vnderstond that Gyesbryght Van Wynsbarge ys

212. 4 wheroff] iij *canc.*    13 rekenyng] off the sale *canc.*    fforsayd] iij M
*canc.*

com to Calles, and soo hee hath taken schew to bye wull, and hytt
ys soo that my Lord Lefftenaunt off thys town off Calles as thys 25
day sent ffor my master Lefftenaunte off þe Stappull, schewyng
vnto hym yn thys wyse, how that sarten town dwellers off Calles
hathe ben at Brugys and hath bowght wyne and oder merchaundyse, the ⌐whych⌐ ys arestyd att Newportte ffor syche goodys that
Englyschemen hathe taken be the see belongyng vnto men off 30
Oostendd and other plases off Flaunders. Wherffor my Lord
schewyd vnto the Lefftenaunt how that thes men that hathe her
gooddys soo arestyd at Newportte desyryth to hawe lysens to rest
Gyesbryght and oder merchauntys off Brugys that be here, ffor
plege ffor the goodys that ys soo arestyd at Newportt. But master 35
Lyefftenaunte ansueryd my Lordd agayne be the avyce off the
Fellyschypp, and sayd vnto hym yn thys wyse: Yff soo be that
Gyesbryght schuld bee arestydd here and trublyd, hytt schuld
cause a grett ynconvenyens to the Stappull, ffor Gyesbryght and
hys ffellow be the men that dothe grettys ffett off any marchauntys 40
that comyth heder, ffor the gooddys that they hawe bowght here
thys ʒere drawythe abowe xxv M¹ li. ster.; wherffor yff they schuld
be stoppyd ther wold come noo moo merchauntys heder, the
whych schuld cause a grett stopp.And yff merchauntys ⌐straungers⌐
myght nott resortt heder that men myght make sale off her 45
gooddys, [166 B] they cowde make noo payment vnto the sowdears
off ther wagys, ⌐andd allsoo⌐ schuld cause men to londd ⌐agayne⌐
syche gooddys as they were ynschyppyng wythall. And allsoo hytt
was answeryd my Lordd yn thys wyse: how that ther ys an entercourse made betwyxte the Kyng off Ynglond and the londd off 50
Flaundders yn Dewke Phyllyppus days, and syns conffermyd be
Dewke Charllys, and syns that conffermyd be Dewke Maxymelyanys, how that any merchaunde off Ynglond, beyng ffree off
Stappell, may goo sayff and come sayff ynto Flaunders, bothe hys
body and goodys at all tymes, wythowte any ynteryppcyon ffor any 55
hurttys doon to any man off Flaunders be see or lond be Englyschemen, and yn lyke wyse all merchauntys off Flaunders or off theke
partyes, comyng to Calleswardd to bye Stappull merchaundyse,
schall goo ffree and come ffree wythowte any ynteryppcyon yn
lyke wyse. And thys entercoursse ys entryd yn the Stappell regester 60

212. 25 Calles] sent canc.      29 arestyd] and canc.      34 ffor] the ples canc.
41 comyth ch. from cam      47 wagys] whyche canc.      54 and] a canc.
55 ynteryppcyon] and lyke canc.      60 Stappell] res rech canc.

off old tyme. W*yth* the whyche my Lordd ys well content, w*yth*
that the Stapp*e*ll wyll sendd ij sadd men off the Fellyschypp vnto
Gaunte to the Councell off Flaunders to know wheder they wyll
abyde be that en*ter*coursse or nott; and soo sartten men schall be
65 apoyntyd to goo to Gaunte w*yth* wrytyng vnder Stap*e*ll seall ffor
to know an answer, etc. but Gyesbryght ys att hys lybbarte, and
he byethe wull here as he hathe don yn tymes past, etc. It*e*m, syr,
I hawe made wrytyng whych yowre masterschyppys schuld a hadd
or thys tyme, but ther hathe noo passage goon thys xiiij days, etc.
70 No more vnto yowre mast*er*schyppys at thys, but allmyghty
Jh*e*su pres*er*ue yow. Wrytten at Call*e*s on Owre Lady Day Anuncyon.

p*er* yowre s*er*ua*u*nte,
Wyll*i*am Cely.

[166 C]
75 M*e*m*orandum*. The xxiiij day off M*a*rche, a*n*no iiij*ˣˣ* iij, sold p*er* me
Wyll*i*am Cely yn the name off my masters Rechard and George
Cely to Gyesbryght Henryckson, Jacob Gye[s]bryghtson, Cornelys
Arnson, Deryck Jacobson, off Dellff, iij M¹ Cott*ys* pell*ys*, prys le
C, xiiij nobull*ys* sterlyng*ys*:

80                                    Argent ------ Cxl li. st*er*.

   Item, the oon hallff amovnt*ys* -  lxx li. st*er*.      ⎫
   Wheroff I receyuedd y*n* redy                          ⎪
   mony ----------------------- xxxiij li. vj s.          ⎪
                                viij d. st*er*.            ⎬ lxx li. st*er*.
85 And lent them be a byll off her                         ⎪
   hond to paye at Sensyon m*a*rt                          ⎪
   nexte ---------------------- xxxvj li. xiij s.         ⎪
                                iiij d. st*er*.            ⎭

   Item, lent them be an oblygacyon to pay the xxiij
90 day off September next ---------------------- xxxv li. st*er*.
   Item, lent them be annoder oblygacyon payabull at
   Cold m*a*rtt nexte -------------------------- xxxv li. st*er*.

[166 D] To my worschyppffull masters Rechardd and George Cely,
m*er*chaunt*ys* off the Stappull at Call*e*s, at London yn M*a*rtt Lane,
95 soo hyt dd. (*Shield.*)

**213.** *William Cely at Calais to Richard and George Cely at London, 27 March 1484*

s.c.1 53/167

Jhesu M¹iiijᶜiiij×× iiij

Ryght worschyppffull syrs and myn especyall goode masters, affter
all [dew] recommendacyon hadd I lowly recommend me vnto yowre
masterschyppy[s]. Furdermore letyng yowre masterschyppys hawe
knowleyge th[at] I hawe receyued a letter lattly ffrom yow beryng
date the xj day off Marche, be the tenour wheroff I vnderstond that   5
yowre m[aster]ᴦschyppisᴨ hathe receyued ij letters ffrom me, conteynyng the twoo sallys made, [one] ᴦv[nto]ᴨ Claysse Peterson and
ᴦþe toderᴨ to John Delowpys, and allsoo that yowre mas[ter]-
schyppys hathe receyuedd ᴦJohn Delowpysᴨ letter off payment,
etc. Item, syr, ᴦIᴨ sent vnt[o yow at] thys passage be Raff Lemyng-   10
ton a letter conteynyng a sale made t[he xxiiij] day off Marche to
Gyesbryght Henryckeson, etc. Item, syr, I vnderstond [be] yowre
sayd letter that yowre masterschyppys be purpossyd t[o schypp]
now at thys ᴦtymeᴨ xx sarppllerys wull. Syr, yff ᴣe cowde hawe
goode schyppys [it] were nott yll ᴦdonᴨ and yowre masterschyppys   15
schyppyd somwhat more, ff[or I trust to] be well ffornyschyd wyth
mony here ffor to paye the costom and subsed[e]. Allsoo syr,
I thyncke as ffar as my symppull reson geyff me, hytt ys more
sewrer schyppyng now than schall be hereaffter, ffor dyuersse
c[auses] etc. Syr, as ffor old Henleys wyddowe, sche hathe ben   20
sowyr syck a grette whyle, but sche ys yett alyue. And sche ffortune
to dye I schall send yow wordd as schorttly as I can, etc. Furdermore, plese hytt yowre masterschyppys to vnderstond that I wrate
yow a clawse yn the letter that Raff Lemyngton bryngyth yow,
how that the Lefftenaun[te] and the Fellyschypp here hath hadd   25
commenycacyon wyth my Lord Lefftenaun[t] off Calles ffor the
entercourse betwyxte Ynglond and Flaunders, and soo my Lordd
ys owre goode lordde yn all matters. And soo oon Satterday the
xxvj day off Marche the Fellyschypp here apoyntyd v persones off
the Stappull to goo as ymbasett ffor the Stappell to Dewke Phyl-   30
lypp and hys Councell off Flaunders, and thes men be poyntyd
to goo: Thomas Amerys, Constabull, Robardd Addlyn, Wylliam
Bentham, Wylliam Dalton, John Ynge; and on Tewysday nexte
they schall departe thederwarddys, and thay schall hawe power

**213.** 9 John Delowpys *over canc.* that        20 old] Henly *canc.*

35 off my Lordd, and allso off the Stappell vnder seall, to hawe
commenycacyon w*yth* the Concell off Flaunders and to conclude
yff they can to gett a savegard vnder the seall off Flaunders that
noo merch*a*unt off the Stappell schall be trubullyd yn Flaunders ffor
any maleffett doon be any oder Englyscheman to any p*er*son off
40 Flaunders, w*ytho*wte hytt be ffor tresspasse be hym don. And yn
lyke wyse my Lord Lefftenaunt off Call*es* schall gewe a sawegarde
to all merch*a*unt*ys* ˹off Flaunders˺ comy*ng* to Call*es* to bye Stappell
merch*a*undyse that noo man sch[all doo] nor saye to them nor her
gooddys at Call*es* nor y*n* the m*a*rchesse, ffor noo maleff[ett doon] be
45 any Flemy*ng* to any Englyscheman, w*ytho*wte hytt be ffor tresse-
passe be hym [don]. [*Dorse*] Item, syr, plese hytt yow to wytt that
I send vnto yowre mast*er*schyppys be the bryng*er* off thys lett*er*,
whoo ˹is˺ name ys James Jarfford, atorney ffor Steven Gybson,
m*er*cer off London, sellyd yn a canvas bagg—xxiiij li. st*er*lyng,
50 wheroff ys yn Carowll*ys* grott*ys* xxiij li. st*er*. and iij angelett*ys*
wrappyd yn pap*er*—xx s., etc. Item, syr, plese hytt to vnder⟨stond⟩
that hytt hath plesyd the Fellysshypp to chese Thom*a*s Noneley
and me collecters ffor thys quarter ensewyng, etc. No more vnto
yowre mast*er*schyppys at thys tyme, but allmyghty Jh*e*su pres*er*ue
55 yow. Wrytten at Call*es* the xxvij day off M*a*rche.

p*er* yowre s*er*ua*u*nt,
Wyll*i*am Cely.

To my worschyppffull masters Rec*hard* and George Cely,
merch*a*unt*ys* off the Stappull at Call*es*, att London yn M*a*rtt Lane,
60 soo hitt dd. (*Shield.*)

**214.** *William Cely at Calais to Richard and George Cely
at London, 10 April 1484*
s.c.i 53/168

Jh*e*su Mˡiiij^c iiij^xx iiij

Ryght worschyppffull syrs *and* my especyall goode masters, affter
all dew recommendacyon had I lowly rec*o*mmend me vnto yowre
mast*er*schyppys. Furdermore, plese hytt yowre mast*er*schyppys to
vnderstond that I hawe sold to Adryan Wyll*i*amson *and* hys

**213.** 50 grottys] xxx *canc.*
**214.** 1 syrs] af *canc.*

ffellows of Layth, xv<sup>c</sup> off yowr Cott*ys* ffell*ys* schyppyd yn Jowlle,  5
a*nn*o M<sup>l</sup>iiij<sup>c</sup>iiij<sup>xx</sup>ij, whych sale ys conteynyd hereaff*ter* yn thys lett*er*,
etc. Furdermore, lyke hytt yowre mast*er*schyppys to wytt that
⌐I hawe⌐ receyued a lett*er* ffro*m* yow beryng datte the second day
of M*a*rche, and yn the same lett*er* the nomb*er* and wayght off
yowre ⌐wull⌐ schyppyd [a]t thys tyme, and allso yn the sayd lett*er*  10
yowre warant off xx s. off the s*a*rpler, conteynyng xxvij li. st*er*.
Item, syr, I hawe receyued anoder lett*er* ffro*m* yowre mast*er*-
schypp*ys* beryng date the ij day off Aprell, the whych lett*er* I hawe
redd and well vnderstond, and acordyng to yowre sayd lett*er*
I schall demene mysellff that schall be ⌐to⌐ yowre plessur, off the  15
whych I schall wryte yow y*n* my nexte lett*er* more at large, etc.
Furdermore, plese hytt yow to vnderstond that thys day the x day
off Aprell the wull fflete came to Call*es*, all yn saffte, thanckyd be
Godd. Ther be Frenschemen on the see, but they sturryd ⌐nott⌐
at thys seson, and wee knowe"noon oder wyse here but wee schall  20
hawe warre be lond w*yth* Fraunce thys somer, etc. Syr, I wold
a wrytt yowre mast*er*schyppys off moo matters, but my space was
but schortt and the passage tarryd ⌐nott⌐ but ȝede at the same tyde
that hytt came ffro*m* Dower, but I schall wrytt yow more at large
w*yth* the nexte passage, etc. No more vnto yowre mast*er*schyppys  25
at thys tyme, but allmyghty Jh*es*u p*re*ser*u*e yow. Wrytten at Call*es*
le x day off Aprell, etc.

p*er* yowre s*er*ua*u*nt,
Wylli*a*m Cely.

M*emorandum*. The iiij day off Aprell, a*nn*o vt supp*r*a, sold p*er* me  30
Wylli*a*m Cely ffor and yn the name off my masters Re*ch*ard *and*
George Cely to Adryan Wylli*a*mson, Deryck Deryckson, Garrad
Laurensson, Garrad Stevenson, Henryck Ottson, Claysse Doo *and*
Gyesbryght Moresson, off Laythe, xv<sup>c</sup> Cott*ys* pell*ys* prys le C,
xiiij nobull*ys*. Argent ----------------------- lxx li. st*er*.   35
    Item, receyued yn hond yn Nemy*n*g grot*ys* -- xxxv li. st*er*.
    Item, lent them be ther oblygacyon payabull
at Senschon m*a*rtt next, s*um* ----------------- xxxv li. st*er*.

*Dorse*: To my worshyppffull masters Re*ch*ard and George Cely,
mer*ch*aunt*tys* of the Stappull at Call*es*, at London yn M*a*rtt Lane,  40
soo hitt dd. (*Shield*.)

**214.** 8 I *over canc.* a     21 warre] wyth *canc.*    24 yow *over canc.* hytt
32 Deryck] Dowsson *canc.*

*In George Cely's writing*:

Item, delyueryd vnto John Veneke yn ffyne gowllde to make a ryng ffor my wyffe, xxvj p[en]ny wayghgh d. qtr., sum—sum liij s. vj d.

## 215. *William Cely at Calais to George Cely at London, 14 April 1484*

s.c.1 53/170

Jhesu M<sup>l</sup>iiij<sup>c</sup>iiij<sup>xx</sup>ii[ij]

Ryght worschyppffull masters, after all de[w recommendacyon hadd I lowly recommend me vnto] yowre masterschypp. Furdermore, plese hytt y[ow to vnderstond that the] wull fflete aryued at Calles the x day off Ap[prell] [. . .] and the moste parte off yowre
5  wull ys londyd and hit [. . .], etc. Furdermore syr, I vnderstond be yowre wrytyng that Pett[er Bayle] hathe ben wyth yowre masterschyppys, and schewed yow howe hee w[old] fynd yow sewerte for syche wullys that John Delowpys schall take of yowrys at Calles. Syr, yf the sewertys be of substaunce and abydyng then
10  I wold avyse yow to take hem, or ellys nott, ffor what world wee schall hawe wyth Flaunders I cannott sey. I feyr me they wyll breke wyth vs, ffor the men that were sent be the Stappell to the Lordys ⟨of⟩ Gaunte to labur a safgard for all the Fellyschypp of the Stappull be come home agayne da[y]lesse, for they were anssweryd
15  how that Flaunders hath susteynyd ma[ny] grett hurttys don be Englyschmen, and noo restytuschon made h[em] agayne, wherffor they can sustayne noo lenger; and as for any sawegard, they wyll gewe non. Wherto thys schall growe I cannott saye, wherffor syr, yf ȝe can hawe goode sewerte of Petter Bayledelett, hytt were well
20  doon, whatsumeuer ffortune hereafter. And syr, I pray yow to wryte me yn what case Peter hath sett yowr masterschyppys ffor syche that I delyuer John Delowppys here, ffor Wyllykyn, John Delowpys man, ys here, and he tellyth me that John Delowpys hath a letter ffrom yowre masterschyppys of the same matter; but
25  I schall delyuer hym noo wull tell I hawe wrytyng ffrom yow agayne, howbehytt the man ys goode inowȝthe were we yn sertente of pes betwyxte Flaunders and vs. But syr, yf ȝe can be sett sewer of yowre mony theyr, hytt were a goode wey, ffor ther ys noo

214. 43 qtr., sum] lvj s. *canc.*

215. 7 schewed] how *canc.*        16 restytuschon *ch. from* restysttuschon
22 ffor] I wull *canc.*        24 matter] how *canc.*

merchaunte that comyth here that payth redy ⌐mony⌐ ffor any new
wull that he byeth here, etc. Furder syr, a⟨s⟩ tochyng the matter   30
that yowre masterschypp wrote ⌐me⌐ of Thomas Whyte, meser;
yn serten syr I spake wyth hym, and hee dynedd at home wyth my
nostys, howbehytt he knew nott me, and theyr he schewyd how
that þat matter ley betwyxte anoder man and yow, howbehytt he
sayd sche hadd yow more yn fawer than the toder man, but syr,   35
ʒe hawe hys goode wyll, etc. Item, syr, Wylliam Sallford ys come,
and I spake wyth hym and wellcomyd ⌐hym⌐, and he tellyd me how
that yowre masterschypp and þat oder gentyllwoman wheyr at
apoynt yn that matter, of the whych I was ryght gladd, and soo
he sayd he was, but hee speryd me noon oder questyons, nott ʒett.   40
And syr, hytt ys sayd here be many persones here, how that ʒe ⌐be⌐
sewer to her, wyth the whych [170 B] [. . . syr, I am] well content
and ryght glad therof, and syr, [. . .] that knowyth yow, both
merchauntys and soudeers, [. . . commen]de yow grettly, sayng yf
that gentellwoman [schuld be worth d]ub[be]ll that sche ys ʒe were   45
wurthy to hawe her. And [as for any] makyng of serche of yowre
delyngys ⌐here⌐, I trow ther ys noo man that makyth any. Yff they
doo they nede goo noo ffarther than the bokys yn the tresery, wher
they may ffynde that yowre sallys made wythyn lesse than ⌐thys⌐
ʒere amovntys above ij M¹ li. ster., where that the person that   50
laboryd for to a be afore yow, he and hys broder hadd nott yn thys
towne thys twellwe monthys the oon hallff of that, etc. Furdermore syr, yowre masterschypp wrytyth me yf theyr were any goode
Gascon wyne here ʒe wold hawe a tonne therof. Syr, here ys noo
goode wyne to gett for noo mony as yett, but I vnderstond ther   55
schall come from Brugys som wythyn x or xij days, wherof I trow
I schall gett a tonne or a pype at leste, whych I schall send yow,
etc. Item, syr, I sent vnto yow at the last passage be oon Thomas
Bland of Boston a letter wheryn ys wrytten the sale made to
Adryan Wylliamson and ⌐his⌐ ffellyschypp of Laythe of xvᶜ Cottys   60
pellys, prys le C, xiiij nobullys: argent lxx li. ster., etc. Item, syr,
thys same day þe xiiij day of Aprell, ther ⌐cam⌐ iij passongers ffrom
Dower, and ther was ij grett schyppys of war of Frenschemen
chasyd them ynto the hawen mowthe; and the passages hadd had
but a myle to a ron farder they hadd be taken. And owre men of   65
warre lyeth all yn Cambre, etc. No more vnto yowre masterschypp

---

**215.** 34 howbehytt] sche *canc.*      37 wellcomyd] hytt *canc.*      40 hee] was
*canc.*      49 thys *over canc.* a      51 yow] hath *canc.*

at thys tyme, but allmyghty Jhesu preserue yow. Wrytten at Calles
the xiiij day of Aprell.

per yowre seruaunt,
Wylliam Cely.

70

To my worshyppffull master George Cely, merchaunt of the
Stappell at Calles, at London yn Martt Lane, soo hyt dd. (*Shield.*)

### 216. *William Cely at Calais to George Cely at London, 23 April [1484]*

s.c.1 53/171

Jhesu [. . .]

Ryght worschyppffull master, a[ffter all dew recommendacyon
I lowly recomend me] vnto youre masterschypp. Fur[dermore
plese hytt yowre masterschypp to] hawe knowlege that I hawe
rec[eyued a letter from yow be Robert] Heryckys man, the whych
5   letter I haw[e redd and well vnderstond] howe that yow wyll that
I schall [. . .] I send vnto yowre masterschypp be [a man whois]
name ys John Burne, draper of Calles, [s]elyd [yn a le]ddern bagg,
[xl li.]. The space was soo schortt I cowde gett no m[ore], but wyth
the ne[xte] sewer passage I schall send ower xx or xxx li. ster. more,
10  but more t[han] that I cannott send yow afore thys martt be don.
Syr, I schall send syche specyalltys of yowrys that be payabull yn
thys martt be Wylliam Hy[ll] to receyue the mony for them,
whyche amovntys an Cx li. ster. Syr, I haw[e] payd partt of yowre
custom and subse⟨de⟩ redy and the rest most [be] payd as sone as
15  the martt ys doon, ffor the sowdears call scharply ffor [ther] wagys,
wherffor ther can be noo resspyte geven to noo man, etc. Item, syr,
as ffor syche ⌈newellys⌉ as ys here, plese hytt yow to comen wyth
the brynger herof and he wyll tell yow, for I darre nott wryght,
etc. No more vnto yowre masterschypp at thys tyme, but allmyghty
20  Jhesu preserue yow. Wrytten at Calles the xxiij day of Aprell
yn hast.

per yowre seruaunt,
Wylliam Cely.

*Dorse*: To my worschyppffull master George Cely, merchaunte of
25  the Stappull at Calles, at London yn Martt Lane soo hitt dd. (*Shield.*)

215. 71 master] s R *canc.*

216. 17 newellys *over canc.* newlys

**217.** *William Cely at Calais to Richard and George Cely*
*at London, 28 April 1484*

S.C.I 53/172

Jhesu M¹iiij°iiij×ˣiiij

Ryght worschyppffull masters, after all dew recommendacyon
I lowly recommend me vnto yowre masterschyppys. Furdermore,
pl[e]se hytt yowre masterschyppys to v[n]derstond that I sent vnto
yow be Joysse, the brynger of thys letter, selyd yn a canvas bagge,
xl li. sterlyng, and allsoo I sent vnto yowre masterschyppys wyth    5
the last passage be oon John Burne, draper of Calles, yn a leddern
baggys oder xl li. ster., etc. Syr, as ȝett I can gett noo more
sterlyng mony, etc. Furdermore, syr, plese [h]ytt yow to vnderstond that Wyllykyn, John Delowppys man, come ower ynto
Ynglond wyth thys pa[ssage], wherfor I thyncke he wyll comen     10
wyth yow for yowre Cottys wull. [Syr], I wyll avyse yow to graunte
hym noon oder wyse than to pay h[ytt] at Calles acordyng to the
ordenance or the wull passe the towne; fo[r] hytt ys known well
inowȝth here that Wyllykyn comyth ower fo[r] noon oder thyng
than to make bargaynys wyth serten persones yn Ynglo[nd] for    15
syche wullys as they hawee at Calles, and allso the delyng of
dy[vers] men yn Ynglond wyth John Delowpys ys known, wherfor
ᵀherᵀ wyll be a g[rett] serche made schorttly and forfettys schall
be levellyd, for hytt ys known well ᵀhereᵀ that Petter Bayle &
Delytt answeryth at days yn Ynglon[d] for myche of the wull that   20
John Delowpys byethe here. But as for yowre delyngys, knowyth
noon man wythowte they serche Petter Baylys bokys, as I thyncke
grett serche schall be made, for the forfett ys levellyd oon som
persones allredy, but they be nott ȝett openly namyd. And as for
yowre wull, I trust to Goodd hytt schall be sold and hawe redy   25
mony for hytt wythyn thys month, for I am yn a goode waye for
hytt allredy wyth goode men, and to paye as they fett hytt, an
to fett hytt wythyn a monthe: Robard Legayneard *and* Collard
Messedawȝth be the men. No more vnto yowre masterschyppys at
thys tyme, but allmyghty Jhesu preserue yow. Wrytten at Calles   30
the xxviij day of Aprell.

per yowre seruaunte,<br>
Wylliam Cely.

Item, syr, plese hytt yow to vnderstond that old Henley ys

**217.** 12 than *ch. from* that          17 Ynglond] ys *canc.*          25 redy] for *canc.*

35 wyddowe hath beyn spechelesse thys day *and* a hallfe, and sche ys
   nott lyckely to leve a day tyll an endd, wherfor here ys oon John Garnett, sowdear. And he hathe ben w*yth* me, and schewyd me howe
   that hee ys bownden w*yth* yong Henley to Harry Francke y*n* an
   oblygacyon of lx li. st*er*. to paye aft*er* Henley moder desseicyth;
40 and hee saythe when hee was at London hee spake to Harry
   Francke [*Dorse*] of the same oblygacyon, and Harry Francke
   tellyd hym how he hadd maded a lett*er* of atorney to yowre mast*er*-
   schypp for to receyue the sayd lx li., whe⟨r⟩for John Garnett saythe
   hee hath gootten as myche goodd*ys* yn hys hondd*ys* of old Henleys
45 wyddows as schall ⌐drawe⌐ the som of lx li. st*er*., for the whyche he
   saythe he wold the oblygacyon were sent ower that the sayd
   goodd*ys* myght answer hytt for hys dyscharge, etc. Item, syr,
   I hawe sold ij s*arplers* of youre fyne Cott*ys* wull that cam last,
   wherof the rekeny*ng* of the sale ys clossyd yn thys lett*er*. I hadd
50 lycens of the Leften*a*nt to make sale as for soo myche as sone as
   hytt was awarddyd, etc.

To my worshyppffull masters Rech*ard* and George Cely, m*er*-
ch*a*unt*ys* of the Stappell at Call*es*, at London yn M*a*rtt Lane, [soo]
hytt dd. (*Shield.*)

## 218. *William Cely at Calais to Richard and George Cely at London, 9 May 1484*

s.c.1 53/174

Jh*e*su M¹iiij°iiij×× iiij

Rygh[t wor]schyppffull syrs and ⌐my⌐ especyall goode masters,
after all dew [recommendacyon] had I lowly reco*m*mend me vnto
yowre masterschypp*ys*. Furdermore, plese hy[t yowre master]-
schypp to vnderstond that I hawe receyued ij letters lattly from
5 yow, oon bery[ng date at] London on Sent Georgeys Day, the
toder wrytten the xxx day of Apre[ll, the whyche] letters I hawe
redd and well vnderstond. And as towchyng John De[l]oppys
matt[er, hyt] ys soo that he *and* Gyesbryghte be come to Call*es*,
and soo they hawe bowghte [here] allredy abowe ij° s*arplerys* end
10 wull, and soo they hawe spoken to me for yowre wul[l]; schewynge
how that they hadd wrytyng fro*m* yowre mast*er*schyppys how that

217. 35 hallfe, and] ys *canc.*     38 Henley] yn *canc.*
218. 1 masters] fur *canc.*          5 London] the *canc.*

Peter de Baylle hadd madde a bargayne wyth yow and was thorow
wyth yow for all yowre wull. Neverthelesse I sayd vnto them
agayne how that I hadd noo syche wrytyng from yowre masterschyppys, wherfor I hadd sold parte of hytt, and promysyd all 15
togeder; wyth the whych answer they were sory; neverthelesse
they labrede styll to me for hytt and desyryng they myghte hawe
⌜hit⌝ that was oonsold, and they wold paye here or þe wull passe,
acordyng to þe ordenaunce as oder men wold do. And þan I sayd
I wold nott wythowte they wuld ⌜take⌝ serten of yowre clyfte 20
⌜wull⌝ wythall; and they ansuerryd me agayne that nowe they
wuld bye as myche end wull as they myght, and noo clyffte wull,
but when they cam nexte agayne they wuld hellpe ⌜me⌝ awaye
wyth all þe clyfte wull. And soo yn conclusyon before a broker
I hawe sold hem xix sarplers and a poke fyne Cottys at þe pryse of 25
þe Plase, and to paye redy mony here or hyt passe. Soo vppon thys
I hawe wayed vnto hym allredy ij sarpllerys, and when I sent to
hym to rekon, he delyuerd me a letter from yowre masterschyppys,
whych letter holdyth yn lyke as he sayd vnto ⌜me⌝ afore, howe that
yowre masterschyppys be thorow wyth Peter de Baylle fore yowre 30
wull. But neverthelesse I sayd vnto John Delowppys I wold doo
noon oder wyse than acordyng to þe bargayne that I made wyth
hym here. Than he answeryd me agayne, yf soo be that yowre
masterschyppys be nott content to ⌜be⌝ payd for yowre wull yn
Ynglond acordyng to þe comenycacon that Peter Debayle hadd 35
wyth yowre masterschyppys ⌜at London⌝; what, he wyll paye me
here acordyng to þe bargayne þat he hadd made wyth me here.
And vppon thys I shalle receyue a byll of hym for þe sayd ij
sarpllerys wull. But syr, yf soo be that yowre masterschyppys maye
be sett sewer for yowre mony at þe day, hyt were as good to 40
receyue ⌜yowr mony⌝ there as oder wyse, howbehytt þe days ar
long, but he sayth he schall sett yow þe best Lombarddys yn all
London to sewerte. Syr, all þe wull þat he hath bowghte here at
thys tyme, he muste paye ⌜hit⌝ yn Ynglond yn lyke wyse. And as
for þe matter that I wrate to yowre masterschyppys of þe or- 45
denaunce, ʒe schall nott nede put noo dowghtys yn hytt. Item,
as for Flaunders, wheder wee schall hawe warr or peese I cannott
seye as ʒett. Meny folckys be goon to þe martt, and noo man doo
nor sayth noothyng to them as ʒett: what they wyll comyng from

50 the mart I wott neyr. Meny men feyr that Flaunders wyll nott be
owre frenddys long, because Englyschemen hathe doon hem soo
many schrowyd tornys on þe see now lattly, etc. Item syr, I praye
yow þat I maye hawe an answer gayne schortly from yowre masterschyppys, for I schall not delyuer to John Delowpys no more of
55 þis wull tell I hawe wryttyng from yowre masterschyppys how
I schall be demenyd wyth hym for hytt. [Dorse] [Item syr, p]lese
hytt yow to vnderston⟨d⟩ that my master Rechard schall [receyue
o]f Hew [Paddley the bryn]ger of þis letter, sellyd yn a lyttyll bagg,
sum xiij li. vj s. viij [d.] ster. for hys [. . .] Crystower Collens, etc.
60 Item syr, the sayd Hew Paddley desyryd me to wryte [yowre]
masterschyppys how that he ys from hys master Wylliam Dalton.
He ys owte of [prentis]hodde, and he departyd from hys master
wyth goode lowe and leve, wherfor he sayth yf [yowre] masterschyppys were destytewyd of a seruaunte, and yf hys seruyce
65 myghte plese yow he w[old do] yowre masterschyppys seruyce
afore all þe men yn þe world, etc. No more vnto yowre [master]-
schyppys at thys tyme, but allmyghty Jhesu preserue yow. Wrytten
at Calles the ix day of M[ay].

per yowre seruaunt,
70 Wylliam Cely.

To my ryght worshyppffull masters Rechard and George Cely,
merchauntys of þe Stappell at Calles, at London yn Martt [Lane,
soo hy]tt dd. (Shield.)

### 219. Thomas Kesten at Calais to Richard and George Cely at London, 17 May [? 1484]

s.c.1 53/175

Jhesu M¹iiijᶜlxxx ijjj[?]

[Reuere]nt syr and syris, I recomaund me vnto you after all dewe
recomendacyon wn [. . .] that I remember full often [yn] myn
enwardely sorow and care that I am indet[y]d w[nto your father
for] pardon, and now the dewte [d]ewe to you his cheldren, etc.
5 The wiche som ys grete [. . .] know nat how [to] content the saide
som / I am faullen into so grete [. . .] etc. John Prout, then Mayre
of the Stapell, and Richard Stokys toke vpon vs for [. . .] the wiche
we toke in honde at the wrytteng and enstance of the Erle of
W[orcester, Tresurer of] Englond, of whom we hadde wrytteng

218. 50 Meny] feyr canc.　　56 demenyd ch. from demynyd

to haue sauyd vs harmeles, but in con[. . .] the Towre Hyll at  10
London, and as he deyed, deyed owre socowre, by the mene [. . .]
vndon by the same // And you wnderstond the curcumstance of my
hurt also we[. . .] as Richard Stockys as by the preyncepall, you
ar any man wolde pety me/ I th[. . .] in the pouerte the wiche
I muste contenew in all my lyffe, the wiche ys to my gr[ete . . .]  15
a gret schorteneng of my lewe dayes // I am nat alone in sorow,
wherffore I g[. . .] for I se dayly kengys, pryncys and oder estattys,
ffrom the heyeste degre to the low[est . . .] wytty and riche that
both hathe fayllid them, wherffore in thes worlde ye [may see
m]en now hey no[we] lowe, nowe riche now pore, now alywe now  20
dedde / he that hathe his lyffe and hathe no goodys ys worst at esse
that euer hadde owght // So mayst⟨er⟩ys yt ys so wyth me that I must,
of fyn force and pouerte and nat of wylle, take on of ij wheyes, of
the wiche neyder ben goode. On ys yf I may haue of you for your
parte longer respitte, I to pay you also sone as I can ar may,  25
I leveng a wery pore lewe, as I myght be abyll to kepe an howsse,
I to be bovnden vpon my feythe and trowthe and as I am a
Christende to pay you and euery man also sone as I can. If you ar
any oder wyll haue my serves I to do them sarves better schep then
any man / ande they that wyll borde wyth me to scape by that  30
mene. And if God and you, my goode maysterys, wolde helpe me
wyth your goode worde and wylle wpon a goode mareage I myght
the soner helpe bothe you and oder, whervpon ys on of my moste
truste // The wiche mareage to my proffet I cannat opteyne, nor
credence, tyll I may be at my leberte and I deeng somwhat in the  35
worlde eyder for myselffe ar som oder men // The wiche I dar nat,
nor oder men wyll nat truste me, tyl I go at large to the moste
menys consentys that I am in whay to contente my credetors //
Wherfore I beseche you for your parte that I may haue your
sewerte and promysse in wrytteng: I to go vntrubeled ffor you ar  40
any for you, the terme of iij yer, and as I delle wyth you in that
tyme to the vttermeste of my power/ so you to delle wyth me
forther / If euer Gode ar the world wyll schew me the worlde
wyth any fauer yt wyl be in that tyme // And as I can stonde in
casse, you schall se me delle wyth you and wyth euery man that  45
you schal be plessed, and after I can abyll myselfe in the saide
terme of iij yer I the more [. . .]ly to assure you to the wttermeste
of my power for your paymentys // And if it wyll plesse you at the

219. 20 pore, now] dedde canc.        22 mast⟨er⟩ys: ms. mastys

reuerence off Jhesu to graunt me this, and the rather that I haue
50 ben an olde sarvaunt and entende to owe you all my sarves my
liwe dewreng, and I and all myn to pray for you, I beseche you to
pety me. Thowe I dede nat allwheys well, I hadde hopid it scholde
nat haue comen to so evell conclevseon / Maysterys if yt wyll plesse
you to graunt me the saide respit th[e]n as abovensaid, I wyll abide
55 in this contre / and ⟨if⟩ nat, then I muste of fyn force take the toder
whey: that ys to departe owght of this contre there and theder
as I schall neuer be abyll to contente you, nor non oder; the wiche
I wolde be [lothe] to do, bothe for myn owne pore name and for
my cheldrenys, as Jhesu deffende. And I com in presson, schold
60 ner com owght I dowte me / Besecheng you of your gode answer
to Calles, at I may know [your] wylle in this, as my gretteste som
that I am indettid. Hopeng of your gode welles / The remenaunt
I h[ope] to h[aue] schortely, wyth the grace of Jhesu, who kepe you
and all yours. Wretton at Calles the xvij day of May,
65            wyth full hewy hart, I kepeng my howsse, etc.
           Per your owne bothe sarvaunt and beddeman,
           Thomas Kesten.

Dorse: To the reuerent syr and syres [Richard C]ely and Gorge
Cely, merchauntys of the Stapell of Calles, dwelleng in London in
70 Marte Lane, soit dd.


**220.** *William Cely at Calais to Richard and George Cely
at London, 22 May [1484]*
s.c.1 53/176. *Very torn and discoloured*

           Jhesu M¹iiijᶜiii[jˣˣiiij]

[Ryght wor]schypf[u]ll syrs and my specy[all good masters, after
all dew recommendacyon had]d, I lowly recommend me vn[to
yowre masterschyppys. Furdermore, plese h]ytt yowr masterschyppys to vnderstond that I ha[we receyued from] yowre
5 masterschyppys ⌈to letters⌉, oon beryng date the xij [day of May
the whyche I hawe] redd and well vnderstond, and how that yowre
[masterschyppys wuld that I schuld] delyuer noo wull to John
Delowpys wythowte hee bry[ng redy mony. . . .] Delowppys
thow3te verylly as thys seson that he schul[d . . .] delyuer hym be

**219.** 60 Besecheng] of *canc.*
**220.** 5 xij *or* ? x[v]ij

yowre masterschyppys commavndement a[. . .] soo Wyllykyn hath 10
ben at Calles all thys seson a[. . .] but now I hawe answeryd hym
that he nor noon oder [man schall not hawe] hytt wythowte he
bryng hys redy mony. And nowe he [desyryth me that] I wull kepe
hytt whyle he gooyth to Brugys, and [ he hath promysyd me that]
he wyll be here agayne wythyn iiij days, and [. . .] I see be them 15
they wyll nott lett þe wull owtt of [. . .] gladd ȝee bee clere wyth
hem, for ⌐yf⌐ they cowde a [browght hyt] abowte, they wold a kept
yowre masterschyppys [. . .] plese them, etc. Syr, I hawe anssweryd
Wyllykyn and yf he co[m nott wythyn] iiij or v days I schall take
my nexte merchaunts, but hee saythe [that he wyll not] fawte, etc. 20
Syr, as for þe v sarpllerys medyll wull that I hawe sold to [John de
Selonder of Mekelyn] they be nott yett delyuerd, for the man ys
nott ȝett comen, but he hat[h] sent me a letter that he wyll be here
wythyn iiij or v days, and [he] hath sent me an C li. Fl. vppon
rekenyng. Syr, as sone as þe wull ys delyuerd I schall send ower 25
the rekenyng therof, and of that John Delowppys schall hawe to,
etc. Syr, yowre masterschyppis wryttyth me for syche mony that
remaynyth be me, yf that I can make hytt ower wyth gode men at
iij or ⌐iiij⌐ monthys ȝe wyll that I schall doo hytt. Syr, here ys ⌐but⌐
few men come ower ȝett þat ben of any substansse that takyth vpp 30
any mony be exchaunge to regarde, but syr, as for þe substance of
yowr mony, ⌐yf⌐ yowre masterschypp ⌐wyll, ye⌐ schall hawe ⌐hyt⌐
yn Ynglond wyth as lyckull aventer and yn schorter space, etc.
Item syr, plese hytt yowre masterschyppys to hawe knowleche here
hathe ben a grett vent of end wull: ther was noon soo grette, nott 35
of a grett whyle, yn ⌐soo⌐ schorte space and soo lyckull mony
receyued yn hondd. Here ys Grafton, Pontessbere, Bettson, Cloppton and oder dyuersse that hath made swepestake. Wherfor, syr,
I thyncke they wyll make wull dere yn Cottyswold ⌐thys ȝere⌐, for
they purpose to doo a grett fett, and for to begyn betymes, but 40
I trow all ther mony schall nott bee soo reddy to them as yowrys
schall be to yowre masterschyppys. Howbehytt they put [no]
dowghtys y[n] Flaunders, syr, hytt ys oonlyckly for to be all well
⌐there⌐ longe, etc. Item syr, John Dawy [whyche] was Cap[teyne]
of the Carvyll of Hew, he ȝede alond yn Selond at Yermevthe and 45
h[e] y[s] taken and se[t] yn preson yn Medyllborow, and was
lyckely for to be put to dethe for serten men that he robbyd oon
þe see of that contrey, but þe men that wastyd Selond flete wer

**220.** 26 of that] to *canc.*          28 men] for *canc.*          48 wer] hath *canc.*

alond at Flyssyng *and* at Camffer and ta[k]en dyuersse men of þe
50 same contrey and hathe them to schypp w*yth* hem, and sayth loke
howe they s*er*ue John Dawy they wyll s*er*ue thes men þe same, etc.
No more vnto mast*er*schyppys but Jh*e*su pr*e*s*er*ue you. Wrytten at
Call*es* þe xxij day of Maye.

p*er* yowre s*er*ua*u*nte,
55                                Wyll*ia*m Cely.

*Dorse*: To my worshyppffull masters Re*ch*ard [and] George Cely,
m*er*chau*n*tys of þe Stappell [of C]all*es*, at London y*n* M*a*rtt Lane
soo hit dd.

### 221. *William Cely at Calais to Richard and George Cely at London, 3 June 1484*

s.c.1 53/177

Jh*e*su M¹iiijᶜiiijˣˣiiij

Ryght worschyppffull syrs and especyall good [maste]rs, affter all
dew recomm[endacyon] had I lowly recommend me vnto yowr
mast*er*schyppys. Furdermore, lyke hytt yowre [master]schyppys
to wytt thatt I hawe rec*eyu*ed a lett*er* fro*m* yowre mast*er*schyppys
5 be Hanykyn, the whych I hawe rede and well vnderstond. And as
towchyng the matt*er* of John Delowppys, Wyllykyn hys man ys
here and I hawe wayed [vnto] hym att thys tyme viij s*arp*l*er*ys
moore of yowre Cott*ys* wull, and soo ther remayn[yth be]hyndd
x s*arp*l*er*ys, wherof ys viij fyne and ij meddyll, whyche at hys
10 c[omyng agayn I schall] delyu*er* vnto hym, whyche, as hee saythe,
schall nott be longge [erst]. And as [for] Jo[hn De Selonder ?]
I hawe delyu*er*d hym. I hawe receyued a byll of hys handd
p[aya]bell [at] plesu[re], whyche I muste kepe by me tyll þe rest
be delyu*er*ed, and then we s[c]hall [hawe both] yn oon rekeneny*n*g,
15 and make þe byll acordyng to þe promysse [ma]de betwyxte yowre
mast*er*schyppys and Pett*er* Vayle & Delyt. And as soon as all þe
wull ys delyu*er*ed I [schall] send ower þe rekeny*n*g and poysse
þerof, and allsoo þe letter of paym*en*t of þe [rekeny]ng; and as for
yowre clyfte wull, he sayth þat John Delowppys wyll doo þeryn
20 þat yowre mast*er*schyppys schall ˹[be] plesed˺, etc. Syr, for any
oder newes here, wee hawe [noon] here but goode as ȝett,

220. 49 *ms.* ben alond

221. 7 here] and I hawe wayed *canc.*     sarplerys] of yow *canc.*     10 vnto
hym] at *canc.*     20 etc.] as for *canc.*

thanckyd be Godd, for all Englys[ch]me[n] were but [cor]t[e]sely
entretyd y*n* Flaunders [and] y*n* theke p*a*rtyes, for þer wa[s] noo
n[oder tru]bblyd but John Dawe yn Selond, and yett I vnderstond
he ys but c[ortesl]y entredyd be þe[m] wherfor meny men 25
thynckythe here that Flaunders nor theke p*a*rtyes entendythe noon
ewyll to noon Englyschemen; for Flaunders ys well satysfyed ⌐for⌐
þat þe Kynge ⌐hath⌐ made restycyon to syche men þat hathe ben
yn Ynglond to la[b]ore for þer god*y*s that was taken on þe see be
Englyschemen, etc. Item syr, plese hytt yowre mast*er*schyppys to 30
vnderstond that ȝe schall receyue be þe John Twyssull, the brynger
herof, an C li. st*er*. sellyd y*n* an bagge: hytt ys Carroll*y*s grott*y*s,
etc. Item ⟨syr⟩, plese hytt yow to vnderstondd that þe byll þat
yowre mast*er*schypp sent ower of þe rekeny*n*g of yowre wull of þe
last schyppyng, yowre mast*er*schypp made yn þe byll but vj 35
s*a*rpll*er* medyll wull, and xxj fyne wull, and þer ys yn dede vij
s*a*rpll*er*ys medyll and but xx fyne, for No. xxvj ys yn þe byll ⌐made⌐
fyne, but hytt ⟨ys⟩ medyll yn dede, as vppon þe s*a*rpl*er*ys makethe
mencyon, bothe be þe M and be þe pat*er*nosters on þe koytt*y*s, and
allsoo I caused to open hytt on þe syde, and hytt ys medyll ⌐wull⌐ 40
yn dede, etc. Item syr, hereafter ys wrytten yn thys lett*er* þe
wayghte a[n]d þe rekeny*n*g of yowre v s*a*rpl*er*ys medyll Cott*y*s
sold to John Delonder, etc. Item syr, I delyuerd to Hanykyn for
hys cos[tys] s*u*m vj s. viij d. Item syr, I hawe delyuerd to Joysse
for yowre jayd v s. Fl. for to bye gere for here, whyche yowre 45
mast*er*schypp muste deducke oon hys wag*y*s, etc. No more vnto
yowre [mas]tersch[ypp at] thys tym[e, b]ut allmyghty Jh*e*su p*re*-
s*er*ue yow. Wrytten at Calles þe iij day of June yn haste.

> p*er* yowre s*er*uau*n*t,
> Wyll*i*am Cely.    50

[177 B]: Jh*e*su M¹iiij°iiij××iiij

M*emor*and*um.* The [x]xv day of Ma[y] sold p*er* me Will*ia*m Cely for
and ⟨yn⟩ þe name of my masters Rechard and George Cely to John
Deselonder, m*er*chau*n*t of Meke[l]yn v s*a*rpll*er*ys medyll Cott*y*s
wull, prys le sacc xiiij m*a*rke. Nomb*er* and poysse herafter followyth. 55

*Sarpler numbers in left margin illegible.*

| [. . .] ss lxv clls. | Sum tot*a*ll yn sacc*y*s— |
|---|---|
| [. . .] ss di. xxxvj clls. | xiij sacc xlj clls. |
| [. . .] ss lxxiij clls. | |

**221. 25** wherfor] eu*er*y man *canc.*    **33** ⟨syr⟩: *ms.* syrye

[. . .]  ss xvj clls.
60 [. . .]  ss di. xxxj cl.          Argent—Cxxv li. xj s. viij d. st*er.*

[*Dorse*] To my worschyppffull masters Rechard and George Cely,
m*er*chaunt*ys* of þe Stapp*ell* at Call*es*, at London yn M*a*rtt Lane,
soo hytt dd. (*Shield*.)


## 222. *Margery Cely to George Cely at Calais* [c. *14 September 1484*]

s.c.1 53/133

### Jh*e*su

Ryght [re]u*er*[en]d *and* worchupfull Ser, [I r]ecomend me vnto
[you wyth] reu*er*ence, as a s[p]ows how to dow to [h]y[r] spow[s],
as [h]artely as [I can], eu*er*more dessyr⟨y⟩ng to her of your wellfar,
þe wyche Jh*e*su p*re*saru[e to his] ple[sure and] your hart desser.
5   *And* [if] it lyke you Ser to send me a lett*er* o[f you]r w[ellfar], that
I dessyr alder[mo]st to her. *And* yf it lyke you ser to h[e]r [o]f my
[h]elt[he, at the] makyng of thys sympyll lett*er* I was in good
helthe of bode, blessyd be J[hesu as] I troste þat ye be, or I wold
be ryght sorye.
10  *And* I pray y[ou] s[e]r that ye well [be of] good cher, for all your
good*ys* ar in safte at home, blessyd be God; *and* [as sone] as ye may
make a nend of your besenes I pray you to sped you ho[me], for
I thyng it a long se⟨s⟩en sen ʒe depart from me, *and* I wott well I
sch[all] n*er*e be mery to I see you agayn. *And* I pray you to send me
15  word in h[aste what] tyme þat ye well be at home yf ye may. Ser,
lattyng you w[ette I] sent you a hart of gold to a tokyn be
Nycklay Kerkebe, *and* ye [schall receyue] in thys lett*er* a feterloke
of gold w*yth* a rebe þerin, and I pray you ser to [t]ake [it] in worthe
at thys tyme, for I knew not wo schold care þe let*er and* þerfo[r]
20  I scent no noder thyng w*yth* thys lett*er*. No mor vnto you at thys
tyme, b[ut] Jh*e*su haue you in hys keppyng.
                                      Be your wyf, Margere Celye.

*Address*: To my ryght worchupfull ho⌈w⌉ssband Gorge Cely,
m*er*chand of þe Stapell at Calys þ*ys* be del[y]uered.

222.  13 se⟨s⟩en: *ms.* senen

**223.** *William Maryon at London to George Cely at Calais,*
*20 September* [*1484*]

s.c.i 53/146

### Jhesu

Ryght worschyppefull syr and [my spec]yall good fren[de, I
recomaund me] vnto you, eueremor desyryng [to he]re of yowre
well[fare]. Plessed you to vnderstond that Y haue ressayve[d
a letter from you wrete]n at Calles the xvj day of Septembere, the
wyc[h I haue rede] and well vnderstond. Also syr, Y vnderstond   5
by youre wryt[tyng that ye] had a fayher passage and a schort to
Calleswarde, thanked [be God, and] Y vnderstord by youre
wrytyng that ye wovld that Y schuld be [com]fortor vnto my
mayesterys yowre wyffe. Syr, y good faythe Y [would that] Y
coude do vnto har any comford ar saruyesse but seche as Y [may   10
ye] schall fynd yt redy at all tymys be the grasse of God. Syr,
s[che ys] sade and nat grettely mery, for that sche ys nat so ase[sted
as] sche was wontte to be; for nowe the nytys begyenyt to [wax]
and sche ys ferfull for to goo into any plasse in har hou[se] in [the]
nytte alon, and sche hat delyue*r*ed Thomas hare man away v[nto]   15
hys modere, and therfor sche prayd yowe that ye would d[elyuer]
yow of anodere ladde a that seyd the see for to be in hys sted[e.
Syr,] my masterys youre wyffe reco*m*aund har harteley vnto you,
sche enformyng you that sche sent a lettere vnto you the last
[we]ke be on Rechard Cartar of Darbey, in the wyche lettere sche   20
sen[t] vnto you a lytell locke of gould y-closed in the sayd lettere,
the wyche sche trust to God ye haue ressayved. Also syr, my
mayesterys youre wyffe prayd yowe harteley as son as ye haue do
youre besene[s] at Calles that ye would com hom, for sche sayd
she thothe neu*er* so longhe for you as sche do nowe, etc. Syr, as   25
for youre broder Rechard, he dep*ar*ted fro London into Cottyswouldward the xiij day of Septe[m]bere: Y pray to God be hys
spede, etc. No mor vnto you at thys tym, but my maysterys yowre
soster and youre brodere Robard recomaund them vnto yow.
Wreten at London the xx day of Septembere, etc.                  30

                            p*er* yowre Wylli*a*m Maryon.

*Dorse*: Wnto my specyall good frend George Cely, marchant of the
Stapull at Calles, thys lettere be delyuerde, etc. (*Shield*.)

**223.** 23 youre] sysse *canc.*

## 224. *John Pasmer at London to George Cely at Calais, 20 September 1484*

s.c.1 53/178

At London, the xx<sup>ti</sup> day of September, anno M<sup>l</sup>iiij<sup>c</sup>iiij<sup>xx</sup>iiij.

Right worshipfull sir, as hertly as I can I recommaunde me vnto
your good maistership, desiryng to here of the welfare and pros-
perite of the same. Sir, please it you to vnderstond that as touchyng
the matier wherof I comoned wyth your maistership at your last
5 beyng at London for myn entre and admyssion into the right worshipfull *and* honourable Felaship of the Staple at Caleys, I am
fully appoynted and condescended in my mynde, and wold be
right gladde to be a poure Brother of the same, yf it woll please
them to accepte and admytte me therto. Wherfore, bycause I may
10 nat be at Caleys in myn owne persone at this tyme, nor am nat
acerteyned whan I shall be there, I beseche therfore your maistership for to breke this matier on my behalf vnto the said worshipfull
Felaship, Desiryng them to accepte and admytte me a Brother of
their said worshipfull Felaship of the Staple aforsaid. Which yf
15 it woll please them so to doo, than I requyre your maistership, yf
it like you, to leye doun and pay there for me to them the Duetie
vsed and accustumed for such entre and admyssion, and I shall
content you agayn therof with Goddys grace; and so vpon the
said admyssion that it woll please them to wryte vnto my maister
20 the Maire of the said Staple beyng in London, that it woll please
hym to receyue myn Othe there, and also the Duetie vsed and
accustumed for my said entre *and* admyssion, yf they woll nat
receyue the Duetie therfore of your maistership at Caleys as is
aforsaid. No more to you at this tyme, but I beseche you to
25 remembre this matier for me; and my maistres your wyf fareth
wele, blessed be God, and she recomaundeth her hertly vnto you,
and Jhesu preserue you, etc.

your owne, John Pasmer of London.

*Dorse*: To my right worshipfull master George Cely, beyng at
30 Caleys.

**225.** *William Cely at Calais to Richard Cely at London,*
*8 October [1484]*

s.c.1 53/152

Ryght ⌜[worsch]yppffull⌝ syr and my reuerent master, af[tyr dew
recommendacyon] had I lowly recommend me vnto yowr master-
[schypp. Furdermore lyke hytt yowr masterschypp] to be enfformyd that my mastyr George [. . . Fland]yrs. He departyd
thederwardys the fyrste day of thys m[onth] of October and ys at  5
Brugys styll, yn gode helth, thanckyd [be God], and I loke aftyr
hym at Calles agayne euery day, for he po[rposyd at] hys departyng
to a ben agayne at Calles at thys day or to[morow], but I thyncke
hee tarryth to come wyth the Imbassett[o]rs of Yng[lond], for they
be comen to Brugys; and they hawe [had] an[swer] of [the] Dewke  10
of Eystryge and of þe lond of Brabond [. . .] wee hawe noo very
knowlege of yett but I [thyncke ytt was] nott soo very plesaunt as
they thowght hytt schuld a b[en . . .]. Syr, they hawe hadd grett
cheyr in Flaunderys and [Englysch]men be cherysched ⌜there⌝ as
well as euer they were. Syr, [mastyr] George goyth noo furder than  15
Brugys, [for] I vnders[tood by hym] at hys departyng that he
purppossyd [to] be [here agayne] schorttly; for as for all syche
thyngys as ys [to do at And]warppe I schall goo theder and do ytt
⌜my selfe⌝ for th[. . .] hath lysenceys þe Fellyschypp of the
Stappell to c[ome to A]ndwarp ffor to receyue her dettys, but  20
theye maye bye no [war]ys, etc. Item syr, John Delowppys hathe
fett the rest of yowre Cottys wull, wyth the whyche [he]e ys
well content, etc. Item syr, hyt ys sayd here that the schyppyng ys
begoon ⌜wyth⌝ yow at London, whyche I pray Godd send hytt
well heder and that hytt maye so bee spedd whyle the wedder ys  25
fayer. No more vnto yowre mastyrschypp at thys tyme, but allmyghty Jhesu pres[erue yow]. Wrytten at Calles the viij day of
October.

> per yowre seruaund,
> Wylliam Cely.        30

*Dorse*: To my ryght worschyppffull mastyr Recherd Cely merchaunt of þe Stappell at Calles, at London yn Martt Lane soo hyt
dd. (*Shield*.)

**225.** 1 Ryght] ryght *canc.*        9 Imbassett *over* Impassett        22 *ms.* the þe
whyche        24 begoon] at London *canc.*

**226.** *William Cely at Calais to George Cely at London,*
*[January] 1486/7*
S.C.1 53/180

Jhesu M¹iiij°iiij×× vj

Ryght worschyppffull syr and myn esspecyall goode mastyr, aftyr
all dew recommendacon precedynge I lowly recommend mee vnto
yowre mastyrschypp. Fyrdyrmore, lyke hytt yowre mastyrschypp
to wytt that I hawe receyued yowre lettyr datyd at London the
5  xxx day of December, the whyche I doo well vnderstand. And ⌈as⌉
towchynge to the matter of Wylliam Smythe, I hawe spoken wyth
hym for the same and he tellyth mee hytt ys nott sold, nor yn noo
bond, but that he maye doo wyth hytt what hytt plese hym. Hee
holdyth hytt at an C marke, and I bad hym sett hytt at l li. and
10  than I wold offer hym, and he sayd he maye hawe above lv li. ster.
but he tellyd mee yff yowre mastyrschypp be wyllynge to byee
hytt yee schall hawe hytt as goode chepe as any man, ffor he sayth he
offerd hytt to yowre mastyrschypp a twelfve monthe agoon; and so
I hawe goon noo ffyrdyr wyth hym yn that matter tyll I knew more
15  of yowre mynde, etc. etc. Item, syr, as for Wylliam Dalton, ys yett
yn Hollond. I hawe conveyd yowre lettyr to Brugys agaynyst hys
comynge, etc. Item, syr, I hawe schewyd vnto Tylbott acordynge
to yowre comavndment that the Margett ys styll at Plemmovth,
wyth the whych he ys nott [we]ll content that sche tarr[y]th soo
20  longe. Allso [. . .] [*Bottom of sheet torn off.*]

*Dorse*: To my ryght worschyppffull mastyr George Cely, merchaunte of the Stappell off Calles, at London yn Martt Lane, soytt
dd. (*Seal and shield.*)

**227.** *William Cely at Calais to George Cely at London,*
*[February] 1486/7*
S.C.1 53/181

Jhesu M¹iiij°iiij×× vj

Ryght worschypffull syr and my specyall goode mastyr, aftyr all
dew recommendacon precedynge I lowly recommend mee vnto
yowre mastyrschypp. Fyrddyrmore, lyke hytt yowre mastyrschypp

---

**226.** 6 towchynge] Wyll *canc.*     7 nor yn] nott *canc.*     10 sayd] *ch. from* sayth
11 wyllynge to] hawe *canc.*     12 man] be *canc.*     20 Allso] yowre *canc.*

to hawe y*n* knowlege that thys day I hawe receyued yowre lettyr
berynge date the xv^th day of Jenyvere, be the tenour wherof 5
I vnderstond the afecte of yowre lettyr that ȝe sente be John
Cooke, whych cam nott to my handd*ys*, and as for syche gere as
yowr mastyrschypp leffte w*yth* Adryan Deffrey, I hawe made noo
conveyaunce therof, ffor I knew nott that yowre mastyrschypp lefft
anythynge w*yth* hym tyll nowe, etc. Item syr, as ffor yowre bavyr, 10
I hawe enqueryd for hytt, and hath fownd hym that hath hytt, the
whych I schall send yow be Peyrs Batton ys schypp w*yth* yowre
sadyll and yowre odyr gere, and alsoo a barell of grene ffysche for
my mastyr yowre broddyr *and* yow, etc. Item syr, I hawe remembyr Syr Raffe Hasty*ng*ys acordynge to yowre wryttynge, and ⌐he⌐ 15
tellyth mee that hee hath wrytten to Syr John Dee to make yow
spedy paym*ent*, etc. And syr, as for Twyssullton, I hawe spoke*n*
vnto hym yn lyke wyse, and hee schewyth vnto mee that hee
ys nott as yett y*n* that case nor ab⟨y⟩lete to make ȝow paym*ent*,
wherffor he beseke yowr*e* mastyrschypp to contenew hys goode 20
mastyr and to geve hym a sparyng ffor a seson, etc. And allso I
hawe remembe*r* Wyll*ia*m Dalton yn lyke wyse, and he tellyth mee
that hee hath wrytten vnto hys man of the same, yn any wyse to see
yow content, etc. Item syr, plese hytt yow to vnderstondd that oon
Thursday the viij day of Feuere the ordena*u*nce made ffor [wullys 25
of] thys last yere scheyr schuld nott come to sale tyll the [... wu]ll
of the tode[r y]ere. [181 B] Allsoo lyke hytt yowre m*a*styrschypp
to vnderstond, as for the Imbassettours of the Kynge of Romayns
and owre Kyngg*ys* comyschoners, cannott growe to noo conclusyon for the entercoursse betwyxte them and vs, noo lenger 30
than tyll Mydsomer nexte, for the Kynge of Romayns comyschoners hath ffully answeryd that ther mastyr hath sent them
a comavndem*ent* ffor to conclude ffor noo pese noo lenger than
Myddsomer nexte; but they comen styll of odyr matters ffor ij or
iij days tyll they dep*a*rte. And syr, the Kynge of Romayns hathe 35
rescewyd hys town of Twrwyn, whych the Lordd Corddys leyde
sege to, but the Lordde Corddys ys ffledd, and all hys cu*m*pany,
and the Kynge of Romayns hath newe veetellyd the town and put
y*n* moo men, and hys armee lyeth styll yett at Sent Omers, etc.
Item, syr, plese hytt yowre masterschypp to vnderstond that yowre 40
boxe ys y*n* safte, but syr, I am purpossyd to be w*yth* yow yn
Ynglond ⌐schortly⌐ wherffor, syr, I pray yow to wryte me yowre

**227.** 7 gere] the *canc.*     20 wherffor] I *canc.*     36 Twrwyn] the *canc.*

mynd whedyr I schall brynge hytt w*yth* me, or ell*ys* to leve hytt
y*n* the chest or w*yth* som schewyr man ⌐at Call*es*⌐. Allsoo syr, yonge
45 Gylys Francke ys nott yett comen ffor yowre wull, nor noo man
ffor hym, nor I here noothynge of hym, wherof I marvell grettly;
wher⟨for⟩, syr, I pray yowre mastyrschyppis to wryte mee yowre
plessyrs whedyr yee wyll I schall kepe yowre wull styll for hym
or sell hytt to som odyr m*er*ch*a*unte, etc. It*em*, syr, Wyll*i*am
50 Smyth, wull packer, hath spoken to mee of the todyr matter,
wherefor, syr, plese hytt yowre mastyrschypp to wryte mee whedyr
ye wyll that I goo any ffarddyr w*yth* hym y*n* that matter or nott,
etc. No more vnto yowre mastyrschypp at thys tyme, but allmyghty Jh*es*u pr*e*ser*u*e yow. Wrytten at Call*es* [. . .] [*Bottom of*
55 *sheet torn off.*]

*Dorse*: To my ryght worschyppffull mastyr George Cely, m*er*-
ch*a*unte of the Stapp*e*ll of Call*es*, at London y*n* Martt Lane, sooytt
dd. (*Shield.*)

**228.** *William Dalton at Calais to George Cely at London,*
*12 March 1486/7*
s.c.1 53/182

### *Christus* 1486

Ryght worshipffull sir, I reco*m*maunde me vnto you. Like it you
to witte that purveid at my beyng in Holond samon of the Mase,
of the wheche all is not co*m*myn, but sithen it is so that I have but
on firkyn co*m*myn, I send it to you be Thom*a*s Bernarde, s*er*vaunt
5 w*yth* John Renold, m*er*cer, to delyu*er* you, p*r*ayng you that it will
plese you for opon it *and* take out therof the on half ⌐for yo*ur* self⌐,
*and* that other half that it will plese you to put su*m* pese of wod in
the seyd firkyn because of bressyng ⌐of þe fyshe⌐ that shal be lefte
ther in that other half, *and* that it may be sent to my Jone *and* this
10 lett*er* therwithe, other be carte if any go to Leyc*ester*, or ell*ys* ⌐by⌐
the carears of Derby that they may cary it vpo*n* horsbake, *and*
that I beseche you in as goodly hast as may be, etc. Plese it you
to vnd*er*stond that Will Cely told me that ye had no knowlege
from me fir p*a*yme*n*t of the xx li. ye of yo*ur* curtesy delyu*er*d vnto
15 Will*i*am Lemster my s*er*uaunte / to my gret m*a*rvel. Sir, ye shal

43 or] le *canc.*
**228.** *Date.* 1486 *ch. from* 1487

be acertened for trouthe, contynent vpon the knowlege of your
curtesy *and* kynd delyng to me of the seid xx li., I made xx li. be
exch*a*unge *and* sent yo*u* the lett*er* of p*a*yme*nt* w*yth* a pronosticacon
*and* an almynake of the makyng of m*a*ster John Laete, *and* this
I sent you all bounden *and* seled toged*er* be Willi*a*m Drynklow /    20
*And* sithen Will Cely told me I delyuerd vnto hy*m* the seconde
lett*er* of p*a*yme*nt* to send ou*er* vnto you, like as I have writon to
you in a lett*er* sent ou*er* at Shorfftyde, the whech I truste ye have
rec*e*y*u*ed / It*e*m if my other samon hade co*m*myn I entended to
have done other, but I p*r*ay to excuse to my gud maistres [*Dorse*]   25
that it is no bett*er*, howbeit it swam sith Candilmasse. W. Ce[ly]
can tell you more then I dar writ*e* / Jh*e*su kepe you. Writ*en* [at]
Call*y*s the xij day of M*a*rche

your W. Dalton.

To the worshipffull Goerge Cely, m*er*chaunt of the Staple  30
[d]wellyng in Marke Lane, set dd. Lond*on*.

## 229. *Richard Cely the younger to George Cely* [*30 April,*
*?1487*]

Ch. Misc. C. 47. 37/13, f. 53

Brother, I recomend me wnto yow, and I send yow the kockett of
ij*c* q*uarter*, and I pray yow that ȝe wyl be heyr tomorrow, for
Tebott has made a byll of xxv li. to yow *and* me *and* to my godfadyr, payabull the fyrste day of May, *and* therfor I pray yow be
her on Tewysday be x a clocke, for ellys Tybott wyl be goon. He  5
sett th' hogyshed of whyn at xxxiij s. iiij d.

*No address or subscription.*

*Dorse, in George Cely's hand*:

xij s. vj d.
Smethe ij s. vj d.
Of John - - - - - - - - - - - - - - - - - - - - - - - - - - - - - - xx d.
Bowght of Jeff*er*ey Aweray iij q*uarter* of wottys xx                    10
q*uarter* - - - - - - - - - - - - - - - - - - - - - - - - - - - - - - - - - v s.
Item of hym iij q*uarter* barley, pris le q*uarter*
iij s. iiij d. - - - - - - - - - - - - - - - - - - - - - - - - - - - - x s.
To my gardener - - - - - - - - - - - - - - - - - - - - - - - - - xx d.

16 trouthe] contend *canc.*     17 of the] sid *canc.*     18 sent] your *canc.*

15 To my ploveman ----------------------------- x d.
   Le rest of wole ------------------------------ iiij s.
   John Carpenter ------------------------------ iij s. iiij d.

## 230. *Richard Cely the younger to George Cely* [? *1487*]
s.c.1 53/91

Riught welbelouyd brother, I recomend me wnto yow, *and* to
my syst*er*. Hyt ys so that her ys Dodlays mane, the bochar of
Eschepe, and I hawe p*a*yd hym aull the mony that I hawhe, ʒeyt
I how hym xxxiij s. iiij d., wheche I pray yow pay hym, and send
5 me a nobyll be Tomas Wade. The iij oxsyn for the Margett comys
to xxxv s.: that ys x s. xx d. a pey at my comynge a Wednysday.
I wantt a lyttyll fardell w*yth* ij craddyll clothys, a tyn basson, w*yth*
odyr geyr. ʒeffe hytt hapyd to be layd in yowr bott I troste hytt
wyl be saffe. I wndyrstonde be Adlyngton at Mydwyntt*er* ys com.
10 God ryd ws of hym. Send me a byll of yowr mynd, I pray yow.
                                                    p*er* Rych*ard* Cely.

*Dorse*: To my brother George Cely.

*In George's hand*: Broder, I recomawnd me to yow and to my.

## 231. *George Cely to Nicholas Best* [? *1487*]
s.c.1 53/150

Nycolas, Y hawe wrett to Allvard and hawe desyryd hym be my
lett*er* to delyuyr to Wyll*i*am Mydewent*er* Cl li. Se that ʒe yndevyr
yow to that Wyll*i*am Mydewent*er* may hawe ytt shorttly. The
plage hasse ben soyche that whe dar nott com ther owrselffe. And
5 ⌐tell hym⌐ yf he he⟨l⟩pe vs nott at thys tyme ytt wholl skathe vs
the byeyng of C sakke of woll at thys sessen.
   And go to Boshope and resseywe my ix m*a*rke of hym, and as
son as Wyll*i*am Mydewent*er* comes make hym p*a*yme*n*t of soyche
mo*n*ny as Y vnderstond ʒe haue resseywyd of Allward, and kepe
10 good rekeny*n*g.
                                                    p*er* George Cely.

Delyuyr to Wyll*i*am Mydewenter Cl li. Yf ʒe resseywe more, kepe
ytt by yow tyll Y come whome.

**232.** *Sir Ralph Hastings at Calais to George Cely at London, 8 May [? 1487]*

s.c.1 53/173

Jhesu

Ryght wyrschypfull sir, I recommend me vnto you as hartely as
I can, etc. Letyng you wnderstond þat I resauyd a letter from you
wherin ʒe wrott for your mone. I pray you þat ʒe take it to no
dysplesour, for I insure you heuer tyll Sir Wylliam com hom I wend
ʒe had ben contentt of Sir John Dye, bote I haw send hym wrytyng      5
vnder syche forum þat ʒe sall be content in all þe hast posybyll
wythowtt fawtt, and I pray you þat ʒe wyll caws hym to hawe
a letter send to hym wyche sall be bownd and sellyd wyth this
your letter, and affter the syʒht of þe byll I wot well ʒe sall not fawt
of your mone. And at my comyng I sall make syche amendys as ʒe      10
sall hold you well contentt, wyche tym sal be ryʒht schortly, be the
gras of God, who preserwf you. At Caleis on þe viij day of Maye.
[*In a different hand*:]

your luffuyng
Rauff Hastyngys.

*Dorse*: To the ryght wyrschypfull Gorge Selye, merchand, dwelyng      15
in Marke Layn in London. [*Sideways in corner*:] Sely.

**233.** *Richard Cely the younger in Essex to George Cely at London, August 1487*

s.c.1 53/183

Riught whelbelouyd brother, I recomend me wnto yow and my
syster in as hartty whysse as I can. Syr, I hawhe ressauyd a letter
be Adlyngton: he bryngys you the same. I wndyrstond hyt ryught
welle, etc. I longe sor to heyr how ʒe hauhe pwrwhayd for Wylliam
Mydwynter. ʒeffe I had spockyn wyth you er ʒe ʒeyd to London      5
whe myhyt [a] made a C li. wyth my brother Awheray: syr, I pray
yow macke hym a byll in bothe howr namus of hys mony to pay
hym at Brogys, as ʒe and he cane agre, for he had neuer the byll at
ʒe tooke me: ʒe remembyr whe hade xl li. at howr comynge, [an]d
I hade xx li. mor, wheyrof ʒeyde xij li. and mor for carryayge of      10

232. 5 bote] yt ys so þat yf yt wyll *canc.*      hym] sy *canc.*      6 syche] wr
*canc.*      9 your] l *canc.*      letter] & at *canc.*

wholl. I pray yow macke hys byll of lx li. st*er*., etc. Syr, I whowlde
awysse my syst*er and* yow to com agayne into Essex, for I wndyrstonde thay dy sor in London.

per yowr brother,

Rych*ard* Cely.

15

*Dorse*: Wnto my brother George Cely at London in Martte Lane.

*In G. Cely's writing*: [. . .]
[d]elyuerd the last day of Agust, a*n*no iiij×× vij.
Item ffor xxiij di. akers, ix d. ob. le aker,

20 nett*ys* and all ---------------------------- xix s. viij d. ob.
    Item, ffor breke to Elles ----------------- xx s.
    Item, delyu*er*yd be my wyffe to Speryng ffor
    the Margett ------------------------- xxx s.

**234.** *William Cely at Calais to Richard and George Cely
at London, 12 September 1487*
s.c.1 53/184

Jh*e*su M¹iiij<sup>c</sup>iiij××vij

Ryght worschyppffull syrs and my reuerent mastyrs, aftyr all dew
recom*m*endacon p*re*cedyng I lowly recom*m*end mee vnto yowre
mastyrschypp*ys*. Fyrdyr, plese hytt yowre mastyrschypp*ys* to
vnderstond that I hawe receyued of John Delowppys vppon pay-
5 me*n*t of the byll the whych yee sent me be Adlyngton, but iij<sup>c</sup> li.
Fl., wherof I hawe p*ay*d to Guyott Strabant iiij××iiij li. vj s. vj d. Fl.
Item, I haue made yow over be exch*a*unge w*yth* Benyngne
Decasonn, Lomberd, an Ciiij×× nobull*ys* sterlyng, p*ay*abu*l*l at
vsaunce. I delyuerd hit at a xj s. ij d. ob. Fl. le nobull: hit amou*n*t*ys*
10 C li. xvij s. vj d. Fl. Item I hawe made yowre ower be exch*a*unge
y*n* lyke wyse w*yth* Jacob Van De Base iiij××ix nobull*ys and* vj s.
st*er*. p*ay*abu*l*l at London at vsaunce y*n* lyke wyse. I delyuerd hit
at a xj s. ij d. Fl. for eu*er*y nobull st*er*.: hit amo*n*t*ys* Fl. l li. Fl. And
the rest of yowr iij<sup>c</sup> li. remayns styll by me, ffor I can make yow
15 over no more at thys ceson, for here ⌈is⌉ no moo that wyll take any
mony as yett. And mony goyth now vppon the Bursse at a xj s.
iij d. ob. the nobull, and non odyr mony but Nenyng grot*ys*,

**234.** 15 for] ther *canc.*

crownys, Andrew gylders *and* Reynysche gylders, and the exchaunge goyth euer the lenger warsse *and* wars. Item syr, I send
yow enclossyd yn thys sayd letter the ij ffyrst letters of pay*m*ent 20
of the exch*a*unge above wrytten: Benyngne Decasons letter ys
derectyd to Gabryell Desuyr *and* Petyr Sauly, Geneways, *and*
Jacob Van De Base ys derectyd to Anthony Corsy *and* Marc*u*s
Strossy, Spaynard—yn Lomberd Strete yee schall here of them,
etc. Item syr, John Lowppys long sore afftyr yowre comy*n*g that 25
he myght make a bergeyne w*y*th yow for yowre wull*y*s. He desyryth to hawe ij sarppll*ery*s to prove hytt bye tyll yowre mastyrschypp*y*s come. He sayth yee schall be to ffar owte of the weye
w*y*thowte yee gree *and* bargeyne togeder. Syr, hytt ys well don
that ye take yowre markett betyme for diuersse consederacons, 30
etc.; allsoo the m*a*rgett wax very slacke here, etc. Item, syr, plese
hytt yowre mastyrschyppys to vnderstond that I hawe sold yowre
ffell*y*s to Jacob Gyesbryghtson *and* John Doo of Dellfe: sum vij*c*
fell*y*s—the rest [be] reffewce—prys le C, xvj nobull*y*s v s. ste*r*.,
s*u*m xxxix li. [j s. viij d.]; the whych to be p*a*yd be a byll of ther 35
handd*y*s yn thys Bam[mys mart]. Item, syr, as tochyng the iij*c* li.
Fl. rec*eyu*ed be me now of Joh[n Lowpys], I hawe wrytten hytt
vppon the byll and hath the byll bye mee sty[ll]; howbe⌈hitt⌉ John
sayth be hys boke thys byll ys p*a*yd owte *and* mor to, ffor [184 B]
he saythe ther was p*a*yd yow yn Ynglond be Allvard vppon the 40
same byll the vj day of Apryll, Clvj li. xvij s. vj d. Fl., besyde the
l li. st*e*rlyng take vpp off Alverd at x s. ix d.; but ⌈he sayth⌉ at
yowre comy*n*g yee and he schall clere that rekeny*n*g. And syr,
I promysyd hym to a delyuerd hym ij sarppll*ery*s of ⌈your⌉ wull tyll
yowr comyng, and he schuld make mee a byll p*a*y*abu*ll at yowre 45
plessyrs for the same at the pryce of the Place. But syr, I cannott
hawe yowre wull yett awarddyd, for I hawe doo cast owte a s*a*rpler
the ⌈whych⌉ ys poyntyd be the Lefftenaunte to be casten owte to
wardd the sortte bye, as the ordenaunce ys now made that the
Lefftenaunte schall poynt the warddyng sarppll*ery*s of eu*e*ry mans 50
wull; the whych s*a*rpler that I hawe casten owte ys No. xxiiij, and
thery*n* ys ffovnd be Wyll*i*am Smyth, paker, a lx myddyll ffl*e*ssys,
and hytt ys a very gruff wull, and soo I hawe causyd Wyll*i*am
Smyth preuely to cast owte anoder s*a*rpler, No. viij, and packyd
vpp the wull of the fyrst s*a*rpler yn the s*a*rpler of No. viij, for thys 55

**234.** 20 of] the *canc.*          36 tochyng] John *canc.*          47 for] I ca *canc.*
55 wull of] thys *canc.*

last sarpler ys ffayr wull inow3th. And therffor Ie muste vnderstond how many be of that sortte *and* the nombyr of the*m*, for
they muste be pakkyd agayne. Hytt ys a very redd leyr and grett
flesys, etc. Item syr, yff yowre mastyrschypp*ys* hawe p*a*yd yowre
60 m*a*rke of the s*a*rpler, I pray yow send mee the waraunt fro*m* the
solyster, that hytt myght be deductyd vppon yowre costom *and*
subs*ede* ⌐here⌐, etc. No more vnto yowre mastyrschypp*ys* at thys
tyme, but allmyghty Jh*e*su pr*e*ser*u*e *and* kepe yow *and* all yowr*ys*
long yn goode helth *and* prossperyte, for allmyghty God vesettythe
65 sore here y*n* Call*es* and the m*a*rchys w*y*th thys grett plage off
syckness that raynyth, I beseche of hys m*e*rcy to serce hytt.
Wrytten at Call*es* the xij jo*ur* de September.

be yowre s*e*ru*au*nte,
Wylli*a*m Cely.

70 Syr, the brynger of thys letter ys John Saunders.

[*Dorse*] To my ryght worschyppffull mastyrs Rech*a*rd *and* George
Cely, m*e*rch*au*nt*ys* of the Stappell of Call*es*, at London yn M*a*rt
Lane, soytt dd. (*Shield.*)

### 235. *William Cely at Calais to George Cely at London, 18 September 1487*
s.c.1 53/185

Jh*e*su M¹iiijᶜiiijˣˣvij

Ryght worschyppffull syrs and my reuerent mastyrs, afftyr all dew
recomendacon pr*e*cedynge I lowly reco*m*mend mee vnto yowre
mastyrschypp*ys*. Fyrdyrmore, plese hytt yowre mastyrschyppys to
vnderstond that I haue receyued yowre lettyr datyd at London the
5 ffyrst day of September, be the tenour therof I vnderstond yowre
mastyrschypp*ys* hath take vpp be exch*au*nge of John Raynold,
m*e*rcer, lx li. st*er*., p*a*y*a*bull the xxv day of thys month, *and* of
Deago Decastron, Spaynard, odyr lx li. st*er*., p*a*y*a*bull the xxvj day
of the same month, the whych schall be both content at the day.
10 And as ffor mastyr Lowys More, Lomberd, ys p*a*yd and I hawe

234. 57 them] that *canc.*    58 muste] be muste *canc.*    59 yowre] make
*canc.*    65 sore] here *canc.*
235. 7 and of] John *canc.*

the byll. Hys atorney ys a wranglyng felow: he wold non odyr
mony but Nemyng grot*ys*, etc. Item, syr, I vnderstond be yowre
sayd lett*er* that yowr mastyrschypp*ys* hath rec*eyued* noo wryttyng
from mee syns Addlynton was here, wherof I marvell, for I wrate
ij letters to yow whyle I was at Brug*ys*, specyfyng of divers matters 15
of Flaunders. The ton was sent from Call*es* be Jam*us* Jarfford,
me*r*cer; the toder be Peryman, packer of clyfte wull*ys*. He ys logyd
at the Crosse Keye. Syr, I hawe ben at Call*es* thys ix days, and
abowte the latt*er* end of thys weke I purpose to Brug*ys*wardde
agayne, and I leue Thom*as* Colton *and* Roberd Hubberd atorneys 20
tyll I com, and I schall leve w*yth* Thom*as* Colton vj li. Fl. for
yowre mastyrschypp yff ye com, and as for yowre black box,
I leve hytt w*yth* Thom*as* Graunger. Syr, as for goyng ynto
Flaundy*rs*, ys goode inow3the as yett, but all the jebardy ys y*n*
comyng home, for and yf owre men of war take ther ffyscher, as 25
I ffeyr they wyll, ther wyll be many Englyschemen stoppyd yn
Flaunders; and allsoo the towne of Donkyrk ys nott content, and
þ*at* wee schall well know yff soo be that they mete w*yth* any
me*r*chaunt*ys* of substaunce. And syr, as for a lettyr of atorney
vnder the Stapp*ell* sell, I can hawe non w*yth*owte I bryng a lett*er* 30
of atorney from yowr*ys* mastyrschypp*ys* owte of Ynglond, for
yowre mastyrschyp hath ben at Call*es* diuersse tymes syns I was
entryd yowre atorney, wherffor yowre p*re*sens hath deffetyd that
entre; and a letter of atorney ys nedffull now at thys tym[e].
[*Dorse*] Item, syr, rec*eyued* of John Saunders a letter wheryn 35
enclossyd ij letters of paym*ent*, on of Benyngne Decason derectyd
to Gabryell Desurle *and* Peter Sauly, Genovo[ise], cont*eynyng*
lx li. st*er*. Item, anoder letter of Jacob Van De Base derectyd to
Anth[o]ny Corsy *and* Marcus Strossy, Spayneardd*ys*, cont*eynyng*
xxix li. xix s. iiij d. st*er*., etc. Item, syr, yowre wull ys awarddyd 40
be the s*ar*pler that I cast owte last, etc. Item, syr, thys same day
yowre mastyrschypp ys alectyd *and* poyntydd here b[e] the courtt
oon of the xxviij the whych schall asyste the Mayer of t[he]
Stapp*ell* now at thys p*ar*liam*ent* ⌐tyme⌐, wheresomeuer hytt be
holden, and to labore s*er*ten matters for the Place wherof ys 45
ynstructons sent to the Mayer be wryttyng, etc. Item, syr, I send
yow enclossyd yn thys lett[er] a byll of the copy of John Delowppys
boke of syche p*ar*cell*ys* as he sayth he hath p*a*yd, to see yff yowre

**235.** 33 atorney] whych *canc.*     40 ster.] Item *canc.*     43 t[he]] mayer
*canc.*

rekeny*ng* and hys agree, etc. No more vnto yowre mastyrschypp at
50 thys, but allmyghty Jh*e*su *pre*ser*u*e yow. Wrytten at Calle*s* the
xviij jo*u*r de September.

*per* yowre ser*u*a*u*nte,
Wylli*a*m Cely.

To my ryght worschyppffull mastyr George Cely, m*e*rch*a*unte of
55 the Stapp*e*ll of Calle*s* at London y*n* M*a*rtt Lane, soyt dd. (*Shield.*)

### 236. *William Cely at Bruges to Richard and George Cely at London, 29 October 1487*

s.c.i 53/187

Jh*e*su M¹iiij°iiijˣˣ vij

Ryght worschyppffull syrs and my reu*e*rent mastyrs, afftyr all dew
recom*m*endacon *pre*cedyng I lowly recom*m*end mee vnto yowr
mastyrschypp*ys*. Fyrdyr, plese hytt yowre mastyrschyppys to
vnderstond that the worlde ys here nowe very caswell, for ther
5 ys many wayns laden w*yth* Englyschemennys gooddys now arestyd
at Ostend *and* at oder dyuersse placys, *and* noo goodd*ys* maye
passe throw as yett noo ways; for Englyschemen hath taken many
of ther fyschermen, whych causeth here a grett rombur. But wee
vnderstond as many as hath sengler safcondut*ys*, ther goodd*ys*
10 schall be delyuerd *and* lett passe throw; but as ffor the gen*e*rall,
they wyll nott obeye, ffor they anull hytt, sayinge that the Englysche
schypp*ys* fforffetyd hytt when they dep*a*rtyd owte of Selond, they
beynge vnder arest. Wherffor the gen*e*rall standyth yn non affecte,
and soo many as be here havynge noo sengler safcondute ar yn
15 jeberdy. Wherffor syr, I pray yow ⌜*þat*⌝ I may hawe yn as goodely
hast as may be yowr lett*er* atorney vnder seall autetyc, that I maye
be yn asewerte be the menys of yowre safcondute as yowre
aturney, for safcondut*ys* ar now put yn vre, etc. Item, ⌜*syr*⌝, as
ffor yowr mony I hawe made over as yett but xxx li. st*er*. w*yth*
20 John Etwell, m*er*cer, at a xj s. *and* iij monthys. Thys rombur
causyth that noo man dar charge here no more as yett. *And* as ffor
heryng, I hawe ben at Dam diuersse tymes: the rone ys at ix li.
x s. *and* yett non to gett yn regard, but ther ys wrack inow3th, *and*
viij li. the last. *And* soo ther ys a schypp at Sclewce that goyth to
25 Calle*s* callyd Ru*m*bold Wylli*a*mson, wherein I hawe leyd ⌜yow⌝

---

236. 3 yowre mastyrschyppys] that *canc.*    12 schypp*ys*] brake *canc.*    16 may
be] a *canc.*    18 now] now *canc.*    22 tymes] & it *canc.*

iiij last heryng, iij wrack *and* on roone. The wrack cost viij li. *and*
the rone ix li., the whych I trust to God schall come ffull well to
Call*es*, for Syr Jam*us* Tyrrell hath goodd*ys* yn the same schyppe,
etc. Item, syr, ther ys a grett rombur at Gaunt; the cheyff of the
town be com *and* fledd to Brug*ys*: I ffere mee Gaunte wyll be 30
Frensche schortly, etc. No more vnto yowre mast*er*schypp*ys* at
thys tyme, but allmyghty Jh*e*su pr*e*ser*u*e yow. Wrytten at Brug*ys*
the xxix day of October.

*per* yowr s*er*ua*u*nt,
Wyll*ia*m Cely.     35

*Dorse*: To my ryght worshyppffull mastyrs Rech*ar*d *and* George
Cely, m*er*chaunt*ys* of the Stappell of Call*es*, at London y*n* M*a*rte
Lane, soyt dd. (*Shield*.)

*Written sideways along the page*: Syr I haue rec*e*yued noo lettyr
fro*m* yow syns your p*ar*tyng hens, wherffor I beseche to wryte 40
mee yowr [plesur in that] behalve, etc.

**237.** *William Cely at Calais to Richard and George Cely
at London, 19 November 1487*

s.c.i 53/189

Jh*e*su M¹iiij<sup>cc</sup>iiij<sup>xx</sup>vij.

Ryght worschyppffull syrs and my reuerent mastyrs, afftyr all dew
recom*m*endacon pr*e*cedynge I louly recom*m*end mee vnto yowre
mastyrschyppis. Fyrddyrmore, plese hytt yowre mastyrschyppis
to vnderstondd that I am com*m*vn to Call*es* yn saffte, thanckyd be
allmyghty Godd, for I was never yn soo grett jebardy comy*n*g owte 5
of Flaunddyrs yn my lyeffe, ffor men a warre lyinge be the waye
waytynge for Englyschemen; *and* allsoo I *and* my cumpany was
arestyd ij days at Dunckyrke, but ffor Syr Jam*us* Tyrrell*ys* sake
wee were lett goo. *And* soo, syr, the world goyth marvyllyusly yn
Flaunddyrs now, for hytt ys open warre betwyxte Gaunte *and* the 10
Kynge of Romayns, etc. Syr, as ffor makyng over of yowre mony,
syns thys trubbull began I cowde nott make over a peny, savyng
an xlviij li. st*er*., wherof I schall send yow the byll*ys* at the nexte
passage. But syr, John Delowppis schewyd mee at my dep*ar*tyng
that I schuld wryte vnto yowr mastyrschyppis to vnderstond 15

**237.** 3 Fyrddyrmore] plese *canc.*     14 Delowppis] was *canc.*     15 yowr] to *canc.*

wheder there schall be any jebardy to brynge warys owte of the
Est partyes ynto Ynglond now ffro hensforth or nott, as he sup-
posyth that þat acte ⌐of þe contrary⌐ schall be put yn susspence
for dyuersse causys; wherffor, syr, he avysyth yow to bestowe yowre
20  mony yn grosse warys now betymys at þis Barow martt; yn syche
warys as yowre mastyrschyppis thynckyth wyll be best at London,
wheder hytt be in madder, wax or ffustyans, but I trow madder be
best. And soo be that ye wyll, Gomers De Sore schall bye hytt for
your mastyrschyppis and schyppyd hytt yn Spaynysche schyppis
25  yn hys owne name, ffor John Delowppis and hee ar purposyd to
bye myche madder to send ynto Ynglond. And yff soo be that ⌐hit⌐
ffallyth to pesse, ther wyll be goode doon vppon madder yf hytt
be bowght betymes, and John Delowppis sayth, yff yowr mastyrschyppis wyll he wull bestowe yowre mony as well as hys owne,
30  and he sayth that þat ys the best ways to make over yowre mony,
for the exchaunge ys ryght nowght, etc. No more vnto yowre
mastyrschyppis at thys tyme, but allmyghty Jhesu preserue yow.
Wrytten at Calles the xix day of November.

per yowre seruaunte,
35                                                  Wylliam Cely.

Dorse: To my ryght worschyppffull mastyrs Rechard and George
Cely, merchauntys of the Stappell off Calles, at London yn Martt
Lane, soyt dd. (Shield.)

In George Cely's writing: George Cely.
40          Rychard per Olowe
            Awerey per Stewen
            George per Pont
            Christoffer per George.


**238.** *William Cely at Calais to Richard and George Cely
at London, 16 December 1487*

S.C.I 53/190. *Very badly stained*

[Jhesu M¹iiijᶜ] iiijˣˣvij

Ryght worschyppffull syrs and my reuerent mastyrs, afftyr all dew
recomendacon precedyng I lowly recommend me vnto yowre
mastyrschyppys. Fyrddyrmore, plese hytt yowre mastyrschyppis

30 sayth] howe *canc.*

to vnderstond that I send yow enclossyd yn thys letter a letter of
payment of John Flewelen, mercer, *and* Wylliam Warner, armerer, 5
payabull at Crystmasse next comyng, conteynyng xxvij li. ster.—
I delyuerd hytt at a xj s. iiij d. Fl. for euery vj s. viij d. ster. Item,
syr, I send yow enclossyd yn thys same letter anoder letter of payment of on Roger Bovser, mercer, of London, payabull the xij day
of Marche nexte comynge, conteynyng xviij li. ster. I delyuerd hytt 10
hym at xj s. Fl. for vj s. viij d. ster. Syr, I can make ower no more
mony as yett: the worlde fa⟨r⟩yth marvelysly nowe yn Flaunders,
ffor all saffcondutys geven afore thys day be dysanullyd, and they
hawe graunttyd *and* gewen a saffcondutt generall duryng the space
of x monthys to all maner merchauntys, of what nacyon or contrey 15
they be off, bryngyng vetell ynto Flaunders, or ellys nott; as yee
schall vnderstond more clerelyar be the copy of the sayd saffcondutt, the whych ys sent vnto mastyr Mayer of the Stapell to
schew vnto all the Fellyschypp at London. Wherffor, syr, I know
noo remedy as yett to make ower the rest of yowre mony wythowte 20
yee wyll bestowe hytt yn ratyd warys be the vyse off John Delowppis, lyke as I wrate vnto yowre mastyrschyppys yn my last letter
be Wylliam Dalton, ffor ther dares noo man here aventer ynto
Flaunders tell wee knowe of a better sewerte than yett ys known.
For ther ys grett warre betwixt the Kynge of Romayns and Gaunt, 25
and ther maye noo man passe be londe to Barow, ffor they of
Gaunte take them presonners, what maner ⌈men⌉ somever they
be, ffor they hawe taken dyuersse Esterlyngys and Coleners lattly,
wherffor ther dars noo merchauntys resorte to nor ffroo. And here
hath comen noo merchauntys straungers of a goode seson, ffor the 30
garyson of Gravenenge hath stoppyd wullys of John Delowppys
and wyll kepe hytt styll at Gravenyng tyll they hawe ther wagys
that the Kynge of Romayns owyth them; byt all yowre wullys
remaynyth yn Calles styll yn my handdys. Syr, wee thynckyth the
world goyth on whelys yn Flaunders, Godd better hytt, etc. Item, 35
plese hytt yowre mastyrschyppis to vnderstond that I hawe
receyued yowr letter [190 B] datyd at London [the] xxvij [day of
November, the] whych I hawe well vnderstond, and ⌈that⌉ yee
purpose nott to meddyll wyth noo warys. Syr, in goode ffaythe,
as yett I know nott how, nor wyth whom, to make over a peny be 40
exchaunge, for ther ys nott yn theke parteys of Englyschemen above

**238.** 16 off] brynger *canc.*       31 garyson of] the *canc.*       40 nor] what
ways to *canc.*

iij or iiij, whych ar porveyd allredy; an[d] as ffor ffyne golddys or
ffyne syluer, hytt ys now to owtragys owt[e] off the waye ffor any
man to brynge over, ffor ye schall nott now gett a ownce of ffyne
45 gold ffor iij li. xij s. gr. and above, ffor I hawe enqueryd ffor the
same, ffor ryallys ar wurthe her[e] now yn Flaunders xx s. Fl., and
other goldys aftyr the rate of the same. Item, syr, I hawe wrytten
to John Delowppys [to fett] yowre wullys, lyke as yowre mastyrschyppys wrate, but he saythe hytt wyll be afftyr Crystmesse or he
50 can ffett hytt, ffor diuersse causys. Syr, wyth the nexte passage
I schall wryte yowre mastyrschyppys of moo thyngys. Syr, the
brynger of thys letter hys name ys Wylliam Iland, seruaunte wyth
Hugh Clopton, etc. No more vnto yowre mastyrschyppys at thys
tyme, but allmyghty Jhesu preserue and kepe yow. Wrytten at
55 Calles the xvj jour of December.

per yowr seruaunte,
Wylliam Cely.

Syr, yff the new grottys of Meclyn wyll goo yn Ynglond hytt were
best, as me thynckyth, to purvey yow of them, ffor I thynckyth
60 I schall gett them vnder xxxij s. the li. Yff they wyll goo yn
Yngland, syr, send me word, and I schall gett as many ffor yowre
mastyrschyppis as I ca[n].

[Dorse] To my ryght worschyppffull mastyrs Rechard and George
Cely, merchauntys of the Stappell of Calles, at London yn Martt
65 Lane, soytt dd. (Shield.)

### 239. William Cely at Calais to Richard and George Cely at London [c. 16 December 1487]

s.c.1 53/188

Jhesu M$^{l}$iiij$^{c}$iiij$^{xx}$ vij

Ryght worschyppffull syrs and my reuerent mastyrs, afftyr all dew
recommendacon precedynge I lowly recommend me vnto yowre
mastyrschyppis. Fyrddyrmore, plese hytt yowre mastyrschyppys
to vnderstond that I doo send yow at thys passage be Wylliam
5 Smyth, packer of wullys, a letter whereyn ys enclossyd ij letters
of payment, on of John Flewelen, sercher, and Wylliam Warner,
armerer, of London, payabull on Crystmesse day nexte, con-

238. 48–9 mastyrschyppys] but h canc.          59 thynckyth to] send canc.
239. 4 yow] wyth canc.

teynyng xxvij li. ster., and anoder of Roger Bowser, mercer, of
London, payabull the iij day of Marche conteynyng xviij li. ster.
Syr, I hawe wrytten yn my letter yn the whyche the fforsayd byllys 10
be clossyd ⌐yn⌐ that oon Wylliam Iland schuld a byn brynger of
the sayd letter, but he toke hys passage yn a crayer laden wyth
gooddys and made sayle yn the nyght, wyth whom I durste nott
aventure the sayd letter at that tyme. Item, syr, I hadd went that
I hadd made yowr mastyrschyppys xxx li. ster. more ower be 15
exchaunge wyth John Ettwell, mercer, but whan thys trubull ffell
yn Flaunders he wold nott of hytt, howbehytt I was throwe wyth
hym beffore ffor hytt, etc. Item, syr, John Delowppys hath send
mee ⌐worde⌐ be hys seruaunte John Deale that yowre mony ys
redy, marvelyng that ye send nott ffor hytt. But syr, I knowe noo 20
waye how to make hytt yow over wythowte grett losse, ffor the
exchaunge goyth very yll, for ther ys noo man to take vpp mony
but straungers, the whych takyth all at vsaunce, and mony goyth
above xij s. viij d. the nobull at vsaunce, wheryn ys grett losse.
And allso ther ys at Barow yn the martt Harold Staunton and oon 25
or ij moo Englyschemen, the whych hath bought [. . .] hytt ys
[. . .] [Bottom of sheet torn off.]

Dorse: To my ryght wurshyppffull mastyrs Rechard and George
Cely, merchauntys of the Stappell of Calles, at London yn Martt
Lane, soytt dd. (Shield.)                                                    30

**240.** *William Cely at Calais to Richard and George Cely
at London, 22 January 1487/8*

s.c.1 53/192

Jhesu M$^l$iiij$^c$iiij$^{xx}$ vij

Ryght worschyppffull syrs and my reuerent mastyrs, afftyr all dew
recommendacon hadd I lowly recommend mee vnto yowr mastyrschyppys, etc. Item, syr, plese hytt yowr mastyrschyppys to vnderstond that I sent vnto yowr mastyrschyppis be Wylliam Smyth,
wull packer, a letter whereyn was enclossyd ij letters of payment, 5
the whych I truste yee hawe receyued. And syr, as ffor all oder
thyngys, ys as yowr mastyrschypp leffte hytt, whych I thyncke
ye schall nott repent, ffor I ffere mee of Flaundyrs: hytt staundyth
marvelyusly wyth Brugys, for the worschyppffull merchauntys of

**239.** 9 Marche *over canc.* Apryll      10 letter] where *canc.*      11 that] I *canc.*
22 noo] tak *canc.*

10 the town hadd lever than myche goode they were owte of the town,
ffor they loke euery owre when the comens of the town schall ryse
and rewle agaynes[t] the Romayns Kynge, for they hawe ben vpp
onys or twyse allredy but they hawe ben pesyd be ffayr menys.
And the Kynge lyeth styll yn Brugys and wold hawe the gydyng of
15 the town but the comyns wyll nott suffur hym, and soo hee hath
sent Phelypp Movnsyr and the Byschopp of Luke ynto Braband
ffor men. What schall com theroff God knowyth, but all the
lorddys of the land takyth the Kyngys parte, etc. Item, syr, plese
hytt yow to vnderstond that Syr Jamus Tyrrell hath ben at Brugys
20 and hath spoken wyth the Kynge of Romayns diuersse tymes, and
the Kynge made Syr Jamus grett chere, and soo dydd the town of
Brugys and all oder towns of Flaunddyrs that he cam throwe; as
grett chere as any man myght hawe. And soo hytt ys thowth yf the
Kynge of Romayns maye subdew Gaunte and rewle Flaunders,
25 as wythyn schortt space wee thyncke hee schall, or ellys muste fflee
hys weye owte of the contrey or be distroyd, that he wull graunte
owre souereyn Lordd Kynge all thyngys that he w[u]ll leffully
desyre, for to hawe pese wyth vs, ffor the contrey wold gladdly
hawe pese wyth vs. For as now wee nor they dar nott resortt to
30 nor ffroo, wyth saffcondite nor oder wyse, ffor Harold Staunton,
Edmond Knyght, Nycolles Taylor, mercer, [Dorse] they hath ben
at Barow martt, and yn ther comyng homward ffrom the martt,
at Sclewce they ben taken presoners and leyd yn the castell of
Sclewce and lyeth styll there and hath doon thys iij wekys, and
35 nott lyckly to come schorttly wyth⟨owt⟩ they ⟨pay⟩ mych mony for
ther raunsom, etc. Item, syr, my Lordd of Sent Jonys comavndyth
hym harttly vnto ⌐yowr⌐ mastyrschyppys and he sayth he longe
sore to see yow, and hys mynd was ffor to a ben yn Ynglond long
or thys, but the Danys ar on the see and euery day afore Calles
40 hawen, wherffor hee dar nott aventur to take passage. Syr, my
Lord sayth he marvell that ye wryte hym noo letters: hee sayth
⟨he⟩ had noo word from yowre mastyrschyppis syns he departyd
owte of Ynglond, wherffor hee fferyth hym yee schuld take som
dysplesyr wyth hym or wyth som of hys, etc. Item, syr, thys same
45 day ys oon come ffrom Brugys and he sayth ther ys an Ymbasett
sent from Brugys and from Ipur vnto Gaun[te] for to make the
pesee betwyxte the Kyng of Romayns and them, whyche ys
thow3te they schall conclude. And that doon ther schall an

**240.** 31 *ms.* I they hath     32 ffrom] Scl *canc.*

Imbasett come from thens ynto Ynglond yn as possybull hast as
maye be to mak[e] a goode pese, as I trust to Godd schall be, who 50
⌜euer⌝ preserue yow. Wrytten at Calles the xxij day of Jenyvere.

By yowr seruaunte,
Wylliam Cely.

To my ryght worschyppffull mastyrs Rechard and George Cely
merchauntys of the Stappell of Calles, at London yn Martt Lane, 55
soytt dd. (*Shield*.)

**241.** *William Cely at Calais to Richard and George Cely
at London, 15 February 1487/8*

s.c.1 53/193

Jhesu M¹iiijᶜiiijˣˣ vij

Ryght worschyppffull syrs and my reuerent mastyrs, afftyr all dew
recommendacon precedyng I lowly recommend mee vnto yowr
mastyrschyppys. Fyrdyrmore, plese hytt yowre mastyrschyppys to
vnderstond that I hawe receyued yowr letter datyd at London the
xviij day of Jenyvere, the whych I doo well vnderston⟨d⟩. And as 5
tochyng John Delowppys, I hawe wrytten hym acordyng to the
tenour of yowr letter, but the ceson ys syche at Brugys now that
noo man there hath noo leyser to goo abowght any thyngys perteynyng merchaundyse; for viij ⌜days⌝ longe the gatys of Brugys
were schytt and noo man sufferyd to com yn nor owte, and euyr 10
syns Candyllmesse Evyn all the comoners of Brugys hath ben yn
harnesse and kepe the markett place. And they hawe sett the Kynge
of Romayns owte of hys place, and put all hys men from hym and
kepyth hym vnder ward, but they saye they wyll doo hym noo
bodyly hurtt. And they hawe taken diuersse that were rewlers 15
abowte hym, whych men thyncke they hawe or schall suffer deth,
and many of hys lorddys beth ffledd. And the cheyffe rewlers of
Gaunte be com to Brugys, and soo ⌜they⌝ wyll playnly hawe peese
wyth Fraunce and to be vnder the abesaunce of the Kynge of
Fraunce yff the town of Brugys wold be agreabull to the samee, 20
but as yett they be nott agreed amongyst hemselffe. Wherffor they
hawe sent ynto Braband and ynto Holond and Zelond that eueryche
of thes contreys doo send to Brugys serten wysemen wyth ffull
auctoryte of ther contrey ffor to coomen and talke wyth the

240. 50 maye be] etc. *canc.*
241. 22 Zelond] to *canc.*          23 wysemen] to *canc.*

25 Gauntenersse *and* them, and that maye take syche wayes *and* con-
cluson amongyst them as they can dryve be reson moste benyffy-
cyall for them *and* ther contreys. But they ar vtterly determenyd
that the Romayns Kynge schall rewle noo longger amongyste them,
for allredy they hawe dischargyd all the old Wytt of Brug*ys*, the
30 whych was sett yn be the Kynge, and made a new Wytt. And they
seye that they wyll hawe the quoyn*us* sett dovn agayne; and soo
they of Brug*ys* sayth all schall be well schorttly, but hytt ys
onlyckly. The imbassettor*us* that schuld a com*m*en ynto Ynglond
beth ffled to Sclewce, etc. Item, syr, I hawe receyued anoder lett*er*
35 fro*m* yow datyd at London the x day of Feuere, the whych I hawe
well vnderstond. And as tochyng makyng over of mony at Brug*ys*
be exch*a*unge, or oder wayis of conveyaunce yn redy mony or
ffyne gold, ther can be none tell thys hete be over, for eu*er*y man
ys yn harnesse yn the makett place, and soo ys John Delowppis *and*
40 Gomers Desors bothe. [*Dorse*] And syr, as for the paym*e*nt of the
nexte halffe yereys wag*ys* at the vj day of Apryll, I truste *and* put
noo dowtt*ys* yn hytt// yowre wull*ys* schall be owte of the town or
any purvyaunce or provyson schal be made for paym*e*nt therof.
For John Delowppis man ys here at Call*es* redy to receyue hytt
45 as sone as he heryth they be at a conclucyon at Brug*ys*, *and*
w*yth*yn viij or x days wee schall knowe at the vttrest what weye
they of Brug*ys* wull take, for they hawe denayed them of Gaunte
diuersse of ther desyrys, etc. Syr, the sayng*ys* ys þat the quoyn*us*
schall be sett dovn at Brug*ys*, *and* yff ⌈it⌉ soo be hytt were best
50 yowre mastyrschypp*ys* taryed yn makyng ower of yowre monys,
ffor hytt ys nowe at to owtrag*ys* losse: the ryall ys wurth xx [s. Fl.]
*and* all oder golдd*ys* affter the rate; and as for new grott*ys*, ar
wurth vij d. a pese y*n* Brug*ys* nowe, etc. Syr, w*yth* the nexte
passage I schall wryte yowre mast[yr]schyppys syche newes as
55 I can here, etc. No more vnto yowre mastyrschyppis at thys tyme,
but allmyghty Jh*e*su pres*er*ue yow. Wrytten at Call*es* the xv day
of Feuere.

p*er* yowr s*er*ua*u*nte,
Wyll*ia*m Cely.

60 To my ryght worschyppffull mastyrs Recherd and George Cely,
m*er*ch*a*untys of the Stapp*e*ll of Call*es*, at London yn M*a*rtt Lane,
soytt dd. (*Shield*.)

25–6 concluson] and *canc.*        35 whych I] do *canc.*        41 nexte] of the
*canc.*        43 therof] and *canc.*        47 hawe] denyed *canc.*

**242.** *William Cely at Calais [to George Cely at London],*
*29 February 1487/8*

s.c.1 53/195

[. . .] the town of [. . .] contenew styll yn ther a [. . . la]st passyd
all the ambawght [. . . to]geder, *and* on ffestyd anoder, and iche
of them swore to o[der] they wold kepe the town of Brug*ys* to the
behooffe of Phelyppe Muns*ir* as Protector of Duke Phelypp. But    5
many men thyncke hit wull ⌈not⌉ be yn ther power to kepe hit
longe, ffor they ⌈haue⌉ hadde many grett displesurs, and moo ar
lyke for to hawe schorttly, for ther ⌈is⌉ myche pepull comen latly
owte of Braband *and* Zelond to New Portt *and* to oder townes that
bee Burgen y*n* Flaunders for to lye yn garyson. *And* moo schall    10
come schorttly, hadd the Kynge of Romayns doon w*yth* his sege
at Rotterdam y*n* Holond, whych he hathe besegyd be water and
be lond soo st[r]ayte that hit muste nedys geve vpp, as they seye
that come lately ffro*m* thens, etc. Syr, here ys nowe mervell*ys*
delynge w*yth* many ffollke, and that I thynke yee schall vnderstond    15
be some men schorttly, etc. Syr, as ffor Sperynge, I hawe schewyd
hym the entent of yowr lett*er*, for the whych he comyth over to
yowr mastyrschypp at this same passage to clere hymselff. And
I pray yowr mast*er*schypp to call vppon Spery*n*ge to gett my gere
ffro*m* mast*er* Hanssis yn Pety Walys, and allmyghty Jh*es*u kepe    20
yow, amen. At Call*es* the last day of Februare.

p*er* yowr s*er*ua*u*nte,
Wyll*ia*m Cely.

*No address.*


**243.** *William Cely at Calais to George Cely at London,*
*12 March 1487/8*

s.c.1 53/194

Jh*es*u M<sup>l</sup>iiij<sup>c</sup>iiij<sup>xx</sup> vij

Ryght worschyppffull syr and myn esspecyall good mastyr, wy*th*
all dew reco*m*mendacon had I vmbly reco*m*mend mee vnto yowr
good mastyrschypp. Fyrdyr plese hytt yowr goode mastyrschypp
to vnderstond that I haue receyued be Thom*a*s Graungers

5  seruaunte yowr letter datyd at London the ij<sup>th</sup> day of Marche, the
whych I hawe well vnderstond. And as towchynge the matter
betwyxte yowr mastyrschypp *and* Sybson, I haue nott as yett
spocken wyth John Hubbard theroff, but wythyn ⌈this⌉ ij days
I wyll goo to Guynesse *and* speke wyth hym therffor, and I dowght
10  nott all the ffavour that hys mastyr and hym bothe can doo yn that
matter, or yn any oder agaynyst hym. I know hytt well, yowr
mastyrschypp schall hawe hytt. And syr, ffor the quetaunce that
Sybson made to Wylliam Strycke of Sentrycasse, I haue nott yett
seyn hytt, but I spake wyth Stryke hys wyffe here at markett, and
15  sche says her husbond hathe a quytaunce of Sybson, the whych
I schall see whan I com theder—wheroff I schall send yowr mastyrschypp the copy schorttly, and tydyngys how ȝe schall spede yn
that matter, etc. Syr, as ffor tydyngys owte of Flaundyrs they contenew styll yn myscheyff, lycke as I hawe wrytten yow yn my last
20  letter be on Thomas Spycer of the Northe Contrey, save on
Satter⌈day⌉ last was behedyd at Brugys the Lordd Dugell, *and*
moo ys lyke to be schorttly. They surmysyd a matter vppon John
Delowppys, but he hath stoppyd them wyth mony. *And* soo syche
men as beth of any substaunce yn Brugys fferyth thys rekenyng,
25  and diuersse off ⌈them⌉ stelyth dayly aweye and goyth to Myddellborow yn Selond; ffor they ffere the end wyll be nawght, whych
I pray allmyghty Jhesu amend hytt, whoo euyr preserue yow.
Wrytten at Calles the xij day of Marche.

                                    per yowr seruaunte,
30                                   Wylliam Cely.

*Dorse*: To my ryght worschyppffull mastyr George Cely, merchaunte of the Stappell of Calles, at London yn Martt Lane, soytt
dd. (*Shield*.)


# UNDATED LETTERS

### 244. *R. Shipden to George Cely or John Dalton*
S.C.I 59/42

My trusty and verry trusty frend and lover, I recommend me vnto
you, to John Elderbek *and* John Dalton, to my maister Wigston
first, *and* all othir. And maister, howbeyt that I have chargid you

                243. 5 the ij<sup>th</sup> *over canc.* xv        24 beth] hathe *canc.*

ofte *and* many tymis w*yth* many thing*ys* wherof as yit no *re*compens
i[n] sothe is made on my partie, yit wot ye wel that I am he which  5
w*yth* all myn hert shal make *re*compens in part, w*yth* all myn hert
*and* se*r*vis. Prayeng to take in pacyens this my request, *and*
accordeng to the same to bie by the help of my broder John Dalton
*and* frend, in the mart ij litil bokis imprintid. On is intitlid or callid
Beliall, *and* anothir Formulariu*m* Instrum*entorum*. And for the  10
love of Jh*e*su forget not this, as ye wil have my se*r*vis whil I lif.
Ther is mat*er* in the ton þat shal do you pleasur*e* as wel as me. If
ye wil not bie he*m*, speke to John Dalton, *and* let me have redy
word.

Yo*ur* trewe lover,        15
R. Shipden p*er*.

*Dorse*: To my trusty frend*ys* and atturneis, George Cely and John
Dalton, marchant*ys*. Or to on of hem, joyntly and seu*er*ally. (*Seal*.)

**245.** *Sir Ralph Hastings at Guines to George Cely,*
*31 October* [*no year given*]
s.c.1 53/179

My ful trusty frende, I recomm*aund* me to you. I haue receiued
yo*ur* kynde and louyng lett*re* and wel vnderstonde alle þing*ys*
þerynne contened, wherof I thanke you, and for youre good and
trewe hert. I am and shal be yo*ur* dettou*r* of as gode a torne ageyne
anoþer tyme, and trusteth þerto trewely / I sende you by John  5
Twiselton þis berer xij li. Fl. in setillers at iiij s. iiij d. I pray you
to take it in gre, and anything þat I cane do vnto plese*r* ye shal
fynde it redy, by God*ys* grace, who eu*er* prese*r*ue you. Writton at
Guysnes the last daye of October.

[*In a different hand*:]                    your tru luffuyng        10
Rauff Hastyng*ys*.

*Dorse* (*same hand as body of the letter*): To my ful good frende
George Cely.

**245.** 5 *ms.* þerto to      9 daye of] N *canc.*      12 frende] John *canc.*

**246.** *John Eldurbek to George Cely at London, 10 April*
*[no year given]*

s.c.1 53/169. *Torn and discoloured*

[Worchepfull syr, as hertely as I] may I r[ecommend me vnto you,
thankyng you of your curtesy] to me [s]chowyd at [. . . Master
George I besek you to] be gud master to Wylliam in h[elping him
. . .] cler mater. Hit was so that John B[arkwey . . .] at Pollus
5 Wharffe was her at Sensa[. . .] that tyme beynge her ix coveryngys
[for] beddys [. . .] wyche coveryngys wer had home ⌈to⌉ London
to þe sa[yd Ba]rk[wey, and] aftur that the sayd Barkwey vndurstood that ther wold [be] trobull for þe same coveryngys, it
fortuneyd that Wylliam my serv[ant] was logeyd wyth hym at
10 London, and becaus þat he was a str[aunger] *and* not knowen,
therfor þe sayd Barkwey causeyd the sayd Wy[lliam] to make salle,
wherfor he is trobuld at this tyme. I besek [you] master George be
his god master, and what poyntment you make hym I well abyd hit.
The master of þe Myss[. . .] of Ospreng hathe wreton a lettur
15 to his cossyn *Christ*ofull Coolenis, [or] in his absenis to his wyff,
to help forthe in this mater. An[d] allmyghty God *preser*ue youre
worchepffull *per*son. Wreton the x day o[f] Aperell.

your*us* to his power,
John Eldurbek.

20 *Dorse*: To the worchepfull George Sele, m*er*chand of þe Stapull
of Calles, in Marke Lane at London.

**247.** *George Cely at Calais to Richard Cely the elder at*
*London, April [1476]. Draft*

s.c.1 63/309

Ry[ght whorshyppfull] ffathyr afft[yr all dew recomen]dacyon
I recome[avnde me vnto] yow yn the most [lowlyest whysse that]
Y can or may // Fordyrmor plesyth yt yow to vndyrst[ond that I
haue ressey]vyd ij lettyrys ffrom ʒow, whon wrytt the [. . .] Apprell,
5 the tothyr wrytt at London the xiij day of Aprell [the wheche]
lettyrys Y hawe rede and do whell vndyrstonde, etc. // Plesythe
[yt yow to] vndyrstond Y hawe resseywyd ancordyng vnto yowr
wryttyng [of Wylliam] Wylsson, mastyr in the George of London,
iij M¹C ffelles, the wheche Y hawe sortyd ancordyng to yowr

247. 4 resseyvyd] ancordyng to y *canc.*

yntente. Ther be of yowr [wynter Cottys] xiiij<sup>c</sup>⌐lx⌐v ffelles, and 10
ther be of yowr somer London ix<sup>c</sup>x ffelles, [and ther be] of yowr
wynter London vij<sup>c</sup>xxv ⌐ij⌐ ffelles. Sum iij M¹C ffelles. // Ytem,
p[ayd by me] vnto Wylliam Wyllson ffor ffraytt off the sayd ffelles
ffor hewry [pack vj s. iiij d.], wherof wher vij pakys iij<sup>c</sup> ffelles. Sum
totall ffraytt—xl⌐ix⌐ [s.] j d. [and] ffor primage of heuery j pake 15
ij d. Sum xvj d. Sum totall—l s. v d. Allso [plesythe yt] yow to
vndyrstond that by the xxiij day off Aprell nex comyng [we most]
ber into the Plasse halffe ⌐yowr⌐ costom in redy mony and ⌐of⌐
the to[dyr] halffe Y most make an byll payabyll ⌐the last day of⌐
Jovne next com a[nd most] make here annothyr byll payabull at 20
London ⌐the last⌐ day ⌐of⌐ May off the x s. off the s[ar]pl[er
wheche] schall be sent vnto John Tate / Plesythe yt yow to vndyrstond the costum of yowr iij M¹C ffelles amovntys to xxv li. vj s.
viij d. ster., wherof 3e most abat to pay at London of vj sarple⟨r⟩s
and a C ffelles, hewry v<sup>c</sup> ffelles ys an sarpler, [and] 3e most pay x s. 25
off le sarpler—sum iij li. ij s. ster. Rest—xxij li. xiiij s. viij d. ster.
The [whec]he [xxi]j li. xiiij s. viij d. most be payd into the Plasse
at xxj s. iiij d. Fl. [le li.] ster. / The losse in Fl. amovntys xxx s. iij
d. ob. quarter. Sum totall [that] Y to pay into the Plasse—xxiiij
li. iiij s. xj d. ob. quarter Fl. Furdyr[mor ples]e yt yow to vndyr- 30
stonde that the Fellyschypp bethe angreyd [that as for s]yche new
wholl as ys comyng, wythyn ⌐a monyth⌐ affter yt co[m vnto Ca]lles
yt schall be set an salle / wherffor ytt whyll be be[st that 3e] schypp
yowr wholl as schortly as 3e may / the sonar 3e s[chypp yowr
who]ll yt schall stonde / etc. / Ther hathe bene moyche a[do at 35
Calles betw]yxt the Kyngys Covnsell and the Fell[y]shyp ffor [the
matter and it had] not come a salle 3ett had not the K[yngys
Covn]sell a be.

18 yowr over canc. the        20 in canc. before Jovne        32 a monyth
over canc. vj whekys

# NOTES

1. This is a typical specimen of an informal bill of exchange. Because the sums are expressed in sterling there is no indication of the actual profit taken. Kesten had in fact paid Dycons not £40 ster. but a sum in Flemish money at an exchange rate artificially calculated to allow interest on the loan, putting it in modern terms.

It is unusual to find one stapler making over money for another, as Wode and his attorney are here doing for Cely: Wode was probably also a merchant adventurer, and indeed may be the John atte Wode alias John Benyngton, grocer of London, who occurs in *CCR 1468–76*, p. 85. The Cely memoranda contain two obligations in the name of John Benyngton, dated Feb. 1485/6 (File 13 ff. 19, 20).

15. *soit doon*: for *soit donné*, which appears in various guises.

2. 3. *the sopesans*: ? 'the substance' (most part), or ? 'the supposition' (that you have sold your fells).

8. *no good rvlys of the Place*: no useful directives from headquarters. *The Place* is used to mean the headquarters of the Staple Company, or its governing body, or the Staple Fellowship as a whole. The expression occurs similarly in *ACM*, p. 311, with reference to the Mercers' Company.

10. *at Geteryng feste on Sonday after Send Peter Day* [3 July]: Kettering, Northants., was still a centre of wool-stapling and combing in the early nineteenth century (Samuel Lewis, *A Topographical Dictionary of England*, 3rd edn., 1835). The four annual fairs mentioned by Lewis do not include one around 29 June, but St. Peter is the patron saint of the parish church, and the *feste* is probably the dedication festival.

12. *John Ranys*: possibly the same as John Raunsse of Guines in 15.

13. *Barton*: the Barton, Northants., where Agnes Cely had property, but it is unclear whether this was Barton Seagrave or Earls Barton.

14. *my mayster Wetyll*:? Adrian Whetehill, comptroller of Calais.

19. *hottymys*: 'betimes' would be an attractive emendation, but Richard 1's letters are clearly formed, and the first character is certainly *h*. (Though in 38. 43 he seems to have misread his own *be* as *he*, changing 'nor be toder men' to 'nor be do toder men'.) Perhaps the word represents an accidental blend of 'betimes' and 'what time'.

3. This letter contains instructions for a double exchange, which amounted, if parity at Antwerp mart did not alter, to a straight loan without interest in return for a reciprocal one on the same terms. George is to repay Eston £14. 2s. Fl. for £12 ster. lent at London, and to lend him a further £14. 2s. Fl., to be repaid at London as £12 ster. The noble at 6s. 8d. here represents a money of account.

4. *Sencyon martte*: the Sinksen or Whitsun mart. The staplers regularly attended four marts in the Low Countries, not to sell wool but to

collect payment from their buyers. These were the Sinksen mart (dial. MDu. for 'Whitsun') and Bamis mart (Bafmis < [Sint] Bavonmisse, from St. Bavon, Baf or Bavo, patron saint of Ghent, whose day was 1 October) at Antwerp, and the Cold mart and Passe or Easter mart at 'Barrow' (Bergen-op-Zoom). There was also an important Easter mart at Bruges.

**4.** 10–12. *I whas at Mekyllyn . . . Kesten and hym*: 'I was at Mechlin and saw it [to be] poor wool. It is this [that forms the quarrel] between Kesten and him'.

16. *Allay*: Aveley, Essex.

18. *the mor sett by thys actys the world*: apparently 'the more shall we be esteemed for these acts [by] the world'.

**5.** 4. *iij M$^l$viij$^c$l fellys*: by the long hundred of six score; see note to **247**.

6–7. *John Tamys fellys*: this is doubtless the celebrated John Tame of Fairford.

7. *the wyche fellys war Thomas Kestenys*: Kesten, who is seen acting as attorney for Richard 1 in **1**, had a long and chequered relationship with the Celys. Further details about these fells emerge from the following letters. Kesten seems to have allowed Maryon to ship them to Calais to avoid arrest by other creditors, but subsequently claimed them again. File 16 f. 6 is a note by George Cely dated 28 November (no year) that he had delivered to Thomas Adam 1,207 winter fells, out of a total of 1,740, valued at £65. 3s. 7d. Fl. (£54. 6s. 3¾d. ster.). Possibly the fells were therefore split up among Kesten's creditors.

18–19. *Hary Seyseld*: probably 'Harry Cecil'.

21–2. *Sent Tolowys scryssche*: St. Olave's Church, Hart St., the Celys' parish church in London.

**7.** This appears from the writing and spelling to be a copy made by George Cely from the original. It seems likely that the author was the Thomas Miller mentioned in **9** as surety in the matter.

7. *by collar*: under cover of Maryon's name. 'Colourable shippings' under false attribution of ownership were strictly forbidden.

8–9. *I wholl nott say the contrary but*: 'I will not deny that'.

9, 14. *do yt(t) good*: a phrase (apparently unrecorded in dictionaries) with a similar range of connotations to 'make good'. Here loosely 'fulfil all obligations'?

20. *takyn wyth henmyys*: captured by enemies.

**8.** 4. *my godfather*: William Maryon.

14. *Kyrstower Brvn*: Christopher Brown of Stamford (*CPR 1494–1509*, p. 169; Wedgwood, p. 119; etc.).

18. The sense of the missing words seems to have been that George must pretend not to know what the letters say.

**9.** 8–9. *no preferment be them in the neyhyng of my mony*: 'no advantage from them in obtaining my money'. Cf. 'Ebalt . . . had no gode to nyghe or to ley hand vppon' (C.47. 25/10(2)); a translation from a Dutch original).

**10.** John Spencer was a fellow stapler (E.101. 197/11). This is another letter of payment with instructions for a double exchange. The exchange rate is 25s. Fl. per £ ster. The only clues to dating are this rate and that of 7s. 10d. Fl. to the noble on the dorse (23s. 6d. Fl. per £), referring to payments at Easter; the note 'Forst to ressewe of Henryc Basler pro John Spensar' at Cold mart, ? 1476 (File 15 f. 45), and another note about £8 Fl. 'written him' on a Bruges money-changer at Sinksen mart 1478 (File 11 f. 40). None of this evidence is conclusive, but on the whole it may point to 1476. 1478 seems ruled out, because at Easter 1479 the exchange rate was well above 23s. 6d. Fl.

**11.** 2. *ty⟨dy⟩ngys*: MS. *tyngys*, as in **23.** 14 *tyyngys* and **90.** 19, 22 *tyyng*.

4–5. *how it stand in the pertys of the Dewke of Borgens londys*: after a series of defeats the Duke of Burgundy, Charles the Bold, was killed at Nancy on 5 January 1476/7. Many of his lands, notably Boulogne and most of Picardy and Artois, were indeed promptly seized by Louis of France.

11–12. *John Tate*: the younger, mercer and merchant of the Staple; treasurer of the Staple at this date.

16. *Byfylde*: William Byfylde or Byfeld(e).

22. *for to doe for hym and wyll hymselve*: 'to help him if he will help himself'.

**12.** 9–10. *sale at long dayys*: with a long term of credit allowed.

11. *John Underhaye*: Jan Vanderheyden of Mechlin, cf. **14.**

15–16. *the pryse kepyt*: no reduction in price allowed (but an artificially low rate of exchange quoted in compensation).

16–17. *money be exchonge at London* . . .: loans at London for repayment at Bruges at usance were being made at an exceptionally low rate of exchange, in expectation of an imminent calling-down of Flemish currency. If there was any reduction in values at this date it was short-lived, since in November 1477 the official Flemish rate went up to 25s. 4d. Fl. (Grierson, table), and it rose even more steeply in the following year.

**13.** 5. *make . . . my prentys freman*: it seems to have been the custom to make an apprentice free of the staple before the expiration of his term. He then obtained certain limited privileges (*Ordinance Bk.*, pp. 142, 150). Fulbourne had apparently served four of his eight years.

**14.** 7. *schoen ghebont*: probably 'good packing' (cf. **50.** 19), a phrase meaning 'of clean wool properly selected'.

**15.** 5. *Rychard Twege*: Richard Twigge, a warden of the London Mercers' Company 1484–5 (*ACM*, pp. 156–80).

6. *John Cowlard*: warden of mercers 1476–7 (ibid., pp. 95–7).

8. *Barmessay Strette*: Bermondsey High Street.

11. *Senttercasse*: S. Tricat or S. Tricaise, Pas-de-Calais.

16. *the Sonday afore the datte of thys letter*: 16 November.

17. *Pollys Crosse*: the sermons delivered by popular preachers from the pulpit-cross in St. Paul's churchyard were often a source of news as well

as edification. It was here that the famous sermon on 22 June 1483 first publicized the Protector's claims to the throne.

18. *howr wncull the Dene of Jorke*: Richard Andrew, Dean of York, formerly secretary to Henry VI, died before 5 November.

**16.** This and the next letter are drafts, starting in a careful and formal hand which becomes cramped and hurried as the writer proceeds, and much corrected. Although in the name of Richard Cely, they are not in his or any other recognizable hand. The place of writing of the first draft of **16** appears to be 'Lee' (? Leigh-on-Sea, Essex), but an abbreviation for London may be meant. The initials T. (or C.) P. at the foot of **16** may be those of the writer or, perhaps more probably, of the recipient. The name of the latter is inserted above the line in **17**.11, but the writing is so cramped that it is impossible to be sure what is intended: the suggested reading 'T. Prout' is very tentative. The tone makes it plain that he was a person of some importance at Calais.

9. *that Y shold report*: a common modal use of *shold* indicating a rejected allegation.

10, 14. *by you*: to your disparagement (*OED* By *prep.* 26 d.); cf. **38.** 43–4 'I here meche thyng sayd be [i.e. against] hym'.

18. *Thomas Blakham*: plate borrowed from Thomas Blacham, 'cousin' of George Cely, is listed in File 12 f. 35. There was a Thomas Blak(e)ham of London, fishmonger, in 1469, who died before 29 September 1487: *PMR 1458–82*, p. 163; *L. Bk. L*, p. 245. *causes vrgent*: a legal phrase perhaps used here more for effect than sense, but possibly 'a vehement quarrel'.

**18.** The Daltons, fellow staplers and close friends of the Celys, occur in various subsidy rolls and merchant guild entries in the *Records of the Borough of Leicester, 1327–1509*, ed. M. Bateson and H. Stocks (1901).

4–5. *j sac di. xviij cl.*: one and a half sacks and eighteen cloves.

6. *redy money*: this was one of the Staple's periodic attempts to forbid credit.

**19.** 9. *a locky man*: lucky for the Celys rather than fortunate himself.

12. *Rychard Prowde*: perhaps the son of an Essex neighbour of that name who witnessed a grant in 1474 (E.R.O. D/DL T1 473).

18. *my Loorde of Sent Jo[nys]*: Sir John Weston, Prior of the Knights of St. John of Jerusalem in England, 1477–89. The prior and order held a good deal of land in Essex in the neighbourhood of Aveley, including More Hall in Aveley, property in Rainham, West Thurrock, and Purfleet, Sutton Temple, and the church of Thurrock Grays (15th cent. cartulary of the Knights Hospitallers, BM. MS. Cott. Nero E. vi).

18. *B. Pasmar*: ? Richard Pasmere, Knight Hospitaller and supervisor of all the order's lands in England, who held land at Aveley, Rainham, etc. (Weever, p. 359; E.R.O. D/DL T1 467). 'B.' in this case may stand for 'brother', as in many of John Dalton's letters.

22. *the wycwr of Awelay*: John Houghton, vicar from 1464 until his resignation in December 1478 (Newcourt, *Repertorium*, ii. 23, and **43**).

26–7. *myn oncles paryche at Gresford*: Richard Andrew became sinecure rector of Gresford some time after 1458, and resigned in 1475 (information kindly supplied by Canon W. V. Lort).

35–6. *owr inbasseturs, and whate ansfor thay haue of the Dewyke*: the Duke is Maximilian of Austria, who married the young Duchess Mary of Burgundy by proxy on 21 April 1477. A commercial treaty was signed by England and Burgundy on 12 July 1478, after a long period of discussions (Rymer, v. iii. 85 ff.).

36. *ansfor*: this curious spelling of *answer* is Richard 2's invariable practice. It probably stems from confusion between *w*, *wh*, *v*, and *f*: cf. Essex place-name treatment of the elements *wood*, *ford*, and *worth*, and such doublets as Inworth and Inforth (*CCR 1468–76*, p. 38). Cf. also the spelling *stowe* 'stuff', **74**. 17. Malden and Zachrisson misread *auffer*: see Hanham, *Medium Ævum* (1957).

38. *do at the next mart . . .*: obtain the best possible rate of exchange in making over your money.

46. *Bottons*: William Botton was a mercer and merchant of the Staple (*PMR 1458–82*, p. 151; *CCR 1468–76*, p. 294).

51. *owr ostes*: Agnes Burnell.

**20.** 3–4. *sterlyng money, xxiiij s. for the li. Were we payd xxj s. iiij d. Flemyche . . .*: for the system whereby the garrison of Calais was maintained by the Staple in return for part of the custom and subsidy on wool, see *Studies in Trade*, pp. 74–5, and for the Staple's manipulation of exchange rates and coin valuations, Hanham, *Bulletin* (1973). Richard's remarks must mean that the soldiers' wages, nominally expressed in sterling, were to be computed in Flemish money at a rate of 24s. Fl. to the £ ster. The staplers had formerly paid their customs and subsidy dues at Calais in currency valued on a scale where two rials (£1 ster.) were worth 21s. 4d. Fl., but this year had to pay either in sterling or in other coins valued on the same scale, the equivalent of 20s. Fl. for £1 ster. The list of coins in which George paid his dues to the Staple *c.* September 1478 (File 11 ff. 21–21ᵛ) shows that these were indeed valued on a 20s. scale. They had been obtained in Flanders at a rate of about 28s. Fl. per £ ster., hence l. 12 'syche goldys as gryte lose ys in at Caleys'.

10. *the acte of Parlement ys to paye them in sterlyng money*: it is not clear what 'act' is meant. The financial arrangements between Crown and Staple are in *Rot. Parl.* vi. 55–61, 100–3. This source does not, as it happens, specify the currency, but presumably sterling was intended.

23. *John Busche*: woolgatherer, of Northleach.

**21.** 8. *Wyttsontyde*: Whitsunday was 10 May.

10. *the xvj s. viij d. of the sarpler hafter the ratte*: for the fixed proportion of custom and subsidy dues payable at London.

16–17. *the weche ȝee schowlde haue*: 'which he says you had'.

**22.** 1–2. *afftyr all dew recomendassyon pretendyng*: there are seven occurrences of this use of *pretend* in George's letters. *OED* cites one instance of *pretend* 'pertain' from Caxton's *Morte d'Arthur*, suggesting it is an error,

but the Winchester MS. (ed. Vinaver, 2nd edn., 1967, i. 41) agrees with
Caxton on this point. It is a possible development of sense.

8–9. *mony ys stylle at Calles ij s. vj d. lowar than ytt ys in Flavndyrsse*:
the English failed to correct the discrepancy because Maximilian kept
promising to call down Flemish currency to the level prevailing at Whitsun
1477. A proclamation to this effect was expected on 16 July 1478 (*Stonor
Letters*, ii. 63: Kingsford got the date wrong), but was not in fact made
until October.

12. *an quyne at Calles*: a mint.

14. *make bettyr shyfft*: ? 'get a better exchange equivalent' (cf. *schyfftyd the mony*, **205**. 25), or 'get along better', a sense also unrecorded in
*OED* but applicable to some of its examples under Shift *n*. 6.

24–5. *the venter ys borne*: ? 'the risk is over'.

27. *make yow houyr*: transfer to you by means of an exchange loan.

38–9. *the iij^{de} peny, vj monthys and vj monthys*: the third part cash
down and the other two-thirds in two payments, ? six months and a year
later respectively.

**23**. 9. *the toder marte*: the Easter mart at Bergen-op-Zoom.

10. *Thomas Bvrgane*: Thomas Burgoyn(e), London mercer—a warden
1479–80 (*ACM*, pp. 116–38) and merchant of the Staple (E.122. 78/4).

17. *there ys moste drede*: of becoming involved in fighting between the
French and Maximilian's troops.

**24**. 4. *Thomas Granger*: stapler, fellow parishioner of the Celys in London
(P.C.C., 34 Bennett), sheriff of London in 1503–4, and a 'viewer' or
'director' (arbiter) in the Chancery suit between Richard and George's
widow *c*. 1490 (File 10 f. 12).

16. *a good pesse*: war had been resumed between France and Burgundy
in the spring of 1478, and troops massed, but there was little major fighting and a year's truce was signed on 11 July.

**25**. 6. *collecturs*: the collectors were Staple officials who saw to the payment of custom and subsidy and registered the staplers' imports of wool
into Calais. George is probably recommended to stay in Bruges to avoid
election: the forecast that the collectors' duties would be heavy was correct, as particularly large shipments of wool were sent in the summer of
1478.

20. *Meandry*[. .]: one or two further letters of the word may have been
lost owing to a tear in the paper. The late Mr. Theodore Veevers-
Thompson, curator of the library of the Order of St. John, Clerkenwell,
suggested to me that the nearest approximation was (Norton) Mandeville,
20 miles north of Aveley, which would be just within possible distance
for a daily visit. Maningtree, earlier Manytre, fits better phonetically, but
seems rather far.

21. *Thomas Folborn*: probably Richard 1's apprentice (**13**), but a
Thomas Fulbourne, gent., lived in the Celys' neighbourhood in Essex
in 1479 (E.R.O. D/DL T1 487, 488). D/DL T1 507 (March 1484) is
a demise at the request of John Petite, goldsmith of London, to Richard

Cely, the rector of St. Olave's, and William Maryon of property in Stifford and South Ockendon formerly held by demise of John Petite and Thomas Fulbourne.

23. *the kenred ys kumbrus*: apparently Richard means that the connection with the Fulbourne family is likely to prove embarrassing, especially as he goes on to mention Fulbourne's involvement in an affray in which the Celys are implicated.

27. *Petyt*: see note to l. 21. *Maudyslay*: unidentified, but there was an Essex family of that name in 1447–8 (Le Neve's 'Index to the Feet of Fines for Essex' [MS. in P.R.O.], Nos. 274, 277). *the gentylm[an]*: Richard's euphemism for some trouble-maker among the local gentry, possibly William Brandon (see notes to **133** and **169**).

30. *to schrape you and me wyth*: ? *shrape* 'scrape', so? 'erase our names from the record'; but there may be confusion with *scape* 'extricate'.

**26. 5.** *John Borsse, marchant of Ryssyll*: 'John Borgesse de Ryssyll' in File 11 f. 43. *Ryssyll* represents the Flemish name for Lille.

10. *at Bamys marte*: it is noteworthy that there was no down payment at all in this sale.

15. *my parthyschom*: a 'partition' was an order for payment of a certain fraction of the pound as an instalment on debts owed by the Staple to individual merchants for loans, for which debentures were issued. They could be used to offset dues.

**27. 15.** *redy mony ... at Brygys*: presumably in account with a banker.

**28. 5.** *Thomas Wygeston*: stapler, son of William Wyggeston, the founder of Wyggeston's Hospital at Leicester.

**29. 3.** *The Pane*: a certain piece of ground outside Calais, cf. Dillon, in *Archaeologia* (1893), p. 321 '[a battery] for the beating of the parke, the pawne, the downes and the contreth all aboutes the same'.

6. *yowr ordyr*: the 'order' of unmarried staplers.

**30. 2.** *neder thy broder nor thyselve*: Richard 2 went to Calais on 2 August and remained there until 23 November (File 16 f. 16).

5–6. *the bacons for to be deperde*: probably the *bacons* are to be shared out among the rest of the fells. The nature of *bacons* is obscure. It was repeatedly agreed in negotiations between the Staple and Leiden merchants that while the Leideners might reject gruff or rotten fells, winter fells wrongly sorted among summer ones, etc., 'vellera, dicta bacons, sint sicut de jure esse tenentur [sic], et si aliter reperiantur esse, quod in illum eventum tunc similiter removeri et excipi possint' (e.g. Posthumus, *Bronnen*, i, No. 500 [1477]). It would seem that the buyer tested fells to see whether they were genuine 'bacons' by tearing them: 'ubi mercatores opidi Leidensis lacerant voluntarie pelles aliquas lanutas nuncupatas vulgariter bacons, quod teneantur easdem sic ruptas penes se retinere aut earum valorem reddere' (ibid., No. 435). Possibly it was the special thickness of the skin that distinguished them, cf. *OED* Back *n.*¹ 18 (a term in the leather trade).

6. *make all sengyll fell*: *make* refers to the mending, i.e. patching, of damaged fells; cf. 'Johnson Letters', p. 549 (1548), 'I dare say there cannot be xl$^{ti}$ felles made, for nothing is lefft of the peltes; only the wull remeyneth'. See also note to **140**. 2–3 below.

7. *London somor fell*: fells bought in London from the butchers. Winter fells are inferior to summer ones since there has been less growth after shearing.

**31.** 14. *a cope of the payyng of the frayfte*: among the memoranda: File 11 ff. 22–3. The spelling *frayfte* beside usual *frayth* or *frayght*, etc., is noteworthy; cf. Edmond De La Pole's *streft* 'straight' in 'I hade hone come streft [printed *strest*] . . . frome the [Dowke]' (Sir Henry Ellis, *Original Letters Illustrative of English History*, third series, i. 130).

34. *Borganys man*: Gilbert Palmer, attorney of Thomas Burgoyn (File 11 f. 34$^v$).

36. *the man of Lyne*: ?Thomas Borwell, brother of William Borwell, described as 'of Lyn' in File 11 f. 39$^v$.

**32.** This may have been written on either 27 August or 24 September. During Richard's stay in Calais George was away 20–30 August and again 18 September–15 October (File 11 ff. 28$^v$, 33), but during the latter period he was probably at Antwerp rather than Bruges.

3. *Redhodys*: Thomas 'Redewhode', burgess of Calais, witnessed a lease of George's in 1481 (File 15 f. 50).

10. *Hary Whayt*: Harry Wayte, merchant of the Staple (E.122. 73/40).

13. *master Lefetenant*: the Lieutenant of the Staple.

**33.** The hawk here requested was probably that delivered to the Vicar of Watford by William Cely about 19 September 1478 (**37.** William left Calais on 18 September: File 16 f. 15). William Maryon had property in Watford.

5–6. *thowe Y be ferre from yow in sythe lette me be ny to 3ou in hert*: a reference to the proverb 'Fere fro iee, fer fro hert', cf. *Paston Letters*, ed. Davis (1971), p. 582. This reference has been missed by Whiting. See B. J. Whiting, *Proverbs, Sentences, and Proverbial Phrases* (Cambridge, Mass., 1968), p. 167.

**34.** 6. *ij partys in hand* . . .: the French merchants proposed to pay two-thirds in hand at 25*s*. 4*d*. Fl. per £ ster., in coin at Calais valuation ('mony corant in Calles'), and the rest in six months in coin at mart valuation ('mony corant in Flandyrs'). Richard wanted the whole price cash down in coin at the favourable Calais valuation, but would allow a concessive exchange rate of 24*s*. Fl. for one-third of the price.

7. *my li.*: the pound sterling in which the price had been quoted.

10. *the Ryan[s i]iij s. iiij d.*: the Rhenish gulden was set at this value by the Duke of Burgundy in November 1477, and that scale was adopted in Calais on 14 May 1478 (Posthumus, *Bronnen*, i, No. 505). The current table of Calais values was displayed in the lower hall of the Staple building (ibid. ii, No. 575). With the spelling *Ryans* compare 'Raynnes gylldorns', File 14 f. 50.

17. *William Gow[ldsmith]*: of Leiden, with whom Maryon had dealings (File 15 f. 38; File 11 f. 41ᵛ).

19. *or not*: 'take it or leave it'. *contre*: fells bought in the country as distinct from London, but in the Celys' usage also distinguished from Cotswold fells.

19–20. *tay wold refewy a scarttayn*: ? for 'they wanted to refuse a certain number'.

26. *Schewstre⟨t⟩*: Show Street, which ran up from the north-west of Staple Hall (Dillon, map).

**36.** 14. *the money in Flanderys schall be sete at a loar pryse schortely*: the ordinance was published two days later, on 12 October, setting down values by 12½ per cent (L. Deschamps de Pas, *Revue Numismatique*, vii (1862), 463–4), but it was ineffective, and such results as George Cely reports on 23 November were only temporary (cf. Rymer, v. iii. 97).

**37.** 26. *a meser alantarn*: ? a measure and a lantern.

28. *a harskob amane*: these words are a puzzle. *Harskob* is followed by another character which may or may not be cancelled, and the final letter (? *e*) of *amane* has been altered, unclearly, from something else. The first word may contain Essex *cob* 'basket', in which case perhaps *hars(k)* may be related to *OED hask* 'fish-basket' and *hassock* 3 'rush basket'. *Amane*: ?'a man', i.e. for each man.

**38.** 6. *Dayys be comyng*: deferred payments ('payments at days') are nearly due.

13. *Flemders*: an aberrant form, perhaps influenced by *Flemings* or *Flemish*.

28. *John Raynolde*: stapler and mercer (E. 101. 197/11 and E. 122. 78/5; *ACM*, passim).

39–40. *conten⟨t⟩ be agremen⟨t⟩ agrete*: contented by a general settlement.

40. *set in a waye*: put in the way of obtaining satisfaction. *in trete*: negotiated with.

44–5. *Intrete for asvrte of a comforde of paymen⟨t⟩*: offered the assurance of some payment.

42; 45. *asvr(e)te*: 'assurety', by confusion between *assure, assurance* and [*a*] *surety*, rather than 'a surety', as *OED* interprets similar occurrences. See also **208.** 30. and **236.** 17, and cf. Med. Lat. *asseuratio* (*Medieval Latin Word-List*, s.v. *assecuratio*).

43–4. *I here meche thyng . . .*: the sense is 'I hear a lot of talk about him, and if he offered me any hope of being paid I could put in a good word for him'.

**39.** 51. *Kay*: George's servant or apprentice John Kay.

54. *postorne*: possibly money paid to be admitted within the gates of Calais after they had been closed for the night, or spent or owed at the house called 'Le Postern' in Hemp St. (*Calendar of Fine Rolls 1461–71*, p. 69).

**40. 25.** *fenanys*: ? pheasants, or some kind of fen birds.

**41. 17.** *by what men heuery [som] vppon*: Staple dues could be met with debentures, which were negotiable. File 11 f. 21 (probably the 'byll' which was enclosed) shows that 19s. 9d. ster. of the total was met with a partition due on a debenture in the name of William Ede. William Dalton's payments (File 15 f. 37) included similar credits in the names of William Wigston and John Thorp.

**30–1.** *Whe wolld an takyn dyvars whays wyth them*: we offered them various methods of payment.

**42.** Robert Radclyff, esq., was the son of Sir John Radclyff of Attleborough, Norfolk. He was squire of the body in 1475 (Myers, p. 264), and captain of the fleet sent against Scotland in 1482 (Rymer, v. iii. 122). He joined Sir Edward Woodville's fleet in 1483, was knighted at the battle of Stoke, 1487, and later executed as an associate of Perkin Warbeck. At this time (1478) he was Keeper (Knight Porter or Master Janitor) of Calais, and is often called 'master Porter'.

The memoranda include a note (File 11 f. 41) of the purchases made by George at Cold mart 1478 for Radclyff: six sugar loaves at 9d. the lb.; 12 lb. of 'raysons corans' for 4s. 6d., and 60 'boge scynys' at 9½d. each. The marten fur is not mentioned.

**12.** *boge skynnes*: budge, i.e. astrakhan, broadtail, or caracul lamb. The name seems to derive from the place-name Bougie, Algeria, cf. Elspeth M. Veale, *The English Fur Trade in the Later Middle Ages* (Oxford, 1966), pp. 216–17. It may have come into English through Flemish *budye*, *budzen* (e.g. Gilliodts-van Severen, *Inventaire des Archives*, ii. 213 (1321).)

**13.** *iij cuet*: three hundredweight, i.e. 300 oz. troy. The loaves bought by George weighed 26 lb. or 312 oz. troy.

**43. 13.** *ij panelles schosyn agaynys ws*: cf. **25.** A *panel* is a list of jurymen, or the jury itself.

**15.** *Torowllde*: ? Thomas Torold, who had been clerk to John Fogge, custos brevium of the Common Pleas, in 1464–5 (Sir Francis Palgrave, *Ancient Kalendars and Inventories of . . . the Exchequer* (1836), iii. 388). *L.Bk. L*, p. 82, mentions a yearly grant to Thomas Torald, gent., for his services to the City in 1468–9.

**15.** *Brandon*: probably the William Brandon mentioned in File 10 f. 19ᵛ as 'prested' 26s. 8d. in ?1482. 'Brandon' seems to have been a local man; in 1481 he accused the Celys of poaching a hart (**136**). By the Cely account, in December 1478 he was 'still' in the Fleet, apparently as a result of an invasion upon the property of one of the Dencourt family in which the Vicar of Aveley was also implicated, and was likely to remain in prison until he came to an agreement with Dencourt.

In August 1478 Sir John Paston retails the news that 'young William Brandon' is in prison for multiple rape, and threatened with execution for marrying a widow (*Paston Letters*, ed. Davis (1971), p. 512). It seems uncertain whether this refers to the same person as the Cely comments, whose tone suggests something less serious. In view of the Essex and

Kentish connections, an obvious identification of the Celys' Brandon is with William Brandon, esq., son of Sir William Brandon of Wangford, Suffolk, and father of Charles Brandon, subsequently cr. Duke of Suffolk; who held the manors of Beckenham, Kent, and South Ockendon, Essex, and land in Stifford by right of his wife Elizabeth Bruyn, widow of Thomas Tyrell, and forfeited them when he was attainted 23 January 1484 (E.R.O. D/DL T1 500; *CPR 1476–85*, pp. 523–4, 530, 550; *Rot. Parl.* vi. 245; *Cal. Inq. P. M. Henry VII*, i. 378–9). He was knighted by Henry VII and killed by Richard III at Bosworth while acting as Henry's standard-bearer. His family were well known to the Pastons.

There are, however, difficulties about identifying the future supporter of Henry VII with either the Paston or the Cely Brandon. The reference to marrying a widow is extremely cryptic: W. Brandon, esq., had indeed married Elizabeth, widow of Thomas Tyrell, but this was over three years before August 1478. And he was a commissioner of the peace for Essex at a period when Richard Cely reports that he had been indicted for poaching (**136**). (Both Paston and Cely may, of course, have been repeating sheer rumour.) The matter is further complicated by the possible existence of a second William Brandon the younger, 'gent.' alias 'esq.', son of Sir William Brandon of Norfolk, knt., who obtained a general pardon for all offences committed before 27 March 1484 (*CPR 1476–85*, p. 423) shortly after the attainder of his apparent namesake.

16. *Dankowrt*: one of the Dencourt or Deyncourt family of Aveley and the vicinity. In 1479 John Selye, citizen and mercer of London, made a gift to, *inter alia*, Robert Molyneaux (see **146** and note) and Robert Dancourt, clerk (*CCR 1476–85*, p. 158. See also *PMR 1458–82*, p. 177).

17. *the Wycur of Awelay*: John Houghton resigned and was succeeded by William Smith D.B. on 31 December 1478 (Newcourt, *Repertorium*, ii. 23). Was it rape or trespass that he instigated?

**44.** 17. *dyschargyd you wyth a tone wyne*: apparently George and William either used up wine provided by the previous treasurer, and failed to replace it, or entered it in their account of disbursements (their discharge) without charging it in their receipts.

**47.** 7. *to lene hym now at hys neyd*: subsequent remarks might suggest the reading *leue* 'leave', but *lene* 'lend' fits better syntactically with *so that* 'provided that'. With the form cf. Richard's *lenyng* 'lending', File 13 f. 4ᵛ.

9. *an offe*: ? offer, ? office (see note to **54**).

14. *Fraynchem*: a mechanical error for *Fraynchmen*.

28–9. *parte of hys felles transporte be the covrt*: some of his fells legally transferred to George.

35. *my Loorde*: Sir John Weston.

37. *Robarde Eryke*: nephew of William Maryon and godson of George Cely; described as both fellmonger and girdler.

41. *he wyll playe wyth a straw*: perhaps a stock expression for friskiness: cf. Chaucer, 'Manciple's Prologue', 44–5, 'I trowe that ye dronken han wyn ape / And that is whan men pleyen with a straw'.

45. *Bawlser*: a horse. The name appears to be a corruption of *bausene*,

OFr. *bausenc, bausent, baussan* 'with a white streak on the forehead' (not *MED*'s 'piebald').

**48.** 3–4. *the iiij$^c$ li. the weche Thomas Kesten howyth to me*: the debt is to be repaid over eight years. Every year Kesten is to sell Cely wool and fell at Calais worth £100 clear, in return for £50 in cash, so that Cely receives £50 worth of free wool annually. There is no evidence that the scheme was carried out.

**49.** No year is given, and it is a little difficult to supply one. From a number of indications 1479 is most likely. Dalton acted as George's attorney in February 1478/9 and then mentions 2,000 fells belonging to Richard 2 at Calais (File 15 ff. 2–6). In File 15 f. 42$^v$ (*c*. May 1479) George refers to payments received from John Clays Heuson on behalf of Richard. In both 1479 (Easter, 11 April) and 1480 (Easter, 2 April) George could have been at the mart at Bergen-op-Zoom in April. The paper shows no watermark, but it has a somewhat distinctive wire-marking of widely spaced lines. The only similar paper among John Dalton's manuscripts in the collection is that of **44**, dated 12 February 1478/9.

The endorsement appears to be the result of a French lesson from a lady, as the feminine form of the adjective betrays in 'je swy hovntesse' (l. 21). Since George had a French-speaking mistress in Calais by 1480 (see note to **54**), it may be supposed that she was the teacher in this instance. The endorsement may well be later than the body of the letter from Dalton (and hence subsequent to **54**); the letter would be kept as a memorandum of the sale.

12. *Je boy Avous . . .*: apparently the words of a drinking song (Hanham, *RES* (1957). The cancellations 'Je nott' and 'Je ssue sseur' seem to represent incidental remarks by the teacher which George started to write down.

14–15. *Je sens lamor rensson estyn selle ke me persse par me le kowre*: 'je sens l'amour en son étincelle qui me perce parmi le cœur'.

17. *vn shavnssovne*: this should be feminine.

**50.** 1. From this date onwards Richard 1 begins his letters to George with 'I grete you wyll' in place of 'I grete the wyll'. **2**, to Robert in 1474, has *the*, and **37**, the earliest to Richard 2, has *you*. (But in the body of his letters he fluctuates between *the* and *you*, e.g. **27**.) George's first surviving accounts start in late 1473; if he became free of the Staple at the age of 16 in 1474 (the minimum age for the sons of freemen, as laid down in the surviving Staple regulations: *Ordinance Bk.*, p. 132) the new mode of address may mark the attainment of his majority in 1479.

4. *lese nor ix s. vj d.*: this rate (28*s.* 6*d.* Fl. per £ ster.) probably represented parity, so that George would get no interest on the loan. By August 1479 loan rates at the mart were down to 8*s.* 6*d.* or 8*s.* 8*d.* Fl. (File 12 f. 9).

6. *Rychard Tywne*: ? for Richard Twigge, cf. **52**.

11–12. *the lose ys grete in the my⟨n⟩te*: the staplers had to deliver part of their foreign currency to the mint in London, being paid the equivalent at the official rate of exchange. The Carolus groat was normally treated as the equivalent of an English groat of 4*d*. (Grierson, pp. 383–6), and George reckoned these to be worth £12 ster. or £15. 6*s*. Fl. (File 11 f. 54).

14. *Hewe Brone, mecer*: also a stapler, and an arbiter in the Cely Chancery suit.

**51.** 8. *Thowff they oder colers* . . .: 'it matters not if they [are] different colours from those mentioned above'.

10. *Raff Lemengton*: a fellow stapler, of Loughborough, Leics.

10–11. *my Laydy Skot*: the wife of Sir John Scott, marshal of Calais 1471–6 (Wedgwood, p. 750).

**52.** 4. *Sotton*: Temple Sutton or Little Sutton, near Prittewell, was a manor of the Knights Hospitallers, but Sutton-at-Hone, near Dartford, was more important and would also fit.

8. *in the Torwer*: at the mint in the Tower of London.

23. *Send Loye*: St. Eligius, Eloi or Loy, patron of goldsmiths, black-smiths, and carriers, and so associated especially with horses. When called upon to shoe a recalcitrant horse, the saint removed its leg, shod it, and replaced it on the animal.

**53.** 2. *John Hosyer*: warden of mercers 1495–6, 1503–4 (*ACM*, pp. 263, 593–9). The transaction is another double exchange loan.

12–13. *Rychard Haynys*: warden of mercers 1487–8 (ibid., pp. 297–304).

13. *John Perys of Norlache*: wool bought from him figures in two notes of purchase among the memoranda: File 11 f. 56 and f. 51.

18–19. *Thomas Cryspe*: another London mercer.

24. *Baras canvase*: probably canvas from the county of Barrois, later (cf. *OED*) confused with Dutch canvas.

24. *Robard Hereke*: Robert Eyryk.

**54.** This letter is probably earlier than **92** (*c*. June 1480), which mentions a fell chamber 'houyr my Lady Clar', and may well antedate the endorse-ment to **49**. I have placed it here on the supposition that Clare's approach to George may be referred to in **55**. After an obscure reference to a poor woman and a maid standing by her father's door, Richard there goes on to say 'I pray you send me word how ȝe do in tho maters, and qwate your profur wos, and wyth hom', suggesting that 'tho maters' and the 'profur' are concerned with a love affair. It is also possible that *offe* in **47**. 9 means 'offer' in a similar sense, but less likely, as the thing in question seems to be burdensome, and Richard continues, apparently in the same sentence, to mention financial matters.

Clare's surname is unknown. The letter may have been written by a professional letter-writer, judging from its rather ornate flourishes and the absence of signature.

17. *vne ainsaigne*: a token. *Bietremeulx*: Fl. *Bietremiu* 'Bartholomew'.

19. The address suggests that the letter was handed to one of George's servants, many of whom were 'Dutch'.

**55.** 20. *Cowldall*: Robert Coldale (cf. **60, 74**), armiger, of Rainham, co-grantee of a lease with George Cely in 1488 (E.R.O. D/DL T1 521a).

**56.** 15. *the wyllys for I haue hyar* . . .: 'I have the wheels for it here from my old Calais cart'.

17. *hexsyd*: possibly a mistake for *hexselyd* (*OED* Axled 1657; *MED* Axelen 1429). It may, however, represent a verbal formation from the n. *ax(e), ȝex* 'axle', quoted by *MED* from 1400.

18. *clotys*: a form of *cleat* 'wedge', probably influenced by MDu. *kloot*. Cf. *Promptorium Parvulorum*, 81 'clyte or clote a wedge', where *OED* (s.v. Cleat) proposed to read *clete*.

19. *John Parcar*: stapler (E.101. 197/11; E.122. 78/5) and burgess of Calais (File 11 f. 50).

28. *Randofe*: Randolf, the Staple Clerk.

30. *for to sve nou*: ? 'to pursue [benefits for the Staple] at present'.

37. *[Ja]cob De Bloke*: Jacob van den Bloke, an Antwerp money-dealer (De Roover, *Money, Banking and Credit*, p. 278).

40. *Huitryshe*: Utrecht gulden. Other forms in the memoranda are *Owterecht, He(w)trytus, Hutryshe, Vtreyshe, Vtritys*, and *Hevtterytus*.

45. *an Gyldars rydar*: a rider of Guelders. Malden, followed by *OED* (s.v. Rider 3), misread this as 'gylden rydar'.

53. *Loyssor Moy*: Lois Syr Moy, alias Lois De May (File 11 f. 36). Probably not the same as 'mastyr Lowys More, Lombard', in **235.**

**57.** John 'Rose' appears as bearer of a letter in **56.** He is described as a mercer in the memoranda (File 10 f. 21), where he is last seen in debt to George for an unpaid obligation for £30 ster.

8–9. *a lletter . . . ffrom your ffather*: ? **53.**

**58.** 7–8. *a town ther that callyt Baltyssall*: *call* in this absolute sense is unrecorded: *callyt* may be a pp. with *is* accidentally omitted. *Baltyssall* is (Temple) Balsall, Warwicks., a preceptory of the Hospitallers. *Contre*: Coventry.

12–13; 17. *we lokt for hem . . . Y thanked God*: present tense, with excrescent final consonant. Cf. *I thankt yow* **149.** 16 and *stomakt* **110.** 7.

25. *Stratford*: in Essex.

33. *my ryng*: 'I hawe payd ffor . . . my cosyn Wylliam Maryon ffor the ffash[on] of an synett . . .', File 14 f. 44ᵛ (July 1479).

**59.** Richard was probably writing from London to his family in Essex. The one-year truce between France and Burgundy of 11 July 1478 was broken when the Burgundians attacked the Château de Selles, near Cambrai. Maximilian defeated the French army commanded by the Sire d'Esquerdes (called 'the Lord Corddys' by the English) in a pitched battle at Enguinegatte (Guinegate) on 7 August 1479, the battle here reported. The victory had little real effect other than the encouragement of Flemish feeling against France.

1–2. *Thomas Blehom*: ?Thomas Blakham or Blacham (see note to **16.** 18).

**60.** Further details of the bankers and cushions here requested are given in **74** (11 November 1479), which fixes the year.

5. *yf yt be gode cheper þare*: an interesting stage in the development of *cheap* from n. to adj. The earliest citation of a properly adjectival use in *OED* is from 1509.

7. *þe ⟨one⟩ to haue xij þe elne*: presumably six ells are to cost 12*d.* each and six to cost 16½*d.*; cf. the entry in File 12 f. 22, 'payd ffor vij ellis of xx le ell, sum xj s. viij d. Fl.'

**62.** It is impossible to date this letter with certainty: references to buying hawks are common in the Papers. But the letters contained in vol. 59 of Ancient Correspondence seem to be not later than 1480, and the hawks mentioned by Tabary may be those in **63**.

'Watkyn Tabere' or 'Tabre' of Gravelines is mentioned several times in the memoranda: in December 1478 (File 11 f. 49) he owed money for hose-cloth, and in October 1487 (File 13 ff. 29ᵛ, 31ᵛ) George lent him 20*s* Fl. and paid him 8*s*. 'for rydeng vyth me to Donkyrke & ffor ffecheng of me'.

3. *hotoirs*: hawks.

4. *iij stoitrez*: stoters, the Flemish name for an English groat (Grierson, pp. 402–3).

4–5. *vng pot de vin*: a pourboire, a tip.

8. *monseigneur de Bewrez*: Philippe de Bourgogne, seigneur de Bèvres (Beveren), captain of Aire in 1482, governor of Artois, and later of Flanders.

14. *Maistre Portier*: ? Robert Radclyff. The letter may have been sent to Bruges; there is no suggestion that George lodged with Radclyff at Calais.

**65.** This letter is placed after **64** on the tenuous ground that both (like File 11 f. 40ᵛ, of 1478) refer to George being lodged at the sign of the Star in Bruges.

2. *Gilbert Hussy*: procurator general of the Castle of Guines (appointed April 1475: *CCR 1476–85*, p. 4), and described as receiver and forester of Guines in 1483–4 (E.101. 198/10).

7. *any goodly fedurs*: File 15 f. 52ᵛ lists feathers bought for various people in 1480: four single feathers, 'an hoystyrs [ostrich] ruyffe', and a thick black feather costing 8*s*. Fl.

**66.** Richard Ryisse was a stapler (E.122. 73/40).

**67.** 7–8. *the Sonday before Alhalon Day*: 31 October.

**68.** *John Sambach*: John Sambach, Sambage or Sambarge, stapler (E.122. 73/40 and *CCR 1468–76*, p. 350). George lent him money at the Cold mart in 1478 (File 11 f. 42).

**69.** **70** contains a request from Maryon for material for sheets 'lyke as Y have wreten vnto yow dyuerys tymes her beforn', and can be dated 1479 on internal evidence.

7. *Haustar sclothe*: otherwise *fyn Halfftar* (**70**) or *Halstar clothe* (File 12 f. 10). Perhaps cloth of Aalst (Alost), but the *-ff-* spelling is curious.

**70.** 8. *youre mader*: a miswriting for *moder*.

27–8. *Feleppe Seller*: see **71, 73, 78.** Philip Celyar, merchant of Tournai, died suddenly in London. His will, dated 25 September 1479, is P.C.C., 12 Logge.

**72.** 8–10. *Ye shall not fawte of your mony in the Colde marte: the be such men as I shall haffe my mony of . . . as I dare make me fast apon*: Postan, 'Private Instruments', p. 44, omitting *the* 'they', read 'You shall not fault of your money in the Cold Mart . . . by such men as I shall have my money of', and used this as an illustration of the assignment of debts. But in this particular case Lemington is plainly promising to repay George in coin when he is himself paid by his customers.

**74.** 31. *goys a* ['on'] *pillgrymage dayly*: Pilgrim's Hatch, with its shrine of St. Thomas, was probably the nearest centre of pilgrimage to Aveley, and a daily visit would be possible.

**75.** John Goldson has not been identified.
3–4. *your man wyth your akys* ['hawks']: William Fawkener.
7. *theparded*: departed.

**78.** 8. *heuer a cam at yow*: this use of *ever* as conj. (which occurs in letters by both George and Richard 2) is not recorded in *OED* or *MED*. It may represent confusion between *ever* adv. and *ere* prep. and conj., or a reduction of *or ever*.

12. *John Jacope, a Lombar*: John Jacoby of Florence, broker, became a denizen in 1484 (*CPR 1476–85*, p. 486).

12–13. *whe bar them on hand at the byll wos prodeste*: 'we maintained against them that the bill had been protested', i.e. a formal declaration had been made that the bill had been presented and payment refused.

19. *the fardell wyth arras*: the 'pawyn' mentioned in **71.**

28. *the cas for the peny*: ? a case for pens; cf. *crowny* 'crowns', l. 15, and *my Lordy byll* 'my Lord's bill', **148.** 13–14.

**80.** 11; 16. *ys faturs*: either a miswriting, or variant, of *facturs*, or *fautors* 'supporters'.

**82.** These are bills of lading carried by the master of the ship (whose name appears on the dorse) for delivery to the consignee at Calais, who would check the wool by them. The seal of 59/29 bears the impression of the edge of a coin rather than the usual signet ring.

**83.** 5–6 *master Thewhaytys*: Thomas Thwaites, Chancellor of the Exchequer 1471–83, Treasurer of Calais from at least 1476 to 1486 (Rymer, v. iii. 72, 182).

6. *the whete of the wolle*: this document is lost, but the weights and details are given in **82.**

8. *Sente Johnys in London*: the Hospital of St. John of Jerusalem in Clerkenwell.

15. *John Rawns*: perhaps the John Raunsse of Guines in **15**. *the Kyngys bowʒer*: probably an official supplier of bows (a title which occurs elsewhere). An alternative reading is *bowzer* 'burser' (OFr. *bowsier*, cf. the name *Brazer/Brasier* in the memoranda). There was no member of the royal household so designated, but a private servant of the King might be meant. The nature of 'John Rawns mater' is unknown. *The syngnete* is probably not the royal signet itself, but a document issued under it.

17. *Lenarde Boys*: ? Leonard Bowes, brother of the Thomas Bowes who was clerk of the King's ordnance in 1475, and one of the keepers of the exchange and mint in the Tower at his death in 1479 (Wedgwood, p. 97), but I have found no other record of Leonard, and the purpose of the visit is not clear.

18. *Bawll*: possibly the same as Bawlser, **47**, but Ball was a common name for a horse, particularly a white-faced one, and remained so in Essex down to modern times (Edward Gepp, *An Essex Dialect Dictionary*, 2nd edn., 1923).

20. *Lontelay*: John Lunt(e)ley, a servant and tenant of the Celys, who also appears in the memoranda as Luntlay and Lottlay.

**84.** 9. *Lokyngton*: John Lokyngton, master of the *Mary Grace* of London.

14–15. *byt for hoype in ws to a whor dyscwmfortys for heuer* . . .: the sense is evidently something like 'please write, if only to encourage our hope to escape unpleasantness for ever more, and so let us endeavour to please, as Jesus give us grace to do, who have us and our good friends [in his] keeping'. A *whor* may represent *a* 'have' and unrecorded pp. of *were* 'ward off', 'check', for which *OED* gives a pt. *wor(e)*, but it seems preferable to take it as an inf. ('to avert any further rows'). It may be *award* (*OED* award v.² 'ward off'), with final -*d* omitted before a following initial *d*-, or *awaren* 'be on guard against' (*MED c.* 1425). With the spelling with -*o*- for -*a*-, cf. 'to Bollen whord' (George Cely, File 16 f. 19), and alternations of the name *Allvard*, *Alvord*, *Alford*, etc., also in the memoranda.

**85.** 9. *Jonne Harthe*: Joan Hart, betrothed to Robert, cf. **83.**

13–15. *sche wyll falle of* . . .: 'she will abandon her claim in return for all the goods Robert has given her, and everything that she has given him'.

15. *Sir John the pryste*: cf. note to **175.** 13.

17–18. *layd aperte wyll noe* . . .: 'if he is wise, all this will be completely put aside now, for he will be undone if he weds her, though I cannot say so to him'.

**86.** 19. *tell hym note of tys ʒend byt of the qwetans*: 'tell him no more of these arrangements than the news of his release from the betrothal'.

23. *Hyt ys not for hyme to come in London ʒeyte*: 'he is not to come to London yet'.

**87.** 7–8. *Wyll Breten*: a well-known woolman and wool packer, and a

member of the Staple (E.122. 76/39). For details of some of his more dis-
creditable activities, see *Studies in Trade*, p. 58.

11–12. *thys halydayys*: Whitsuntide.

14. *se and caste a sorte of fell*: view and appraise a consignment of fells.
With *cast* in this sense cf. Fl. *uteworpen* v.tr. 'examine and select wool'
(Poerck, iii, No. 778).

23–4. *scharege me wyt fell* . . .: 'he will buy heavily for me if he likes the
offering, wherefore I have sent him to gain experience'.

**88.** This seems most probably to belong to 1480, when the Thursday
in Whitsun week was 25 May, and when the wool fleet left England on
2 June. If the Sinksen mart ran for six weeks at this date, i.e. from 6 May
to 17 June, it would be over well before Midsummer Day ('be that tyme
the marte wull be don'). The two other extant letters from John Cely,
also referring to George's aunt, are dated in September 1480.

6. Richard Bowell: formerly associated with Richard 1 and John Felde
(*CPR 1446–52*, p. 315; E.101. 197/11). He died in 1478 (will in P.C.C.,
33 Wattys). It is not clear what relation the 'sister' bore to either John
Cely or Bowell. Money due to Bowell and Fethyan from a Staple partition
is noted in File 13 f. 51 (undated, but *c.* 1482 ?).

12; 15. *Fythian, Fidyan*: William Fethyan, alderman of Calais and
merchant of the Staple (**208.** 44).

**89.** 9. *M*: middle wool.

20. *Myllhall*: ? Millwall, Isle of Dogs. The name appears as Myllalle
or Myhall in File 11 f. 24, and as Milhawe in E.122. 78/2.

**90.** 4. *John De Sclermer of Gante*: otherwise John Descyrmyr, etc. For his
complaints about this wool see **93.**

7. *clotys*: cloths, i.e. sarplers, bales of wool; cf. Fl. *cleet, clede*, the
equivalent of Fr. *serplier* in the same sense (Poerck, iii, No. 313).

15–16. *prathy rond canvase*: 'good [*pretty*] thick canvas'.

**91.** 23. *Edwhard Lenawllys*: George left £6 at Calais with 'Edewharde
Lenallys' in Dec. 1478 (File 11 f. 41ᵛ).

24–5. *Lontelays whoddyng*: Luntley's wedding. The word *whoddyng*
occurs in a stained patch, but examination under an ultra-violet lamp
shows that it is clearly spelt with an *o*.

**92.** These memoranda were written for Thomas Granger as attorney for
George Cely when the latter was at the Sinksen mart.

4–5. *my Lady Clar*: see **54** and note.

17. *theras Thomas Kesten dewellyth now*: see **76.**

24. *John Vandyrhay*: **87** notes that the middle wool had been asked for
by De Schermere and Vanderheyden. A memorandum made by George,
? at Sinksen mart (File 15 f. 51ᵛ), runs 'Item the Fryday the same day
I com to Andewharpe I made an bargen wyth John Vandyrhay, merchant
of Mekelyn, ffor all my medell woll, and hawe resseywyd an Godys peny
of hym'.

**93.** The absence of address, signature, and signs of folding suggests that George did not in fact send his father this strongly worded letter.

9. *better medyll yowng Cottys*: young wool is shorter in the staple than wool from the fully grown sheep, and of less value for most cloth manufacture. There was a difference of nine marks between the price per sack of good Cotswold and middle young Cotswold.

**94.** Robert or Robin Good was the servant or apprentice of Richard 1.

**95.** 7. *a byll of master Rychardys hand*: master Richard was apparently a Staple official: ? Richard Noneley, solicitor of the Staple in March 1482/3 (File 10 f. 13).
20. *Berwyke*: Berwick, Essex.
21. *the iiij li. ster. of hour brother*: see **91.**

**96.** 15. *Wylliam Browell*: William Borwell or Burwell, warden of mercers 1511–12 (*ACM*, pp. 394–404).
16. *Cowlton*: Thomas Colton, stapler and burgess of Calais (File 15 f. 50) and friend of the Celys. **171** is a letter from him.
23. *my Lady Marget*: the Dowager Duchess of Burgundy, sister of Edward IV.

**97.** The P.R.O. may be right in placing this among letters of 1482, but there seems no obvious reason to do so, and in File 15 f. 51 (1480) the name 'Harrowld Stavnton' appears in a list of various commissions to be done.
2. *Flemmyngys Dame*: the Vlamincdam (Rue S. Georges) in Bruges (Malcolm Letts, *Bruges and its Past*, Bruges and London, 1926, p. 156). There was also a tavern of that name (Gilliodts-van Severen, *Inventaire des Archives*, vi. 478). On Gheeraert's map of 1562 (Letts, p. 20) 'hoedemakers straete' is two streets east of 'Flaminicdam'. The armourers were in Candlemakers' Street near the Place S. Jean, the area where the English merchants lodged.
4. *by the same tokyn that*: the sense, probably already rather imprecise at this date, seems to be 'in the same way as', 'as, in connection with the same matter,'. Later it shaded into 'and by the way,' or 'I might add in parenthesis'. It perhaps originated in the idea of one token authorizing several different actions on the part of an agent.
6. *William Kenett*: merchant of Bruges, who bought wool from the Celys on several occasions.

**98.** 9. *wyt my Lorde . . . into Franse*: Sir John Weston and Thomas Langton, Treasurer of Exeter Cathedral, were appointed on 24 August 1480 to treat with the King of France for the marriage of the Dauphin with Edward IV's daughter Elizabeth of York (Rymer, v. iii. 112).
15. *Mondedanell*: alias Mondanyell or Hemonde Danyall (File 12 f. 4ᵛ; **104.** 3), master of the *Thomas* of Rainham.
16. *a grane*: ? some unidentified part of a horse's harness.

**99.** 3. *your crosse*: perhaps 'money', from the cross which often figured on coins (*OED*, Cross *n.* 20).

9. *Plomtton*: ? one of the family of the *Plumpton Correspondence*. Edward Plumpton of Furnival's Inn was secretary to Sir John Weston in 1483 (*Stonor Letters*, No. 329) and may well be intended here. *Nowell*: if this is a surname he was presumably Plumpton's brother-in-law. A 'Nowell, soldier of Calais' is mentioned in the arbiters' accounts as lent 20*s*. on 28 February ?1481/2 (File 10 f. 8ᵛ). *Thys byll* referred to an enclosure.

**100.** 2. *my sistir youre avnte*: see note to **88.** On 31 August 1480 George noted that he had £91 Fl. of his aunt's in ready money (File 12 f. 2).

7. *maystur Ylam*: Thomas Ilam or Ilom, mercer, stapler, and sheriff of London 1479–80.

9–10. *hath made her exchange . . . for the iiijˣˣxj li.*: R. H. Tawney (introduction to Thomas Wilson, *A Discourse upon Usury*, 1925, p. 77) misunderstood this transaction as a case of 'an outsider' securing an advance in sterling in return for a bill on Antwerp. In fact the aunt was not borrowing, but agreed to lend the mercer £91 Fl. at the mart, to be repaid as £75. 16*s*. 8*d*. ster. at days at London.

**101.** A second version of **100.** John Cely was unsure whether his nephew was at Antwerp or Calais and sent to both places.

**102.** 10. *amendynde*: an unusual form of the pr. p. for the Celys.

**103.** Edmond Bedyngfeld married the daughter of Sir John Scott. He was cr. Knight of the Bath at the coronation of Richard III, and died in 1496. 'Beyngffeldys quarellis' are mentioned among 'thyngys to be done at the [Sinksen] marte' in 1480 (File 15 f. 52ᵛ). This letter would therefore seem to be of the following September.

7. *worn long gowne*: ? a mistake for *won* 'one', but possibly 'one second-hand' gown is meant.

16. *Bondeman*: William Bondman of Calais.

**104.** 6. *xxx⟨ᶜ⟩ fell*: miswritten *xxx fell* in MS., but compare 3,000 in File 12 f. 4ᵛ.

10. *Rebate*: for the weight of canvas and the 'draught' at weighing.

17. *Mallyng*: ? West Malling, bordering on the Medway, or South Malling, Sussex, on the River Ouse.

43. *se scharly to hym*: ? for 'see sharply to him', but *scharly* may be *charily* 'carefully' (*OED*, 1579).

48. *delyng wyt worde*: 'conducting business by letter'.

51–2. *I hadde so many sayyng of men that cam from Caleys*: 'I heard so many reports of men arriving here from Calais'—who might be expected to carry letters.

52. *gryly*: ? for *grytly* 'greatly'.

**105.** Evidently later than **92,** much of the wool there mentioned having now been sold. File 12 ff. 4–5 is William Cely's account of his activities while helping Granger in October–November, and confirms the date for **105.**

Although the first part is ostensibly written by George to Granger, most of the document is in William's hand. George's original instructions were no doubt given to Granger after William had made this copy for his own reference.

20. *John Eldyrbecke*: a stapler who held various positions at Calais during the course of the letters, and was an appraiser at this time (File 12 f. 15).

**107.** 7. *the byll*: File 12 f. 3.

16. *Berelay*: ? Beverley, Yorks.

23–4. *the woll of Cottyswold ys bogwyt be Lombardys*: the King's Italian creditors were often recouped with licences to buy and export wool, and were highly unpopular with their English rivals as a result.

**108.** 5. *to Helttame*: Eltham Palace, one of the royal houses repaired and enlarged by Edward IV.

7. *Bregyt*: tenth and youngest child of Edward IV, christened 11 November 1480. Sir John Weston carried a spice-plate at the ceremony (BM. Add. MS. 6113 f. 74; Harl. MS. 364 f. 1).

14. *Py j*: Pye the first—George had two horses so named. *Syr Vmf[ry] Tawlbot*: Lord Marshal of Calais, younger son of John, Earl of Shrewsbury.

18. *xij tyde*: Twelfth tide, Epiphany.

**109.** 11. *my cossyn Maryons*: this letter, referred to in **110,** has disappeared.

18. *yowr good so lond*: the cargo was apparently damaged in transit: *made ffellis* (l. 19) are fells that have been repaired, so *lykewhysse arayd:* in a similarly bad state.

24–5. *that at Y desyryd long to se*: not further elucidated. *Y toke this seson* suggests that George took time off from his duties at Calais to join his brother and Sir John. George seems to have left Calais *c.* 16 October (if the letter mentioned in **107** was really written there), leaving William and Robin to land the shipment of wool by themselves, unknown to his father. Robin may have revealed what had happened on his return to England. George's attempt to shift the blame on to William and Robin seems a little unfair.

32–3. *dat of the xiiij day of Septembyr*: Richard's list of his shipments (**104**) is dated 25 September, but it seems to have been sent on 13 October (**106**), which may have been the date that the wool fleet actually left. William's first freight payments to ships' masters at Calais were made on 18 October (File 12 ff. 4–5). The intention had apparently been to cocket the wool in before the end of the customs year (29 September): failure to do so seems to have meant that the wool missed qualifying as 'old' stock—i.e. that cocketed in between 29 September 1479 and 29 September 1480?—and counted as 'new'. As George goes on to explain, it was in fact agreed that this shipment should 'passe appon yt selffe': that is, it would be exempt from the normal rule of selling 'free out', which meant that for every three sarplers of new wool the buyer had to purchase one of old. The rule made 'new' wool more difficult to sell than unrestricted older stock, hence the staplers' alarm over the mistake.

Malden's statement (*Cely Papers*, p. xii) that at the Celys' time 'old' wool was that 'taken to Calais in or before the February of any year, and remaining unsold by April 6 following' is due to a misunderstanding of a temporary ordinance quoted in Rymer (v. iii. 91; see further note to **247** below). E. E. Rich (*Ordinance Bk.*, p. 164 n.) in turn misinterpreted Malden's statement as meaning that in the Celys' time old wool was that of 'the spring shipment only'.

50. *long lyyng*: in the ships.

52. *myn howllde Lady*: Margaret, Dowager Duchess of Burgundy.

55–6. *the very grovnde most come howght of Ynglond*: ? 'the real lead must come from the English'.

**110.** Malden dated this letter 1482, but it obviously belongs with **111.**

16–17. *anythyng . . . hoderwysse then good*: cf. Fl. *anders dan goet* 'some calamity', Gilliodts-van Severen, *Inventaire des Archives*, vi. 334.

17–18. *a grete parte of my mastys gey in thys world wayere y-do*: 'most of my master's pleasure in this world would be at an end'. No n. *gay* is recorded in *OED* or *MED* in this sense. Probably, in view of Maryon's spellings *ley(e)n* 'loin' (File 12 f. 41), 'joy' is meant.

**111.** 8. *hys condyssyon*: ? their father's proclivity to worry.

23–4. *a marte . . . not . . . heyllfull*: the Cold mart.

**112.** 6. *an byll closyd herin*: not in fact sent, see **114.**

12–13. *cast howght*: separated.

21. *the ordynavnsse*: that after Candlemas the minimum exchange rate in sales was to be 26s. Fl. per £ ster., cf. **109.**

**114.** 15. *Bongay*: unidentified.

20. *Hane*: Heyne, MDu. dim. of Heinrik.

24. *the Lorde Master*: the Grand Master of the Order of St. John.

27. *the Rodys*: the island of Rhodes, which had withstood one attack by the Turks the previous summer and expected a new one. Two wings of the triptych allegedly given to the priory church at Clerkenwell by Sir John Weston to commemorate the successful defence hang over the altar in the restored church (*The Times*, 14 October 1958).

28. *my Lord Rewars*: Anthony Woodville, Earl Rivers. *my Loord Schambyrlen*: William, Lord Hastings, Chamberlain of the Exchequer from June 1471, Keeper of the Exchange in the Tower and at Calais, etc., and Lieutenant-General of Calais; executed in June 1483.

33. *Geoys*: George's Flemish servant Joyce (Goes) Parmenter.

51. *Hynys*: Heyne's.

52. *mostyrdewyl[l]*: Malden read *mostyrdewyk*, reproduced, but queried, by *OED*, s.v. Musterdevillers.

**115.** 9–10. *warantys off xv s. off the pownde*: warrants of payment to the holders of obligations and debentures, setting out the fraction of the pound to be paid as the next instalment (*Studies in Trade*, p. 76).

15. *Federston*: William Fedyrston or Fetherston, a captain in the

King's service (Scofield, ii. 87–8, 284, 414 n. 3; *CPR 1476–85*, p. 317). *John Dave*: of Fowey, in the King's service and also a pirate himself. He seized a Breton ship in 1483 (*CPR 1476–85*, p. 356), and was later imprisoned in Zealand for his depredations (**220**).

17. *master Marschall*: the Marshal of Calais.

18. *Syr Thomas Eueryngham*: Knight of the Body, one of the King's Council resident in Calais in 1482 (Posthumus, *Bronnen*, i, No. 1953). *master Nesseffylde*: John Nessefeld, armiger. He and Everingham were captains of two of the King's ships taken by the French in 1484 (Crowland Chronicle, ed. W. Fulman, *Rerum Anglicarum Scriptorum Veterum*, i (Oxford, 1684), 571).

22. *my Lorde*: William, Lord Hastings.

28. *Serche and the Water Baylys*: the houses of the Searcher and the Water Bailiff stood on the pier. It was necessary for travellers and others to remain outside the walls of Calais if they arrived, or business detained them, after the gates had been shut for the night.

45. *the Scape ys Clawe*: a hostelry name, Fl. *de schaepsclaeuwe* 'sheep's foot'.

**116.** 5–6. *the ʒeueyng of money was ix s., ix s. ij d.*: perhaps '27s. Fl. per £ ster. was the rate quoted for exchange loans to England while parity was 27s. 6d. Fl.'

10. *the weche mater in aspeschall*: proposals for George's marriage with John Dalton's sister.

**117.** 6. *Plomton*:? Edward Plumpton, as in **99**, perhaps acting for Robert, son and heir of Sir William Plumpton. Sir William died 15 October 1480. His estates had been conveyed to feoffees, of which the chief was Richard Andrew ('my noncle'), and resettled on Sir William for life, with remainder in tail to Robert (*Plumpton Correspondence*, p. lxxvii). In December 1480 inquisitions were held on the feoffment to Andrew and on Robert Plumpton's right to the property.

25–6. *the dethe of the sch⟨y⟩lde*: this must be 'Margery''s first child, cf. **181.** 8–10 (13 August 1482), 'Margery . . . schulde hawe rayment . . . agaynest her chyrchyng, as sche hadd the toder tyme'.

30–1. *Schestyrs dowter*: the Chesters were a notable merchant family. Richard Chester, skinner, alderman, and sheriff of London 1484–5, is mentioned in **167** and may be meant here.

**118.** 6. *the Turkepler*: the *Turcoplerius Rhodi*, Lieutenant to the Grand Master of the Order of St. John: Sir John Kendall at this date.

**119.** 8. *cownter candyll*: candle for the office counter.

**120.** 7. *scoostely*: ? a miswriting for *schortely+hastily*.

**121.** Misplaced by the P.R.O., 'Sent Tanys [Anne's] Day' having been misread as 'St. David's Day'.

11. *lettyrs myssyue*: less formal letters than the letters of payment; in this case possibly letters of advice from the Lombards' London associates.

M. M. Postan ('Private Financial Instruments', p. 64 and n. 2) wrongly thought that the expression was used in the Cely Papers to mean a letter of payment, but in File 10 ff. 2, 3ᵛ **168** and **230** are so described.

19. *the Coletry*: the Staple collectors were a source of foreign currency, since the clerk was paid dues in a variety of coin.

19–20. *docettys Wenycyans*: Venetian ducats.

22. *Syr Wyllyam Wheston*: commanded the English defences at the siege of Rhodes, and was Prior of the English house of St. John at the dissolution. According to some accounts he was Sir John's brother, but by others, and more plausibly, he was his nephew. *Syr Thomas Dane*: ? Prior of Berden, Essex. There is a letter to him, dated September 1463, in Anc. Corr. 62/114, and Newcourt gives 'Thomas Dawe' as vicar of Berden up to July 1474 (*Repertorium*, ii. 55).

**122.** 5. *John London*: the *John* of London.

14. *for vij s. the nobyll ster.*: Richard probably means that he proposes to charge Sir John a shilling in the pound interest, treating the transaction as a straight loan at interest rather than an exchange loan as normally operated. £100 Fl. lent at a rate of 21s. Fl. to the £ ster., would, at this date, mean that interest of 26⅔ per cent over two years was being charged. It is more likely that the Celys gave Sir John the Flemish equivalent of £95 ster. at the current rate of conversion, to be repaid as £100 ster. at London in two years' time.

**123.** Sir Roland Thornburght: evidently one of the Knights of St. John, but not otherwise traced. Stow mentions a *Thomas* Thornburgh buried in the priory church (*Survey*, ii. 85).

2. *Derford*: ? Dartford.

14. *the church within Newgate*: not, despite Malden, St. Nicholas Shambles, but St. Audoen (Ewen). Robert Bradford, who had been presented by the Prior of St. John's and died in 1481, was succeeded by William Ball on 12 September, patrons Oliver King, secretary to the King, and Thomas Rogers, armiger (Hennessy, pp. 97–8).

**124.** 21. *non sarpler cast howght but sen in þe showe*: certain 'show days' were appointed when the foreign merchants could inspect the wool for sale. On this occasion the Staple appraisers awarded the grades at the same time—normally they directed that certain sarplers should be specially 'cast out' as samples for their inspection.

**125.** 5. *the Cottysold* [MS. Cottys old] *wooll, that freeth hymsellff*: 'the Cotswold [not 'Cots. old'] wool, that frees itself.' A memorandum of the sale (File 12 f. 26) shows that five of these six sarplers were those shipped in early October 1480 (**104**), when the wool was specially classed as neither 'new' nor 'old', but to 'pass upon itself', in other words to 'free itself' (**109** and note).

25. *Prestun*: ? John Preston, mentioned in a list of specialities held by George, File 15 f. 15.

26. *anwardys*: ? towards, in part payment of a debt.

**126.** 2. *my bowhay*: ? *boy*, servant; but both George and Richard elsewhere spell this *boy(e)* (e.g. **112.** 38 and File 13 f. 4), and it would be more natural to give the lad's name in writing to another member of the household. ? Fl. *boe*, MDu. *boeier* (Gilliodts-van Severen, *Inventaire des Archives*, vi. 277), a medium-sized vessel, originally a coaster and riverboat, which was very popular in the 16th cent. for trading between Britain and the Low Countries; so ? a ship in which Richard was expecting goods from Calais. ? Fr. *boie*, *buie*, appearing in Scots as *bowy*, *buye*, and *bawhoy* (*DOST*, i, Addenda, sub Bed *n.* 2), a bowl, vessel for liquids or tub; possibly here used to mean a barrel in which goods were packed. In either of the two latter cases, the sense is that Joyce's coin may be with some of Richard's belongings.

14. *my brothers letter*: the next.

**127.** 12–13. *howr father and ȝe and I ar indyttyd*: this is a different affair from the one mentioned in **25** and **43**. As subsequently appears, the Celys had the indictment quashed before the matter came to court, so that no record remains.

14–15. *Syr Tomas Tyrryll, scherefe*: sheriff of Essex 5 November 1480–5 November 1481 (Wedgwood, p. 892). The missing name is probably Brandon (**133** et seq.).

17 *Myhyllys [wyfe]*: Alison Myhell [Michael], cf. **117.**

**128.** 6–7. *vᶜ xxxviij cast small tale wynter ffellys off London*: described in **131** and **133** as 556 winter country fells, discrepancies which are unexplained. *Cast* here means specially sorted. Five hundred 'small tale' evidently means reckoning by the 'long hundred' of six score, so that the total in modern terms is 638. Both in **247** and in *Ordinance Bk.* p. 149, 'five hundred' fells ('smalle tale' is specified in the *Ordinance Bk.*) are made the equivalent of a sarpler of wool, that is two and a half sacks at the standard equivalent of 240 fells to the sack = 600 fells by the hundred of five score.

**129.** Holograph (no secretary could afford to write as badly as the Prior does). Malden misread the date as '1487'.

3–4. *euer nobleman saying thay sawe not thys C yer so lequelly a felychyppe for so manny and in þat aray come howte of Ynglonde*: 'every nobleman saying that so handsome ['so likely'] a fellowship, so large and so well equipped, had not come from England these hundred years'.

9–10. *I treste do be the sonner at ome*: 'I trust to be at home the sooner'.

11–12. *Ryscharde Herron*: for Heron's twenty years' litigation with the Staple over wools seized at Calais in 1459, see W. I. Haward in *Studies in Trade*, pp. 318–20, and *Cal. Papal Letters 1471–81*, pp. 227–35, 252. *Remedyis and demandys* (16–17) refers to Heron's appeal against the Pope's relinquishment of the case, and annulment of a previous verdict, in November 1479 [Haward, and Scofield (i. 223), have confused the dating of the papal year]. The King's procurator (*proctor*) at Rome was John Shirewode.

15–16 *I dede in is as messe* . . .: 'I did in this as much as I should have done if they had given me a great reward'.

**131.** 13–14. *Wylliam Lyndys man off Northhampton*: William Lynde was mayor of Northampton in 1484 (*CPR 1476–85*, p. 434).

**133.** 4; 10. *Brandon, Brarddon*: see note to **43. 15.**

7. *mastyr Mwngewmbre*: Sir Thomas Montgomery, member of Edward IV's Privy Council, ambassador, and Steward of the Royal Forest of Essex—so interested in an accusation of poaching.

20. *howt of the whystelers handys*: this must refer to the financial difficulties of Collard de May (Nicolas de Man) or William Roelandts, two Bruges money-dealers with whom the Celys dealt, who both went bankrupt about this time (*Studies in Trade*, p. 371 n. 136; De Roover, *Money, Banking and Credit*, p. 332; Gilliodts-van Severen, *Consulat d'Espagne*, i. 135–6).

22. *Whykyng*: William Wiking, sheriff of London, died 19 October. Sir Richard Chawry ('Chary'), salter, was elected in his place. Both Wiking and Chawry were also free of the Staple (E.122. 73/40 and 78/5).

35. *to plesse that genttyllman*: perhaps *that genttyllman* here means George himself, but cf. the use in **25.** 27 and **169.** 20. Sir Thomas Tyrrell would seem to be one possible candidate. If George is not meant, it is not clear whether one of the whelps was destined to be a present, or whether Richard is saying ironically that the dead bitch gave their enemy a pretext to accuse them of poaching, and he hopes soon to get another which may serve him equally well. Richard 1 evidently regarded keeping a greyhound as dangerous (**136.** 30).

41. *howr pensyon in Fornyngwhallys In*: an annuity or other periodical payment due from Furnival's Inn.

85. *Charlly[s] Wyllars*: Charles Villars or Villiers of Leicester, merchant of the Staple. A later member of the family was George Villiers, Duke of Buckingham.

87–8. *Claysse Demowll*: Clays de Moll, 'man of the lawe', acted for George in the preliminaries of a lawsuit at Bruges. Five men of Ypres, two of them schepens, stood surety for a total of £367. 16s. 11d. ster., and the 'procuraryes' at Ghent were paid 20s. 'to sue the seid matir accordyngly', but the account (File 12 f. 21) has been extracted from George's books by the Chancery arbiters, and 'the seid matir' is not defined.

**134.** Presumably the letter sent by Kay on 14 November 1481 (cf. **136** and **137**).

19. *that ʒe gebart not . . .*: 'do not expose yourself to danger by going too often to Bruges'.

22. *a Parlemente*: there is no record of such a Parliament.

27. *Plumar*: Robert Plomer or Plummer, gent., a collector, and later comptroller, of the custom and subsidy of wool for London (E.R.O. D/DL T1 498; P.R.O. E.122. 73/40; *CPR 1476–85*, p. 421). According to Wedgwood (p. 688) he was also a lawyer and M.P. for Maldon borough 1478 and 1491–2, and a servant of the Earl of Essex.

28. *my Loorde of Essex*: Henry Bourchier, Earl of Essex, Master of the Royal Forests south of Trent.

28–9. *that my Loorde gaue me at Barwyke*: Richard obtained some sort of protective document before Sir John Weston left for Rome.

34–5. *master [Depu]te*: Sir John Dynham, deputy of the Lieutenant of Calais.

36. *vᶜ Doche pepwll*: ? expelled in case they should collaborate with the French in a possible attack on Calais.

**135.** The dating of this letter is complicated. It is apparently connected with the transactions recorded on one side of **200**, and also with a list of debentures in File 13 f. 51. Bryan was not a stapler, but had evidently obtained Staple obligations in discharge of a debt. It appears that he held two debentures or obligations in the name of Nicholas Bristol which were worth £41. 12s. 8d. ster. On these a partition of 15s. in the £ was declared, payable at a rate of 26s. Fl. per £ (**200.** 17). On the remainder (£10. 8s. 1d. [*sic*] ster.) a later partition of 10s. fell due (File 13 f. 51). This was payable, surprisingly, at the lower rate of 25s. Fl., but George received payment in coins valued on a scale representing 26s. 8d. Fl. per £ ster., i.e. that current in Calais from about March 1482. As Bryan was offered payment at a rate of 26s. 6d. Fl. (l. 10), it was probably the first partition that was due at this date. The debt of £50 said in **200.** 21–4 to be due to Bryan at Sinksen mart seems to be that recorded as paid on the dorse of **157** (23 April 1482—Whitsun was 26 May in that year), so that a date of 1481 best fits this letter for both reasons.

11. *John Hatfeld*: merchant of the Staple, treasurer in 1481 (File 12 f. 16).

14. *in yowr custum*: George might either have received cash for the partition or used the obligations to offset his custom dues.

**136.** 10 *sormyse*: false accusation.

29–30. *in recwmpense of yow⟨r⟩ beche*: cf. **133.** Was George or the Lieutenant being recompensed? Possibly George was to have Hector and the Lieutenant the other dog. *Grauenyng* is Gravelines, MFl. *Greveninghe*. Waterin Tabary is mentioned specifically in connection with Gravelines in the memoranda, and the Lieutenant said by him to be buying hawks in **62** may be this man, not otherwise identified.

36. *not hawlfe insamyde*: not nearly enseamed (rid of superfluous fat).

41. *my ʒeunge lady of ʒeurke*: Lady Anne Mowbray, only daughter and heir of John Mowbray, Duke of Norfolk, married Richard, Duke of York, second son of Edward IV, in January 1477/8 at the age of five. The *Complete Peerage* puts the date of her death between 25 January and 10 November 1481, but it must have occurred near the end of this period for Richard to give it as recent news on 23 November.

**137.** 6. *Benet Trotter*: Benedict Trotter, grocer and stapler (*L.Bk.L*, p. 229; E.122. 78/5).

22. *Schepe dys wpe in Engelonde*: 'sheep are dying further north', not, as Laetitia Lyell translated it, 'sheep dye is up in England' (*Mediaeval Post-Bag*, pp. 182–3).

**138.** Probably the letter referred to in **139.**

2. *my Lorde*: the Lord Chamberlain, Lord Hastings.

3. *Wynsour*: the King spent Christmas at Windsor (Scofield, ii. 324).

**139.** 6. *Andrew*: Andrew Hawes (**140.** 7). Dalton paid him £9. 13s. 3d. for the property (File 12 f. 13ᵛ).

9. *Neweresday*: although the year began officially on 25 March, 'New Year's Day' always meant 1 January.

**140.** 2–3 *we lack pelltys her*: 'pelts' were required for mending damaged fells according to the note in File 10 f. 36 of pelts (costing 3s. 4d. ster.) and packthread bought for this purpose.

3. *Sent Tomos*: St. Omer, Fl. Sint Omaers.

6. *Robert Byngam*: alderman of Calais and merchant of the Staple, cf. **208.** File 12 f. 17 records Dalton's payment to him of 26s. 8d. Fl. for quit rent.

6–7. *the grovnd ȝe haue bowght of Andrew Hawes*: File 15 f. 47 is a draft document in George's hand setting out that on 24 August 'Handrew Hawesse' sold George Cely a wool house and yard next to George's stable, and two tenements next the two houses previously bought from Hawes.

9. *Botrell*: the comment in **185.** 20–1 suggests that the dispute was over the ownership of the wool house.

**141.** 4. *your grett hevenes of your faider*: R. Cely senior died 14 January 1481/2.

5–6. *Gysbreth Van Winbragh*: alias Gysbryght Van Wenysbarge, Wynbarow, etc.

12. *no syn*: 'now since'.

19. *no mane may be gense*: ? 'no man may be against', i.e. oppose; cf. early ME. *gains* prep. 'against'.

30–1. *Caroldys . . . at xvj d. þe pond*: earlier Dalton had paid a premium of 18d. Fl. per £ (File 12 f. 13ᵛ).

37. *the Irysch skeyne*: an Irish dagger, a skene. In 1491 a resident of Dartmouth was accused of assaulting another *cum uno cultell' hibern'* (Hugh R. Watkin, *Dartmouth . . . Pre-Reformation* (Devonshire Association, 1935), p. 196).

**142.** This letter is exceptionally well written and carefully punctuated; a scribe may have been employed. 'Joisius Permanter, theotonicus' was one of three foreign servants for whom George Cely paid alien subsidy dues in London in 1484: E.179. 242/25 f. 7.

15. *John Ekynton*: John Ekyngton. The account for the breakfast given by John Dalton is in File 12 f. 14, 'Item j breckeffast on Robard Torney, John Elderbecke, Charles Vellers, wyth oder as Joyes can tell you, for to se wat Botreell hayd don in breckyng of your hosse and thraweng dongg among ffellys—ij s. vj. d.'.

33. *Hankyn*: the same as Hane.

**143.** 4. *Wylliam Brerely*: the mutual indebtedness of Thomas Kesten and William Bryarley is confused. For Kesten's pledges to Bryarley see **145** and note. But Kesten appears in the role of creditor in a letter from Bryarley to Thomas 'Kestven', dated only 17 October, in the P.R.O. (S.C.1 51/2—probably originally part of the Cely collection). This runs in part:

> Sir, I am for yow ryght evy, for I haue had vnderstondyng ffrom Fyz John that he had of yow lx li. gr. Flemysche. God knowyth I am ther-fore ryght sory þat euer he schuld take ony money of hym þat whas my frend and to paye hym þat is not my ffrend. But sir, sen that it is so I beseke yow of a litill paciense, and syr, I trust to God . . . þat I schall content euery man wyth a respeyth and þer schall no man lese on peny by me. . . . Wherefore, goode brother, I pray yow cast not me all away, for I trust in ouer Lord ye schall not lese on peny by me, to sell all þat I haue into my schyrte. . . .

10. *Saynt Laurence Pouteny*: St. Lawrence Poultney, in Candlewick or Candlewright St. (now Cannon St.) at the east end of Great Eastcheap.

**144.** 3–4. *the same man that he whas in his sayeng* . . .: 'he holds by his previous statement, that the debt is Bryarley's, and not his own'.

**145.** 3. *a bylle of Wylliam Bereley is honde*: it appears that George took over the debt and the pledges as requested. Dalton notes the payment of £6 5s. on his behalf 'Vnto Wylliam Breleay wyff for [cer]ten pleggys of Thomas Kestevens' (File 12 f. 13ᵛ). The list of goods in pledge for house rent of £6. 5s. Fl., due on 25 March 1482, was drawn up on 12 December 1481 (File 12 f. 29). The goods were household linen and clothing, and had been appraised by the 'preysers of þe town, John Whete, Saunder Wynde, sergeants'.

**146.** 7. *Bryan*: Harry Bryan.

**147.** 12–13. *Lombardys wholl at Hamton*: the *Mary de la Towre*, belonging to the King, left Southampton with a cargo of wool and cloth for Italy on 28 May 1482 (*Studies in Trade*, p. 45).

15. *Low Sonday*: the Sunday after Easter Day—14 April in 1482.

20. *John Croke of the Tempyll*: John Croke of London, gent. (dead by March 1478), was a feoffee of lands in Aveley which Richard I acquired from Richard Andrew in 1462 (E.R.O. D/DL T1 441, 479). This was probably the father of Elizabeth Stonor, who died in October 1477 leaving two sons named John, one of whom may be 'John Croke of the Temple'.

21. *the Exchetter*: no escheators' records for Essex at this date have survived.

25. *master Molenars*: ? Robert Molyneux or Molyners, common pleader or sergeant of the City of London (*PMR 1458–82*, p. 131; *ACM* p. 103 [both 1477]). Cf. File 10 f. 25 (April 1482), 'to master Molyneux to be off councell—vj s. viij d.'.

26. *Malyns*: George's Essex residence, Mallins, Little Thurrock; evidently inherited from his father.

**37.** *toke the manttell and the rynge*: i.e. took vows of widowhood; to the disappointment of potential suitors? For a description of the ceremony, see *Lincoln Diocese Documents*, ed. Andrew Clark, E.E.T.S. o.s. 149, 1914, p. 245.

**148.** 12–13. *Syr Wylliam*: ? Sir John Weston's chaplain, William Ball, or Sir William Weston.

**149.** 29. *Palm Sonday*: 31 March. *the Frensche inbaset*: the embassy was headed by Etienne Pascual, one of Louis XI's councillors; cf. Scofield, ii. 332–9.

**150.** 3–4. *the dethe of my yow⟨n⟩ge Lady of Borgen and of the treson at Sent Tomors*: Mary, Duchess of Burgundy, died 27 March. St Omer was supposedly betrayed to the French.

**151.** 13. *hys plasse in Hesext*: Bretts Place, Aveley.

20. *har leghe ys nat yt all holl*: 'her leg is not yet all whole'. File 10 f. 16 has the entry, '[paid by Richard] to master Norton, surgeon, for helyng off his moders sore leg—xxvj s. viij d.'.

49. *at the howyser in Barow*: cf. the address to **154**, 'beyng in the howeyser at Barow'. *How(e)yser* may be for MDu. *huushere* 'conductor domus', the *concierge* who, among other functions, took care of money and valuables for the merchants of his nation; perhaps misunderstood, or extended, in the second instance to mean the house under his care, which was set apart for the use of the English merchants at Bergen-op-Zoom.

56. *rydars Gyll.*: riders of Guelders.

**152.** 12–13. *Bryggys mart*: this started the Thursday before Easter, 4 April in 1482, and was a rival to the Passe mart at Bergen—'Barow mart' of line 25.

**153.** 23–4. *my Lord of Canterbery ys cortte*: the probate court, in connection with the will of Richard 1.

25. *Marynar(e)*: ? Molenars or Molyneux (**147.** 25 and note), with substitution of medial *r* for *l*.

**155.** Evidently of approximately the same date as the three preceding letters.

**156.** 13–14. *they can hawe no olde wull but where they bye new wull*: William probably means that the foreign merchants were being required to buy both new wool and the old wool necessary to 'free it out' from the same dealer, contrary to the agreement made in 1478 (Rymer, v, iii. 92).

**157.** Apparently of 1482: cf. **163** (7 May 1482) ll. 6–8, 'I vnderstonde that yowre masterschypp wold [th]at John Dalton schuld bye the horsse that he wrote to yow off'.

9. *Hary Bryan*: see note to **135**.

**159.** Two men called Nicholas Knyveton (alias Knyfton, Kneveton) seem to have been indentured retainers of William, Lord Hastings

(William Huse Dunham, jnr., 'Lord Hastings' Indentured Retainers 1461–
1483', *Transactions of the Connecticut Academy of Arts and Sciences*, xxxix
(September 1955), 1–175). Nicholas Knyfton, sheriff of Nottingham and
Derby, in 1489 is described as 'the elder' (ibid., p. 144). The writer of this
letter may have been the younger and less distinguished of the two, since
he addresses George as 'brother'. The dating depends on a note by
George (File 15 f. 49, ? *c*. June 1482), 'to by ffor Kneffton an bed of varder
of an xiiij d. an Fl. ell. Testor, selor and vallansse and cow⟨er⟩eng ffor the
bed of the same whorke'.

5. *þe strangyusst warke*: ? 'strangest', i.e. rarest, most unusual pattern.

**160.** 22. *surplysage*: the surplus left over from the custom and subsidy
after the Staple had met its various obligations, which had to be paid to
the Exchequer (*Studies in Trade*, p. 77).

28. *master Stoker*: Sir William Stocker, draper and stapler; brother-in-
law of Elizabeth Stonor.

**161.** The document which dates **159** also refers to George's purchases for
Bryan: 'Thyngys to be bowght ffor Bryan as his remembravnsse makys
mensyon' (File 15 f. 49). He notes the purchase of twelve dozen gloves
at 3*s*. 4*d*. the dozen in File 16 f. 24.

2–3. *laboure mad ayenst you*: ? about the debt from 'pore Henley', **162**.
File 10 f. 25 notes 'Paide by Richard Cely in Feuerer anno iiij$^{xx}$j to Bryan
to be good soliciter to the Lord Chambrelayn ffor the saide Richard and
George—xx s.'.

5. *my Lord*: Lord Hastings, who had returned to Calais the previous
day.

8. *all men recervid*: ? 'all men reserved', i.e. setting aside all others.

13. *iiij dosin of the mark of ij*: sic.

**162.** 17. *master Debyte*: the Deputy Lieutenant of the staple?

19. *pore Henley*: 'old Henleys wyddowe' figures in **213** and **217**.

21. *yowre gode detters here*: apparently members of the Calais garrison.

**163.** 8. *Synt Telen Day*: not St. Helen's Day on 18 August, but the In-
vention of the Cross, 3 May. William started to write *Holy Rood Day*, but
cancelled it.

9. *Odenborow*: Oudenbourg.

17. *kockyttyd yn affore the vj day off Aprell last past . . .*: it is not clear
whether a false date was entered in the customs accounts themselves or
only on the certificates of entrance.

**165.** 8. *the Byschopys ofesars*: cf. File 10 f. 14, 'Item paide . . . for certeyn
vytayle which, as the saide Richard sayth, was ffor the Bysshoppys offycers
. . . vij s. x d. and v d., an⟨d⟩ to þe coke—xx d.'

16. *wyth blottys*: including packs containing less than one sack weight;
cf. 'Johnson Letters', 70 (1544), 'j blott good Cottes, weyng here ix tod,
and at yowr commyng to Callys John Crante shall delyver yow as moche
fyne Cottes as shall make yowr blott a juste sacke.' The word probably
derives from MDu. *bloot, blote* 'bare; lacking'.

27. *Lemryke*: Thomas Limrick or Lymeryke of Cirencester and Stowell, Worcs., M.P. for Gloucestershire, J.P., etc. His daughter's name was Elizabeth (Wedgwood, pp. 544–5).

36–7. *be the mene of Pettyt, for inwynde and grete markyng*: in 1484 John Petite, merchant, and John Bolle, woolman, were appointed to make search through the realm for defective wool (*CPR 1476–85*, p. 494), and this was probably a similar inquiry into the packing of wool. *Inwinding* was the illegal practice of winding inferior wool among the locks of good fleeces.

77. *the byll of xiij s. iiij d.*: for the payment of a mark per sarpler as part of the custom and subsidy.

84–91. *the Kyng has sente to the mercars . . .*: no such proposals are mentioned in *ACM*.

90–1. *the mony . . . at viij s.*: that is, 8s. Fl. for 6s. 8d. ster.

**166.** This letter from William Adam is referred to in **170**. There is nothing to indicate which of several Langhams he wrote from.

**167.** 6–7 *they wyste where to abyde*: they knew where to stop, i.e. with whom to deal. In other words, there was some such illegal bargain made in advance as that between George and Vanderheyden in 1480 (**92.** 24 note, above).

11–12. *men talke yn Caleys marvellysly*: cf. **168.** 11–12 'Wylliam Cely wrat that whe be lyke to hawhe whar wyth Frawns'.

**168.** 13. *Rawson[s] dowttyr*: Anne, daughter of Richard Rawson, mercer and alderman, whom Richard Cely married before January 1483/4. After Rawson's death in 1487 Harry Bryan entered, with others, into a bond for £400 which he was to pay to Rawson's younger daughters upon their marriage or majority (*L.Bk.L*, p. 247).

**169.** Much of this letter is badly stained and patches are exceptionally difficult to read, even under an ultra-violet lamp, because the paper had been left folded and a portion of another letter became off-printed on to the left margin through damp.

15. *Schrofe ʒeuyn*: the eve of Shrove Tuesday, 18 February, or Shrove Tuesday itself. *Em* is otherwise unknown.

20. *the genttyllmane ys byt strayngely dysposyd*: possible identifications are discussed in notes to **43** and **133**. The next extant letter from Richard, **174**, makes no further mention of the matter. **175**, written nearly a month after **169**, describes false rumours at Calais about their mother and attacks on a priest by enemies who are again anonymous.

22. *my Lady Mary*: Mary, second daughter of Edward IV, died 23 May 1482, aged 15.

28. *my gostely brother*: a humorous analogy to *ghostly father* 'father confessor', in reference to the confession in the earlier part of the letter.

**170.** 9. *John Lemyngton*: of Leicester, stapler.

10. *Raff*: John's brother Ralph.

44. *payne off lesyng off the benyffete*: *the benyffete* is the preference

given to old wool, called 'the benefite of olde wolle' in *Ordinance Bk.*, pp. 150, 167.

**171.** 10–11. [*my*] *Lorde off Gloceter and my Lorde of Northomberlonde*: commanders of expeditions against Scotland in support of the claims of the Duke of Albany, brother of James III of Scotland. Albany landed from France at Southampton on 25 April. Edward IV returned to London, from a visit to Dover, on 23 May and took up his residence at the Tower.

14. *Frydey last past*: 24 May.

**172.** The dating depends on a note by George Cely of wool sold to 'Mavryn Clayson and hys ffellowys' (cf. l. 17) on 1 December 1481 (File 12 f. 30). This states that £26. 16s. 3d. Fl. was due to him and £22. 10s. 8d. Fl. to Maryon on the last day of May next coming, and 'at Bamus next'. Colton was selling wool for George early in 1482 (File 12 f. 38; File 16 f. 50).

2. *Wylliam Norton . . . draper*: described as a merchant of the Staple in E. 122. 78/4.

5–6. *my schyp and my presoners*: probably 'my ship and its crew that were taken prisoner' rather than indicating piracy on Colton's part.

**173.** This appears to refer to the same debt of John Williamson as the dorsal note to **172**, while the values assigned to the coins also suggest the date of 1482. Hugh Paddley, mentioned in **218** as having left his apprenticeship with William Dalton and being anxious to enter the Celys' service, may be this Hugh. 'Hugh' also collected a debt for George in January 1484/5 (File 10 f. 1).

4; 12. *di. lymvn grotys*; *lymon grotys*: this name seems to be a variant of *nemyng* groats. They appear as *lymmyn* groats in a note by an employee (File 10 f. 33), when George describes the same actual coins as *nynehegyn* or *nymeryn* groats (File 13 ff. 41, 41ᵛ). Other spellings in the memoranda are *nynhegyn* and *nymhekyn* (File 13 f. 64; File 15 f. 14). These names, appearing only from ?1480, for what were generally known in the Low Countries as *double briquets*, *double stuivers*, *patards*, or *vuurijzer*, are apparently unrecorded outside the Cely papers. Identification with the place-name (or surname) Nijmegen presents grave difficulties (Grierson, pp. 392, 393–4); are the various Cely forms perhaps corruptions of MDu. *limegnon*, *lemignon* 'match', alluding, like *briquet* and *vuurijzer*, to the badge which appeared on the coin?

**175.** 8. *Corpys Kyrste Day*: 6 June.

13. *Syr John*: ? 'Sir John the pryste' in **85**, perhaps John Wendon, 'soule prest' (File 10 f. 14ᵛ, etc.), who was paid an annual salary to sing for the soul of Richard 1, and later his wife. His successor in that office had business transactions with the Celys and was one of the feoffees of Bretts Place in 1487 (E.R.O. D/DL T1 516).

15. *them that whe gawhe gownys to*: for the practice of giving gowns at funerals or a month mind see Sylvia L. Thrupp, *The Merchant Class of Medieval London* (1948), p. 153.

**176.** 6. *the Kyng at Dower*: Edward visited Dover again on 9 July (Sco-field, ii. 340).

13. *to borow x or xij li.*: i.e. obtain free credit for.

**177.** 4. *the town off Ary*: Aire was surrendered, reportedly by the treachery of the commander, on 28 July 1482 (F. Godefroy, ed., *Mémoires de Philippe de Commynes* (Brussels, 1723), v. 260).

7. *my toder letter*: this is lost.

**178.** For a discussion of the dating of this letter see H. E. Malden, 'An Unedited Cely Letter of 1482', *Transactions of the Royal Historical Society*, 3rd ser. x (1916), 159–65. Malden concludes that it must have been written in July or early August. I have placed it in July, but it may be earlier.

5. *an lettyr . . . beryng datte at Napullus*: several letters from Sir John are mentioned about this time, but the only one extant is **129,** from Rome.

10–11. *the Dewke of Abany*: Albany left for the north of England on 29 May—the *terminus a quo* of this letter. Sixty thousand men is a con-siderable exaggeration of the size of the English force.

14. *Wythyn an mony⟨th⟩*: within a month of the writing of the letter, or of the army's arrival in Scotland? Successes by Gloucester and Northumberland were already being reported by 24 May (**171**—Malden did not print or refer to this letter, which he may have found illegible), and George's information may be mainly based on the news then current. Plainly he does not yet know of the surrender of Berwick, or of Edinburgh on 2 August, which reached Calais not long before 16 August. Dumfries was burnt in a separate raid on the western marches.

18. *grett rombyr*: with the cross and circle over these words compare the markings in the note made by George of rumours perhaps communicated by Weston, **200** and plate V, especially the similar symbol above the word *romber*.

**181.** 5. *hallff passage and brege money*: half passage money seems to have been a freight charge on goods shipped from Calais (*ACM*, pp. 200, 206). Bridge money was a toll paid on goods other than wool passing over Newnham (Neuillet) Bridge, west of Calais.

8. *Margery*: the date is consistent with her being the lady of the good puddings in **141** and **142**. She is not, of course, George's wife Margery, whom he married in 1484.

**184.** 12–13. *to ffollow the carttys*: the usual practice, to see that no harm came to the contents.

**185.** 4. *Syr Wylliam Stocker*: the mayor of the Staple, cf. **160**. 28.

14–21. *they that were beffore yn the wagys off master Robardd Radd-clyffe*: a contemporary chronicle mentions that about 10 August 1482 there was a scandal about a plot to duplicate the keys of Calais (*A Chronicle of London from 1089–1483*, ed. N. H. Nicolas and Edward Tyrrell (1827) p. 147). Suspicion would naturally fall on the Master Porter's servants, with whom Botterell (for whom see also **139**) seems to have been associated.

This incident may be connected with the bitter (but obscure) quarrel between Lord Hastings and the Marquess of Dorset in which each is said to have fabricated capital charges against the other through suborned informers (Dominic Mancini, 'De Occupatione Regni Anglie', ed. C. A. J. Armstrong, *The Usurpation of Richard the Third*, 2nd edn., Oxford, 1969, p. 68). Radclyff was a supporter of the Woodvilles (ibid., p. 122) and had previously been denounced to the council of Calais, together with Dorset and Anthony, Earl Rivers, by a man called John Edward, perhaps suborned by Hastings. Edward confessed on 8 May 1482 that his accusation was false (J. Gairdner, *History of the Life and Reign of Richard the Third*, 2nd edn., Cambridge, 1898, pp. 338–9), and was himself condemned to death for conspiracy, sedition, and treason early in December 1482 (P.R.O. Anc. Corr. 44/60). According to the Latin version of More's history of Richard III printed in 1565 (*The Complete Works of St. Thomas More*, ii, ed. R. S. Sylvester, New Haven, 1963, p. 51) Rivers in turn accused Hastings of planning to betray Calais to the French. Was Botterell, who had also fallen foul of Hastings (**188**), an informant on the Woodville side?

**187.** 21. *affore the Doches dyedd ffyrst*: 'immediately before the death of the Duchess'. These were to be the official valuations operative at Calais for the payment of custom and subsidy, etc. The values assigned to the coins are much lower than the official rates in the Low Countries for July: see Grierson, table facing p. 404, and Hanham, *Bulletin* (1973).

**189.** 7–8. *Andryan yowre oste*: Adrian Deffrey of the 'Sheep's Foot' in Bruges: 'Atryan yn the Scapys Claw, my nost', File 13 f. 27; 'Adreon in the Skapslaw of Brugys', File 12 f. 13.

21. *redy mony yn Calles*: this rule caused much evasion.

30. *yowre byllys . . . whych be abelyd yn courtt*: cf. *Ordinance Bk.*, pp. 115–16, 'he shalle not departe . . . before his accomptes ben vieued by the companie . . . and abled in court'.

**191.** 8. *the Boschoppe off Lewke*: the Bishop of Liège, cousin of Charles the Bold, was murdered by Guillaume de la Marck, allegedly supported by French troops of Louis XI.

**192.** 4–5. *the wycche I wolde Y hadde sleppyd the wylys*: perhaps 'I wish I had spent the time sleeping instead', or 'I wish it were only a dream', but more probably 'I wish I had slipped [out of] the bargain before now'.

5. *costemerys*: customary suppliers (sense not in *OED* or *MED*).

12. *bey and bey*: immediately.

**193.** 5–6. *take hym wpe*: put him in a stable. *ser*: clip. *stand*: remain indoors.

7. *he schawll be sawhe whell he ys hors*: 'he will come to no harm while his hoarseness continues'.

**195.** 7. *howr fathers towmbe*: in the chapel of St. Stephen in St. Olave's Church. Payments of £6. 3s. 4d. and 40s. by Richard 2 to Roger Egge, freemason or 'marbelar', are mentioned in File 10 ff. 14ᵛ, 15.

**196.** 29. *in plakkys—xxvj d.*: Malden, and so *OED*, printed 'iij plakes xxvj d.', which grossly inflates the value.

73. *Nycolas Hont*: London mercer. File 12 f. 7 is an unfinished letter of payment to him from George in 1480.

**197.** 4. *the whar*: the rebellion against Maximilian centred on Utrecht.

15–16. *howr detturs ar sclow payars*: absurdly printed by Malden, and so reproduced by other writers and in *OED* (s.v. Slow *adj.* 4), as 'goude detturs ar sclow payars'.

20. *Levynge*: a servant of George's. The accounts mention shoes bought for him *c.* 1481 (File 10 f. 18ᵛ).

**199.** 11–12. *dyd call the lest hawke that ys nott reclamyd wyth a creaunce*: a creance or cranes was a long thin cord attached to a hawk's leash during the process of training or 'calling to reclaim', that is, to come back at call when loosed.

16. *Syr Raff Hastyngys*: brother of William, Lord Hastings, knighted at Tewkesbury and described as Knight of the Body from 1474 (Myers, p. 263).

28. *I plehytt*: ? for 'I pledge it'.

**200.** This vague note of events and rumours evidently reflects the doubts and confusions prevalent immediately after the execution of the popular Lord Hastings, Lord Chamberlain and Lieutenant of Calais, about noon on Friday, 20 June 1483. (The formerly accepted date of 13 June appears to be an error: Alison Hanham, 'Richard III, Lord Hastings and the Historians', *English Historical Review*, lxxxvii (1972), 233–48.) The news here recorded must have been communicated to George Cely before the wilder stories could be dispelled, and before Richard's claims to the throne were first propagated on 22 June. It seems to derive from Sir John Weston, 'De Movnsewr Sent Jonys' being perhaps a naïve attempt to disguise the name. Two curious features further connect the document with Weston. Although the note is in the hand of George Cely, the pp. endings in -*t(t)* are not typical of George's usage, but do occur in Sir John's letter, **129**, e.g. *premysset*, *favorret*. And the signs or markings over certain words (see plate V) are of the same type as that over the word *rombyr* in **178**, the draft of a letter from George to Weston. It looks as though George was in the habit of substituting agreed ciphers for particular words in his correspondence with Weston.

The first five items in the note are stated as fact. The next five, being prefixed by 'if', were apparently recognized as doubtful stories. It seems possible that many of these rumours were put about by Richard's supporters in an effort to suggest that Hastings and his companions had taken part in a widespread conspiracy to destroy the protector's party and to seize the persons of the king and his brother. In fact, as far as we can tell, Hastings, Morton, and Rotherham seem to have been trapped by Richard before they could effectively prevent his plans to depose his nephew.

At the head of the page is a modern pencilled note dating it 'August

1478', and accordingly the document has been bound up as no. 19 of the volume. A cataloguer must have taken the bishop of Ely whose death is (falsely) reported to be William Grey, d. 4 August 1478. The document comprises a whole sheet of paper, which has been folded in two to form four pages. The bottom half of the first leaf (19 A) has been torn off. In fact, the binders placed leaves A and B in the wrong chronological order. The notes on what is now 19 B dorse were written first: in late 1481 or early 1482 (see note to **135**). **182** (13 August 1482) refers to attempts to get payment on 'warantys off xv s. off the pownde' like those listed here. Lines 10 ff. cannot have been written in June 1483, as 'Syngsyon' (Whitsun) (l. 22) was 18 May in that year. It therefore appears that George jotted down the news of 20 June 1483 on the back of an old memorandum that lay to hand.

1. *The Scottys*: according to Malden (p. 132 note b), Albany had reopened negotiations with England in January 1482/3, and there was some recrudescence of border fighting. It is possible, however, from the prominence here given this item, that stories about a Scottish invasion and general unrest in England were put about by Richard to emphasize the need for strong government, and to capitalize on the popularity he had earned by his signal victory against the Scots the previous summer.

2–3. *the Chavnseler ys dyssprowett*: Thomas Rotherham, Archbishop of York, had been replaced as Chancellor by John Russell, Bishop of Lincoln, early in May, but is probably the person meant. *Dyssprowett*: either 'deprived of office' or, more relevantly to Rotherham at this date, 'proved false', 'found traitor'.

3. *the Boshop of Ely ys dede*: this was untrue. Morton was arrested with Hastings and Rotherham and sent to Wales in Buckingham's keeping. He escaped to the Continent at the time of the Buckingham rebellion in the autumn of 1483.

4. *dessett*: apparently for *dessesset* 'deceased', as in l. 2.

4–5. *the Dewke of Glosetter*: the official proclamation about Hastings's execution apparently charged Hastings with treason against Richard as protector.

5. *my Lorde Prynsse*: the Duke of York, brother of Edward V. He was surrendered from sanctuary at Westminster on Monday, 16 June so that he might attend his brother's coronation, and had joined him in the royal apartments at the Tower, where the arrests were made.

6. *my Lord of Northehombyrlond*: Henry Percy, Earl of Northumberland, commander of the troops being mustered to Richard's support in the north. Killed in fact in Yorkshire in April 1489.

7. *my Lorde Haward*: John Howard, created Duke of Norfolk shortly after Richard's accession on 26 June.

**201.** 11. *Petter Bayle & Delete*: this gentleman, also known simply as Peter Bayle, is the Petter Valle de Let [Valladolid], Spaniard, of File 13 f. 43$^v$. De Lopez was illegally paying in England for wool bought in Calais, through his factor in London; see especially **217**.

**202.** 11. *Peyrs Joye . . . Crystower Collyns*: Peyrs or Peter Joye was a draper and merchant adventurer (*ACM*, p. 157, etc.; there was also a woolman of the same name: *PMR 1458–82*, p. 164). Collyns was a well-known London draper (*L.Bk.L*, pp. 145, 148, etc.).

34. *the preste mony*: possibly the 2s. 8d. per sarpler paid to John Narsbye (**204.** 45–6). It is unclear whether *prest money* here bears its later sense of 'earnest money paid to sailors on their engagement' (*OED*, Press-Money 3), or refers to ordinary wages, or arrears of wages, paid by the Staple on the King's behalf. The second seems more likely.

**203.** 6. *ij letters lattly from me*: no longer extant; written before **201** and **202** (which may be the two referred to in **204** as sent at the last shipping). The lost letters containing 'lewde and ontrewe Englysche' were evidently written during William's illness, mentioned in **201,** and one must be the letter entrusted to Benet Trotter (**201.** 23).

**204.** 45–6. *John Narsbye*: ? John Naseby, master of the King's ship *La Clement* (*CPR 1476–85*, p. 264 [April 1481]).

**205.** The date heading this letter is lost, but the trouble over sales to John De Lopez places it in the group of 1483–4.

4. *schett owte*: 'shot out', rejected. The sense, apparently misunderstood by *OED*, parallels that of *cast out*. Compare File 15 f. 3, 'a vᶜ ffellys, the wych the Holondys hayd schowt owt', and 'Johnson Letters', p. 633 (1550), 'shootyng owte le reffewse and myddell wulles'.

21–2. *receyue the mony affter the rate*: *mony* here means 'coins', valued at Calais on a scale of 15s. Fl. to the rial (30s. Fl. per £ ster.) (File 12 f. 40), but at a higher rate at the mart ('nott soo goode as xxx s. the li.'). Possibly William was able to change his groats at Bruges for coins that bore a more favourable valuation.

27. *master Graffton*: either John or Thomas Grafton, both mercers and staplers. Thomas was Lieutenant of the Staple in 1486 (Rymer, v. iii. 182).

46. *redy mony all gr.*: payment cash down in Flemish currency.

48. *Sonday beffore Twellffeday*: 4 January.

50–51. *the Carvyll off Hewe*: the *Carvell de Ewe* (Eu, Seine inférieure). Scofield suggests that she was the same as the *Trinity* of Eu bought by Edward IV in 1481 (Scofield, ii. 303 n.).

**206.** 31–2. *the schyppys that were taken to Sandwyche whyle yowre masterschypp was theyr*: various visits to Sandwich are alluded to in the memoranda, but none of this date. In the next letter the ships are said to have been brought to Sandwich when the King was there. Malden notes that Richard III was at Canterbury on 12 January and may have visited Sandwich about the same time. Reprisals had been encouraged against the Bretons in return for acts of piracy against English ships (*CPR 1476–85*, pp. 366, 547).

66. *sum argent—lxxix li. xviij s.* ○ ● *ster.*: the final cipher represents an *english*, originally a Flemish synonym (*engelsc*) for *sterling* with reference to weights (1 dwt. troy) or coins (a Flemish penny, later superseded by the *gros* or *groot*), but adopted by wool merchants as an accounting device

for the most convenient fraction of a penny ster. in reckoning the price of a clove of wool. The *point* (●) stands for a fraction of an *english*. (Explanations and tables are given in BM. MS. Cott. Vesp. E. ix, ff. 103, 106, and Balliol MS. 354, ff. 10$^v$, 20–20$^v$).

Here the clove is Calais weight, with ninety cloves to the sack. At twenty marks (£13. 6s. 8d.) per sack, the clove costs 2s. 11⅝d., and the correct total here is £79. 17s. 0⅘d. The fraction of a penny in the total is treated as one-third (○) plus one-ninth (●). With English wool weights where there were fifty-two cloves to the sack, the *english* was taken as one-thirteenth of a penny, and the *point* as one-quarter (instead of one-third) of the *english*.

**207.** 26–7. *the yong Dewk Phellyppus*: Maximilian's son, the nominal ruler of the Low Countries, who was in the custody of the Gantois at this time.

41. *the Regent*: Anne de Beaujeu, as regent of Charles VIII, since the Flemish towns had put themselves under the suzerainty of France. Charles concluded a treaty with the towns on 25 October 1484 (Gilliodts-van Severen, *Inventaire des Archives*, vi. 251).

43. *ij townes off Flaunders*: apparently Roubaix and Lille.

**208.** 39. *crossyd the Plase*: dismissed from membership of the Staple Company. Cf. *Ordinance Bk.*, p. 171, 'for his thirde suche offence he shalbe crossed this place for ever'.

**209.** 39. *Tewysday the xxv day off Feuere*: the 25th was in fact a Wednesday; at l. 52 the 27th is correctly described as Friday.

**210.** 5. *Harry Kebyll*: grocer, sheriff of London 1502–3, mayor 1510–11.
33, 34. . . . *vj d.* ○● ; *v d.* ○●● : 6⅘d. and 5⅝d.

**211.** 28. *Fryday last past*: 12 March.

28–9. *Rychard Awrey*: the capture of his ship by the French is referred to in *CPR 1476–85*, p. 529. 'Richard Aurey', late of Sandwich, yeoman, mariner, or shipman, was given a general pardon in March 1477 (ibid., p. 19).

29. *my Lord Dennam*: John, Lord Dynham, who succeeded Lord Hastings as Lieutenant of Calais.

**212.** 12. *as they were schyppyd twyse*: cf. the note in File 10 f. 36 of payments to labourers for attending to fells which 'were londid ayen at London because of the trouble vpon the see and heer in England'. They were first shipped on 26 March 1483, and reshipped on 5 June (File 10 f. 30).

17. *master Donsta[l]*: Sir Richard Tunstall, who appears as 'Ssyr Rychard Donstall' in a note by George Cely to buy him 'ij grett chaffyrs' in 1480 (File 15 f. 52$^v$).

20. *master Yorcke*: Richard York, merchant of the Staple and fishmonger, mayor of the Staple 1486 and knighted 1487 (E.101. 197/11; Rymer, v. iii. 182; Shaw, ii. 26).

21. *master Wymbysche*: Thomas Wymbissh of Kesteven (E.101.

197/11; named in various commissions for the county of Lincoln, *CPR 1476–85*, passim).

41. *that comyth heder*: I formerly read *camyth* (*Medium Ævum* (1957), p. 194), but enlargement of the microfilm copy suggests that *-o-* was intended.

51. *Dewke Phyllyppus*: Philip the Good.

**213. 32.** *Thomas Amerys, Constabull*: of the Staple. *Robardd Addlyn*: stapler and mercer (*L.Bk.L*, p. 277), and writer of the challenge, **29**.

50. *iij angelettys*: an *angelet* was properly half an English angel noble, but here the name is applied to the whole angel of 6s. 8d. (Grierson, p. 384).

**214. 42–3.** *a ryng ffor my wyffe*: George married about 13 May 1484— the dorsal note is later than the letter itself.

**215. 14.** *da[y]lesse*: 'without redress' (*OED*), or, in the original sense of the expression, 'no continuation of the case being granted' (*MED*).

36. *Wylliam Sallford*: London mercer and stapler.

38. *þat oder gentyllwoman*: Margery, widow of Edmond Rygon, citizen and draper of London, and also of Calais (will dated 19 January 1483/4, P.C.C., 22 Logge), whom George married in May. Much of the passage is deliberately obscure. It is impossible to identify the other lady mentioned, or George's rival.

**217. 12–13.** *to pay h[ytt] . . . or the wull passe the towne*: 'to pay before the wool leaves Calais': it was illegal at the time to give the traditional credit on wool sales, cf. **218**.

22. *Petter Baylys bokys*: it would appear that William feared a search of Valladolid's books in England rather than of his own at Calais because the latter were being deliberately falsified to frustrate any such inquiry. This emerges from study of an arbiter's correlation of two sets of Cely accounts for wool sales in 1483–5, many to De Lopez and his partners (File 10 ff. 30–1, and Alison Hanham, '"Make a careful Examination"; Some Fraudulent Accounts in the Cely Papers', *Speculum* xlviii (1973), 313–23). In one set of George's accounts weights and prices are systema-tically distorted so that they will bear no obvious resemblance to the real figures involved in transactions with his customers.

28–9. *Collard Messedawȝth*: also known in the memoranda as 'Collard Mesdowhe of Bryggys'.

**218. 9–10, 22.** *end wull*: ? remaining stocks of old wool, ? clean wound wool, as distinct from *clift wool*. *OED* mistakes the sense.

25–6. *at þe pryse of þe Plase*: William's repeated use of this phrase is a little suspicious, since there should have been no question of any de-parture from the fixed price, but I can find no evidence that he broke the rules in this respect.

**219.** The year in the heading is not clearly written: 1482 may be intended, and this is the date assigned in the second edition of *Lists and Indexes* xv, but the original P.R.O. cataloguer evidently also read it as 1484. The purpose of the letter seems to be to obtain an extension of immunity from prosecution, and in early 1482 Kesten had letters of protection from the King (**143**). Moreover, George was not in London in May 1482.

6. *John Prout*: mayor of the Staple in 1469. Prout, Richard Stokes, and Kesten had redeemed Edward IV's jewels from Thomas Portinari, to whom they were in pawn, and were given obligations for £2,700 ('duarum millium septingentarum librarum') from the mayor and fellowship of the Staple. The Staple in turn was recouped by grants from the customs made in 1472 and for sixteen years thereafter. (Georges Daumet, *Calais sous la domination anglaise*, Académie d'Arras, Arras 1902, pp. 185–8; *CCR 1468–76*, pp. 287–8, 341; *CCR 1476–85*, pp. 326–7; *CCR 1485–1500*, pp. 2–3. In the two latter calendars the figure is given as £27,000.)

8–9. *the Erle of W*[. . .]: if it is the Earl who died on Tower Hill, John Tiptoft, Earl of Worcester, executed by the Lancastrians in October 1470, must be meant. Richard Neville, Earl of Warwick, and James Butler, Earl of Wiltshire, were respectively killed at the Battle of Barnet, 1471, and executed at Newcastle, 1461. Tiptoft was Treasurer of England at various times, and lastly from July to October 1470. Apparently his death is alleged to have rendered the 'wrytteng to haue sauyd vs harmeles' [from what?] inefficacious. Kesten seems also to be claiming that Richard Stokes had cheated him in some way, but the letter is too badly damaged for reliable reconstruction, and it probably suited Kesten to be rather vague about his liabilities and excuses.

30–1. *they . . . to scape by that mene*: 'they may recoup themselves', ? by lodging free.

39–40. *your sewerte and promysse*: there is an example of the kind of 'letter of licence' sought in *Arnold's Chronicle* (ed. 1811), pp. 113–16.

59–60. *And I com in presson* . . .: 'if I get into prison I fear I shall never come out again'.

**220.** 21–2. [*John De Selonder of Mekelyn*]: this is the name given in the arbiter's account, File 10 ff. 30–1.

37. *Pontessbere*: Richard Pontisbury, merchant of the Staple and mercer. He was Constable of the Staple in 1490, and a warden of mercers 1496–7 and 1502–3 (E.122. 78/4; Posthumus, *Bronnen*, ii, No. 643; *ACM*, pp. 254–62, 606–31). *Bettson*: Thomas Betson of the Stonor correspondence and Eileen Power's *Medieval People*. *Cloppton*: Hugh Clopton, an important mercer, sheriff of London 1486–7, and builder of the great stone bridge at Stratford on Avon.

45. *Yermevthe*: Arnemuiden, Zealand; the port for Middelburgh.

48–9 and fn. *þe men . . . wer alond*: William originally wrote *wer hath ben alond*, and then cancelled *hath* by mistake for *wer*, so that the MS. now reads *wer ben alond*.

50–1. *loke howe they serue*: OED (commenting on its lack of any instances between the 12th and 16th cents.) explains 'look how' as 'however', 'just as'. The sense here seems stronger: 'consider carefully how you treat Davy, because we will treat your people the same'. Cf. 'lok what I maye do . . . and hyt schall be redde', **75.** 11–12, where the stress is on the verb, not the relative.

**221.** 16. *Petter Vayle & Delyt*: William Cely here achieves a rather more accurate rendering of Valladolid's name than before.

31. *John Twyssull*: John Twyssullton.

39. *þe paternosters on þe koyttys*: in the absence of any detailed description or picture of such markings, one can only guess at the meaning. The *paternoster* may be a stamped device resembling a rosary, and *koyttys* are probably *quoits*; perhaps flat discs of metal like those now used to seal wire-bound packing cases. Bales of cloth were certainly sealed with lead.

**222.** The letter mentioned as sent in **223** (20 September [1484]). The year may be fixed as 1484 because George was married in May of that year, and Robert Cely, mentioned in **223,** seems to have died in February 1484/5. Margery's letter is apparently holograph. There are a few further lines in her hand in a domestic account in File 14 ff. 61ᵛ–62.

13. *a long se⟨s⟩en*: MS. has *senen*, probably by anticipation of the following *sen* 'since'.

17. *Nycklay Kerkebe*: formerly 'servant' (apprentice) of Margery's first husband (will of Rygon, 22 Logge), and probably the Nicholas Kirkeby described as a merchant of the Staple in 1488, and as a skinner and merchant adventurer in 1490 (*CCR 1485–1500*, p. 76; *ACM*, p. 206).

18. *a feterloke of gold wyth a rebe þerin*: an ornament in the shape of a D with bar in the centre. There is an example of a small gold fetterlock in the 15th cent. Fishpool Hoard in the British Museum.

**223.** 7. *Y vnderstord*: probably a miswriting for *vnderstond*.

8–9. *my mayesterys yowre wyffe*: Margery was probably pregnant with her first child. George left four sons and a fifth unborn at his death in June 1489.

12–13. *nat so ase[sted as]*: the sense seems to be that Margery is short of servants.

15. *Thomas hare man*: *man* here means a very young servant.

**224.** John Pasmer was a skinner and prominent merchant adventurer; one of eleven citizens chosen by the Common Council to attend the Chief Butler at the coronation of Richard III (*Stonor Letters*, ii. 103; *L.Bk.L*, pp. 208, 246). He was shipping wool as a member of the Staple in 1487 (E. 122. 78/5). The accounts note various transactions with him, including a loan from him of £30 on 30 August 1484 (File 10 f. 1). The punctuation and capitalization of this letter are those of the original.

**225.** The P.R.O. placed this with letters of 1482, but it is clearly of 1484. Among weightier evidence is the fact that William Cely concludes with 'allmyghty Jhesu pres[erue yow]', his regular ending in 1484. In 1482 he used the formula 'Jhesu kepe yow'.

9. *the Imbassett[o]rs of Yng[lond]*: to Maximilian (the 'Dewke of Eystryge') to discuss the extension of the treaty of intercourse of 1478.

A commission had been given to Sir Thomas Montgomery, Dr. John Coke, Hugh Clopton, and John Wendy on 11 August 1484 (Rymer, v. iii. 148). Meanwhile, the merchant adventurers were boycotting the Duke's dominions, hence the embargo on buying goods mentioned in l. 21. Many of William's subsequent letters refer to the difficult progress of the negotiations over the next few years.

**226.** This letter, written more than two years after the preceding one, shows a remarkable change in the character of William's writing, which in **226** and **236** is now much more expansive and ornate.

6. *Wylliam Smythe*: wool-packer. The nature of the goods for sale never appears.

17. *Tylbott*: Tylbott or Tebott Ollyver of Calais. He shipped 48 tuns of wine from Bordeaux in the Celys' ship *Margaret Cely* in 1486–7 (File 13 f. 52, etc.).

**227.** 8. *Adryan Deffrey*: the account of George's expenses on his visit to the Continent in October–November 1486 is in File 13 ff. 26–9. He left 'wyth my nost Atryan at the Shepys Clawe an lyttyll ffardell wyth crossebowys and an long barell wyth mattrassys', both marked with the Cely family mark, which were to be sent to London by the next ship.

16. *Syr John Dee*: probably a clerk, not a knight.

28. *the Kynge of Romayns*: Maximilian returned to his Burgundian dominions in June 1486, having been elected King of the Romans in February.

36. *the Lordd Corddys*: Philippe de Crèvecœur, Sire d'Esquerdes, Marshal of France; earlier in the service of Charles the Bold.

**228.** 18–19. *a pronosticacon . . . of master John Laete*: John Laet and his son Jasper were celebrated authors of prognostications in the late 15th and early 16th centuries: Caxton published a translation of one by Jasper Laet of Antwerp in 1493.

26–7. *W. Ce[ly] can tell you more then I dar write*: ? about the activities of John de la Pole, Earl of Lincoln, who was in the Low Countries plotting the invasion of Lambert Simnel. Rumours about Simnel had been rife for some time.

**229.** 1–2. *the kockett of ij$^c$ quarter*: this probably refers to part of a delivery of a total of 620 quarters of wheat which George and Richard bought to be sold to Spaniards for export in February 1486/7 (File 14 f. 46; File 13 f. 39).

3. *Tebott*: see note to **226.** 17. File 13 f. 59 refers to freight paid or owed by him on 16 March 1486/7.

**230.** Early 1487, according to File 10 f. 2, where the arbiter notes, 'Item sent to . . . Richard Cely by . . . George Cely vpon a lettir myssyf by the handys of Thomas Wade . . . vj s. viij d.'.

2. *Dodlay*: John Dudley, butcher, appears in a bond in *L.Bk.L*, p. 271 (1489).

5. *Tomas Wade*: goldsmith, farmer of customs, and a neighbour of the Celys in Essex (E.R.O. D/DL T1 478). *the Margett*: the Celys' ship.

9. *Adlyngton*: John Adlyngton, servant of George Cely.

**231.** Nicholas Best was one of George's servants. He acted as steward of the household in George's absence (File 16 ff. 30 seq.), and as purser of the *Margaret Cely* on a voyage to Bordeaux in 1488 (File 14 ff. 49–58).

1. *Allvard*: Albaro or Alfonso De Cisneros of Spain, a London broker with whom the Celys had extensive dealings at this period. Known in the accounts as Alvard de Sysseneros, and apparently associated with John De Lopez.

**232.** Later than **227,** which mentions Dee and a debt of Sir Ralph Hastings. While he was at Bruges in October–November 1486 George bought goods for Sir Ralph to the value of £3.12*s*. 3*d*. Fl., including a gold tassel, black satin, and black velvet (File 13 ff. 27–27ᵛ). **232,** like **245,** is written by a secretary, apart from the closing words and signature.

**233.** 6. *my brother Awheray*: Avery Rawson, Richard's brother-in-law, a mercer like his father.

22. *Speryng*: John Speryng, George's servant, who acted as purser of the *Margaret* on some of her voyages.

**234.** 8–9. *payabull at vsaunce*: that this is the first instance of the phrase in the *OED* probably goes to show the paucity of surviving English commercial documents before the Celys' time. The Celys do not use it in connection with their normal transactions, however. In exchange dealings between England and the Low Countries, it indicates that a period of thirty days was allowed for repayment.

16. *the Bursse*: this, the original 'Burse', was at Bruges. For other, erroneous, views see *OED*'s note sub Burse 3.

23–4. *Anthony Corsy and Marcus Strossy, Spaynard*: in fact both are described as 'of Florence' in contemporary records.

53. *gruff wull*: apparently the earliest recorded use in English of *gruff*, from Fl. *groof* 'coarse'.

58. *a very redd leyr*: *leyr* (*OED* Lair *n*.¹ 4 and 5; Lear³) meant the pasture on which animals, esp. sheep, were bred, and by transference the characteristics thought to be conferred on the fleece by the nature of the soil. For the first sense cf. [? Clement Armstrong], 'A Treatise concerning the Staple . . .', *Tudor Economic Documents*, ed. R. H. Tawney and Eileen Power (1924), iii. 101–2:

> In old tyme the erth was . . . openyd by tillage, that the shepe myght fede of the inward leyre of the erth and therupon nyghtly lay and was foldydd. Then receyvid the shep ther naturall fedyng of the leyre of fyne staple wolle.

For Armstrong, a 'heyry corse leyr' referred not to a fleece, but to the ground that bred such a fleece.

**235.** 10 *Lowys More*: Lodowic Moro, merchant of Venice (*CCR 1468–76*, p. 195).

22. *yff ye com*: George arrived in Calais on 30 September (File 13 f. 31).

25. *ther ffyscher*: fishing boats.

44. *thys parliament tyme*: writs were sent out in September 1487, to meet in November at Westminster.

**236.** 16. *seall autetyc*: authentic seal.

22–3. *rone . . . wrack*: these names for two categories of herring are evidently Flemish; cf. L. Gilliodts-van Severen, *Cartulaire de l'ancienne estaple de Bruges*, ii (Bruges 1905), No. 1234, July 1486 '[Forty last of herring] te wetene xx last roone ende xx last wracke vanden Damme'. The *wrack* were herring of inferior grade, the *rone* apparently those gauged with a special measuring rod (also called *rone*); cf. Verwijs and Verdam, *Middelnederlandsch Woordenboek* (s'Gravenhagen 1885–1952), s.v. Rone, Ronen.

28. *Syr Jamus Tyrrell*: one of the English ambassadors appointed to treat with Maximilian (Rymer, v. iii. 182).

**237.** 18. *þat acte of þe contrary*: ? the restraint on trade with the Low Countries.

20. *grosse warys*: 'all maner of warys that be sold by the C, as wode [woad], mader, alym, wax, . . . and such odyr be called Grete Warys, . . . and other warys that be sold by the lb., as peper, saffryn, clowys . . . thes be called Sotyll Warys' (BM. MS. Cott. Vesp. E. ix, f. 87).

23. *Gomers De Sore*: Gomes de Sorye [Soria], merchant of Spain and Bruges (Gilliodts-van Severen, *Consulat d'Espagne*, i. 181, 183).

41; 43. *Awerey . . . Christoffer*:? Avery and Christopher Rawson.

**238.** 5. *John Flewelen*: John Lewelen, mercer (File 10 f. 2ᵛ and *ACM*, *passim*). Lewelen and Warner were well-known merchant adventurers.

9. *Roger Bovser*: Roger Bowser, Bowcer, or Bourghchier (e.g. *L.Bk.L*, p. 206; *PMR 1458–82*, p. 178).

34. *wee thynckyth*: ? by false analogy with *me thynckyth*; cf. also *I thynckyth*, l. 59.

34–5. *the world goyth on whelys*: everything is in upheaval. Although the modern sense of 'go on wheels' is 'go smoothly and rapidly', as in *OED*'s definition sub Wheel *n*. 12 b, the earlier connotation seems to have been that of the American idiom 'be on marbles', the wheel (like the wheel of fortune) being seen as something proceeding by constant reversal. *OED*'s examples, like the pun in Swift's *Polite Conversation*, plainly suggest disordered functioning of some kind. Similarly, Backbiter's expression in *The Castle of Perseverance* (*Macro Plays*, ed. Mark Eccles, E.E.T.S, 1969, ll. 664–7), 'To speke fayre beforn and fowle behynde . . . /Trewly, Lordys, þis is my kynde, / þus I renne upon a whele', probably means 'thus I keep reversing myself', not 'so I go on continuously'.

58. *the new grottys of Meclyn*: the mint of Mechlin was reopened in 1487. The new coins were much heavier than previous issues (Grierson, pp. 392–3).

**239.** 24. *above xij s. viij d. the nobull at vsaunce*: normally the Celys apparently preferred to make loans for longer than a month, since these brought them more profit. Superficially, lending at a rate of about 38s. Fl. per £ ster. when the current exchange at Bruges was 40s. Fl. (the rial being worth 20s.) would seem to give a good profit of about 2s. Fl. in the £. But the Celys had obtained their money at a much less inflated rate, and would lose by lending it at the higher one.

**240.** 11–12. *ryse and rewle agaynes*[*t*] *the Romayns Kynge*: *rewle,*? 'rebel' or 'riot' (but it means 'rule' in l. 24); cf. *revel* n. 'riot', and mod. dial. *rule* 'be unruly'. But perhaps 'rule the town in opposition to Maximilian' as in fact happened shortly.

   16. *Phelypp Movnsyr*: Philip of Cleves, Seigneur de Ravestein, the principal Lord of the Blood.

**241.** 19. *vnder the abesaunce of the Kynge of Fraunce*: Charles VIII took Ghent under his protection in January 1488 and it set up as an autonomous republic under his suzerainty.

   21. *amongyst hemselffe*: William Cely gradually replaces the older southern forms *hem* and *her* by the modern *them* and *the*(*i*)*r*. In the 35 extant documents written by him between 1479 and October 1482 he has 30 instances of the *h*- type to 28 of the *th*- type. In the second group of 23 documents of 1483 and 1484 there are 22 *h*- type to 43 *th*-, and in the third group of 12 letters, after an interval of two years, this is the only occurrence of *h*- beside 28 *th*- forms.

   31. *the quoynus sett dovn agayne*: the currency called down to a former level.

**242.** 2. *ambawght* [. . .]: apparently a borrowing of MDu. *ambacht* or *ambachter*.

   20. *Pety Walys*: now Lower Thames Street.

**243.** 7. *Sybson*: William Sybson the elder was 'cousin' to Edmond Rygon, Margery Cely's first husband, and also a draper (will of Rygon, 22 Logge; *CCR 1476–85*, p. 266).

   13. *Wylliam Strycke*: unidentified.

   20. *Thomas Spycer*: merchant of the Staple (E.122. 73/2), and possibly of a Leicester family.

   21. *Satterday last*: 8 March. *the Lordd Dugell*: Jacob Van Dudzeele, Seigneur de Ghistelle, a former burgomaster of Bruges.

   26. *the end wyll be nawght*: a peace treaty between Bruges and Maximilian was signed on 16 May 1488 (Gilliodts-van Severen, *Inventaire des Archives*, vi. 303).

## Undated Letters

**244.** Since this letter formed part of what is now vol. 59 of Ancient Correspondence, it is probably not later than 1480, like the rest of the letters therein. The *Formularium* may possibly be the purchase referred to in the arbiters' accounts (File 10 f. 8ᵛ, no date), 'per consanguinem suum [sc. of

George] de Northampton pro libro de lege empto—liij s. iiij d.'. R. Shipden is unidentified.

9. *ij litil bokis imprintid: Reverendi Patris Jacobi de Theramo compendium perbreve consolatio peccatorum nuncupatum: et apud nonnullos Belial vocitatum*, by Palladinus (Jacobus) de Theramo; printed in Augsburg 1472, Louvain 1474, Cologne 1475, and Gouda 1481, etc., also in Dutch, French and German versions; and *Formularium Romae Curiae*, or, as here, *Formularium Instrumentorum*, a widely published legal work. A glance at its sensational illustrations will readily suggest that it was the *Belial* that George was expected to find attractive.

**245.** As this letter was written at Guines, it is likely that at the time Sir Ralph Hastings was still Lieutenant of Guines. Unfortunately, the exact dates of his tenure are by no means clear. He was required to surrender the custody of Guines castle to Sir John Blount, Lord Mountjoy, as a condition of his pardon of 18 August 1483 (*Letters and Papers of the Reigns of Richard III and Henry VII*, ed. J. Gairdner, i (1861), 46; *CPR 1476–85*, p. 365). But on 4 March 1484 he received a grant of the captaincy contingent on the death, surrender, or forfeiture of Blount, who was said to be dying on 14 August (ibid., p. 385; Rymer, v. iii. 149). Deputies probably acted for John, bastard son of Richard III, when he was made nominal Captain of both Calais and Guines on 11 March 1485 (Rymer, p. 162).

The *setillers* (l. 6) may give some clue to the date. MDu. *setelaer*, like Fr. *chaise*, was applied to coins bearing an enthroned figure, and especially to the French *écu à la chaise*, first struck in 1337, and its many imitations in the Low Countries. Grierson (pp. 401–2) points out that since the sum is so large it is likely that the coin used by Hastings was a contemporary issue, and suggests that the Martinusgulden of Utrecht, first struck in 1483, best fits the value given. This coin did bear a seated figure. Grierson feels that in appearance the new gulden was 'so unlike the old *écus à la chaise* that a transfer of the name is scarcely possible', but I do not find this objection of great weight, especially as the name does not appear elsewhere in the Cely papers, which suggests that the earlier coin was no longer in general use.

**246.** There is no indication of date, since no other reference to this incident has come to light. One John Berkeway 'seruaunt with the Kyng' had to apologize for slandering the mayor and wardens of the Mercers' Company on 8 April 1479 (*ACM*, pp. 112–13).

15. *Christofull Coolenis*: ? Christopher Collyns.

**247.** This damaged and incomplete draft of a letter which is separated from the rest of the Cely correspondence in the Public Record Office and incorrectly calendared as written to William Cely *c.* 1480 (P.R.O. *Lists and Indexes No. XV*, revised edition, 1968), came to my notice too late to be included in its proper chronological place. It was almost certainly written in April 1476: File 11 f. 20, dated [14]76, is a fragmentary note of George's payments for a shipment of fells belonging to Robert Cely which similarly mentions a rebate of 10s. per sarpler paid at London and dues paid to the Place at the same exchange rate of 21s. 4d. Fl.; and File 11 f. 17ᵛ records three sales on 24 April 1476 of fells which correspond very closely with those here described.

9. *iij M¹C felles*: this total omits the two winter London fells added as an afterthought.

25. *hewry vᶜ ffelles ys an sarpler*: the 'hundred' used throughout this letter is the long hundred of six score; thus 'three thousand and one hundred fells' (l. 9) is 3,720 fells which, at the official rate of 240 fells (two hundreds of six score) per sack, makes for customs purposes six sarplers of 2½ sacks each and 120 odd fells (ll. 24–5). Similarly, 3,720 fells make up a freight of seven packs and 360 fells (three hundreds of six score) at the equivalent of 480 fells per pack (l. 14).

31. *the Fellyschypp bethe angreyd* [i.e. agreed]: this agreement seems to refer to an ordinance of April 1476 (Rymer, v. iii. 91), which, as a temporary expedient to clear stocks of old wool at Calais, laid down that no wool shipped to Calais between March 1476 and 6 April 1478 should ever be classed as 'old' wool and so obtain the customary preference over the 'new' wool of later shipments. The effect would be that the buyer of any wool shipped after February 1476 was forced to 'free out' his purchase with wool from the old stock stored in Calais before that date. There must have been a sufficient supply of this to last for three seasons. It seems from this letter that the Staplers had wanted to keep the spring shipment of 1476 off the market until some of the old wool was disposed of, but were overruled by the Council at Calais.

# BIBLIOGRAPHY AND ABBREVIATIONS

E.R.O. D/DL    Essex Record Office, Barrett Lennard documents

P.R.O.         Public Record Office
  C.47         Chancery Miscellanea
  E.101        Exchequer Accounts, Various
  E.122        Exchequer, Customs Accounts
  S.C.1        Ancient Correspondence

P.C.C.         Prerogative Court of Canterbury (probate registers in Public Record Office)

*ACM*    *Acts of Court of the Mercers' Company 1453–1527*, ed. Laetitia Lyell, Cambridge, 1936.

*Arnold's Chronicle*    *The Customs of London, otherwise called Arnold's Chronicle*, ed. F. Douce, 1811.

*CCR*    *Calendar of Close Rolls*.

*Complete Peerage.*    G. E. Cokayne, *Complete Peerage of England, Scotland, Ireland* . . ., rev. edn., 12 vols., 1910–59.

*CPR*    *Calendar of Patent Rolls*.

Dillon, Hon. H. A., 'Calais and the Pale', *Archaeologia*, liii (1893), 289–388.

*DOST*    *Dictionary of the Older Scottish Tongue*, Chicago and London, 1937 —.

Edler, Florence, *Glossary of Mediaeval Terms of Business, Italian Series*, Cambridge, Mass., 1934.

Gilliodts-van Severen, L., *Cartulaire de l'ancien consulat d'Espagne à Bruges*, i, Bruges, 1901.

—— *Inventaire des Archives de la Ville de Bruges: Inventaire des chartes*, 9 vols., Bruges, 1871–85.

Godefroy, F., *Dictionnaire de l'ancienne langue française*, Paris, 1880–1902.

Grierson, Philip, 'Coinage in the Cely Papers', *Miscellanea Mediaevalia in Memoriam Jan Frederik Niermeyer*, Groningen, 1967, pp. 379–404 and table.

Hanham, Alison, 'The Cely Papers and the Oxford English Dictionary', *English Studies*, xlii (1961), 129–52.

—— 'Foreign Exchange and the English Wool Merchant in the late Fifteenth Century', *Bulletin of the Institute of Historical Research*, xlvi (1973), 160–75.

—— 'The Musical Studies of a Fifteenth Century Wool Merchant', *Review of English Studies* (N.S.) viii (1957), 270–4.

—— 'The Text of the Cely Letters', *Medium Ævum*, xxvi (1957), 186–96.

Hennessy, G. L., *Novum Repertorium Ecclesiasticum Parochiale Londinense*, 1898.

Höhlbaum, K., *Hansisches Urkundenbuch*, 3 vols., Halle, 1876–86.

'Johnson Letters 1542–1552', ed. Barbara Winchester (unpublished Ph.D. thesis. University of London, 1953).

*L.Bk.L*     *Calendar of Letter Books . . . of the City of London, Letter Book L*, ed. R. R. Sharpe, 1912.

Lyell, Laetitia, *A Mediaeval Post-Bag*, 1934.

Malden, H. E., ed., *The Cely Papers*, Camden, Third Series, i (1900).

*MED*     *Middle English Dictionary*, ed. Kurath and Kuhn, Ann Arbor, 1952 —.

*Medieval Latin Word-List*, ed. R. E. Latham, 2nd edn., 1965.

Myers, A. R., *The Household of Edward IV*, Manchester, 1959.

Newcourt, Richard, *Repertorium Ecclesiasticum Parochiale Londinense*, 2 vols., 1708–10.

*OED*     *Oxford English Dictionary*, 1933.

*The Ordinance Book of the Merchants of the Staple*, ed. E. E. Rich, Cambridge, 1937.

*Paston Letters and Papers*, ed. Norman Davis, Pt. 1, Oxford, 1971.

*Paston Letters A.D. 1422–1509*, ed. J. Gairdner, 6 vols., 1904.

*The Plumpton Correspondence*, ed. T. Stapleton, Camden Society, 1839.

*PMR 1458–82*     *Calendar of Plea and Memoranda Rolls, 1458–82*, ed. P. E. Jones, Cambridge, 1961.

Poerck, G. de, *La draperie médiévale en Flandre*, 3 vols., Bruges, 1951.

Postan, M. M., 'Private Financial Instruments in Medieval England', *Vierteljahrschrift für Sozial-und Wirtschafts-Geschichte*, xxiii, Stuttgart, 1930, 26–75.

Posthumus, N. W., ed., *Bronnen tot de Geschiedenis van de Leidsche Textielnijverheid*, 2 vols., The Hague, 1910–11.

Roover, Raymond de, *Money, Banking and Credit in Mediaeval Bruges*, Cambridge, Mass., 1948.

*Rotuli Parliamentorum*, 6 vols., 1767–77.

Rymer, T., ed., *Foedera, conventiones, literae et cuiusque generis acta publica . . .*, 3rd edn., 10 vols., The Hague, 1739–45.

Scofield, Cora L., *The Life and Reign of Edward the Fourth*, 2 vols., 1923.

Shaw, W. A. *The Knights of England*, 2 vols., 1906.

Smit, H. J., ed., *Bronnen tot de Geschiedenis van den Handel met Engeland, Schotland en Ierland*, 2 vols., The Hague, 1928–42.

*The Stonor Letters and Papers*, ed. C. L. Kingsford, Camden, Third Series, 2 vols., 1919.

Stow, John, *The Survey of London*, ed. C. L. Kingsford, 2 vols., Oxford, 1908.

*Studies in English Trade in the Fifteenth Century*, ed. Eileen Power and M. Postan, 1933.

Wedgwood, J. C., ed., *History of Parliament*: i. *Biographies of the Members of the Commons House 1439–1509*, 1936.

Weever, John, *Antient Funeral Monuments*, 1767.

Zachrisson, R. E., *Pronunciation of English Vowels, 1400–1700*, Göteborg, 1913.

—— *The English Pronunciation at Shakespeare's Time as taught by William Bullokar*, Uppsala, 1927.

# GLOSSARY

REFERENCES are to letter and line, and are usually confined to no more than two examples of any particular use or spelling. Vocalic *y* is treated as *i*, vocalic *v* and *w* as *u*, consonantal *u* as *v*, and initial ʒ as consonantal *y*. No distinction is made between initial *ff* and *f*, initial *ss* and *s*, or *þ* and *th*. For convenience, a few headwords are supplied (in square brackets) in forms that do not occur in the letters, e.g. [cocket], **kockett**.

**a** *adj.* all 43/21, 95/25.

**a** *pron.* he 19/37, 34/28, 117/24; I (?) 91/8.

**a** *v.* have (as unstressed aux.) 7/21, 22/39, 110/8, 155/10.

**a** *prep.*[1] of 41/33, 147/34, 237/6, *a clokt* o'clock 39/3.

**a** *prep.*[2] on 74/11, 31, 117/9; with *vbl. n.* 148/10, 168/25, 195/7.

**a** *prep.*[3] to [Fr. *à*] 3/12, 4/27, 15/24, 19/56; *x s. xx d. a pey* to pay 230/6.

**abaft(e)** *prep.* behind 5/6, 130/6, 7.

**abat(te)** *v. tr.* deduct 21/21, 247/24; *pp.* **abatyd** 163/42.

**abawe** *adv.* above 92/10.

**abedyensses** *n. pl.* matters of obedience 129/6.

**abesaunce** *n.* jurisdiction 241/19. [Blend of *abaisance* and *obeisance*.]

**abyd(e)** *v. intr.* remain, wait 88/16; **abydyn** 44/12; *where to ~* with whom to deal 167/7; *tr.* await 165/10; *pr. 3 sg.* **abydythe** 165/65; *3 pl.* **abydys** 168/24, 174/8; meet 198/20; **abyd hit** abide by it 246/13.

**abydyng** *adj.* ?permanent, ?resident 215/9.

**abyll** *v. tr.* make competent, habilitate 219/46; *pp.* **abelyd** warranted 189/30.

**abowte** *adv.* about 220/17, **abhowte** 114/31, **abohut** 117/29, **anbowght** 22/12; *prep.* 19/29, 235/19, **anbowt** 4/16, **abohut** 108/18, **abot** 165/33; *goo abowght* attend to 241/8; *there abode* thereabouts 56/13.

**abowe** *prep.* above, over: *houyr and ~*

that 22/26, **abouhe** 168/26, **aboweff** 49/3, **aboffe** 192/7, 9.

**aboven** *adv.* above (*~ said*) 219/54; *prep.* **anbovyn** 92/28.

**abrood** *adv.* around 140/12.

**aburdde** *adv.* aboard 115/17.

**acerteyned** *pp. adj.* sure 224/11; *pp.* **acertened** assured 228/16.

**acertynyng** *pr. p.* certifying 161/2.

**acord(e)** *v. tr.* reconcile 44/25; *intr.* agree 9/15; *pp.* **acordyd** 88/9.

**acordyng** *pp. adj.* *~ to* matching 60/3, 159/7; in accordance with 56/4.

**acostom** *pp. adj.* accustomed 22/33.

**acovmpt** *n.* accounts 41/37.

**acteon** *n.* legal suit 6/4, **acschon** 38/38.

**ader** *adj.* other 139/6; *n. pl.* others 125/26.

**ado(e)** *v.* to do 98/12; *n.* bustle; fuss 85/9, 109/31, 124/7, **adoo** 211/17.

**adwisse** *n.* advice 6/5; **hadvysse** 109/44. Also **avyse**.

**affardde** *pp.* and *pp. adj.* afraid 211/25, **a(f)ferd(d)** 38/32, 167/10, 211/20.

**af(f)ecte** *n.* tenor 227/6; effect 236/13.

**affore, afor** *adv.* and *prep.* formerly, before 22/8, 12/6; in front of 211/18; in presence of 47/26, 170/38; with precedence over 206/20; *to a be afore yow* 215/51.

**affte(r)warde** *adv.* towards the stern 128/5, 131/45.

**after** *prep.* according to 8/12; at the rate of 141/23.

**agayn(e)** *adv.* again 43/7, 199/14,

**agayn(e)** (*cont.*):
  **agane** 23/7, **ageyn(e)** 47/31, 245/4, **agen(e)** 22/12, 84/11, **aȝe(y)n** 107/17, 28, **aȝyn** 39/20, **ayen** 58/13; *prep.* against 143/4, 175/15; in preparation for 133/34; *conj.* 114/52.
**agaynste** *prep.* in time for, ready for 43/13, **agaynest** 181/10, **ayenst** 40/12; against, contrary to: *ayenst me* 16/16, **agaynys** 43/13, **agaynyst** 199/20, **anȝenst** 93/20, 109/38; in return to, 149/20, 153/7; in ratio to: *iij old agaynest on new* 212/10.
**ago(o)n** *pp. adj.* past 202/25, 226/13.
**agrete** *adv.* altogether, generally 38/40.
**Agust** *n.* August 180/23, 233/18.
**akeayntyd** *pp. adj.* acquainted 19/16. Also **aqwaynttyd.**
**aker** *n.* acre 233/19.
**akys** *n. pl.* hawks 75/4, 10. Also **hawke.**
**albeit**, *conj.* although 140/13.
**alder[mo]st** *adv.* most of all 222/6.
**alecschon** *n. putt yn ~ off* put up for election as 212/20.
**alectyd** *pp.* elected 235/42.
**alemetyd** *pp. adj.* fixed, designated 170/21. Also **lemetyd.**
**Alhalon Day** *n.* All Saints' Day, 1 November 67/8, **Aulhalonday** 74/3, **Alhalowhyn Heuen** (31 October) 70/7, **Hawlhalon Heuyn** 133/84.
**Allmaynus** *n. pl.* Germans 112/26; **aulmen** *adj.* German 126/9.
**allmythy** *adj.* almighty 94/3, **allmyty** 21/22.
**al(l)s** *adv.* as 29/5, 145/5. Also **also.**
**all togeder** the whole lot 218/15–16.
**allway(e)** *adv.* at all times 100/3, 48/7, 180/21; *lokyth allwey when* expects constantly that 176/7.
**allw(h)eys** *adv.* always 167/18, 219/52.
**almynake** *n.* almanac 228/19.
**alond(e)** *adv.* on (to) land 182/11, 115/16, 211/31.
**alowaunce** *n.* permission 204/42.
**alowyd** *pp. ~ ffor* reckoned as 132/5; *anlowyd appon* deducted from 109/7.
**also** *adv.* as 64/8, 219/25; *also well . . . as* both . . . and 143/3–4.
**alsoy** *adv.* also 18/11, 28/5, 44/6.

**ambassett(ors)** *n. pl.* embassy, ambassadors 109/58, 53. Also **ymbassett, imbassettorus.**
**ambawght[ers?]** *n. pl.* embassy 242/2. [Cf. MDu. *ambacht, -er.*]
**ambelyng** *pp. adj.* ambling 170/56, **amblynge,** 171/3, **haumlyng** 57/15, 22.
**amende** *v. tr.* better 15/15, **amente** 31/32; *pr. p.* **amendynde** 102/10.
**amenyng** *vbl. n.* amending 73/2.
**amyt** *v.* appoint 114/30; *pp.* **amyttyd** 160/28.
**amongyst(e)** *prep.* amongst 206/23, 241/21, **anmongeyst** 93/20.
**amowntys** *pr. sg.* amounts to *~ l s.* 114/22, *amovntys an Cx li.* 216/13, **amontys** 234/13, **amovntyth** 189/32, **amontys vnto** 141/15; *pt.* **amontyd** 18/6.
**an** frequently used by George Cely for *a-* prefix, and *a, indef. art.* before consonants as well as vowels, e.g. 4/3, 9.
**an** *prep.* on 124/16.
**an** *v.* have, as unstressed aux. 22/36, 41/31, 109/27.
**ancordyng** *adv.* accordingly, appropriately 7/15, 109/7; *~ vnto* conformably to 247/7.
**and** *conj.* and; if 8/9, **an** 151/17, **ant** 84/15, *and iff* 159/2, *and yf* 235/25.
**Andreus** *n.* and *adj.* the Burgundian florin of St. Andrew, struck from 1466 to 1485 56/38, 151/45, 196/34, **Andrus** 151/34, *the Andreus gyldern* 187/23, *Andrew gylders* 234/18.
**anffor(e)** *adv.* previously 41/35, 93/23.
**angelettys** *n. pl.* angelets (see note) 213/50.
**angreyd** *pp.* agreed 247/31.
**anythyng** *n.* (as *adv.*) *and they be ~ wurth* if they have any value 189/16.
**an(n)oder** *adj.* another 177/5, 155/12, **annodyr** 41/13, **anodur** 159/1; **anodere** 223/17; *n.* 180/19.
**ansfor** *n.* answer 19/36 and note, 74/35, 114/25, 41, 136/4, 147/16, *a nansfor* 74/37.
**ansfor** *v. tr.* and *intr.* answer 43/14, 195/7; *pt.* **ansford** 34/8, 55/8; *pp.* **ansforde** paid 47/39.

**answar(e)** *n.* answer 109/66, 27/2, **answher** 29/8; **aunswer** 161/6, **onswer** 140/9.

**answer** *v.* repay someone; pay, meet costs 22/25, 172/9, **onswer** 140/8; *pr. 3 sg. answeryth at days for* pays for on delayed terms 217/20; *pt.* **answar(d)** replied to 39/12, 20; **answerd** 64/7, **ansuerryd** 218/21; *pp.* **ans(s)weryd** 205/14, 215/14, **onsward** 159/8.

**Anuncyon, Owre Lady Day** 25 March 212/71-2.

**anwardys** *adv*(?) 125/26 and note.

**anwhardyd** *pp.* see **awarde.**

**apayard** *pp.* impaired 179/10.

**apenyon** *n.* opinion 209/49.

**aperyt** *pr. 3 sg.* appears 13/6, 106/4.

**aperte** *adv. layd* ~ put aside 85/17.

**apoynt** *n. at* ~ in agreement 215/38-9. [OFr. *appoincte*.]

**apon** *prep.* upon, in var. senses ~ *the Sonday* 15/15-16; ~ *the see* 47/14; ~ *v*ᶜ *li.* about £500 121/8; *appon (h)yt selffe* separately 109/36 and note, 170/46; *I shall* ~ *hym ffor them* I shall tackle him 170/38; *apond* upon it 51/7. Also **vpon.**

**aponte** *v.* ~ *me* arrange to act 20/28; *pp.* **appoynted** ready 224/7; **apwoyntydd, apoynt(t)yd** prescribed; nominated 187/15, 212/65, 187/20. Also **poynt.**

**apparteyneth** *pr. 3 sg. as* ~ as is fitting 16/2.

**appert** *adv.* openly 16/19 fn.

**apwnttemente** *n.* arrangement or resolution 134/7. Also **pontment.**

**aqwaynttyd** *v. tr. pt. 3 sg.* ~ *me wyth* introduced me to 133/11; *pp. adj. as ȝe ar aqwayntyd* with your circle of friends 111/19. Also **akeayntyd.**

**aqweyntans** *n. pl.* acquaintances 117/5.

**aquytte** *v. tr.* requite 42/19.

**ar** *conj.* or 22/34, 69/8, 99/4, 129/25, 28.

**aray** *n. in ƥat* ~ so fitted out 129/4.

**arayd** *pp. adj. lykewhysse* ~ in similar condition 109/20; *with ffowle* 198/12; *ffowllest arayyd* 112/15.

**areste(d)** *pp.* arrested, of goods or people 38/37, 5/8. Also **rest.**

**argent(e)** *n.* cash price; argent comptant 31/5, 149/7; *sum (totall)* ~ 107/7, 206/66, 210/24.

**arndys** *n. pl.* see **erand.**

**Arnovldes** *n.* gold coin(s) of Arnold, Duke of Guelders (1423-73) 56/44, pl. *Arnowldys* 196/40.

**arnst** *n.* earnest 97/5.

**arras** *n.* cloth from Arras, tapestry 78/19, 22; *ares clothes* 64/14.

**as** *adv.* (*rel., rel. conj.*) as: of time 15/15, 212/25; ~ *now* 112/20; ~ *for* (with omission of *pron.*) as regards: 8/5, 136/8-9; ~ *for Pyyswhell mendyd* 126/5; ~ *of* for 149/28, *good as of that contre* good, for that district 111/10; so that, in order that 129/16; since, inasmuch as, because 148/7, 212/11.

**as** *pr. 1 pl.* have 129/12.

**ascuse** *v.,* **ascwysyd, askewyshyd; askvse** *n.* see **excuse.**

**aseye** *v. intr.* try 201/28.

**asemlyd** *pp.* assembled 212/16.

**ase[sted]** *pp. adj.* supplied with servants 223/12.

**asyn(e)** *v.* allot 186/17; direct 63/8. Also **synyd.**

**asollet** *pt.* absolved 129/6. [*Assoiled.*]

**aspecyaull** *adj.* especial 25/1; *in aspessyaull adv.* especially 111/36; *in aspeschall* 116/10.

**assyse** *n.* size 103/12.

**astonyd** *adj.* amazed 104/53.

**asvrete** *n.* security, guarantee 38/42 and note, **asvrte** 38/45; *be yn asewerte be* be protected by 236/17; *sett yow yn asewerte* secure you 208/30. Also **sewerte.**

**at** *prep.* at, in various senses: *at losse* 22/8; *at afternon* 39/3; *at thys* (time of writing) 212/70; *com at London* 58/20; *heuer a cam at yow* before he reached you 78/8; *at iij or iiij monthys* payable in 3 or 4 months 220/28-9; *at makyng* being made 189/7; *at the reuerence off* for love of 219/48-9.

**at** *rel. pron.* that 25/26, 105/29, 129/17, 146/7; *that* ~ that which 6/10, 7/5, 19/38, 34/28, 109/24.

**at** *conj.* that 25/17, 22, 129/7, 133/23, 146/7, 219/61.

**atendyt** *v.*+*pron.* attend to it 149/25.

**at(t)orney** *n.* legal representative 58/30, 1/3 **aturney** 236/18, **atornay** 91/30; *pl.* **atturneis** 244/17; *letter (of) atorney* 236/16, 217/42, 235/29.

**auctoryte** *n.* authority 241/24.

**aull** *adj.* all 19/32, **awll** 86/4, **hawlle** 91/19, **halle** 192/14.

**a(u)ll** *adv.* quite, completely 149/33, 96/2.

**aul(l)thyng** *n.* everything 84/7, 147/5, **aulleth⟨y⟩ng** 86/18, **all thyngys** 155/5.

**awmbeler** *n.* an ambling horse 174/5.

**awne** *adj.* own 10/17, 86/7.

**awnys** *n. pl.* ells 136/40. [Fr. *aune.*] Also **e(y)lle.**

**autetyc** *adj.* authenticated 236/16.

**awalyd** *pp.* avaled, sailed on an ebb tide 113/9.

**aventer** *v. tr.* risk 12/8, **aventure** 239/14; *intr.* venture 238/23, **aventur** 240/40.

**aventer(e)** *n.* risk 220/33; **aventture** 115/32 (see **stand**); *put yowre body in* ~ imperil yourself 110/15–16. Also **venter.**

**avyse** *n.* advice 20/28, **avyce** 212/36, **awyse** 147/31. Also **adwisse, vyse.**

**avyse** *v. tr.* advise 107/17 **avysse** 233/12, **awys(e)** 8/7, 114/33, **awyes** 58/19; *pp. I am avysyd* I intend 20/21, 50/8; *pp. adj. wylle avysyd* sensible 85/16–17.

**away(e)** *adv.* away 142/23, **awhay** 109/14; *put* ~ sell off 149/12, *hellpe me* ~ *wyth* rid me of 218/23–4.

**awarde** *v. tr.* appraise: determine the quality of wool and fell shipped to Calais *pr. 3 pl.* 105/9; *pp.* **awhardyd** 92/27, **awarddyd** 191/5, **awardd** 190/5; *anwhardyd ffor contre ffellis* designated country fells 46/18, *anwhardyde ffor Cottys* designated Cotswold wool 93/19–20; *intr.* **awardyt** *pp.* adjudicated 78/17. Also **whardyd.**

**a whor** see note to 84/14.

**axith** *pr. 3 sg.* asks 100/18; *pt.* **axyd** 46/6, **askyd** 47/15.

**axys** *n.* ague fit 95/30, **axsys** 169/16.

**B.** *abbrev.* for brother 18/18, 19/18 and note, 125/35, 138/7.

**bachelerys** *n. pl.* bachelors 29/19.

**bacons** *n. pl.* some kind of woolfell 30/5 and note.

**Bamys marte** *n.* the mart held at Antwerp around St. Bavon's Day (1 October) 26/10, **Bamyse** 38/7, **Bammys** 96/17, **Bal(l)mus** 176/13, 177/15.

**banker(y)s** *n. pl.* chair or bench covers 74/17, 19, 60/2, **bankars** 34/31.

**Baras(e) canvase** *n.* canvas from Bar 53/24, 56/26, 67/15.

**bare** *adj.* unfurnished 56/15; *barr wytthehowte money* short of cash 192/20, ~ *yn plyght* in poor condition 179/13; ? scant, ? poor quality 205/7.

**bargayne** *n.* commercial agreement 218/32; **bargin** 197/14, **bargan** 48/14, **bergeyne** 234/26; **bergen** purchase 165/15; *pl.* **barganys** 27/13.

**bargeyne** *pr. 2 pl.* make a bargain 234/29.

**Bartyllmewys tyd** *n.* the season around 24 August 91/10, **Barttyllmew Tyde** 169/27.

**basson** *n.* basin 230/7.

**bastard** *adj.* of abnormal shape or size 146/7, 150/13.

**battelles** *n. pl.* divisions of an army 178/13.

**bavyr** *n.* beaver: lower part of the face-guard of a helmet 227/10.

**be** *v.* ~ *ther* marry her 117/31; *hayd they not bene* had it not been for them 125/9, *had not [they] abe* 247/37–8; *pr. 1 sg.* **am(e)** 2/3, 74/21, **ham(me)** 21/9, 102/7, 192/19; *3 sg.* **is, ys** 2/11, **hyse** 180/8; *1 pl.* **be** 154/6, **bene** 140/3, **ar** 25/26; *2 pl.* **be** 2/9, **ar(e)** 169/5, 189/42; *3 pl.* **be(e)** 19/24, 242/10, **by** 94/9, **beth(e)** 7/4, 13, **beythe** 208/57, **ben(e)** 15/4, 141/21, **ar** 19/26, **ys** 43/7; *pr. subj.* **be** 2/22, **by** 94/7; *pt. sg.* **was(se)** 19/46, 88/5, **whas** 4/10; **w(h)os(se)** 19/18, 39/6, 114/7, 127/14; **v(h)os** 96/9, 95/10, **wher** 126/10; *pl.* **wer(r)** 15/4, 192/12, **whe(y)r** 7/6, 215/38, **war** 5/7, **whos** 165/7; *pt. subj.* would be **w(h)er** 19/34, 7/8, **whor** 95/30, 117/29, **warre** 70/7, **war(e)** 40/18, 58/31, **wayer** 110/18; **vher** 108/17;

*pp.* **be** 34/34, **ben(e)** 7/10, 21, 41/19, **beyn** 19/17, **byn** 100/6; *pr. p.* and *vbl. n.* **beeng** 143/20, **beyng(e)** 146/19, 192/3, 166/2; *I hawe ben wyth [hym] ffor her* I went to ask him for her 199/15–16; with *pr. p.* in periphrastic constr. *he ys owyng* 5/13.
**be, by(e)** *prep.* by, in various senses. ~ *me (the)* in hand 21/10, 36/15; from: *bey yowre wrytyng* 58/14, *be her moter* 165/28; approximately: *by a vj personys* 58/23–4; ? by as much as: ~ *xx li.* 7/16; concerning 16/10, 38/44, 165/64, 68; with regard to 134/15.
**be affte** *adv.* behind, towards the stern 131/21; *prep.* 131/7, 12, 132/6. Also **affte(r)warde**.
**because** *adv.* ~ *of* for fear of 228/8; *becaws of* 55/12; *for becawys of* on account of 111/35–6; *conj.* for the reason that: **becawis** 109/32, **becavsse** 93/13, **bycause** 66/7, 224/9.
**beche** *n.* bitch 126/6, 133/31.
**becomen** *pp. war the bell ys* ~ what has become of the bill 39/15.
**beddeman** *n.* one who prays for someone 219/66.
**bed(e)** *n.* bed 159/2, 109/26.
**bedfelow(e)** *n.* companion in bed 123/1, 16, 17, 40/15.
**befe** *n.* beef 119/10, 18.
**befor** *prep.* in front of 113/6, **beffore** 131/17; in preference to 57/25.
**beforn** *adv. her* ~ already 70/20.
**begyllyd** *pp.* cheated 168/23.
**begyn** *v.* begin 220/40; *pr. 3 sg.* (?) 111/34; *3 pl.* **begynys** 111/39, **begyenyt** 223/13; *pt.* **begane** 59/4, **begon** 109/15; *pp.* **begon(e)** 98/18, 20/13, **begoon** 225/24, **begwn** 165/81.
**behalf, behalve** *n. in þat* ~ in that matter 16/28, 236/41.
**beheldyng** *pp. adj.* beholden 168/14, **beholdyng** 47/21–2.
**behyndd** *adv.* late 204/48, *behynde wyth* in arrears with 170/33.
**beho(o)ffe** *n.* use, benefit 57/24, 242/4.
**bey and bey** *adv.* immediately 192/12.
**bey** *v.* buy 5/20; *(absol.* 70/15); **bhey** 40/21, **bie** 244/8, **by(e)** 10/28, 12/2,

**byee** 226/11; *pr. 3 sg.* **byethe** 190/10, **beyth** 189/16, *bye hem vpp* 190/9; *3 pl.* **bye** 156/11, **byeth** 203/34; *pt.* **bowght** 93/14, **boute** 103/17, **bogwyt** 24/12; *pp.* **bowte** 84/10, **boghte** 142/9, **bogwyt** 20/26, 31/25, **bohyt** 165/19, **bohut** 91/6, **bohwt** 146/4, **bovt** 25/21, **bowyt** 25/9, **y-boght** 40/13; *bowght yt vp* purchased all available 109/47; *boght hym of you* bought him from you 166/4. Also **whelbhowte**.
**beydys** *n. pl.* rosary 139/5.
**beyere** *n.* buyer 130/13.
**beyr** *n.* beer 198/18.
**bell** *n.* see **bill**.
**beluffyd** *pp. adj.* beloved 125/39, **beluffid** 140/21. Also **whelbelouyd**.
**benyffete** *n.* advantage 170/44 and note.
**benyveysse** *n.* church benefice 115/39.
**ber(e)** *v.* carry 127/5; sustain **bare** 31/31, 24/9; *beyr record* witness 142/18; *pr. 1 sg.* **bere** 16/26; *3 sg.* **beryth** 105/16; *3 pl.* **bers** 105/18, **bere** 105/28; *pt.* **bare** 109/32, **bar** 78/12 (see **hand**); *pp.* **born(e)** 34/28, 22/25, 203/17, **boren** 153/22; *born(e) yn* submitted to the Staple 170/47–8, 189/29, 31, *ber into the Plasse* pay to the Staple 247/18.
**berer** *n.* carrier 65/5.
**beryed** *pt.* and *pp.* buried 58/24, 25; **beryd(d)** 115/38, 188/4, **berryd** 147/37, **bereed** 75/8, **y-beryed** 58/23.
**beseche** *pr. 1 sg.* beseech 61/11, **besek(e)** 7/2, 170/65; *3 sg.* **beseke** 227/20.
**besecheng** *pr. p.* beseeching 143/15, 219/60.
**beseg(h)yd** *pp.* besieged 242/12, 191/11.
**besene** *pp. adj. better* ~ better dressed or equipped 78/30.
**besy** *adj.* busy 49/16, **byssy** 94/9.
**besyd(e)** *prep.* near 57/26, 59/3, **beseyd** 58/8; as well as 47/18, **bysyde** 202/20.
**besynes(e)** *n.* activity 2/19, 10/4, 37/4, **besenes** 222/12, **beysones** 44/25; preoccupation with or pres-

**besynes(e)** (*cont.*):
sure of business 63/5, **besynesse** 46/9; commercial undertakings 104/53.

**bespeke** *v. tr.* order 161/11; *intr. pt.* **bespake ffor** 97/8.

**bestow(e)** *v.* invest 77/14, 205/42, 237/19, 29; **bestowhyd** bestow it 70/13; *pp.* **bestowyd** 203/29; **bystowyd** stowed 130/5.

**bet** *compar. adv.* better 171/5.

**betyme** *adv.* in good time 36/17, 234/30; **betymes** in good time; early 154/12, 184/9, **betymus** 109/65, **betymys** 117/30.

**betors** *n. pl.* bitterns 71/18.

**betryste** *pp.* trusted 55/9.

**better** *v. tr.* improve 238/35; *intr.* 12/20.

**bettyn** *pp. adj.* compacted 112/10.

**betwen** *prep.* between 25/26, **bytwene** 16/18, **betwhene** 133/10, **betwheyn** 175/19, **betwyne** 88/6.

**bytwyn(e)** *adv.* from one place to the other 72/16, *com* ~ 61/13.

**betwyxt(e)** *prep.* between 141/26, 115/34, **betwyx** 29/4, **betwext** 41/29, **bytuyxt** 4/9.

**bycoket** *n.* peaked casque 114/37.

**byd** *pr. 3 sg.* makes an offer 91/27; *pt.* **bad** 55/23; **bed** *pr. 3 sg.* asks 40/10; *pt.* **badd** 202/15; *pp.* **byd** wished 19/49.

**by(e)** *prep.* see **be**.

**bye** *adv.* near 199/11.

**by(e)** *v.* see **bey**.

**byell** *n.* bell: *iij of the* ~ 3 o'clock 153/19.

**byeng** *vbl. n.* purchasing 25/13, **by(e)yng** 26/16, 231/6.

**byldyng** *vbl. n.* building 26/17, 47/11.

**bill, byll(e)** *n.* memorandum, letter, note 49/5, 116/16, 33/7, 230/10, 235/47; letter of payment or obligation 1/9, 4/6, 234/5, **bell** 39/8; ~ of one's hand: obligation 3/7, 100/13–14, ~ *at plesur* 141/14, *byllys off plessur* 204/27, ~ *payabull at sye[t]* 47/37–8 bill(s) payable on demand; *byllis of xviij monthis and xviij* bills payable in 18 months and 3 years 124/5–6.

**bytys** *n. pl.* horses' bits 119/9.

**blak(e)** *adj.* black 103/9, 43/4, 69/3; *in* ~ in mourning 175/9.

**blankys** *n. pl.* silver coins 173/6. [MDu. *blanc*, after Fr. *blanc*].

**blemeschyd** *pp. adj.* blemished 212/11.

**blesbe** worn down form of *blessed be* 57/6, 8.

**blessud** *adj.* blessed 152/3; *pp.* 154/6, **blissid** 64/15, 142/34, **blyssyd** 35/3.

**blew** *adj.* blue 51/5.

**blyssyng** *n.* blessing 169/4.

**blodeschede** *n.* (?) bloodshed 59/5–6.

**blottys** *n. pl.* packs of wool weighing less than 364 lbs. 165/16 and note. [? MDu.]

**bochar** *n.* butcher 230/2.

**bode** *n.* body 222/8; *be the faythe of ther bodys* on their honour 117/6–7. Also **whelbodyd**.

**boge** *n.* see **bugge**.

**bogke** *n.* account book 31/15, **boke** 38/31.

**bogwyt** *pp. and pt.* see **bey**.

**boye** *n.* servant lad 112/38; also note to 126/2.

**bokyll** *n.* buckle 86/9.

**bollewarkys** *n.* bulwarks 183/11.

**bond** *n.* contract 226/8.

**bonotys** *n. pl.* bonnets 97/8.

**booyth** *adj.* both: ~ *of vsse* 28/5, *the wyche boothe letterys* 9/5; *adv.* **bothe** too, also 104/47, 117/15, 165/34, *buthe for woll and fell* 37/15, **boyth** 125/13, *off oottys … and … bothe of whete* 142/29–31.

**bord** *n.* board and lodging 86/13, **burdd** 204/54.

**borde** *v. intr.* board 219/30.

**borell** *n.* barrell 119/6, **barell** 119/10.

**Borgan** *adj.* belonging to territories of the Duke of Burgundy; from the Low Countries: ~ *canvase* 67/15, **Burgen** 242/10.

**borow** *v.* borrow 40/11; have free credit for 176/13.

**boshop** *n.* bishop 200/3, **boschoppe** 191/8; *poss.* **Byschopys** 165/8, **beschepys** 85/8; *pl.* **bochoppys** 15/20.

**bott** *n.* boat 230/8; *pl.* **botys** 115/17.

**bowllde** *adj. makys hym* ~ is em-

# GLOSSARY

307

**boldened** 112/32; [*be*] *bold to* venture to 103/5.

**bo(v)nden** *pp.* obliged 10/19, 219/27; *bownden to H. F. yn* indebted to him by 217/38, **bu⟨n⟩de** 53/11; tied, attached 228/20, **bownd(e)** 232/8, 64/11, **bonde** 158/3.

**bowhay** *n.* 126/2 (see note).

**bowȝer** (?) *n.* bowyer 83/15 and note.

**box(kys)** *n.* box 120/2, 38/10, 56/3, **boxkt** 39/6.

**Braboners** *n. pl.* men of Brabant 191/10.

**brasse pensse** *n. pl.* small silver coins 173/9. [After MDu. *braspenninc.*]

**braste** *pt. sg.* burst 147/40.

**bravthe** *pt.* see **brynge**.

**brede** *n.* breadth, width 67/16, 90/14.

**bredurne** *n. pl.* see **brodere**.

**brege money** *n.* bridge money, a toll 181/5 and note.

**bregenders** *n. pl.* briganders, plated body-armour 114/36.

**breke** *n.* brick 233/21.

**breke** *v. intr.* ~ *wyth* cause a rupture (with) 206/39, 208/32; *tr.* broach a matter *to* someone 224/12; *pt.* **brake** 165/42, 199/12; *pp.* **brokyn** 165/42; *brok(en) vp(p)* broken; destroyed 142/10, 191/10; *pp. adj.* **broken** in pieces 186/4.

**brenar** *n.* bringer 73/11, **brenger** 51/2.

**brent** *pp.* burnt 149/11, 212/11, **byrnyd** 169/23; **burnyd** 115/33; *pp. adj.* 149/14.

**bressyng** *vbl. n.* bruising 228/8.

**Brettens** *n. pl.* Bretons 205/52; *poss.* **Brettayns** 206/33.

**bryng(e)** *v.* bring; ~ *yn* submit to the Staple 170/43-4; ~ *(in)* escort 134/27, 96/23; *breng hym appon the way* see him started 124/14-15; *pr. 3 pl.* **breng** 22/17; *pt.* **broght** 39/28, **browt(e)** 19/19, 57/8, **browyt** 47/31, **brohut** 117/12, 133/11, **bravthe** 37/19; *pp.* **browhyt** 81/7, 86/8, *browght an bowght*, *brohut abohut* brought about 22/11-12, 117/29, *have browght ytt that* arranged that 41/32, *browght vpp* raised to a good position 208/47.

**brynyng** *vbl. n.* bringing 135/3.

**brocar** *n.* broker 78/11; **broker** 218/24.

**brod(e)** *adj.* broad 133/54, 67/16.

**broder(e), brother** *n.* brother 5/18, 19, 3/1; brother-in-law, wife's brother 233/6; friend; (fellow-) member of the Staple Company 224/8, 13; 138/1; **brod(d)yr** 10/28, 29/18, 227/14, **brodir** 142/8, **brodur** 88/10, **broth(e)yr** 4/1, 28/1, **brothir** 49/1, **brothur** 42/1, 65/11, **brothe⟨r⟩** 34/1, 165/1, 193/10; *abbrev.* **B.** 19/18, 125/35; *pl.* **bredurne** 152/5, 154/5, **brethyrn(e)** 117/18, 142/33, **brethern** 138/5, **brethon** 80/5, **breon** 67/3.

**broderhod** *n.* brotherly affection: *of yowr good* ~ 102/12, **brotherhod** 117/2.

**brokyn,** *pp.* see **breke**.

**bromus** *n. pl.* brooms 37/27.

**bug(g)e** *n.* budge, i.e. broadtail or astrakhan 60/11, 196/22, **boge** 42/12 and note, 123/4, *bugyschankys* budge from the legs of the animal 60/4. [Bougie, Algeria].

**Burgen** adj. see **Borgan**.

**burgys** *n. pl.* ?fortified towns, applied specif. to towns in the Low Countries after MDu. *burch* 191/10.

**Bursse, the** *n.* the Bourse, the exchange at Bruges 234/16 and note.

**but(t)** *conj.* but, except 4/13, **bot(e)** 10/14, 156/11, **bott(e)** 15/20, 21/8, **byt** 8/7, **bud** 94/12; only 3/7, ~ *yong* 163/10, 170/58, ~ *on* only on 189/11; unless, without that 21/15, 33/4, **byt** 134/14; *byt for, saue* ~ *ffor* except for 43/5, 15/8; if only for 84/14; ~ *onely* except 142/5; ~ *yff* unless 22/18-19; *not ȝeyt byt, no(o) mor(e) but* no more than 95/14, 22/37, 204/54.

**C¹** *abbrev.* for hundred, either 100 or, for certain commodities, 120, e.g. 49/4, 91/6, 129/3.

**C²** mark on London winter fells 128/8, 133/58; on country winter fells 131/25; ?for Cely, on pelts 131/35.

**caye** *n.* key 19/48, **kay** 72/13, 105/41, **key** 105/21; *pl.* **cayys** 92/35, 37.

**Caleys** *n.* ~ *trede* thread from Calais 67/17; ~ *carthe* 56/16.

**cal(l)abyr** *n.* squirrel fur 60/4, 165/73. [Calabria.]

**call(e), cawll** v. call; train a hawk to return 199/11; ~ *on me for* ask me for 15/9; ~ *vppon S.* to require him to 242/19; *3 sg. pr.* **cawlthe** 15/12; *pp.* **callyt** (?) [is] named 58/8 and note; *called* (*callyd*) *vpon* applied to 7/21, 103/5; *kawlyd apon* urged 133/23.

**callyng** *vbl. n.* demand 11/12, *the scharpe* ~ *on* the sudden demands for payment 38/26.

**can** v. know 56/20; *pr. 1 sg.* **cane** 136/41; **con** am able 4/2, **kan** 159/2, **kon** 124/22, 168/22; *I can no mor to yow* I write no more 142/31; *I* ~ *thynke* I would guess 12/20, 36/19; *neg.* **cannat** 16/20, **cannatte** 21/8, **conott** 41/26, **connot(t)** 195/10, 109/54, **connat** 192/8; *3 sg.* **con(e)** 4/12, 86/2; *pt. and pt. subj.* **covd(e)** 39/34, 40/21, **cowd(e)** 22/11, 16/22, **code** 38/45, **kowde** 212/9, **kod** 141/10.

**Candellmase** *n.* Candlemas, 2 February 10/21, **Candyllmesse Evyn** (1 February) 241/11, **Candelmese** 67/19.

**canvase** *n.* canvas 53/24, 56/26, **canw(h)as** 197/25, 136/39, **canuas** 34/30.

**Carolus** *adj.* ~ *grot(t)ys* double patards of Charles the Bold, issued from 1467 to 1474 133/16, **Carrollys** 221/32, **Carowllys** 205/19, 213/50, **Caruluss** 142/24, **Carleche** 50/10, **Carlyche** 52/7, **Carlys** 134/12, **Carroldus** 72/3; *n.* **Caroldys** 141/30, **Carowllys** 209/33. [Lat. *Carolus, -d-* in one form unetymological.]

**cart(h)e** *n.* cart 57/12, 56/14, 85/2, *haue to* ~ put to cart work 52/20; **cartt** cart-load of people 142/20.

**cas(e)** *n.* container 78/28; matter, state of affairs, condition 22/15, 30/5, 38/42, **kasse** 109/38, **casse** 124/7, 151/21, *yn what* ~ *P.* hath set [*you*] *ffor* how P. has placed you regarding 215/21; *be in* ~, *stonde in casse* be in a favourable position 227/19, 22/23–4, 219/44–5; *in* ~ *be that* if 141/31–2; *I pott an casse* I pose a question, instance an example 7/19.

**cast(e)** v. throw 142/12; appraise fells 87/14, 92/36; *pp.* 168/7; **scast** *pp.* ? turned 58/28; ~ *howght* separated 112/12–13; ~ *owte* put out as a sample 234/47; *pt.* 235/41; *pp.* ~ *howght*, *cast(en) owte* 112/16, 190/3, 234/48; *cast owte* rejected 209/58 (see also **schett**); *pp. adj.* selected 128/6 and note.

**caswell** *adj.* risky 205/26; unsettled 236/4.

**caulluys** *n. pl.* calves 136/12, **cawluys** 127/14, 136/14.

**caws** v. cause 232/7.

**caws(se)** *n.* cause, reason 47/16, **cauys** 8/2, **cawis** 112/9; ~ [*necess*]*ery* impelling reason 21/5; *causes vrgent* ?vehement accusations 16/18 and note.

**cellyssytor** *n.* see **solyster.**

**cepeyd** *pp.* kept, celebrated 83/7.

**ceson** *n.* see **ses(s)on.**

**chamberyng(e)** *n.* chamber hangings 198/13–14, 189/7.

**chammelet** *n.* camlet, material of silk and ?Angora goat hair 103/7, 9.

**change** *n.* charge for changing money 142/24.

**chapelayne** *n.* chaplain 33/10 (fig.); **chapelen** 123/13.

**chard** *n.* charge 70/26.

**charge, scharge** *n.* request to make payment 2/5, 41/9, 205/34; stock, investment 107/25; *maters of* ~ important things 66/7; **chargys** *pl.* expenses 22/26; responsibilities 25/7.

**charge, scharge** v. burden financially 25/12, 197/12; **scharege** load with goods 87/23; *pp.* **chargid** burdened 244/3; **(s)chargyd** indebted 206/14, 30/3; *chargyd me* (*hym*) *so sor(e)* undertaken so much 24/10, 47/10–11; *stondyth chargyd . . . to* is bound to 7/12.

**chavke** *n.* chalk 131/33.

**chawns** *n.* event, accident 169/10.

**cheyff(e)** *adj.* chief, head 241/17; *my chef comyng* my main reason for coming 57/14; *n.* chief men 236/29.

**cheyr** *n.* (with *good* or *great*) hospitality, entertainment 10/3, **(s)chere** 240/21, 116/10, **sche(y)r** 19/21, 108/2; *good cher* cheerfulness 222/10.

**chepe** *n. goode* ~ cheap; cheaply 201/25–6, 226/12; *gowd schepe* 136/38;

*better schep* more cheaply 219/29; *quasi-adj. gode cheper* cheaper 60/5.

**chepynge** *vbl. n.* shipping 21/6. Also **schepyng.**

**cherysched** *pp.* treated well 225/14.

**chese** *v. intr.* choose 208/18, **chesse** 22/11; *tr.* elect 213/52; *pp.* **chos-(s)yn** 78/15, 22/43, **choosen** 212/21; **schosyn** 25/7, 43/13, **i-chosen** 160/29.

**chese** *n.* cheese 88/21, **cheys** 126/3, **chesys** 131/30.

**chyld** *n.* boy servant 47/30, **chelde** 144/11, **schyld(e)** 70/17, 28/6, 106/7; **sch⟨y⟩lde** child 117/26; *pl.* **chyldern** 185/19, **cheld(e)ren** 219/4, 76/8; *withe child, wyth schyl(l)de, gret wyt chylde* (far) pregnant 142/28, 141/36–7, 169/13, 39/41–2.

**chyrchyng** *n.* service after childbirth 181/10.

**Christende** *n.* a Christian 219/28.

**cl., cll(ys)** *abbrev.* for *clove(s)*, a weight of wool: 7 lb. avoird. ($\frac{1}{52}$ sack) in England, and 4 lb. of 14 oz. ($\frac{1}{90}$ sack) at Calais 18/5, 89/9, 205/5.

**clarett** *adj.* light red, of wine 201/25.

**clausse** *n.* sentence, passage dealing with a particular matter 110/6, **claws(e)** 81/11, 213/24, **clawys** 47/20, **clase** 38/49; *pl.* **clavsys** 109/7.

**Clementys ʒewyn, Sente** 22 November 111/43.

**clenly** *adj.* neat; proper 4/16. Also **sclen** *adv.*

**cler(e)** *adj.* and *adv.* plain 246/4; net, after deduction 104/11; entirely 149/14; without encumbrance (?) 169/12; *bee ~ wyth hem* have settled accounts with them 220/16–17.

**clere** *v.* pay (a bill) 38/29; *pp.* **cleryd** ? approved, passed 176/21; *cleryd the bill owt of the tresory* paid it and had it returned 66/8–9; ~ *(cleyr vp) my boke* balance accounts 38/31, 41/37; ~ *that rekenyng* adjust the (disputed) account 234/43; ~ *hymselff* ?exculpate himself 242/18.

**clerely** *adv.* plainly 31/6; net 48/11; *compar. more cleyrly* 41/48; *more clerelyar* 238/17.

**cler(e)nesse** *n.* complete statement 112/19; settlement of accounts 26/3, **clerenese** 38/30, **clernes** 96/19; **cle(y)rnesse** 184/14, certificate that dues have been paid 41/35.

**clyf(f)te wull** *n.* soiled wool from the breech of the sheep, crutchings 218/20, 22, 221/19; *pl.* **clyfte wullys** 235/17. [*Clift* 'fork of the legs'.]

**cloke** *n.* clock: *iiij of the ~* 4 o'clock 59/5, *a clokt* 39/3.

**closse** *adj.* private 143/15.

**clos(s)yd** *pp.* and *pp. adj.* ~ *in* enclosed in 8/10, 15/4, **i-closed** 9/4; **y-clowsyd** wrapped or securely fastened 112/14.

**clotys** *n. pl.*[1] 'cloths': sarplers 90/7.

**clotys** *n. pl.*[2] cleats, wedges 56/18 and note.

**[cocket], kockett** *n.* certificate of entry of goods in the customs register 229/1; *pl.* **cokyys** 90/7.

**cokettyd, kockyttyd** *pp.* ~ *yn* certified as entered in the customs register 163/21, 163/17.

**cold(e), covld** *adj.* cold 49/19; ~ *mart(t) (marte)* the winter mart at Bergen-op-Zoom 37/5, 70/12, 176/11–12, 212/92, **Cowlld Marte** 34/11; *n.* **kowlde** 43/5.

**Coleners** *n. pl.* men from Cologne 238/28.

**coler** *n.* collar 60/11.

**coler, colo(w)r** *n.* colour 103/10, 51/5, 60/3; *pl.* **colors** 97/8; *by collar* as a cloak for another 7/7 and note.

**col(l)ectors** *n. pl.* collectors of Staple dues at Calais 135/16, 41/18, **collecturs** 25/6 and note, **collecters** 213/53.

**collectry** *n.* collectors' office 66/9–10, 156/10, **Coletry** 121/19.

**com, cum** *v.* come 11/21, 78/24, **covm** 40/6, **cowm** 114/41, **cwm(e)** 165/57, 174/6; *to ~ se hym* 78/24; ~ *to* befall one 110/16 *that wull comme theroff* the consequences 191/18–19; ~ *thereto* prove necessary 12/13; *neste ~* next 26/10; *Fryday ~ viij dayys* Friday week 124/16; *pr. 3 sg.* **com(m)ys** 114/42, 160/9, **cwmys** 136/32, **cums** 72/16, **comyt(h)** 9/11, 207/17; *comyth even owyth*

**com, cum** (*cont.*):
tallies with 179/7–8; *3 pl.* com 86/22, **com(m)ys** 92/38, 190/8, **comyth** 212/41, *comme on* advance 183/13; *subj.* **cum** 19/9, *pt.* **cam** 78/8, **com(e)** 165/60, 19/42, **comme** 158/4; *pp.* **com(e)** 20/26, 129/4, **comme** 198/8, **coum** 120/2, **cwm** 165/54, **com(m)en** 68/5, 170/55, **com(m)yn** 88/14, 111/9, **common** 196/9, **com(m)vn** 77/6, 237/4, **y-comen** 39/12, 40/18.

**comande** *v.* commend, recommend 129/21; *pr. 1 sg.* **comaund(e)** 42/1, 21/1, **commaunde** 60/1; *3 sg.* **com(m)avndyth** 100/2, 181/8. Also **comende**.

**combyrd** *pp.* ~ *wyth* incommoded by 74/22.

**comeavndyd** *pt.* ordered 46/11.

**comen** *v.* talk (with) 216/17, **coomen** 241/24; *pr. 3 pl.* ~ *of* discuss 227/34; *pt.* **comoned** 224/4, **comende** 117/23. [OFr. *comuner*.]

**comende** *v.* commend 126/11; *pr. 3 sg.* **commende** 84/20; *pt.* **commend** 190/4, **commendyd** 19/50. Also **comande**.

**comens** *n. pl.* commons 240/11, **comyns** 240/15.

**comforte** *n.* help, encouragement, consolation 47/11–12, **comeffortt** 22/22, **cumfortte** 150/16, **comford** 30/4, **cumforde** 19/34, **conford** 20/29; *do vnto har any comford* give her any aid 223/10; *comffortte of paymentte, comforde of paymen⟨t⟩* something on account 21/11–12, 38/45. [comfort], **cownfort** *subj.* comfort 76/5; *pp.* **comforttyd** reassured 133/3.

**comyng** *vbl. n.* coming 204/16, **cowmyng** 122/24, 165/65, **cum-myng** 43/17, **cwmyng** 165/10; *long of comyng* slow to come 20/14; *pl. at my commyngys howte of* when I arrived from 91/12–13.

**com(m)yng, commenyng** *n.* *hadd(e)* ~ *wyt(h)* talked with 50/3, 182/13; *in* ~ under discussion 36/18.

**comunicacon, com(m)enycacyon** *n.* talk 213/26; **comynycasyon** 46/4,

**commynnecaschon** 162/4, **com-myngaschon** 12/7; *hadd* ~ *for* talked about 166/3; news, information 117/32; *as be the fyrst comynycacyon* ?on first appearances 165/62–3.

**conclude** *v.* arrange 213/36; ~ *ffor* agree to settle on 227/33; *pp.* **con-clewdyd** agreed 22/6; *be concludyd apon* have agreed to 162/8.

**conclusyon** *n.* *yn* ~ in the end 218/24, result: **conclevseon** 219/53; agreement 227/29–30, **conclu-cyon** 241/45, **conclesyon** 38/16, **concleseon** 20/19; *take syche con-cluson* reach such agreement 241/25–6.

**condessendyd** *pp.* agreed 124/4; **condescended** decided 224/7.

**condyssyon** *n.* condition; cast of mind; physical characteristics 111/8; *pl.* **condyscyons** 117/18.

**condyte mony** *n.* fee paid for the convoy of the wool fleet 204/43, 206/8.

**conowthe** *pr. 3 sg.* knows 35/11.

**consayt** *n.* opinion 36/21.

**consederacons** *n. pl.* considerations 234/30, **consederraschons** 170/16.

**contaynynge** *pp. adj.* of letter of payment: for the amount of 15/5, 7, **contanyng** 91/21.

**content(e)** *v.* satisfy a creditor 60/8, 219/38; pay a bill, etc., 204/19; *pp.* **content** 1/7, **contentt(e)** 232/5, 102/14; *adj.* not *conttent*, nott *content*, unhappy; disaffected 165/91, 200/3.

**contynent** *adv.* ~ *vpon the knowlege* immediately on hearing 228/16.

**contynewans** *n.* continuance 84/21.

**contrary** *adj.* opposing 209/49; (of wind) 194/11; contradictory 170/37; *n. I wholl nott say the* ~ *but* I will not contradict the fact that 7/7–8; *of þe* ~ to the opposite effect 237/18; *adv.* 206/11; *prep.* **contrey** against 208/49.

**cont(t)re** *n.* countryside 52/5, **cwn-ttray** 168/19, **contrey** 131/25; *in that* ~ in those parts 165/28–9, **con-terey** 58/12; *the* ~ people of the district 165/64; wool from a specified district 170/46, 93/24; *pl.* **contrey** 111/39; *adj.* *con*[*tr*]*ay men* 19/26;

*contre*(*y*) (*fells*) fells from country areas (other than the Cotswolds) 34/19, 46/18, 92/9, 156/12.

**conuey** *v.* convey 63/3, **conw(h)ay** 43/6, 114/47; *pp.* **conveyd** 205/24, 226/16, *whell convhayd* managed with secrecy or carried to a successful end 169/29.

**Coraynce, raysens off** currants 42/14.

**cordyall** *adj.* heartfelt 17/3.

**Corpys Kyrste Day** *n.* Corpus Christi, the Thursday after Trinity Sunday 175/8.

**cor(r)ant** *pp. adj.* current; at specified valuation 187/20, 189/28, 26; *mony ~ in Flandyrs (Calles)* 34/8 and note, 34/9.

**corrected** *pp.* punished 16/23.

**corsse** *n.* ornamental girdle 51/7; *pl.* **corssys** 51/2.

**corten** *n.* curtain 189/11.

**cortesy** *n.* courtesy 192/14, **curtesy** 228/14.

**c[or]t[e]sly** *adv.* politely 221/22.

**cortte** *n.* Staple court 5/10, **courtt** 208/36.

**corttes** *adj.* polite; obliging; gracious 21/12, **curtes** 10/13, 25/25.

**cosyn** *n.* nephew 88/1, 101/1, **cosen** 88/4; relation (kinship unascertained) 60/7, 74/15, **cossyn** 60/1, 109/11, 246/15, **cousan** 7/16; ?as an indication of friendship 123/5, **coyssyn** 129/1, 11, 23.

**cossars** *n. pl.* horse dealers 193/3.

**cos(s)yons** *n. pl.* cushions 74/21, 18.

**cost(e)** *n.* expense 109/10; costly entertainment 19/2, 108/2; *pl.* **scostys** 5/16, **sostys** 130/14.

**costom(e)** *n.* custom dues (esp. of 6*s.* 8*d.* per sack of wool or 240 fells), often linked with **subsede** 7/21, 111/12, **costum** 7/14, 41/15, **custem** 72/7, **custon** 20/2, **kustum** 84/8.

**costomer** *n.* customs officer 132/5; **costemerys** *pl.* people from whom one customarily buys 192/5.

**Cot(t)ys** *abbrev.* for 'Cotswold' *n.* Cotswold wool: *medyll yowng ~* 93/9; *ffyne ~* 211/9–10; *good ~* 112/5; Cotswold fells 92/6, 105/2; *adj. ~*

*fellys* 25/10, 41/41; *~ woll* 67/11, 105/15.

**Cottyswold(e)** *n.* Cotswold fells or wool 34/18, 18/5, 30/6, **Cottys(s)-owlde** 133/52, 113/4, **Cottsowlde** 127/10; *adj.* 34/5, 90/6, 26/7, **Cotts-oulde** 133/62, **Cottysold** 125/5, 201/16, **Cotsolde** 19/6, **Cutsewout** (Du.) 13/7.

**cowmpeny** *n. in ~ of* with 136/25.

**covnsell, counssell** *n.* advice 47/7, **consell** plan 140/16; body of councillors: of Calais 201/26, **councell** 212/18; of Flanders **concell** 213/36; the King's Council 22/7, **Cons(s)ell** 20/7, 182/14; assembly of a council 111/34, *in cwnsell* 197/11; secret: *kepe no cwnsell frome yow* 169/11; *gewhe me cownsell to* advise me to 193/4.

**co(w)nter** *n.* counting house or locked desk 72/13; *~ candyll* large candles for use on or in the counter 119/8.

**cower** *n.* coffer 84/7.

**craddyll clothys** *n. pl.* sheets, etc., for a cradle 230/7.

**craftys** *n. pl.* Trade Guilds 149/31.

**cray** *n.* disease of hawks, stone 71/15. [Fr. *craie* 'chalk'.]

**crayer** *n.* small trading boat 198/13, 15, 239/12.

**creaunce** *n.* long line attached to a hawk's leash in training 199/12.

**credence** *n.* good financial standing, credit 219/35, *yn grett credens* 206/22; *gyffeth ~ to* trust 65/10.

**crem(y)syn** *adj.* crimson 165/71, 175/9.

**crye** *v.* proclaim 207/38.

**Cristen man** *n.* Christian 16/17, **Crestyn–** 7/9, **Cresten–** 61/18.

**Crystemas** *n.* Christmas 78/25, **Crystmesse** 112/21; **Cyrstemes** 136/26, **Kyrstemas** 114/51, **Kyrstemes** 43/9, 71/12, **Screstemas** 70/24.

**crosse** *n. pl.* (?) ? money 99/3.

**crossyd** *pp. be ~ the Plase* be dismissed from membership of the Staple 208/39 and note, 208/57.

**crown(e)** *n.* French gold coin: *the old ~* the *écu à la couronne*, struck before 1475 187/22, *owlld crovnus pl.* 151/36;

**crown(e)** (*cont.*):
*the new* ~ the *écu au soleil*, struck from Nov. 1475 187/22; **crovnus** *pl.* 151/35; without specification: 78/16, **crovne** 41/34, **crone** 80/10; *pl.* **crownys** 151/44, **crownus** 196/36, **cronys** 80/10, **crowny** 78/15.
**cuet** *abbrev.* for hundredweight, a hundred ounces troy 42/13 and note.
**cursar** *compar. adj.* coarser 93/24.
**cwstelew** *adj.* costly 134/11.

**d.** *abbrev.* for *penny* (*pence*) 2/12; for *pennyweight* 159/13, 14; for *dimidium* 'half' 5/4, **di.** 18/4.
**day** *n.* date set for payment 1/7, 3/8, 31/35, 95/21; *pl.* **dayys** 38/6; term of credit 12/13, 22/40, *pl.* **dayes** 151/10; *iij ʒere* ~ 12/15; *hawe Passe* ~ *off payment* have credit till Easter 207/52; respite or renewed appointment 165/37, 195/4; *at day(y)s* (*dais*) on credit terms; in instalments 12/10, 163/18, 100/12, 217/20; *off a monyth* ~ for a month 201/7, *at a monyth* ~ *after* a month later 12/19.
**da[y]lesse** *adj.* without redress, or sine die 215/14 and note.
**dame** *n.* wife 60/4.
**danger** *n.* make yt ~ to be obstructive about 8/15.
**dar(e)** *pr. 1 sg.* dare 25/11, 219/36, 72/10, **darre** 216/18; *3 sg.* 96/12, 240/40, **dar(e)s** 238/29, 23; *3 pl.* **dar** 8/5, 240/29; *pt.* **durste** 239/13.
**Davyd** *n.* gold coin of David of Burgundy, Bishop of Utrecht 1456–96 196/57, **Dawethe** 196/39.
**dd.** *abbrev.* for *donné*, or *delivered* 28/13: (*be*) *thys* ~ be it delivered 32/20, 34/38, 146/19. Also **done, soit(t)**.
**debenters** *n. pl.* vouchers for payment issued by the Staple for loans made by individual members to the government 115/5, 167/16, **debentyrs** 124/5.
**debyte** *n.* deputy; *master* ~ the deputy lieutenant of the Staple? 162/17; *pl.* **debyteyys** 109/23.
**dede** *n.¹ in* (*yn*) ~ in fact 109/13, 221/36; **deyd(e)** legal instrument 111/31, 147/26.

**dede** *n.²* see **det(t)he.**
**ded(e)** *adj.* dead 39/31, 11/8, **dedde** 76/8, **deyd** 74/23, 75/7; *n. the* ~ *of wynter* 109/50, 193/6.
**deducke** *v.* ~ *oon* deduct from 221/4; *pp.* *deductyd off* (*vppon*) 162/14, 206/6, 234/61.
**defaut** *n.* shortcoming 10/11; **defayte** lack 26/17, 37/18.
**deffende** *pr. subj.* forfend 219/59.
**deffetyd** *pp.* annulled 235/33.
**deyd** *adj.* dead 165/27.
**delyng(e)** *n.* conduct 10/13, 142/14, **dellyng(e)** 96/15, 21/13; commercial transactions 38/30, 104/54, 217/16; *pl.* **delyngys** 215/47; ~ *wyt worde* transacting business by letter 104/48; *mervellys* ~ astonishing goings-on 242/15.
**delyuer** *v.* (re)pay 12/18, 50/15; *pt.* **delyueryd** lent 10/26, **delyuerd** 234/9; *pp.* **delyuer** conveyed to 2/22, 11/26, **delyuyrt** 192/24.
**del(l)e** *v.* ~ *wyth* do business with 31/34, 22/33, **deyll** 168/8; treat 93/10, 219/41; handle 104/46, **dell** 25/24; *pp.* **i-delt** 7/10.
**dem** *pr. 1 sg.* deem 92/33.
**demene** *v. refl.* conduct oneself 214/15; *be demenyd* (*wyth*) behave (towards), treat 25/13, 55/27.
**demenyng** *n.* behaviour, actions 26/3.
**demy** *adj.* half- or less than full-sized 189/11.
**deny** *v.* refuse 18/4; *pp.* **denayed** 241/47.
**depart(te)** *v.* leave; ~ *into Ynglond* leave for England 18/12; ~ *frome* abandon 197/13; ~ *from* (*wyth*) part with 199/18, 72/5; *pt.* **depart** 222/13, **depertyd** 90/8; **departyd** parted 18/11; *pp.* *theparded to God* dead 75/7. Also **deperde.**
**depart(t)yng** *n.* leaving 19/3; parting 19/33, **depattyng** 136/28.
**depected** *pp.* for *derected* 'directed' 16/7.
**deperde** *pp.* divided out 30/6.
**deppe** *adj.* wide 159/6.
**dere** *adj.* expensive 190/10, **deyr** 55/24; *compar.* **derar** at higher valuation 41/33.

**derectyon** *n.* ~ *takyn* a ruling given
109/34; *take noo derecsch*[*on*] *ffor*
make no arrangements for 189/43.

**derect(t)yd** *pp.* directed 78/19, 146/3,
**derecked** 58/4, **derckyt** 53/9,
**dyrectyd** 148/13, **dyrect(e)** 15/4, 6.

**derge** *n.* matins in the office of the
dead 75/8.

**desarue** *v.* merit 121/7; **dyssaruf** requite 10/5; *deserue it to* [*you*], *deseruit vnto 3ou, dessaruytte to yow, deserved ayenst yow* repay you 17/9,
33/6, 102/17–18, 153/7–8, 149/20;
**desarwyd** deserve it 169/14.

**descreschon** *n.* discretion 160/20.

**desen** *n.* dozen 60/5.

**desyar** *n.* desire 24/9, **deysyre** 57/4,
**desser** 222/4.

**desyar** *v.* wish; request 122/17, **de-
s(s)yer** 8/11, 121/14, **dysyr** 51/10;
*deseyere yowte of the toun* invite you
out of town 110/20; *desyryd forthe*
summoned out 111/20; *pr. 3 sg.* **dyssyers** 74/26, **dessirethe** 144/5,
**desyer** 71/11; *3 pl.* **desywr** 78/5; *pt.*
**desyerd** 25/16, **desyret** 129/7, **desered** 125/14, **desseryd** 18/3; *pr. p.*
**dyssyeryng** 135/2.

**desseicyth** *pr. 3 sg.* dies 217/39; *pp.*
**deses(s)yd** 70/28, 169/22, **dessesced** 123/15, **dessesset** 200/2,
**dessett** 200/4, **discesyd** 142/3, **dyssessyd** 71/5.

**destytewyd** *pp. adj.* ~ *of* lacking
218/64.

**det(t)he** *n.* death 111/21, 136/13;
(mortality from) plague 39/24, 64/16,
66/13, **deythe** 43/10, [d]ede 38/33,
**dehet** 40/4.

**dettour** *n.* debtor 245/4; *pl.* **detturs**
197/15, *gode detters* those likely to repay 162/21.

**Dew(y)ke** *n.* Duke 11/5, 19/36.

**dewt(t)e** *n.* see **dute.**

**devars** *adj.* various 7/4, **deuersse**
115/19, **deyueres** 143/3.

**de[w]e[llys** *n. poss.* devil's 9/21.

**deuysyon** *n.* disagreement 83/12.

**dy** *v.* die 110/39; *pr. 3 pl.* **dey** 58/14,
**dys** 137/22; *pt.* **dyed(d)** 66/14, 187/
21, **deyed** 58/25; *pp.* **y-deyed** 58/17.

**dys** *n.* dice 32/12.

**dysanullyd** *pp.* cancelled 238/13.

**dyscharge, descharge** *v.* pay a debt
145/6–7; ~ *them off ther towne* re-
nounce their civic office 208/54–5;
*pp.* **dyschargyd** relieved 212/19; dismissed 208/53; released 8/3, 207/32,
**y-dysscharged** 9/14; unloaded 104/
44, 198/16.

**dys(e)charge** *n.* release; receipt; ac-
quittance 95/8, 217/47, 80/17.

**dyshease** *v.* annoy, molest 185/20;
*pp.* **dys(s)esyd** ill, unwell 95/29,
201/30, **desshessyd** 102/7–8.

**dyspend** *v.* have as income 165/28.

**dysspleser** *n.* offence 206/36; *take displesur*(*e*) take offence, be angry
180/20, 112/27; *take displesir ayenst*
(*wyth*) *me* 16/15–16, 17 fn.; *take noon
dysplessur off myn Englysche* 203/7–8;
*take it to no dysplesour* 232/4; *pl.* **displesurs** grievances 242/7.

**dysses** *n.* decease 81/8, 147/34.

**dysspontyd** *pp.* refused payment
10/14.

**dyssprowett** *pp.* ?deprived, ?proved
false 200/3 and note.

**do** for **to** *prep.* 129/10.

**do** *n. makys any* ~ *ffor* makes an offer
for 156/18.

**do** *v.* do, act 16/17, **doo** 9/21, 68/8,
**dow** 222/2, **doe** 2/11, **doy** 28/7,
**done** 6/10; *doo þeryn þat* act in the
matter so that 221/19; ~ *wyth* deal
with 19/38, 77/7; ~ *for* assist; support 11/22, 19/25, 25/22, 73/7; ~
*whel by* treat generously 168/16; ~
*moche therto* do good business by it
109/39 (also **gode**); cause to: *to* ~
*seyell them* to sell them 58/30. As aux.
4/4, 95/6, 143/5, 202/5; as substitute
*v.* 205/34, 212/67, 242/21; *pt.* **dyde**
41/34; *pp.* **done** 16/17 fn., 19 fn.

*pr. 3 sg.* **doyt(h)** 151/23, 139/5,
**doys** 19/7, **dos** 197/18, **do(o)** 133/40,
218/48; *dothe esse* makes for leisure
2/20; *3 pl.* **doyth** 125/22, **dothe**
22/34, **doys** 158/14, **don** 141/33; *pt.*
**dyd(e)** 142/12, 136/12, **deydde**
192/3, **ded(e)** 117/14, 41/18, **dod**
110/19; *the* (*your*) *coste that 3e dyd on*
(*to*) *me* what you expended on me
19/2, 108/2–3; *pp.* **don(e)** 88/18,
152/12; **doon** 68/3; **doyn** 55/38; **doe**
27/10; **doo** 234/47, **y-do** done away

**do** (*cont.*):
with 110/18; **done** *intr.* over 18/12; *tr.* finished 92/36; *doon wyth* finished with 242/11; *done grett* performed great feats 200/1; *pr. p.* **doyng** causing 94/4, 128/2; dealing 111/40, **deeng** doing 219/35. Also **whell don(e).**

**doblet clothys** *n. pl.* cloth for doublets 114/50; *sg.* **dublett clothe** 160/33.

**docatys** *n. pl.* (Venetian or Hungarian) ducats 56/46, **doketys** 118/10, **docettys** 121/19.

**Doche** *adj.* from the Low Countries 134/36; *Dowche myle* the German mile (*OED* s.v. *mile n.* 2) 177/5, *Dewche meyll pl.* 209/45-6.

**Doches** *n.* Duchess (of Burgundy) 187/21, **Dowches(se)** 189/26, 178/18.

**doket** *n. in* ~ in abstract 38/23; **dokatys** *pl.* dockets, abstracts of entries in the customs register 109/32.

**done** *pp.* delivered 149/43; in the address of a letter: *soit* ~ be it given 22/51, 66/19, **don** 125/40, **doon** 1/15; *this don* 72/24. Also **dd.** and **soit(t).** [Fr. *donné pp.*]

**dong(e)** *n.* dung 142/11, 13, **dongke** 140/11, 12; ~ *forke* 37/30, 142/12.

**dosseren** *n.* for 'dozen' 141/21.

**dowghter** *n.* daughter 188/3, **dowter** 108/7, **dowt(t)yr** 78/10, 168/13.

**dowyn** *adv.* down 197/5, **done** 36/23, 37/12, 125/13.

**dowte** *v.* fear ~ *theroff* fear it 153/26; *pr. 1 sg.* **dowght** 243/9; *I* ~ *me* (*that*) I fear 219/60, 145/1-2.

**dowttys, dowghtys** *n. pl.* doubts: *I put noo* ~ *yn hytt* I am sure 241/42; *ʒe schall nott nede put noo* ~ *yn hytt* you need not fear it 218/46.

**draper** *v.* make into cloth 93/15. [Fr. *draper.*]

**drapery** *n.* cloth manufacture 93/14.

**draw(e)** *v. intr.* ~ *vnto* extend to 209/22; *pr. 3 sg.* **drawys** to 60/7; *tr.* amount to 208/17, 217/45; *pr. 3 pl.* **drawythe** 212/42.

**dryke** *n.* drink 73/4.

**dryve** *v.* negotiate 241/26; *pp.* **dreuyn** driven 133/5; *he hath dreven vs off* he has put us off 164/5.

**drovnyd** *pp.* sunk 7/20.

**duryng** *pr. p.* lasting 17/15; throughout 238/14, *my liffe devreng, my lewe dewreng* all my life 145/14, 219/51.

**dute** *n.* debt 88/6, **dwete** 71/6, **dewt(t)e** 4/12, 21/21; **duetie** charges 224/16; *pl.* **dewtes** 170/16; moral obligation: **duty** 4/20; *pl.* **devteys** 109/23.

**dwell** *v.* live 58/26; *pr. p.* **dwelyng** 232/15, **dewellyng** 22/50, **dwyllyng** 57/26.

**eder** see **hyddyr.**

**eyder** *conj.* either 219/36.

**e(y)lle** *n.* ell, 45 inches in England, 27 inches in Flanders 90/14, 55/31, **elne** 60/6; *pl.* **ellys** 55/30; **yellys** 70/21, *elnys Ynglysche* 60/5. Also **awnys.**

**elle** *n.* see **heyll.**

**els** *adv.* else; otherwise 152/13, **(h)ellys** 180/19, 120/3, **hels(e)** 58/28, 192/19; *and nat elles* and nothing more 143/6.

**em** *n.* uncle 152/6, **heyme** 195/8, *my neme* 92/8, **neym** 96/3.

**end(d), ʒend** *n.* end 125/19, 217/36; remnant 92/13, *the laste* ~ *off* 131/48; final agreement, outcome: **ende** 85/16, **heynd** 165/22; purpose 86/19; *made an* ~ *of* finished 112/7; *make a neynd wyth hym* conclude the business 117/8.

**end wull** *n.* ? old stock, ? wound lock wool 218/9-10 and note, 22, 220/35.

**Englys** *adj.* English 55/30, **Ynglyssche** 60/3, **Englysch** 115/19. Also note to 206/66.

**eny** *adj.* any 16/10, 25/16. Also **onny.**

**enmys** *n. pl.* enemies 175/13, **henmyys** 7/20.

**enqwer** *v.* inquire 71/9, **inqweyr** 114/31; *pp.* **enqueryd** 227/11.

**enqwery** *n.* inquisition post mortem 147/22.

**entent** see **intent.**

**entercours(s)e** *n.* agreement for exchange of trading rights 212/49-50, 60, 227/30. [OFr. *entrecours* 'exchange'.]

**entermete** *v.* meddle 191/18.

**entredyd, entretyd** see **intret.**

**entter** *v.* ~ *hys name to* enlist with
207/40; *pp.* **entryd** entered 212/60,
*entyrdyd in* incorporated with 112/11.

**enwardely** *adj.* inward 219/3.

**er** see **ʒeyr.**

**erand** *n.* message, errand 64/4; *pl.*
**arndys** 57/11.

**erst** *adv.* before 77/17.

**es(e)** *v.* assist, accommodate 170/57,
**ʒese** 4/14, **hese** 122/18; *to* ~ *hym* to
relieve himself 34/29; *pp.* *better hessyd*
more settled 86/16–17.

**esse** *n.* leisure 2/20, 106/10, **ease**
76/4; **hesse** convenience 80/8,
**yeasse** 171/9; *worst at* ~ the most
discommoded 219/21.

**essynglar** *adj.* especial 178/1. Also
**sengler.**

**estapell** *n.* see **Staple.**

**Ester** *n.* Easter 40/12, **Estyrn** 83/8,
**Estorn** 92/23; ~ *wheke* the week be-
ginning with Easter Sunday 148/9,
**Estyrwyeke** 10/24, *Hester weke*
149/28, *Esterne, Esturne weke* 152/11,
154/11; ~ *martt* the Easter mart at
Bruges or Bergen-op-Zoom (see also
**Passe**) 209/29–30.

**Esterlyngys** *n. pl.* Germans from the
Hanse towns 238/28.

**ete** *v.* eat 179/11, **hett** 133/33; *pr.* (?)
*1 pl.* **ette** 141/35; *2 pl.* **ete** 142/
28.

**ewre** *n.* *put in* ~ make use of 143/8,
**vre** 236/18. [ure; AFr. *\*eure*, OFr.
*(u)evre*, etc.]

**ewe** *conj.* if 8/10; *eve so be that* 8/14.
Also **heffe, yeff(e).**

**even** *adv.* exactly 179/7, *ʒeuyn next*
right next 133/54.

**euer** *adv.* always, ever ~ *the lenger* as
time goes on 234/19; *ewer syn* since
19/17; *for heuer* for ever 84/14–15;
*heuyrmor* evermore 174/2; *prep.* before: *heuer thys* 136/8, *heuyr any
wryttyng* 109/28; *conj.* (h)euer 78/8
and note, 78/29, **heuyr** 93/6, **heuir**
93/19, 133/8, **hewyr** 165/31; *heuyr
that* 196/72, *heuer tyll* 232/4.

**euery** *adj.* every, each 3/5, **hewry**
4/21, **heuyry** 150/15, **yeuery** 172/5,
**effyry** 192/11, **euer** 129/3.

**eueryche, euerychon** *adj.* (*n.*) each
one 241/22, 64/15.

**euerythyng** *quasi-adv.* in every way
189/10.

**evydensse** *n. pl.* legal documents,
title-deeds 176/23.

**euyll** *adj.* bad, hurtful; unfortunate
197/12; **evell** 219/53, *hewell well*
ill-will 110/24; *n.* **ewyll** misfortune, mischief 74/23, 221/27.

**ewyn** *n.* see **ʒewyn.**

**exchaunge** *n.* rate of exchange between sterling and Flemish money
234/18–19, **exs(c)hange** 31/31, 22,
**exschonge** 36/12; *make (one's)* ~
*with* make an exchange agreement
with 10/11, 100/9, **exschaunge**
122/16; ~ *makyng* exchange loans
77/12; receive (have, take (up)) *by
(be)* ~ borrow for repayment abroad
1/2, 205/15, **excheaunge** 53/2, **exschounge** 122/13, **exchonge** 118/8;
deliver (make, give (over)) *by (be)* ~
lend, for repayment abroad 228/17,
**excheunge** 53/22, **exschanchege**
87/19, **exschonge** 38/8, **exschange**
122/4. Also **speceaulte.**

**Exchetter** *n.* escheator 147/21, 32.

**exchettyd** *pp.* escheated 147/29.

**excuse** *n.* denial 17/11; **askvse**
ground for excuse 30/8.

**excuse** *v.* *I pray to* ~ *to* [*her*] *that*
please give my excuses to her for the
fact that 228/25; *pr. 3 pl. ascuse hem
that* make the excuse that 162/22;
*pt. ascwysyd me* refused politely
165/57–8; *pp. has askewyshyd hyr
that* refused because 47/13.

**excuse** *n.* denial 17/11; **askvse**
ground for excuse 30/8.

**exprest** *pp.* stated 208/38.

**face** *n.* *make a ffayer* ~ feigns good
will 170/35–6.

**fader(e)** *n.* father 5/17, 9/12, **ffadyr**
22/1, **faider, fayder** 141/4, 125/32,
**fadur** 88/6, **fathe(r)** 108/12, 133/2,
**ffathyr** 4/4 *poss.* **father** 133/42.

**fay(e)r** *adj.* good of its kind, in good
condition, handsome; of weather:
favourable 19/30, 114/37, **fayar**
38/32, **fayʒe(y)r** 43/11, 108/4, **fayher**
223/6, **ffayyr** 41/38, **fayre** 37/6,

**fay(e)r** (*cont.*):
**far(e)** 19/31, 107/14, **ffeyr** 162/24, **feyer** 39/26; due 121/15; soothing 240/13; *superl.* **fayreste** 134/4; *adv.* promisingly 109/16, 183/6, **ffeyr** 184/10; 'decently' 197/13.

**fay(y)t** *n.* faith 110/18, 151/23, **faythe** 168/22.

**falle** *v.* ~ *of* withdraw 85/13; ~ *yn* incur 169/27; *ffallyth to* turns out to be 237/27; *pt.* **ffell** occurred 239/16; *pp.* **fawl(l)yn** 133/31, 83/12, **ffall** 204/51.

**fardell** *n.* bundle 34/26, 78/19.

**farder** *compar. adv.* further 25/12; *ffardyr go, goo seke farther* apply elsewhere 4/13, 72/16–17; *go fardar* (*goo any ffarddyr*) *wyth* deal further with 147/12, 227/52; *hawe goon noo ffyrdyr wyth hym* 226/14; *superl.* at the fardest (*ffarthest*) at latest 121/21, 209/24.

**farys** *pr. 3 sg.* fares 19/8, **faryt** 39/40, **fareth** 224/25; *pr. 3 pl.* **faren** 154/5, **faryn** 152/6; *pt.* **fard** 25/3; *for* went 2/11; *pp.* **fore** 87/15, 98/8.

**farthermore** *adv.* furthermore 15/2, **fferthermore** 3/1–2, **forthermore** 64/11, **firthermore** 88/4, **ferdermor** 5/2, **ferdermo** 40/1, **fordyrmor** 4/2, **fyrdyrmore** 226/3, **furdermore** 176/8, **furdurmorr** 192/2.

**Fast** *n.* Lent 141/26.

**fast** *adj.* dependable 72/12, 209/25.

**fast(e)** *adv.* steadily 20/21, 111/39; urgently 15/9, 12; *make me* ~ *apon* depend upon 72/10.

**faturs** *n. pl.* ? factors 80/11, 16 and note.

**fawghte** *pt.* fought 211/33.

**fawkener** *n.* falconer 137/19, **ffawckener** 199/10.

**fawte** *n. for the* ~ *of* for lack of 39/30; *wythowtt fawtt* without fail 232/7. Also **defaut.**

**fawt(e)** *v.* fail 220/20; ~ *of* lack 72/8–9, 232/9.

**fauer** *n.* favour: *wyth any* ~ in a favourable light 219/44; *hadd yow yn fawer* favoured you 215/35; *be yn ffawer to hawe* be favoured with 201/27.

**Februare** *n.* February 242/21,

**Feuere(r)** 207/46, 1/6, **Feuerell** 143/13, **Feueruell** 44/20.

**fedurs** *n. pl.* feathers 65/7.

**fefes** *n. pl. poss.* feoffees' 147/27.

**feynd** *v.* find 123/4, **fende** 12/4; *pt.* **fond** 114/19, **fand** 123/2; *ffownd them grewyd* were aggrieved 208/46; *pp.* **fond(e)** 10/12, 12/8, **fwnde** 84/7.

**feyr** *n.* fair, market 162/23, **ffaȝer** 163/9.

**fekerey** *n.* see **vekery.**

**felbyndars** *n. pl.* binders of fells 34/29.

**fele** *pr. 1 sg.* perceive, infer, 'gather', 12/10, 27/2, **ffelle** 22/6, **fely** 122/7; *I feyll by hym* I gather from him 108/17.

**Felyppys** *n. pl.* see **Phellypus.**

**felyschepe, feloship** *n.* companionship 23/16, **felleschype** 83/19; company of associates 123/10, **felychyppe** 129/4, **fellyschyp** (in a lodging) 19/51–2, **ffellyschypp** 204/52; the Company of the Staple: **Felychepe** 12/14, **Felaship** 224/6, **Feleschyppe** 39/27–8, **Fellyshyp** 22/19; partnership, esp. of Dutch merchants: **felyschip** 44/4, **felyschype** 34/17, **feleschype** 149/6; *pl.* **ffellyschyppys** 167/8.

**fell** *n.* wool-bearing sheepskin 168/6; *pl.* 20/26, **fellys** 2/3, **felles** 7/6, **ffeellys** 44/4. Also **pell.**

**fellmen** *n. pl.* dealers in fells 15/8.

**fenanys** *n. pl.* ? pheasants, ? fen birds 40/25.

**ferde** *adj.* afraid 168/12; *compar.* **ferdar** 169/25.

**fer(e)** *pr. 1 pl.* fear 25/7; *I* ~ *me of, Y feyr me that* I fear 12/3, 11/7–8, 110/14; *pt.* **ferryd** 117/18.

**fferyaunce** *n.* see **varyavnsse.**

**fferme** *n.* dues for a lease 15/11.

**ferre** *adv.* far 33/5.

**fesaunte** *n.* pheasant 19/30.

**fessychons** *n. pl.* doctors 73/4; *sg.* **vesyschon** 77/22.

**fet** *v.* fetch 108/20, **fet(t)e** 136/15, 78/22; *pp.* **fett** 225/22. Also **fyech.**

**ffett** *n.* 'feat of merchandise', business, sale, deal 112/20, 212/40, 220/40, **fette** 149/21; *pl.* **ffettys** 206/23.

**fette** *n.* fit. attack 70/9.

**Feuerell** see **Februare.**

**fyech** *v.* fetch 141/7; **feche** 55/42. Also **fet.**

**fylde** *n.* field: *hathe the* ~ has won the battle 59/6.

**fyne** *adj.* synonym for *good*, as grade of wool 206/47, 221/9, 36, *compar.* **fynar** better quality 87/9.

**fir** *prep.* and *conj.* for 138/2, 228/14.

**ffyrdyr** see **farder.**

**firkyn** *n.* cask 228/4, 8, **wyrkyn** 119/10, 120/6; *pl.* **wyrkyns** 114/12.

**first, ffyrst** *adj.* of letters of payment, the first of two or more copies 1/8, 234/20; *adv.* at earliest 194/10; *affore the Doches dyedd ffyrst* immediately before the death of the Duchess 187/21.

**ffyscher** *n. pl.* fishing boats 235/25; **fyschermen** fishermen 236/8.

**fytyng** *n.* litigation 85/8.

**Fl.** *abbrev.* for Flemish (currency) 4/7, 6/6, 247/28.

**flankardys** *n. pl.* armour for the thighs 114/48.

**fle** *v. intr.* fly 137/20.

**fol** *adj.* foul 129/19.

**for** *prep.* despite 37/6; to avoid 133/77; because of 43/5; *hyt ys not* ~ *hyme to* he must not 86/23.

**force** *n. of fyn* ~ by sheer necessity 219/23, 55.

**fore** *adv. as it gothe* ~ as it proceeds 98/18.

**for(e)** *pt.* and *pp.* see **farys.**

**forgeet** *pr. 1 sg.* forget 125/36; *2 pl.* **forgete** 2/18; *pp.* **fforgotyn** 161/5, **forgettyn** 81/13, **forgetton** 125/16.

**fforhowsse** *v. tr.* move wool from one store to another 105/26; *vbl. n.* **fforhowssyng** rehousing 105/54. [? Adapt. from Fl., cf. Du. *verhuizen.*]

**for-rom** *n.* the forepart of a ship 5/5.

**fforst** *num.* and *adj.* first 22/4, **furste** 96/12, **furest** 125/37; *adv.* **fforste** 15/18, **forst** 92/2.

**fforten** *pr. subj. tr.* send you the chance of 203/12; *intr.* happen 213/21.

**fortewyn** *n.* chance 111/20.

**forth** *adv. and so* ~ *to* and then go on to 140/16.

**foster** *n.* forester 133/10.

**fowld** *n.* paunce, apron of plate 114/38; *pl.* **fowlldys** 114/48.

**fowle** *adv.* badly; ? dirtily 198/12; *superl.* **fowllest** 112/15.

**foull** *adj.* full 114/47.

**ffox** *n.* ~ *gowne* gown furred with fox 64/12.

**ffrayght** *pp. adj.* laded 206/33.

**frayte** *n.* freight charge 84/9, **frayght** 26/14, **freyght** 5/16, **frayth(e)** 27/6, **frayfte** 31/14 and note.

**freeth** *pr. 3 sg.* ~ *hymsellff* frees itself (see note) 125/5.

**Frenscheman** *n.* French ship 115/24; *pl.* **Frenschemen** 115/20, **Fraynchem** 47/14.

**frere** *n.* friar 129/15, 18, **Freyr** 117/15.

**Frynche** *adj.* French 59/4.

**frynd** *n.* friend 42/20, **ffreend** 68/12.

**fryse** *n.* coarse woollen cloth 119/9.

**fryst(e)** *adj.* first 98/21, 20/30, **frysth** 38/3. Also **fforst.**

**fro** *prep.* from 15/2, **from:** *he ys* ~ *hys master* he has left his apprenticeship 218/61.

**fuill** *adv.* very 24/15; **ffull** fully 41/15. Also **foull,** *adj.*

**fulle** *adj.* ?foul, ?full 107/9.

**furre** *n.* fur lining 196/22.

**ffustyans** *n. pl.* coarse cloths 237/22.

**gayne** *adv.* again 218/53.

**garnettys** see **pound** ~.

**gadryth** *v. intr. pr. 3 pl.* increase in numbers 182/28; *tr. pp.* **gadered** collected from the growers 67/12, **gatheryd** 197/7; *vbl. n.* **gaderyng** wool-gathering, collection 20/23, 122/8.

**Gauntenersse** *n. pl.* people of Ghent 241/25.

**gebarddys** *n. pl. stand yn no* ~ *off* run no risk for 206/21. Also **jebardy.**

**gebart** *subj. pl.* ~ *not yowrselfe to* do not risk a journey to 134/19–20.

**geffe** *conj.* if 200/5. Also **ewe, yeff(e).**

**gey** *n.* ? joy 110/17 and note.

**gene** *v.* make a profit of 111/10.

**Geneways** *n.* Genoese 234/22, **Genovo[ise]** 235/37.

**Geneuer** *n.* see **Jenuar.**

**gense** *prep.* be ~ oppose 141/19 and note.

**gentyll** *adj.* obliging 76/12.

**George, Sent** ~ *ys day, Sent Jorge day* 23 April 218/5, 157/6–7.

**ger(e)** *n.* goods, 'things' 8/25, 103/15, **geyr** 95/18, **geyhyr** 114/14.

**ges[t]** *n.* guest 133/84; *pl.* **gestys** lodgers 115/26.

**gett(e)** *v.* buy; obtain 63/5, 118/9, **geyte** 47/27, **geet** 125/27, 141/31, **gehet** 165/21, **gehyt** 136/38; *to gett* obtainable 190/8, 215/55; *get frome leave* 55/15; *pt.* **gote** 115/17; *pp.* **gottyn** 112/31, **goten** 191/7, **goot-(t)en** 207/42, 217/44, **getyn** 121/20, **gityn** 108/23, **gette** 59/7; **gettyn** begotten 169/14, 15.

**geve** *v.* give 103/20, **gew(e)** 7/2, 8/16, **geyff** 18/9, **giff** 72/6; **gewhe** give away 169/19; ~ *vpp* surrender 242/13; *pr. 3 sg.* **gyffyth** 170/37; *as ffar as my symppull reson geyff me* as far as I can tell 213/18; *2 pl.* **gyffeth** 65/10; *pt.* **gaave** 39/30, **gaw(h)e** 19/54, 136/20; *pp.* **geven** 16/19 fn., **gewyn** 117/44, **gyffyn** 135/10, **geffun** 140/12, **gyn** 129/16; *has geuyn hyr ower* has given her up 83/13. Also **ʒeue**.

**gevyng** *vbl. n.* ~ *hower off mony* lending by exchange 77/11. Also **ʒeueyng**.

**gydyng** *n.* behaviour 38/47; control 70/26, 240/14, **gydeng** 64/19.

**Gyldars** *adj.* of Guelders: *an* ~ *rydar* gold rider of Duke Arnold of Guelders 56/45; *abbrev.* **Gyll.** 151/56.

**gyldern(e)** *n. pl.* gulden: various gold coins current in the Low Countries (see also **Rynysche, Andreus**) 187/23, 41/34, **gyldorn** 151/47, **gyldyrns** 118/10, **gylders** 234/18. [Corrupt. of MDu. *gulden*.]

**Gylhellmus** *n.* gold coin, prob. the *scild* of William VI of Holland (1404–17) 187/24. [fr. Lat. inscription.]

**Gyll.** *abbrev.* for **Gyldars**.

**gyn** *pp.* see **geve**.

**gyu** *pron.* you 117/24. Also **iou, ʒou**.

**gode** *adj.* good 17/1, **god(d)** 102/3, 162/16, **goyd(e)** 43/21, 47/42, **gowd**

136/38, **gud(d)** 72/2, 100/18; creditworthy 162/21, **goode** 215/26; first grade (of wool) 18/4, 26/7; *godd lordd, good master* patron, protector 162/16, 19/14, 137/14; ~ *lordshipe* 161/8; ~ *mastership* 16/19 fn.; *do yt(t) good* see note to 7/9; *doe (hony) good (therewyt)* deal profitably (with) 26/16, 27/16; *ther whoulde be done good ouer, ther wyll be goode doon vppon* there is a profit to be made on 114/49, 237/27; *don any goode* achieved anything 205/53; *dothe lyttyll good* 2/19. Also **gud**.

**golde** *n.* gold; gold coinage 36/23, **goulde** 86/4; *an pesse gowld* a gold coin 196/42; *pl.* **gol(l)dys** 238/47, 20/5, **gowldys** 34/11, 41/33.

**gonars** *n. pl.* gunners 114/30.

**gone** *n.* gun, cannon 147/38; *pl.* **gonnes** (changed to **gvnnes**) 183/11.

**goo** *v.* go 55/19, **goe** 56/17; *pr. 3 sg.* **gothe** 37/5, **go(o)yth** 188/8, 196/15, **goys** 120/4; *3 pl.* **goys** 74/31, 118/6; *pp.* **go(o)n** 182/32, 212/69, **goyn** 43/19; ~ walk 102/10; of coin: circulate, pass as currency 22/13, 238/58; be valued at 239/23; of horses: **goynge** *ppl. adj.* running loose 195/12; *as the markyt gothe* at market rate 53/15; *go thorow wyth hym* conclude the bargain 109/61; *go to that pryse* pay so much 165/18; *goo vppon* attack 186/14–15. See also **farder, fore** *adv.*

**Good(e)** *n.* God 55/20, 41/36, **Godde** 169/13, **Gud** 125/16; **Goddys man** see **mane**; *a God(d)ys peny* earnest money 141/9, 209/19.

**good** *n. pl.* goods 5/15, 7/17, **godis** 88/13, **godys** 160/23, **good(d)ys** 5/13, 203/18.

**goodly** *adj.* good 228/12, 29/7; laudable 42/7; fine quality 65/7; *adv.* well 44/24.

**gornay** *n.* journey 117/40.

**goshavke** *n.* goshawk 33/3, **gosshavke** 39/29, **govshawke** 39/34, **gos(s)ehawke** 37/17, 189/14; *pl.* **goshaukys** 81/9, **gosehawkys** 169/18.

**gosse, gossep** *n.* friend; also used to

the godfather of one's child 6/2, 76/2, 143/1, 145/13.

**gostely** *adj.* spiritual: *my ~ brother* 'brother confessor' 169/28.

**gow(y)n clothe** *n.* cloth for a gown 25/19, 114/51; **govn–** 40/9.

**gr.** *abbrev.* for **gret(ys), groot** 97/4, 173/13.

**grayne** *n. clothe in ~* cloth dyed with 'grain' or kermes 40/12.

**grandam** *n.* grandmother 58/25.

**grane** *n.* appar. some (?forked) part of a horse's equipment [cf. *OED grain n.²*] 98/16.

**gre** *n. take it in ~* take it in good part 245/7.

**g⟨r⟩eabyll** *adj. be ~ to* agree to 136/31.

**gree** *v.* agree 53/17; *pr. subj.* **gre** 43/16; *pp.* **greyd** 162/7.

**grefe** *n.* distress 74/12, **greve** 111/6.

**grehyt** *v.* greet 126/1, **gret(e)** 2/1, 90/1.

**grene** *adj.* fresh, unsalted 227/13; *greyn gynger* ginger preserved in syrup 136/44–5, 169/5.

**gret(e)** *adj.* great 25/7, 2/18, **grett(e)** 4/25, 19/34, **greit** 10/4, **greyt** 19/10, **grehyt(e)** 74/3, 147/38, **greht** 10/3, **gryte** 20/12; *done grett* see **do;** *adv.* **gretly** 16/10, **grehytly** 78/2.

**gretys** *n. pl. deniers groot* or *gros:* the unit of one-twelfth shilling Flemish 173/6; hence, Flemish currency, *abbrev.* **gr.** 173/13, 205/46.

**grewandys** *n. pl.* greyhounds 136/30.

**gryly** *adv.* ? for 'greatly' 104/52.

**grosse** *adj. ~ warys* wares distinct from spicery 237/20 and note.

**grote** *n.* groat, Netherlands or English coin 85/11, **grott** 22/16, *Englysche grotys* 205/19; *(the) new grottys (of Meclyn)* Malines groats 238/58, 241/52. Also **Carolus, lymon, nemyng.**

**growe** *v. wherto thys schall ~* what will develop 215/18; *~ to noo conclusyon* reach no result 227/29–30; *pp.* **grow(y)n** accumulated 22/25, 189/43; due to be paid 19/38, 203/20, 21, 204/26, 211/41.

**grovnde** *n.* ground for agreement 109/56.

**gruff** *adj.* coarse 234/53 and note. [MDu. *groof.*]

**gud** *n.* reward 129/16.

**3- see y-.**

**ha** *pron.* he 43/18.

**hack(e)ney man** *n.* hirer of riding horses 203/25, 199/3.

**hagyshed** see **hog(g)yshed.**

**hayre** *n.* heir 147/30.

**haythe** *n.* height 117/21.

**halfe** *adj.* and *n. ~ quarter* one-eighth 90/15; *nott . . . the oon hallff of* not even half 215/52; **haillwe** half 41/29, **hawlue** 78/34; *adv.* **hal(l)ff** partly; almost 77/15, 167/10; **hawlfe** 134/15, *not hawlfe* not nearly 136/36; *hallffe see ower* half across the channel 194/11. Also **passa(y)ge.**

**Halfftar** *n.* see **Haustar.**

**halydayys** *n. pl.* holidays 87/12, **hallydayes** 111/37.

**Hal(l)ontyd** *n.* the first week of November 74/5, 91/10, 193/5.

**halpeny** *n.* halfpenny 22/17.

**hand** *n. in ~* immediately; in cash 12/18; under way 36/18; *howlld ~* forbear 109/45; *bar them on ~ at* maintained against them that 78/12; *toke in honde* undertook 219/8; *be in ~* (with someone for something): negotiate with 34/17, 207/50; *a byll of ys honde* an obligation 3/7; *of my honde* in my writing 144/7.

**hany** *adj.* any 42/15, **hony** 23/12, 57/25.

**har** *pron. obl.* her 108/10, 149/29; *poss.* **hare** 223/15, **harys** 149/30. Also **heyr.**

**hardd** *adj. ~ mette* hay 179/12; *superl.* **harddeste** most stubborn 34/15.

**harm** *n. take ~* suffer damage 58/29.

**harm(e)les** *adj. save ~* free from liability 7/13–14, 5/10, 219/10.

**harnes(se)** *n.* body armour 114/34, 207/39, 241/12; **harnys, harnyss(e)** metal ornamentation 51/8, 7, 6.

**harnest** *pp. adj.* equipped with armour 114/39; mounted with metal decoration **(vn)harnys(s)yd** 51/2, 3.

**harskob** see note to 37/28.

**haskys** *pt. 3 sg.* asks 84/9.

**hassche** *n.* ash wood 56/16.

**hast(e)** *n.* haste: *in all þe ~ posybyll, yn as possybull ~ as may be, in all (the)* ~ with all speed 232/6, 240/49–50, 135/27–8, 23, 120/3.

**haste** *adj.* hasty 96/5.

**haufeter** *adv.* after 21/9; *prep.* **haf(f)ter** 3/8, 192/18.

**hawke** *n.* hawk 37/19, **havke** 39/32; *pl.* **akys** 75/4, 10.

**Hawlhalon Heuyn** *n.* see **Alhalon Day.**

**hawltyd** *pt.* limped 47/39.

**haumlyng** *adj.* ambling 57/15, 22. Also **ambelyng.**

**haunsse** *n.* hance, membership of the Staple company 208/41.

**Haustar sclothe** *n.* ?cloth from Alost 69/7 and note, **Halfftar** 70/21.

**hawhe, haue** *v.* have 146/4, 2/14, **hauhe** 146/8, **(h)affe** 129/15, 72/8, **haueff** 18/10; *haue howt* remove 133/8; *pr. 1 sg.* **ha(y)th** 227/11, 234/38, 125/25, **heue** 15/2, **haf(f)e** 102/9, 72/17, **haue** 1/2, **haave** 9/6; *3 sg.* **has(se)** 19/5, 28/6, **hase** 140/10, **hat(t)** 5/9, 21, **hayth(e)** 18/4, 171/9, **ha** 71/13, **hawe** 93/5, **haue** 9/24; *1 pl.* **as** 129/12, **hafe** 147/31; *2 pl.* **hath** 70/3; *3 pl.* **hath(e)** 167/19, 142/8, **haue** 12/6, **hawee** 217/16, **has** 83/17, 109/46; *pr. subj.* **hawe** 45/12, **hath** 77/17, 82/19; *pt.* **hadde** 2/16, **had(e)** 19/20, 21/18, **hat** 70/7; *pt. subj.* **hade** 7/9, 20, **ad** 129/16, 19; *pp.* **hayd** 18/7; *after all reuerence had* respectfully 16/1–2; *wer had home* were taken home 246/6; *wold an hade ytt* maintained that it was 109/33; in pleonastic cmpd.: *Y wold haue had corrected her* 16/23, *and I had natte haue hade þat mony* had I not had 102/15. Also **a, an.**

**hed(d)ys** *n. pl.* leaders 209/49; *schew ther* ~ ?venture abroad, ?pursue their claims 8/5–6.

**heey** *n.* hay 125/23.

**hef(f)e** *conj.* if 165/25, 147/19, **heve** 120/1. Also **ewe, yeff(e).**

**hey** *adv.* high 219/20; *adj. superl.* **heyeste** 219/18.

**heyll** *n.* health 19/4, **heell** 152/7,

**hell(e)** 8/25, 35/3, **hele** 64/19, **elle** 53/26; ~ *full* salubrious 111/24.

**heyme** *n.* uncle 195/8. Also **em.**

**heyr** *pron. obl.* her 137/20, **hyr(e)** 57/21, 61/10; *the frendes of here* her friends 85/10; *poss.* **hyr** 47/29. Also **har.**

**help(e)** *v.* ~ *forthe* give assistance 246/16; *ytt conott* ~ , *hyt* ~ *not* there is no help for it 41/26, 74/22; *halpe (hellpyt) to* help(s) out 26/15–16, 31/17; *to* ~ *yow of l li.* help you with £50 142/24; ~ *me wpon* help me to 219/31–2; *pp.* **holpyn** 47/5. Also **away(e).**

**hels(e), hellys** see **els.**

**hem** *pron.*[1] them 115/6, 23, 131/26; ~ *sel(l)ffe* themselves 241/21 and note, 191/15.

**hem** *pron.*[2] him 5/19, 20, 9/24.

**henmyys** *n. pl.* see **enmys.**

**her** *pron.* their 77/14, 225/20.

**her** *prep.* ere 117/7.

**her** *adv.* here 5/10, **heyr** 19/12, **heere** 180/5, **hyar** 56/15.

**herd** *pt.* see **hyr.**

**her(e)** *v.* hear 39/11, 15/17, **heyr** 55/9, **herre** 57/2, **heer** 152/2, **ʒer** 94/3; *pt.* **hard(e)** 19/30, 38/13, **herde** 15/17.

**heryng(e)** *n.* herring 202/27, 236/22, 203/28.

**herly** *adv.* early 147/37.

**heronsew** *n.* young heron 165/60.

**hert** *n.* heart 33/6.

**hertly** *adv.* cordially 16/24, **herttely** 3/1, **hart(t)eley** 5/20, 8/1.

**hes(s)e** *n. and v.* see **ese, esse.**

**Hester** *n.* see **Ester.**

**het** *pron.* see **hit.**

**hete** *n.* excitement 241/38.

**hett** see **ete.**

**Hettry(t)us** see **Huitryshe.**

**hewell** *adj.* see **euyll.**

**hevy** *adj.* downcast; grave 67/4, **hewy** 219/65; **hewe** 8/19, **heve** 111/7; onerous 31/31.

**heuynese** *n.* trouble; grief 12/2, **hewynesse** 143/5, **hevenes** 141/4.

**hewyng** *n.* urgent discussion 41/28.

**hexsyd** *pp. adj.* axled 56/17 and note.

**hy** *v. refl.* hasten 4/5, *tr.* 86/19.

**hyar** *adv.* see **her.**

**hyd(d)yr** *adv.* hither 43/12, 23, **hyder** 44/24, **(h)eder** 103/18, 40/17, 42/17, **hythyr** 174/11.

**hyr** *imper.* hire 92/32; *pt.* **herd** 75/5; *pp.* **hyrryd** 174/8.

**hysyng** *n.* hoisting, raising goods from a ship with tackle 184/7.

**hyssyn** *pron.* his 92/26, **hessen** 144/5.

**hystyrday** *n.* yesterday 148/14.

**hyt** *adv.* yet 165/82. Also **yett(e)**.

**hit** *pron.* it 1/2, **hytt(e)** 77/13, 192/17, **het(t)** 42/5, 188/2.

**hyt** *pt. 3 sg.* promised 43/7.

**ho** *pron.* who 33/9, 35/11, **hoo** 102/18; **how** 75/12; *obl.* **hom(e)** 55/38, 108/5; *poss.* **hos** 78/10, 11. Also **qwou, wo.**

**hoape** *v. tr.* require, desire 67/14; *intr. pr. p.* **hopeng** *of* hoping for 219/62.

**hoby** *n.* small or ambling horse 134/23, 174/7.

**hoder(e)** *adj.* other 2/8, 5/16, 149/26, **hodyr** 22/13, **hother** 86/11, **hothyr** 22/24; **hodyrwhysse,** *in hoder wyse* otherwise 2/8–9, 93/13; *hoderwysse then* other than 110/16 and note. Also **othyr.**

**hoffes** *n.* office 137/11.

**hoft(on)** *adv.* often 58/28, 134/20.

**hog(g)yshed** *n.* large cask; hogshead (63 wine gallons) 114/47, 229/6, 196/75, **hagyshed** 111/10.

**hoype** see **hoppe.**

**Holanderys** *n. pl.* men from the province of Holland 141/9, **Holondorys** 70/11, **Hollonders** 156/11, **Hollendars** 124/10, **Howllonders** 77/5.

**holl** *n.* hull 133/46.

**Hol(l)ond (s)clothe** *n.* linen cloth from Holland 55/30, 69/6–7, **Holand clothe** 60/6.

**hond** *n.* hound 19/31.

**hon(e)** *adj.*[1] one 112/5, 14. Also **whone.**

**hone** *adj.*[2] own 57/24.

**honest** *adj.* worthy 4/16.

**honeste** *n.* reputation, credit 91/12, 134/16, **onest(i)e** 169/11, 172/7; *pl.* **honesteys** 4/15.

**hooll** *adj.* entire, complete 149/31, **hole** 133/39; well, cured 19/31, **hoyll** 47/41, **hoy⟨l⟩** 74/35, **holl(e)** 70/10, 73/10.

**hoom** *n.* home 74/13, **whom(e)** 145/2, 231/13, **howom** 57/17, **ome** 129/10. Also **hawhe, make.**

**hoppe** *n.* hope; expectation 22/27, **hoype** 84/14.

**hopper** *adj.* upper 92/13.

**hordenans** *n.* ordnance 114/29.

**hors** *adj.* hoarse 193/7.

**hor⟨s⟩harnese** *n.* horse harness 161/15.

**horsyn** *n. pl.* horses 141/34, **horson** 125/22, **horsse** 181/4.

**hors(se)** *n. pl.* mounted soldiers 186/11, **horssys** 209/40.

**hosbanry** *n.* husbandry 104/46.

**hos(s)e** *n.* house 180/17, 141/36; **howsse** boarding-house 219/26; **hows** household 137/20.

**hosse** *v.* store in a wool-house 28/6, **hovsse** 130/11; *imper.* **howsse** 92/31; *pp.* **howssyd** 105/29.

**hoss(e) cloth(e)** *n.* cloth for hose 10/25, 47/36.

**hos(s)yn** *n. pl.* hose 84/23, 55/28.

**hossyng** *n.* the action of housing wool 27/6, 7, **howssyng** 186/7; **howssyng(e)** storage room 105/32; house property 115/29.

**hottely** *adv.* intensely 192/19.

**hotterans** *n.* see **vttravnsse.**

**hottymys** see note to 2/19.

**hottys** *n. pl.* see **oottys.**

**how** *adv.* ~ *that 3e heyr of* what news you have of 19/35.

**how** *pron.* who 75/12.

**how(e)yser** *n.* 151/50 and note, 154/22.

**hovld** *v.* hold: ~ *me* consider myself; promise to be 9/18, 151/9; *holdyth yn* indicates 218/29; *holdyth hytt at* prices it at 226/9; *absol. holldys of the Kynge* is held of the King 147/31; *pp.* **holde** 64/6, **holden** 235/45, **holdyn** 147/28, **howl(l)dyn** 147/29, 24.

**howmly** *adj.* uncivil 97/10.

**howr** *pron.* our 15/18, **hour** 95/3, **howyr(e)** 22/43, 111/2, **howr(r)e** 147/8, 21/2, **howur** 117/31; **howrys** ours 91/19. Also **ow3re.**

**howre** *n.* hour 123/15, **owr** 4/21; *pl.* **owrse** 29/8.

**howsehold** *n.* household goods

**howeshold** (*cont.*):

142/33-4; **hows(h)owlde** people of the household 165/3, 111/3, **howssowld** 78/4, **howssowllde** 127/3, **hovssold** 152/6, **houssould** 151/24, **howseold** 123/9, **howswold** 141/38, **hossolde** 50/23, **hosseso⟨l⟩d** 37/9; *hys howssold mayne* 196/16.

**howssband** *n.* husband 222/23, **husbond** 243/15.

**howssers** *n. pl.* people employed to house wool or fell 105/53.

**houst** *n.* host 39/44.

**hoversyth** *n.* supervision 73/7.

**houyr** *adv.* over 22/26, **howyr** 41/12, **howre** 58/20; *prep.* 92/32, **hover(e)** 39/34, 28. Also **ouyr**, and see **make**.

**Huitryshe** *n. pl.* gulden struck by David of Burgundy, Bishop of Utrecht 56/40 and note, **Hettry(t)us** 151/51, 196/26, 53. [Utrechts.]

**hundyr, hondor** see **wndyr**.

**hus(se)** *pron.* us 91/6, 44/13, **hws** 81/8, **hvse** 104/58. Also **wus**.

**i-, y-** enclitic particle with *pp*. *y-boght* 40/13; *y-wreten* 5/9; *y-yeuen* 5/21; *i-ressayued* 9/24, etc.

**i, y** *prep.* in 74/9, 223/9; on 109/15.

**ych** *adv.* also 125/14.

**ych(e)** *adj.* each 141/40, 187/8, **iche** 242/2.

**Ie** *pron.* I 234/56.

**yll** *adj.* inferior 4/11; *adv.* badly 239/22; [*it*] *were nott ~ don and* it would be a good idea to 213/15.

**ymbasett** *n.* embassy 206/30, 240/45, **inbaset** 149/29, **inbassette** 111/33. Also **ambassett(ors)**.

**imbassettor(u)s** *n. pl.* ambassadors 225/9, 241/33, **inbas(s)eturs** 148/14, 19/35, **inbassetorys** 102/6, **inbassyturs** 114/40; *sg.* **inbassador** 129/9. Also **ambassett(ors)**.

**indewer** *v. refl.* exert oneself 84/15; *se that ʒe yndevyr yow to that* make sure that 231/2-3; *pp.* **endev[eryd]** 41/23.

**inforttewin** *n.* misfortune 133/31. [Fr. *infortune*.]

**ynow(e)** *adj.* enough 25/11, 22/8, **inowʒth** 236/23; *as n.* **ynowghe** 211/40; *adv.* 58/28, **inow** 47/27,

**inowth** 167/24, **inowʒth(e)** 203/21, 215/26, **inowʒght** 202/36.

**inportansse** *n.* importance 129/9.

**insamyde** *pp. adj.* enseamed; caused to lose superfluous fat 136/36.

**ynschyppyng** *v. tr. pr. p.* embarking 212/48. [Cf. MDu. *inscepen*.]

**insure** *pr. 1 sg.* assure 232/4. [AFr. *enseurer*.]

**inteyrly** *adv.* entirely 44/1, **interl(l)y** 55/1, 119/1.

**intent, entent** *n.* desire, intention 8/12, 85/22; purport 242/17; reason, purpose 36/20, 142/16; *to the ~ he shall* that he may 92/35-6.

**intret** *v. tr. ~ hym* induce him 8/16; *pp.* **intredyd** treated 21/9, **entretyd** 221/23, **entredyd** 221/25; **intrete** negotiated with 38/40; *intrete for* offered terms of, or the inducement of 38/44; *there as he ys intreted to* where he is offered an accommodation 11/17.

**inuiatory** *n.* list 165/6. [Corrupt. of *inventory*.]

**inwynde** *vbl. n.* (?) inwinding, incorporating inferior wool in the wound fleece 165/37.

**iou** *pron. obl.* you 38/50 (2); *poss.* **iowr** 41/22. Also **ʒou, yovre**.

**ys, is** *pron. poss.* his 2/13, 44/3, 129/7, 9.

**is** *pron.* this 129/15.

**yt(te)** see **yett(e)**.

**ithryftyle** *adv.* immoderately 142/14.

**jayd** *n.* nag 221/45.

**japys** *n. pl.* trifles 19/32.

**jarre** *n.* dissension 88/5.

**jebardy** *n.* danger 235/24, 237/5, **jeberdy** 236/15. Also **gebarddys**.

**Jenuar** *n.* January 140/18, **Jeneuer** 11/24, **Jenyvere** 206/55, **Jenyveyr** 205/59, **Geneuer** 114/16, **Genewer** 114/44.

**jepardes** *adj.* risky 109/51.

**Jovlle** *n.* July 58/24.

**jour** *n.* day 238/55, 234/67, 235/51.

**jurdyccyon** *n.* administrative office, legal authority 208/48, 52. [Fr. *juridiction*.]

**juste** *adv. ~ to* right beside 132/7.

**justely** *adv.* punctually 143/12.

**kay** *n.* key 72/13, 105/41, **key** 105/21.
Also **caye.**

**ken** *pr. 3 pl.* ~ *of* know about 137/20.

**kenred** *n.* ?relationship, ?family 25/
23 and note.

**kepe** *n.* keeping 75/13.

**kepe** *v.* defend 114/39; *pr. 3 sg.* looks
after 105/39; ~ *in hys honde* retains
21/16; *pr. subj.* preserve 6/12; *pt.*
**keped** 75/4; *pp.* **kepyt** maintained
12/16; *kepte my bedde* was confined
to bed 102/9; *pr. p.* **kepeng** not
moving from 219/65.

**Kesten wull** *n.* wool from around
Kesteven 205/4.

**Kyrstemes** *see* **Crystemas.**

**kyrstynd** *pp.* christened 108/7.

**know** *v.* ~ *an answer* obtain an answer
212/66; *pr. 3 sg.* **know** 47/19,
**knowys** 28/8, **knoweys** 97/12,
169/14, **knowyth** 217/21, **knowthe**
64/18, **conowthe** 35/11; *pt.* **knew**
140/7; *pp.* **known** 217/13, **novne**
38/13.

**knowlege** *n.* acknowledgment 228/
13; **knowleche** information 16/23;
*haue knowlec, hawe yn* ~ *that* be
informed 58/15, 65/2, 227/4.

**koce** *n.* cock 19/30.

**kockett** *n. see* **[cocket].**

**koyttys** *n. pl.* ?quoit-shaped objects
221/39 and note.

**kow** *n.* cough 83/19.

**kumbrus** *adj.* obstructive, awkward
25/23. See also **combyrd.**

**labor(e)** *n.* exertion 10/4, 73/5, 135/3;
*take the* ~ *to Bregys* trouble to go to
Bruges 122/22, **lab(o)ur** 100/4,
103/6; exertion of influence; supplication 19/53, 161/2, *has made* ~ *to
me* 19/13.

**labor(e)** *v. refl.* exert oneself 73/10,
81/14; *tr.* work (a horse) 158/8; *pp.*
**laboryd** 179/14; *labers me to* urges
me to 168/13; work to achieve: *labur
a safgard* 215/13; *pt. subj. labyrde hyt*
117/30; *intr.* work for or against
someone: *to labour ffor them* 207/37;
*labors agayne hym* 175/15; ~ *(vn)to*
make representations to 9/12, 127/12;
*pt.* **labrede** 218/15; ~ *for* work to get
221/29; *pp.* **labord** 78/14; *laboryd for*

*to a be afore yow* tried to best you
215/51; ~ *to* travel to 73/8; ~ *nowher*
go nowhere 74/34.

**laborus** *adj.* troublesome 134/10.

**Lade** *n. Owre* ~ *Day* 25 March
145/2.

**lay** *v.* place 133/76; ~ *owte, ley owth*
expend 42/3, 161/14–15; *leye doun
pay* 224/16; ~ *in* put in as lining
165/73; *they* ~ *vnto me* they accuse
me of 93/9–10; *pt. leyde arndys on*
charged with messages 57/11; *pp.* **leyd**
236/25; *layd aperte* put aside 85/17.

**laysar** *n. see* **leyser.**

**lantarn** *n.* (?) see note to 37/26.

**large** *adj.* wide 159/3; lavish 86/17;
*by* ~ *mony* by a generous amount
61/14; *n. at* ~ fully 214/16, 24; un-
molested 219/37.

**largely** *adv.* roundly, unreservedly
93/8.

**last** *n.* measure for herring 202/27,
203/28, 236/24.

**laste** *pt.* lasted 59/5.

**lat** *v.* last 32/16.

**lat(e)** *v.* allow; cause 22/12, 135/16,
**lett(e)** 61/9, 33/6, **lete** 27/14;
*lett crye* proclaim 207/38; ~ *ytt alon*
let it be 92/23–4; **leet**, *lett owt*
rent 180/19, 10; *pr. p.* **lattyng, laytyng** causing 142/1, 57/6; *pp.* **lett(e)**
207/38, 165/84, **leyt** 75/10; *vbl. n.
latyng owte* lending at interest 153/
10.

**law** *n. menystyr yowr* ~ *vnto me* dispense me justice 7/23.

**lawmprays** *n. pl.* lampreys 19/19–20.

**le** *def. art.* the 214/27, 229/16; in
commercial use, 'per', each: *pryse le
C* 25/10, 109/43, ~ *pesse* apiece 196/
44 [Fr.]

**leberte** *n.* liberty 219/35, **lybbarte**
212/66.

**leddern** *adj.* leather 217/6, **leyder**
139/4.

**leet** *v. see* **lat(e).**

**leffe** *n.* permission 149/27, **leve** 42/4,
218/63.

**leffe** *v.* leave 192/12, **leyff** 18/14,
**lewe** 10/28; *pt.* **leyfft** 18/15, **lefete**
79/5, **leuyd** 19/43; *pp.* **leyeft** 18/8,
**leffyt** 78/20.

**Lefftenaunt** *n.* Lieutenant (esp. of

# GLOSSARY

324

**Lefftenaunt** (*cont.*):
Calais or the Staple) 160/14, **Lefe-tena(u)nt** 32/13, 34/32, **Leffeten-navnt** 22/43, **Lyeftenaunt** 16/7, **Levetenaunt** 44/15, **Levetenanthe** 90/9, **Leutenaunt** 103/4, **Lew-tenant** 140/16, **Lewetenaunt** 34/32, **Lewhetenawnt** 137/12, **Lewheuf-tenaw⟨n⟩t** 136/29.
**leffully** *adv.* legitimately 240/27.
**leghe** *n.* leg 151/20.
**leyke** *adv.* like 151/4.
**leyr** *n.* 234/58 and note.
**leyser** *n.* leisure 241/8, **laysar** 46/10, 147/34.
**leyste** *n. the ~ of bothe* ? the slightest hint of either, ? the result of either, at best, 111/21.
**lekys** *n. pl.* leagues 109/59.
**lemetyd** *pp.* appointed 170/42. Also **alemetyd.**
**lene** *v.* lend 47/7 and note, 47/25.
**lenger** *compar. adv.* longer 137/18, 227/30; *euer the ~* as time goes on 234/19. Also **long** *adj.*
**lenght** *n.* length 29/3, **lengkhe** 159/7.
**lent** *pt.* and *pp.* allowed on credit (*by a byll,* etc. on the strength of a bill) 52/19, 204/37, 209/70.
**lequelly** *adj.* handsome 129/3. Also **lyckely.**
**leryng** *n. for ys ~* so that he may learn 87/24.
**lesyng** *vbl. n.* losing 170/44.
**les(s)e** *v.* lose 31/29, 93/22, 192/10, **leys** 43/18, **leyesse** 149/14; *pp.* **y-lost** 39/32; *loste for kowlde* dead of cold 43/5.
**les(s)e** *compar. adj.* smaller 76/9, 95/19; less 50/4, 5; *superl.* **lest** 199/11.
**lest(e)** *pr. 3 sg. if yow ~* if you wish 76/11; *if hy[t] ~ you bet* if you prefer it 171/4.
**let** *n.* hindrance, delay 152/11.
**letter** *n. ~ (lettyr) of atorney* power of attorney 217/42, 235/29; *lettre of payement* obligation 1/8; *~ of pass-ayge* 'passport' 121/17; *pl. lettyrs of exchonge* bills of exchange 121/9; *lettyrs myssyue* personal letters 121/11 and note.
**lettyd** *pp.* hindered 177/8.
**lettyll** *adj.* little 21/20; *adv.* **lytyll**: *re-*

*member ~* have forgotten 202/14–15. Also **lyccwll.**
**lettyng** *n.* hindrance; delay 104/53, 153/16, 154/11.
**lewde** *adj.* inadequate 203/7; *~ pay-ment* ? by paltry sums, ? unpunctually 21/14; **lvde** sorry, or ? scandalous 85/9.
**lew(e)** *n.* the Burgundian *lion d'or,* struck by Philip the Good between 1454 and 1466 173/11, 56/41, 187/23; *pl.* **lewis** 151/33, **lewys** 151/41, 43. [MDu. *leeuw* 'lion'.]
**lewe** *n.* see **lyue.**
**leve** *v.* live 217/36; *pr. p.* **leveng** 219/26.
**levellyd** *pp.* levied 217/19, 23.
**leueray** *n.* livery 25/19, 114/52.
**lever(e)** *compar. adj. have ~* prefer 39/32, 240/10, **lewer** 163/30, **leuyr** 134/20, **leyuer** 44/11; *~ a grette dell* much rather 39/18–19; *superl.* **leuest** 103/9.
**li.** *abbrev.* for *pound,* in money or weight 1/6, 103/14.
**ly** *v.* sleep; lodge 19/21; *pt.* **lay** 19/24; *pr. subj. that hyt ~ be yow* that it re-main in your hands 117/36; *pr. 3 sg.* **lythe** 104/37, **lye** 202/28; *lyes ap[on] myne oneste, thes . . . lyethe my pore onestie apon* threatens my reputation 169/10–11, 172/6–7; *my honeste lyes ther apon* my credit depends on it 91/12; *hit lyse not in me* it is not in my power 97/11; *pr. 3 pl.* **lyeth** lie 131/48, **leyyt** 5/5, **ley** 89/6, **lyes** 113/6; *pt.* **ley(e)** 115/15, 176/9; *ley betwyxte* was in the balance between 215/34; *pp.* **lyne** 109/25.
**lyccwll** *adj.* and *adv.* little, small 158/11, **lyc(c)ull** 77/13, 170/58, **ly(c)kull** 201/30, 220/33, 36; *lykyll inowe, lykull inow3ght* little enough 202/30, 36.
**lyck(e)ly** *adj.* likely 217/36, 220/47; with ellipsis of *be*: 191/12; *lyeth styll and nott ~ to come* 240/34–5. Also **lequelly.**
**lyek** *pr. 3 pl. ~ wyll* thrive 75/11; *subj. lyke yt you* please 8/2.
**lyght** *adj.* bright 40/8.
**lyghtly** *adv.* casually 167/6.
**lyke** *adj.* likely 168/11; *~ of* equal in

96/7; *adv.* **lycke** 243/19; *conj.* ~ *as*
as 8/4.

**lyklyhod** *n.* *be* ~ in all probability
110/12.

**lymon grotys** *n.* *pl.* 173/12, **lymvn
grotys** 173/4: 'nemyng groats' (see
note).

**lynys pynys** *n.* *pl.* linch pins 56/18.

**lyue** *n.* life 19/29, **lyeffe** 237/6, **lyff**
161/11, **lewe** 219/16, 26; *on lyve*
alive 66/11.

**lyvelodd** *n.* evidence of income or
property, deeds 176/22, **lyvelode**
176/21.

**lyuerd** *pp.* delivered 18/21, 28/13.

**loar** *compar. adj.* lower 36/14.

**lo(c)ke** *n.* ornament in the shape of a
lock 223/21; ? padlock 37/29.

**locky** *adj.* promising 19/9.

**loge** *v.* lodge 115/35; *pp.* **lo(w)gyd**
34/24, 28/12; **logged** deposited
151/49.

**loke** *n.* lock of wool 107/23.

**lok(e)** *v.* look: ~ *(app)on* peruse
105/37, 134/17; *imper.* ~ *howe*, ~
*what* consider how (what) 220/50-1
and note, 75/11; *pr. 1 sg. I lokt for*, ~
*aftyr*, ~ *that* I expect 9/26, 225/6,
38/35; *3 sg.* **lokys** 78/28, **loked** 40/5,
*lokyth . . . when*, ~ *when* expect that
176/7, 240/11; *1 pl.* **lokt** 58/13, **loke**
177/12.

**lokeley** *adv.* fortunately 149/20.

**Lombard(e)** Italian; *n.* Italian banker
(not nec. from Lombardy) 56/7, 5,
**Lomberd** 234/8, 235/10, **Lombar**
78/12; *pl.* **Lombard(d)ys** 107/24,
119/11, 121/8, 218/42.

**London** *n.* (*adj.*) (fells) bought from
the butchers in London 92/2, 156/12,
~ *somor fell* 30/7, *somer* ~ 127/10,
*somer ffellys* ~ 92/18, 149/6.

**long** *adj.* thynke ~ *for* (*tyl, to, after*)
await impatiently 40/19, 13/1, 161/18,
48/17-18; *thothe neuer so longhe for
you* never so longed for you 223/25;
~ *of comyng* slow to come 20/13.
Also **lenger**.

**long** *v.* ~ *to* concern 90/17; *pr. p.*
**long⟨in⟩g** 50/20.

**losse** *n.* absence 47/16, **lose** loss 12/22,
*whe wher at* ~ we were losing money
22/8.

**Low Sonday** *n.* the Sunday after
Easter 147/15.

**lowe** *n.* affection, esteem 218/63.

**Loven** *adj.* of Louvain 161/12.

**lover** *n.* affectionate friend 244/1, 15,
**louer** 66/16, **lowar** 169/31.

**lowyngly** *adv.* affectionately 4/1,
147/2.

**lvde** *adj.* see **lewde**.

**luffuyng** *adj.* affectionate 232/13,
245/10.

**M** *abbrev.* for 'middle wool' 89/9,
221/39.

**M¹** *abbrev.* for thousand; either 1,000
or 1,200 1/11; 5/4.

**ma** *pron. obl.* me 192/11.

**mader** *n.¹* mother 70/8.

**mader** *n.²* madder 70/14.

**mayde** *n.* young girl 55/35; maid servant 76/8; *pl.* **madys** 169/6.

**mayll** *n.* metal plates for armour
114/38.

**mayne, mayny** see **mene¹**.

**ma(y)ster** *n.* master 5/4, 1/1, **maystur** 88/6, **mester** 97/1, **moster**
94/16; title of a priest 123/13; *good* ~
patron 133/9, 136/17; *pl.* **maysturys**
142/33.

**ma(i)stres** *n.* mistress 143/5, 224/25,
**mastras** 152/5, **masters** 94/6, 8,
**may(e)sterys** 9/24, 149/32, **mas(s)-
terys** 39/23, 40/2.

**make** *v.* make 50/17, draw up 8/12,
**macke** 233/7, **makt** 40/9, 58/30;
*mayke vnto yowe* write you 10/19;
*pr. 3 sg.* **makyt** 11/16, *makethe
mencyon* is stated 221/38; *wherof he
makys hym bowllde* which emboldens
him 112/32; *pt.* **mad** 19/21; *pp.*
**mayd(e)** 142/22, 11/18, **maid** 97/3
**mad(de)** 147/39, 144/6, **maded**
217/42; **made** caused to 47/40;
set down as 221/37; *laste madedys* for
'last made deeds' 147/26; ~ [a sum]
(*wyth* a borrower), ~ *houyr*, ~ *home*
lend money by exchange 50/5,
114/9, 22/26, 56/22 (see also **ex-
cha(u)nge**); of damaged fells, re-
pair 30/6 and note, 107/11; *pp.* and
*pp. adj.* **mad(e)** 149/11, 15, 107/10,
109/19, 186/8.

**malardys** *n.* *pl.* mallards 40/25.

**male** *n.* bag, pack 131/30.

**maleffett** *n.* offence 213/39, 44. [OFr. *malfait*.]

**man(e)** *n.* servant 8/14, 154/16, 19/42; of a child 223/15; *neydere Goddys ~ nayder manys* serviceable to neither God nor man 9/20.

**manerly** *adj.* fashionable 103/19; *manarly fellows* 'decent chaps' 19/25.

**manyr** *n.* sort 41/32; *any maner persone* anyone at all 16/13–14; *maner off a gray coler* a kind of grey 163/10; *in thys manar forme* in this fashion 53/10.

**mant(t)ell** *n.* set of furs 117/45; *the ~ and the rynge* the symbols of widowhood 147/37 and note.

**marches(se)** *n. pl.* the land bordering a frontier 185/19, 186/19, 213/44.

**margett** *n.* market 234/31, **makett** 241/39.

**mark(e)** *n.*[1] mark to indicate size or quality 161/12, 128/8; merchant's mark 131/31, 33, 34.

**marke** *n.*[2] money of account, 13*s.* 4*d.* 55/41; *pl.* 31/4, 160/22, **markt** 39/32.

**marschaunt** *n.* merchant 33/12, **mershaund** 66/18, **marchand** 35/16; *marchant beyere* customer 130/12–13.

**marsse** *n.* mercy 75/7, **marsy** 81/7, 188/5, **mersy** 50/24.

**marvele** *n.* *haue (grete) ~* be surprised 56/27, 11/1.

**marvel(l)ysly** *adv.* surprisingly; alarmingly 238/12, 167/12, **mervyllyusly** 237/9, **marvelyusly** 240/9.

**Mathew, Sen** St. Mathew's Day, 21 Sept. 61/20.

**mecer** *n.* mercer, dealer in textiles 2/6, 23/10, **meser** 215/31; **mercer** 15/5, **mersar** 3/3; *pl.* **mersers** 122/4, **mercars** 165/84.

**meche** *adj.* and *adv.* much 11/3, 24/10, **mesche** 70/19, **messe** 129/15. Also **mycche**, **moche**, **much**.

**Mechelmesse** *n.* Michaelmas, 29 Sept. 52/20, **Mehellmas Day** 151/12, **Myhel(l)mas** 192/19, 95/24, **Myhellmes** 117/7.

**med** *n.* reward 175/16.

**med(d)yll** *adj.* see **myd(d)yll**.

**meddyll** *v.* *~ wyth* concern oneself with 238/39; *pp.* **med(d)yllyd wyth**

mingled with 133/52, 62.

**meyll** *n. pl.* miles (see **Doche**) 209/46.

**meyrth** *n.* merriment 44/13.

**me(y)t** *v.* (*wyth*) meet 147/14, 10/6, 29/2, **mehyt** 174/7; *pr. subj.* **met** 57/17.

**mekell** *adj.* much 110/13, **mekull** 42/18, *yn so mekyll that* in so much as 191/15.

**mendys** *pr. 3 sg. intr.* heals, recovers 55/26; *pp.* **mendyd** 74/24, **mendyt** 95/30; **mend** amended 169/7.

**mene** *n.*[1] household, attendants 55/21, **mayny** 175/9, **mayne** 196/16.

**men(e)** *n.*[2] mean(s) 5/10, 12/4; *by (be) the ~ of* because of, through 7/12, 165/36, by way of 12/5, **meyn** 78/11, **mein** 127/14; *pl.* **menys** 83/17, 133/4.

**men(e)** *adj.* *in the ~ sesun, in that ~ tym* meanwhile, in the interim 84/5, 149/25.

**menystyr** *v.* dispense 7/23.

**mensyon** *n.* *as makys ~ , as makethe mencyon* as it is stated 112/7, 221/ 38–9.

**merchaundyse** *n.* trade 241/9; *doo her merchaundyes* do their buying and selling 191/17–18; merchants' wares 212/28–9, 58.

**mercha(u)nt** *n.* buyer 57/18, merchant 1/14; *merchauntes strangers n. pl.* foreign customers 194/5–6; *merchaunt(t)ys straungers* 212/44, 196/6, *marchauntys strangers* 12/5–6. Also **marschaunt**.

**mery** *adj.* cheerful, lighthearted, pleasant 31/37, 70/6, **myr(r)y** 25/5, 55/20, 95/17; *make ~* enjoy oneself 133/37.

**mervellys** *adj.* astonishing 242/14.

**meser** *n.* ?measure, object for measuring 37/26.

**met** *adj.* convenient 130/12.

**met** *v.* see **me(y)t**.

**met** *pp.* *~ owt* measured 29/4.

**met(t)e** *n.* solid food 73/4, 133/33, 179/12. Also **hardd**.

**mewd** *pp. adj.* of a hawk: that has moulted 63/10.

**mewyll** *n.* mule 108/15, 23.

**meve** *v.* broach a subject 116/12; *pp.* **meuyd** 165/32.

myc(c)he *adj.*, *n.* and *adv.* much 19/54, 56/24, 211/17, 192/9. Also meche, moche.

myd(d)yll *adj.* the second grade of wool 165/13, 16, 234/52, 36/3, medyll 92/25, 109/16, medell 36/4, medle 107/4.

mynd *n.* intention 240/38; *monthis* (*monthys*) ~ memorial service held a month after death 143/15, 175/11.

mynkys *n. pl.* mink pelts 165/75.

myscheyff *n. yn* ~ in a bad state 243/19.

myse *n. haue* ~ *of, haue a gret myesse of* miss 104/45, 44/11.

myssedeme *v. absol.* take it amiss 164/14.

myssyd *pp.* done without 106/8.

mystruste *n. put noo* ~ *yn* do not mistrust 207/53, *putt hem yn noo myssetruste* 209/28.

myt(e) *pt.* (*indic.* and *subj.*) might; could 9/16, 25/17, 147/12, myth(e) 153/21, 90/17, myth(e)t 9/15, 71/10, 96/11, myght(e) 18/3, 142/17, mygth 106/7, myhyt 136/24, 233/6.

moch(e) *adj.* much 42/6, 21/18, moyche 247/35; large 163/11. Also meche, mycche.

moder(e) *n.* mother 37/1, 9/24, modyr 43/7, moter 165/28, mothe(r) 111/22, 114/3, 136/44; *mother-i-law* stepmother 165/50.

moyr *adj.* and *n.* more 71/15, morre 9/26, 135/18, moor 96/13; *and lytyll moor* ? a little over 141/24.

mone *n.* moon 40/8.

mon(e)y *n.* money in general 9/9, 12/16, mone 100/14; coins, specie 22/13, 34/7.

monyth(e) *n.* month 12/19, 45/9; moneth 16/6; *pl.* monyht 26/11, monyhtys 36/10, monythys 36/11.

mo(o) *adj.* and *n.* more 4/19, 25/13, 131/26, 211/14.

mornyd *pt.* moped 83/18.

morow tyd(e) *n.* a morning tide 39/26, 40/8.

most *adj.* greatest 57/4; *moste partte* for most of the time 102/8–9.

most(e) *pr.* must, be obliged to, require to 10/27, 42/3, 15/14, mowste

147/33, mwste 47/18, mvst 44/16; *pt.* moste 21/15.

mostyrdewyl[l] *n.* musterdevillers, kind of woollen cloth 114/52. [OFr. *mostier* 'monastery'+*de Villers*.]

mothe, mowthe *n.* mouth: *be* (*by*) ~ verbally 48/3, 57/11, 124/18.

motte *pr. subj.* might 129/7, 8, 13, mowte 63/5.

mowro *n.* morrow 61/20.

much *adv.* a great part of the time 94/10; mwche much 86/15.

nacyon *n.* assembly of merchants of a particular nationality 238/15, naschon 191/16.

nan in *mor* ~ more than 112/12.

(n)ansfor see ansfor.

nar *compar. adv.* see ner(e) *adv.*[2]

narow *adv.* narrowly 175/19.

nat *n.* naught: *ande* ~ *elles* and nothing else 143/6.

nat(t) *adv.* not 9/19, 157/3, natte 102/15. Also no(o)t.

nawght *adj.* ?negligible, profitless 77/13; ?disastrous 242/26. Also nowght.

ne *conj.* nor 16/19 fn., 47/25, 74/36, 180/15.

nede *v.* require 7/23; *pr. 3 sg.* neddys 86/17; *2 pl.* neyd 117/18, ned 153/26.

neder *adv.* neither 24/13, nedyr 109/34, nether 34/22, nethyr 126/2, nayder 2/8; nor 110/21; neydere ... nayder neither ... nor 9/20; as *n.* with *pl. v. ij wheyes of the wiche neyder ben goode* 219/23–4.

nedes *adv.* of necessity 42/3, neydys 41/38.

nedy *adj.* short of money 15/9.

nedyr *adj.* lower 92/4.

neffyr *adv.* never 192/20, nevyr 7/10, newer 124/10; *nevyr a hone* not one 112/14. Also ner(e)[1].

neyhyng *n.* obtaining 9/9 and note.

neyte *n.* night 34/34, nyte 19/20, 108/8, nytte 223/15, nyght 59/5.

(n)eme, neym see em.

nemyng grot(t)ys *n. pl.* Burgundian silver groats (double briquets) 182/17, 20, 187/26, 209/33, 77, 214/36, 235/12, nenyng–234/17, Nyme Egyn–

196/31. Also **lymon** and note to
173/4. [Etym. obscure: ? not recorded elsewhere.]

**ner** *conj.* nor 19/44, 110/25.

**ner(e)** *adv.*[1] never 53/23; *I wotte* ~
(*neyr*) I have no idea 205/46, 218/50;
*nerthelese* nevertheless 36/13.

**ner(e)** *adv.*[2] nearly 27/10, 88/17;
*compar.* **nar** nearer 114/41.

**neste** *adj.* next 23/6, 104/38; *n. the
next* my next letter 112/13; the next
messenger 161/17; *adv. nexte beffore*
immediately in front of 131/17; *prep.*
**nex** 128/4.

**new(e)** *adj.* new, in technical application to wool and fell: see note to
109/32–3: 36/8, 92/21.

**newellys** *n.* (*pl.*) news 216/17.

**Neweresday** *n.* New Year's Day, 1
Jan. 139/9.

**newes** *n.* (pl.) news 221/21, 241/54,
**newis** 46/20.

**ny** *n.* (an) eye: *haue a* ~ *to* consider
111/23.

**ny(e)** *adv.* and *prep.* near 33/6, 95/
24; almost 112/17; *as* ~ *as ye* (*I*) *can*
? as close to instructions as possible
105/2, 189/6, 199/28; *adj. a* ~ *mane to*
a close associate of 133/12.

**nyste** *adj.* next 100/16.

**no** *adv.* now 49/10, 140/15, **noo** 28/2,
**noe** 12/20, **nou(e)** 56/30, 104/50,
**nowye** 192/7.

**nobull** *n.* 1. *þe olde* ~ the English
noble struck from 1412 to 1464,
originally 6*s.* 8*d.* ster. but raised to
8*s.* 4*d.* in 1464: 187/26. 2. The angel
noble struck from 1465, with a value
of 6*s.* 8*d.* ster., *pl.* **nobullys** 55/5.
3. A money of account representing
6*s.* 8*d. the* ~ *starllyng* 55/40, **nobyll**
3/5, 24/8, **nobell** 70/15, **noboll**
192/10; *pl.* **nobill** 103/8, **noblys**
34/16, **nobelys** 110/10.

**noder** *adv.* neither 163/24.

**noyn** *adj.* no; none 43/10, 55/29,
**no(o)n** 124/21, 194/10; *none hodyr*
no other 7/23–4.

**noysse** *n. a gret* ~ *theroff* much talk
about it 143/9.

**non(e)** *adv.* not: ~ *ffardyr* no further
4/13; *or* ~ or not 40/18.

**none dayes** *n.* noon 19/29.

**no(o)t** *adv.* not 18/4; *or* ~ take it or
leave it 34/19(2). Also **natt.**

**nor** *conj.* than 36/21, 37/11, 12,
56/25, 87/9; neither, and ... not
170/35; **norhowyr** for *moreover*
7/11.

**nothyng** *adv.* not at all 39/18, **notyng**
20/20.

**noticion** *n.* haue ~ be informed 16/5.

**nou** ?*adv.* ?now 56/30.

**now** *adj.* no 22/9, 47/41.

**nowght** *adj.* worthless 237/31; *n.*
**notgh** nothing 85/20. Also **nawght.**

**novne** *pp.* known 38/13.

**Nowhembyr** *n.* November 136/42,
192/17.

**O** mark on fells 113/6, 128/9, 131/9,
19, 28, 133/53.

**o** used to indicate an 'english' 206/66
and note, 210/33, 34.

**ob.** *abbrev.* for *obolus* 'halfpenny'
37/27.

**oblygacyon** *n.* bill of payment containing the clause 'I (we) bind me
(us)' and sealed: 173/2; *pl.* **oblygaschons** 105/43; *oblygacions of the
Stapyll* (for debts to members) 135/4
(cf. 185/9), **oblyggacyons** 200/16;
*obyllygacyons of whollis* ?for custom
and subsidy 124/6.

**occupy(e)** *v. tr.* make use of 42/3,
181/16; employ money 203/26; *intr.*
**ocupye** practise one's trade 160/25.

**oder** *adj.* and *pron.* other 34/31,
143/4, 209/18, **odyr** 34/11, **odur**
10/20, **othur** 65/6; **other** otherwise
228/25; *ffor none othyr* ?for no other
reason ?for no other person 7/5;
*ovder ... or, odir ... or els, other ...
or ellys* either or 135/14, 154/12,
228/10.

**of** *prep.* ~ *the est* (*weste*) *syde of*(*f*) on
the east (west) of 29/2, 142/10.

**offe** *n.* ? offer, ? office 47/9, and note to
54.

**offer** *v. intr.* make one an offer (of
the stated amount) 226/10; *tr. pp.*
**offerd** 226/13, **offyrd** 142/25.

**olde** *adj.* old: ~ *wooll* (*wull*) 18/3,
156/13, *owld fellys* 34/16: see note to
109/32–3, **wolde** 56/16, **howld**
22/38; not of the current issue: see

**crowne, nobull;** *myn howllde Lady* the Dowager Duchess of Burgundy 109/52.

**ome** *n.* home 129/10.

**on-** see also **un-.**

**on** *pron.* one 40/11, **oon** 199/4.

**onys** *adv.* once 240/13; *at* ~ at one time 91/29. Also **whons.**

**onyvn** *n.* onion 208/66.

**on(n)y** *adj.* any 28/7, 37/6, 61/9; *in onny wyse* by all means 73/8–9, 107/18. Also **eny.**

**onschod** *pp. adj.* without tyres 57/12, **unschoide** 56/15.

**onstofyd** *pp. adj.* unstuffed 74/20.

**onswer** see **answare, answer.**

**ontrewe** *adj.* incorrect 203/7.

**oon** *prep.* on 204/22, 208/33.

**o(o)nlyckly** *adj.* unlikely 241/33, 220/43.

**oottys** *n. pl.* oats 142/29, **ot(t)ys** 37/26, 180/13, **hottys** 55/24, **wottys** 229/10.

**oppe** *adv.* up 50/8 (see **ta(c)ke**).

**opteyne** *v.* obtain 219/34.

**or** *prep.* and *conj.* before 18/10, 24/11, 167/7, 8; ~ *that* 107/18.

**orden** *v.* ~ *for* make provision for 87/12.

**ordenons** *n.* ordnance 59/8.

**ordyr** *n.* condition (of bachelorhood) 29/6.

**or-haste** *adj.* over-hasty 11/7, **ouer haste** 96/4–5.

**os** *conj.* as 135/3, 14.

**ost(e)** *n.*[1] army 182/30, 179/21.

**oste** *n.*[2] host 88/21; *at* ~ *wyth* boarding with 19/57, 47/48, **osthe** 40/32.

**ostes** *n.* hostess 19/51, 32/11, **ostys** 75/4; *my nostes* 43/21, *my nostys* 215/32–3.

**otterst** see **uterst.**

**ottyrans** see **vttravnsse.**

**owe** *v.* bear (good will, etc.) to 16/26, 166/7; *pr. 3 pl.* **hows** 117/27; **howe** be indebted to 21/21; *pr. 3 sg.* **how** owes 7/9, **owith** 16/17 fn., **howyth** 48/4, **howys** 111/29.

**owght** *n.* anything 219/22.

**ovns** *n.* ounce 159/13; **unse** 50/11; *pl.*, 56/12.

**owr** *n.* hour 4/21; *pl.* **owrse** 29/8. Also **howre.**

**owth** *adv.* out 153/18, **howt(e)**

78/16, 91/13, **howght** 93/11; **owght** outside 145/12; *pwt hut of* expelled from 134/36; *tryd howt* see **tryd.**

**owtragys** *adj. to* ~ immoderate, intolerable 241/51; *adv.* excessively 238/43.

**ow3re** *pron.* our 47/10, **owyr** 74/30. Also **howr.**

**ouyr** *adv.* and *prep.* over; across the channel 28/6, **(h)owyr** 198/7, 136/28, **ower** 203/11; *ouer seye, hover the se* 61/8, 107/20; *ower an nyght* overnight 115/35; *owyrburdd* overboard 198/10. Also **houyr, make.**

**pacyenly** *adv.* resignedly 141/18.

**pacyens** *n. take in* ~ receive with good humour 244/7.

**pack(e)** *n.* a pack of 480 fells 131/40, 7, **pake** 247/15; *pl.* **packys** 5/4.

**packe t(h)rede** *n.* pack thread 67/16–17, 85/2.

**payis owt** *pr. 3 sg.* disburses 135/15; *pp.* **payd owte** discharged 234/39.

**payment** *n. good* ~ a punctual payer 31/36; reliably repaid 53/17. Also **letter.**

**payne** *n. take the* ~ *as to* go to the trouble to 42/1; *(vppon)* ~ *off* on the penalty of 187/7, 208/40.

**panelles** *n. pl.* juries 43/13.

**pang** *n.* sudden spasm 188/5.

**parcellys** *n. pl.* items, particulars 42/11, 235/48, **passelys** 31/15; *sg.* **passell** sample, lot 87/23.

**parell** *n.* peril 200/5; *pl.* **parellys** legal liabilities 147/33.

**parsaue** *v.* perceive 111/18.

**pars(s)on** *n.* parson 123/14, 15/12; *pl.* **parsonys** people 121/18.

**parte** *v.* divide 88/11.

**party** *n.* faction 191/18; *on my partie* for my part 244/5; *in* ~ *of payment* in part payment 5/12; *pl.* **partyes** parts 212/58; *ij part(t)ys* two-thirds 34/6, 196/41. Also **pert(e).**

**partys(c)hon** *n.* dividing line 131/14, 22; dividend of a Staple debenture, etc. [sense not in *OED*], 200/11, 115/8, **partysseon** 124/5, **parthyschom** 26/15 and note, **pertyschon** 31/16. Also **warant.**

**passa(y)ge** *n.* conveyance, esp. across

**passa(y)ge** (*cont.*):
the channel; passage of the channel 66/6, 78/24, 156/16; ship making the passage 194/11, 209/52; passengers: *toke yn* ~ 211/31; *pl. the passages* 215/64; *hallff* ~ a freight charge 181/5 and note. [These senses exemplified in *OED* poorly, or not at all.]

**Passe** *n.* Easter 207/52; ~ (*martt*) the Easter mart at Bruges or Bergen-op-Zoom 176/12, 155/8. [MDu.]

**passe** *v.* of wool, see note to 109/32–3; *pr. subj.* **pase** leave Calais 218/26; *pp.* **passyd**: ~ *to God* dead 15/18.

**passy** *adj.* past 121/7.

**passyng** *adv.* extremely 198/12; ~ *well sesid* almost over 64/17.

**passonger(s)** *n.* (*pl.*) passenger ship(s) 209/53, 215/62.

**past(e)** *prep.* more than 51/5, 55/15.

**pattyschyd** *pp. ys* ~ *to* have made treaties with 169/24. [*Patish,* after OFr. \**patiser,* mod. Fr. *pactiser.*]

**pawyn** *n.* pledge 71/7.

**peese** *n.* peace 218/47, **peys** 32/15, **pesee** 240/47, **pesse** 24/16, 237/27.

**pey** *v.* pay 230/6.

**peyny** *n.* penny 159/9; *iij^{de} (v^{th}) peny* the third (fifth) part of the whole sum 22/38, 26/9, 41/20; *p[en]ny wayghgh* dwt. 214/43; *a Godys peny* earnest money 141/9.

**peys** *n.* length of cloth 55/30, 114/50, **pyesse** 69/6; **pes(s)e** piece of money 151/56, 41/33.

**peke** for **poke** 117/35.

**pell(ys)** *n. pl.* fells 131/12, 91/6, **ppellys** 21/7, **peles** 92/9.

**pelt** *n. pl.* skins 142/5, **pel(l)tys** 140/5, 113/8, **peelltys** 141/27.

**peny** ? for 'pens' 78/28 and note.

**pensyon** *n.* periodical payment by an official body 133/41.

**penwalte** *n.* penalty 160/27.

**per** *prep.* by 2/21, 3/11, 163/44, 237/40. [Fr.; *OED* 1588.]

**perfformyd** *pp.* fulfilled 156/8.

**pert(e)** *n.* part 11/14; *doe youre* ~ act 13/7, **parte** some 175/15; *pl.* **pertys** parts of a country 11/4, **parties** 59/6.

**pertecseon** *n.* grant of immunity from legal action 143/8.

**perteynyng** *pp. adj.* belonging to 241/8–9.

**pesyd** *pp.* appeased 240/13.

**Peter, Send** ~ *Day* St. Peter and St. Paul, 29 June 2/10.

**pewyke** *n.* puke, fine grade of woollen cloth 146/4, 148/5. [MDu. *puuc, puyck,* best grade of cloth or wool.]

**Phellypus** *n.* coin struck by Philip the Good before 1434 196/28; *pl.* **Felyppys** 173/10.

**pyle** *n.* heap 133/54; *in* ~ of wool, stored before packing 67/11, 104/37.

**pype** *n.* cask holding half a tun (126 wine gallons) 85/1, 133/7, 215/57.

**place, plas(s)e** *n.* residence 60/9, 58/10; *The Place* the Staple hall at Calais 44/16, 189/40; hence, the Staple fellowship or its governing body 2/8, 15/13, 135/14, 235/45; *men of yowr* ~ 135/9; *the pryce of(f) the* ~ the price fixed by the Staple 234/46, 209/19.

**plack** *n.* Burgundian half groat, usually called *patard* or *stuiver: the old sengull* ~ a half Carolus groat 187/27; *pl.* **plak(k)ys** 56/47, 196/29. [MDu. *plack.*]

**playd** *pp.* gambled away 32/12.

**playne** *adv.* plainly, clearly 146/17.

**plehytt** ? for 'pledge it' 199/28.

**ples** *v.* please: *to* ~ *you* to meet your price 57/23; **pleyse** 29/1; *pr. 3 sg.* **plesse** 39/18; *pp.* **ples(s)yd** recouped; paid 11/19, 208/27; *pr. subj. and yt plesse you* (*pleaseth hit you, plesythe yt yow, pleesse yt yow, plessed you*) please 5/2, 1/2, 4/2, 15/2, 40/2, 110/2; *pt.* **plesetheyde** 165/62, **plesehyd** 117/39.

**plesaunt** *adj. nott soo very* ~ *as* less cordial than 225/12.

**ples(s)er** *n. do* [*one*] ~ do (one) a favour 159/2, 204/20; *at* [*one's*] ~ on demand 208/17, 209/22–3, **plesere** 153/14, **plesyr** 187/11, **plesur** 141/14, **plessure** 6/10, **pleseur** 25/18, **plesor** 57/4, **pleasure** 244/12; *byllys off plessur* bills payable on demand 204/27.

**plete** *n.* for 'fleet' 20/25.

**plyte** *n.* physical condition, of animals 19/8, 47/39, **plyght** 179/13, 14.

**pluckyd down** *pp.* pulled down 115/33.

**poch** *n.* pouch 139/4.

**po(y)er** *n.* *to ~, to my ~ (poeier)* to my ability 139/10, 28/8, 141/43, 140/19. Also **powhere.**

**poynt** *n. apon the ~ of* almost, about 165/20; **ponte** detail 24/3; *yn gode pwoynte* in good condition 158/7.

**poynt** *v.* appoint 234/50; *pt.* **powyntyd** intended 61/8; *pp.* **poyntyd** 213/31; *I pwynte my tyme* I dispose my time 148/11; *poynttyd vpp* made ready 196/11. Also **aponte.**

**poys(s)e** *n.* weight 31/5, 107/7, 206/46.

**poke** *n.* pack of wool smaller than a sarpler 20/22, 22/30, 82/23.

**polesy** *n. be ~* with prudence or contrivance 169/11.

**ponchys** *n. pl.* daggers 103/20. [*Punch.*]

**pontment** *n.* arrangement 11/16, **pwoyntment** 131/27, **poyntment** 246/13. Also **apwnttemente.**

**porffett** *n.* profit 41/25.

**porpos** *n. to no ~* not effectively 55/23; *apone a schorte pwrpos* on the spur of the moment 91/13; *kepe your ~* carry out your plan 95/16.

**porpos(e)** *pr. 1 sg.* intend 8/21, 152/12, **pwrppos** 78/25; *3 sg.* **powrpos** 95/23, **porpos** 55/28, **porposythe** 109/58, **porposet** 149/27, **porposed** 151/17; *pp.* **y-porposed** 39/28, 151/14, **porpossyd** 93/25; **purpose** *pr. 1 sg.* intend to go 125/19–20; *be purposid to the marte* *pp.* 88/16; *refl.* *I purpose me to more esse* I am determined on more leisure 106/9–10.

**pors** *n.* purse 86/14.

**porvay** *v. ~ for* provide 27/7, **purvey** 208/66, **purvae** 67/18; *porvay me off* obtain 109/65; *tr.* obtain, furnish: **pwrwhay** 133/34, **purway** 95/19, **pwruay** 95/18; *pt.* **purveid** 228/2; *pp.* **pwrwhayde** 134/12 **pwrwayd** equipped 111/17; **purveyd, porveyd** furnished with money 103/4, 238/42.

**porveons** *n.* provision 27/5, **pwrwyans** 134/24, **purvyaunce** 241/43.

**postlatys** *n. pl.* coins issued by Rudolf of Diepholt when *postulatus* of the see of Utrecht, or later imitations 56/42, 151/37, 50, 196/38. [MDu. *postula(e)t*; Lat. *postulatus* 'claimant to a see'.]

**postorne** *n.* see note to 39/54.

**pott** *pr. 1 sg.* propound 7/19. Also **put.**

**pottell** *n.* half a gallon, or a vessel containing about that 165/53.

**powher(e)** *n.* authorization 134/30; **power** 213/34; ability 75/12, **pover** 76/20. Also **po(y)er.**

**pound (powd) garnettys** *n. pl.* pomegranates 32/4–5, 43/23.

**praysyd** see **prese.**

**praysment** *n.* price set on fells, valuation 34/21, **prayssementte** 35/6, **prasement** 49/3.

**prayssers** *n. pl.* appraisers 105/8, 205/8; **praysayrs** 146/16.

**prathy** *adj.* 'pretty': good, properly 90/15.

**precedyng(e)** *pp. adj.* first given, premised 234/2, 226/2, etc.

**preferment** *n.* ?advantage, ?prior claim 9/8.

**premer** *n.* prayer book 199/24.

**premysset** *pp. adj.* stated first 129/1.

**prentes** *n.* apprentice 8/26, **pryntys** 13/4, **prentys** 13/5; [*prentis*]*hodde* apprenticeship 218/62.

**presarffe** *v.* preserve 57/3; *subj.* **preserwf** 232/12.

**preschesyon** *n.* procession 175/8, **proseschon** 183/9.

**prese** *v.* appraise 190/6; *pp.* **presyd** 191/4, **praysyd** 44/5, 92/3.

**preste** *v.* lend money, esp. **to the** government 15/14; *pp.* **prestyd** 202/34, 211/43; *prest(e) mony* (see note) 202/34, 206/6, 211/43.

**pretendy(i)ng** *pp. adj.* extended, having been put forward (cf. **precedyng(e)**) 22/1–2 and note, 41/2, 45/2, 93/2, 109/2, 124/2, 178/2.

**preve** *adj.* private 85/21; *adv. prevy ne appert* secretly or openly 16/19 fn.

**prevely(e)** *adv.* privily 85/21, 234/54, 123/14.

**prevyt** *pr. 3 sg. ~ well* is turning out

**prevyt** (*cont.*):
well 40/24. Also **prove**.

**prye** *pr. 1 sg.* for 'pray' 192/15.

**prykys** *n. pl.* marked targets 29/3, 6.

**primage** *n.* fee for loading or unloading a ship 247/15.

**prynspall** *adj.* ~ *sum* principal 170/34; *n.* **preyncepall** ?principal cause, or contributor 219/13.

**pryste** *n.* priest 85/15, **preste** 19/22.

**proctor** *n.* procurator 129/12.

**prodest** *n.* protest: action taken to fix liability for a dishonoured bill 78/21.

**prodest(e)** *pp.* subjected to protest 78/23, 13.

**profur** *n.* proposal 55/37.

**profurd** *pt.* offered 55/23.

**promesse** *pr. sg. I* ~ *ʒow* I assure you 129/18; *pp.* **y-promesed** promised 151/18.

**promyse** *n. mayd* ~ promised 142/22.

**pronosticacon** *n.* astrological forecast 228/18.

**prosses** *n.* narrative, series of events 165/21.

**prove** *v. to* ~ [the bargain] *bye* as earnest 234/27. Also **prevyt**.

**puddyngys** *n. pl.* kind of sausage, as black or white puddings 142/28, **podyngys** 141/35.

**pwr** *adj.* poor, humble 134/16.

**put** *v.* ~ *away* sell off 149/12; ~ *me away from* do me out of 9/7; *puttys me off* fobs me off 167/17–18; *pp.* **pwte** 81/9; *pwt hut of* expelled from 134/36; ~ *owte off wagys*, ~ *from hym* dismissed from service 185/15–16, 241/13.

**qwayntans** *n. cwm in* ~ *of* become acquainted with 136/19.

**quarell** *n. pl.* square-headed bolts for a cross-bow 103/13, 15.

**qwat(e)** *pron.* what 47/19, 55/37.

**qwedyr** *conj.* whether 55/32, **qwhether** 147/23, **qwhethyr** 147/23. Also **wheyder**.

**Qwehyn** *n.* queen 150/9.

**queyt rent** *n.* quit-rent 140/6.

**qwen** *adv.* when 84/11. Also **whan**.

**qweryng** *n.* cover 56/13.

**question** *n.* (?) *whan it was* ~ ? when the matter came up 161/4.

**quetaunce** *n.* quittance 243/12, **qw(y)etans** 86/19, 7, **quytaunce** 243/15, **quytons** 80/16.

**qwhattyrn** *n.* quarter (ounce or pound) 136/45.

**qwhe(y)r** *adv. and conj.* where 74/11; ~ *as* although 111/17; ~ *by* 147/4; *qw(h)erfor* 55/36, 9; ~ *in* 84/7; *qw(h)erof* 111/6, 74/7. Also **were**.

**qwhessy** *adj.* unsettled 134/18.

**qwych(e)** *pron.* which 42/4, 34/26, 65/4, **qw(h)eche** 47/4, 133/6, **qweych(e)** 78/15, 19/7. Also **w(h)yche**.

**qwyhet** *adj.* quiet in mind 111/25; *nott quyett* disturbed 203/8–9.

**quyne** *n.* mint 22/12; *pl.* **quoynus** coins 241/31, 48. [Fr. *coin* 'wedge', hence 'die'; 'mint'; 'coined money'.]

**quysschyns** *n. pl.* cushions 60/2.

**quyt(e)** *pp. and pp. adj.* repaid 159/10; ~ *wyth* clear with 68/4; *qwyte of* rid of 47/10, 74/6.

**qwou** *pron.* who 42/6. Also **ho, wo**.

**rader** *adv.* preferably 31/38; *radar nor* rather than 73/10; *the rather that* the more readily that 219/49.

**raynyd** *pr. 3 sg.* prevails 56/30, **raynyth** 234/66.

**raysens off Coraynce** *n. pl.* currants 42/14.

**rasar** *n.* measure of about 4 bushels 37/26, **rasur(ys)** raser(s) 142/30, 31.

**rate** *n.*[1] *affter the same* ~ on a proportionate scale of valuation 238/47, 187/25, 241/52; *after the* ~ *of ster.* as the coins are valued in England 20/4–5; **ratte** rate of exchange 3/7, 20/5; proportionate charge 21/11.

**rate** *n.*[2] for 'rebate' 104/20.

**ratyd** *pp. adj.* subject to specific customs duty 238/21.

**rattons** *n. pl.* rats 74/9.

**rebe** *n.* rib, bar 222/18.

**receyf** *v.* receive 10/8, **ressayue** 5/14, **resseve** 64/11, **ressaue** 121/13; *recayue vppon* have deducted from 204/42–3; *pr. 3 pl.* **recheyuyth** 160/18: **resayue** borrow money 12/18; **resayuyd, ressayved** receive it 26/10, 70/13; *pp.* **res(s)ay-**

**uyd** 2/1, 3/3, **resseywyd** 4/3, **i-ressayued** 9/24.

**recervid** *pp.* ?reserved 161/8 and note.

**reclamyd** *pp. adj.* taught to return at call 199/11.

**recomaund(e)** *pr. 1 sg.* recommend 3/1, 1/1, **recomeavnde** 4/1, **recomend** 8/1, **recommeund** 110/1, **reykecommand** 192/1; *3 sg.* **recomaund** 151/21, **recomavnd-ytys** 160/31.

**reconeng** see **rekenyng**.

**record(e)** *n.* witness 47/26, 129/14, 142/18.

**recvryng** see **reqvreng**.

**red(d)e** *adj.* ready 112/11, 75/12, **red(d)y** 112/9, 192/18, **rydy** 56/17; *adv.* **redy** already 177/17.

**rede** *pp.* see **reyd(e)**.

**rede** *n.* reed 131/23, 133/59.

**refewy** ~ *a scarttayn* ? for 'refuse a certain' 34/20 and note.

**reffelyd** *pp.* rifled 198/14, **ryffylyd** 198/15.

**refforme** *v.* correct 179/9; *pp.* **reformede** improved 38/16.

**refvse** *adj.* rejected, leftover; (of wool), composed of small pieces, scrap 36/5, 104/55, **refussche** 69/2, **reffewse** 209/58; as *n.* **reffewys** 105/8, **reffewce** 234/34, **reffys** 192/10.

**regard(e)** *n.* **yn** ~, **to** ~ worth speaking of 236/23, 220/31.

**reyd(e)** *v.* ride 58/12, 149/27, **ryed** 8/11; *pt.* **rod** 165/49; *pp.* **ys rede** has ridden 87/13.

**reydyng govnne** *n.* gown for riding 40/10.

**rekenyng** *n.* reckoning; written account 19/6, 111/41; **reconeng** 6/6, **reconyng** 10/27, **rekenenyng** 221/14, **riknyng** 88/13; *reke⟨n⟩yng vp* 135/24; payment 41/26; *take ryknyng of* reckon with 88/20; *vppon* ~ ? on account 220/24–5; *thys* ~ 'the day of account' 243/24.

**rekewer** *n.* recovery 170/6. Also **reqvreng**.

**rekon** *v.* reckon up *intr.* 218/28; *pp.* **recond** 41/17; *tr.* **recckyn** take into account 192/10.

**remayng** *pr. 3 pl.* remain 149/11.

**reme** *n.* realm 200/1.

**remedy** *n.* redress; counteraction 22/19, 37/14, 129/19; *noo* ~ *to* no means to 238/20; *pl.* **remedyis** 129/16.

**remember, rememyr** *v. tr.* remember 165/92, **rembor** 38/49; *remembre me for* remember to get me 33/2–3; *refl.* ~ *you for* don't forget to 69/2; *intr.* ~ *ffor* remember about 196/7; *pp.* **remember** 202/16; *and 3e be remembyrd* if you recall 117/16–17; remind: *pt.* **rememberyd** 161/4–5; *pp.* **remember** 202/16; **remembyr** 227/14–15; *remembred therof* mindful of it 16/19 fn.

**rememb(e)raunce** *n.* memory 144/7; *haue in rememborans* (*remembrans, remem(e)rans*) remember 11/18, 74/37, 91/12, 116/12; reminder 161/6; memorandum: **remembravns** 92/1, 105/1, 144/8–9; *of any* ~ recorded 144/10.

**remenand** *n.* remainder 91/18, **remena(v)nt** 5/6, 46/17, **rembenant** 111/11; **rembnant** 34/9, 113/5.

**remeve** *v.* remove 115/29; *pp.* *I am remevid* I have moved 76/9.

**ren, ron** *v.* run: *let (lette hym)* ~ leave him at large 193/4–5, 6; *pr. 3 sg.* **ronys** is at liberty 197/19; ~ *vpon them* be applicable to them 130/14; *ryn to* be applied to 163/19, 24; *pt.* *ran wyth* sailed along 205/55–6; *pp.* **ron** sailed 215/65; *ren Frenchemen* turned French supporters 112/30.

**rent** *pp.* torn 186/7.

**repayryd** *pp.* resorted 12/6.

**report** *v.* spread, repeat 16/9.

**requer(e)** *pr. 1 sg.* request 65/7, 42/17, **requyre** 224/15; *3 sg. as the casse requered* in these circumstances 149/16.

**reqvrede** *pp.* recovered 67/7.

**reqvreng** *n.* recovery 67/1, **reqvryng** 73/2, **recvryng** 80/1.

**resayyng** *n.* receiving 98/7, 10.

**resaytys** *n. pl.* amount of money received 24/14.

**rescewyd** *pp.* rescued 227/36; *pt.* **rescudyd** 115/19.

**rese** *pp.* risen 37/16.

**res(e)nabyll** *adj.* fair, appropriate, moderate 63/8, **reasonable** 68/7,

**res(e)nabyll** (*cont.*):
**ressenabull** 133/39, **resvnabyll** 166/5; *adv.* reasonably 165/20, 168/8, **ressnabell** 58/16, **resonnabull** 184/10.

**reson** *n. be ~* ?by discussion ?in their opinion 241/26; *as ffar as my ~ geyff me* as far as I can judge 213/18.

**resonably** *adv.* reasonably, sufficiently 201/25, **resenably** 47/34; *so resson-abeley* as much as can be expected 149/32–3.

**resspyte** *pp. a ~ hym off* have given him a respite for 206/51.

**rest** *n.*[1] remainder 200/9, 247/26.

**rest** *n.*[2]? arrest 7/15.

**rest** *v.* arrest 212/33; *pr. 1 sg.* **reyst** 32/8.

**reste** *n.* peace 169/19.

**restytyschon** *n.* restitution 207/31, **restytuschon** 215/16, **restycyon** 221/28.

**rewle** *v.* 240/12: see note.

**reuerence** *n.* respect 16/1; *atte þe ~ of, in the reverens of* from respect for 16/25, 93/21.

**rewiwid** *pp. adj.* recovered 76/5.

**ryall** *n.* the rial, or rose noble, first struck by Edward IV in 1465, to a value of 10s. ster. 187/27 241/51; *pl.* **ryallys** 20/5, 196/27, 63, 238/46.

**ryall** *adj.* princely 178/7. [OFr. *rial*, var. of *real*, *roial*.]

**Ryan[s]** see **Rynyshe.**

**ryder** *n.* Burgundian gold coin, struck between 1434 and 1454 187/27; *pl.* **rydars** 196/35, 55; **Gyldars rydar** the rider of Guelders 56/45; *pl.* **rydars Gyll.** 151/56, **r[y]darus** 151/46. [MDu. *rider*, from figure of horseman.]

**rydy** *adj.* see **red(d)e.**

**ryghtys** *n. pl.* funeral rites 75/9.

**ryn** *v.* see **ren.**

**Rynyshe** *adj. ~ gyldorn* (etc.) one of the uniform gulden issued by the Rhineland electors 151/47, *pl.* **Rynysche gyldyrns** 118/10; **Ryn[ysh]**— 41/34, **Reynysche gylders** 234/18; *n.* (*sg.* and *pl.*) (a) Rhenish gulden 56/39, 196/37, 54, 59, **Ryan[s]** 34/10. [Adapt. of Fl. *rins*, *rynsche gulden*.]

**ryt** *adv.* right; very 129/2, **ryght** 12/2, **ryghyt** 170/5, **ry3ht** 232/11, **ryught** 19/1, 25/1, **riught** 55/11.

**ryvall** *n.* arrival 211/47.

**ryvyng** *n. ~ alond* disembarking 182/10–11.

**rombyr** *n.* commotion 178/18, **rombur** 236/20, 29; ?outcry 236/8; **romber** disturbance, upheaval 200/1.

**romnay** *n.* sweet wine from Greece or Spain 165/54.

**ron** *v.* see **ren.**

**rond** *adj.* made of thick thread 90/15.

**ro(o)ne** *n.* graded, of herring (see note) 236/22, 27, 26. [Fl.]

**s.** abbrev. for shilling 3/5; for sack 210/28; **ss.** two sacks 89/9.

**sacke** *n.* weight (not container) of wool: 364 lbs. avoirdupois in England, 360 lbs. of 14 oz. at Calais 18/4, 31/4; *pl.* 197/7, **sacc** 206/61, **sakke** 231/6, **saccys** 206/65.

**sad(e)** *adj.* serious 19/32, 223/12; **sadd** responsible 212/62; *compar.* **sadder** 206/12.

**ssaffe** see **sawhe.**

**saffyng** *prep.* and *conj.* except for 151/6; except that 151/10. Also **sauyng.**

**sayeng** *n.* speech 140/14; *the same man that he whas in his ~ that* he holds to his statement that 144/3–4; *pl.* **seyingys** reports 16/28, **sayngys** 241/48.

**sayyng** *pr. p. I hadde so many ~ of* so many people told me about 104/51; *I wrote of the money saiyng of . . .* saying concerning it 38/12. Also **sayt(he).**

**sayle** *n. made ~* set sail 239/13; *pl.* ships 208/33, **sayllys** 205/51.

**sayt(he)** *pr. 3 sg.* says 40/25, **says** 162/19; *~ yow lettyll worchepe* speaks of you disrespectfully 21/20; *3 pl.* **seye** 241/31; *pt. 3 sg.* **sayed** 153/23, **sayyt** 153/25; *pp.* **seyde** 16/22; *I have sayd yow* I have told you 49/20; *has sayd ffor hymselff* has put his case 7/1–2; *pp. adj.* **sade** aforesaid 16/14.

**sale** *n.* opportunity of selling 52/22, 87/25; **sall** sale 147/10; *make salle* (*of*) sell 31/28, 96/11; *come to* ~, *come a salle, be set an salle* come on the market 227/26, 247/37, 33; *pl.* **sayellys** 125/12, 13.

**salers** *n. pl.* salt cellars 56/12.

**salew(e)** *n.* the *salut d'or* struck by Henry VI as King of France 187/25, 196/56; *ij parttys of an sallewe* the angelet or two-thirds salut 196/41.

**sammyd** *pp. adj.* see **schamyd**.

**sarmon** *n.* sermon 15/17.

**sarpler** *n.* canvas covering 234/55; bale of wool, usu. holding a little over 2 English 'sacks' (728 lb.) 21/10, **sarplere** 11/11, **sarpeller** 18/3, **sarppler** 39/10, **serpler** 82/23; *pl.* **sarpelerys** 9/25, **sarplers** 4/10, **sarp(p)ellys** 117/35, 201/16, **sapplers** 89/4. [*OED* wrongly defines as 80 tods, i.e. 2240 lb.]

**sart(t)en** *adj.* certain 160/13, 127/13, **sartte** 136/13; *n. ffor* ~, *yn serten* certainly 64/8, 182/27, 215/32. Also **scarttayn**.

**sarvand** *n.* servant 135/29, *hawhe to my sarwhant* employ 169/18; *pl.* **sarwanttys** 55/31; **sarvaunt** ?apprentice, ? provider of services 219/50.

**sarwe** *v.* profit 7/16; *pp.* **sarvyd** treated 106/9; **seruyd** dealt with, attended to 167/18; **y-serued** provided for 9/13, 16.

**sarves** *n.* service 219/29, **ssaruys** 57/25, **sarfys** 192/15, **saruyesse** 223/10, **servis** 66/10, **serves** 219/29; **sarwes** employment 19/15, 53.

**saulwe** *n.* salve 134/6.

**save** *adj.* safe 26/20; **sawhe** secure from further ill 193/7.

**sawe** *prep.* except 184/8, ~ *hone* but one 178/17, **sawhe** 165/82; *conj.* 189/10, 81/18.

**sawegarde** *n.* safeguard 213/41.

**savete** *n.* safety 31/12, **sauety** 142/34, **sawete** 78/29, **safet(t)e** 95/27, 147/5, **saffte** 45/5.

**sawhe** *v.* preserve 169/12, **saff** 5/10, *subj. 3 sg.* **ssaffe** 200/4. See also **harmles**.

**sauyng** *prep.* except 137/8; *conj.* 65/7, **sawyng** 41/32, *saweng only*

211/25, **sauynd** 153/11. Also **saffyng**.

**scape** *v.* escape 219/30 and note; *pt.* **schapyd** 175/19; *pp.* **scapydd** 205/52.

**scarttayn** *n. a* ~ a fixed quantity 34/20.

**scast** *pp.* see **caste**.

**scent** *pt.* sent 222/10.

**s(c)hall** *v. pr.* shall 22/7, 5/2, **schaull** 19/8, **schawlle** 91/33, **sal(le)** 129/16, 192/10, **s(c)hull** 110/22, 111/37, **schol(l)** 20/9, 11/11; *pt. subj.* **showld** 7/17, **s(c)hold(e)** 16/9, 64/6, 63/2, **sch(o)uld** 5/10, 34/11, **shuld(e)** 166/5, 170/17, **showd** 4/5, **solde** 192/6, **sode** 46/14; **schowlde**, **schulld** are (is) alleged to 21/16, 20, 175/6, 8.

**s(c)hamyd** *pp.* and *pp. adj.* dishonoured 134/15; ?bashful 49/22; **sammyd** shamed 192/19.

**schambyr** *n.* chamber 197/22.

**Schambyrlen** *n.* the King's Chamberlain 114/28, 146/8, **Schamberlayne** 200/2, **Chamberleyn** 158/12.

**schankys** *n. pl.* (fur from) shanks 60/4, 117/45, 127/17.

**schapeman** *n.* purchaser 52/23–4.

**scharge** *v.* see **charge**.

**scharly** *adv.* see note to 104/43.

**scharpe** *adj.* sudden 38/26; **sharp** strict 16/19; **scharply** *adv.* firmly 15/10.

**schasyd** *pp.* ~ *wyth* pursued by 175/18.

**sche** *pron.* she 6/10, 40/6.

**scheyr** *n.* shearing 227/26. Also **ser** *v.*

**schep** *n.* see **chepe**.

**schepe** *n.*[1] *pl.* sheep 108/19, **scheype** 111/39.

**schepe** *n.*[2] ship 85/1, **scheppe** 130/6, **schyp(p)e** 127/9, 5/5.

**schepe** *v. tr.* and *intr.* ship 20/21, 23/5, **shyp(e)** 22/22, 109/49, **seppe** 67/21; *pr. 3 sg.* **schype** 111/26; **schyppyth** 196/11; *pt.* **schepede** 87/10, **sheppyd** 22/23; *pp.* **schepyt(h)** 26/19, 107/9, **schyp(p)yd** 91/14, 5/3.

**schepyng** *n.* act or time of shipping 20/13, 23/3, **sheppyng** 22/29, **chepynge** 21/6, **shyppyng** 131/4; goods

**schepyng** (*cont.*):
shipped 106/6; ship(s): *nexte shippyng þat comys betwene* 142/7.

**scher(e), scheyr** *n.* see **che(y)r**.

**scherefe** *n.* sheriff 127/15, **scheryfe** 133/24.

**scherewde** see **shrowd**.

**schertys** *n. pl.* shirts 69/7.

**schest** *n.* chest 32/4.

**schetys** *n. pl.* sheets 69/8, 70/22. Also **sterne**.

**schett** *pp.* fired 183/11; ~ *owte* removed as rejected 205/4, 5 and note. Also **shot**.

**schew** *n.* see **showe**.

**schew(e), shew** *v.* display 16/28; acknowledge, 208/53; **schow** display for sale 55/22; **s(c)how** tell, explain 124/18, 140/15, **sche⟨w⟩** 133/14; *pr. 3 sg.* **schewyth** 227/18; *pt.* **schewyd(e)** 56/7, 5, **shewde** 17/4, **[s]chowyed** 246/2; *pp.* **shewed** 103/3.

**schyfftyd** *pp.* changed for other coin 205/25. Also **shyfft**.

**schyld(e)** see **chyld**.

**schytte** *pt.* shut 209/41; *pp.* **schytt** 241/10.

**scho** *pron.* miswritten for *sche* 'she' 165/74.

**scho** *v.* furnish with tyres 57/13. Also **onschod**.

**schortly** see **scorttly**.

**schosyn** *pp.* see **chese**.

**schotterys** *n. pl.* shooters 19/24.

**schrape** *v.* see note to 25/30.

**Schrofe ʒeuyn** *n.* ?Shrove Monday, ?the night of Shrove Tuesday 169/15.

**scle** *v.* slay 136/11; *pp.* **sclayn** 111/21, 136/11, **slayne** 59/8; *vbl. n.* **scleyng** killing 127/13, 133/5.

**sclen** *adv.* entirely 9/7.

**scleuys** *n. pl.* sleeves of mail 114/37; **sleuys** sleeve linings 60/11.

**sclothe** *n.* cloth 69/7 (2).

**sclow, sloe** *adj.* dilatory 197/16, 2/9.

**scorttly** *adv.* quickly; briefly; soon 74/35, **schortlay** 39/17, **schorteley** 9/10, **schortly** 8/21; *compar.* **schorttlyer** 208/21.

**scoostely** *adv.* ?for 'shortly' 120/7.

**scostys** *n. pl.* see **coste**.

**Screstemas** *n.* Christmas 70/24.

**scryssche** *n.* church 5/22.

**se** *v.* wait for 37/6; ~ *a way therin* find a means to settle 95/26; *imper., subj.* read 147/41; make sure 56/16; ~ *wyll to* be prepared 11/10; ~ (*well vn*)*to* look after 81/21–2, 58/27; *pt.* **se** saw 108/10, 133/6, **saw(e)** 19/47, 34/30, **sau** 19/29, **save** 34/29; *pp.* **sen** 109/24, 124/21; *seyn by hyr* evident from her state 71/19; *pr. p.* *seyng T.A. y-serued* making sure that T.A. is provided for 9/13.

**seche** *adj.* such 5/13, 39/12, **scheche** 130/13, **schey⟨c⟩he** 135/14. Also **syche, soche**.

**secutorys** *n. pl.* executors 21/11.

**seye** *n.* sea 61/8, **se** 46/9.

**seye** *v.* say 218/48.

**se(y)t, seth** see **sith**.

**seke** *adj.* ill 67/2, **seyk(e)** 75/4, 74/5, **syke** 8/26, **syck** 213/21.

**sekenes(s)e** *n.* illness, plague, 50/23, 66/14, **seykenes** 74/7, **seckenys** 74/4, **sycknesse** 188/6.

**sell** *n.* seal 235/30, **seell** 3/9, **sele** 137/11.

**sel(l)e** *v.* sell 98/4, 20/25, **seell** 125/10, 141/10, **seyell** 58/30; *to* ~ on sale 20/23; *pr. 3 sg.* **sele** 2/13; *pt.* **solde** 192/9, **sowlde** 93/7, **selld** 126/10; *pp.* **soold** 49/2, 125/9, **soullde** 34/16, **sowlld** 149/5, **sowyld** 192/6, **sovud** 149/17, **y-sould** 58/31, 70/24.

**sellere** *n.* canopy for a bed 159/3.

**sel(l)ffe** *n. appon yt* ~ on its own (see note) 109/36; in *cmpd. prons. them* ~ *were* 115/16; *youreselve* 2/18; *yoursell* 141/18; *hymseve* 90/12.

**semble** *n.* assembly 163/15.

**Sencyon**, etc. see **Synksen**.

**sengell** *adj.* unlined 97/7; **sengyll** single 30/6, **sengull** 187/27.

**sengler** *adj.* individual 236/9; **syng-(e)ler** special 25/14, 86/1, **synggular** 61/22. Also **essynglar**.

**senyght** *n.* week 187/7.

**sent** *v.* send 93/24; *pr. 1 sg.* 45/11; *3 sg.* **sendys** 114/31, **send** 151/22, **sendyt** 149/29, 153/28; *3 pl.* **sen⟨d⟩** 61/5, **sendys** 19/5, 25/3; *pt.* **send**

37/1, 52/6, **scent** 222/20; *pp.* **send(e)** 2/5, 114/23, **sent** 103/15.

**ser** *v.* clip 193/6.

**serce** *v.* put an end to 234/66. [For 'cease'.]

**serche** *n.* (customs) examination, search 121/17, 205/27; the Searcher's house 115/28; *make* ~ seek 121/18.

**sercher** *n.* customs officer appointed to search ships or goods 239/6.

**sertente** *n. be at* ~ know for sure 160/12; *yn* ~ *of* sure of 215/26–7.

**sertyffyeng** *pr. p.* notifying 18/1, **serteffyyng** 75/3, **certefyn[g]** 17/5.

**sesid** *pp.* ceased 64/17; **sesyd** *pr. subj.*+'it' 56/31; **sessyde** 50/24.

**sesyd** *pp.* ~ *in* seised of 147/23.

**ses(s)on** *n.* particular time 12/10, 109/24, **sesun** 74/7, **sessen** 231/6, **seysyn** 192/4; stretch of time 189/44, 227/21; ?break from work, ?opportunity 109/25; term of office 211/49; *the ceson ys syche* times are such 241/7.

**set** *adj.* settled 39/26.

**set don** see **soitt.**

**Sete** *n. the* ~ the city of London 52/5.

**setillers** *n. pl.* coins bearing a seated figure (see note) 245/6.

**sett(e)** *v.* fix 63/10, 105/10; price (*at*) 226/9, 229/6; **set** enter 10/27; esteem: *the les wyll sche* ~ *by ws* 47/23; *the mor sett* (*pp.*) *by thys actys* 4/18 and note; *set asyde* disregard 16/27; *sete done* (~ *(pp.)*) *dovn*) set down money 37/11–12, 241/31, 49; *pp.* prepared (? stacked), of fells 190/6, 191/3; ~ *yn* installed 241/30; *seet on* affixed 51/7; ~ *vppon* (*apon*) deducted from 115/12, 156/7, 164/9; ~ *owte of hys place* deposed 241/12–13. See also **sewer, sewerte, whaye.**

**settyng(e)** *vbl. n.* ~ *done* calling down currency 36/23; *a* ~ *wp* being erected 195/7.

**sewer** *adj.* reliable 209/81, **soore** 135/23, **schewyr** 227/44, **svre** 12/5; safe, secure 8/17, **sewyr** 114/48; ~ *to* contracted to 215/42; *be sewyr of, be sett* ~ *of* (*for*) obtain security for 5/11, 215/27, 218/40; *compar.* **more sewrer** 213/18–19; *superl.* **sewreste** 193/12. Also **stand.**

**sewer** *adv.* surely 55/9; **svre** with security 20/24.

**s(e)werte** *n.* assurance, guarantee 219/40, 238/74; security for a debt 125/28, 206/52; person standing surety **sewyrte** 8/3; *pl.* **sewyrteys** 5/12, **suyrteys** 7/12, **suyretys** 7/15; *sett yow* [*them*] *to* ~ appoint them your surety 218/42–3. Also **asvrete.**

**sewge(y)ttys** *n. pl.* subjects 207/33, **sewgyettys** 207/30.

**sewgyr** *n.* sugar 71/11, **sugurre** 42/13.

**sewyd** *pp.* sued 25/26, 43/12.

**shake** *pp.* shaken 64/15.

**sheff** *n.* sheaf 103/13.

**shyfft** *n. make bettyr* ~ ?get on better 22/14 and note. Also **schyfftyd.**

**Shorfftyd** *n.* Shrovetide 228/23.

**shot** *v. intr.* shoot 29/6; *pp.* **schott, schett** fired off 147/39, 183/11. Also **schett** *pp.*

**showe** *n.* display of wool to customers 124/21; *hath taken schew to bye wull* has viewed the wool for sale 212/24. Also **schew(e),** *v.*

**shrowd** *adj.* bad; serious; difficult; annoying 4/10, **schrowyd** 218/52, **schrode** 177/14, 182/19, **scherewde** 15/15.

**sych(e)** *adj.* such 10/5, 11/2, 31/31, **siche** 16/27. Also **seche, soche.**

**syd** *n. a thys* ~ *Northehamton* on this side of N. 117/9, *a that seyd the see* 223/17.

**syke** *adj.* see **seke.**

**synd** for 'side' 97/6.

**syn(e)** *adv.* since, after 55/34; ~ *that* 165/8; *prep.* 19/22, **sen** 124/9; *conj.* 43/10, 63/11; in as much as 61/13, 141/17.

**syne** *n.* attestation 80/17; (shop) sign 97/2.

**syngnet(e)** *n.* signet 137/15, 83/16 and note.

**synyd** *pp. adj.* assigned 115/28. Also **asyne.**

**synistre** *adj.* malicious 16/11, **sinstre** 16/27.

**Synksen** *n.* Whitsun, esp. of the Antwerp Whitsun mart 154/12, **Syncyon** 18/9; with *mart:* **Synxon** 68/5, **Syn(s)chon** 53/15, 52/10; **Synsson**

**Synksen** (*cont.*):
23/8, **Syngsyon** 22/32, 93/4, 200/22,
**Sensyon** 212/86, **Sencyon** 3/4,
117/36, **Senschon** 214/38, **Senchan**
96/18. [Dial. MDu. and Fl. *Sinksen*
'Whitsun'.]

**syns** *adv.* after, since 92/23, 196/6;
*prep.* **sens** 161/2; *conj.* 179/10;
**sennes** as, seeing that 129/8.

**syr** appellation of a priest 115/36,
175/13.

**syrplys(s)age** *n.* money due to the
King from the surplus of custom and
subsidy after the Staple had taken its
share 160/31, 163/13, 185/6, **surplysage** 160/22.

**syster** *n.* sister; brother's wife 8/25,
**sistur** 88/8, **sistir** 100/2, **soster**
223/29.

**sith** *prep.* since, later than 228/26,
**seth** 10/4; *conj.* **shyt** 104/48, **se(y)t**
40/4, 151/23.

**syt(h)e** *n.* sight 33/6, **syʒht** 232/9,
**syhyt** 121/11; *hawhe a ~ of* get a look
at 165/45; *at the syght, at sye[t],
after the syt* at (after) sight, of a letter
of payment [*OED* 1617] 10/14, 41/14,
47/37–8, 119/12.

**sithen** *conj.* because 228/3; after
228/21.

**skante** *adj.* in short supply 148/8.

**skathe** *v.* *~ vs the byeyng of* cost us
the purchase of 231/5–6.

**skeyne** *n.* *the Irysch ~* skene, Irish
(? or Highland Scots) dagger 141/
37.

**skyl(l)e** *n.* expert knowledge: *can
(con) lytyl (good) ~ of* know(s) little
(much) about 56/20, 75/10.

**skyllys** *pr. 3 sg.* (*impers.*) *it ~ not* it
matters not 51/5, 9.

**slacke** *adj.* of the market, sluggish
234/31.

**sleppyd** *pp.* ? slept, ? slipped 192/5 and
note.

**slytte** *v.* cut 189/12.

**small** *adj.* low (price) 103/8; thin,
narrow 131/15; *superl.* **the smaleste**
finest 90/15.

**so** *adj.* such: *my besynes ys ~* 63/5; *adv.*
**soo** at that price 203/34.

**sobsyde** see **subsede**.

**soche** *adj.* such 22/33, 109/13, **soyche**

4/13, 7/10, 185/6, **souche** 105/2,
**suche** 16/11. Also **seche, syche.**

**sodears** see **sowdear.**

**sodenly** *adv.* suddenly 126/7.

**soffyr** *v.* put up with 22/10; **suffer**
allow 201/26, **suffur** 203/33.

**soyn** *adv.* soon 95/27. Also **sonner.**

**soit(t)** *pr. subj.* [Fr.] *~ don(e), ~ doon,
~ dd., ~ delivré* be it given 125/40,
22/50–51, 1/15, 4/28, 97/17, 6/14; *set
dd.* 228/31; *so hyt dd.* 19/58; *soo
(h)it dd.* 68/13, 128/14–15; (*so thys
dd.* 147/47); *so dd.* 84/26, 133/93.
Also **dd.**

**solyster** *n. the ~* the official who
transacted business in England for
the Staple 160/29, 189/35, 205/16,
234/61; **s[ol]esseture** 205/20; **cellyssytor** advocate 136/23.

**somar** *n.* summer 95/21; *adj.* of fells,
from sheep killed in summer: **somer**
92/18, 113/5, **somor** 30/7.

**som(e)** *n.* total of 179/9, 53/9, **sum**
104/9; sum of money 5/8, 165/66;
*pl.* **somys** 22/18.

**sonner** *compar. adv.* sooner 129/10,
194/10, **sonar** 247/34.

**soor** *n.* sore 19/31.

**soper** *n.* supper 163/41.

**sopesans** *n.* see note to 2/3.

**soppeowse** *pr. 1 sg.* suppose 39/27,
**soppose** 23/7, **sopos(s)e** 37/5, 102/6,
**suposse** 44/23; *pt.* **sophosed** 110/12.

**sor** *adj.* not yet mewed 134/4.

**sore** *adj.*[1] *~ of* sorry for 141/39.

**sore** *adj.*[2] in pain 102/9; severe 52/5.

**sor(e)** *adv.* grievously; hard; greatly
8/26, 11/8, 47/11, **soor** 74/27, 168/13,
**sorre** 212/11, **sowyr** 213/21, **sowre**
75/4; *taked ~ at yowre stomakt* were
annoyed by 110/7.

**sorell** *adj.* bright chestnut 52/19.

**sormyse** *n.* formal allegation, information 136/10. Also **surmysyd.**

**sort(e)** *n.* batch 112/8, 87/14, **sortt(e)**
92/20, 234/49, **soorte** 91/16; *pl.*
**sortys** varieties 113/6.

**sortyd** *pp.* classified 247/9.

**sostys** *n. pl.* costs 130/14.

**sothe** *n. for (in) ~* truly 21/6, 244/5.

**sow** *conj.* so 75/4, 6.

**sowdear** *n.* soldier 217/37; **sowdoer**
199/13, **sauldiour** 66/7; *pl.* **sowdyar**

22/7, **sodears** 20/2, 24/7, **sowdeers** 115/19, **sowdyerys** 110/14.

**sowl(l)e** *n.* soul 142/4, 75/7, **sowyll** 81/7, 175/9, **sole** 141/4; *a my sowll upon my soul* 74/11.

**sowme** *adj.* some 19/15, **sum(me)** 78/27, 103/20.

**sowndyng** *pp. adj.* referring to 137/6.

**soweren** *adj.* sovereign 112/29.

**sovud** *pp.* see **sel(l)e.**

**space** *n.* time 214/22; *in schort ~* soon, promptly 44/24–5.

**Spaynard** *n.* Spaniard 234/24; *pl.* **Spayn(e)arddys** 208/33, 235/39.

**sparyng(e)** *n.* respite 227/21, 203/14.

**speceaulte** *n.* letter of payment or obligation 96/16; *pl. specyal(l)tys (off exchaunge)* 205/17, 206/19.

**speche** *n.* ~ *of* talk about 11/3; *the ~ ys grete of* there is much talk about 36/18–19; *in ~ wyt* negotiating with 50/14.

**sped(e)** *n.* helper 85/7, 21/7.

**spede, speyd** *v. intr.* prosper 243/17; *pr. 1 sg.* 127/16; *tr.* assist 114/9; *pr. subj. sg.* **sped** 150/12; *refl. speed you, sped yow* hasten 44/25, 168/24; *pp.* **sped(d)** accommodated 72/12, 167/9; accomplished 225/25.

**speke** *v.* speak 22/32, **spekt** 39/14; *pt.* **spake** 34/5, 55/36, **spakt** 149/26; *the mater that spake vnto* what I spoke about [OED 1639] 152/17; *pp.* **spo(c)kyn** 32/5, 233/5, **spoke** 38/40, 85/10.

**spekyng** *vbl. n. strange ~* disturbing talk 11/6.

**spent** *pp.* crippled by loss of masts or other fittings 137/8.

**spere** *pr. 3 pl.* ask 38/46; *tr.* with cognate obj. *pt.* **speryd** 215/40.

**spor rowell** *n.* the revolving wheel of a spur 111/42.

**spredyd** *pt.* spread 140/12.

**stablysch** *v.* establish 160/16; *pp.* **stablyschyd** 165/91.

**stand, stond** *v.* be stabled 193/6; stand 55/35; ~ *sewyr (of)* be secure (for) 47/8, 27, 34; ~ *there to* keep a bargain 48/15; *pr. 3 sg.* **standys(s)** 163/24, 162/24; *how it ~, as the casse stondythe* how (as) matters are 11/4, 22/15; *hytt staundyth wyth* it

fares with 240/8–9; *stondyd in good casse* goes on well 151/21; *stondyth chargyd . . . to* is bound to 7/12; *3 pl.* **stonde** remain untouched 76/8; ~ *you to coste* put you to expense 91/27–8; ~ *at hys owne aventture* bear the risk 115/32. Also **case.**

**standarde** *n.* collar of mail 114/37; *pl.* **standardys** 114/48.

**staple** *n.*[1] the fibre of a fleece 125/8.

**Staple** *n.*[2] *the ~ of (at) Calles* the staple for wool at Calais; hence the Company of wool merchants; its headquarters at Calais (also **Place**) 1/15, **Stap(p)ell** 22/50, 77/22, **Stap-(p)ull** 5/26, 115/45, **Stapyll** 12/3, **Estapell** 25/36; *Stappull (Stappell) merchaundyse* wool, fell, hides and lead 212/58, 213/42–3.

**starlyng(e)** *adj.* sterling, English currency 22/7, 3/7, **starleng** 22/10; **sterlyng** 20/3; *pl.* **sterlyngys** 1/4, 212/79.

**stekyng** *n.* ~ *anჳenst ytt* opposition 93/20. [OED has only (*sticking vbl. n.*[1] 1 e) 'hesitation, scruple' 1528].

**ster.** *abbrev.* sterling 1/6.

**ster** *n.* star 97/2.

**sterne schete** *n.* stern portion of a boat 131/18.

**Steuyn, Sent** ~*s Day,* 26 December 114/6.

**styc** *n. le (the) ~* apiece 182/17; each item 185/9; *pl.* **styk(k)ys** measures (?Flemish) of cloth 133/25, 161/22. [West Fl. *stik.*]

**stydffast** *adj.* steadfast 170/35.

**styl(l)e** *adv.* still (as before) 107/11, **styell** 39/38, 44/12, **stelle** 76/11; without movement: *kepe ~* be inactive 22/34; *sett styll* keep out of it 191/17.

**stofe** *n.* 'gear', things, goods 34/31, 74/33, **sthofe** 38/37, **stoufe** 111/41, **stuff(e)** 42/2, 145/4, **stowe** 74/17.

**stomakt** *n.* stomach (as seat of emotion) 110/7.

**stope** *n.* stoppage of trade 109/43, **stopp** 212/44.

**stovyd** *pp.* stowed 133/45, **stowyd** 130/7.

**strayght(e)** *adj.* stringent, strict 211/20, 205/27.

**strayngely** *adv. byt ~ dysposyd* not friendly 169/20.

**st[r]ayte** *adv.* closely 242/13.

**strange** *adj.* unexpected, surprising 11/6; *superl.* **strangyusst** rarest 159/5.

**streydly** *adv.* stringently 53/12.

**stripys** *n. pl.* strokes 140/13.

**stryte** *n.* trust 31/22. Also **tryst(e)**.

**strywe** *v. ~ wyth* quarrel with 93/13.

**stroke** *adj.* strong 73/6.

**sturryd** *pt.* budged 214/19.

**subsede** *n.* the tax of 33s. 4d. per sack of wool or 240 fells 115/12, **sub(e)sete** 20/2, 48/8, **sobsyde** 7/21, 41/15.

**subseryvyd** *pp. adj.* ?for *subscryvyd* 'subscribed', or confused with *subserved* 137/15.

**substa(u)nce** *n.* main part 220/31; **sobstons** amount 109/47; *of ~ (substansse)* prosperous 235/29, 243/24, 220/30. Also? **sopesans**.

**suche** see **soche**.

**sve** ?sue *v.*: see note to 56/30.

**svere** *adv.* without risk 20/24. Also **sewer**.

**suggestion** *n.* false representation 16/11, 17/11.

**sum** see **some**, **sowme**.

**supersedyas** *n.* writ staying legal proceedings 136/27, **sewpersedyas** 137/11.

**surmysyd** *pt. ~ a matter vppon* made a (?trumped-up) charge against 243/22. Also **sormyse**.

**susspence** *n. put yn ~* suspended 237/18.

**swefft** *adj.* hasty 109/39.

**swepestake** *n. hath made ~* have taken everything 220/38.

**swete** *v.* sweat (of fells) 184/11.

**swherd** *n.* sword 146/7, 8.

**ta(c)ke** *v.* take 10/18, **taake** 5/11; *~ hit att* consider it 164/15; *~ wpe* stable 193/5; **take**, *~ oppe (vpp)* borrow money 118/7, 50/8, 239/23, 22; *pt.* **to(o)ke** 3/9, 74/7, **tuke** 142/13; *toke hem oonly to* gave sole allegiance to 208/55; *pp.* **takyn** 41/31; captured 7/20; **takon** 141/8, **take** 52/11, 87/19; **takyt** *pr. 3 sg.+* 'it' 90/19;

**taked** *pr. 2 pl.+* 'it' 110/7, 29; *pp.+* 'it' 110/8.

**taht** *conj.* that 12/11; **tat** 19/39.

**tayllour ȝardys** *n. pl.* cloth yards of 36 in. 29/4.

**tal(l)e** *n.* full number 182/5, 186/6, 105/49; *small ~* by the hundred of six score, see note to 128/7.

**tangyllyd** *pp.* entangled 86/6.

**Tanys Day, Sent** St. Anne's Day, 26 July 121/25.

**tar(y)yng** *vbl. n.* tarrying 134/14, 112/9; *tarryng on* waiting for 136/8.

**tar(r)y** *v.* delay, wait, remain 81/28, 112/22; *~ May Day* wait until 165/45, **tare(y)** 152/12, 153/22; *pr. 1 sg.* **tary** 52/10; *3 sg.* **tarryth** 225/9; *pt.* and *pt. subj.* **taryd** 25/6; **taryed** 241/50, **tarryd** 108/6; *pp.* **tarryd** 137/2. [Forms like *taryd* for *taryed* not noted in *OED*. *OED* says spg. with *rr* is rare before 1500.]

**tarsel** *n.* tercel, male hawk 33/3, **tassellys** 169/17.

**Telen Day, Synt** St. Helen's Day, 3 May 163/8 and note.

**tell** *imper.* count 105/49; *pp.* **told** 179/3; *told hem ower* 186/5; *inf.* tell: [t]*ell off* give information about 202/12; *pr. 3 sg.* **telles** 141/7, **tellyth** 181/9; *pt.* **tellyd(e)** 34/32, 108/13, **telde** 165/42, **tyllyd** 202/18, **to(w)lde** 18/9, 117/25; **towllyd** 108/14; *pp.* **tellyd** 175/6, **teld** 8/24, **towllyd** 117/30.

**tell** *prep.* and *conj.* till 189/43, 241/43; *~ tyme* until 202/29. Also **tyell**.

**tend** *v. ~ to* attend to 73/13.

**tendyr** *v. tr.* have consideration for 111/22.

**Tenebyr Weddynysday** *n.* the Wednesday in Holy Week 55/13.

**teno(u)r** *n.* purport 17/9, 213/5; contents 209/5; details 210/11.

**Ternyte** *n.* Trinity 81/23, **Trenyte** 5/22.

**tester** *n.* hanging for a bedhead 159/2.

**thackyd** *pp. adj.* thatched 44/7.

**thay(e)** *pron.* they 5/7, 179/22, **þay** 142/9; **tay** 34/19; *obl.* **tha(y)m** 135/6, 65/9, **þayme** 142/23; *poss.* **thayr** 111/22.

**thake** *subj. pr. 3 sg.* thank 35/7.

**than** *adv.* then 22/14, 164/10, þan 142/20.

**thancke** *n.* myche ~ many thanks 199/19.

**thankefully** *adv.* gratefully 19/20, 165/54.

**thankt** *pr. 1 sg.* thank 149/15, 19, **thanked** 58/17; *pp.* **thanckyd** 77/5, **thaunkyd** 158/14.

**thar(e)** *adv.* there 135/18, 60/5.

**that** *pron.* ~ *that* that which 163/20. Also **at** *rel. pron.*

**thaulkyd** *pt.* talked 117/17.

**the** *pron.* they 20/21, 41/22; *poss.* **ther(e)** 19/5, 11/14, **thyr** 160/19.

**theder** *adv.* thither 219/56, 243/16, **thyedyr** 34/33; ~ ward(d)ys 225/5, 213/34; ~ ward 58/9.

**thefe** *n.* thief 34/27; *pl.* **theuys** 34/27, 134/33.

**they** *conj.* even if 151/12. Also **thow(e)**.

**they** *def. art.* the 28/5, 44/16, 180/3.

**theyns** *adv.* frome ~, ffrom thenns thence 44/24, 63/6.

**theke** *adj.* those 46/12, 17, 93/15, 105/28.

**then** *conj.* than 8/12, 39/19.

**theng** *n.* thing 28/7; *pl.* 6/9, 141/27; **tyngke** 73/3, **then(g)kys** 145/11, 18/14, **thynkys** 70/29.

**theparded** *pp.* departed 75/7.

**ther** *adv.* where 142/28, 144/11; ~ *as* wherever 63/7.

**thes** *adj.* and *pron.* this 63/21, 110/33, **theis** 41/35, **thys** 7/1, **tys** 21/6, 84/23; *pl.* **thes** these 7/19, 91/8, **thesse** 41/36, **theys** 91/11, **thys** 23/7, 31/21.

**thym(e)** *pron. obl.* them 8/19, 75/10.

**thyn(c)ke** *v.* think: hytt ys to ~ it may be supposed 207/53; as hart cane ~ as can be imagined 174/2; ~ apone remember 150/12; *pr. 1 sg.* ~ 206/14, **thyng** 30/3, 222/13, **thyngke** 48/17, **thynckyth** 238/59; *3 sg.* **thyng** 2/17, **thynket** 40/19, **thynkys** 134/18; *1 pl.* ~ 206/35, **thynckyth** 238/34; *3 pl.* **thynckythe** 221/26; *impers.* me thynk 25/23, me thynkys hyt wel done 47/7, as me thynckyth 238/59, me thynky 47/22; *pt.* **thowʒte** 220/9, 240/48, **thothe** 223/25; *pp.* **thowth** 240/23. Also **long** *adj.*

**thyne** *adv.* then 75/5.

**tho(w)** *adj.* and *pron.* those 55/37, 141/21.

**thowchand** *num.* thousand 160/21, **thowsand** 163/13.

**thowe** *n.* thought 31/23.

**thow(e)** *conj.* though, although 22/8, 33/5, **thowff(e)** 51/8, 4, **thoff** 138/3, **thowʒth** 170/35. Also **they**.

**thrawen** *pp.* thrown 140/10.

**throw(e)** *adv.* through 236/10; whe be thoro (thorow) we are quit 137/10, 147/32–3; go thorow wyth, be ~ wyth [one] ffor reach final agreement (about) 109/61, 239/17–18; *prep.* **thorrow** 136/19, **thurgh** 16/14 fn.

**tydyng** *n. pl.* news 165/80, **tytyng** 59/1, **ty⟨d⟩yng** 90/19, 20, 22, **tydyngys** 8/20, **tythyngys** 171/9, **ty⟨d⟩(y)ngys** 11/2, 23/14.

**tyell** *conj.* till 40/7, 151/16, **tyll** 8/20. Also **tell**.

**tymy** *n.* time 121/23.

**typete** *n.* tippet 86/11.

**tyre** *n. pl.* iron rims for wheels 57/12.

**to** *prep.* and *conj.* till 161/17, 222/14; ~ *that* so that 22/10.

**tochyng** *pp. adj.* as ~ as regards 114/23, 234/36, **towchyng(e)** 55/33, 125/24; as towchynge to 226/6; **tossyng** 129/11.

**tod** *n.* weight of wool in England: two stone (one-thirteenth sack) 192/7, **to(o)de** 122/11, 67/13.

**toder** *adj.* and *pron.* other 156/17; with *the*: 20/17, **todyr** 92/27, **todir** 88/10, **todor** 18/8, **tother** 8/5, **tothyr** 22/37.

**toffore** *prep.* in front of 205/49.

**togeder(e)** *adv.* together 64/13, 9/15, **togedder** 203/22, **togedure** 10/6, **togeydder** 96/9, **togyd(d)yr** 117/17, 34/33, **togyder** 51/8, **togedyr** 92/21.

**to(y)n** *adj.* and *pron.* the one 18/8, 28/5, 74/19.

**tokyn** *n.* keepsake 222/16; means of identification 117/11; **token** mark 196/75; by the same ~ that as, in the same connection, 97/4 and note.

**Tomas, Sente** ~ tyde around 29 December 134/8.

**ton(e)** *n.* cask or measure of wine (252

**ton(e)** *(cont.)*:
wine gallons) 201/24, 44/17, **tonne**
215/54.

**tony** *n.* tuna 114/13.

**torne** *v.* ~ *vs to losse* result in loss for
us 22/14–15; *pp.* **tornyd** turned over
34/13.

**tornys** *n. pl. schrowyd* ~ injuries
218/52.

**tother** see **toder.**

**toward(e)** *adv.* in prospect, ap-
proaching 41/38, 109/49; *prep.* towards (of time) 67/19; to be put to
211/42.

**traywe** see **trow(e).**

**transporte** *pp.* transferred to another
owner 47/27.

**trede** *n.* thread 67/17.

**treser(r)y** *n.* the Staple treasury
215/48, 170/32, **tressery** 156/10,
**tresory** 66/9, 189/44.

**tress(e)passe** *n.* offence 213/40, 46.

**treste** see **tryst(e).**

**trew(e)** *adj.* faithful 16/17, 245/4,
**tru** 61/18.

**trewly(e)** *adv.* faithfully 42/4, 123/7,
**trwely** 48/16, **treulle** 159/8; *whell
and* ~ punctiliously 95/21–2.

**trybelassyon** *n.* tribulation 74/14.

**tryd** *pp.* ~ *howt* ascertained 175/11.

**tryst(e)** *n.* trust 8/18, 50/20, **stryte**
31/22. Also **truste.**

**tryst(e)** *pr. 1 sg.* trust 152/14, 11/17,
**treste** 25/29, 114/11; *pr. p.* **trystyng**
74/4; *pp.* *(passive)* **betryste** 55/9.
Also **trost(e).**

**trysty** *adj.* trusty 152/23. Also **trosty.**

**trobuld** *pp.* and *pp. adj.* in trouble
with authority 246/12; **trobellytt**
200/7, **trobellett** 200/6, **trub(ul)lyd**
molested 206/37, 212/38, 213/38.
Also **vntrubeled.**

**trobull** *n.* trouble, esp. that caused an
offender by authority 175/14, 246/8,
**trobell** 100/2; **trub(b)ull** disturbance, disorder 239/16, 237/12. Also
**trublyng.**

**trost(e)** *pr. 1 sg.* trust 7/16, 57/23,
**trvst** 125/21, **trwste** 95/12; *3 sg.*
**trust** 223/22; *pt.* **trostyd** 192/6.
Also **tryst(e).**

**trosty** *adj.* trusty 4/23, 21/1, **trwsty**
78/28; in terms of address: *ryght*

**trusty** 68/1, *trusti sir* 72/1. Also
**trysty.**

**trothe** *n.* faith *by (be) my* ~, *vpon my
trowthe, as my* ~ *helpe ma* on my
faith 63/4, 192/10, 219/27, 192/11.

**trow(e)** *pr. 1 sg.* think, suppose; expect 4/13, 100/18, 141/29, **traywe**
56/19; *pt.* **trowyd** 203/10.

**trublyng** *vbl. n.* molestation 207/79.
Also **trobull.**

**trublys** *adj.* turbulent 194/11.

**trust(e)** *n.* 9/22; *whervpon ys on of my
moste* ~ ?which is one of my chief
hopes 219/34. Also **tryste.**

**Turkepler** *n.* the Turcopolier, commander of lightly armed soldiers of
the Order of St. John 118/6; *master
Twrkepler* 121/22.

**twayn** *num.* two 65/8.

**Twellffeday** *n.* Epiphany, 6 January
205/48; *xij tyde* 108/18.

**twelfve** *num. a* ~ *monthe* a year
226/13.

**un-** see also **on-.**

**vncurtes(e)** *adj.* churlish 140/14, 10,
**vncurtesse** 142/14.

**understande** *v.* hear, learn, perceive 24/11, **vndyrstond(e)** 46/20,
4/2, **vnderstond** 5/9, **onderstond(e)**
44/3, 47/4, **ondyrstond** 71/9, **vnder-
ston⟨d⟩** 58/2, 149/14, **wndyr-
ston⟨d⟩** 91/24, 168/3–4, **vnderstondon** 94/5; *pr. 1 sg.* **honderstonde** 15/13; *3 sg.* **onderstond**
8/7–8, *vndyrstondys of* knows about
96/14; *pt.* **understande** 67/2, **understonde** 31/24, **vndurstood**
246/7–8, **vnderstode** 17/10, **vnderstord** 223/7; *pp.* **vnderstond** 9/6,
**understonde** 35/6, **understand(e)**
2/2, 23/2.

**vnderstondyng** *n.* knowledge 16/20,
**vnderstan⟨d⟩yng** 11/4.

**wndyr** *adv.* and *prep.* below a price
165/18, 21, **onder** 142/6, **ondir**
142/30, **hondor** 192/8; **hundyr** be-
neath 137/15; *vnder this maner* in
this way 93/10–11.

**vndo** *pp.* left undone 110/29; **undoe**
ruined 85/17, **vndon** 219/12, **ondone**
47/30.

**vngodely** *adj.* unfitting 16/9.

vnkyndenesse *n.* bad faith 93/10, onkyndnesse 164/15.

unschoide *pp. adj.* see onschod.

unse *n.* see ovns.

vnto *prep.* up to, until 142/19; onto to 8/1.

vntrubeled *pp.* free from prosecution 219/40. Also trobuld.

vpon *prep.* nearly, about 40/25, wppon 72/4; on top of 5/6; in account with 56/53. Also apon, wryt(t).

vpp *adv. they hawe ben ~* have been in tumult or revolt 240/12; *wpe in Engelonde* further north 137/22.

vp(p)rest *adv.* uppermost 131/48, 8; *~ off* above 132/8.

wpwrmwste *adv.* uppermost 133/46, wpurmoste 133/63, wppurmwste 133/76.

vre *n.* see ewre.

vrgent *adj.* see cawsse.

vsaunce *n. at ~* at the usual length of time (30 days in these cases) 234/9, 239/23, 24. [It. *a usanza*.]

vsed *pp. adj.* customary 224/17.

vterst *superl. adj.* utmost 180/16; otterst 125/13; *at the vttrest* at the latest 241/46.

vttermeste *n.* limit 219/42.

vttravnsse *n.* sale 124/8, ottyrans 197/13, hotterans 36/20, hottravnsse 124/9.

vayage *n.* voyage 129/8. [OFr. *veiage*.]

valve *n.* valuation 20/6, whalew value, price 133/7.

varyavnsse *n.* dispute 112/25, veryavns 4/9, veryaunce 204/51, verians 88/5; *at a fferyaunce* contending 191/15.

vekery *n.* vicar 37/20, fekerey 40/24, 25. Also wycwr.

velaygys *n. pl.* villages 178/15.

vent *n.* sale, 'utterance' 220/35, wente 147/19. [Fr. *vente*; OED 1545.]

venter *n.* risk 22/24. Also aventer(e).

verdure *n.* green 60/3.

ver(e)y *adj.* true, certain 31/21, 159/11, whery 122/23, 165/63; *adv.* truly, very 225/12, verry 244/1, wery 219/26, were 111/25.

vernakelys *n. pl.* representations of Christ's face from the sudarium of St. Veronica 5/20.

vesettythe *pr. 3 sg.* inflicts illness 234/64.

vesyschon *n.* physician 77/22; *pl.* fessychons 73/4.

vet(t)ell *n. pl.* victuals 238/16, 177/12.

vetellyd *pp.* victualled 179/22, veetellyd 227/38.

vher, v(h)os see be.

vyelett *adj.* violet 161/23, vyolet 51/6.

vyse *n.* advice 238/21, vyce 170/41. Also avyse.

vyth *prep.* with 19/46, 57.

voyde *v.* quit 185/16.

wayer, war(re) see be.

waythe see weythe.

waytynge *pp. adj.* in ambush 237/7.

wald, wallde see whyll.

walur *n.* value 10/13.

wantt *pr. 1 sg.* am missing 230/7.

warant *n.* voucher for payment 109/6, waront(e) 106/4, 5, 107/15, whar(r)ant 114/22, 200/23; *pl.* warantys 115/9, 202/34, warrant(t)ys 164/5, 156/4, war(r)auntys 182/22, 167/13.

wardd *v.* award, appraise 234/49. Also awarde.

warddyng *pp. adj. the ~ sarppllerys* the samples by which wool was awarded 234/50.

warddysmen *n. pl.* ?arbitrators, ?representatives of wards [cf. OED *wardman, wardsman n.*²) 176/21.

ward(e) *n.*¹ *in (under) ~* under arrest 38/39, 241/14.

warde *n.*² ?award, ?ward of the town 176/26.

warde *quasi-adv. to ~* to; towards, on the way to 23/16, 97/6–7; *to Bregyswhard* 150/11; *into Cottysowldewhard* 146/9–10; ?aphetic for *toward* 'forthcoming': *wyll be no good marchantys ~* 24/17.

warde day *n.* day for 'awarding' wool 190/5.

ware *adj.* careful 36/17, 15.

ware *n.* see warre.

**warffare** *n. 3ede fforthe a* ~ went to wage war 211/29–30.

**warke** *n.* work: *for the schortter* ~ as a quicker expedient 115/33–4; *a scherewde werke* a sorry business 15/15; *made a fol werke* brought things to a bad pass 129/19; **whorke** difficulty 93/19; **w(h)arke** pattern, embroidery 159/5, 74/19, 21; *rydy for goe to worke* ready for use 56/17; *pl.* **warkus** 159/4; *wharke (whork) mene* workmen 174/10, 168/25.

**warled(e)** *n.* see **whorlld(e)**.

**war(r)e** *n.* war 11/8, 98/19, **whar** 111/19, 168/11; *men a (of)* ~, *men of whar* soldiers 237/6, 112/25, 31–2, 215/65–6; fighting ships 211/32, 235/25; *schepys of war* 56/23.

**wars(se)** *compar. adv.* worse 234/19(2). Also **whorsse**.

**warthe** *n.* see **whorlld(e)**.

**wastyd** *pt.* despoiled 220/48; *pp.* spoilt 205/9.

**wat** *pron. and adj.* what 2/18, 11/15, 180/7; ~ *tyme* when 106/5; **what** any, such 165/86, 87.

**wat(e)** *v. tr.* await 38/31; *intr. wayte on (vpon)* await 61/17, 143/12; ~ *on* attend on, or to 73/13; *whaytt vppon* 4/19, *whayght appon* 112/38, *whate apon* 136/16, *wayte vppon* 105/40; call upon, visit 199/22. Also **waytynge**.

**Water Baylys** *n. poss.* house of the Water Bailiff 115/28.

**wax** *pr. 3 sg.* is becoming 234/31, **wext** 149/28; *3 pl.* grow 19/30; *pt.* **whaxyd** 114/34.

**weder(e)** *n.* spell of particular kind of weather 37/6, 39/26, **wedder** 225/25, **whed(d)yr** 22/30, 41/38, 111/36.

**wey** *v.* weigh 52/14; *pp.* **wayed(d)** 218/27, 209/20.

**weythe** *n.* weight 56/12, **whet(t)e** 83/6, 91/32, **wayght(e)** 210/9, 221/42, **waythe** 26/8, 50/11.

**wekerayge** *n.* benefice 43/18.

**wel(le)** *n.* welfare, prosperity 129/13, 20/20, **whell** 111/23.

**welth** *n.* interests, prosperity 208/49.

**wene** *pr. 3 pl.* suppose 77/14; *pt.* **wend** 232/4; *pp.* **w(h)ent** 239/14, 46/8, 109/36; *pr. p. wen(e)yng (whenyng) to me (hym) that* supposing 125/6, 37/11, 96/17.

**Wenesday** *n.* Wednesday 171/7, **Wedon(y)sday** 194/4, 143/13, **Wedunsday** 65/12.

**wenson** *n.* venison 19/13.

**wente** *n.* see **vent**.

**were** *v.* wear 65/8.

**were, w(h)ery** see **ver(e)y**.

**were** *adv. and conj.* where 56/9; whereas 20/3; *where that* 215/50; *war the bell ys becomen* what has become of the bill 39/15; *wher as(e)* in the place where 97/2, 141/35, 180/8; *wer(e)of, wheroff* whereof 102/6, 27/8, 198/9; *whersumeuyr* wherever 125/18. Also **qwheyr**.

**wery** *n.* ~ *of* tired of 104/47.

**werke** see **warke**.

**west** *pp.* see **wyste**.

**wet** *v.* see **wyt(t)**.

**wettnes** *n.* witness 3/9.

**wh-** see also **qw(h)-**.

**w(h)ay(e)** *n.* road 237/6; *by (be) the* ~ on the journey 7/20, 134/33; *owt[e] off the* ~ expensive 238/43; *be to ffar owte of the weye* be left in the lurch, miss the market 234/28; *be yn a wey wyth, in whay wyth, yn a goode* ~ *with* be in negotiations with 160/15, 109/60, 217/26–7; *fflee hys weye* escape 240/25–6; *in good* ~ *(of)* in good course 197/6; well on with 109/29; *sete in a* ~ given means (of recovering a debt) 38/40; *in (a)* ~ *to, in the* ~ *of* in prospect of 169/17, 219/38, 165/25, 175/7; course, means (also **se**) 5/10, 41/31, **whey** 219/56, **weye** 241/46; *pl.* **w(h)ays** 7/24, 41/31, **wheyes** 219/23; *noo ways* in no direction 236/7; *pl. as sg. þat ys the best ways to . . .* 237/30.

**whaygys** *n. pl.* wages 41/30.

**whalew** *n.* see **valve**.

**w(h)an** *conj.* when 9/11, 22/24, **whane** 147/41, **wen** 21/14, 25/15. Also **qwen**.

**whar** *n.* ware 165/88 (2); *pl.* **warys** 237/20.

**whardars** *n. pl.* awarders 46/18.

**whardyd** *pp.* awarded 112/16–17. Also **awarde**.

**wharf(f)or** *adv.* wherefore 142/26, 155/9, **werfor** 33/5.

**wharke** see **warke**.

**what** *interj.* well then 218/36.

**whe** *pron.* we 4/18, 22/7, 126/4.

**whedow(e)** *n.* widow 19/57, 55/48, **wedew** 40/32, **wyedow** 28/13, **wyddowe** 217/35.

**wheyder** *pron.* which of two 51/4; *conj.* whether 180/14, **w(h)eder** 104/55, 40/18, **wether** 21/17, **whedyr** 135/6, **whethyr** 118/5. Also **wher**, **qwedyr**.

**w(h)eke** *n.* week 77/8, 195/14, **wyeke** 10/24; *pl.* **whekys** 165/12.

**w(h)elbelouyd** *adj.* well beloved 3/1, 126/1, **whell(e)-** 136/1, 86/1, **welbelufed** 29/18, **welbeluffyd** 18/1, 28/1, **wheylbelouyd** 81/1.

**whelbhowte** *pp. adj.* bought at a reasonable price 114/48-9.

**whelbodyd** *adj.* of good physique 117/20.

**whelcom** *pp. adj.* welcome 45/5, **whelcum** 108/6.

**whelfar** *n.* welfare, well-being 71/2, **wellfar** 130/2, **wel(le)fare** 16/3, 192/2, **wyllfare** 75/3; entertainment 117/15, **welfayr** 10/2.

**whelys** see **wyllys**.

**whell** *adv.* well 4/4, 7/2, **wheyll** 71/17, **weyll** 44/9, **wel(l)e** 17/10, 108/14, **weell** 125/22, 139/5, **wyll** 2/1, 23/13.

**whellcwmyd** *pt.* greeted 165/55-6, **wellcomyd** 215/37, **wyllcwmyd** 165/24.

**whell don(e)** *pp. adj.* prudent, advisable 46/14, 22/23, **weldone** 47/7, **well doon** 215/19-20; *hyt wher whell doyn to, hytt ys well don that ye* it would be a good idea to 71/9, 234/29-30.

**whellfauyrd** *adj.* handsome 165/63.

**whenso** *adv.* whensoever 152/14.

**Whenysyans** *n. pl.* Venetians 114/26-7; *adj. pl. docettys Wenycyans* Venetian ducats 121/19-20.

**w(h)ent** *pp.* see **wene**.

**whent(e)** *pt.* went 165/35, 117/8; was dressed 175/10.

**wher** *conj.* contracted from *whether* 93/18, 109/44, 62.

**wher?** *pr. subj.* ?were 125/30.

**wheryng** *n. of hyr* ~ from her wardrobe 165/72.

**whete** *n.* wheat 19/29, 142/31.

**whet(t)e** see **weythe**.

**whexsasyon** *n.* vexation 74/14-15.

**w(h)ych(e)** *rel. adj. and pron.* which 18/6, 5/5, 7, 64/2, **w(h)eche** 2/2, 4/3, **whyhch** 184/4, **wysch(e)** 57/3, 17, 63/11, **wycche** 192/4; **wiche** who 161/5; as *rel. conj.* 206/24, ?192/4. Also **qwich**.

**whyle** *n. (of) a grett* ~ for a long time 167/16, 220/36; *the wylys* the while 192/5; *conj.* while 220/14; **whyll** 91/31; **whell** ?as long as 193/7; *the wylys (that)* whilst 70/26; when, seeing that 110/29.

**w(h)yll** *pr.* will 7/15, 22/20, **wyell** 125/16, **well** 246/13, **w(h)oll** 5/15, 7/7, **whowl** 122/21, **wull** 77/8, **vyll** 111/10; *I woll vnto, I wyll into* I will go to 22/31-2, 63/15; *tr.* desires 179/12; *pr. p.* **wyllyng** 37/2; *pt. and subj.* **wylld** 199/20, 209/44, **wylled** 23/10, **wyllyd** 136/44, **wald** 34/20, **wallde** 129/5, **wold(e)** 4/5, 34/5, **wolld(e)** 8/9, 93/13, **woold** 44/14, 51/6, **woul(l)d** 58/19, 25/6, **wuld** 207/14, **wholde** 95/11, **wholld(e)** 137/14, 109/66, **whould(e)** 114/46, 96/8, **whowllyde** 136/44; *wold nott of hytt* refused it 239/17.

**whyn(e)** *n.* wine 133/7, 165/57, **whyen** 111/9, **wyne** 203/31.

**whyntter** *n.* winter 193/6; *adj.* (fell) collected in winter 133/71, **w(h)ynter** 30/7, 131/24, 92/10, **wenter** 70/23.

**whysdom(e)** *n.* prudence, (prudent) discretion 147/17, 105/52, **wysdome** 81/21, **wysdum** 19/37.

**Whisson, Whytt(e)son** *n.* Whitsun 88/23, 155/13, 165/77, **Whytsuntyd** 84/24, **Whyttsontyde** 21/8; *Wysson marte* (see also **Synksen**) 50/7; **Whesensondey** Whitsunday 171/16.

**whystelers** *n. pl. poss.* money changers' 133/20. [MDu. *wisseler*.]

**whystyllys** *n. pl.* exchanges, official money changers' offices 165/85; *sg.* **wystyll** 165/89. [MDu. *wissel*.]

**whyte mony** *n. pl.* silver coins 187/19, **whyght** 151/57.

**w(h)ytty** *adj.* clever, intelligent 219/18, 165/64.

**whyttys** *n. pl. poss.* wits' 195/10.

**whoddyng** *n.* wedding 91/25.

**w(h)oll** see **whyll, whooll.**

**wholl getherars** *n. pl.* middlemen who collected wool from the growers 165/36.

**whom(e)** *adv.* home 145/2, 231/13 Also **hoom.**

**whonde** *pp.* wound 112/10.

**whon(e), won** *num.* one 91/29, 78/8, 18/4; ~ *wyth anothyr* ?mingled 113/6.

**whons** *adv.* once 169/14, **wonys** 194/11. Also **onys.**

**w(h)ooll** *n.* wool 18/3, 91/18, **vooll** 108/16, **w(h)oll** 2/11, 92/25, **wo(o)lle** 83/6, 141/8, **wull** 82/4; *pl.* **wollys** 21/7, **whollis** 124/6, **wullys** 215/8. Also **wol-, woll.**

**whor** see **be**; *a whor* see note to 84/14.

**whord(e)** *n.* word; information 126/2, 111/14, **whoord** 96/20, **wurd(e)** 161/14, 16.

**whorke** see **warke.**

**whorlld(e)** *n.* state of affairs 109/54, 134/18, 197/12, **world(e)** 208/31, 215/10, 238/12, **warled(e)** 31/22, 29, 56/30, **warthe** 23/14; *the world goyth marvyllyusly* things are in a pretty pass 237/9. Also **wyllys.**

**whorsse** *compar. adj.* worse 124/10, **worsse** 58/32; *superl.* **the whorste** 74/4. Also **wars(se).**

**whos** see **be.**

**whothe** *conj.* with 165/44.

**whow(e)** *adv.* how 135/19, 5.

**whryttyng** *vbl. n. a* ~ *of* engaged in writing 148/10.

**whrongefowlly** *adv.* unjustly 175/14.

**wycwr** *n.* vicar 19/22, **wycur** 43/17. Also **vekery.**

**wyll** *adj.* see **whell;** *v.* see **w(h)yll.**

**wyll(e)** *n. pwt on yowr* ~ at your disposal 136/35–6; *of* ~ by choice 219/23; *hewell well* malice 110/24; *wyth a good* ~ willingly 165/46–7;

*good(e)* ~ *(whyll)* favour 35/8, 215/36, 117/26; *pl.* **gode welles** 219/62.

**wyllys** *n. pl.* wheels 56/15; *the world goyth on whelys* see note to 238/25.

**wyndas** *n.* winch for a cross-bow 103/14.

**wynne** *v.* gain 64/9.

**wyrkyn** *n.* see **firkyn.**

**wyse** *n.* manner, way 212/27, **whys(e)** 91/2, 86/2, **whisse** 45/3, **whyes** 118/2, **wyisse** 66/2; *in no wys(s)e* on no account; by no means 104/38, 39/25; *in onny wyse* by all means 107/18; *in any whysse* in any case 22/27; *noon oder* ~ *(but) (than)* nothing else but (than) 214/20, 217/12, 218/32; *yn lyke wyse* similarly 227/22.

**wysemen** *n. pl.* councillors, members of *wits* 241/23.

**Wysson** see **Whysson.**

**wyste** *pt.* knew 167/6, **whyst** 93/24, **woust** 69/4; *pp.* **west** 110/8. Also **wyt(t).**

**wyth** *prep.* by 7/20.

**wyt(h)all** *adv.* in addition 211/16, 212/9; therewith 44/19, 105/24; with 77/7, 110/15.

**wythhov[te]** *adv.* outside 49/16; *prep.* **wythowt(e)** 125/34, 115/27; **wytthehowte** lacking 192/20; *conj.* **wyth(h)owte,** *wythowt that* except that, unless 186/16, 57/17, 180/18.

**wyth that** *conj.* provided that 205/44, 209/8.

**Wytt** *n.* the Council of Bruges 241/29, 30.

**wyt(t)** *v.* know 10/6, 1/2, **witte** 171/2, **wyte** 52/17, **w(h)et(t)** 8/2, 61/2, 165/85, 22/21, **wette** 15/2, **w(h)ete** 39/2, 137/2; *that is to witt* to be exact 49/4; *pr.* **wot(t)** 34/12, 51/4, **wot(t)e** 33/4, 34/21, **whot(te)** 74/11, 195/6; *pt.* see **wyste.**

**wo** *pron.* who 222/19. Also **ho, qwou.**

**wolde** *adj.* see **olde.**

**wole** sense unclear 229/16.

**wol flet** *n.* fleet of woolships 120/6, **woll flete** 83/4, **wull fflete** 183/4, 214/18.

**wollers** *n. pl.* woolships 181/19.

**wol(l)packar** *n.* packer of wool 43/6, 87/7, **wull packer** 227/50.

**woll schepys** *n. pl.* wool ships 90/10 **whol(l)schypys** 136/40, 169/8, **whowlschypys** 137/7, **wull shippis** 88/22.

**wollhovsse** *n.* store for wool 140/11, **wolhowse** 142/11, **-hus** 34/26, **w(h)ollhowsse** 105/21, 92/31, **wullhowsse** 182/9.

**worn** ? for 'one' 103/7 and note.

**wor(s)chepe** *n.* battle honours 59/7; *for ys* ~ helpful to his reputation 38/46, 49; *spekys of yow myche whorschype, saythe yow lettyll* ~ speaks (dis)respectfully of you 114/15–16, 21/20.

**wor(s)chepf(f)ull** *adj.* worthy of respect; reputable; honoured 63/1, 57/1, 143/19, 76/1, **worchypfull** 129/1, **worchupfull** 192/1, 222/1, **worschipf(f)ull** 1/1, 135/1, **worschypp(e)full** 77/1, 223/1, **whorshyp(p)ffull** 45/1, 4/14–15, **whowrschypfull** 136/19–20, **wyrschypfull** 60/1, 12, 232/1, **wurshipfull** 100/1, **wurs(c)hyppffull** 156/1, 202/1. Also **wursull.**

**worschyppefull-ley** *adv.* with honour 149/30.

**worthe** *n. take it in* ~ be content with it 222/18.

**worthe** *adj.* worth: *as sche ys* ~ whatever her value 61/10, **whorthe** 114/32, **wurthe** 238/46; *anythyng wurth* of any value 189/16.

**wottys** *n. pl.* see **ootys.**

**woust** see **wyste.**

**wrack** *n.* inferior grade of herring 236/23, 26. [MDu. *wrac* 'inferior'.]

**wryt(e)** *v.* write 8/21, 19/14, **wrytte** 8/15, **whryte** 114/40, **wryet** 25/17, **wreet** 180/5, **whrayt** 165/72, **wryght** 109/51, 216/18, **wrytythe** 206/40; *pr. 1 sg.* **wryt** 8/20, **wrytyth** 201/6, **whryte** 165/21; *3 sg.* **wrytys** 170/51, **whryttys** 134/17, **wryttyth** 170/8, **wrytytyth** 202/14; *pt.* **wrott(e)** 112/18, 155/11, **w(h)rot(e)** 52/6, 114/50, 111/14, **w(h)rat(e)** 8/9, 81/12, 133/83, 134/12; *pp.* **wryt(t)** 2/17, 4/4, **wryte** 2/1, **whryt** 114/44, **wrote** 16/19 fn., **wrhryt** 165/92, **wrete** 20/17, **wrett(e)** 231/1, 15/3, **w(h)ryttyn** 19/40, 136/42, **wrytyn**

114/5, **wryttun** 10/15, **writon** 228/22, **wret(t)yn** 1/9, 25/31, **wret(t)on** 246/17, 18/16, **y-wreten** 5/9; with *direct obj.:* ~ *me answere, he wrytys me he was . . .* 11/15, 155/8; *write* (a sum) *vppon* (a bill) enter for deduction from 170/41–2, 234/37–8; *wrytten vppon yowre byll* 189/33.

**writtyng** *n.* letter; written instructions 142/3, **whryt(t)yng** 126/4, 134/32; *pl.* **wrytyngys** 55/8; *at the wrytteng of* at the written behest of 219/8.

**wrothe** *adj.* displeased 25/19.

**wull** see **whyll, whooll.**

**wursull** *adj.* ?contracted from 'worshipful' 88/1, 25.

**wurthy** *adj.* deserving 215/46.

**wus** *pron. obl.* us 34/24. Also **husse.**

**ʒard** *n.* (court)yard 34/29.

**ʒeardys** *n. pl.* yards (measure) 74/20, 146/4, **yardus** 159/6, **yerdus** 159/7, **yerdys** 60/2.

**yeasse** *n.* see **esse.**

**yede** *pt.* and *pt. subj.* went 138/3, **ʒede** 115/17, 198/13, **ʒed** 34/29, **ʒeyd(e)** 165/33, 150/13; *ʒeyde for* was spent on 233/10; *as thay ʒeyd* as they were current 34/11. See also **goo.**

**ye(e)** *pron. nom.* you 142/18, 209/34, **ʒe(e)** 8/7, 15/13, 21/4; *obl.* **ʒe** 19/9, 44, 32/18, 109/10, 49.

**yeff(e)** *conj.* if, whether 9/12, 70/23, **ʒeff(e)** 208/21, 230/8; **ʒefe** 126/10, 133/29, **ʒeyf(f)e** 81/28, 55/8, **ʒeue** 47/28, **geffe** 200/5. Also **ewe, hef(f)e.**

**yeff(e)** *v.* see **ʒeue.**

**ʒe(y)r** *conj.* and *prep.* ere, before 99/10, 43/19; **er** 15/9, **her** 117/7.

**ʒeystyrday** *n.* yesterday 147/25, **hystyrday** 148/14.

**yellys** *n. pl.* see **eylle.**

**ʒend** *n.* see **endd.**

**ʒenge** *adj.* see **yong(e).**

**ʒer** *v.* see **here.**

**ʒer(e)** *n. sg.* and *pl.* year 34/7, 48/5, **ʒeere** 3/2, **ʒeyr** 91/17, **ye(e)r** 219/41, 1/11.

**ʒerely** *adv.* yearly 48/12.

**ʒese** *v.* see **ese.**

**ʒetys** *n. pl.* acquisitions 85/13.

**yett(e)** *adv.* and *conj.* as yet; yet 77/12,
125/27, **yete** 20/27, **yit** 244/4, 5,
**yt(te)** 9/26, 125/10, **ȝett(e)** 45/10,
21/16, **ȝete** 23/6, **ȝe(h)yt** 19/8,
168/23, **ȝyt** 152/12, **hyt** 165/82; *and
ȝet . . . and ȝett* although . . . nevertheless 63/10–12.

**ȝeue, yeff(e)** *v.* give 48/4, 70/25,
40/26; ~ (*owte*) lend for profit 36/23,
70/16, 153/12–13; *pp.* **y-yeuen** given
5/21; *ȝeue hover* lent by exchange
122/4. Also **geve**.

**ȝeueyng** *vbl. n. the* ~ *of money* the
rate of exchange for loans 38/8,
116/5–6, **ȝeyng** 24/5. Also **gevyng**.

**ȝeuyn** *adv.* see **even**.

**(ȝ)ewyn** *n.* evening 55/14, 111/43,
**euyn** 19/30, **ewe** 55/16.

**yeuery** see **euery**.

**yong(e)** *adj.* young 163/10, 162/24,
**ȝeung(e)** 55/36, 136/41, **ȝewng(e)**
165/34, 26, **ȝenge** 117/20, 28,
197/19; *yowng* (*wool*) wool from the
first (?) shearing of the animal 93/9;
*compar.* **the ȝongar** 37/24, **ȝeungar**
126/13.

**ȝou, you** *pron. obl.* you 33/2, **yowe**
10/9, **yowu** 121/3, **yew** 152/10,
154/7, **gyu** 117/24, **iou** 38/50(2);
*nom.* **you, yow** 31/23, 44/12, 61/3;
*pl.* 219/1; *yowte* for 'you out' 110/20.

**yovre** *pron. poss.* your 145/6, **youere**
110/21, **ywr** 174/8, **yor** 43/23, 148/4,
**yur** 117/22, **yewre** 40/2, **ȝowr(e)**
114/34, 204/20, **ȝor** 150/18, **ȝewr**
169/6; *you ande all your* you and
yours 144/13; *all your* yours entirely
143/17. Also **iou**.

**yourys** *pron. poss.* yours: *yow and all
yowr(y)s* 109/67–8, 234/63; *any of
yours* 16/15; at your service: ~
*Bryan* 161/21, *I am yours* 28/7.

**yt(te)** *adv.* see **yett(e)**.

# INDEX OF NAMES

PLACE NAMES, English (but not foreign) personal names, and some surnames are given in their modern spelling. A cross-reference is supplied where the form in the Letters may make identification difficult, e.g. Yermevthe for Arnemuiden

Abingdon, Berks. (Abynton, (H)abendon), 147/10; 149/23; rector of, 40/14; 87/8.
Abram, Thomas, grocer, 10/7, 18.
Achamber, Harry, 208/42.
Adam, Thomas (Hadam), 5/8 & n.; 7/13; 9/13, 16; 32/6.
— — the elder, 6/5.
— William, 6/7; 7/13; 32/10; 170/50. Letter from: 166.
Adderbury, Oxf. (Addyrbery, Attyrbery), xii; 84/10; 136/33.
Ad(d)lyn, Robert, 29/11; 213/32.
Adlyngton, John (Addlynton), 230/9 & n.; 233/3; 234/5; 235/14.
Aire (Ary), 177/4 & n.; 179/23.
Albany, Duke of, 171/10–11 n.; 178/10–11 & n.; 200/1 n.
All Souls, Oxford, xii.
Allbryghtson, Allbryght, 204/35.
Allvard, see De Cisneros.
Allwynson, Cleyss, of Leiden, 105/45.
Almains, 112/26.
Alost, 69/7 n.
Amerys, Thomas, 213/32.
Andrew, see Hawes.
Andrew, John, xii.
— Lucy, xii.
— Richard, xii; xiv-xv; xviii n. 2; xxi & n. 1; 15/18 & n.; 19/26 & n.; executors of, 117/6 & n.; 147/20 n.
Andryan, see Deffrey.
Antwerp (Andwarp, And(e)warpe, Anwarp, Andewharp, Andwarppe), xx; 3/4; 4/24; 72/4; 81/4; 92/24 n.; 101/13; 125/19; 163/39; 197/2; 225/18, 20; Bamis Mart at, 3/4 n.; 38/7; 96/17; 101/13; 176/13; 177/15; 196/8; 234/36; Sinksen Mart at, 3/4 n.: 18/9; 22/32; 23/8; 50/15; 52/10; 53/9; 68/5; 88 n.; 93/4; 96/18;

117/36; 154/12; 200/22; 212/86; 214/38.
Ardson, William, of Delft, 208/6; 209/66.
Arnemuiden (Yermevthe), 220/45 & n.
Arnold, Isabel, wife of Robert. xviii n.
Arnolde, Thomas, shipman, 104/22.
Arnson, Cornelys, of Delft, 212/77–8.
Asschelay, baker, 111/15.
Austria, Archduke of, see Burgundy, Maximilian Duke of.
Aveley, Essex (Allay, Awelay, Hawelay, Auvelay, Alluelay, Aluerley, Aulay, Auwheley, Awhelay), xviii; xxi; 4/16; 19/17, 18 n.; 55/14; 74/31 n.; 83/11, 20; 86/16; 102/8; 110/31; 111/11; 114/20; 147/20 n.; 150/14; 169/9; 174/9; More Hall, 19/18 n. (see also Bretts Place). Priest of, 19/22; vicar of, 19/22; 43/17 & n.
Aweray, Geoffrey, 229/10.
Awheray, see Rawson.
Awrey, Richard (Aurey), 211/28 ff. & n.

Bacar, see Asschelay.
Baker, John, xviii.
Ball, William, priest, 123/14 n.; 148/12–13 n.
Balsall, Temple, Warw. (Bawlsall, Baltyssall), 58/8 & n.; 78/30
Bar, County of, 53/24 n.
Barkwey, John (Berkeway), 246/4, 7, 11 & n.
Barnet, battle of, 219/8–9 n.
Barow, etc., see Bergen-op-Zoom.
Barthelomeo, John Domynyco, Lombard, 56/5.
Barton, Northants., xii; 2/13 & n.
Basler, Henryc, 10 n.
Batton, Piers, shipman, 227/12.

Bayle, Bayle & Delyte, etc., *see* Vallodolid.
Beckenham, Kent, 43/15 n.
Bedyngfeld, Edmond (Beyngffeld), letter from: 103 & n.
*Belial*, 244/10 & n.
Benett, Thomas, 208/43.
Bentham, William, 115/6; 167/15; 213/32.
Benyngton, John, al. atte Wode, 1 n.
Berden, Essex, prior of, 121/22 n.
Berelay, *see* Beverley.
Bereley, *see* Briarley.
Bergen-op-Zoom (Bergghen, Barow, Barowgh, Barrowe), 14/9; 49/11; 77/4; 138/5; 151/49 & n.; 154/22; 168/3; 238/26; Cold Mart at, 3/4 n.; 34/11; 37/5; 70/12; 72/9; 111/23 n.; 176/11; 204/34; 205/14, 28; 212/92; 237/20; 239/25; 240/32; Passe Mart at, 3/4 n.; 23/9; 49 n.; 152/15, 25; 155/8; 156/25; 160/33; 176/12; 216/12, 15; 218/48–50.
Bermondsey (Barmessay), 15/8 & n.
Bernarde, Thomas, 228/4.
Berwick, Essex (Barwyke, Berwyke, Berweke), 95/20; 134/29; 168/25; priest of, 19/23.
Berwick, Northumb., 178/14 n.
Best, Nicholas, xxv; 231 & n.
Besten, Robert, 29/14.
Bettson, Thomas, 131/44; 132/7; 133/67; 220/37 & n.
Bèvres, Seigneur de (Bewrez), 62/8 & n.
Bietremeulx, 54/17.
Binche (Bynus), 109/52.
Bingham, Robert (Byngam, Byngham) 140/6 & n.; 208/44.
Blakham, Thomas (Blacham, Blakeham), 16/18 & n., 21; 59/2 n.
Bland, Thomas, of Boston, 215/59.
Blehom, Thomas, 59/2 & n. (*see also* Blakham).
Blunden, Walter, xiii n. 2.
Bolle, John, 165/36–7 n.
Bond(e)man, William, 29/11; 32/3; 76/10; 103/16; 105/21; 170/59–60; 171/4, 6; 176/9.
Bongay, 114/15.
Bordeaux, xx; 226/17 n.; 231 n.
Bordon, Laryns, shipman, 104/5.
Borgan, Thomas, *see* Burgane.
Borgayne, Borgen, *see* Burgundy.

Borgesse, John, of Lille (Borsse), 26/5 & n.
Bornell, *see* Burnell.
Borwell, Thomas, 31/36 n.
— William (Browell, Burwell), xix; 15 & n.; 31/36 n., 102/13, 16; 117/37; 133/19.
Boshope, 231/7.
Boston, 103/15, 18; 203/16; 204/26, 47; 215/59.
Botrell (Bottrell, Botreell, Botterell), 140/9 ff. & n.; 142/10 ff., 15 n.; 185/17 ff. & n.; 188/6; wife of, 188/8.
Botton, (?William), 19/46 & n., 49.
Boulogne (Bol(l)en), 99/2, 10; 104/49.
Bourgneuf, Bay of, xx.
Bourgogne, Philippe de, *see* Bèvres.
Bowell, Richard, xii; 88/6 & n.
Bowser, Richard (Bovser, Bowcer, Bourghchier), 238/9 & n.; 239/8.
Boys, Leonard (?Bowes), 83/17 & n.
Brabant (Brabon, Brabond, Braband), 183/13; 191/10; 225/11; 240/16; 241/22; 242/9.
Bradford, Robert, 123/14 n.
Brandon, Charles, 43/15 n.
—, William (Brarddon), 25/27 n.; 43/15 & n., 127/14 n.; 133/4, 10, 38; 134/30; 136/10 ff.; wife of, 43/15 n.
— — Sir, 43/15 n.
— — the younger, 43/15 n.
Brasier, Harry (Brazer), 83/15 n.
Brekellyssay, *see* Brightlingsea.
Bret(t)en, William, 87/8 & n.; 124/20; 147/11; 149/24; 151/15; 165/13, 51, 61.
Bretts Place, Aveley (Brettys, Bryt(t)ys, Byrttys), xviii; xxi & n. 1; 52/2; 53/27; 55/43; 56/25; 96/20; 107/27; 116/14; 147/26; 151/13; 175/13 n.; 197/10.
Briarley, William (Brerel(e)y, Bereley, Bryerley, Bryarley, Breleay), 143/4 & n.; 144/3–5; 145/3 & n., 9; 211/37; wife of, 145/3 n.; letter from: 143/4 n.
Brightlingsea (Bryckyllsaye, Brekellyssay), ship of, 82/12; 104/32.
Bristol, Nicholas (Brystall), 135 n.; 200/10, 15.
Brittany, 205/48–57; 206/31 & n., 33.
Browell *see* Borwell.

Browmer, 55/23.

Brown, Christopher (Brvn), 8/14 & n.; 168/21; 204/60.

— Hugh (Brone), 50/14 & n.; 52/15.

— Robert (Brone), ship's purser, 122/6.

Bruges (Brege(s), Bregys, Bryg(g)ys, Byrgesse, Brogys, Brugys), xx; xxii; 12/18; 24/7; 25/5; 27/15; 31/20; 64/5; 85/6, 8; 87 n.; 93/16; 114/8, 26; 119/11; 120/4; 121/8; 123/4; 125/19; 133/20–1 & n.; 134/20; 140/4; 141/23; 142/22; 150/11; 152/13; 154/8, 12; 165/85; 169/23; 179/17; 183/12; 186/10 ff.; 189/7; 191/14–19; 205/11, 25, 42; 206/17, 34, 37, 61; 207/49; 209/40 ff.; 210/7; 211/18 ff., 26; 212/28, 34; 215/56; 220/14; 225/6, 10, 16; 226/16; 232 n.; 233/8; 235/15, 19; 236/30; 240/9 ff.; 45 ff.; 241/7 ff.; 242/4; 243/21 ff.; 26 n.; Burse of, 234/16 & n.; marts at, 3/4 n.; 151/12–13 & n.; 154/12; 155/8; satin of, 161/23; 'Scapys Claw' (Scape ys Clawe, Shepys Clawe, Skapslaw), 115/45 & n.; 189/7–8 n.; 227/8 n.; 'Star', 64/24; 65 n.; 65/3; 97/2; 170/59; streets in, 97/2 & n.; Wytt of, 241/34–5 n.

Bruyn, Elizabeth, 43/15 n.

Bryan, Harry, xv; 135 n., 146/7; 157/9; 161 n.; 161/2–3 n., 168/13 n.; 169/25; 170/62; 200/21. Letter from: 135.

Buckingham, Henry Stafford, Duke of, 161/15; 200/3 n.

Bumpsted, Aveley, xxi.

Burford (Burforde), 165/23.

Burgane, Thomas (Burgan, Borgan), 23/10 & n.; 31/34 & n.; 50/3; 87/20.

Burgundy (i.e. Burgundian Netherlands), 19/35 ff.; 24/16; 109/55; 178/18; 225/9 n. See also Flanders.

— Charles, Duke of, 11/4 n., 8; 112/25 ff.; 191/8 n.; 212/52; 227/36 n.

— Margaret, Duchess of, 96/23; 109/52 & n., 57; 136/16.

— Mary, Duchess of, 19/35 n.; 150/3 & n.; 178/18; 187/21; 189/22, 26.

— Maximilian, Duke of, 19/35 n.; 22/8 n.; 59/3; 112/25 ff.; 179/21; 182/29–32; 183/12; 186/11 ff.; 197/4 n.; 207/41; 209/37 ff.; 80; 211/17–22; 212/52; 225/10; 227/28 & n., 31, 35–9; 237/11; 238/25, 33; 240/12–29, 47; 241/12, 28, 30; 242/11; 243/26 n.

— Philip, Duke of, son of Maximilian, 207/26 & n.; 213/30–1; 242/5.

— Philip the Good, Duke of, 212/51.

Burne, John, 216/7; 217/6.

Burnell, Agnes (Bornell the widow), 19/51; 57; 28/13; 40/32; 43/21; 47/48; 55/48.

Burton, Thomas, 72/15.

Burwell, see Borwell.

Busche, John, 20/23 & n.

Bushey, Herts. (Bwschay), 134/26.

Byfelde, William (Byfylde), 11/16; 39/45; 147/36; wife of, 147/37.

Byllsby, John, 206/4.

Calais (Cal(l)es, Calese, Callys, Callyes, Cal(l)eys, Caleis, Calice, Calys, Calis, Calais), xi; xiv; xx; 18/10; 20/12; 22/9 ff.; 34/9; 39/25, 35; 45/8; 55/33; 56/14; 57/12, 14; 58/14; 59/2; 61/3; 63/10; 67/17; 72/4; 75/4; 83/16; 85/8; 96/13; 104/52; 109/46; 110/14; 112/28; 115/14, 16, 21, 27 ff.; 118/7; 134/36 & n.; 165/86; 167/11; 170/43 ff.; 175/6; 177/4; 185/14 ff. & n.; 189/15, 21; 203/34; 205/49–50; 212/27; 213/44; 216/7, 17; 240/39; aldermen of, 208/36 ff.; appraisers of, 145/3 n.; bishop's court at, 85/8; council of, 115/18 n.; 201/26; 212/18; 247/31 n.; garrison of, 20/2 ff. & n.; 22/7; 24/7; 41/30 ff.; 110/14; 115/19; 160/11; 162/5, 21; 163/26 ff.; 182/15; 187/18; 202/36; 203/17; 211/41; 212/46; 215/44; 216/15; 217/37; 241/41; Lieutenant of (see also Hastings, Dynham), 90/9; 201/28; 212/17, 25 ff., 61; 213/26. 27, 35, 41; Marshal of, 51/10 n.; 108/14 n.; 115/17; 134/35; 212/17; mint at, 22/12; porter of, see Radclyff; treasurer of, 83/5 n.

— places in: East Watch House, 182/9; St. Nicholas Church, 182/10; the Pane, 29/3 & n.; le Postern 39/54 n.; Searcher's house, 115/28 & n.; Show St., 34/26 & n.; Water

Calais (cont.):
  Bailiff's house, 115/28 & n.; Staple Hall, 34/10 n., 26 n.
— Staple at: admission to, 13/4 ff.; 224/5 ff.; appraisers of, 105/8, 124/21 n.; 146/16; 205/8; clerk of, 56/28 n.; 137/4; collectors of, 25/6 & n.; 41/18; 135/16; 213/53; collectory, 66/9–10; 121/19 & n.; 156/10; constable, 213/32; 220/37 n.; court of, 109/42; 163/15 ff.; 170/15, 42; 182/23 ff.; 185/4, 11; 187/4, 15; 189/20, 30, 41; 204/12, 23; 208/36, 40; 212/16, 62; 213/29, 30, 52; 215/12; 235/42; 247/31, 36; Lieutenant of, 16/7, (letter to, 17); 22/43; 32/13; 34/32, 39/27; 40/7; 44/15; 72/7; 103/4; 115/10; 140/16; 156/4; 160/14, 30; 162/3, 7, 15, 17; 163/14; 164/4; 167/13; 170/27 ff.; 182/12; 187/14; 196/4; 205/27 n.; 208/45; 211/49; 212/26, 32, 36; 213/25; 217/50; 234/48, 50; Deputy Lieutenant, 162/17; Mayor of, 20/6; 22/19; 38/14; 52/16; 95/7; 106/3; 124/15; 160/13, 28; 185/4; 207/28, 36; 212/19–22; 219/6 & n.; 224/20; 235/43, 46; 238/18 (see also Stocker, Sir William); solicitor of, 95/7 n.; 160/29; 189/35; 205/16, 20; 234/61; treasurers of, 44/16; 135/11 n.; treasury, 66/9; 156/10; 170/32; 189/44, 215/48.
Cambrai (Cambre), 215/66.
Camden, see Chipping Campden.
Camfer (Veere), 220/49.
Canterbury, 206/31–2 n.; court of Archbishop of, 153/23–4 & n.; Archbishop's officers, 165/8 & n.
Carpenter, John, 229/17.
Carter, Richard, 223/20.
Caxton, William, xxii.
Cay, see Kay.
Cecil, see Seyseld.
Cely family (Cele, Cel(l)y, Sely(e), Selle, Seely, Sele, Sellay, Siliat, Silait), vi; x–xii; badges of, x; language of, xxii; xxiv–v.
Cely, Agnes (née Andrew), xi n. 3; xii; xv; 9/24; 16/18 ff., 37/1; 39/23, 37; 40/5, 9, 16; 43/22; 52/2; 55/18; 58/11, 19; 59/11; 70/8; 71/10; 74/30 78/28; 94/8; 108/10, 21; 110/21;

126/3; 136/44; 143/5; 147/21; 149/32; 151/19, 20 n.; 152/5; 153/27; 154/4; 165/2, 69–71; 168/10; 169/4 ff., 24; 175/6 ff., 13 n.; 180/2; 195/2; 197/9; maids of, 169/13 & n.; letter to: 59.
— Anne (née Rawson), xiii; xv; xvi; xvii; xx n. 2; 168/13 & n.; 223/29.
— Barbara, xi n. 3; xvii.
— George, ix; xi & n. 3; xiii; xiv; xvi–xvii; xxi; sued for affray, 25/25; 43/12 ff.; treasurer of staple at Calais, 44/15–16; matrimonial affairs, 117/16 ff.; 215/30 ff.; sickness, 67/2 ff.; 70/3 ff.; 73; 74/3 ff.; 170/4; 174/4; family quarrel, 108 to 111; complaints against at Calais, 161/2 ff.; 162/17–20; Staple representative, 235/42; servants of, 54/19 n.; 105/39; 134/35; 142 n.; 144/11 (see also Best, Hayn, Kay, Paddley, Parmenter); George, son of, xii and n. 4; xvi & n. 5; other children of, xiv & n. 5; 117/26; 141/35–7; 142/28; 181/8–11; 188/3–6. Letters from: 4, 22, 41, 45, 46, 92, 93, 105, 109, 112, 124, 173, 178, 190, 231, 247; memoranda by: 49, 151, 157, 196, 200.
— Isabel, xvii–xviii.
— John, xi & n. 1; xxiv; 9/25; 20/26; 31/27; 39/10, 13; 43/16 n.; 67/12; 92/8; 96/3; 105/44; 122/8; 195/8; 197/6; John, son of, xi n. 1; sister of, 88/6 n., 8; 100/2 ff. & nn.; 101/3 ff. Letters from: 88, 100, 101.
— Margaret, xvii; xviii n. 1.
— Margery, viii; xv–xvii; 214/43; 215/38 & n., 45; 222 n.; 223/9 ff. & n.; 224/25; 228/25; 230/2; 233/2, 12, 22. Letter from: 222.
— Richard, senior, x; xi; xii; xiii; xviii n. 2; xxi; 4/5; 40/13; 47/10, 33, 34; 55/7, 11, 22; 74/30; 84/13; 88/6 ff.; 94/8; 95/29; 108/12 ff.; 110/11 ff.; 117/23 ff.; 118/8; 127/12; 133/4, 22, 24; 136/9; 141/4; 143/14–15, 20; 147/20 n.; 23, 26 n.; 165/7; 175/10, 13 n.; 195/7 & n.; 219/3; apprentice of, see Fulborn. Letters from: 2, 11, 12, 13, 16, 17, 20, 23, 24, 26, 27, 30, 31, 36, 37, 38, 48, 50, 52, 53, 56, 59, 67, 73, 79, 80, 85, 87, 90, 98, 104, 106, 107, 116, 122.

— — junior, viii; x; xii; xiii; xiv–xv;
xvi–xvii; xx; xxi; xxiii; xxiv–v; 15/
16; 27/9; 38/31; 39/21; 41/41; 49/2;
52/3, 18; 58/6; 61/6; 70/8; 85/3;
87/13, 22; 88/10; 90/10; 94/10;
98/8; 102/5; 104/45, 64; 109/64;
110/25; 123/5; 146/15; 149/22;
151/13; 152/5; 153/18; 154/5; 161/
3; 170/49, 51; 196/11; 199/4, 26;
203/28; 204/6; 208/65; 218/57;
223/26; 227/14; daughters of, xi n.
3. Letters from: 8, 19, 25, 32, 34, 43,
47, 55, 71, 78, 81, 83, 84, 86, 91,
95, 96, 108, 111, 113, 114, 117, 118,
119, 120, 121, 122/20–5, 126, 127,
133, 134, 136, 137, 146, 147, 148,
150, 165, 168, 169, 174, 175, 193,
195, 197, 229, 230, 233.
— Robert, x; xi; xii–xiv; xxiv; 4/23;
5/21; 6/2; 11/13; 13/3; 19/43 ff.;
25/25; 32/6 ff.; 34/22; 39/9, 40;
47/5 ff.; 55/7; 58/22 ff.; 83/12; 85/7
ff.; 86/6 ff.; 91/2; 95/22; 96/14;
108/9; 151/24; 152/5; 153/29; 154/
5; 165/3; 222 n.; 223/29; 247 n.;
grandmother of, 58/25; wife of, 2/
17; 8/25; 39/41; 47/13, 20; 58/24
(see also Harthe, Joan); apprentice of,
8/26. Letters from: 3, 15, 21, 35,
102.
— William, ix n. 3; xiv; xvi; xxiii;
xxiv–v; xxvi; 19/45; 34/4; 35/5; 37/
19; 39/ 38; 73/6, 13; 74/28; 78/7; 80/
6; 87/15; 98/8; 104/45; 105/1, 34;
106/8, 107/8, 10; 109/24 n., 27; 133/
40; 137/18; 147/8; 150/6; 154/10;
165/78; 168/11; 174/3; 180/6; 197/
22; 213/53; 228/13, 21, 26; 237/7;
241/26 n. Letters from: 77, 82, 89,
115, 128, 131, 132, 155, 156, 158, 160,
162, 163, 164, 167, 170, 176, 177,
179, 181, 182, 183, 184, 185, 186,
187, 188, 189, 190, 191, 194, 196,
198, 199, 201, 202, 203, 204–18,
220, 221, 225–7, 234–43.
Celyar, see Seller.
Chamberlain, my lord, see Hastings,
William.
Chanon, William, priest, 115/37.
Charlys, 142/25.
Chawley, John, 208/42.
Chawry, Sir Richard (Chary), xii;
133/23 & n.

Chester, Richard (Schestyr), 117/30 n.;
167/20; daughter of (?), 117/31.
Chipping Campden (Camden), 165/
15, 39.
Chipping Norton (Chepyng Nortton,
Nortten), 168/6; 170/52; 197/5.
Clare, 49 n.; 54 n.; 92/5; 105/33, 41.
Letter from: 54.
Clarke, Thomas, 154/16; 204/60–1.
Clays, servant of George Cely, 196/74.
Clays(s)on, Mauryn, of Leiden, 172/
17 & n.
Cleves, Philip of, see Monsieur
Clop(p)ton, Hugh, 220/37 & n.;
225/9 n.; 228/53.
Clyffton, John, 210/4; 211/8.
Coke, Dr. John, 225/9 n. See also
Cook(e), Koke.
Colchester, ship of, 104/27.
Coldale, R. (Coldall, Cowlda(y)ll),
55/20 & n; 74/15 ff.; 111/41; wife
of, 55/21; 60/4, 11; 74/16. Letter
from: 60.
Collyns, Christopher (Collens, Cool-
enis), 202/11 & n.; 204/38; 218/59;
246/15; wife of, 246/15.
Cologne, men of, 238/28.
Colton, Thomas (Cowlton), 96/16 &
n.; 172 n.; 235/20, 21. Letter from:
172.
Contre, see Coventry.
Cook, Antony (Coke), xviii.
Cooke, John, 227/7. See also Coke,
Koke.
Corddys, the Lord (Sire d'Esquerdes),
59 n.; 227/36, 37 & n.
Corsy, Antony, 234/23; 235/39.
Costentyne, John, shipman, 89/16.
Cotheridge, Worcs., xvii.
Cotswolds (Cotyswold, Cottyswolde,
Cottysswold Cot(t)yswould, Cot-
tysso(u)ld, Cottys(s)owlde, Cotes(s)-
owlde, Cottsowld, Cotsold), 24/12;
31/26; 37/16; 47/35; 50/18; 52/12,
13; 55/11; 67/13, 20; 83/11; 84/4; 87/
23; 90/11; 91/6; 107/23; 118/11;
122/10; 133/17; 134/13, 27; 136/7,
33; 146/10; 148/8; 149/27; 150/10;
151/14; 153/18; 165/5; 195/9; 220/
39; 223/26.
Cottyn, John, shipman, 82/15.
Coventry (Contre), 58/8.
Cowlard(e), John, 15/6 & n.; 21/11.

Crante, John, 165/16 n.
Croke, John, gent., 147/20 n.
—— — of the Temple, 147/20 & n.
Crysp(e), Richard, 53/20; 56/49.
— Thomas, 53/18–19 & n.
Cutte, John, xvii.

Dagenham, xxi.
Dalton family (Dallton, Dawlt(t)on, Daul(l)ton, Dawlltom), xxiii; 18 n.
Dalton, Joan, 228/9.
— John, xv; xxv; 22/35; 49 n.; 72/13; 117/18; 133/46; 139/6 n.; 140/6 n.; 142/8, 15 n.; 21, 145/3 n.; 146/3; 148/6; 149/17; 156/3; 162/23; 163/7; 164/3, 14; 166/2; 167/9; 176/18; 181/11; 244/2, 8, 13; father of, 117/18; mother of, xv; 117/12, 13, 19, 32; sister of, xv; 116/10 n.; 117/17 ff. Letters from: 18, 28, 44, 49, 51, 125, 139, 140, 141, 157, 180. Letter to: 244.
— Ralph, 117/12, 18.
— William, 18/15; 28/4; 34/22; 41/17 n.; 44/5, 15, 22; 64/13; 72/17; 117/11, 18; 131/9; 133/82; 139/3; 141/22, 28; 147/18; 148/5; 168/20; 170/38, 41; 179/18; 204/59; 213/33; 218/61; 226/15; 227/22; 238/23; servants of, 189/5; 227/23; 228/15. Letters from: 138, 171, 228.
Damme (Dam(e)), 202/28; 236/22 & n.
Dancourt, see Dencourt.
Dane, Sir Thomas, 121/22 & n.
Danes, 240/39.
Danyell, Hemonde, shipman (Monde Danell, Mondanyell, Mwndanyell), 98/15 & n.; 104/3; 113/7; 119 fn.
— John, shipman, 82/4, 11; 130/4; 131/29; 133/73.
Dartford (Darteford, Derford), 123/2; 136/11.
Dartmouth, 141/37 n.
Dave, John (Dawe, Dawy), 115/15 & n.; 220/44 ff.; 221/24.
Dawe, Thomas, 121/22 n.
Deale, John, 239/19.
Debayle, see Vallodolid.
De Bloke, Jacob (Van den Bloke), 56/37 & n.
De Bott, John, of Bergen-op-Zoom, 196/75.

Decason(n), Benyngne, 234/8, 21; 235/36.
Decastron, Deago, 235/8.
De Cisneros, Albaro (De Sysseneros; Alfonso, Allvard, Allward, Alverd), 231/1 & n., 9; 234/40, 42.
Dee, John (Dye), 227/16 & n.; 232/5.
Deffrey, Adrian (Andryan, Atryan), 189/7 & n.; 227/8 & n.
De La Marck, Guillaume, 191/8 n.
De La Pole, Edmond, 31/14 n.
— John, Earl of Lincoln, 228/26 n.
Delft (Delff(e), Dellff(e), Dellfe, Deffe), 41/40; 44/3; 141/10; 167/5; 172/14; 176/10; 189/24; 208/6; 209/67; 212/78; 234/33.
Delopys, John, of Bruges (Delopis, Delowp(p)ys, Delowppis, Lowppys), xx; 26/5; 31/7; 41/7; 157/10; 201/10 ff. & n.; 202/15; 204/13–21; 205/29–46; 206/13–25; 207/4–20; 208/16; 209/6 ff.; 210/6, 18; 211/8, 11; 212/40; 213/8, 9; 215/8, 22, 23; 217/9, 17, 21, 22 n.; 218/7 ff., 54; 220/8 ff., 26; 221/6 ff.; 225/21; 231/1 n.; 234/4, 25, 37; 235/47; 237/14 ff.; 238/21, 31, 48; 239/18; 241/6, 39, 44; 243/22; servants of, see Deale, Wyllykyn.
De May, Collard (De Man), 133/20 n.
De Moll, Clays (Demowll), 133/87–8 & n.
Demorres, Harry (Demorys, Demorrs), 78/11; 79/2 ff.; 80/18; 81/18.
Dencourt (Danko(w)rt, Deyncourt), 43/15 n., 16 & n., 17.
— Robert (Dancourt), 43/16 n.
Deram, John, 208/44–5.
Derby (Darbey), 223/20; 228/11.
Derford, see Dartford.
Derlyngton, William, 2/13.
Deryckson, Deryck, of Leiden, 214/32.
Descermer, John, of Ghent (De Sclermer, Descyrmyr, De Schermere), 36/2; 87/4; 90/4; 92/24 n.; 93/5.
De Selonder, John, of Mechlin (Delonder, Deselonder), 220/21–2; 221/11, 43, 54.
De Sore, Gomers (Desors, Gomez de Soria), 237/23 & n.; 241/40.
D'Esquerdes, see Corddys.
Des(s)all, Romenett, 208/43, 56.

Desuyr, Gabryell, of Genoa (Desurle), 234/22; 235/37.
Donstal, Master (Sir Richard Tunstall), 212/17 & n.
Doo, Claysse, of Leiden, 214/33.
— John, of Delft, 234/33.
Dorney, see Tournai.
Dorset, Thomas Grey, Marquis of, 185/14 n.
Dover (Dowyr, Dower, Douer, Douyr), 99/5; 133/30; 158/12; 171/10–11 n.; 174/7; 175/19; 176/6; 198/20; 209/52, 54; 211/31; 214/24; 215/63.
Downs, The, 39/3; 205/56.
Drynklow, William, 228/20.
Dudley, John (Dodlay), 230/2 & n.
Dugell, the Lord (Jacob van Dudzeele), 243/21 & n.
Dumfries (Donfryss), 178/14 n., 16.
Dunkirk (Donkyrk(e), Donckyrcke, Dunckyrke), 62 n.; 209/55; 211/26, 36; 235/27; 237/8.
Dyars, John, 29/12.
Dycons, John, Letter from: 1.
Dye, see Dee.
Dynham, John, Lord (Dennam), 136/34–5 n.; 201/28; 211/29; 212/17.

East parts, the (? of the Netherlands), 237/17.
Easterlings, 238/28.
Ede, William, 41/17 n.
Edinburgh, 178/14 n.
Edward, John, 185/14 n.
Egge, Roger, mason, 195/7 n.
Ekyn(g)ton, John, 29/12; 142/15 & n.
Elderbecke, John (Eldurbek, Eldyrbecke, Elderbek, Ellyrbek), 105/20 & n.; 142/15 & n.; 244/2. Letter from: 246.
Elles, brick seller, 233/21.
Eltham (Eltam, Helttame), 108/5 & n.; 150/9.
Ely, John Morton, Bishop of, 200/3 & n.
Em, 169/13–16.
England, kings of:
Edward IV, 108/5; 109/62 ff.; 112/29; 114/24, 27, 41; 117/43; 133/8; 143/7; 147/14, 28 ff.; 150/9; 160/15, 21 ff.; 163/13 ff.; 165/48, 84; 171/10 n., 12, 13; 176/6;

178/11–12; 185/5; 197/10; 205/50–1 n.; 219/6 n.; 246 n.; wife of, 150/9; Bridget, dau. of, 108/7 & n.; Elizabeth, dau. of, 98/9 n.; Mary, dau. of, 169/22 & n.; 178/17; Edward, son of, 150/9 (also Edward V); Richard, son of, 136/41 n.; 200/5 & n.
Edward V, 200/4, 5 n.
Richard III (see also Gloucester, Duke of), xvi, 43/15 n.; 103 n.; 200 nn.; 202/34 n.; 206/30 & n.; 207/25, 29 ff.; 221/28; 224 n.; 225/9; 227/29 ff.; John, son of, 245 n.
Henry VII, 43/15 n.; 240/27.
king's council, 20/7; 22/7; 38/15; 41/29; 111/34; 133/7 n.; 134/22; 162/5, 8; 182/14; 187/16; 197/11; 247/36–8.
Essex (Esexkys, Esex, Hes(s)ex, Hesext), 25/20; 52/2; 55/20, 25; 58/10, 15, 16, 20; 94/9; 108/10, 20; 147/22 ff.; 148/16; 151/13; 169/20; 193/12; 197/20; 233/12; Cely property in, xvi; xxi; 147/22 ff.; Hospitallers' property in, 19/18 nn.; 25/20 n.; 52/4 n.; royal forest of, 133/7 n.; escheator of, 147/21, 32.
Essex, Henry Bourchier, Earl of, 134/27 n., 28 & n., 29; 136/28 & n.; 137/11, 15.
Este, Friar, 117/16.
Eston, John, 211/27.
— William, 3/3, 6; 47/19; 67/8.
Eton, John, 100/17.
Et(t)well, John, 236/20; 239/16.
Eueryngham, Sir Thomas, 115/18 & n.
Ewen, Robert, shipman (Hewan), 131/44; 132/4; 133/65.
Eyryk, Robert (Eryke, Hereke, Heryke, Heryck(e)), xi n. 3; 47/37 & n.; 53/24; 55/39; 58/33; 146/6; 151/8; 153/12; 155/7; 160/9; 165/76; 175/3, 6, 18; 197/16; 199/6; daughter of, xi n. 3; servant of, 216/4. Letters from: 152, 154.
Eystryge (Austria), Duke of, see Burgundy, Maximilian, Duke of.

Fawkener, Watkin (Fawkyner, Faukenar), 134/26; 136/32; 137/19; 169/17; 174/8.

Fawkener, William (Fawkenar), 71/14; 74/22, 24, 27; 75/3 ff. & n.; 81/6, 9.

Feders(s)ton, William (Fedyrston, Fetherston), 115/15 & n., 23.

Felde, John, xii; 88/6 n.

Fethyan, William (Fythian, Fedyan, Fidyan, Fydian), 88/6 n., 12 & n., 15, 18; 100/17, 19; 208/44, 56.

Flanders (Flawndyr(y)s, Flaunder(e)s, Flavndyrsse, Flemders), 22/9 ff.; 36/14; 37/11–12; 38/8 ff.; 41/28; 142/9; 206/25 ff.; 207/22, 44, 53; 208/31; 209/27, 37; 211/22 ff.; 212/31, 49 ff.; 213/27; 215/11, 27; 218/47, 50; 220/43; 221/23, 26–30; 225/14; 235/16, 24 ff.; 237/6–11; 238/12, 16, 24 ff., 46; 239/17; 240/8 ff., 45 ff.; 242/10; 243/18; council of, 207/27, 38; 212/63; 213/31, 36; Flemish pirates, 47/14; 198/15.

Flemyng, Robert, 134/9; 137/5.

Flewelen, John, 238/5 & n., 239/6.

Florde, 196/72.

Florence, merchants of, 78/12 n.; 114/27.

Flushing (Flyssyng), 220/49.

Fogge, John, 43/15 n.

*Formularium Instrumentorum*, 244/10 & n.

Forner, John, 78/10; 79/1; 80/18.

Fowey, 115/15 n.

Fowlle, John, 115/37.

France (Fraunce, Frauns, Franse, Frawnce), 32/15–16; 47/14; 98/9; 102/6; 104/51; 107/17; 109/54 ff.; 111/32; 115/14 ff.; 148/15; 149/29; 168/12; 169/23, 24; 171/10–11 n.; 177/5 ff.; 179/22; 182/27–9; 183/14; 186/15, 18, 20; 191/7, 11; 205/48–57; 209/54; 211/25, 32 ff.; 214/19, 21; 215/63; 236/31; 241/19; Louis XI of, 11/5, 9; 59/4; 98/9 n.; 109/56; 112/31; 149/29 n.; 191/8 n.; Charles VIII of, 98/9 n.; 207/41 n.; 241/19 & n.; Regent of, 207/41 & n.

Francke, Giles, 227/45.

— Harry, 217/38, 40–1.

— Jois, of Mechlin (Franke), 18/7; 41/8.

Frost, Walter, xvii.

Froste, John, forester, 133/10.

Fulborn, Thomas (Folbord, Folborn(e)), 13/4, 5; 25/21 & n., 26.

Fulbourne, Thomas, gent., 25/21 n.

Furnival's Inn (Fornyngwhallys In), 99/9 n.; 133/41 & n.

Fyz John (?Robert Radclyff), 143/4 n.

Gaines, Essex, xxi.

Garnett, John, soldier, 217/36–7, 43.

Gascon wine, 201/25; 203/31, 33; 215/54.

Genoa (Gean), 147/13; Genoese in London, 234/22; 235/37.

'Gentleman, the', 25/27 & n.; 133/35 & n.; 169/20.

Geoys, etc., *see* Parmenter.

Geteryng, *see* Kettering.

Ghent (Gent, Gawnt, Gaunt(e), Gante), 36/2; 90/4; 93/5, 16; 133/87–8 n.; 163/41; 169/23; 186/12 ff.; 191/14–19; 206/38; 207/26–7 n.; 209/47; 211/19; 212/63, 65; 215/13; 236/29–30; 237/10; 238/25, 27; 240/24, 46; 241/18, 25, 47; 242/1 ff.

Gladman, servant to Sir John Weston, 55/31, 42; 95/19.

Gloucester, Richard Duke of (Gloceter, Glosetter), 171/11 & n.; 178/14 n.; 200/4–5 & n. *See also* England, Kings of.

Golbrond, servant of Robert Radclyff, 65/10.

Goldson, John, letter from: 75.

Good, Andrew (Goodys), 131/40; 133/61.

— Robert (Robyn), 104/42; 105/51; 106/7; 107/13; 108/12; 109/9, 24 n.; 111/7. Letter from: 94.

Gowldsmith, William, 34/17 & n.

Grace, mercer, 2/6.

Graf(f)ton, Master, 205/27 & n.; 220/37.

Granger, Thomas (Graunger, Grawng, Graynger, Grayng(e)ar), 24/4 & n., 7; 25/4; 39/45; 56/19; 63/2; 70/25; 81/7; 91/30; 92 n.; 105 n.; 124/8; 128/6; 131/22; 133/59; 204/52–3; 206/10; 235/23; 243/4; wife of, 64/14; 215/33 (?). Letter from: 64. Letters to: 82, 89, 92, 105, 113.

Grantham, Simon, 29/14.

Gravelines (Grauenyng(e), Graveny⟨n⟩g, Grawenyng, Gravenenge), 177/8, 15; 205/27; 211/27; 238/31, 32; Lieutenant of, 62/8; 136/29 & n.

Gravesend (Grauys End), 96/22.
Grene, Richard, shipman, 89/12.
Gresford, 19/27 & n.
Grey, William, Bishop of Ely, 200 n.
Guinegate, 59 n.
Guines (Gynys, Gynese, Guysnes, Guynesse), 15/11; 65/2 n.; 171/8; 243/9; 245/9; Lieutenant of, 245 n.
Gybson, Stephen, 213/48.
Gyesbryght, see Van Wynsbarge.
Gyesbryghtson, Jacob(b), of Delft, 204/36; 212/77; 234/33.

Halwell, Sir John (Haleghwell), xvi.
Hamton, see Southampton.
Hans (?), Master, 242/20.
Harmanson, Jacob, 204/37.
Harry, George Cely's boy, 112/38.
Harthe, Joan, xiii; 83/3; 85/9 ff.; 86/6 ff.
Hastings, Sir Ralph (Hastyngys), 199/16 ff. & n.; 227/15; 232 n.; 245 n. Letters from: 232, 245.
— William, Lord (my lord chamberlain, my lord lieutenant, my lord), 114/28 & n., 42; 115/22, 39; 138/2; 146/8; 158/12; 159 n.; 160/3, 20; 162/4, 16, 18; 171/7, 9; 176/7; 177/9, 10, 11; 182/14; 183/8; 185/14 n.; 187/16; 188/10; 189/15; 190/8–10; 196/15; 198/19; 200/2 & n.; household of, 196/16.
Hatfeld, John, 135/11 & n.
Hawelay, see Aveley.
Hawes, Andrew (Hawesse), 125/28; 139/6 & n.; 140/6–7 & n.
Hawllus, John, shipman, 89/20.
Hayn(e) (Hyne, Hane, Han(y)kyn), 114/20, 51; 119/4, 6; 120/5; 142/33; 155/4; 221/5, 43.
Haynys, Richard, 53/13 & n.; 14, 16.
Hayward, Thomas (Heywarde), 170/56; 171/2, 5.
Helttame, see Eltham.
Henley, poor, 161/2–3 n.; 162/19; 'old Henley's widow', 213/20; 217/34–5, 39, 44–5.
— young, 217/38, 39.
Henryck(e)son, Gyesbryght, of Delft, 212/77; 213/12.
Hereke, etc., see Eyryk.
Her(r)on, Richard, 129/11 ff. & n.
Hew, see Paddley.

Hewson, John Cleys (Heuson), 49 n., 49/3.
Higham Ferrers, Northants. (Hyham Ferrys), 57/27.
Hobard, see Hubberd.
Holland (Hollond(e), Holond, Holand), 150/7; 172/5; 226/16; 228/2; 241/27; 242/12; Hollanders, 34/42; 70/11; 77/5; 124/10; 125/12; 141/9; 142/19; 156/11; 167/4; 194/6; 197/4; 205/4 n.; 211/14.
Hont, Nicholas, 196/73 & n.
Horne, Thomas, shipman, 104/12.
Horses: Bale, Bawll, 83/18 & n.; 87/24; Bawlser 47/45 & n.; Bayard(e), Bayerd, 142/26; 156/16; 158/7; 197/18; Great Bayard, 163/12; Great Sorell, 179/14, 181/4; Little Bayard, 158/11; Py I, 44/9; 108/14; Py II, 126/5; 133/38; 137/18; 168/22.
Hos(s)yer, John (Hosyar), 53/2 & n.
Houghton, John, vicar of Aveley, 19/22 n.; 43/15 n., 17 & n.
Howard, John, Lord, 200/7 & n.
Hubbard, John, 243/8.
Hubberd, Robert (Hobard), 186/9; 235/20.
Hull (Holl), ship of, 131/40; 133/61.
Hussy, Gilbert, 65/2 & n.
Hyll, William, 142/15; 202/10; 216/12.

Ilam, Master (Ilom, Ylam), 100/7 & n.
Iland, William, 238/52; 239/11.
Ipswich (Ypyswyche, Ypysweche), 182/18; 183/5; 187/5.

Jacob, Master, the Physician, 77/22.
Jacobson, Deryck, of Delft, 212/78.
Jacoby, John (Jacope, Jakopy), 78/12 & n., 14, 17.
James, servant of Robert Stocker, 211/27.
Jarfford, James, 213/48; 235/16.
Jocobson, Jacob Yong, 72/11.
John, Sir, priest, 85/15; 175/13.
'Johnson Letters', vii; 30/6 n.; 165/16 n.; 205/4 n.
Johnson, Arnold, of Antwerp, 125/10.
— Derycke, of Delft, 209/67.
— John, of Delft, 176/10.
— Peter, of Delft (Johnsun), 44/3; 77/7.

Jon, Harry, 124/21.
Joye, Piers, 202/9 ff. & n.; 204/39.

Kay, John (Cay), 39/51 & n.; 92/35; 105/26, 38; 134/3, 31 ff.; 136/5; 137/3.
Kebyll, Harry, 210/5 & n.
Kendall, Sir John, Turcopolier of the Hospitallers, 118/6 & n.
Kenett, William, of Bruges (Kynett), 97/6 & n.; 206/41, 48, 60; 209/32.
Kent, 55/22, 25; 133/5.
Kesten, Thomas (Kesteyn, Kestven, Kesteven, Kestevyn), xi; 1/3; 2/5,10; 4/8, 9, 11, 28; 5/7 & n., 9; 7/8 ff.; 8/8; 9 passim; 11/10 ff.; 38/35 ff.; 39/44; 41/44 ff.; 44/6; 46/5 ff.; 48/2 ff. & n.; 69/4; 92/17; 105/12; 143/4 n.; 145/3 n.; 147/6; 219 nn.; wife of, 6/4, 8, 9; 39/44; 76/8; children of, 76/8; 219/59; maid of, 76/8. Letters from: 6, 76, 143, 144, 145, 219. Letter to: 143 note.
Kesteven, Lincs. (Kesten), 212/21 n.; wool from, 205/4.
Kettering, Northants. (Geteryng), 2/10 & n.
Kettleby, John (Ketylby), xvii.
King, Oliver, 114/23 n.
King's Lynn, see Lynn.
King's Sutton, Northants. (Kyngys Sotton), 168/6.
Kirkeby, Nicholas (Kerkebe), 222/17 & n.
Knyght, Edmond, 240/31.
— Robert, 29/17.
Knyveton, Nicholas (Kneveton, Knyfton, Kneffton), 159 n. Letter from: 159.
— — senior, 159 n.
Koke, Michael, of York, 165/69; wife of, 165/70–4.
Kynton, Roger, 211/5.

Laete, Jasper, 228/19 n.
— John, 228/19 & n.
Lambe, John, woolpacker, 43/6, 19.
Lambryghtson, Laurans, 72/11.
Langham, 166/10.
Langton, Thomas, 98/9 n.
Lasse, 150/14.
Laurensson, Garrad, of Leiden, 214/32–3.

Lausson, Harry, shipman (Lawson), 131/16; 133/51.
Layne, Thomas, 29/15.
Laythe, see Leiden.
Legayneard, Robert, 217/28.
Leicester (Leycetter, Leyce(s)ter, Laysetter), xiv; 28/8, 11; 116/9; 117/10, 12; 133/83; 170/9 n.; 180/4; 211/48; 228/10; Newarke College, xv; Wyggeston's Hospital, 28/5 n.
Leiden (Layth(e)), 30/5–6 n.; 105/46; 149/6; 167/4; 172/16, 17; 189/24; 214/5, 34; 215/60.
Leigh-on-Sea, Essex (Lee), 16 n.
Lemster, William, 228/15.
Lemyngton, John, 170/9 & n.
— Ralph (Lemengton), 51/10 & n.; 72 n.; 170/10; 204/59; 213/10, 24. Letter from: 72.
Lenawllys, Edward (Lenallys), 91/23 & n.
Levynge, servant of George Cely, 197/20 & n.
Lewelen, see Flewelen.
Lewke, see Liège.
Leyche, John, shipman, 82/26.
Liège (Lewke, Luke), 191/8, 9, 11; Bishop of, 191/8 & n.; 240/16.
Lille (Lyell, Ryssyll), 26/5 & n.; 207/43.
Limrick, Thomas (Lymryke, Lymeryke, Lemryke, Lemeryke), 165/27 ff.; dau. of, 165/26 ff. & n.; wife of, 165/27–8.
Lincoln, Bishop of, see Russell; Earl of, see De La Pole.
Lokyn(g)ton, John, shipman, 84/6, 9; 85/1; 128/4; 131/20; 133/56.
Lombards, 56/7, 10; 107/24 & n.; 109/46; 119/8 ff.; 121/8, 12; 147/12 & n.; 218/42; 234/8; 235/10.
London: defence of, 114/39; exchanges at, 1/5; 2/7, etc.; 12/17; 50/5; 52/8, 10; 53/2 ff.; 165/86; plague at, 38/33; 40/24; 50/24; 52/5; 56/30; 58/20 ff.; 233/13; wool at, 104/37; 109/48; wool fleets from, 20/13; 21/6, etc.; mayor and crafts of, 149/31; recorder of, xviii; 20/8; sergeant of City of, 147/25 n.; sheriff of, 133/21 ff.; 'Crosse Keye', 235/18; Eastcheap (Eschepe), 230/3, Fleet prison, 43/16; Leadenhall

(Ledehalle), 52/14; Lombard St., 234/24; Mark Lane (Marke Layn(e), Marcke Layne, Martt(e) Lane, Mart(e) Lan(e)), xiii; xvi; 22/50, etc.; 58/26; Mincing Lane, xvi; Old Fish St. (Howlde Fysche Strette), 133/85; Paul's Cross, 15/17 & n.; Paul's Wharf (Pollus Wharffe), 246/4–5; Petty Wales (Pety Walys), 242/20; St. Audoen, Newgate, 123/14 n.; St. Lawrence, Poultney (Saynt Laurence Pouteny), 143/10 & n.; St. Olave's, Hart St. (Sent Tolowys scryssche), x n. 2; xiv & n. 3; xviii & n. 2; 5/21; 195/7 n.; rector of, 25/21 n.; Smithfield (Smethe Fellde), 193/4; the Temple, 147/20; the Tower, 114/29; 147/39, 171/10 n., 13; 197/10; 200/5 n.; Tower Hill, 219/10; Tower mint, 52/8 & n.; 78/102.

Lont(t)elay, John (Lontlay, Lunt-(e)ley, Luntlay, Lottlay), 83/20 & n.; 91/24; 136/9; 150/14.

Lord, my, see Hastings; Weston.

Loughborough, Leics., 51/10 n.

Louvain (Loven), 161/12.

Lowick, Northants. (Lowyke), 57/26.

Loye, Saint, 52/23 & n.

Lynd, William, of Northampton, 131/13–14 & n.

Lynn, King's (Lyn(n)e), 31/36 & n.; 103/15, 17.

Macro Plays, 238/34–5 n.

Maidstone (Mayd(e)ston), 131/15; 133/51.

Maldon, 134/27 n.

Malines (Mechelen, Meclyn, Meke-lyn, Mekyllyn), 4/11; 13/11; 36/7; 41/8; 92/24; 107/6; 220/22; 221/54; groats of, 238/58 & n.

Malling, ship of (Mallyng), 104/17 & n.

Mallins, Little Thurrock (Malyns), xxi; 147/26 & n., 28; 150/15.

Manhall, manor of, xxi.

Maningtree (?Meandry), 25/20 n.

Margaret, my Lady, see Burgundy, Margaret Duchess of.

Margery the pudding-maker, 117/25–6 n.; 141/36; 142/28; 181/8 & n.; 188/3.

Markeson, John, shipman, 113/3.

Marshall, Thomas, 72/15.

Martson, Peter, 72/11.

Marttyson, John, of Leiden, 167/9.

Maryett, John, shipman (Marrett), 82/24, 25.

Marynar(e), see Molenars.

Maryon, William, xi & n. 3; xvi; xx; xxii; xxiv; xxv; 7 passim; 8 passim; 11/13; 25/21 n.; 33 n.; 34/2, 16; 37/4; 38/2, 22, 32; 44/6; 46/7; 47/15; 52/3; 55/6; 67/3; 74/31; 83/4; 85/19; 91/25; 92/8; 98/17; 104/63; 105/5, 44; 108/9, 11; 109/11, 40; 110/17 n.; 111/6 ff., 12, 29; 117/41; 125/15; 131/33; 133/79; 152/6, 8; 154/6; 155/11; 160/6; 165/3; 172 n.; 179/6; 203/22; 204/7, 32; 205/6, 13; 229/3–4. Letters from: 5, 9, 39, 40, 58, 69, 70, 110, 130, 149, 151, 153, 223.

Mathew, John, 100/9 ff.; 101/3 ff.

Maudyslay, 25/27 & n.

Maximilian, see Burgundy.

Mayhew, hackney man, 199/3; 203/25.

'Meandry', 25/20 & n.

Meg (a hawk) (Mege, Meyge, Mehyg), 71/14, 18; 74/7; 134/25.

Melchbourne, Beds. (Melcheburne), 134/25.

Mell, John, 56/50.

Mercers' Company, 165/84–91 & n.; 246 n.

Messedaw3th, Collard (Mesdowhe), 217/28–9 & n.

Meuse (Mase), 228/2.

Middelburgh (Myddellborow, Medyll-borow), 220/46; 243/25.

Midwinter, William (Mydwynt(t)er, Mydwy(n)ttyr, Mydewenter, Myd-wytter, Medwynter, Medwenter), xxiii; 67/9, 11; 85/5; 87/6; 90/12; 91/10; 122/9; 147/16; 148/10; 149/25; 165/12, 17, 23 ff.; 168/8; 170/53; 195/6; 197/7, 14; 230/9; 231/2 ff.; 233/5. Letter from: 192.

Mile End (Myll3end, Myle3eynde), 25/27; 147/39.

Miller, Thomas (Mylar, Myller, Mellere), 8/2, 6; 9/14. Letter from (?): 7.

Millwall, ship of (Myllhall, Mylale, Myllalle, Myhall, Milhawe), 89/20 & n.; 104/22.

Molenars, Master (Molyners, Marynar(e); ? Robert Molyneux), 43/16 n.; 147/25 & n., 32; 153/25 & n.
Mondedanyell, see Danell.
Montgomery, Sir Thomas (Mongewnbre, Mongewmbre, Mwngewmbre, Mongehowmbre), 127/12; 133/7 & n., 13; 136/14, 25; 137/13; 195/16; 225/9 n.
More, Master Lowys (Lodowic Moro), 235/10 & n., 11.
More Hall, Aveley, 19/18 n.
Moresson, Gyesbryght, of Leiden, 214/34.
Morton, John, see Ely.
Mountjoy, John Blount, Lord, 245 n.
Mowbray, Lady Anne, 136/41 & n.
Moy, Loyssor (Lois Syr Moy, Lois De May), 56/53 & n.
Mvncke, Robert, shipman, 82/20.
Mvnstron, Allysaunder, of Bruges, 206/60.
Muston, William, 208/44.
Mychellson, Patrick, shipman (Mechelson), 89/7; 104/7.
Myhell, Alison (Myhyll), 117/45; 127/17.

Naples (Napwllys, Napullus), 147/41; 178/5, 8.
Narsbye, John, 202/34 n.; 204/45 & n.
Nesseffylde, John (Nessefeld), 115/18 & n.
Newcastle, 114/42; 219/8-9 n.
New Hythe, Kent, ship of, 131/44; 132/3; 133/65.
Newnham Bridge, Calais, 181/5 n.
Nieuport (Newportt(e)), 212/29, 33, 35; 242/9.
Noneley, Richard, 95/7 n.
— Thomas, 213/52.
Normandy, canvas of, 67/16; 136/39.
Northampton (Northehamton), 117/9; 131/14 & n.; 244 n.
Northamptonshire (Norhamtonscheyr), 57/27.
Northleach, Glos. (Northelacche, Nortlacht, Norla(y)che, Norlayge, Norlagh, Norlay), 53/13; 67/9, 12; 85/4; 87/6, 14; 91/14-15; 122/9; 147/15; 149/24; 151/17; 165/23, 40, 51; 192/22.
Northumberland, Henry Percy, Earl of (Northomberlonde, Northehombyrlond), 171/11 & n.; 178/14 n.; 200/6 & n.
Norton, Master, surgeon, 151/20 n.
— William, draper, 172/2 & n.
Norton Mandeville, Essex, 25/20 n.
Nowell, 99/9 & n.

Ockendon, South, Essex, 25/21 n., 43/15 n.
Ollyver, Tylbott (Olowe (?), Tebott, Tybott), 226/17 & n.; 229/3 & n., 5; 237/40.
Ospringe, Kent, ship of (Ospreng), 246/14.
Ostend (Oste End, Oostendd), 198/10; 202/27; 212/31; 236/6.
Ottson, Henryck, of Leiden, 214/33.
Oudenbourg (Odenborow), 163/9.
Owerton, Thomas, 115/15.

Paddley, Hugh (Hew), 173 n.; 218/58, 60 ff.
Page, Henryc, of Leiden, 149/5.
Palmer, Gibert (Pamar, Paulmar, Paullmar), 23/11; 31/34 & n.; 50/3; 56/52; 66/5; 87/21; 114/13; 117/37.
Parker, John (Parcar), 56/19 & n.; 88/21; 176/24; 204/33.
— Richard, 204/32; 205/16, 23.
Parmenter, Joyce (Joys(s)e, Joyes, Geos, Geoos, Geyos, Geoys, Goos), 114/33 & n.; 117/39, 44; 118/4; 126/8, 15; 134/20; 139/5; 142 n.; 156/19; 158/9; 160/31; 164/13, 16; 167/12, 23; 169/7; 170/4, 7, 49, 56, 60; 171/2; 181/4, 14; 194/3, 15; 196/13, 21; 198/4, 6; 199/8, 25; 201/31; 202/24, 25, 28; 203/24, 26; 208/65; 217/4; 221/44. Letter from: 142. Letters to: 120, 126.
Pascual, Etienne, 149/29 n.
Pasmar, Richard, 19/18 & n.
Pasmer, John, 224 n. Letter from: 224.
Paston family and correspondence, vii; xxiv n. 1; 33/5 n.; 43/15 n.
Penmarcke, xx.
Peryman, woolpacker, 235/17.
Perys, John, 53/13 & n.
Petter, 111/30.
Pet(t)erson, Claysse, of Delft (Cleys), 151/30; 204/35; 208/5; 209/56, 66; 211/6; 213/7.

Pettyt, John (Petite), 165/36 & n.
—— goldsmith, 25/21 n.
Petyt, 25/21 n., 27.
Phelypp Movnsyr (Phelyppe Munsir; Philip of Cleves), 240/16 & n.; 242/5.
Phylpott, William, shipman, 82/22.
Picardy (Pecardy), 11/9.
Pilgrim's Hatch, Essex, 74/31 n.
Plumar, Robert (Plomer, Plummer), 134/27 & n.
Plumpton family and correspondence, vii; 99/9 n.; 117/6 n.
Plumpton, Edward (Plomt(t)on), 99/9 & n.; 117/6 & n., 14.
— Robert, 117/6 n.
— Sir William, 117/6 n.
Plymouth (Plemmovth), 226/18.
Pont, 237/42.
Pontessbere, Richard, 220/37 & n.
Pope, the (Sixtus IV), 129/5.
Porter, Master, see Radclyff, Robert.
Portinari, Thomas, 219/6 n.
Pottry, Jacob, of Bruges, 36/3.
Prestun, (? John), 125/25 & n.
Prowd, John (Provd), 92/31; 105/27.
Prowde, Richard, 19/12 & n., 53.
Prout, John, 219/6 & n.
— Thomas, 16 n., 17/11 (?)
Purfleet, Essex, 19/18 n.

Radclyff, Sir John, 42 n., 42/10; 65/13.
— Robert (Raddclyffe), 42 n.; 62/14 & n.; 185/15 & n.; 199/15 ff. Letters from: 42, 65. See also Fyz John.
Rainham, Essex (Raynam(e)), 19/18 n.; 55/20 n.; ships of, 82/3; 104/3; 130/3; 131/11, 29, 32; 133/48, 73; 137/9.
Ramston, 133/12; 136/21.
Randolffe (Randofe, Randowlfe), 56/28; 105/43; 137/4.
Raunsse, John, of Guines (Ranys, Rawns), 2/12; 15/11; 83/15.
Rawson, Avery (Awheray), xvii; 233/6 & n.; 237/41 (?).
— Christopher, 237/43 (?).
— Isabel, xvii.
— Richard, xv; 168/13 n.; Anne dau. of, see Cely, Anne; younger daus. of, 168/13 n.
Rayleigh, Essex (Raylay), 195/4.

Raynold(e), John (Renold), 38/28 & n.; 228/5; 235/6.
Rechirdley, William, shipman (Recherdlay), 82/13; 104/32.
Redeman, Alan, 208/43.
Redhode, Thomas (Redewhode), 32/3 & n.
Redryth, see Rotherhithe.
Reede, George, 204/5.
Rhodes (the Rodys), 114/27 & n.; 117/43; 118/6; 121/22 n.
Richard, servant of R. Eyryk, 70/17.
Rivers, Anthony Earl (Rewars, Reuerys), 114/28 & n., 31; 185/14 n.
Robardys, William, 34/24.
Robert, John, 68/3.
Robyn, see Good.
Roelandts, William, 133/20 n.
Rogers, Thomas, 123/14 n.
Romans, King of, see Burgundy, Maximilian Duke of.
Rome, 129/2; king's proctor at, 129/12.
Roo, William, 206/18.
Roosse, John (Ros(e)), 56/12, 13, 21; 57 n.; 64/4; 67/2. Letters from: 57, 61, 63.
Rotherham, Thomas, Archbishop of York, 200/2 & n.
Rotherhithe, Surrey, ship of (Redryth), 82/28.
Rotterdam, 242/12.
Roubaix (Rovbey), 207/43.
Rouen (Roon), 34/4.
Rover, Robert, 184/12.
Russell, John, Bishop of Lincoln, 200/2 n.
Rychard, Master (? Richard Nanfant or Richard Noneley), 95/7 & n.
Rygon, Edmond, xv; 215/38 n.; 222/17 n.; 243/7 n.
Ryisse, Richard, 66 n. Letter from: 66.
Ryken, factor of Joes Wranx, 14/4.
Ryssyll, see Lille.

St. John of Jerusalem, order of; prior of, 121/22 n.; 123/14 n. (and see Weston, Sir John); Lord Master of, 114/24, 25; Turcopolier of, 118/6 & n.; 121/22; priory church at Clerkenwell, 83/8 & n.; 123/11; 114/27 n.
St.-Omer (Sent Tomers, Tomors, Tomos, Thomers, Thomar, Omers),

St.-Omer (*cont.*):
109/53, 58; 136/15; 140/3; 150/4 &
n.; 177/6, 9; 182/31; 208/66;
227/39.
St.-Tricat (Senttercasse, Sentrycasse),
15/11; 243/13.
Sallford, William, 215/36.
Sambach, John (Sambage, Sambarge),
68 n. Letter from: 68.
Sandwich (Sandwych(e)), 140/5; 198/
9; 206/32 & n.; 207/24; 211/28–9 n.
Sauly, Peter, of Genoa, 234/22; 235/37.
Saunders, John, 234/70; 235/35.
Scotland (Skoteland, Scottlond), 114/
40 ff.; 171/10 ff.; 178/12–16; 183/8;
James III of, 171/10–11 n.; Scots,
115/23; 175/18; 200/1 & n.
Scott, Sir John, 51/10 n.; dau. of,
103 n.
— Lady (Skot), 51/11 & n.
Segon, William (Segeon), 144/2; 145/
10.
Seller, Philip, of Tournai (Celyar,
Selar, Sellar), 56/8; 70/28 & n.;
71/5 ff.; 73/12; 78/9, 20; 79/2, 5;
80/10, 14; 81/17, 19; wife of, 71/8;
dau. of, 78/10; factors of, 78/9–11;
80/11, 16 ff.
Sely family, skinners, xii.
Sely, Robert, fishmonger (Sele), xiii
n. 2.
Seyseld, Harry, 5/19.
Sharpe, Thomas (Scharpe), 29/15;
39/15.
Shipden, R., letter from: 244.
Ships: the king's, 115/18 n.; 147/12–
13 n.; 202/35; 204/45–6; 205/50–1
& n.; 211/44; 220/45; Anne of
London, 89/7; 104/7; Anne Cely,
xx; Antony of London, 82/
15; Antony of Myllhall, 89/20;
Battowll, 204/48; Blythe of London,
82/20; 104/5; Carvyll of Hewe,
205/50–1 & n.; 220/45; Clement of
London, 82/22; Crystover of Lon-
don, 82/26; 89/12; Crystover of
Raynam, 131/11, 31; 133/48; 137/9
(Crystowyr); Edward of Mylale,
104/22; Fortune of London, 82/24;
George of London, 5/3, 247/8;
Grase à Dew of Calais (Grace à De),
113/3, 8; John of London, 122/5;
La Clement, 204/45–6 n.; Margett

(Margaret Cely of London), xvi;
xx; 226/17 n., 18; 230/5; 231 n.;
233/23; Mary de la Towre, 147/12–
13 n.; Mary of Bryckyllsaye, 82/12;
104/32; Mary of London, 82/17;
131/6; 133/44; Mary of Malling,
104/17; Mary of Raynam, 82/3;
130/3; 131/29; 133/73; Mary of
Redryth, 82/28; Mary Grace of
London (Mary Grasse), 128/3; 131/
20; 133/56; Mary John of London,
89/16; Myhell of Hull, 131/39; 133/
61; Myss[. . .] of Ospreng. 246/14;
Nicolas of Colchester, 104/27;
Rumbold Wylliamson, 236/25;
Thomas of London, 104/12;
Thomas of Maydeston, 131/15;
133/51; Thomas of New Hythe,
131/44; 132/3; 133/65; Thomas of
Raynam, 104/3; Trinity of Eu,
205/50–1 n.
Shirewode, John, 129/11 n.
Simnel, Lambert, 228/26 n.
Sion College, xii.
Sluis (Sclewse, Sclewce), 205/49; 236/
24; 240/33, 34; 241/34.
Smethe, John, 56/36.
Smith, William, vicar of Aveley,
43/17 n.
Smythe, John, shipman, 104/27.
— William, woolpacker, 226/6 ff.;
227/50; 234/52–4; 239/5; 240/4.
Sordyvale, William, shipman (Sordy-
woll), 131/6; 133/44.
Southampton (Hamton), 147/12–13 n.;
151/15; 171/10–11 n.
Spain, merchants of, xx; 229/1–2 n.;
234/24; 235/8, 39 (*and see* De
Cisneros, Delopys, De Sore, Val-
lodolid); ships of, 208/33; 237/24.
Spencer, John (Spensar), 10 n. Letter
from: 10.
Speryng, John (Sperynge), 233/22 &
n.; 242/16, 19.
Spycer, Thomas, 243/20 & n.
Spyngyll, John, Lombard, 56/7.
Stamford, 204/60.
Stappell, Sir William, priest, 115/38.
Stawntoyn, Harold (Stawnton,
Staunton, Stanton), 114/17; 139/4;
239/25; 240/30–6. Letter from: 97.
Stevenson, Garrad, of Leiden, 214/33.
Stewen, 237/41.

Stifford, Essex, 25/21 n.; 43/15 n.

Stocker, Robert, 206/45; 211/27.

Stokar, John, 52/7.

Stoker, Sir William (Stocker), 52/15; 106/2; 160/28 & n.; 185/4; 205/16; 212/20, 21.

Stokys, Richard (Stokes), 219/6 n., 7, 13.

Stonor family and correspondence, vii; 99/9 n.; 220/37 n.

Stonor, Elizabeth, 147/20 n.; 160/28 n.

— Sir William, vii.

Strabant, Guyott, 234/6.

Stratford (? Langthorn, Essex), 58/25.

Stratford-on-Avon, 220/37 n.

Strossy, Marcus, Spaniard, 234/24; 235/39.

Stry(c)ke, William, 243/13; wife of, 243/14.

Sutton (Sotton): Temple Sutton, 19/18 n.; ?Sutton-at-Hone, 52/4 & n.

Sybson, William, 243/7 & n., 10, 13, 15.

Tabary, Waterin (Tabere, Tabre), 62 nn.; 136/29–30 n. Letter from: 62.

Talbot, Sir Humphrey (Tawlbot), 108/14 & n.

— John, Earl of Shrewsbury, 108/14 n.

Tame, John, 5/6 & n.

Tate, John (Tatte), 11/12 & n.; 38/27; 39/8, 11; 196/3; 247/22.

— Robert (Taatte), 22/43; 40/7.

Taylor, Nicholas, 240/31.

Tebott, Ty(l)bott, see Ollyver.

Tewkesbury, battle of, 199/16 n.

Thames (Temys), 8/25; 136/10.

Thérouanne (Tyrwyn, Tyrwhyne, Tyrwhenyng, Twrwyn), 59/3; 109/59; 169/23; 227/36.

Thomas, Staple carter, 64/12.

— servant of Margery Cely, 223/15.

Thornburgh, Thomas, 123 n.

Thornburght, Sir Roland, 123 n. Letter from: 123.

Thorp, John, 41/17 n.

Thundersley Park, Essex (Thondyrlay), 195/11; parker of, 195/13 ff.

Thurrock, Little, Essex, xxi; Socketts Heath, xxi.

— West, 19/18 n.

Thurrock Grays, 19/18 n.

Thwaites, Thomas (Thewhaytys), 83/6 & n.

Tomson, 55/42.

Torney, Robert (Turney), 142/15 & n.; 204/59.

Torowllde, Thomas (Torald), 43/15 & n.

Tournai (Dorney), 56/9; 70/28 n.

Trotter, Benedict (Benett), 137/6 & n.; 201/23.

Tunstall, see Donstal.

Twege, Richard (Twigge, Twge, Tewek, Tywne), 15/5 & n.; 21/12; 50/6; 52/15.

Twesylton, John (Tweselton, Twhessylton, Twiselton, Twyssullton, Twyssull), 43/19; 108/15; 126/10, 11; 156/17; 157/5; 164/12; 221/31; 227/17; 245/6.

Tymanson, Jacob, of Leiden, 149/5.

Tyrrell, Sir James, 236/28 & n.; 237/8; 240/19–23.

— Sir Thomas (Tyrryll), 127/15 n.; 133/35 n.

— — — senior, 43/15 n.

Underwode, John, shipman, 104/17.

Upminster Hall, xxi.

Utrecht, 197/4 n.; coins of, see Glossary under Huitryshe.

Vallodolid, Peter (Vayle & Delyt, Valle de Let, Bayle & Delete, Bayle & Delyt(t)e, Bayle & Delytt, Bayledelett, De Bayl(l)e, Bayle), 201/11 ff. & n.; 202/16 ff.; 204/14, 16; 205/37; 206/17; 207/5, 9, 12; 208/11, 28; 209/6 ff.; 215/6, 19, 21; 217/19, 22 & n.; 218/12, 30, 35; 221/16.

Van De Base, Jacob, 234/11, 23; 235/38.

Vanderheyden, Jan, of Mechlin (John Underhay(e), Van Underhay, Vandyrhay, Vanderhay, Wandyrhay), 4/9; 12/11; 22/33; 36/6; 87/4; 92/24 & n.; 96/10; 107/6; 124/12; 167/6–7 n. Letter from: 14.

Van de Rade, Daniel, of Bruges (Van the Rayde), 18/2; 31/4–5.

— Peter, of Bruges, 31/4.

Vandorne, Cornelius, of Bruges, 26/6; 31/7.

Van Dudzeele, Jacob (the Lordd Dugell), 243/21 & n.

Van Wynsbarge, Gysbryght, of Bruges (Van Wynesbragh, — Wenysbarge, Whennysbarge, Wehnysbarge, Wynbarow, Winbragh, Whynsbeyg, Wan Wynsbarge; Gyesbryght, Gysbreth, Gysherybyrt), 26/6 31/7–8; 109/60; 112/4; 125/4; 141/6, 30; 201/17; 204/10–21; 208/9 ff.; 209/11, 14 ff.; 210/6, 18; 211/9, 12; 212/23 ff., 66; 218/8 ff.

Veneke, John, goldsmith, 214/42.

Venetians in Bruges (Whenysyans), 114/26.

Villars, Charles (Villiers, Vellers, Wyllars), 133/85 & n.; 142/15 n.

Vlissingen, see Flushing.


Wade, Thomas, 230/5 & n.

Warbeck, Perkin, 42 n.

Warham, Robert, xvii.

Warner, William, 238/5 & n.; 239/6.

Warwick, Richard Neville, Earl of, 219/8–9 n.

Warwickshire (Warwykescher, Wharwykeschyre), 58/7; fells from, 133/76.

Watford, vicar of, 37/20; 40/24–6. Letter from: 33.

Wayte, Harry (Whayt), 32/10 & n.; 205/20.

Wellson, William, shipman, 5/3 (see also Wylson).

Wendon, John, priest, 175/13 n.

Wendy, John, 225/9 n.

Wennington, Essex, xxi.

West Country, 38/34; seamen from, 205/54.

West Ham, xvii.

Westminster (West(e)myster, Whestemynster), 25/26; 43/12–13; 111/25; 144/10.

Weston, Edmond, xv n. 1.

— Sir John (my Lord, my Lord of Sent Jonys, — Jhonys, Jonns, Sente Jhons, Sentt Johns, Sentte Johnys, Send Johnys, — Jonnys, Johnns, Sen Jonys; Movnsewr Sent Jonys), xv & n. 1; 19/18 & n.; 25/14; 37/18; 39/30; 40/16 ff.; 47/35, 36, 45; 52/3; 55/15, 27; 58/7, 9; 74/24; 78/24; 83/7; 84/20 ff.; 90/18 ff.; 94/10; 95/17; 96/22;

98/9 & n.; 99/2, 9 n.; 102/5; 104/49; 108/6, 7 n.; 109/24 n., 64, 66; 111/29, 32, 41; 114/23, 25, 27 n., 29, 52; 117/42; 118/6 ff.; 119/10; 121/3 ff., 22 n.; 122/13 ff., 14 n.; 123/9, 15; 124/13; 134/23, 28 & n.; 136/32; 137/16; 19; 147/40; 148/12–14; 158/4; 165/79; 178/5; 200/8 & n.; 204/5; 240/36–44; chaplain of, 123/13; 148/12–13 n.; household of, 40/15; 55/21, 31; 83/9; 123/9. Letter from: 129. Letter to: 178.

— Sir William (Wheston), xv n. 1; 121/22 & n.; 148/12–13 n.

Westwell, Oxf. (Westewell), 85/5; rector of, 87/8.

Wetherfyld, servant of William Lynde, 131/13.

Wetyll, Master (?Adrian Whetehill), 2/14 & n.

Whete, John, 145/3 n.

Whyte, Thomas, 215/31.

Wigston family (the Whegystons), 117/27.

Wigston, Master 244/2.

— John (Wyxston), 176/19; servant of, 176/18.

— Roger (Wyxton), 117/9; 211/48; wife of, 117/10.

— Thomas (Wigeston, Wygeston), 28/3, 5 & n.

— William (Wyggeston), 28/5 n.; 41/17 n.

Wiking, William (Whykyng), 133/22 & n.

William, apprentice of Robert Cely (Wylliam), 8/26.

— Master, chaplain to Sir John Weston, 123/13, 14 n.

— servant of John Elderbeck, 246/3 ff.

— Sir, 148/13 & n.; 232/4.

— the parson's man 15/11.

Williamson, Philip, 29/13.

Wiltshire, James Butler Earl of, 219/8–9 n.

Winchcomb, Glos. (Wynchecwme), 165/49.

Windsor (Wynsour), 138/3 & n.

Wode, John (atte Wode), 1 & n.

Woodville family, 185/14 n.

Woodville, Sir Edward, 42 n.; danger from fleet of, 212/12 n.

Worcester, John Tiptoft Earl of, 219/8–9 & n.

Wranx, Joes, 14/4.

Wryght, John, 29/16.

— Thomas, 29/18.

Wurme, John, 105/41.

Wylkyns, Harry, shipman, 131/11, 32; 133/48.

Wylliam, Dave, shipman, 82/28.

Wylliamson, Adryan, of Leiden, 214/4, 32; 215/60.

— John, of Delft, 209/66.

— John, of Leiden, 172/16; 173/1 & n.

Wylliamsone, Jacob, of Delft, 172/14, 19; 196/25.

Wyllykyn, John Delopys' man (Wylykyn), 205/41; 206/24; 207/4, 9, 13; 209/11, 15; 215/22; 217/9, 14; 220/10, 19; 221/6, 19.

Wylowly, Richard, 29/13.

Wylson, William, shipman (Wylsson, Wyllson), 82/17; 247/8, 13 (see also Wellson).

Wymbysche, Master (Thomas Wymbissh), 212/21 & n.

Wynde, Alexander, 145/3 n.

Wyytte, servant of Richard Twege, 21/17.

Yermevthe, see Arnemuiden.

Ynge, John, 213/33.

Yorcke, Richard, 212/20 & n.

York (Ʒorke, Ʒeorke, Ʒeurke), xiv; 52/21; 116/9; 117/44; 165/70; Dean of, 15/18; Anne, Duchess of, 136/41 & n., Richard, Duke of, 200/5 & n. Archbishop of, see Rotherham.

Ypres (Ypur, Iper, Ipur), 133/87–8 n.; 179/21; 182/30; 209/48; 240/46.

Zeeland (Zelond, Selond), xx; 114/14; 115/15 n.; 186/12; 220/45, 48, 50; 221/24; 236/12; 241/22; 242/9; 243/26.

# EARLY ENGLISH TEXT SOCIETY

The Early English Text Society was founded in 1864 by Frederick James Furnivall, with the help of Richard Morris, Walter Skeat and others, to bring the mass of unprinted Early English literature within the reach of students and to provide sound texts from which the New English Dictionary could quote. In 1867 an Extra Series was started of texts already printed but not in satisfactory or readily obtainable editions. In 1921 the Extra Series was discontinued and all publications were subsequently listed and numbered as part of the Original Series. In 1970 the first of a new Supplementary Series was published; unlike the Extra Series, volumes in this series will be issued only occasionally, as funds allow and as suitable texts become available.

In the first part of this list are shown the books published by the Society since 1938, Original Series 210 onwards and the Supplementary Series. A large number of the earlier books were reprinted by the Society in the period 1950 to 1970. In order to make the rest available, the Society has come to an agreement with the Kraus Reprint Co. who reprint as necessary the volumes in the Original Series 1–209 and in the Extra Series. In this way all the volumes published by the Society are once again in print. The prices of books reprinted by Kraus are shown in dollars.

―――――

Membership of the Society is open to libraries and to individuals interested in the study of medieval English literature. The subscription to the Society for 1976 is £5·00 (U.S. members $14.00, Canadian members Can. $14.00), due in advance on 1 January, and should be paid by cheque, postal order or money order made out to 'The Early English Text Society', and sent to Dr. Anne Hudson, Executive Secretary, Early English Text Society, Lady Margaret Hall, Oxford. Payment of this subscription entitles the member to receive the new book(s) in the Original Series for the year. The books in the Supplementary Series do not form part of the issue sent to members in return for the payment of their annual subscription, though they are available to members at a reduced price; a notice about each volume is sent to members in advance of publication.

Private members of the Society (but not libraries) may select in place of the annual issue past volumes from the Society's list chosen from the Original Series 210 to date or from the Supplementary Series. The value of such texts allowed against one annual subscription is £7·50, and all these transactions must be made through the Executive Secretary. Members of the Society may purchase copies of books O.S. 210 to date for their own use at a discount of 25% of the listed prices; private members (but not libraries) may purchase earlier publications at a similar discount. All such orders must be sent to the Executive Secretary.

Details of books, the cost of membership and its privileges, are revised from time to time. The prices of books are subject to alteration without notice. This list is brought up to date annually, and the current edition should be consulted.

*June 1975*

# ORIGINAL SERIES 1938–1974

O.S. 210  **Sir Gawain and the Green Knight**, re-ed. I. Gollancz, with £2·00
introductory essays by Mabel Day and M. S. Serjeantson.
1940 (*for* 1938), *reprinted* 1966.

211  **The Dicts and Sayings of the Philosophers**: translations made £5·75
by Stephen Scrope, William Worcester and anonymous
translator, ed. C. F. Bühler. 1941 (*for* 1939), *reprinted* 1961.

212  **The Book of Margery Kempe**, Vol. I, Text (*all published*), ed. £5·40
S. B. Meech, with notes and appendices by S. B. Meech and
H. E. Allen. 1940 (*for* 1939), *reprinted* 1961.

213  **Ælfric's De Temporibus Anni**, ed. H. Henel. 1942 (*for* 1940), £3·20
*reprinted* 1970.

214  **Forty-Six Lives translated from Boccaccio's De Claris** £4·00
**Mulieribus by Henry Parker, Lord Morley**, ed. H. G. Wright.
1943 (*for* 1940), *reprinted* 1970.

215, 220  **Charles of Orleans: The English Poems**, Vol. I, ed. R. £4·75
Steele (1941), Vol. II, ed. R. Steele and Mabel Day (1946 *for*
1944); *reprinted as one volume with bibliographical supplement*
1970.

216  **The Latin Text of the Ancrene Riwle**, from Merton College £3·40
MS. 44 and British Museum MS. Cotton Vitellius E. vii, ed.
C. D'Evelyn. 1944 (*for* 1941), *reprinted* 1957.

217  **The Book of Vices and Virtues**: A Fourteenth-Century English £5·75
Translation of the *Somme le Roi* of Lorens d'Orléans, ed.
W. Nelson Francis. 1942, *reprinted* 1968.

218  **The Cloud of Unknowing and The Book of Privy Counselling**; £3·75
ed. Phyllis Hodgson. 1944 (*for* 1943), *corrected reprint* 1973.

219  **The French Text of the Ancrene Riwle**, British Museum MS. £4·00
Cotton Vitellius F. vii, ed. J. A. Herbert. 1944 (*for* 1943),
*reprinted* 1967.

220  **Charles of Orleans: The English Poems**, Vol. II; *see above*
O.S. 215.

221  **The Romance of Sir Degrevant**, ed. L. F. Casson. 1949 (*for* £3·75
1944), *reprinted* 1970.

222  **The Lyfe of Syr Thomas More, by Ro. Ba.**, ed. E. V. Hitch- £4·75
cock and P. E. Hallett, with notes and appendices by A. W.
Reed. 1950 (*for* 1945), *reprinted* 1974.

223  **The Tretyse of Loue**, ed. J. H. Fisher. 1951 (*for* 1945), £3·20
*reprinted* 1970.

224  **Athelston: a Middle English Romance**, ed. A. McI. Trounce. £3·20
1951 (*for* 1946), *reprinted* 1957.

225  **The English Text of the Ancrene Riwle**, British Museum MS. £3·75
Cotton Nero A. xiv, ed. Mabel Day. 1952 (*for* 1946), *reprinted* 1957.

226  **Respublica**: an interlude for Christmas 1553 attributed to £2·25
Nicholas Udall, re-ed. W. W. Greg. 1952 (*for* 1946),
*reprinted* 1969.

O.S. 227  Kyng Alisaunder, Vol. I, Text, ed. G. V. Smithers. 1952 (for £5·75
1947), reprinted 1961.

228  The Metrical Life of St. Robert of Knaresborough, together £3·20
with the other Middle English pieces in British Museum MS.
Egerton 3143, ed. Joyce Bazire. 1953 (for 1947), reprinted
1968.

229  The English Text of the Ancrene Riwle, Gonville and Caius £2·75
College MS. 234/120, ed. R. M. Wilson with an introduction
by N. R. Ker. 1954 (for 1948), reprinted 1957.

230  The Life of St. George by Alexander Barclay, ed. W. Nelson. £3·00
1955 (for 1948), reprinted 1960.

231  Deonise Hid Diuinite and other treatises related to The Cloud £3·75
of Unknowing, ed. Phyllis Hodgson. 1955 (for 1949), reprinted
with corrections 1958.

232  The English Text of the Ancrene Riwle, British Museum MS. £2·25
Royal 8 C. i, ed. A. C. Baugh. 1956 (for 1949), reprinted
1959.

233  The Bibliotheca Historica of Diodorus Siculus translated by £6·00
John Skelton, Vol. I, Text, ed. F. M. Salter and H. L. R.
Edwards. 1956 (for 1950), reprinted 1968.

234  Paris and Vienne translated from the French and printed by £3·20
William Caxton, ed. MacEdward Leach. 1957 (for 1951),
reprinted 1970.

235  The South English Legendary, Corpus Christi College £4·75
Cambridge MS. 145 and British Museum MS. Harley 2277,
with variants from Bodley MS. Ashmole 43 and British
Museum MS. Cotton Julius D. ix, ed. C. D'Evelyn and A. J.
Mill. Vol. I, Text, 1959 (for 1957), reprinted 1967.

236  The South English Legendary, Vol. II, Text, ed. C. D'Evelyn £4·75
and A. J. Mill. 1956 (for 1952), reprinted 1967.

237  Kyng Alisaunder, Vol. II, Introduction, commentary and £3·75
glossary, ed. G. V. Smithers. 1957 (for 1953), reprinted with
corrections 1969.

238  The Phonetic Writings of Robert Robinson, ed. E. J. Dobson. £2·25
1957 (for 1953), reprinted 1968.

239  The Bibliotheca Historica of Diodorus Siculus translated by £2·25
John Skelton, Vol. II, Introduction, notes and glossary, ed.
F. M. Salter and H. L. R. Edwards. 1957 (for 1954), re-
printed 1971.

240  The French Text of the Ancrene Riwle, Trinity College Cam- £4·00
bridge MS. R. 14. 7, with variants from Paris Bibliothèque
Nationale MS. fonds fr. 6276 and Bodley MS. 90, ed. W. H.
Trethewey. 1958 (for 1954), reprinted 1971.

241  Þe Wohunge of Ure Lauerd and other pieces, ed. W. Meredith £3·40
Thompson. 1958 (for 1955), reprinted with corrections 1970.

242  The Salisbury Psalter, ed. Celia Sisam and Kenneth Sisam. £6·75
1959 (for 1955–6), reprinted 1969.

243  The Life and Death of Cardinal Wolsey by George Cavendish, £3·40
ed. R. S. Sylvester. 1959 (for 1957), reprinted 1961.

244  The South English Legendary, Vol. III, Introduction and £2·25
glossary, ed. C. D'Evelyn. 1959 (for 1957), reprinted 1969.

O.S. 245 **Beowulf**: facsimile of British Museum MS. Cotton Vitellius £7·50
A. xv, with a transliteration and notes by J. Zupitza, a new
reproduction of the manuscript with an introductory note by
Norman Davis. 1959 (*for* 1958), *reprinted* 1967.

246 **The Parlement of the Thre Ages,** ed. M. Y. Offord. 1959, £3·00
*reprinted* 1967.

247 **Facsimile of MS. Bodley 34: St. Katherine, St. Margaret,** £4·75
St. Juliana, Hali Meiðhad, Sawles Warde, with an introduction by N. R. Ker. 1960 (*for* 1959).

248 **Þe Liflade ant te Passiun of Seinte Iuliene,** ed. S. R. T. O. £3·00
d'Ardenne. 1961 (*for* 1960).

249 **The English Text of the Ancrene Riwle: Ancrene Wisse,** £3·75
Corpus Christi College Cambridge MS. 402, ed. J. R. R.
Tolkien, with introduction by N. R. Ker. 1962 (*for* 1960).

250 **Laȝamon's Brut,** Vol. I, Text (lines 1–8020), ed. G. L. £7·50
Brook and R. F. Leslie. 1963 (*for* 1961).

251 **The Owl and the Nightingale**: facsimile of Jesus College £3·75
Oxford MS. 29 and British Museum MS. Cotton Caligula
A. ix, with an introduction by N. R. Ker. 1963 (*for* 1962).

252 **The English Text of the Ancrene Riwle,** British Museum MS. £3·75
Cotton Titus D. xviii, ed. F. M. Mack, and the Lanhydrock
Fragment, Bodleian MS. Eng. th. c. 70, ed. A. Zettersten. 1963
(*for* 1962).

253 **The Bodley Version of Mandeville's Travels,** ed. M. C. £3·75
Seymour. 1963.

254 **Ywain and Gawain,** ed. Albert B. Friedman and Norman £3·75
T. Harrington. 1964 (*for* 1963).

255 **Facsimile of British Museum MS. Harley 2253,** with an £7·50
introduction by N. R. Ker. 1965 (*for* 1964).

256 **Sir Eglamour of Artois,** ed. Frances E. Richardson. 1965. £3·75

257 **The Praise of Folie by Sir Thomas Chaloner,** ed. Clarence H. £3·75
Miller. 1965.

258 **The Orcherd of Syon,** Vol. I, Text, ed. Phyllis Hodgson and £7·50
Gabriel M. Liegey. 1966.

259 **Homilies of Ælfric, A Supplementary Collection,** Vol. I, £7·50
ed. J. C. Pope. 1967.

260 **Homilies of Ælfric, A Supplementary Collection,** Vol. II, £7·50
ed. J. C. Pope. 1968.

261 **Lybeaus Desconus,** ed. M. Mills. 1969. £3·75

262 **The Macro Plays**: The Castle of Perseverance, Wisdom, £3·75
Mankind, ed. Mark Eccles. 1969.

263 **The History of Reynard the Fox translated from the Dutch** £3·75
**Original by William Caxton,** ed. N. F. Blake. 1970.

264 **The Epistle of Othea translated from the French text of** £3·75
**Christine de Pisan by Stephen Scrope,** ed. C. F. Bühler. 1970.

265 **The Cyrurgie of Guy de Chauliac,** Vol. I, Text, ed. Margaret S. £7·50
Ogden. 1971.

266 **Wulfstan's Canons of Edgar,** ed. R. G. Fowler. 1972. £2·25

267 **The English Text of the Ancrene Riwle,** British Museum MS. £5·40
Cotton Cleopatra C. vi, ed. E. J. Dobson. 1972.

O.S. 268  Of Arthour and of Merlin, Vol. I, Text, ed. O. D. Macrae-  £3·75
Gibson. 1973.
269  The Metrical Version of Mandeville's Travels, ed. M. C.  £3·75
Seymour. 1973.
270  Fifteenth Century Translations of Alain Chartier's Le Traite  £3·75
de l'Esperance and Le Quadrilogue Invectif, Vol. I, Text, ed.
Margaret S. Blayney. (1974.)
271  The Minor Poems of Stephen Hawes, ed. Florence Gluck and  £3·75
Alice B. Morgan. (1974.)
272  Thomas Norton's The Ordinal of Alchemy, ed. John Reidy.  £3·75
(1975.)
273  The Cely Letters, 1472–1488, ed. Alison Hanham. (1975.)  £5·75

## SUPPLEMENTARY SERIES

S.S. 1  Non-Cycle Plays and Fragments, ed. Norman Davis with an  £4·60
appendix on the Shrewsbury Music by F. Ll. Harrison. 1970.
2  The Book of the Knight of the Tower translated by William  £4·00
Caxton, ed. M. Y. Offord. 1971.
3  The Chester Mystery Cycle, Vol. I, Text, ed. R. M. Lumiansky  £6·90
and David Mills. (1974.)

## FORTHCOMING VOLUMES

O.S. 274  The English Text of the Ancrene Riwle, Magdalene College
Cambridge MS Pepys 2498, ed. A. Zettersten. (1976.)
275  Dives and Pauper, Text Vol. I, ed. Priscilla H. Barnum. (1976.)
S.S. 4  The Winchester Malory, a facsimile with introduction by
N. R. Ker. (1976.)
O.S. 276  Secretum Secretorum, Vol. I, Text, ed. M. A. Manzalaoui.
(1977.)
277  Laȝamon's Brut, Vol. II, Text (lines 8021–end), ed. G. L.
Brook and R. F. Leslie. (1978.)

# LIST 2

## ORIGINAL SERIES 1864–1938

O.S. 1 Early English Alliterative Poems . . . from MS. Cotton Nero A. x, £4·00
ed. R. Morris. 1864, *revised* 1869, *reprinted* 1965.

2 Arthur, ed. F. J. Furnivall. 1864, *reprinted* 1965. 75p

3 William Lauder Ane conpendious and breue tractate concernyng ye £1·50
Office and Dewtie of Kyngis, ed. F. Hall. 1864, *reprinted* 1965.
*Also available reprinted as one volume with* O.S. 41 $8.00
William Lauder The Minor Poems, ed. F. J. Furnivall. 1870, *reprinted*
Kraus 1973.

4 Sir Gawayne and the Green Knight, ed. R. Morris. 1864. Superseded
by O.S. 210.

5 Alexander Hume of the Orthographie and Congruitie of the Britan £1·50
Tongue, ed. H. B. Wheatley. 1865, *reprinted* 1965.

6 The Romans of Lancelot of the Laik, re-ed. W. W. Skeat. 1865, *re-* £3·20
*printed* 1965.

7 The Story of Genesis and Exodus, ed. R. Morris. 1865, *reprinted* $12.00
Kraus 1973.

8 Morte Arthure [alliterative version from Thornton MS.], ed. E. Brock. £1·90
1865, *reprinted* 1967.

9 Francis Thynne Animadversions uppon Chaucer's Workes . . . 1598, £4·00
ed. G. H. Kingsley. 1865, *revised* F. J. Furnivall 1875, *reprinted* 1965.

10, 112 Merlin, ed. H. B. Wheatley, Vol. I 1865, Vol. IV with essays $29.00
by J. S. S. Glennie and W. E. Mead 1899; *reprinted as one volume*
Kraus 1973. (See O.S. 21, 36 for other parts.)

11, 19, 35, 37 The Works of Sir David Lyndesay, Vol. I 1865; Vol. II $24.00
1866 The Monarch and other Poems, ed. J. Small; Vol. III 1868 The
Historie of . . . Squyer William Meldrum etc., ed. F. Hall; Vol. IV
Ane Satyre of the Thrie Estaits and Minor Poems, ed. F. Hall.
*Reprinted as one volume* Kraus 1973. (See O.S. 47 for last part.)

12 Adam of Cobsam The Wright's Chaste Wife, ed. F. J. Furnivall. 1865, 75p
*reprinted* 1965. (See also O.S. 84.)

13 Seinte Marherete, ed. O. Cockayne. 1866. Superseded by O.S. 193.

14 King Horn, Floriz and Blauncheflur, The Assumption of our Lady, £3·75
ed. J. R. Lumby. 1866, *revised* G. H. McKnight 1901, *reprinted* 1962.

15 Political, Religious and Love Poems, from Lambeth MS. 306 and £4·75
other sources, ed. F. J. Furnivall. 1866, *reprinted* 1962.

16 The Book of Quinte Essence . . . Sloane MS. 73 c. 1460–70, ed. F. J. 75p
Furnivall. 1866, *reprinted* 1965.

17 William Langland Parallel Extracts from 45 MSS. of Piers Plowman, $7.00
ed. W. W. Skeat. 1866, *reprinted* Kraus 1973.

18 Hali Meidenhad, ed. O. Cockayne. 1866, *revised* F. J. Furnivall 1922 $5.00
(*for* 1920), *reprinted* Kraus 1973.

19 Sir David Lyndesay The Monarch and other Poems, Vol. II. See
above, O.S. 11.

20 Richard Rolle de Hampole English Prose Treatises, ed. G. G. Perry. $3.00
1866, *reprinted* Kraus 1973.

21, 36 Merlin, ed. H. B. Wheatley. Vol. II 1866, Vol. III 1869; *reprinted* $27.00
*as one volume* Kraus 1973

22 The Romans of Partenay or of Lusignen, ed. W. W. Skeat. 1866, $14.00
*reprinted* Kraus 1973.

O.S. 23  Dan Michel Ayenbite of Inwyt, ed. R. Morris. 1866, *revised* P. Gradon,   £4·00
reprinted 1965.

24  Hymns to the Virgin and Christ ... and other religious poems, ed. F. J.   $7.00
Furnivall. 1867, *reprinted* Kraus 1973.

25  The Stacions of Rome, The Pilgrims Sea-Voyage etc., ed. F. J. Furni-   $3.00
vall. 1867, *reprinted* Kraus 1973.

26  Religious Pieces in Prose and Verse from R. Thornton's MS., ed. G. G   $18.00
Perry. 1867, *reprinted* Kraus 1973.

27  Peter Levins Manipulus Vocabulorum, ed. H. B. Wheatley. 1867,   $17.00
*reprinted* Kraus 1973.

28  William Langland The Vision of Piers Plowman, ed. W. W. Skeat.   £2·75
Vol. I Text A 1867, *reprinted* 1968. (See O.S. 38, 54, 67, and 81 for
other parts.)

29, 34  Old English Homilies of the 12th and 13th Centuries, ed. R. Morris.   $16.00
Vol. I. i 1867, Vol. I. ii 1868; *reprinted as one volume* Kraus 1973. (See
O.S. 53 for Vol. II.)

30  Pierce the Ploughmans Crede etc., ed. W. W. Skeat. 1867, *reprinted*   $4.00
Kraus 1973.

31  John Myrc Instructions for Parish Priests, ed. E. Peacock. 1868, *re-*   $6.00
*printed* Kraus 1973.

32  Early English Meals and Manners: The Babees Book etc., ed. F. J.   $23.00
Furnivall. 1868, *reprinted* Kraus 1973.

33  The Book of the Knight of La Tour-Landry (from MS. Harley 1764),   $12.00
ed. T. Wright. 1868, *reprinted* Kraus 1973.

34  Old English Homilies of the 12th and 13th Centuries, Vol. I. ii. See
above, O.S. 29.

35  Sir David Lyndesay The Historie of ... Squyer William Meldrum etc.,   £1·50
ed. F. Hall. 1868, *reprinted* 1965. *Also available reprinted as one*
*volume with* O.S. 11, 19, and 37. See above, O.S. 11.

36  Merlin, Vol. III 1869. See above, O.S. 21.

37  Sir David Lyndesay Ane Satyre ... Vol. IV. See above, O.S. 11.

38  William Langland The Vision of Piers Plowman, ed. W. W. Skeat.   £3·20
Vol. II Text B 1869, *reprinted* 1972. (See O.S. 28, 54, 67, and 81 for
other parts.)

39, 56  The Gest Hystoriale of the Destruction of Troy, ed. G. A. Panton   £8·00
and D. Donaldson. Vol. I 1869, Vol. II 1874; *reprinted as one volume*
1968.

40  English Gilds etc., ed. Toulmin Smith, L. Toulmin Smith and L.   £7·50
Brentano. 1870, *reprinted* 1963.

41  William Lauder The Minor Poems. See above, O.S. 3.

42  Bernardus De Cura Rei Famuliaris, with some early Scottish   £1·50
Prophecies etc., ed. J. R. Lumby. 1870, *reprinted* 1965.

43  Ratis Raving, and other Moral and Religious Pieces in prose and verse,   $7.00
ed. J. R. Lumby. 1870, *reprinted* Kraus 1973.

44  Joseph of Arimathie: the Romance of the Seint Graal, an alliterative   $7.00
poem, ed. W. W. Skeat. 1871, *reprinted* Kraus 1973.

45  King Alfred's West-Saxon Version of Gregory's Pastoral Care, ed. H.   $15.00
Sweet. Vol. I 1871, reprinted with corrections and an additional note
by N. R. Ker 1958, *reprinted* Kraus 1973. (See O.S. 50 for Vol. II.)

46  Legends of the Holy Rood, Symbols of the Passion and Cross-Poems,   $12.00
ed. R. Morris. 1871, *reprinted* Kraus 1973.

47  Sir David Lyndesay The Minor Poems, ed. J. A. H. Murray. 1871,   $10.00
*reprinted* Kraus 1973. (See O.S. 11, 19, 35, 37 for other parts.)

48  The Times' Whistle, and other poems; by R. C., ed. J. M. Cowper.   $10.00
1871, *reprinted* Kraus 1973.

O.S. 49 An Old English Miscellany : a Bestiary, Kentish Sermons, Proverbs of $15.00
Alfred and Religious Poems of the 13th Century, ed. R. Morris. 1872,
*reprinted* Kraus 1973.

50 King Alfred's West-Saxon Version of Gregory's Pastoral Care, ed. H. $11.00
Sweet. Vol. II 1871, reprinted with corrections by N. R. Ker 1958,
*reprinted* Kraus 1973. (See O.S. 45 for Vol. I.)

51 Þe Liflade of St. Juliana, ed. O. Cockayne and E. Brock. 1872, *re-* £2·80
*printed* 1957. (See O.S. 248 for more recent edition.)

52 Palladius On Husbandrie, ed. B. Lodge. Vol. I 1872, *reprinted* Kraus $10.00
1973. (See O.S. 72 for Vol. II.)

53 Old English Homilies of the 12th Century etc., ed. R. Morris. Vol. II $14.00
1873, *reprinted* Kraus 1973. (See O.S. 29, 34 for Vol. 1.)

54 William Langland The Vision of Piers Plowman, ed. W. W. Skeat. £4·00
Vol. III Text C 1873, *reprinted* 1959. (See O.S. 28, 38, 67, and 81 for
other parts.)

55, 70 Generydes, a romance, ed. W. A. Wright. Vol. I 1873, Vol. II $12.00
1878; *reprinted as one volume* Kraus 1973.

56 The Gest Hystoriale of the Destruction of Troy. Vol. II. See above,
O.S. 39.

57 Cursor Mundi, ed. R. Morris. Vol. I Text ll. 1–4954, 1874, *reprinted* £3·00
1961. (See O.S. 59, 62, 66, 68, 99, and 101 for other parts.)

58, 63, 73 The Blickling Homilies, ed. R. Morris. Vol. I 1874, Vol. II £5·40
1876, Vol. III 1880; *reprinted as one volume* 1967.

59 Cursor Mundi, ed. R. Morris. Vol. II ll. 4955–12558, 1875, *reprinted* £3·75
1966. (See O.S. 57, 62, 66, 68, 99, and 101 for other parts.)

60 Meditations on the Supper of our Lord, and the Hours of the Passion, $3.00
translated by Robert Manning of Brunne, ed. J. M. Cowper. 1875,
*reprinted* Kraus 1973.

61 The Romance and Prophecies of Thomas of Erceldoune, ed. J. A. H. $6.00
Murray. 1875, *reprinted* Kraus 1973.

62 Cursor Mundi, ed. R. Morris. Vol. III ll. 12559–19300, 1876, *reprinted* £3·00
1966. (See O.S. 57, 59, 66, 68, 99, and 101 for other parts.)

63 The Blickling Homilies, Vol. II. See above, O.S. 58.

64 Francis Thynne's Emblemes and Epigrames, ed. F. J. Furnivall. 1876, $6.00
*reprinted* Kraus 1973.

65 Be Domes Dæge, De Die Judicii: an Old English version of the Latin £2·25
poem ascribed to Bede, ed. J. R. Lumby. 1876, *reprinted* 1964.

66 Cursor Mundi, ed. R. Morris. Vol. IV ll. 19301–23836, 1877, *reprinted* £3·00
1966. (See O.S. 57, 59, 62, 68, 99, and 101 for other parts.)

67 William Langland The Vision of Piers Plowman, ed. W. W. Skeat. $23.00
Vol. IV. 1 Notes, 1877, *reprinted* Kraus 1973. (See O.S. 28, 38, 54,
and 81 for other parts.)

68 Cursor Mundi, ed. R. Morris. Vol. V ll. 23827–end, 1878, *reprinted* £3·00
1966. (See O.S. 57, 59, 62, 66, 99, and 101 for other parts.)

69 Adam Davy's 5 Dreams about Edward II etc. from Bodleian MS. Laud $6.00
Misc. 622, ed. F. J. Furnivall. 1878, *reprinted* Kraus 1973.

70 Generydes, a romance, Vol. II. See above, O.S. 55.

71 The Lay Folks Mass Book, ed. T. F. Simmons. 1879, *reprinted* 1968. £6·75

72 Palladius On Husbandrie, ed. B. Lodge and S. J. Herrtage. Vol. II £3·20
1879. (See O.S. 52 for Vol. I.)
*Also available reprinted as one volume with* O.S. 52.

73 The Blickling Homilies, Vol. III. See above, O.S. 58.

74 The English Works of Wyclif hitherto unprinted, ed. F. D. Matthew. $28.00
1880, *reprinted* Kraus 1973.

75 Catholicon Anglicum, an English–Latin Wordbook 1483, ed. S. J. H. $22.00
Herrtage and H. B. Wheatley. 1881, *reprinted* Kraus 1973.

O.S. 76, 82  Ælfric's Lives of Saints, ed. W. W. Skeat. Vol. I. i 1881, Vol. I. ii   £4·60
1885; *reprinted as one volume* 1966. (See O.S. 94 and 114 for other parts.)

77  Beowulf, autotypes of Cotton MS. Vitellius A. xv. 1882. Superseded by O.S. 245.

78  The Fifty Earliest English Wills . . . 1387–1439, ed. F. J. Furnivall.   £3·75
1882, *reprinted* 1964.

79  King Alfred's Orosius, ed. H. Sweet. Vol. I Old English Text and Latin  $12.00
Original (*all published*) 1883, *reprinted* Kraus 1974.

80  The Life of Saint Katherine, from Royal MS. 17 A. xxvii etc., ed.  $12.00
E. Einenkel. 1884, *reprinted* Kraus 1973.

81  William Langland The Vision of Piers Plowman, ed. W. W. Skeat.  $25.00
Vol. IV. 2 General Preface and indexes. 1884, *reprinted* Kraus 1973.
(See O.S. 28, 38, 54, and 67 for other parts.)

82  Ælfric's Lives of Saints, Vol. I. ii. See above, O.S. 76.

83  The Oldest English Texts, ed. H. Sweet. 1885, *reprinted* 1966.   £8·00

84  [Adam of Cobsam] Additional Analogs to The Wright's Chaste Wife,
ed. W. A. Clouston. 1886, *reprinted* Kraus 1973. (See also O.S. 12.)

85  The Three Kings of Cologne, ed. C. Horstmann. 1886, *reprinted* Kraus  $15.00
1973.

86  The Lives of Women Saints etc., ed. C. Horstmann. 1886, *reprinted*  $12.00
Kraus 1973.

87  The Early South-English Legendary, from Bodleian MS. Laud Misc.  $25.00
108, ed. C. Horstmann. 1887, *reprinted* Kraus 1973.

88  Henry Bradshaw The Life of Saint Werburge of Chester, ed. C. Horst-  $12.00
mann. 1887, *reprinted* Kraus 1973.

89  Vices and Virtues [from British Museum MS. Stowe 240], ed. F.   £3·00
Holthausen. Vol. I Text and translation. 1888, *reprinted* 1967. (See
O.S. 159 for Vol. II.)

90  The Rule of S. Benet, Latin and Anglo-Saxon interlinear version, ed.  $9.00
H. Logeman. 1888, *reprinted* Kraus 1973.

91  Two Fifteenth-Century Cookery-Books, ed. T. Austin. 1888, *reprinted*   £3·20
1964.

92  Eadwine's Canterbury Psalter, ed. F. Harsley. Vol. II Text and notes  $13.00
(*all published*) 1889, *reprinted* Kraus 1973.

93  Defensor's Liber Scintillarum, ed. E. W. Rhodes. 1889, *reprinted*  $12.00
Kraus 1973.

94, 114  Ælfric's Lives of Saints, ed. W. W. Skeat. Vol. II. i 1890, Vol. II.   £4·60
ii 1900; *reprinted as one volume* 1966. (See O.S. 76, 82 for other parts.)

95  The Old English Version of Bede's Ecclesiastical History of the English   £4·00
People, ed. T. Miller. Vol. I. i 1890, *reprinted* 1959.

96  The Old English Version of Bede's Ecclesiastical History of the English   £4·00
People, ed. T. Miller. Vol. I. ii 1891, *reprinted* 1959. (See O.S. 110,
111 for other parts.)

97  The Earliest Complete English Prose Psalter, ed. K. D. Bülbring.  $10.00
Vol. I (*all published*) 1891, *reprinted* Kraus 1973.

98  The Minor Poems of the Vernon MS., ed. C. Horstmann. Vol. I 1892,
*reprinted* Kraus 1973. (See O.S. 117 for Vol. II.)

99  Cursor Mundi, ed. R. Morris. Vol. VI Preface etc. 1892, *reprinted*   £2·75
1962. (See O.S. 57, 59, 62, 66, 68, and 101 for other parts.)

100  John Capgrave The Life of St. Katharine of Alexandria, ed. C. Horst-  $20.00
mann, forewords by F. J. Furnivall. 1893, *reprinted* Kraus 1973.

101  Cursor Mundi, ed. R. Morris. Vol. VII Essay on manuscripts and   £2·75
dialect by H. Hupe. 1893, *reprinted* 1962. (See O.S. 57, 59, 62, 66, 68,
and 99 for other parts.)

102  Lanfrank's Science of Cirurgie, ed. R. von Fleischhacker. Vol. I Text  $16.00
(*all published*) 1894, *reprinted* Kraus 1973.

O.S. 103   History of the Holy Rood-tree, with notes on the orthography of the   $7.00
           Ormulum etc., ed. A. S. Napier. 1894, *reprinted* Kraus 1973.

104   The Exeter Book, ed. I. Gollancz. Vol. I Poems I–VIII. 1895,   $14.00
      *reprinted* Kraus 1973. (See O.S. 194 for Vol. II.)

105, 109   The Prymer or Lay Folks' Prayer Book, ed. H. Littlehales. Vol. I   $9.00
           1895, Vol. II 1897; *reprinted as one volume* Kraus 1973.

106   Richard Rolle The Fire of Love and The Mending of Life . . . translated   $7.00
      by Richard Misyn, ed. R. Harvey. 1896, *reprinted* Kraus 1973.

107   The English Conquest of Ireland, A.D. 1166–1185, ed. F. J. Furnivall.   $9.00
      Vol. I Text (*all published*) 1896, *reprinted* Kraus 1973.

108   Child-Marriages, Divorces and Ratifications etc. in the Diocese of   $16.00
      Chester 1561–6 etc., ed. F. J. Furnivall. 1894 (*for* 1897), *reprinted*
      Kraus 1973.

109   The Prymer or Lay Folks' Prayer Book, Vol. II. See above, O.S. 105.

110   The Old English Version of Bede's Ecclesiastical History of the   £4·00
      English People, ed. T. Miller. Vol. II. i 1898, *reprinted* 1963.

111   The Old English Version of Bede's Ecclesiastical History of the   £4·00
      English People, ed. T. Miller. Vol. II. ii 1898, *reprinted* 1963. (See
      O.S. 95, 96 for other parts.)

112   Merlin, Vol. IV. See above, O.S. 10.

113   Queen Elizabeth's Englishings of Boethius, Plutarch and Horace,   $9.00
      ed. C. Pemberton. 1899, *reprinted* Kraus 1973.

114   Ælfric's Lives of Saints, Vol. II. ii. See above, O.S. 94.

115   Jacob's Well, ed. A. Brandeis. Vol. I (*all published*) 1900, *reprinted*   $15.00
      Kraus 1973.

116   An Old English Martyrology, re-ed. G. Herzfeld. 1900, *reprinted*   $13.00
      Kraus 1973.

117   The Minor Poems of the Vernon MS., ed. F. J. Furnivall. Vol. II   $16.00
      1901, *reprinted* Kraus 1973. (See O.S. 98 for Vol. I.)

118   The Lay Folks' Catechism, ed. T. F. Simmons and H. E. Nolloth.   $8.00
      1901, *reprinted* Kraus 1973.

119, 123   Robert of Brunne's Handlyng Synne [and its French original],   $18.00
           ed. F. J. Furnivall. Vol. I 1901, Vol. II 1903; *reprinted as one volume*
           Kraus 1973.

120   Three Middle-English Versions of the Rule of St. Benet and two   $13.00
      contemporary rituals for the ordination of nuns, ed. E. A. Kock.
      1902, *reprinted* Kraus 1973.

121, 122   The Laud Troy Book, Bodleian MS. Land Misc. 595, ed. J. E.   $25.00
           Wülfing. Vol. I 1902, Vol. II 1903, *reprinted as one volume* Kraus
           1973.

123   Robert of Brunne's Handlyng Synne, Vol. II. See above, O.S. 119.

124   Twenty-Six Political and other Poems . . . from Bodleian MSS. Digby   $11.00
      102 and Douce 322, ed. J. Kail. Vol. I (*all published*) 1904, *reprinted*
      Kraus 1973.

125, 128   The Medieval Records of a London City Church (St. Mary at   $26.00
           Hill), 1420–1559, ed. H. Littlehales. Vol. I 1904, Vol. II 1905;
           *reprinted as one volume* Kraus 1973.

126, 127   An Alphabet of Tales, an English 15th-century translation of the   $25.00
           Alphabetum Narrationum, ed. M. M. Banks. Vol. I 1904, Vol. II
           1905; *reprinted as one volume* Kraus 1973.

128   The Medieval Records of a London City Church, Vol. II. See above,
      O.S. 125.

129   The English Register of Godstow Nunnery . . . *c.* 1450, ed. A. Clark.   $18.00
      Vol. I 1905, *reprinted* Kraus 1971.

130, 142   The English Register of Godstow Nunnery . . . *c.* 1450, ed. A. Clark.   $23.00
           Vol. II 1906, Vol. III 1911; *reprinted as one volume* Kraus 1971.

O.S. 131  The Brut, or the Chronicles of England . . . from Bodleian MS. Rawl.  £4·00
B. 171, ed. F. W. D. Brie. Vol. I 1906, *reprinted* 1960. (See O.S. 136
for Vol. II.)

132  The Works of John Metham, ed. H. Craig. 1916 (*for* 1906), *reprinted*  $10.00
Kraus 1973.

133, 144  The English Register of Oseney Abbey . . . *c*. 1460, ed. A. Clark.  $14.00
Vol. I 1907, Vol. II 1913 (*for* 1912); *reprinted as one volume* Kraus
1971.

134, 135  The Coventry Leet Book, ed. M. D. Harris. Vol. I 1907, Vol. II  $27.00
1908; *reprinted as one volume* Kraus 1971. (See O.S. 138, 146 for
other parts.)

136  The Brut, or the Chronicles of England, ed. F. W. D. Brie. Vol. II  $15.00
1908, *reprinted* Kraus 1971. (See O.S. 131 for Vol. I.)

137  Twelfth Century Homilies in MS. Bodley 343, ed. A. O. Belfour.  £2·00
Vol. I Text and translation (*all published*) 1909, *reprinted* 1962.

138, 146  The Coventry Leet Book, ed. M. D. Harris. Vol. III 1909, Vol.  $19.00
IV 1913; *reprinted as one volume* Kraus 1971. (See O.S. 134, 135 for
other parts.)

139  John Arderne Treatises of Fistula in Ano etc., ed. D'Arcy Power.  £3·30
1910, *reprinted* 1968.

140  John Capgrave's Lives of St. Augustine and St. Gilbert of Sempring-  $9.00
ham and a sermon, ed. J. J. Munro. 1910, *reprinted* Kraus 1971.

141  The Middle English Poem Erthe upon Erthe, printed from 24 manu-  £2·25
scripts, ed. H. M. R. Murray. 1911, *reprinted* 1964.

142  The English Register of Godstow Nunnery, Vol. III. See above, O.S.
130.

143  The Prose Life of Alexander from the Thornton MS., ed. J. S. West-  $5.00
lake. 1913 (*for* 1911), *reprinted* Kraus 1971.

144  The English Register of Oseney Abbey, Vol. II. See above, O.S. 133.

145  The Northern Passion, ed. F. A. Foster. Vol. I 1913 (*for* 1912),  $12.00
*reprinted* Kraus 1971. (See O.S. 147, 183 for other parts.)

146  The Coventry Leet Book, Vol. IV. See above, O.S. 138.

147  The Northern Passion, ed. F. A. Foster. Vol. II 1916 (*for* 1913),  $10.00
*reprinted* Kraus 1971. (See O.S. 145, 183 for other parts.)

148  A Fifteenth-Century Courtesy Book, ed. R. W. Chambers, and Two  £2·25
Fifteenth-Century Franciscan Rules, ed. W. W. Seton. 1914, *reprinted* 1963.

149  Lincoln Diocese Documents, 1450–1544, ed. A. Clark. 1914, *re-*  $17.00
*printed* Kraus 1971.

150  The Old English Versions of the enlarged Rule of Chrodegang, the  $6.00
Capitula of Theodulf and the Epitome of Benedict of Aniane, ed.
A. S. Napier. 1916 (*for* 1914), *reprinted* Kraus 1971.

151  The Lanterne of Liȝt, ed. L. M. Swinburn. 1917 (*for* 1915), *reprinted*  $16.00
Kraus 1971.

152  Early English Homilies from the Twelfth-Century MS. Vespasian D.  $7.00
xiv, ed. R. D.-N. Warner. 1917 (*for* 1915), *reprinted* Kraus 1971.

153  Mandeville's Travels . . . from MS. Cotton Titus C. xvi, ed. P.  $11.00
Hamelius. Vol. I Text 1919 (*for* 1916), *reprinted* Kraus 1973.

154  Mandeville's Travels . . . from MS. Cotton Titus C. xvi, ed. P.  £3·00
Hamelius. Vol. II Introduction and notes. 1923 (*for* 1916), *reprinted*
1961.

155  The Wheatley Manuscript : Middle English verse and prose in British  $7.00
Museum MS. Additional 39574, ed. M. Day. 1921 (*for* 1917), *re-*
*printed* Kraus 1971.

156  The Donet by Reginald Pecock, ed. E. V. Hitchcock. 1921 (*for* 1918),  $14.00
*reprinted* Kraus 1971.

O.S. 157 The Pepysian Gospel Harmony, ed. M. Goates. 1922 (*for* 1919), $9.00
*reprinted* Kraus 1971.

158 Meditations on the Life and Passion of Christ, from British Museum $6.00
MS. Additional 11307, ed. C. D'Evelyn. 1921 (*for* 1919), *reprinted*
Kraus 1971.

159 Vices and Virtues [from British Museum MS. Stowe 240], ed. F. £2·00
Holthausen. Vol. II Notes and Glossary, 1921 (*for* 1920), *reprinted*
1967. (See O.S. 89 for Vol. I.)

160 The Old English Version of the Heptateuch etc., ed. S. J. Crawford. £5·75
1922 (*for* 1921), reprinted with additional material, ed. N. R. Ker
1969.

161 Three Old English Prose Texts in MS. Cotton Vitellius A. xv, ed. S. $8.00
Rypins. 1924 (*for* 1921), *reprinted* Kraus 1971.

162 Pearl, Cleanness, Patience and Sir Gawain, facsimile of British £15·00
Museum MS. Cotton Nero A. x, with introduction by I. Gollancz.
1923 (*for* 1922), *reprinted* 1971.

163 The Book of the Foundation of St. Bartholomew's Church in London, $4.00
ed. N. Moore. 1923, *reprinted* Kraus 1971.

164 The Folewer to the Donet by Reginald Pecock, ed. E. V. Hitchcock. $12.00
1924 (*for* 1923), *reprinted* Kraus 1971.

165 The Famous Historie of Chinon of England by Christopher Middleton, $9.00
with Leland's Assertio Inclytissimi Arturii and Robinson's translation, ed. W. E. Mead. 1925 (*for* 1923), *reprinted* Kraus 1971.

166 A Stanzaic Life of Christ, from Harley MS. 3909, ed. F. A. Foster. $19.00
1926 (*for* 1924), *reprinted* Kraus 1971.

167 John Trevisa Dialogus inter Militem et Clericum, Richard Fitzralph's $12.00
'Defensio Curatorum', Methodius' 'þe Bygynnyng of þe World and
þe Ende of Worldes', ed. A. J. Perry. 1925 (*for* 1924), *reprinted* Kraus
1971.

168 The Book of the Ordre of Chyualry translated by William Caxton, ed. $9.00
A. T. P. Byles. 1926 (*for* 1925), *reprinted* Kraus 1971.

169 The Southern Passion, Pepysian MS. 2334, ed. B. D. Brown. 1927 $10.00
(*for* 1925), *reprinted* Kraus 1971.

170 Boethius De Consolatione Philosophiae, translated by John Walton, $17.00
ed. M. Science. 1927 (*for* 1925), *reprinted* Kraus 1971.

171 The Reule of Crysten Religioun by Reginald Pecock, ed. W. C. Greet. $22.00
1927 (*for* 1926), *reprinted* Kraus 1971.

172 The Seege or Batayle of Troye, ed. M. E. Barnicle. 1927 (*for* 1926), $10.00
*reprinted* Kraus 1971.

173 Stephen Hawes The Pastime of Pleasure, ed. W. E. Mead. 1928 (*for* $14.00
1927), *reprinted* Kraus 1971.

174 The Middle English Stanzaic Versions of the Life of St. Anne, ed. R. E. $8.00
Parker. 1928 (*for* 1927), *reprinted* Kraus 1971.

175 Alexander Barclay The Eclogues, ed. B. White. 1928 (*for* 1927), £4·00
*reprinted* 1961.

176 William Caxton The Prologues and Epilogues, ed. W. J. B. Crotch. $14.00
1928 (*for* 1927), *reprinted* Kraus 1973.

177 Byrhtferth's Manual, ed. S. J. Crawford. Vol. I Text, translation, £4·75
sources, and appendices (*all published*) 1929 (*for* 1928), *reprinted* 1966.

178 The Revelations of St. Birgitta, from Garrett MS. Princeton Uni- $5.00
versity, ed. W. P. Cumming. 1929 (*for* 1928), *reprinted* Kraus 1971.

179 William Nevill The Castell of Pleasure, ed. R. D. Cornelius. 1930 $6.00
(*for* 1928), *reprinted* Kraus 1971.

180 The Apologye of Syr Thomas More, knyght, ed. A. I. Taft. 1930 $17.00
(*for* 1929), *reprinted* Kraus 1971.

181 The Dance of Death, ed. F. Warren. 1931 (*for* 1929), *reprinted* Kraus $6.00
1971.

O.S. 182  Speculum Christiani, ed. G. Holmstedt. 1933 (*for* 1929), *reprinted*  $22.00
Kraus 1971.

183  The Northern Passion (Supplement), ed. W. Heuser and F. A. Foster.  $7.00
1930, *reprinted* Kraus 1971. (See O.S. 145, 147 for other parts.)

184  John Audelay The Poems, ed. E. K. Whiting. 1931 (*for* 1930), *re-*  $14.00
*printed* Kraus 1971.

185  Henry Lovelich's Merlin, ed. E. A. Kock. Vol. III. 1932 (*for* 1930),  $14.00
*reprinted* Kraus 1971. (See E.S. 93 and 112 for other parts.)

186  Nicholas Harpsfield The Life and Death of Sr. Thomas More, ed.  £7·75
E. V. Hitchcock and R. W. Chambers. 1932 (*for* 1931), *reprinted*
1963.

187  John Stanbridge The Vulgaria and Robert Whittinton The Vulgaria,  $9.00
ed. B. White. 1932 (*for* 1931), *reprinted* Kraus 1971.

188  The Siege of Jerusalem, from Bodleian MS. Laud Misc. 656, ed. E.  $7.00
Kölbing and M. Day. 1932 (*for* 1931), *reprinted* Kraus 1971.

189  Christine de Pisan The Book of Fayttes of Armes and of Chyualrye,  $14.00
translated by William Caxton, ed. A. T. P. Byles. 1932, *reprinted*
Kraus 1971.

190  English Mediaeval Lapidaries, ed. J. Evans and M. S. Serjeantson.  £3·75
1933 (*for* 1932), *reprinted* 1960.

191  The Seven Sages of Rome (Southern Version), ed. K. Brunner. 1933  $11.00
(*for* 1932), *reprinted* Kraus 1971.

191A  R. W. Chambers: On the Continuity of English Prose from Alfred to  £1·90
More and his School (an extract from the introduction to O.S. 186).
1932, *reprinted* 1966.

192  John Lydgate The Minor Poems, ed. H. N. MacCracken. Vol. II  £5·75
Secular Poems. 1934 (*for* 1933), *reprinted* 1961. (See E.S. 107 for
Vol. I.)

193  Seinte Marherete, from MS. Bodley 34 and British Museum MS.  £3·75
Royal 17 A. xxvii, re-ed. F. M. Mack. 1934 (*for* 1933), *reprinted* 1958.

194  The Exeter Book, ed. W. S. Mackie. Vol. II Poems IX–XXXII. 1934  $12.00
(*for* 1933), *reprinted* Kraus 1973. (See O.S. 104 for Vol. I.)

195  The Quatrefoil of Love, ed. I. Gollancz and M. M. Weale. 1935 (*for*  $4.00
1934), *reprinted* Kraus 1971.

196  An Anonymous Short English Metrical Chronicle, ed. E. Zettl. 1935  $12.00
(*for* 1934), *reprinted* Kraus 1971.

197  William Roper The Lyfe of Sir Thomas Moore, knighte, ed. E. V.  £2·75
Hitchcock. 1935 (*for* 1934), *reprinted* 1958.

198  Firumbras and Otuel and Roland, ed. M. I. O'Sullivan. 1935 (*for*  $12.00
1934), *reprinted* Kraus 1971.

199  Mum and the Sothsegger, ed. M. Day and R. Steele. 1936 (*for* 1934),  $8.00
*reprinted* Kraus 1971.

200  Speculum Sacerdotale, ed. E. H. Weatherly. 1936 (*for* 1935), *re-*  $13.00
*printed* Kraus 1971.

201  Knyghthode and Bataile, ed. R. Dyboski and Z. M. Arend. 1936 (*for*  $12.00
1935), *reprinted* Kraus 1971.

202  John Palsgrave The Comedy of Acolastus, ed. P. L. Carver. 1937 (*for*  $12.00
1935), *reprinted* Kraus 1971.

203  Amis and Amiloun, ed. MacEdward Leach. 1937 (*for* 1935), *reprinted*  £3·75
1960.

204  Valentine and Orson, translated from the French by Henry Watson,  $17.00
ed. A. Dickson. 1937 (*for* 1936), *reprinted* Kraus 1971.

205  Early English Versions of the Tales of Guiscardo and Ghismonda and  $14.00
Titus and Gisippus from the Decameron, ed. H. G. Wright. 1937
(*for* 1936), *reprinted* Kraus 1971.

206  Osbern Bokenham Legendys of Hooly Wummen, ed. M. S. Serjeantson.  $14.00
1938 (*for* 1936), *reprinted* Kraus 1971.

O.S. 207  The **Liber de Diversis Medicinis** in the Thornton Manuscript, ed.   £3·20
M. S. Ogden. 1938 (*for* 1936), *revised reprint* 1969.

208  The **Parker Chronicle and Laws** (Corpus Christi College, Cambridge   £12·00
MS. 173); a facsimile, ed. R. Flower and H. Smith. 1941 (*for* 1937),
*reprinted* 1973.

209  **Middle English Sermons**, from British Museum MS. Royal 18 B.   £5·75
xxiii, ed. W. O. Ross. 1940 (*for* 1938), *reprinted* 1960.

# EXTRA SERIES 1867–1920

E.S.  1  The **Romance of William of Palerne**, ed. W. W. Skeat. 1867, *reprinted*   $17.00
Kraus 1973.

2  **On Early English Pronunciation**, by A. J. Ellis. Part I. 1867, *reprinted*   $10.00
Kraus 1973. (See E.S. 7, 14, 23, and 56 for other parts.)

3  **Caxton's Book of Curtesye**, with two manuscript copies of the treatise,   $4.00
ed. F. J. Furnivall. 1868, *reprinted* Kraus 1973.

4  The **Lay of Havelok the Dane**, ed. W. W. Skeat. 1868, *reprinted* Kraus   $10.00
1973.

5  **Chaucer's Translation of Boethius's 'De Consolatione Philosophiæ'**, ed.   £3·00
R. Morris. 1868, *reprinted* 1969.

6  The **Romance of the Cheuelere Assigne**, re-ed. H. H. Gibbs. 1868,   $3.00
*reprinted* Kraus 1973.

7  **On Early English Pronunciation**, by A. J. Ellis. Part II. 1869, *reprinted*   $10.00
Kraus 1973. (See E.S. 2, 14, 23, and 56 for other parts.)

8  **Queene Elizabethes Achademy** etc., ed. F. J. Furnivall, with essays on   $9.00
early Italian and German Books of Courtesy by W. M. Rossetti and
E. Oswald. 1869, *reprinted* Kraus 1973.

9  The **Fraternitye of Vacabondes** by John Awdeley, Harman's Caveat,   $6.00
Haben's Sermon etc., ed. E. Viles and F. J. Furnivall. 1869, *reprinted*
Kraus 1973.

10  **Andrew Borde's Introduction of Knowledge and Dyetary of Helth**, with   $18.00
Barnes's Defence of the Berde, ed. F. J. Furnivall. 1870, *reprinted*
Kraus 1973.

11, 55  The **Bruce by John Barbour**, ed. W. W. Skeat. Vol. I 1870, Vol. IV   £4·75
1889; *reprinted as one volume* 1968. (See E.S. 21, 29, for other parts.)

12, 32  **England in the Reign of King Henry VIII**, Vol. I Dialogue between   $19.00
Cardinal Pole and Thomas Lupset, ed. J. M. Cowper (1871), Vol. II
Starkey's Life and Letters, ed. S. J. Herrtage (1878); *reprinted as one
volume* Kraus 1973.

13  **Simon Fish A Supplicacyon for the Beggers**, re-ed. F. J. Furnivall,   $6.00
A Supplycacion to . . . Henry VIII, A Supplication of the Poore
Commons and The Decaye of England by the great multitude of shepe,
ed. J. M. Cowper. 1871, *reprinted* Kraus 1973.

14  **On Early English Pronunciation**, by A. J. Ellis. Part III. 1871, *re-*   $17.00
*printed* Kraus 1973. (See E.S. 2, 7, 23, and 56 for other parts.)

15  The **Select Works of Robert Crowley**, ed. J. M. Cowper. 1872, *re-*   $10.00
*printed* Kraus 1973.

16  **Geoffrey Chaucer A Treatise on the Astrolabe**, ed. W. W. Skeat. 1872,   £3·00
*reprinted* 1968.

17, 18  The **Complaynt of Scotlande**, re-ed. J. A. H. Murray. Vol. I 1872,   $15.00
Vol. II 1873; *reprinted as one volume* Kraus 1973.

19  The **Myroure of oure Ladye**, ed. J. H. Blunt. 1873, *reprinted* Kraus   $20.00
1973.

20, 24  The **History of the Holy Grail by Henry Lovelich**, ed. F. J. Furnivall.   $22.00
Vol. I 1874, Vol. II 1875; *reprinted as one volume* Kraus 1973. (See
E.S. 28, 30, and 95 for other parts.)

E.S. 21, 29   The Bruce by John Barbour, ed. W. W. Skeat.  Vol. II 1874, Vol.   £6·75
III 1877; *reprinted as one volume* 1968. (See E.S. 11, 55 for other part.)

22   Henry Brinklow's Complaynt of Roderyck Mors, The Lamentacyon of a   $7.00
Christen agaynst the Cytye of London by Roderigo Mors, ed. J. M.
Cowper. 1874, *reprinted* Kraus 1973.

23   On Early English Pronunciation, by A. J. Ellis. Part IV. 1874, *re-*   $21.00
*printed* Kraus 1973. (See E.S. 2, 7, 14, and 56 for other parts.)

24   The History of the Holy Grail by Henry Lovelich, Vol. II. See above,
E.S. 20.

25, 26   The Romance of Guy of Warwick, the second or 15th-century   £5·75
version, ed. J. Zupitza. Vol. I 1875, Vol. II 1876; reprinted as one
volume 1966.

27   John Fisher The English Works, ed. J. E. B. Mayor. Vol. I (*all pub-*   $21.00
*lished*) 1876, *reprinted* Kraus 1973.

28, 30, 95   The History of the Holy Grail by Henry Lovelich, ed. F. J.   $18.00
Furnivall. Vol. III 1877; Vol. IV 1878; Vol. V The Legend of the Holy
Grail, its Sources, Character and Development by D. Kempe 1905;
*reprinted as one volume* Kraus 1973. (See E.S. 20, 24 for other parts.)

29   The Bruce by John Barbour, Vol. III. See above, E.S. 21.

30   The History of the Holy Grail by Henry Lovelich, Vol. IV. See above,
E.S. 28.

31   The Alliterative Romance of Alexander and Dindimus, re-ed. W. W.   $6.00
Skeat. 1878, *reprinted* Kraus 1973.

32   England in the Reign of King Henry VIII, Vol. II. See above, E.S. 12.

33   The Early English Versions of the Gesta Romanorum, ed. S. J. H.   £7·50
Herrtage. 1879, *reprinted* 1962.

34   The English Charlemagne Romances I: Sir Ferumbras, ed. S. J. H.   £4·00
Herrtage. 1879, *reprinted* 1966.

35   The English Charlemagne Romances II: The Sege of Melayne, The   $10.00
Romance of Duke Rowland and Sir Otuell of Spayne, ed. S. J. H.
Herrtage. 1880, *reprinted* Kraus 1973.

36, 37   The English Charlemagne Romances III and IV: The Lyf of   £4·00
Charles the Grete, translated by William Caxton, ed. S. J. H. Herrtage.
Vol. I 1880, Vol. II 1881; *reprinted as one volume* 1967.

38   The English Charlemagne Romances V: The Romance of the Sowdone   £3·75
of Babylone, re-ed. E. Hausknecht. 1881, *reprinted* 1969.

39   The English Charlemagne Romances VI: The Taill of Rauf Coilyear,   £3·20
with the fragments of Roland and Vernagu and Otuel, re-ed. S. J. H.
Herrtage. 1882, *reprinted* 1969.

40, 41   The English Charlemagne Romances VII and VIII: The Boke of   $29.00
Duke Huon of Burdeux translated by Lord Berners, ed. S. L. Lee. Vol. I
1882, Vol. II 1883; *reprinted as one volume* Kraus 1973. (See E.S. 43,
50 for other parts.)

42, 49, 59   The Romance of Guy of Warwick, from the Auchinleck MS.   £8·00
and the Caius MS., ed. J. Zupitza. Vol. I 1883, Vol. II 1887, Vol. III
1891; *reprinted as one volume* 1966.

43, 50   The English Charlemagne Romances IX and XII: The Boke of   $12.00
Duke Huon of Burdeux translated by Lord Berners, ed. S. L. Lee.
Vol. III 1884, Vol. IV 1887; *reprinted as one volume* Kraus 1973.

44   The English Charlemagne Romances X: The Foure Sonnes of Aymon,   $15.00
translated by William Caxton, ed. O. Richardson. Vol. I 1884, *re-*
*printed* Kraus 1973.

45   The English Charlemagne Romances XI: The Foure Sonnes of Aymon,   $17.00
translated by William Caxton, ed. O. Richardson. Vol. II 1885, *re-*
*printed* Kraus 1973.

46, 48, 65   The Romance of Sir Beues of Hamtoun, ed. E. Kölbing. Vol. I   $22.00
1885, Vol. II 1886, Vol. III 1894; *reprinted as one volume* Kraus 1973.

E.S. 47 The Wars of Alexander, an Alliterative Romance, re-ed. W. W. Skeat. $23.00
1886, *reprinted* Kraus 1973.

48 The Romance of Sir Beues of Hamtoun, Vol. II. See above, E.S. 46.

49 The Romance of Guy of Warwick, Vol. II. See above, E.S. 42.

50 The English Charlemagne Romances XII: The Boke of Duke Huon of Burdeux, Vol. IV. See above, E.S. 43.

51 Torrent of Portyngale, re-ed. E. Adam. 1887, *reprinted* Kraus 1973. $7.00

52 A Dialogue against the Feuer Pestilence by William Bullein, ed. M. W. $7.00 and A. H. Bullen. 1888, *reprinted* Kraus 1973.

53 The Anatomie of the Bodie of Man by Thomas Vicary, ed. F. J. and $16.00 P. Furnivall. 1888, *reprinted* Kraus 1973.

54 The Curial made by maystere Alain Charretier, translated by Caxton, 90p ed. P. Meyer and F. J. Furnivall. 1888, *reprinted* 1965.

55 The Bruce by John Barbour, Vol. IV. See above, E.S. 11.

56 On Early English Pronunciation, by A. J. Ellis. Part V. 1889, *reprinted* $42.00 Kraus 1973. (See E.S. 2, 7, 14, and 23 for other parts.)

57 Caxton's Eneydos, ed. W. T. Culley and F. J. Furnivall. 1890, *reprinted* £3·75 1962.

58 Caxton's Blanchardyn and Eglantine, ed. L. Kellner. 1890, *reprinted* £4·75 1962.

59 The Romance of Guy of Warwick, Vol. III. See above E.S. 42.

60 Lydgate's Temple of Glas, ed. J. Schick. 1891, *reprinted* Kraus 1973. $14.00

61, 73 Hoccleve's Works: The Minor Poems, Vol. I ed. F. J. Furnivall £4·75 (1892), Vol. II ed. I. Gollancz (1925 *for* 1897); reprinted as one volume and revised by Jerome Mitchell and A. I. Doyle 1970.

62 The Chester Plays, ed. H. Deimling. Vol. I 1892, *reprinted* 1967. (See £2·75 E.S. 115 for Part II.)

63 The Earliest English Translations of the De Imitatione Christi, ed. J. K. $15.00 Ingram. 1893, *reprinted* Kraus 1973.

64 Godeffroy of Boloyne, or the Siege and Conqueste of Jerusalem by $18.00 William, archbishop of Tyre, translated by William Caxton, ed. M. N. Colvin. 1893, *reprinted* Kraus 1973.

65 The Romance of Sir Beues of Hamtoun, Vol. III. See above, E.S. 46.

66 Lydgate and Burgh's Secrees of old Philisoffres: a version of the $7.00 Secreta Secretaorum, ed. R. Steele. 1894, *reprinted* Kraus 1973.

67 The Three Kings' Sons, ed. F. J. Furnivall. Vol. I Text (*all published*) $10.00 1895, *reprinted* Kraus 1973.

68 Melusine, ed. A. K. Donald. Vol. I (*all published*) 1895, *reprinted* $19.00 Kraus 1973.

69 John Lydgate The Assembly of Gods, ed. O. L. Triggs. 1896, *reprinted* £3·20 1957.

70 The Digby Plays, ed. F. J. Furnivall. 1896, *reprinted* 1967. £2·25

71 The Towneley Plays, re-ed. G. England and A. W. Pollard. 1897, $20.00 *reprinted* Kraus 1973.

72 Hoccleve's Works: The Regement of Princes and fourteen minor poems, $13.00 ed. F. J. Furnivall. 1897, *reprinted* Kraus 1973.

73 Hoccleve's Works: The Minor Poems, Vol. II. See above, E.S. 61.

74 Three Prose Versions of the Secreta Secretorum, ed. R. Steele and $14.00 T. Henderson. Vol. I (*all published*) 1898, *reprinted* Kraus 1973.

75 Speculum Gy de Warewyke, ed. G. L. Morrill. 1898, *reprinted* Kraus $14.00 1973.

76 George Ashby's Poems, ed. M. Bateson. 1899, *reprinted* 1965. £2·25

77, 83, 92 The Pilgrimage of the Life of Man, translated by John Lydgate $37.00 from the French by Guillaume de Deguileville, Vol. I ed. F. J.